Based on extensive archival research, this volume examines the early growth of Barcelona and the formation of its ruling classes and challenges many traditional assumptions about the nature of Mediterranean towns.

Because the city emerged as a commercial centre later than its rivals, the transformation of the urban economy from a regional agricultural market into an international trading emporium is well documented and places the take-off of the European economy in a new light. Barcelona's growth consisted of two distinct phases, interrupted by a long period of stagnation: the first phase was based on market-oriented agriculture and tribute from Islamic Spain, the second on craft production, finance, and trade.

Barcelona's patriciate did not emerge at the beginning of the urban revival but only during its second stage. Its rise formed part of a profound restructuring of territorial power in response to the "feudal crisis" that challenged traditional authority throughout Catalonia. As the comital dynasty gained strength, barons and knights loosened their ties to the city. Unlike many Mediterranean towns, Barcelona never fell under the sway of an urban aristorcracy. Patrician families did not model themselves after noble patrilineages, but forged marital alliances in which the wife's dowry played a fundamental role.

Cambridge studies in medieval life and thought

BARCELONA AND ITS RULERS, 1096–1291

Cambridge studies in medieval life and thought
Fourth series

General Editor:

D. E. LUSCOMBE

Professor of Medieval History, University of Sheffield

Advisory Editors:

R. B. DOBSON

Professor of Medieval History, University of Cambridge, and Fellow of Christ's College

ROSAMOND MCKITTERICK

*Reader in Early Medieval European History, University of Cambridge,
and Fellow of Newnham College*

The series Cambridge Studies in Medieval Life and Thought was inaugurated by G. G. Coulton in 1920. Professor D. E. Luscombe now acts as General Editor of the Fourth Series, with Professor R. B. Dobson and Dr Rosamond McKitterick as Advisory Editors. The series brings together outstanding work by medieval scholars over a wide range of human endeavour extending from political economy to the history of ideas.

For a list of titles in the series, see end of book.

BARCELONA AND ITS RULERS, 1096–1291

STEPHEN P. BENSCH

Swarthmore College, Pennsylvania

CAMBRIDGE
UNIVERSITY PRESS

Published by the Press Syndicate of the University of Cambridge
The Pitt Building, Trumpington Street, Cambridge CB2 1RP
40 West 20th Street, New York, NY 10011-4211, USA
10 Stamford Road, Oakleigh, Melbourne 3166, Australia

First published 1995

Printed in Great Britain at the University Press, Cambridge

A catalogue record for this book is available from the British Library

Library of Congress cataloguing in publication data

Bensch, Stephen P.
Barcelona and its rulers, 1096–1291/Stephen P. Bensch.
p.   cm. – (Cambridge studies in medieval life and thought; 4th ser., v.)
Includes bibliographical references and index.
ISBN 0 521 43511 0 (hardback)
1. Barcelona (Spain) – Economic conditions.
2. Barcelona (Spain – Commerce) – History.
3. Barcelona (Spain) – History.
4. Nobility – Spain – Barcelona – History.
I. Title.   II. Series.
HC388.B3B3 1994
946'.7202 – dc20   93-4251 CIP

ISBN 0 521 43511 0 hardback

For Margaret and Anselm

CONTENTS

FIGURES

MAPS

TABLES

PREFACE

The following study deals with a period of rapid urban growth in the Latin Mediterranean. A long-standing interest in the sophisticated environment created by the expanding towns of medieval Europe first drew my attention to the topic, and the partially exploited wealth of Catalonian archives enticed me to undertake an examination of Barcelona. Both the subject and the location have revealed new and unexpected perspectives to me over the decade in which this work has matured. From the perspective of urban studies on the medieval Mediterranean, it quickly became clear that many of the models of early urban development and social organization I had been prepared to employ failed to capture the nature of the world that slowly opened up before me as archivists dutifully carried out stacks of parchments and thick notarial registers. On my first day of investigation in the splendid viceregnal palace that houses the Arxiu de la Corona d'Aragó, the better part of an afternoon was spent (with occasional breaks to observe with romantic fascination the guitarist playing Albéniz outside and avid youngsters intent at soccer in the ancient Plaça del Rei) struggling over the cramped hand of a royal scribe, who must have intended to confound the uninitiated with inexplicable strokes and indecipherable contractions. One document, however, held my attention. It contained a splendid account of an urban feud, full of intimidation, insults, bloodshed, and simmering hatred; in short, just what a generation of studies of Italian towns had taught me to expect. Relieved, I seemed to have stumbled onto a promised land of social conflict. Yet thousands of more folios and tall stacks of parchments did not present a comparable example of an urban feud. Months of patient work with the source materials were required to overcome my initial impression, and through reflection and reevaluation to arrive at a rather different framework in order to explain the distinctive qualities of Barcelona's patriciate. As a result of these initial encounters with

xiii

the sources, the original time frame for my research was also moved back another half century[1] in order to search for the emergence of a particular form of medieval urbanism whose outlines, however malleable, could already be seen in 1150.

While the present work concentrates on Barcelona's first great period of expansion, it was written during a period of sustained and highly self-conscious, not to say self-adulatory, urban renewal. Three energetic periods of growth have given the city its current texture: the confirmation of its urban plan from the twelfth to the fourteenth century, the filling up of the Eixample district with its splendid architectural expressions of *modernisme*, and the exuberant renovation and experimentation in the late twentieth century to dispel from the city any remaining shadows of Francoist gloom. At the dawn of the second millennium Barcelona began to look out to the rest of Europe, which, in the apt phrase of Raoul Glaber, was donning a white mantle of churches; at the beginning of the third millennium it will have taken its old cloak to the cleaners and added many elegant contemporary embellishments to enhance its beauty. As the electronic tribe slowly gathers its forces to lay siege to the city for the celebration and the promotion of the 1992 Olympic Games, surely as significant a marker in the city's identity as that great festival of *modernisme*, the 1888 World Exhibition, one can only applaud the invigorating optimism of this revivalist affirmation in urbanism past and future.

As a work devoted to Catalonian history, proper names are rendered in modern Catalan whenever they involve the Principate of Catalonia except in a handful of instances for which English usage is solidly established (thus Catalonia rather than Catalunya); proper names that reveal a non-Catalan identity are rendered accordingly (Toulouse and Marseilles rather than Tolosa and Marsella). While the appearance of Catalan forms in areas now part of France may produce some initial disorientation for English-speaking readers (Rosselló and Perpinyà rather than Roussillon and Perpignan), this system has the advantage of bringing out the coherence of a medieval culture at the expense of modern state divisions. Modern Catalan-Castilian bilinguilism

---

[1] Controversy surrounds the date chosen to begin this study, namely the year Ramon Berenguer III began to act as sole ruler. I prefer the traditional date of 1096, the last year for which we have a clearly sovereign diploma issued by Berenguer Ramon II "the Fratricide," who was subsequently deposed. For a detailed discussion of the issue, see Santiago Sobrequés i Vidal, *Els grans comtes de Barcelona* (Barcelona, 1961), 145–49, who opts, however, for 1097.

presents another complication, for many Catalan authors employ both forms of their personal name. In addition, Catalan spelling has been standardized only recently, so that titles and proper names from earlier in the century appear odd to a contemporary reader (today Montjuïc for the older form Montjuich). Names of authors and titles are given in their original form before the regularization of spelling, and I have been guided by the author's presentation of his or her name in major works. While this will inevitably lead to seeming inconsistencies in spelling, it should nevertheless facilitate bibliographic identification.

Like many twelfth-century debtors, I have drawn on human and material resources that will be difficult to repay fully in a lifetime. A Fulbright-Hayes Scholarship provided the opportunity to spend an initial year of research in Barcelona, and stipends from a University of California Humanities Graduate Research Grant, the Committee for Faculty Research at Swarthmore College, and the National Endowment for the Humanities allowed my investigations to go forward. The materials collected were first worked into a dissertation submitted to the University of California, Berkeley thanks to the support of a Mabelle McLeod Lewis Fellowship, and a Mellon Faculty Fellowship at Harvard University provided the intellectual companionship and the splendid resources of Widener Library that helped transform the dissertation into a book.

Throughout my periods of investigation in Catalonia, the staffs of archives and libraries have responded to the incessant demands I placed on their time with generosity and courtesy. The kindness and patient help extended by Drs. Josep Baucells i Reig and Àngel Fàbrega i Grau at the Arxiu Capitular de la Catedral de Barcelona proved invaluable in my research and bring to mind many pleasant mornings passed in the sun-drenched reading room, perched on the roof of the medieval cloister high above the noisy streets of the Barri Gòtic. Prof. Federico Udina Martorell, retired director of the Arxiu de la Corona d'Aragó, introduced me to that splendid repository, whose fine staff under the able new direction of Rafael Conde y Delgado de Molina has continued to track down even the most obscure series and provide microfilms promptly. In addition to offering an initial orientation to the modern city and delightful tours of its medieval remains, Dr. Philip Banks generously pointed me toward many unexplored corners of the urban documentation with his superb knowledge of the city's early topography and archeology. Maps 4 through 6 are based on his plans and have recently been published by Enciclopèdia Catalana,[2] which has graciously permitted their reproduction here. Philip Banks, Paul Freedman, Gene Brucker, Susan M. Stuard, Edward Muir, and Robert Duplessis have read parts of the manuscript in various forms and the project has greatly benefited from their comments and criticisms. Chris Salvatico has prepared the maps and patiently incorporated numerous revisions. Finally, I wish to thank above all Thomas N. Bisson, who stood behind what often seemed an overly ambitious thesis topic while my director at Berkeley and helped see the project through at Harvard.

I owe the greatest debt both to my wife Margaret for her support during long absences overseas, for reading numerous versions of the manuscript, and for constantly challenging me to make my thoughts as clear as possible, and to my son Anselm for waiting a lifetime to see the book completed and hear his father talk endlessly of a far-off city. This book is dedicated to them.

[2] *Història de Barcelona*, II. *La formació de la Barcelona medieval*, ed. J. Sobrequés i Callicó (Barcelona, 1992), 67–68. This work was unfortunately received too late to be consulted for the present study.

ABBREVIATIONS

ACA	Arxiu de la Corona d'Aragó
ACB	Arxiu Capitular de la Catedral de Barcelona
ADB	Arxiu Diocesà de Barcelona
ADPO	Archives départementales des Pyrénées-Orientales
AEM	*Anuario de estudios medievales*
AESC	*Annales: économies, sociétés, civilisations*
AHCB	Arxiu Històric de la Ciutat de Barcelona
AHDE	*Anuario de historia del derecho español*
AM	*Annales du Midi*
APR	Arxiu de Palau de Requesens, Sant Cugat del Vallès
ARM	Arxiu del Regne de Majorca, Palma de Majorca
ASPP	Arxiu de Sant Pere de les Puel·les
Bisson, *Fiscal accounts*	Bisson, Thomas N. *Fiscal accounts of Catalonia under the early count-kings (1151–1213)*, 2 vols., Berkeley and Los Angeles, 1984
B. R.	Berenguer Ramon
BRABLB	*Boletín de la Real Academia de Buenas Letras de Barcelona*
Capmany	Capmany y de Monpalau, Antonio de. *Memorias históricas sobre la marina, comercio y artes de la antigua ciudad de Barcelona*, 4 vols., Madrid, 1779–92. 2nd ed., revised and introduced by E. Giralt i Raventós and C. Batlle i Gallart, 3 vols., Barcelona, 1961–63
CHCA	*Congreso de historia de la Corona de Aragón*
CHEC	*Cuadernos de historia económica de Cataluña*
CODIN	*Colección de documentos inéditos del archivo general de la Corona de Aragón*, eds. P. de Bofarull y Mascaró et al., 42 vols., Barcelona, 1847–1973
Cortes	*Cortes de los antiguos reinos de Aragón y de Valencia y principado de Cataluña*, 26 vols., Madrid, 1896–1922

List of abbreviations

CSC	*Cartulario de "San Cugat" del Vallés*, ed. J. Rius Serra, 3 vols., Barcelona, 1945–47
d.	denarius, denarii
EEMCA	*Estudios de Edad Media de la Corona de Aragón*
EHDAP	*Estudios históricos y documentos del Archivo de Protocolos de Barcelona*
extrainv.	extrainventari(s)
GAKS	*Gesammelte Aufsätze zur Kulturgeschichte Spaniens*
Huici-Cabanes, Documentos	*Documentos de Jaime I de Aragón*, eds. A. Huici Miranda and M. Desamparados Cabanes Pecourt, 5 vols. to date, Valencia, 1976–
LA	Libri antiquitatum, 4 vols. (in ACB)
lb.	libra, libre
LFM	*Liber feudorum maior: cartulario real que se conserva en el Archivo de la Corona de Aragón*, ed. F. Miquel Rosell, 2 vols., Barcelona, 1945–47
Llib. bl.	*El "Llibre blanch" de Santas Creus (cartulario del siglo XII)*, ed. F. Udina Martorell, Barcelona, 1947
Mas	Mas, Josep. *Notes històriques del bisbat de Barcelona*, 12 vols., Barcelona, 1906–15
mbt(s).	morabetin(s)
MCV	*Mélanges de la Casa de Velázquez*
MRABLB	*Memorias de la Real Academia de Buenas Letras de Barcelona*
Oliveras Caminal	Oliveras Caminal, José. *Archivo Capitular de la Santa Iglesia Catedral de Barcelona. Cartas reales (siglos XII–XV). Catálogo*, Barcelona, 1946
parch.	parchment(s)
perg.	pergamin(s)
Poblet	*Cartulari de Poblet*, ed. J. Pons i Marquès, Barcelona, 1938
R. B.	Ramon Berenguer
s.	solidus, solidi
Santa Anna	*L'arxiu antíc de Santa Anna de Barcelona del 942 al 1200 (Aproximació històrico-lingüística)*, ed. J. Alturo i Perucho, 3 vols., Barcelona, 1985
unnumb. parch.	unnumbered parchment
VL	*Viage literario a las iglesias de España*, ed. J. Villanueva, 22 vols., Madrid and Valencia, 1806–1902

INTRODUCTION

During the 1160s an adventurous rabbi named Benjamin of Tudela set out from Zaragoza in the upper Ebro Valley on an ambitious journey that would eventually take him to the eastern rim of the Mediterranean and beyond to distant Khurasan.[1] After several days sailing down the broad, slow-moving Ebro and skirting the beaches and rugged hills of the Catalan coast on the first leg of his trip, he arrived at Barcelona. When he described the city many years later in his travel log, Benjamin, by then a seasoned traveler thoroughly conversant with the nuanced idioms of Mediterranean urban life, recalled it as a small but dynamic port, attracting merchants from Genoa, Pisa, Sicily, Alexandria, Greece, and the Levant. Although neither as self-assured or domineering as the bustling Italian communes nor as cosmopolitan as the exotic Greek and Islamic cities he had visited, Barcelona nevertheless seemed to him full of energy and promise. Benjamin of Tudela's terse description captured a medieval city undergoing rapid transformation.

During the twelfth century the maritime powers of the Latin Mediterranean were vying to dominate the sea lanes that Christian galleys had secured from Islamic attacks.[2] As the lines of commercial, naval, and diplomatic communication grew denser among cities on or in contact with the coasts of Italy, Occitania, and Catalonia, patterns of cooperation and competition emerged that would leave their imprint on the rest of the Middle Ages and beyond. In comparison to its principal Italian and Occitanian

---

[1] Benjamin of Tudela, *The travels of Benjamin of Tudela*, in *Early travels in Palestine*, ed. and trans. T. Wright (London, 1848), 64.

[2] On the technological and economic reasons for the reassertion of Christian naval power, see John H. Pryor, *Geography, technology and war: studies in the maritime history of the Mediterranean 649–1571* (Cambridge, 1988), 108–11; Archibald R. Lewis, *Naval power and trade in the Mediterranean A.D. 500–1100* (Princeton, 1951), 225–49; Robert S. Lopez, "The trade of medieval Europe: the South," in *The Cambridge economic history of Europe* (2nd ed., Cambridge, 1941–87), II, 344–50.

competitors, Barcelona was a late bloomer. Until the mid-twelfth century the city had grown in synchronization with its small hinterland and had firmly established itself as the hub of regional life, but it had not yet projected itself as a major commercial and naval force on the Mediterranean. In Benjamin of Tudela's eyes Barcelona still appeared as a passive point of exchange, not a generator of commerce. By 1300, however, the Catalan capital had forced its way into the leading ranks of Southern European towns. Its merchants competed with the Genoese for economic domination of the Western Mediterranean, its municipal council supervised Catalan trading outposts stretching from Seville to Alexandria, and its financiers held lucrative administrative positions in the extensive dynastic confederation known as the Crown of Aragon. During the two centuries covered by this study, not only had Barcelona itself grown into the largest city in eastern Iberia, but it had come to form an integral part of a vast, interconnected, and highly competitive Mediterranean world.

It would be deceptive, however, to see in overseas trade the only impulse that stimulated the urban economy and set social change in motion. The vitality of Mediterranean towns has long been judged by the face they presented to the outside world rather than by their internal evolution. Ever since the pioneering synthetic works of Adolf Schaube and Wilhelm von Heyd, trade in the medieval Mediterranean has been thought of as an integrated and relatively self-contained system, in which commercial privileges, treaties, tariffs, and private business contracts traced out the stature and defined the position of the major cities.[3] The stimulus to Mediterranean studies provided by Fernand Braudel, S. D. Goitein, and Eliyahu Ashtor has deepened and expanded the view that the region formed an interdependent whole, enclosed by the dictates of climate and geography and linked by reliable, cheap shipping and economic interdependence.[4] The larger the city, the greater the need to keep abreast of its competitors. Braudel's sixteenth-century Mediterranean in particular is a tightly bound,

---

[3] Adolf Schaube, *Handelsgeschichte der romanischen Völker* (Munich and Berlin, 1906); Wilhelm von Heyd, *Histoire du commerce du Levant au moyen-âge*, trans. F. Raynaud, 2 vols. (Leipzig, 1885–86).

[4] Fernand Braudel, *The Mediterranean and the Mediterranean world in the age of Philip II*, trans. S. Reynolds, 2 vols. (2nd ed., New York, 1973); S. D. Goitein, *A Mediterranean society: the Jewish communities of the Arab world as portrayed in the documents of the Cairo Geniza*, 5 vols. (Berkeley and Los Angeles, 1969–88); Eliyahu Ashtor, *Levant trade in the later Middle Ages* (Princeton, 1983).

even a claustrophobic world. Bolts of brightly colored cloth, bags
of aromatic spices, exotic drugs, bushels of grain, fine brocades,
and delicate silks circulated through the great ports in ceaseless
motion, at times slowing to form eddies and at others moving
rapidly along a swift current together with merchants, sailors, sail-
makers, riggers, carpenters, armorers, and other craftsmen and
adventurers whose livelihood depended on the sea. In undulating
cycles of rise and decline, one town's difficulties worked to
another's advantage. As individual cities became enmeshed in the
dense web of exchange and the commercial culture that underlay
it, they assumed a common profile: their character was therefore
largely imposed by the cosmopolitan world in which they were
forced to compete. One inevitably approaches Braudel's Mediterranean towns as a traveler.

Although it is impossible to deny that a sailor or merchant in
the late medieval Mediterranean would have felt quite at home as
he gazed upon the outlines of ships anchored offshore, strolled
along the docks, or peeked into the warehouses in one of his ports
of call, less familiar scenes, more idiomatically framed by regional
traditions, awaited as he made his way to the seats of urban power,
the local marketplace, the houses of the well-to-do, or neighborhood churches, mosques, and synagogues. The picture of a
unified Mediterranean world depends in large part on the function
of towns as highly charged relay points, concentrating, transforming, and redirecting the human and material resources grudgingly
provided by a stingy environment. Yet they also faced inland,
where they drew upon the products of their hinterlands and
established their place in a complex matrix of local power relations. Owing to the very limitations imposed by climate and
geography, the fragmentation of the coastline, the dispersion of
the strips of vineyards and olive groves, and the frequent separation of coastal plains from large towns, all parts of an historical
landscape painted in such brilliant colors by Braudel, towns
proved particularly sensitive to the ability of municipal leaders or
their lords to organize these dispersed resources through compul-
sion as well as through commercial exchange for the benefit of the
urban community. This is above all true before maritime trade
became the lifeblood of urban economies. In the twelfth and
thirteenth century the sea itself seemed larger, less secure, and
more fragmented than in subsequent periods, for the great ports
on its Latin shore were just beginning to stake out and defend their

spheres of influence. In order to understand how they projected naval power and sustained commercial networks, it is first of all necessary to examine the underlying social transformations and the forms of urban leadership upon which the commercial economy rested. During the period considered here, the individual pieces of a broad Mediterranean community were only beginning to be locked into place.

The purpose of the present study is to look inside the city of which Benjamin of Tudela has provided only a passing glimpse. It will analyze the economic forces that transformed Barcelona from an isolated provincial center into a major commercial emporium, identify the emergence of the patriciate that commanded and profited from urban expansion, and explore how patrician families consolidated their influence and reproduced their power. While the intricacies of local authority and the control of the urban economy will provide the principal focus of the following chapters, the character of the city and the nature of its patriciate can, as Benjamin of Tudela realized, only be understood when set against a broad Mediterranean background.

Barcelona provides a splendid vantage point from which to reconsider the resurgence and early structuring of urban societies in Southern Europe. Because the city emerged rather late as a commercial and maritime power, its rich local documentation permits a detailed examination of the first blossoming of long-distance trade and the internal adaptations required to sustain it. The most dynamic cities of northern Italy had already developed viable commercial structures by the time archival material begins to swell in the twelfth century; in most cases the precociousness of cities south of the Alps makes it possible to study in detail only the results, not the process, of early urban expansion. Catalonia's isolation held back the first surge of growth in Barcelona, but this in a sense allowed the documentation to catch up with the city's development. Yet an investigation of the rise of medieval Barcelona and the consolidation of its leading families into a patriciate has more to offer than a distinctive chronology and an unusually rich archival basis: it presents a vivid contrast to the urban history of medieval Italy.

The towns of the medieval Mediterranean have usually been viewed through the stylishly tinted lenses of Italian glasses. By their antiquity, number, and fierce independence, the city-republics of northern Italy have certainly merited the attention lavished on them by generations of historians, but the problems raised by their study have rather presumptuously been equated with those of Mediterranean towns generally. In order to contrast urban life in Northern and Southern Europe, it has become an historiographical commonplace to fix the early Italian city–republics and the towns of the Low Countries as two poles of development, forming an axis around which European urbanism revolved.[5] While no one will dispute the remarkable density of urban networks in these two areas, it is far from clear whether they possessed enough common characteristics or sufficient weight to justify this geographical dualism in European town development. Recently Susan Reynolds has questioned Italian urban exceptionalism by insisting upon common, deeply embedded forms of European communal organization, while Paul M. Hohenberg and Lynn H. Lees, arguing from the perspective of widespread urban networks, insist that the revival of towns after 1000 represented a complete reworking of previous patterns, sweeping up and reordering the remnants of earlier urban societies into a distinctive, cohesive new system.[6] Barcelona offers an opportunity to explore the nature of a Mediterranean town from an original perspective, for many of the characteristic themes of Italian urban history simply do not apply, or need considerable retooling to be useful. First, in contrast to northern Italy, public authority did not shatter into tiny pieces which fell into the hands of individual towns and seigniories but remained focused on an assertive, expansionist dynasty. Second, the internal restructuring of urban society in Barcelona had little to do with the territorial expansion of the city, which would never control a *contado*. Finally, aristocratic clans played only a marginal role in the Catalan capital; as a result, the city's political life was not dominated by the factional struggles that overwhelmed many Italian towns. The relative stability of Barcelona's municipal regime and its pivotal role in the expansive confederation of the Crown of

[5] The approach was most thoroughly articulated in the stimulating comparative study by Jean Lestocquoy, *Aux origines de la bourgeoisie: les villes de Flandres et d'Italie sous le gouvernement des patriciens, XIᵉ–XVᵉ siècles* (Paris, 1952). Cf. Edith Ennen, "Les Différents types de formation des villes européennes," *Le Moyen âge*, 62 (1956), 397–412; Robert Fossier, *Enfance de l'Europe* (Paris, 1982), II, 980–86; Jacques Le Goff, "L'Apogée de la France urbaine médiévale, 1150–1330," in *Histoire de la France urbaine*, ed. G. Duby (Paris, 1980–85), II, 276–79.

[6] Susan Reynolds, *Kingdoms and communities in Western Europe, 900–1300* (Oxford, 1984), 197–98, 204–6; Paul M. Hohenberg and Lynn H. Lees, *The making of urban Europe* (Cambridge, MA, 1985), 59–62.

Aragon present the problem of Mediterranean urban development in a distinctive and little-explored setting.

Urban historiography has in general shied away from dealing
with the ongoing relations between early towns and the feudal
and territorial powers that surrounded them.[7] Because traditional
approaches to medieval towns have placed them outside the bonds
that held feudal society together, both royal and feudal influences
on developing urban communities are usually treated only in
terms of an external force legitimizing local municipal institutions
or confirming urban autonomy. But officeholding, credit, and
military involvement also created many opportunities for urban
lords to influence the internal organization of the urban community as well as its external relationships. The more thoroughly
medieval towns are integrated into the power structures of the
medieval world, the greater the importance accorded their lords in
determining their character. This is particularly true of early
Catalan towns. Without reference to the resilient territorial
authority of the counts of Barcelona and, after the dynasty acquired
a crown by marriage into the Aragonese royal house, the daring
expansionism of the count-kings, the history of medieval Barcelona would be incomprehensible. Rather than plot the formation of a city-state, the following chapters will therefore
explore the expansion of a regional capital within the dynastic
confederation known as the Crown of Aragon.

In order to grasp the distinctive contours presented by urban
society in medieval Catalonia and understand why the conjunction of dynastic, commercial, and family interests do not fit the
traditional model of Mediterranean towns, one must first turn to
the historiographical assumptions upon which that model rests.

THE TYPOLOGY OF THE MEDITERRANEAN CITY

In the heated nineteenth-century debates about the origin of
European towns, historical interest first focused on Germany,
France, and the Low Countries. Although national pride certainly
influenced the choice, so too did the ideological cast of liberalism.

---

[7] For some recent exceptions, see R. H. Hilton, *English and French towns in feudal society: a
comparative study* (Cambridge, 1992), 87–104; Christian Guilleré, "Ville et féodalité
dans la Catalogne au bas moyen-âge," in *La formació i expansió del feudalisme català. Actes
del col·loqui organitzat pel Col·legi Universitari de Girona (8–11 de gener de 1985)* [*Estudi
General. Revista del Col·legi Universitari de Girona, 5–6*] (Girona, 1986), 447–66.

In order to find a reassuring historical pedigree for the triumphant bourgeoisie of industrial Europe, scholars turned their attention to the formation of the medieval communes in search of ancestors. Because of their association with commerce, craft production, and representative municipal councils, medieval towns seemed the harbingers of capitalism, rationality, and representative democracy; in short, they embodied the forces of progress in the face of agricultural backwardness, clerical obscurantism, and feudal oppression. Towns thus presented an anomaly in feudal Europe. By setting up urban communities as an antithesis to feudalism, it seemed evident that modern industrial societies emerged in those areas where burghers had completely freed themselves of seigniorial control in order to pursue an economic and political agenda of their own; the fullest embodiment of medieval urbanism therefore lay in the North, the future engine of Western industrial development. Mediterranean towns seemed the poor relations of the novel, forward-looking Northern communes. Voicing the predilections of the German, French, and Belgian pioneers of early urban history, Henri Pirenne declared that the medieval town attained its "most classic form" in Flanders, for there neither nobles nor clerics impeded the free development of urban communities, which owed their existence to commerce alone.[8] In a similar vein, Max Weber asserted that the Western city developed its "purest form" north of the Alps, for there burghers completely severed the "magical taboos" of clannish exclusivity and formed new communities based on individual, contractual responsibilities rather than on family bonds: the new pattern of civic association presented a sharp turn on the road leading to the Protestant ethic.[9]

What disturbed both these influential scholars of European urban societies when they looked over the Alps was the high profile of aristocratic families and knights in the early Italian city-states. Urban communities in the South seemed to emerge almost too effortlessly in a landscape littered with the physical ruins and distant memories of a Roman civic past; without the pressure of hostile, overbearing feudal lords, burghers did not have to organize themselves quite so tightly, assert their claims so forcefully, or see themselves so far removed intellectually and

---

[8] Henri Pirenne, *Early democracies in the Low Countries*, trans. J.V. Saunders (New York, 1963), 68.

[9] Max Weber, *The city*, trans. D. Martindale and G. Neuwirth (New York, 1958), 91, 98–99.

politically from the seigniorial world surrounding them as did their counterparts in the North. If merchants and an egalitarian legal community lay at the heart of the Western town, then the presence of a privileged aristocratic element in urban society indicated a stunted social evolution in the South: from this perspective an urban nobility undermined the very nature of the medieval town. In spite of the grandeur and sophistication of Italian civic life, the traditions of medieval urban historiography have burdened the study of Mediterranean towns with a psychology of imputed underdevelopment.[10]

Since the Second World War this perspective has slowly changed not so much through direct comparative studies among towns in different regions as through a reevaluation of the ties between town and country. In Northern Europe the bonds forged by immigration, credit, and investment between burghers and villagers in the urban hinterland have attracted considerable attention over the past generation. As a result, towns of the North no longer appear to have served primarily as commercial relay stations dominated by long-distance merchants; urban communities possessed deep, firm roots in their hinterlands.[11] In Italy, on the other hand, aristocratic elements now do not seem embarrassingly out of place in an urban setting. Because the increased productivity of the countryside lay behind the reanimation of urban life in the Po and Arno Valleys during the tenth and eleventh centuries, nobles resident in the ancient *civitates* but still possessing strong ties to the countryside helped concentrate agricultural surpluses for the burgeoning urban marketplace. The tables have thus been completely turned. Rather than retarding or, at best, disdainfully ignoring trade, nobles are now credited with transforming agricultural profits into commercial capital and, through ship construction in the great ports, directing their aggressiveness to piracy and its twin, overseas trade.[12] The closer

---

[10] For a similar perspective in ethnology, M. Herzfeld, *Anthropology through the looking glass: critical ethnography in the margins of Europe* (Cambridge, 1987), 64–76.

[11] Fundamental among the works reorienting urban historiography toward the connections of the city to its hinterland is Jean Schneider, *La Ville de Metz aux XIIIᵉ et XIVᵉ siècles* (Nancy, 1950). Cf. André Chédeville, *Chartres et ses campagnes, XIᵉ au XIIIᵉ siècles* (Paris, 1977), 393–504; R. Fietier, *La cité de Besançon de la fin du XIIᵉ au milieu du XIVᵉ siècle*, 3 vols. (Lille, 1978); David Nicholas, *Town and countryside: social, economic, and political tensions in fourteenth-century Flanders* (Bruges, 1971); Léopolde Genicot, "Villes et campagnes dans les Pays-Bas médiévaux," *Acta mediaevalia*, 7–8 (1986–87), 163–92.

[12] The reorientation of Italian urban studies toward the countryside was initiated by Cinzio Violante, *La società milanese nell'età precomunale* (Bari, 1953). For recent appraisals of the

medieval towns are brought to their countrysides, the narrower the historiographical gap that separates Northern and Southern Europe.

This *rapprochement*, however, has come at the expense of denying medieval urban communities much of the institutional originality and social cohesiveness that earlier generations of scholars had so admired in them. Philip Abrams has trenchantly pointed out the methodological weakness of treating the town as an abstract, generic social entity in itself; urban communities assume their character and functions depending upon their place in larger systems of economic and political organization rather than from a transhistorical, reified "townness."[13] This general criticism has left a deep mark on medieval scholarship. In economic terms, the reanimation of urban life after the year 1000 now seems more the product than the cause of Europe's broad advance in productive capacity, which was still overwhelmingly agricultural in nature. Long-distance trade, once considered the lifeblood of the urban revival, has now taken a back seat to the emergence of a market-oriented agriculture and local craft production.[14] In conjunction with a reevaluation of the economic functions of early towns, doubts have been raised about the distinctiveness of their communal cohesiveness and social structure. In a recent refurbishing of von Below's *Landgemeinde* theory, which found in medieval urban communes a projection of an older village solidarity, Reynolds argues that the character of medieval communes differed little from other forms of medieval lay collectivities.[15] By means of such criticism towns have therefore been stripped of the

economic and social impact of urban nobles in Italy, Georges Duby, *The early growth of the European economy*, trans. H.B. Clarke (London, 1974), 260–63; Giovanni Tabacco, *Egemonie sociali e strutture del potere nel medioevo italiano* (Turin, 1974), 226–36; Philip Jones, "Economia e società nell'Italia medievale: il mito della borghesia," *Economia e società nell'Italia medievale* (Turin, 1980), 51–61; M. Tangheroni, "Famiglie nobili e ceto dirigente a Pisa nel XIII secolo," in *I ceti dirigenti dell'età comunale nei secoli XII e XIII* (Pisa, 1982), II, 323–46; Gerhard Rösch, *Der venezianische Adel bis zur Schließung des Großen Rats* (Sigmaringen, 1989), 69–80.

[13] Philip Abrams, "Towns and economic growth: some theories and problems," in *Towns in societies: essays in economic history and historical sociology*, eds. P. Abrams and E.W. Wrigley (Cambridge, 1978), 9–33.

[14] Charles Verlinden, "Marchands ou tisserands? A propos des origines urbaines," *AESC*, 27 (1972), 396–406; Adriaan Verhulst, "The 'agricultural revolution' of the Middle Ages reconsidered," in *Law custom, and the social fabric in medieval Europe: essays in honor of Bryce Lyon*, eds. B.S. Bachrach and D. Nicholas (Kalamazoo, 1990), 23–24.

[15] Reynolds, *Kingdoms and communities*, 155–218. Cf. M. von Below, *Der Ursprung der deutschen Stadtverfassung* (Dusseldorf, 1892).

revolutionary merit badges of political equality, democratic representation, and lay communal solidarity that had once distinguished them within "feudal" Europe. Their "bourgeois" character has even been put in doubt.[16] In contrast to a model of social stratification that emphasizes horizontal classes marked off by levels of wealth, economic occupation, and shared, self-conscious political interests, vertical solidarities based on family, neighborhood, and religious corporations that encompass individuals of varied economic levels have for a generation received the greatest attention, especially in northern Italy.[17] The corporate solidarity which to Max Weber appeared to provide the essence of the Occidental city has been gradually evaporating; medieval towns have virtually taken on the appearance of uncomfortable, volatile agglomerations of villages.

In an act of "ethnic revenge," the shift of scholarly interest away from the North to Mediterranean societies has created new models that have challenged traditional assumptions about the Middle Ages worked out in England, Germany, and northern France.[18] Fundamental to the reevaluation of medieval urban life has been the stress on aristocratic clans in the formation of Italian cities. In a direct assault on the relevance of modern social categories to the study of precapitalist societies, Jacques Heers has denied the usefulness of class analysis for medieval urban communities and has tossed the medieval "merchant class" on the scrap heap of historiographical anachronisms.[19] Not associations of long-distance traders, he argues, but aristocratic clans provided the framework for Italian urban societies and politics. Strongly agnatic in character, cohesive groups of rural nobles entrenched themselves in urban soil as the cities began to revive in the tenth

[16] Jones, "Economia e società," 6–11.

[17] The same can be said for Renaissance cities, whose distance from their medieval predecessors is rapidly diminishing; for an historiographical overview of work on two of the most thoroughly studied Italian towns, see Gene Brucker, "Tales of two cities: Florence and Venice in the Renaissance," *American historical review*, 83 (1983), 599–616.

[18] Thomas N. Bisson, "Some characteristics of Mediterranean territorial power in the twelfth century," *Proceedings of the American Philosophical Society*, 123 (1975), 143 [repr. in *Medieval France and her Pyrenean neighbours: studies in early institutional history* (London and Ronceverte, WV, 1989), 257].

[19] Jacques Heers, *Le Clan familial au moyen âge: étude sur les structures politiques et sociales des milieux urbains* (Paris, 1974) [*Family clans in the Middle Ages: a study of political and social structure in urban areas*, trans. B. Herbert (Amsterdam, London, and New York, 1977)] and *Les Partis et la vie politique dans l'Occident médiéval* (Paris, 1981) [*Parties and political life in the medieval West*, trans. D. Nicholas (Amsterdam, London, and New York, 1977)].

and eleventh century, promoted family cooperation in economic and military affairs, and built defensive strongholds at the very center of ancient, partially deserted towns. Although not unique to Italy, defensive towers dominated the civic skyline south of the Alps: Florence possessed 135 towers in 1180, Pisa 60, and more than 100 are recorded in Bologna and Verona.[20] Some still serve as monuments to the enduring strength of aristocratic kinship in emerging civic societies. The factionalism for which Italian towns are famous therefore had its roots in feuds among competing noble families rather than in conflicts among commercial and craft groups with articulate economic and political interests. Based on his familiarity with the Italian urban scene, Heers has attempted to generalize his findings to towns throughout medieval Europe. Urban aristocracies, once thought a Mediterranean deviation from the "true" development of Western cities, have now been offered as a key to unlock the underlying family structures that provided the framework for all medieval towns. Especially in Southern Europe, urban life now seems dominated by tall towers, long knives, and short tempers.

Outside Italy, however, little work has been done on family structure to confirm or modify these conclusions. Particularly problematic for the present study is the assumed continuity between rural and urban family organization, in itself a critical element in the reevaluation of the relationships between town and country. In order to make medieval towns more at home in a predominantly agricultural society, a long proto- or preurban phase, sometimes plunged into the murky past of pre-Roman settlements, is posited to smooth the way for their integration into a regional context.[21] Recent historiography has done its best to rub away the once dazzling novelty of European towns.

Often lost, however, in the attempt to break down the dialectic between feudal and bourgeois categories are the structural adjustments required of families and factions within the nascent towns to come to terms with their new social environment. The most challenging criticism to the continuist model comes from a sociologist, Yves Barel.[22] Drawing upon theories of social reproduction

---

[20] See the summary in Fossier, *Enfance*, II, 93.

[21] Anne Lombard-Jordan, "Du problème de la continuité: y-a-t-il une protohistoire urbaine en France?" *AESC*, 25 (1970), 1121–42.

[22] Yves Barel, *La Ville médiévale: système social, système urbain* (Grenoble, 1977), esp. 69–119.

taken from contemporary urban studies, Barel avoids the pit-
falls of both traditional urban historiography, which views
towns as out of place in medieval Europe, and a recent, continuist approach, which denies them a clear identity. Auto-
reproduction provides the key to autonomy. Barel argues that
towns did not emerge in opposition to a seigniorial, agrarian
regime, but as its by-products. As defensive, administrative, and
ecclesiastical centers and places of aristocratic consumption,
early towns served the dominant system of authority and social
organization grounded in the countryside, here presented in
terms of a "feudal system." Even though the urban population
began to increase and its economic activities diversified, the
internal organization of the community depended ultimately on
external forces beyond its control; the basic structures of urban
life were therefore reproduced over time by the feudal system
rather than by the power of the burghers themselves. A distinct
urban system could only emerge when a patriciate coalesced as
its leading element and identified its interests with those of the
town as a whole in order to promote its commercial potential.
The basic structure of urban society matured and began to
reproduce itself over generations, rather than being recreated as
an unstable product of a feudal regime. Although Barel tends to
look upon fully developed urban societies in terms of systemic
abstractions, this approach nevertheless has considerable advantages in understanding the processes by which medieval towns
took shape. The "birth" of European towns has painted medievalists into a conceptual corner, for they have been forced to
offer abstract, ahistorical, and ultimately unsatisfactory definitions of what a town is in order to fill out its birth certificate
properly. The transition from "reproduction" to "auto-
reproduction" of an urban society provides for a much more
subtle transformation since it does not present town and
country as inherently opposed worlds yet at the same time
allows for the creation of a civic self-consciousness and for considerable variety in the forms of urban life. The following
chapters will argue that Barcelona did not consolidate its social
structure and assume its distinctive place in the medieval
Mediterranean during the first phase of urban growth but only
later, when a patriciate emerged to lead the town in new
directions and to give the city the basic character it would
retain throughout the *ancien régime*.

Introduction

Even though the towns of the Crown of Aragon have not received the same degree of scholarly attention as the Italian city–republics, Barcelona has certainly not lacked its historians. Because of its centrality to Catalan identity, few medieval cities have received such partisan and impassioned treatments of their pasts as Barcelona.

While the erudite sixteenth- and seventeenth-century works on Catalan history by Zurita, Pujades, and Bosch showed a passing interest in the city, the groundwork for the modern study of Barcelona was laid in 1779–92 with the publication of *Memorias históricas sobre la marina, comercio y artes de la antigua ciudad de Barcelona* by Antonio de Capmany y de Monpalau.[23] Capmany turned to the medieval past of his native city in order to stimulate interest in Spanish commercial and industrial development. His explorations of Barcelona's royal and municipal archives produced a magnificent collection of commercial documents, principally from the fourteenth and fifteenth century, accompanied by an insightful discussion of the expansion of the city's medieval trade; carefully reedited and annotated, Capmany's work remains the vade mecum for explorers into the city's past and has oriented subsequent research toward commerce.

Unfortunately, the early impetus to medieval urban studies provided by Capmany did not carry over into the nineteenth century. Little of note appeared either in terms of specialized monographs or the publication of local sources until around the turn of the twentieth century. The nineteenth-century revival of Catalan literature and culture, the *Renaixença*, eventually spilled over into other fields as well, but the early history of the Catalan capital was approached obliquely. The philologist José Balari Jovany probed the early charters of Catalonia for evidence of naming patterns, family ties, and local customs, which bore indirectly on urban life.[24] With the publication of *Les monedes catalanes* by the numismatist Joaquím Botet y Sisó, a solid basis was laid for an investigation into the medieval economy,[25] but the exploration into the

---

23 Antonio de Capmany y de Monpalau, *Memorias históricas sobre la marina, comercio y artes de la antigua ciudad de Barcelona*, 2nd ed., revised and introduced by E. Giralt i Raventós and C. Batlle i Gallart, 3 vols. (Barcelona, 1961–63).

24 José Balari Jovany, *Orígenes históricos de Cataluña*, 2 vols. (2nd ed., San Cugat del Vallés, 1964) [original edition 1899].

25 Joaquím Botet y Sisó, *Les monedes catalanes: estudi y descripció de les monedes carolingies, comtals, senyorials, reyals y locals propries de Catalunya*, 3 vols. (Barcelona, 1908–11).

formation of the city itself began in earnest with Francesc Carreras Candi, a geographer. Of the six volumes comprising the *Geografia general de Catalunya*, a compendium of Catalan civilization published under his direction, his study, appearing in 1916, was devoted to Barcelona and its hinterland.[26] Still the most synthetic treatment of the city in the premodern period, it was cast in the mold of *urbanismo*, an evocation of the city's past through its building history. His approach led to a proliferation of studies on urban monuments and antiquities, but, with little connection to the more general historiographical debates beyond the Pyrenees, this framework for investigation had only a provincial appeal.

Only in the mid-twentieth century did two scholars, José María Font Rius and Jaume Vicens Vives, break away from a restrictive local perspective to reorient the study of Catalonian towns toward larger themes. With the publication of his doctoral dissertation, *Orígenes del régimen municipal de Cataluña*, in 1940, Font Rius, a legal historian, amply filled a glaring gap in local historiography: the emergence of Catalonian municipal constitutions.[27] Grounded in a solid understanding of the debates about urban origins that shaped German and French historiography in the nineteenth and early twentieth century, his investigations rapidly made up for the methodological insufficiencies of earlier scholarship on Barcelona. As Font Rius was establishing the foundations of municipal institutional history, Jaume Vicens Vives turned the attention of an entire generation of Spanish historians toward economic and social questions in the late Middle Ages. In an early work, he examined the relations between Barcelona and Ferdinand the Catholic in order to determine the impact of the Catalan Civil War (1462–65) on the city;[28] increasingly drawn into the orbit of the French *annalistes*, he put forward a series of bold and controversial hypotheses that inspired historians to look carefully at the economic and social difficulties facing the city in the fifteenth century in an effort to explain and determine the chronology of Catalan decline. With the works of Claude Carrère, Mario del Treppo, and Carme Batlle i Gallart, the city's commercial contraction and political instability have emerged in a new light,

---

[26] Francesc Carreras Candi, *Geografia general de Catalunya. La ciutat de Barcelona* (Barcelona, nd [1916]).

[27] José María Font Rius, *Orígenes del régimen municipal de Cataluña* (Madrid, 1940) [repr. in *Estudis sobre els drets i institucions locals en la Catalunya medieval* (Barcelona, 1985), 281–560 (subsequent references will be to the latter)].

[28] Jaume Vicens Vives, *Ferran II i la ciutat de Barcelona*, 3 vols. (Barcelona, 1936).

making the fifteenth century the most thoroughly investigated period in the city's medieval past.[29] In addition to the problem of Catalan decline in the late Middle Ages, a theme haunting local historiography during the waning decades of Franco's Spain, the nature of the city's early growth has recently attracted considerable attention. In his meticulous investigations culminating in a magisterial *thèse d'Etat*, Pierre Bonnassie touched upon early urban growth in a sweeping study of Catalonia from the mid-tenth through the eleventh century and devoted an earlier article to the subject.[30] In several short studies José Enrique Ruiz Doménec also examined the city's eleventh-century economic growth and arrived at conclusions similar to those of Bonnassie.[31] Stressing an increase in agricultural production, the planting of market crops, and a dynamic local land market, both scholars look for the seeds of urban growth in the countryside and present an urban economy that by 1100 had already undergone the basic transformation that would produce its subsequent commercial blossoming.

Thus, early growth in the eleventh century and the time of troubles in the fifteenth have provided the two major themes dominating the historiography of medieval Barcelona. Because the city emerged so late on the Mediterranean stage and suffered decline and stagnation on the eve of Spain's golden age, some suspect that the city and its patriciate failed to fulfil their potential: André Sayous and, more recently, Geo Pistarino have emphasized Barcelona's "historical retardation"; Ruiz Doménec has expressed doubts that it achieved a coherent "urban system"; and in evaluating the city's late medieval economy Robert S. Lopez asserted that the "Catalan coast was like the gilt façade of a building of mud and

---

[29] Claude Carrère, *Barcelone: centre économique à l'époque des difficultés 1380–1462*, 2 vols. (Paris, 1967); Mario del Treppo, *I mercanti catalani e l'espansione della Corona d'Aragon nel secolo XV* (Naples, 1972) [*Els mercaders catalans i l'expansió de la Corona catalano–aragonesa al segle XV*, trans. J. Riera Sans (Barcelona, 1976)]; Carme Batlle i Gallart, *La crisis social y económica de Barcelona a mediados del siglo XV*, 2 vols. (Barcelona, 1973).

[30] Pierre Bonnassie, *La Catalogne du milieu du Xe à la fin du XIe siècle: croissance et mutations d'une société*, 2 vols. (Toulouse, 1975–76); "Une famille de la campagne barcelonnaise et ses activités économiques aux alentours de l'an mil," *AM*, 75 (1964), 261–307 ["A family of the Barcelona countryside and its economic activities around the year 1000," in *Early medieval society*, ed. and trans. S. Thrupp (New York, 1967), 103–25].

[31] The most important of which are José E. Ruiz Doménec, "El origen del capital comercial en Barcelona," *Miscellanea barcinonensia*, 31 (1972), 55–88 and "The urban origins of Barcelona: agricultural revolution or commercial development?" *Speculum*, 52 (1977), 265–86.

straw."[32] Because these judgments largely rest on comparison with the Italian city–republics, they tend to dismiss the distinctive relationship between Barcelona and the Crown of Aragon as an aberrant deviation from urban independence and patrician self-confidence.

Only scattered work has been done on Barcelona's social and economic structure from the twelfth to the fourteenth century in order to test the proposition that the patriciate suffered a collective failure of will.[33] Social history in particular is in need of further exploration. As recently as 1977 Robert I. Burns pointed out that the extensive royal registers of the Crown of Aragon remained an untapped resource for the study of small-group dynamics, collective biographies, and naming patterns.[34] Some patches in the forest have been cleared since then, but little has been done to chart the overall evolution of the city and analyze its social and family structure during these formative centuries. The present work will attempt to fill part of the gap. It begins during the reign of Count Ramon Berenguer III (1096–1131), under whom Catalonia began to emerge from its provincial isolation, and ends with that of King Alfons II (1285–91), who consolidated the gains brought by the incorporation of Sicily into the Crown of Aragon and secured its defense against Angevin opposition. During the two centuries that separate these two sovereigns a patriciate emerged to structure and direct the course of Barcelona's history.

THE SOURCES

"In a large chest I have found two bolts of linen cloth, one helmet, one silk tunic, one green vest of silk, one dagger, one silk jacket,

---

[32] André Sayous, *Els mètodes comercials a la Catalunya medieval*, trans. and intr. A. Garcia i Sanz and G. Feliu i Montfort (Barcelona, 1975), 85–86; Geo Pistarino, "Genova e Barcelona: incontro e scontro di due civiltà," *Atti di 1.° congresso storico Liguria–Catalogna* (Bordighera, 1974), 106–7; José E. Ruiz Doménec, "La ciudad de Barcelona durante la Edad Media: de los orígenes a la formación de un sistema urbano," *Quaderns d'arqueologia i història de la ciutat*, 18 (1980), 95; *Cambridge economic history*, II, 395.

[33] Josefa Mutgé Vives, *La ciudad de Barcelona durante el reinado de Alfonso el Benigno (1327–1336)* (Barcelona, 1987); Teresa-Maria Vinyoles i Vidal, *La vida quotidiana a Barcelona vers 1400* (Barcelona, 1985); Carme Batlle i Gallart, "La burguesía de Barcelona a mediados del siglo XIII," *X CHCA* (Zaragoza, 1980–82), II, 7–19.

[34] Robert I. Burns, "The realms of Aragon: new directions in medieval history," *The Midwest quarterly*, 18 (1977), 235 [repr. in *Moors and crusaders in Mediterranean Spain* (London, 1978)].

one leather belt, six ledgers, and six bags of charters."[35] This extract from the postmortem inventory of Burget de Banyeres, a wealthy cloth merchant, in 1256 vividly conveys the type of sources upon which this study rests and their state of organization. To recreate the formation of Barcelona's patriciate, one must in essence rummage through family chests, tossing aside the cluttered debris of the past in order to retrieve the sacks haphazardly stuffed with parchments. The chests, of course, have long since disappeared, but the precious bundles of documents they contained (somewhat pretentiously referred to as family archives today) have often found their way piecemeal or by the sack-full into local Barcelona archives. The charters present a rather disorderly assembly of information, expressed in curt, abbreviated Latin penned onto sheep skins of various dimensions and shapes. The ledgers (*capudbrevia*) contained accounts of business transactions; by the mid-thirteenth century they were certainly written on paper and intended for private use. Unfortunately, they have not survived, but the stiff pieces of parchment remain in impressive numbers. Through pious donations or land sales, an individual transferred not only the possession of property but all documents ensuring title, such as previous sales or donations, wills, dowries, pledges, records of dispute, or even business contracts; they survive in large part because they provided authentication in a world long accustomed to the manipulation of written acts and duly respectful of scribal formulas. Barcelona's archives contain one of the most extensive parchment collections relating to early urban development in Europe.

In contrast, private notarial registers begin to appear only at the end of the thirteenth century. The first fragments from the register of a Barcelona notary date from 1292, and the collection, still only partially explored by scholars, does not attain substantial proportions until the fourteenth century. More concentrated, systematic, and diverse than the random survival of individual parchments, notarial registers have proved the staple source of medieval urban history. Besides Genoa's six notarial registers, however, none survive in Mediterranean towns before 1200. The unusual richness of Barcelona's parchment collections therefore partially compensates for a documentary gap unbridgeable in

[35] Carme Batlle i Gallart, "La família i la casa d'un draper de Barcelona, Burget de Banyeres (primera meitat del segle XIII)," *Acta mediaevalia*, 2 (1981), 90, ap. 2.

many towns; when brought together, the extant charters provide a rare glimpse into the early formation of an urban society. Beginning in a steady stream from 985, the date the city was put to the torch by an Islamic army and its early documentation destroyed, the source material swells to a raging torrent by the late thirteenth century, overwhelming even the most intrepid researcher. Although the large number of surviving parchments can not completely compensate for the loss of thirteenth-century registers, by their antiquity, continuity, and diversity one has the unusual opportunity of probing into the distant urban past.

For the period covered by the present study, the Arxiu Capitular de la Catedral de Barcelona and the Arxiu de la Corona d'Aragó offer the most abundant materials. The massive four-volume cartulary known as the *Libri antiquitatum* provides the solid core of the cathedral's collection: it alone has preserved copies of over 2,700 documents, all but a few dating from 985 to 1220.[36] The medieval canons, however, took care to preserve a far larger number of parchments related to their properties and rights. The massive documentation of the cathedral and its poor organization discouraged early researchers from exploiting it effectively; the heroic work of reorganization undertaken by Àngel Fàbrega i Grau and Josep Baucells i Reig, still proceeding today, together with the completion of a new building, opened in 1969, to house the materials, has made many treasures of the Mediterranean past accessible for the first time.[37] The archives of Barcelona's cathedral still hold many secrets. To this point research has focused on the cartulary and the rich *Diversorum* series, both made easier to manipulate through the notes of Josep Mas, the archivist during the early twentieth century. As its name implies, the *Diversorum* series contains a potpourri of parchments, particularly the largest and most interesting division, section C; the canons who originally organized the material must have considered it a waiting-to-be-filed tray, for it contains many charters with little direct connection to the properties held by the church. Although marginal to the canons, modern investigators have found its records extremely valuable since it contains documentation relating to

---

[36] Brief summaries of the entries can be found in Mas, IX–XII.

[37] For a brief history of the archive and the organization of its holdings, Josep Baucells i Reig, *El Baix Llobregat i la Pia Almoina de la Seu de Barcelona: inventari dels pergamins* (Barcelona, 1984), 6–28 and *Guia dels arxius eclesiàstics de Catalunya-València-Balears* (Barcelona, 1968).

trade, credit, and administration. Other series more central to the interests of the medieval church, however, have received little attention. The uncatalogued subseries entitled Morabetins of the Pia Almoina, for instance, has been largely ignored even though the thousands of parchments it encompasses refer to the canons' urban property; in essence it is the continuation of the cathedral cartulary for the city. Other substantial and underutilized collections are housed in local religious houses, especially the Arxiu Diocesà de Barcelona, Sant Pere de les Puel·les, Santa Maria del Pi, and Santa Maria del Mar, whose collection was badly damaged during the Spanish Civil War.

In addition to local ecclesiastical archives, the Arxiu de la Corona d'Aragó provides considerable additional material and presents Barcelona from the perspective of the early counts of Barcelona, later the count-kings of Aragon. The counts had long housed many of their records in the Palau Comtal, adjacent to the present location of the archives in the viceregnal palace. The chancery series contains early records of administration, castleholding, finance, and diplomacy touching all parts of Catalonia and Aragon and, as the dynasty expanded, the realms of Aragon, Valencia, Majorca, Sicily, and Sardinia. Although charters relevant to the history of Barcelona represent only a fraction of the records, when sifted and carefully collected they nevertheless make up a considerable cache for urban history. For any study of the Crown of Aragon after 1257, the impressive series of royal registers begun that year, the earliest of its kind in Europe, provides a wealth of detail not always available in parchments.[38] Virtually all evidence, for instance, of urban violence derives from investigations and fines recorded in the registers, which show the wheels of royal justice turning. Although some of the more important pieces dealing with Barcelona from the royal registers have been known and a handful published, no systematic investigation has yet been undertaken to evaluate what the thousands of entries directed toward the magistrates, officials, and citizens of Barcelona reveal about royal influence in the city.

An abundance of private charters and administrative documents

---

[38] A splendid introduction to the registers is now available in the initial volume to the edition of the Valencian documentation under Jaume I, Robert I. Burns, *Diplomatarium of the Crusader Kingdom of Valencia. The registered charters of its conqueror Jaume I, 1257–1276*, I. *Introduction. Society and documentation in Crusader Valencia* (Princeton, 1985), 48–58. For a general introduction to the holdings of the ACA, see Jesús M. Martínez Ferrando, *El Archivo de la Corona de Aragón* (Barcelona, 1944).

exist to trace the activities of well-to-do Barcelonans, but there is a dearth of narrative sources revealing how they perceived their world. While many towns beyond the Pyrenees can boast of extensive medieval urban chronicles, Barcelona possesses none exclusively devoted to its civic past. Through the twelfth century narrative records in Catalonia, and southern Frankland generally, remained closely tied to stiff, dry forms of institutional and dynastic commemoration; strong respect for legal tradition and wide-spread familiarity with the use of prosaic written records may well have worked against the creation of celebratory civic chronicles.[39] Chivalric, heroic, and courtly themes from the *chansons de gestes* and the *planys* of the troubadours transformed Catalan historical writing in the thirteenth century. With its four *grans cròniques* by King Jaume the Conqueror, Desclot, Muntaner, and King Pere the Ceremonious, each a masterpiece of vernacular historical narrative, medieval Catalonia hardly lacks for rich chronicles, but their authors boast of military adventures and display aristocratic tastes.[40] The world of shipbuilders, entrepreneurs, and merchants hardly receives even passing notice; the leading figures of the Catalan towns appear only in relation to the place they fill in a society of orders presided over by the monarchy. Barcelona provides a backdrop for splendid royal courts in the great Catalan chronicles, not a stage for presenting the struggles of patrician houses. Civic pride was largely absorbed by dynastic history.

Complementing the rather brief view of towns presented from the aristocratic perspective of the chronicles, the charter evidence provides an abundance of information about the day-to-day activities of townspeople. Individually dry, stiffly formulaic, and

[39] Thomas N. Bisson, "Unheroed pasts: history and commemoration in south Frankland before the Albigensian crusades," *Speculum*, 65 (1990), 307–8; Bernard Guenée, *Histoire et culture historique dans l'Occident médiéval* (Paris, 1980), 311.

[40] The chronicles are most easily accessible in the collective volume *Les quatre grans cròniques*, ed. F. Soldevila (Barcelona, 1971). On their literary orientation, Martí de Riquer, *Història de la literatura catalana* (Barcelona, 1964–72), I, 373–501. For King Jaume's autobiography, see the evaluation of Robert I. Burns, "The spiritual life of James the Conqueror, King of Arago-Catalonia, 1208–1276: portrait and self-portrait," *The Catholic historical review*, 62 (1976), 1–35 [repr. in *Moors and crusaders*]. The presentation of the urban population in these aristocratic works is considered by Joan Pau Rubiés and Josep M. Salrach, "Entorn de la mentalitat i la ideologia del bloc de poder feudal a través de la historiografia medieval fins a les *Quatre grans cròniques*," in *La formació i expansió del feudalisme català. Actes del col·loqui organitzat pel Col·legi Universitari de Girona (8–11 de gener de 1985)* [*Estudi General. Revista del Col·legi Universitari de Girona*, 5–6] (Girona, 1986), 502–4.

coldly impersonal, when examined in large quantities early urban charters nevertheless can be forced to reveal their intricate and often abstract patterns, the shifting relationships among individuals and groups, and the movement of economic trends that, taken together, chart the evolution of prominent families and the entire urban community. Although scholars have delved into portions of the available sources before, there has to date been little attempt to treat the available documentation for the twelfth and thirteenth century as a whole. Except for the investigations of Philip Banks into urban topography, most studies on the city's history during its early period of growth have relied upon one archival collection, or even a single series within an archive.[41] Because data lie scattered in dispersed collections, only by carefully gathering all available bits of information, many left by medieval scribes in the documents they drafted for purposes quite different from those which interest us today, and by relating them to one another does a broader perspective emerge. While the following chapters will devote considerable attention to urban notables and the emergence, organization, and cohesiveness of patrician houses, the goal of the study is not the history of individual families but an analysis of family structure within the context of a young, expansive urban environment.

Owing to the remarkable richness of Barcelona's archives and the consistency of its scribal traditions, the overall movement of social and economic forces can best be captured through a serial analysis. The use of quantitative methods in a prestatistical age poses delicate problems of interpretation, but David Herlihy, Robert Fossier, Pierre Toubert, and Pierre Bonnassie have marked off a path through what once seemed an inhospitable, barren landscape of charter collections.[42] While most serial analysis has concentrated on regional agricultural societies from the eleventh to the thirteenth century, the rich source material avail-

---

[41] Philip Banks, "The topography of Barcelona and its urban context in eastern Catalonia from the third to the twelfth centuries," 5 vols. Unpublished Ph.D. thesis, University of Nottingham, 1980. Banks includes a valuable summary of 967 documents relating to urban topography from 919 to 1200.

[42] David Herlihy, "Church property on the European continent, 701–1200," *Speculum*, 36 (1961), 81–105 and "Land, family and women in Continental Europe, 701–1200," *Traditio*, 18 (1962), 89–120 [both repr. in *The social history of Italy and Western Europe, 700–1500* (London, 1978)]; Robert Fossier, *La Terre et les hommes en Picardie jusqu'à la fin du XIIIᵉ siècle*, 2 vols. (Paris, 1968); Pierre Toubert, *Les Structures du Latium médiéval: le Latium méridional et la Sabine du IXᵉ siècle à la fin du XIIᵉ siècle*, 2 vols. (Rome, 1973); Bonnassie, *La Catalogne*, II, 881–984.

able for Barcelona offers a rare opportunity to apply these techniques to an early urban environment. Only by understanding the long-term trends of the economy, institutional development, and evolving structure of family organization do the individual choices made by patrician houses reveal their full meaning.

Chapter 1

THE CITY AND ITS REGION

By the time Cervantes visited Barcelona in the early seventeenth century and placed words of praise for that "archive of courtesy" in the mouth of Don Quixote, who extolled its citizens for their refined manners, gallantry, and generosity, the city had already long dominated the province of Catalonia and enjoyed an enviable international reputation.[1] The solid hub of regional communication, production, and culture, Barcelona was already known in a homespun phrase as the *cap i casal de Catalunya*, the head and hearth of Catalonia, or, to use the architecturally dignified metaphor of King Joan I, the *caput et columna totius Cataloniae*, the capital and pillar of all Catalonia.[2] History has made Barcelona the heart of Catalan identity. By the later Middle Ages its place was already secure. Geographically, the city lay squarely in the middle of the Catalan coast; politically, it served as the seat of the provincial parliament, the *Generalitat de Catalunya*; culturally, it provided a causeway for Mediterranean and European learning and tastes to enter Iberia. At once confidently international and proudly regional, its prosperous citizens took their place among the leading circles of Catalonian society. Because Barcelona has exercised such a decisive role in the formation of Catalonia, its rise often seems inevitable, a natural expression of regional and cultural self-awareness, an event in need only of description and admiration, not explanation.

If, however, we can manage to close our eyes to the approach of the third millennium and retrace our steps, blindly stumbling backward a thousand years before opening them again, the future preeminence of Barcelona would have been hard to predict. In the year 1000 the city was not situated at the center of a coherent regional culture; rather, it stood as an isolated, threatened outpost at the furthest edge of Frankish influence, anchoring the southern

---

[1] Miguel Cervantes, *El ingenioso hidalgo Don Quijote de la Mancha* (Madrid, 1976), II, 72.
[2] Carreras Candi, *La ciutat*, 330.

23

flank of Latin Christendom against Islam. Its tight, stout walls still afforded the tiny population huddled within them a degree of protection, but, in spite of its formidable stone ramparts, the Roman past did not leave the city with a tradition of local leadership. Under the Caesars Barcelona was a minor *colonia*, a second- or third-rate administrative outpost, subject to the sophisticated and domineering provincial capital, Tarragona. Barcino, as the Romans called it, had no special status or function to set it apart from a group of other small settlements; indeed, Empúries, Lleida, and Tortosa were larger than Barcelona, and all seemed to possess greater potential for expansion. But the sudden collapse of the sub-Roman Visigothic kingdom under the lightening attacks of Berber and Arab warriors in the early eighth century completely reshaped the Iberian urban grid traced out by the Latins. As the second millennium approached, a formidable and unbending opponent, separated by religion, language, and blatant hostility, lay just beyond the ancient ramparts of Barcino.

The very survival of Christian Barcelona had recently been cast in doubt. A sector of the walls, probably to the southeast near the *turris ventosa*, the "breezy tower," would have shown hasty repairs, patching up the breach in the stout Roman stonework opened by an invading Islamic army in 985. Stone buildings within the walls still bore the scorch marks from the fires set by the marauding Saracens; the scattered, ramshackle houses and sheds below the walls lay in ruins. Many local Christians who had sought shelter inside the seeming safety of the city's walls were still serving their victorious Muslim masters in al-Andalus, praying for relatives to arrange ransom in order to deliver them from captivity. With the assurance of hindsight, it is easy enough to dismiss the physical damage to the city as of minor consequence, for Barcelona quickly recovered from its wounds and exhibited a restless, new vitality in the decades after 1000. Yet the psychological trauma endured for generations. Not only did it recall the continuing instability caused by the menacing proximity of Islam, but the sack of the city also produced a sharp rupture with the traditional security provided by the Frankish protectorate. According to the bitter recollections of later chroniclers and scribes, the appeal of the count of Barcelona to the king of the Franks for aid in defending the city against the Moor went unheeded. After the disaster, urban residents and those whom its defenses shielded realized they would have to dig in and fend for themselves.[3] The very survival of the city in the face of a traumatic Islamic triumph created a new, cathartic foundation myth, liberating the city at once from both the polluting hands of the infidel and the impotent guard of the Franks. The identification of urban resistance with a self-conscious, regional independence came about through the violent confrontations in an early medieval frontier society, not the lingering traditions from the Roman past. In all essentials Barcelona is a product of the Middle Ages.

A CONSTRICTIVE HINTERLAND

The site of Barcelona stands center stage in a compact geological amphitheater.[4] To the north, the low, rugged, scrub-covered hills called the Collserola running parallel to the coast marks off the urban hinterland from the interior. Two formidable natural obstacles flank the city on either side: to the northeast, an extension of the coastal range, which presses toward the sea and leaves below it a narrow plain above the beach known as the Maresme; to the southwest the Garraf, a massive limestone block broken by numerous fractures and small streams. The small, fertile coastal plain gently sloping toward the sea lies nestled among enveloping hills, which shield it from the harsh Pyrenean winds and chilling fogs of the interior. Barcelona and its adjacent plain therefore form a privileged, compact opening in the rugged Mediterranean coast but they do not provide a natural link for inland communication, which passes through the Vallès, a narrow valley above the Collserola, and along a broad prelittoral depression spreading out below the Pyrenees from the Perthus Gap in Rosselló to the Ebro Valley. This artery provided the invasion route for the waves of conquering armies that passed from southern Gaul to eastern Iberia, whether Carthaginian, Roman, Visigothic, Arab, or Frankish. Even as Barcelona was assuming its place as the administrative focus of the Catalan counties, Count Ramon Berenguer IV in the mid-twelfth century relied upon Sant Pere de Vilamajor and Caldes de Montbui in the Vallès for his supply and

---

[3] Michel Zimmerman, "La Prise de Barcelone par Al-Mansûr et la naissance de l'historiographie catalane," *Annales de Bretagne et des pays de l'Ouest*, 87 (1980), 191–218.

[4] For a brilliant evocation of the human geography of Catalonia, see Pierre Vilar, *La Catalogne dans l'Espagne moderne* (Paris, 1962), I, ch. 2, esp. 251–58. Also useful are the sections by Pau Vila, *Geografia de Catalunya*, III. *La ciutat de Barcelona* (Barcelona, 1974), ch. 15; and, although dated, Carreras Candi, *La ciutat*, 21–32.

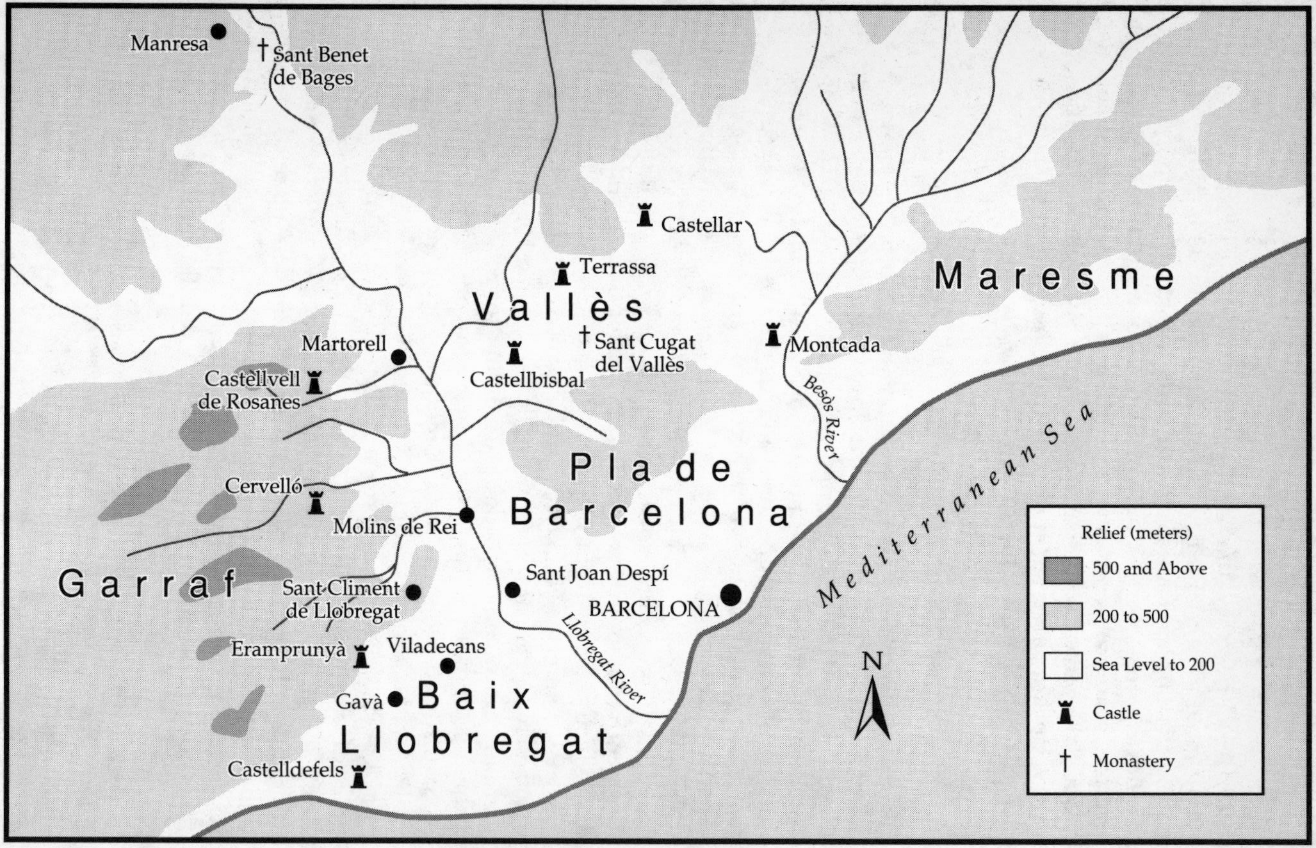

Map 1   Barcelona and its region

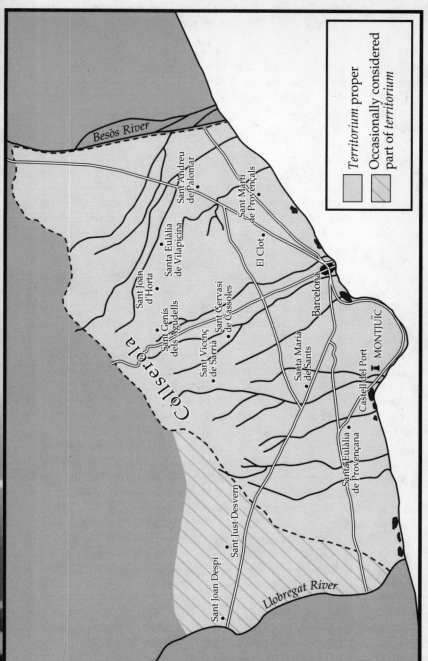

Map 2   *Territorium* of Barcelona

communication centers, not his largest city just to the south.[5] The protection offered by a mantle of low mountains at the same time made the city peripheral to the main line of inland communications.

Barcelona was not, however, isolated from the interior, for two rivers pierce the Collserola range. To the northeast, the Besòs carves out a steep gorge at Montcada to reach the coastal plain; to the southwest, the Llobregat passes through the prelittoral chain below Martorell as it makes its way to the sea. With their sources in the lower reaches of the Pyrenees, the banks of both rivers allow access to the interior, but neither is easily navigable upstream. Through the natural gateways opened by the Besòs and Llobregat the ancient Roman highway entered and exited the coastal plain; this route formed the axis of land communication until dynamite, steel rails, and asphalt roadways opened the coastal route. The difficulty and expense of overland transport did not, however, facilitate a creeping encroachment of the town over inland farmland. Thirteenth-century tenurial contracts from the Vallès did occasionally demand that a peasant cart his produce all the way to the city, but such a stipulation indicated an unusually onerous charge.[6]

The sea, the Collserola range, the Besòs, and the Llobregat provide the rough natural boundaries for Barcelona's compact hinterland, today called the Pla de Barcelona but known as the *territorium* during the Middle Ages. The origins of the term *territorium*, as well as its precise boundaries, are unclear.[7] Although not formally part of classical Roman administrative vocabulary, *territorium* probably derives from an administrative unit centered on the *colonia* Barcino. During the ninth and tenth century it appears to be used interchangeably with *pagus*, an archaizing word, or *comitatus*, all of which could refer to the entire county, an area considerably larger than the Pla de Barcelona proper. After 1000 the use of the term *territorium* stabilized to indicate the confined plain surrounding the city. Its dimensions, however, were not completely clear, for it did not follow the course of the Llobregat to the point at which it entered the coastal plain but turned eastward, toward a location known as Codines or

---

[5] Bisson, *Fiscal accounts*, 1, 30–31.   [6] ACB 1–2–1079; 1–6–1731, 3018; ASPP, 339.

[7] For the sketchy early history of the area, see Philip Banks, "The Roman inheritance and topographical transitions in early medieval Barcelona," in *Papers in Iberian archaeology*, eds. T. F. C. Blagg, R. F. J. Jones and S. J. Keay (Oxford, 1984), 602–12; Marina Mitjá Sagué, "Condado y ciudad de Barcelona: capítulos de su historia en los siglos IX y X," *EHDAP*, 3 (1955), 267–81; Carreras Candi, *La ciutat*, 285–328.

Inforcats, although scribes occasionally included the villages of Sant Just Desvern and Sant Joan Despí to the west in the *territorium*. A considerable portion of the Llobregat delta, the Baix Llobregat, therefore did not form part of the *territorium*, nor did the strip of land just across the Besòs. These were mostly marshy, low-lying areas, less attractive to the urban population than the land between the rivers. Parts of the Baix Llobregat, choked with reeds, were given over to grazing; from their bailiff of Sant Boi de Llobregat the nuns of Sant Pere de les Puel·les in the city could expect cheeses and ninety sheep annually.[8] As Barcelona rapidly expanded in the thirteenth century its citizens found obtaining and developing properties in the Baix Llobregat and even in the Maresme attractive, but earlier these areas were of minor interest in comparison to the valuable, carefully tilled land between the Llobregat and the Besòs. The compact *territorium*, only 4 miles wide and 8 miles long, formed Barcelona's true hinterland.

Within these narrow limits, the Pla de Barcelona encompasses two zones distinguished by the type of water supply. At the foot of the Collserola easily controlled *rieres*, seasonal streams and gullies, provided irrigation for the vineyards, orchards, gardens, and fields at the elevated rim of the coastal plain. A series of prosperous villages ringed its edge and supplied the city with produce: Sants, Sarrià, Sant Gervasi, and Horta. This higher table became known simply as the city's "garden and vineyard," the *ort i vinyet de Barcelona*.[9] Toward the shore, however, lower elevations produce poor drainage for the *rieres*, which can form stagnant pools, especially on either side of Montjuïc, the "Jew's Mountain," an anticlinal granite protrusion just to the west of the walls. Les Rambles, today the city's pedestrian thoroughfare, was still a seasonal gully in the thirteenth century, terminating in a stagnant pool below Montjuïc. Because of poor drainage and the attendant malaria, the western suburbs developed slowly and have remained the poorer quarter of the old town to this day.

Because of the irregularity of the water supply from the *rieres*, medieval urban development depended upon harnessing the waters of the Besòs and Llobregat for irrigation and milling. In order to supply the city with water, the Romans had constructed

---

[8] ASPP, 123.
[9] In the thirteenth century scribes refer to the *ortum* and *vinetum* independently but not yet in conjunction, e.g. ACA perg. varis, Marquès de Monistrol, 198; ADB perg. Santa Anna, Carp. 2a, 277.

two stone aqueducts, one leading north toward Tibidabo, the highest point of the Collserola range, and the other to the Besòs. Owing to the decline of the urban population and lack of maintenance, both aqueducts had collapsed during the early Middle Ages. Once urban life revived after the year 1000, however, a new channel, the Rec Comtal, was dug by the 1040s along the line of the old aqueduct from the Besòs toward the city, but before it reached the eastern suburbs it turned sharply toward the sea. Along its course water mills were soon grinding the city's grain and irrigation canals were supplying water to the plots below it; the area on its lower course quickly became known by the name *orta maris*, the Sea Garden. By the late twelfth century the needs of a growing population for irrigation and water power encouraged the count to undertake the construction of a similar channel from the Llobregat to the western limits of the city, but the slope of Montjuïc caused the project to be abandoned.[10] As a result, the Rec Comtal would provide the city's main power source throughout its medieval history.

Nature provided Barcelona with a compact, insulated, and potentially lush agriculture cradle for its economic infancy, but its meager dimensions could not easily accommodate continued growth. The laborious but futile effort to extend the water and power supply from the Llobregat suggests that the city was already feeling the constrictive pinch of the limited resources in its hinterland. The Rec had difficulty meeting the demands placed on it for the capacity of the Besòs, its source, can fluctuate by as much as 95 percent between wet and dry months. By 1200 its flow turned water wheels in four clusters of mills (*casale molindinorum*) in the suburbs, containing twelve grain mills in all, but this did not suffice for the ballooning thirteenth-century population. By 1267 the number of Clot mills just beyond the suburbs had grown from four to six, and the king authorized the construction of other new mills downstream.[11] The more mill wheels impeding the flow of the Rec, the slower their speed. The immediate consequence of the spate of thirteenth-century mill construction was not necessarily an increase of water power but a rash of lawsuits complain-

---

[10] On the dating of the Rec Comtal, see the revision by Banks, "Roman inheritance," 612–13. The abandoned channel from the Llobregat appears in ACA perg. Alfons I, 502; Gran Priorat, armari 1, 66.

[11] ACA Reial Patrimoni, Batllia General, Classe 3ª, vol. 6, fols. 16 v.–17 r., 54 r.–v.; Reg. 9, fols. 13 v.–14 r.; Reg. 10, fol. 60 r.; ACB 1–1–1095, 1493; 1–6–175.

ing that the proliferation of mills reduced the Rec's flow. The limitations on hydraulic power had reached such a point that one enterprising burgher sought a royal license to construct a mill driven by water hoisted from a well with a mule-driven wheel.[12] Whatever the outcome of this project, the demands of the city were quickly outstripping the ability of the urban hinterland to supply those needs.

The mantle of low mountains that surround the city's narrow coastal plain offered protection and secure resources for the fledgling urban society emerging from its early medieval cocoon by 1000, but by the thirteenth century it also discouraged the expansive, profit-driven city from extending its influence and jurisdiction further into the interior. Constricted within its narrow coastal plain, medieval Barcelona would have to look toward the sea for new resources. Yet even if nature did not offer clear advantages in location over those of its competitors, the convergence of a rich, compact plain, communication with the interior, and access to the sea allowed Barcelona to assume a central role in medieval Catalonia.

THE EXTENSION OF URBAN SPACE

The urban area itself consisted of two clearly distinguished zones: the *civitas* or *urbs*, the area enclosed by the Roman walls, and the *suburbium* or *burgus*, the settled region spreading out below the walls. Even as new buildings pressed against and gradually swallowed up the ancient Roman ramparts, scribes continued to mark off the city from the suburbs consistently, even though inhabitants of both areas possessed the same rights and obligations and called themselves *cives et habitatores*, citizens and residents, no matter in which zone they lived. The difference between the two was historical rather than administrative or legal. That the memory of the ancient city still mattered more than eight centuries after the empire had disintegrated reveals the deep imprint the Romans left on the medieval town; the ancient line of defenses and the original grid street plan are still readily identifiable on the metropolitan map.

---

[12] On the seasonal capacity of the Besòs, see Vilar, *La Catalogne*, 1, 310. Disputes about the impeded water flow on the Rec begin in the 1250s: ACB 1–1–2541; ASPP, 358; ACA perg. Jaume I, 1259, 2145; Reg. 15, fol. 52 r. ACA Reg. 12, fol. 44 r.–v.: "quod molat de aqua putei cum bestia sive bestiis vel sine bestiis et quibus aliis artificiis volueris," probably a reference to a *noria*, an Islamic water wheel.

The most important legacy of the Roman past was the stout girdle of walls studded with seventy-four defensive towers, which enclosed a raised area at its center known as Mons Tabor. Unlike the sprawling maze of fortifications at Tarragona, splendid defensive works meant for a provincial capital but unmanageable given the limited resources and manpower of the early Middle Ages, Barcelona's ramparts enclosed a small area of 10.4 hectares, roughly 400 m. by 180 m. at its widest and narrowest points. It therefore proved possible to defend and maintain the ramparts with relatively limited resources during the centuries of Visigothic, Arab, and Frankish rule. In keeping with the defensive requirements of an unsettled age, an *intervallum* street just inside the walls was kept clear of obstructions in order to facilitate the rapid deployment of troops along threatened sections of the battlements. The expansive optimism of the eleventh century, however, gradually overshadowed defensive requirements. Clerics, provincial notables, and prosperous burghers constructed curtain walls inside the old Roman ramparts, spanned the space between towers with vaults, erected staircases to their upper-story rooms, and opened windows in the stonework in order to create impressive rampart-homes on the defenses, the "penthouses" of the intramural zone.[13] According to a fifteenth-century chronicler, several of the great baronial families of Catalonia carved up the defenses among themselves soon after the city had been retaken from the Moors.[14] While details of the story are in error and the amount of the walls controlled by a single family exaggerated, nevertheless the tradition does reflect the fragmentation of the Roman walls into the hands of aristocrats and influential local figures, who turned the towers and walls, which had remained under comital control in the tenth century, into private residences. Yet the wall-towers with their attached accommodations did not evolve into private fortresses comparable to the massive, austere towers that cast such long shadows over Italian urban history. In Barcelona the pressures of urbanization overwhelmed defensive needs as new construction first encumbered and then swallowed up large portions of the city's ancient walls.

Two lords commanded the city in the ninth and tenth century:

---

[13] Banks, "Roman inheritance," 614–15. For early examples of buildings on the defenses, *Santa Anna*, II, no. 170; ACA perg. R.B. III, 253; ACB LA IV, fol. 18, Mas IX, no. 44.

[14] M. Coll i Alentorn, "El Llibre de les nobleses dels reys," *Estudis universitaris catalans*, 13 (1928), 508.

the count and the bishop. The stable balance between them left its impression on urban topography and on the city walls themselves. Two main roads pierced the elliptical pattern of the defences at their widest and narrowest points, then crossed at a perfect right angle at the center of the intramural area, once the site of the forum. Of the four turreted castle-gates commanding the entrances to the old city, Castellvell, to the east, and Castellnou to the west, belonged to the count and his representative; Bishop's Gate, to the north, and the Regomir Gate to the south were subject to episcopal control. Each gate provided a center of power for the armed clients of the count and bishop. Both Castellnou and the Regomir had small fiefs in the *territorium* attached to them, and a valuable Jewish oven stood at the foot of Castellnou.[15] Although without attached fiefs, Castellvell overlooked the main entrance to the city and the marketplace at its base. During the early phase of urban growth it formed the hub of local power, first held by the viscounts of Barcelona and later by the urban vicar. Neither the bishop nor the count, however, allowed the men who commanded the castle-gates to use them as centers of banal lordship. By the thirteenth century only Castellvell retained its earlier importance; the rights attached to Castellnou were slowly dismembered and the Regomir became buried under private dwellings.[16]

With the crossroads dividing the walled space into four equal quadrants, the remaining streets were originally laid out parallel to the two main roads leading out of the city according to the typical Roman grid pattern. The basic plan survived to shape the medieval *civitas*, even though in the early Middle Ages collapsed buildings and new constructions caused detours on once straight streets and blocked off others. The cathedral and the comital palace, both located in the northeastern quadrant, dominated the intramural space. The comital residence probably stood on the site of the ancient prefecture; in front of it lay a *freginal*, an open yard employed as a corral for the horses of distinguished visitors at court. Today the Plaça del Rei, it formed the only open, public space within the walls. The romanesque cathedral, demolished by

---

[15] On the castle-gates themselves, *Els castells catalans*, ed. R. Dalmau (Barcelona, 1967–80), I, 516–31 and Philip Banks, "The north-western gate of the city of Barcelona," *Cuadernos de arqueología e historia de la ciudad*, 17 (1977), 117–27. The fiefs attached to Castellnou and Regomir appear in ACB 1–1–1229; 4–49–152; LA I, fol. 66, Mas XI, no. 1989, and the following note.

[16] ACB 1–1–359, 2136; ACA perg. varis, Marquès de Monistrol, 131.

1298 for the Gothic structure that replaced it, stood nearby, providing the focus for clerical life. The cathedral canons owned the bulk of property in the northwestern quadrant of the old city. Here relatively large houses were built for the aristocratic enclave of clerics, who had only a short walk to reach the cathedral. A small but important Jewish community also lived in this zone; by the eleventh century it had become concentrated in the area known simply as the Call, "the street," which began at Castellnou and wound its way toward the cathedral.[17] Until its destruction in the pogrom of 1391, the Call was one of the leading centers of Jewish life in the peninsula and by far the largest Hebrew community in Catalonia.

While the northern half of the compact intramural space remained densely settled in the early Middle Ages, the southern half was largely underdeveloped and open, given over to garden plots, small vineyards, orchards, fields, and scattered dwellings. Sants Just i Pastor, Sant Jaume, and Sant Miquel, the three tiny parish churches of the *civitas*, lay in this zone, huddled near the old forum; they languished under the shadow of the cathedral. During the eleventh and twelfth century the southern half of the old city gradually filled with houses of nobles, churchmen, and religious orders interested in securing access to the comital court and the cathedral. The bishop of Vic, the archdeacon of Tarragona, the bishop of Solsona, the Templars, and the monks of Sant Benet de Bages obtained residences in this zone, many of which contained storage spaces (*cellaria*) for the grain and wine they received from rents in the Pla de Barcelona.[18] Throughout the Middle Ages the tranquil, smug atmosphere of an affluent residential area pervaded this lower half of the inner city.

Thus, by 1200, virtually all available space within the old Roman walls had been filled. Priests and warriors dominated early medieval Barcelona and left a deep impression on the ancient *civitas* throughout its subsequent history. The defensive fortress blended smoothly with the holy city, promoting a large degree of topographic continuity within the venerable shell of the old Roman fortifications. While outside the walls the marketplace, the shipyards, and workshop complexes provided the new focal points of wealth and power, the ancient nucleus of urban settle-

---

[17] Carreras Candi, *La ciutat*, 273–75.
[18] On the properties owned by churches from outside the city, infra, 51, n. 15.

ment retained its archaic dignity against the encroachments of entrepreneurs, money changers, and artisans.

Long before the new construction had filled the small intramural area, intensive settlement had begun below the walls.[19] The first known reference to suburban property (*in burgo*) occurs in 966, a generation before an Islamic army breached the city's defenses, but intense occupation of sites beyond the walls began in earnest just before 1000. The earliest extramural settlements seem spontaneous extensions of the most active intramural locations, not planned communities on unoccupied sites. The first areas to develop lay to the north and east of the walls, the former opening onto the city's *ort i vinyet* and the latter centered on the road leading from Castellvell to the Montcada gap and beyond to Occitania. By 1000 the first houses had been built in the area known as Arcs Antics above Bishop's Gate, so called because of the ruins of the Roman aqueduct leading to Tibidabo, remains of which can still be seen today. Scattered stalls had also sprung up in the market area at the foot of Castellvell, already in existence by 987. The market must have had a ramshackle appearance at first, resembling a shantytown crammed haphazardly with wooden stalls, workshops, and protruding tables, but the area later received clearer definition; permanent stone structures (*case*) had been built by 1076, and a meat market (*macellum*) and cloth hall (*draperia*) erected by the close of the twelfth century.[20] Further from the walls, settlers clustered around the old Benedictine cloisters of Santa Eulàlia del Camp and Sant Pere de les Puel·les, a female monastery, the parish church of Sant Cugat del Rec, founded in 1023, and Santa Anna, constructed around 1140 and part of the military order of the Holy Sepulchre. Early suburban development therefore occurred spontaneously around a number of independent nucleated sites. Yet the early occupation of Arcs Antics and the market zone oriented subsequent expansion, for the most densely settled area lay to the north and east of the Roman walls, radiating out in an arc formed by the Roman fortifications

[19] Early suburban growth is now well covered by Philip Banks, " 'Burgus,' 'suburbium' and 'villanova': the extramural growth of Barcelona before A.D. 1200," in *Història urbana del Pla de Barcelona. Actes del II Congrés d'Història del Pla de Barcelona celebrat a l'Institut Municipal d'Història els dies 6 i 7 de desembre de 1985* (Barcelona, 1989–90), II, 106–33.

[20] *El archivo condal de Barcelona en los siglos IX–X*, ed. F. Udina Martorell (Barcelona, 1951), no. 222; Arxiu de Montserrat, perg. Sant Cugat del Vallès, 121; *Llib. bl.*, no. 372; ACB 1–5–287.

beginning at Bishop's Gate, passing by Castellvell, and gradually thinning out toward the Regomir Gate.

To the west and along the coast, however, extramural development proceeded slowly. Except for the area just outside Castellnou, where baths, a royal meat market, and shops were built not long before 1200, most residents lived dispersed among vineyards, gardens, and orchards. The most prominent structures were the tiny, impoverished monastic house of Sant Pau del Camp and the parish church of Santa Maria del Pi, where one could receive a final resting place for a few pennies. The open spaces provided ample room to house the poor, the sick, and the ascetic; the Lepers' House, the Hospital of En Colom, and the Franciscan community found their place in this marginal zone of urbanization. Poor drainage and an unhealthy environment partly explain the backwardness of the area, yet Barcelona's economic orientation during its early development was toward its immediate hinterland and Occitania, not toward Aragon and the sea. Through the early modern period the western suburbs remained sparsely settled.

Once the initial phase of spontaneous, unplanned suburban growth had gained momentum, landowners began to develop substantial tracts of land systematically by tracing out a regular street plan and leasing adjacent lots one after another for construction. Before 1300, seven planned developments, called *vilanovae* or *vilae*, can be identified, all but two begun by 1225. The canons should receive credit for the earliest attempt to build up a suburban zone as a unit. During the 1080s they subdivided a tract of land in the eastern suburbs above the church of Santa Maria del Mar, but their initiative did not have immediate imitators because of difficulties in the real estate market and the uncertain nature of leasehold, which made it difficult for the landlord to retain control.[21] By the early thirteenth century, however, real estate developers had established several *vilanovae* and *vilae* in order to subdivide these areas systematically and secure valuable rents. Because large tracts of open suburban land were rapidly disappearing in the thirteenth century, development of large *vilanovae* tended to give way to building up individual streets. Soon after 1200 a new word for street appeared, *vicus*, at first connoting

[21] On the early development of the area, see Banks, " 'Burgus,' 'suburbium' and 'villanova'," 116–20. Although certain features of emphyteutic tenure appear in the eleventh century, as Banks notes, only in the late twelfth does this system of leasehold mature to ensure the landlord's firm control over tenants, infra, 306–8.

a private road built up under a single developer.[22] Although the units were smaller, the pace of construction was more intense. A "new street" near the shore built by Arnau Burgès in the mid-thirteenth century brought in rents from ten tenants, while Bernat Eimeric held leases from twenty householders on another complex developed above the shore to the west.[23] As the pace of growth quickened in the late twelfth and thirteenth century, suburban expansion passed from the initiative of small, individual freeholders into the hands of distinguished citizens who came to dominate suburban real estate development.

The coastline experienced the most spectacular surge of construction in the thirteenth century. Developers literally parted the waters to erect new houses and shops. In the early Middle Ages, the shoreline came close to the parish church appropriately named Santa Maria del Mar; by 1200, however, the sea had receded by as much as 200 m. The geological cause for the extension of the shore is far from clear, but the digging of the Rec Comtal and the blockage of a *riera*, rudely called the Merdança ("excrement stream") just to the east of the Roman walls, evidently shifted the pattern of alluvial deposits left by the currents moving east to west along the shore. In order to determine precisely where the beach lay for the purposes of real estate development, urban magistrates and judges had to become amateur geologists; they settled a dispute about property title by digging a trench along the coastline in 1251 to see where the sand deposits ended and "land" began.[24]

The coastal area around Santa Maria del Mar eventually emerged as the center of Barcelona's mercantile quarter. Carreras Candi and others following him have assumed that the suburb around the church was one of the first to expand since it was nourished by overseas trade, but Banks has recently shown that the area developed rather late and largely in response to the establishment of a *vilanova* by the bishop and canons in the 1080s; what is more, the early structures that filled the area provided spacious residences for clergy and urban landlords, not merchants, sailors, and artisans.[25] Topography therefore suggests that Bar-

---

[22] ACB 1–6–71 (15 x 1205): "in vico novo ... in alio vico novo." Cf. ACB 1–6–1206, 2414; ADB perg. Sant Anna, Carp. de la creu, unnumb. parch. [29 iv 1203]. *Vicus* was added to the other current words for street, *carraria, platea, via*.

[23] ACB 1–1–379; 4–32–605.   [24] ACB 4–40–456.

[25] Banks, " 'Burgus,' 'suburbium,' and 'villanova'," 116–23.

celona was late in developing overseas trade. Because of the shallow bottom near the beach, the city does not possess a natural harbor. Only in the early fifteenth century did the town council erect a stone jetty and pier, at considerable expense and difficulty, to provide a welcoming port to large ships; until then boats had to be dragged upon the shore below the Regomir gate or a flotilla of skiffs had to unload the cargo from large ships anchored offshore. Yet in spite of the difficulties posed by a shallow bottom, just after 1200 the coastal district expanded rapidly. The king established two compounds for foreign merchants (*alfóndecs*), the royal ship-yards (*drassanes*), and a fish and meat market, while influential burghers systematically subdivided and leased out lots for construction. By the 1250s the coastal district, popularly known as the Ribera, formed the center of Barcelona's booming commercial economy.

By the close of the thirteenth century, the dispersed nuclei of suburban settlements were fusing into a relatively continuous and densely occupied space far larger than that contained within the ancient Roman fortifications. By 1260 new gates at Santa Anna and Portaferrissa were constructed in the western suburbs;[26] these marked off the parameters of a vastly enlarged second ring of walls which would eventually enclose the expanding suburbs and integrate newly settled areas into a burgeoning urban community. The second ring of walls went up in several stages, but most of the construction was due to the initiatives of King Pere II (1276–85) and King Alfons II (1285–91); by 1293 all but the eastern section of the defenses had been completed, but work on the final length of fortifications did not resume until 1358. Typically both the king and the municipality worked in conjunction to build the new ramparts, for in 1287 King Alfons II promised 100,000s. collected

---

[26] The *portale* at Santa Anna is mentioned in November, 1260 (ADB perg. Santa Anna, Carp. 2b, 495) and in February, 1261 the nearby gate at Portaferrissa is recorded (ACA Reg. 11, fol. 194 v.). This reference to Portaferrissa caused Carreras Candi, *La ciutat*, 340 to conclude that the section of the new walls on Les Rambles was completed by that time, but the gates may well have been built long before large sections of the walls in order to guarantee the safety of the two heavily settled streets which they commanded. The growing menace of the French during the reign of Pere II may have provided the greatest stimulus to the extensions of the walls; only in 1289 is there a clear indication that the western walls were standing, ASPP, 433: "prope viam de molis et prope portalem muri novi." Further, in 1286, the city magistrates were urged to complete the walls, a sign that work on them had been particularly intense in the previous few years, ACA Reg. 66, fol. 85 r. Carreras Candi therefore seems to exaggerate when he calls the second ring of fortifications the "muralles de Jaume I."

from the city in order to support the cost of construction and in the following year permitted the town to collect a defense tax (*cisa*) from the rest of Catalonia for that purpose; the king's failure to supply the promised funds in large part accounts for the long delay in the completion of the project.[27] The commitments expressed in the subsidy, although partially a dead letter, nevertheless equated the defense of Barcelona with the defense of Catalonia. Under the watchful eye of the dynasty of Barcelona, by the thirteenth century the city had grown from a provincial Roman backwater into a vibrant Mediterranean emporium and the political fulcrum of an expansionist monarchy. Even though a burgeoning commercial economy had shifted the weight of population to the *suburbium*, the ecclesiastical and political center remained fixed in the *civitas*. Yet urban space did not fragment into a multiplicity of competing jurisdictions and lordships as a result of explosive growth; Barcelona would not be counted among the many European *Doppelstädte* taking shape during these centuries. Rather its character as an administrative and economic center blended smoothly, allowing the *civitas* and *suburbium* to fuse into a coherent, self-confident, and vibrant new community that would at once embody local Catalan identity and spearhead overseas expansion.

BARCELONA AND THE CROWN OF ARAGON

While topographic changes provide clear evidence for the pace of the city's expansion, it is impossible to arrive at anything more than a rough estimate of population growth before the hearth tax surveys (*fogatges*) of the late fourteenth century. Based on a careful topographic analysis, Banks places the urban population in the year 1000 around 1,500, for only the northern portion of the tiny intramural area was densely occupied during the early Middle Ages; with the burgeoning suburbs, by 1200 the city covered roughly 60 hectares, which places the population at about 10,000 to 12,000.[28] Even though demographic growth was vigorous during the eleventh and twelfth century, and, as will be argued in

---

[27] Carreras Candi, *La ciutat*, 340–45. The promised subvention was still outstanding in 1300, but the municipality at that time forgave the debt in return for a tax exemption: ACA Reg. 197, fols. 66 r.–68 r. On the *cisa*, ACA Reg. 75, fols. 63 r.–64 v.
[28] Banks, "Roman inheritance," 618 and "The inhabitants of Barcelona in 1145," *Acta mediaevalia*, 9 (1988), 149, n. 35.

Map 3 Catalonia from the tenth to the twelfth century

chapter 4, particularly after 1140, it nevertheless pales in comparison to the explosive expansion during the next century and a half. The first *fogatges*, recorded soon after the Black Death had decimated the urban population, list 6,668 households in 1365 and 7,648 in 1378; in the imperfect science of medieval demography, the city contained 30,000 to 34,000 in the late fourteenth with a conservative multiplier of 4.5 individuals per household.[29] This suggests a pre-plague population of well over 40,000. Since the

[29] The tangled chronology of the *fogatges* is set in order by Josep Iglésies Fort, "El fogatge de 1365-70," *Memorias de la Real Academia de Ciencias y Artes de Barcelona*, 34 (1962), 247-356; "La cursa demogràfica de les principals ciutats catalanes," *Memorias de la Real Academia de Ciencias y Artes de Barcelona*, 43 (1977), 458-59.

second ring of walls encompassed most of the settled area in late medieval Barcelona, the greatest surge in numbers surely occurred in the thirteenth century. The city may well have trebled or even quadrupled in size between 1200 and 1300.

However approximate the figures may be, it is clear that a decisive phase in urbanization began after 1200 and that the city's tiny hinterland could no longer support the needs of the booming urban population. Already in the 1190s grain imports had begun from Empúries to the east; a century later Barcelona depended upon a complex Mediterranean supply system stretching from Sicily to the Ebro. Both the Crown and the municipality carefully monitored the grain trade in order for the city to secure its daily bread.[30] By 1260 the city's butchers were already traveling to the livestock market of Puigcerdà high in the Pyrenees, where they found the meat to put on Barcelona's tables.[31] For its very survival the city came to depend upon its economic influence throughout Catalonia and the Mediterranean.

Because of its growing size and wealth, the city became critical to the monarchy as both an administrative center and a source of income. The best indication of the weight Barcelona carried in the Crown of Aragon toward the close of the thirteenth century comes from an emergency tax levied during the reign of King Pere II. Faced with the impending invasion of Catalonia by Philip the Bold of France, Pere ordered the collection of an extraordinary aid (*auxilium*) in February, 1284. Because of the gravity of the situation and the infrequency of the levy, exemptions and cheating were rare; the amounts collected therefore provide a rough indication of the size and wealth of the communities involved. Barcelona contributed 160,000s., Lleida 120,000, Tarragona 60,000, and Girona 30,000; only Valencia, assessed at 200,000s., exceeded Barcelona in its fiscal liability, but the heavy royal exploitation of the reconquered city skews the comparative value of the tax burden.[32] The largest single imposition demanded of the city during the period covered by this study, the *auxilium* of 1284 shows that among the towns of Catalonia Barcelona already stood in a class by itself. Only Lleida, near the border of Catalonia and

---

[30] ACB 1–5–330; infra, 333–34. For the importance of the grain trade for the city in the fourteenth and fifteenth century, Mutgé Vives, *La ciudad de Barcelona*, 41–96; Carrère, *Barcelone*, 1, 326–41.

[31] Arxiu Històric Comarcal de Puigcerdà, Protocols, Reg. 1, fol. 7 r.

[32] ACA Reg. 51, fols. 6 r.–8 r. Numerous cities other than those cited here also contributed.

Table 1.1 *Presence of the royal court in the principal cities of the Crown of Aragon (1162–1276, 1285–1291), percent.*

	Barcelona	Lleida	Zaragoza	Huesca	Valencia
Alfons I	4	10	10	9	—
Pere I	7	11	10	9	—
Jaume I	13	13	13	2	14
Alfons II	21	6	12	6	5

Aragon, provided any serious competition, but through its wealth, size, and broad Mediterranean contacts, Barcelona clearly established its preeminence among Catalan towns by the end of the thirteenth century.

Traditional ties with the ruling dynasty also gave the city a crucial political role in the Crown of Aragon, but its function as the Catalan capital is more problematic than usually assumed. The dynasty of Barcelona originally ruled over a conglomeration of administrative districts established by the Carolingians: the counties of Barcelona, Osona, and Girona. During the twelfth century the comital family extended its control over the majority of the independent Pyrenean counties in Old Catalonia, pushed the frontier westward into what is now called New Catalonia, and, through a dynastic marriage arranged in 1137, acquired the kingdom of Aragon, less wealthy than Catalonia but with a powerful, aggressive baronage. During the thirteenth century, the count-kings, as they would now be known, added new kingdoms to their title through Mediterranean conquests from Muslim and Christian rulers alike: Valencia, Majorca, and Sicily. Because of its breathtaking territorial expansion, the dynasty felt pulled in a number of different directions at once, for each realm possessed its own political center and autonomous traditions. As table 1.1 demonstrates,[33] rulers moved incessantly among their domains old and new; despite what is often rather casually assumed, the

[33] The figures above represent the proportion of diplomas issued from the major cities of the Crown for the reigns of Alfons I and Pere I, but the total time spent at a site for the richly documented reigns of Jaume I and Alfons II; no itinerary for Pere II has yet appeared. Jaime Caruana, "Itinerario de Alfonso II de Aragón," *EEMCA*, 7 (1962), 73–298; Joaquím Miret i Sans, "Itinerario del rey Pedro I de Cataluña, II en Aragón" *BRABLB*, 3 (1905–6), 79–87, 151–60, 238–49, 265–84, 365–87, 435–50, 497–519; 4 (1907–8), 15–36, 91–114 and *Itinerari de Jaume I "el Conqueridor"* (Barcelona, 1918); Francesc Carreras Candi, "Itinerari del rei Anfós II," *BRABLB*, 10 (1921–22), 61–83.

early count-kings tended to spend more time in Zaragoza, Lleida, and Valencia than in Barcelona. Only during the relatively tranquil reign of King Alfons II (1285–91) did the king settle down to rule from his largest Catalan city.

Until late in the thirteenth century count-kings ruled on horseback, moving throughout the domains because they relied upon dispersed centers of regional power; government did not stay fixed at one location. As a result, Barcelona would never truly serve as an imperial capital. Even the political preeminence it enjoyed within the early Aragonese-Catalan union was problematic. True to ancient precedent, the only archbishop in eastern Iberia had his seat in the old Roman provincial capital, Tarragona, even though the city was subject to Islamic control for four centuries. Moreover, geography did not always work to the advantage of Barcelona. To the swashbuckling chronicler Ramon Muntaner, it seemed clear that his homeland possessed a binary core: "Barcelona was the capital of maritime Catalonia and Lleida the capital of inland Catalonia."[34] Located on the border of New Catalonia and Aragon, Lleida had the advantage of easy communications with both regions for the first count-kings, Alfons I and Pere I, who felt as comfortable with their Aragonese barons as with their Catalan financiers. The mantle of kingship did not hang comfortably on Barcelona. Bonifacio Palacios Martín has argued that Zaragoza possessed a certain primacy over all the realms because of its connection to the Aragonese royal title, but his case is strongest for King Pere II "the Great" (1276–85) and his successors because of their inflated royal rhetoric.[35]

Yet what Catalonia's largest town lacked in royalist pomp and archiepiscopal dignity it made up for with cool efficiency and organization. Barcelona provided the memory bank for dynastic rule. From an early date the counts had made a habit of depositing their most important documents in the comital palace of Barcelona. Under Ramon de Caldes, the orderly and efficient dean of Barcelona's cathedral, the royal archives were put in order in the 1180s, a reorganization culminating in the *Liber feudorum*, the great book of fiefs for both Catalonia and Aragon. As the realms expanded and royal administration blossomed, the remarkable

---

[34] Ramon Muntaner, *Crònica*, c. 24, in *Les quatre grans cròniques*, 688: "així con Barcelona és cap de Catalunya en la marina e en la terra ferma Lleida."

[35] Bonifacio Palacios Martín, *La coronación de los reyes de Aragón* (Valencia, 1975), 105–12. Cf. the comments by Burns, *Diplomatarium*, II, 18, n. 8.

series of royal registers, providing a documentary skeleton of royal power shaping the different realms, was housed in the ancestral palace of the counts of Barcelona. Even though medieval authors rarely theorized about the political importance of Barcelona, it was in fact the only vantage point, in the Middle Ages as well as today, from which it is possible to survey the Crown of Aragon as a whole.

CONCLUSION

To sum up, neither geography nor historical tradition gave medieval Barcelona significant advantages over other old Roman towns in eastern Iberia. Its compact, fertile plain provided a reassuring cocoon in which urban society could grow in relative safety from the turbulent baronial world of upland Catalonia, but once the city had matured and opened its wings, its sheltering ring of low mountains constricted its territorial expansion. Barcelona would not carve out its own *contado*. Although the urban population had increased significantly in the eleventh and twelfth centuries, the most intense growth came after 1200. The city's development moved in synchronization with the expansion of the Crown of Aragon, led by a dynasty which had begun its rise as minor marcher lords of the tiny, isolated county of Barcelona. A convergence of regional and dynastic factors, the products of a vibrant frontier society, propelled Barcelona into its commanding position in Catalonia, not a transcendent, preordained geographical, historical, or ethnic imperative. In order to explore the distinctive contours of urban society during its formative period, it is first of all necessary to examine the relationship between Barcelona and its lord.

Chapter 2

THE CITY AND ITS LORD

Medieval urban communities carved out their distinctive judicial and administrative outlines from the block of rights and privileges held by their lords. Whatever its size, economic importance, or *de facto* sphere of collective action, a town possessed no natural right to judge its residents, regulate its market, levy taxes, build mills or ovens, oversee municipal construction, or select representatives to direct its affairs: sovereign or seigniorial authority had to relinquish these prerogatives, or at least formally acknowledge a *fait accompli*. The form this transfer assumed, the timing of municipal grants, and the extent of liberties conferred on individual towns varied tremendously, yet charters of urban privileges were always highly prized and frequently reaffirmed. The contents of these documents had a lasting impact on regulating not only the subsequent relationship between townspeople and their lords but also in establishing balances within urban communities themselves.

The latter point needs special emphasis, for it can easily be overlooked due to the laconic nature of the sources and the assumption that the bestowal of privileges directly reflects a singleness of purpose espoused by the community. The diplomatic nature of municipal charters makes it tempting to see in them a simple tug-of-war between the community as a whole and its lord or lords. In a reductionist dialectic, the lord who possessed rights in the town typically conceded all or part of them "freely" or "benevolently" to the entire faceless body of townspeople, the *universitas*, *populus*, or *comune*. The constituent elements represented in the formula, however, were far from homogeneous. Certain factions within the town may well have stood to gain more by the transfer of authority than others, while the person making the concession, often under pressure or for strategic purposes, in fact possessed numerous agents working on his behalf, some of whom were usually townsmen. Through experience gained by *ad hoc* participation in judgments, military operations, or revenue collection as well as in service as administrators to urban lords, influential burghers first learned to rule their community and articulate its interests. Episcopal courts in precommunal Italy served as prep schools in lordship for the influential townsmen who served in them, and seigniorial agents often formed a part of early patriciates in the Rhineland and the Low Countries.[1] As the most dynamic elements within the urban population asserted their power, the early urban privileges conceded by lords represented neither a simple formalization of time-honored habits of communal action nor the drafts of a precise blueprint for the organization of urban societies; rather they record the cumulative experience gained by urban leaders through participation in traditional forms of lordship and the recognition, however grudging, that such participation was legitimate. Municipal charters and privileges were experiments in redefining authority, not final declarations of a new order.

If the first person singular conceals the array of administrators and supporters standing behind the donor in early town charters, the collective noun used to designate the recipient of the grants obscures the diversity and tensions within the urban community. The cozy solidarity some have found in early towns depends largely on taking the legal terminology of the charters at face value.[2] In some instances, especially in Northern Europe, there is nowhere else to turn. In the richer documentation of the South, however, one can detect sharp divisions within urban communities long before the establishment of autonomous municipal institutions and the transfer of extensive liberties to burghers. Throughout the Latin Mediterranean, early towns took shape against a background of barroom rowdiness and simmering factionalism. Milan offers a classic example of the explosive pressures building in a precommunal urban setting, yet other towns in northern Italy also experienced violent confrontations in

[1] Eugenio Dupré-Theseider, "Vescovi e città nell'Italia precomunale," *Atti del II convegno di storia della Chiesa in Italia* (Padua, 1964), 80–91; Tabacco, *Egemonie*, 419; K. Schulz, "Stadt und Ministerialität in rheinischen Bischofsstädten," in *Stadt und Ministerialität. Protokoll der IX. Arbeitstagung des Arbeitskreises für südwestdeutsche Stadtgeschichtsforschung*, eds. E. Maschke and J. Sydow (Baden-Württemberg, 1973), 16–42; Lestocquoy, *Aux origines de la bourgeoisie*, 57–64.

[2] Reynolds, *Kingdoms and communities*, 155–83 and for Catalonia, Font Rius, "Orígenes del régimen," 377–462.

the early eleventh century.[3] When autonomous municipal
regimes did emerge in twelfth-century Provence and Languedoc,
urban consuls sometimes represented separate seigniorial districts
within the town rather than the community as a whole.[4] Even in
Catalonia, noted for its peaceful elaboration of municipal governments, the first explicit authorization to establish consuls at
Cervera in 1182 specifically excludes twenty men from joining the
confratria et fraternitatis unanimitas, presumably because they threatened the stability of the community.[5] These examples hardly
reveal a steady trajectory of increasing urban solidarity peaking
with the foundation of representative governments. Long before
the appearance of consular regimes and municipal councils, factionalism profoundly marked civic life. The communal or consular
movement in the Latin Mediterranean did not flow smoothly
from an innate collective solidarity already in play; rather, it was
forged through the cooperation of diverse urban groups in order
to exercise rights of lordship collectively.[6]

Even after the appearance of municipal regimes, urban lords
and their agents could still have considerable impact on urban
society. The first mention of consuls does not necessarily signal a
hasty, disorderly retreat on the part of all lords from urban soil.
Indeed, if urban associations and the drive for autonomy now
appear more typically medieval than ever before, if towns and
municipal institutions have justifiably lost much of their revolutionary edge in recent historiography, then we should expect
that prominent burghers conceived of power in terms similar to
those of their lords. The implications of this reappraisal have yet to
be drawn out fully, for urban lords are still frequently portrayed as
clinging parents meddling in the affairs of their maturing offspring, but in many cases urban communities had yet to set up
their own households. In order to reevaluate the relationships
between the evolution of lordship and the formation of urban
institutions, it will be necessary to take into account the influence
lords possessed in determining the balances among urban factions,

---

[3] Hagen Keller, *Adelsherrschaft und städtische Geschichte in Oberitalien 9. bis 12. Jahrhundert*
(Tübingen, 1979), 270–91; Tabacco, *Egemonie*, 226–33.
[4] Of the twelve consuls at Arles, four represented the Vieux-Bourg, two the Bourg Neuf,
two the market district, and four were knights, Louis Stouff, *Arles à la fin du moyen-âge*
(Aix-en-Provence, 1986), I, 159. Cf. *Histoire de la France urbaine*, II, 278–79.
[5] Font Rius, "Orígenes del régimen," 478, n. 798.
[6] Tabacco, *Egemonie*, 230–34; John H. Mundy, *Liberty and political power in Toulouse,
1050–1230* (New York, 1954), 63–73.

the prestige of competing families, and the articulation of common interests within the community.

If these preliminary remarks have stressed the ongoing interaction of lordship and municipal institutions rather than sudden ruptures, the traditionally close ties between the House of Barcelona and its most dynamic Catalan town make such a perspective useful. Throughout Catalonia independent municipal institutions took shape slowly, hesitatingly, and, for the most part, peacefully. The wave of consular regimes began to build in northern and central Italy in the 1080s, reached the shores of Languedoc and Provence in the 1120s, and finally swept into Catalonia only in the 1180s.[7] Attempts to account for this delay have ranged from criticizing Catalonian urban societies for a lack of cohesion to crediting the count-kings with a benevolently efficient administration which offered citizens security against fiscal and judicial abuses that townspeople elsewhere had to seek through the creation of new institutions.[8] Did the close bonds between Barcelona and its lord dampen or deflect the impulse for urban autonomy? Or, to put the question in current terms of discussion, did a viable *système urbain* fail to mature in Barcelona because the city became integrated into a larger organism, the territorial state, which partially absorbed it?

To explore these and related problems, whatever terminology one prefers, the points of contact between Barcelona and its lords must be identified and the pressure exerted on urban society at those points measured.

A UNIFIED LORDSHIP

After more than eighty years of Islamic rule, the last, wearied Muslim defenders of Barcelona surrendered to the Frankish army sent to conquer the city on April 3, 801.[9] On the following day, Easter Sunday, its commander, Louis the Pious, Charlemagne's

---

[7] The chronology of the consular movement in Italy and southern France is summarized by Daniel Waley, *The Italian city-republics* (New York and Toronto, 1969), 60 and André Gouron, "Diffusion des consulats méridionaux et expansion du droit romain aux XIIe et XIIIe siècles," *Bibliothèque de l'Ecole des Chartes*, 121 (1963), 52.

[8] Philippe Wolff, "Barcelone et Toulouse au XIIe et XIIIe siècles: esquisse d'une comparison," *VII CHCA* (Barcelona, 1962), II, 591–92.

[9] On the chronology of the siege, complicated by divergent chronicle accounts, see Josep Maria Salrach i Marés, *El procés de formació nacional de Catalunya (segles VIII–IX)* (Barcelona, 1978), I, 14–26.

son and future emperor, triumphantly entered the city's gate. At that moment the Carolingian advance beyond the Pyrenees reached its climax. Despite some initial resistance by restored Gothic aristocrats, Barcelona and the reorganized Pyrenean territories were securely placed in the Frankish orbit. Soon after the victory, Charlemagne sent a capitulary to the Goths and *Hispani*, immigrants from non-Frankish Spain and the Pyrenees, residing in the "renowned city of Barcelona" (*Barchinona famosi nominis civitas*) and the castle of Terrassa, a critical frontier fortification to the north.[10] Military security and the foundation of comital authority were the overriding concerns in Barcelona's first privilege. Placed under the "protection and defense" of the emperor, all free men owed military service to the count in order to ensure that the "cruel yoke of the Saracens" might not weigh down upon them again. As to judicial organization, the count reserved for himself the three major pleas of high justice, murder, kidnapping, and arson, but allowed the inhabitants to deal with all other infractions according to local custom. A capitulary issued by Charles the Bald in 844 confirmed the earlier provisions and added new clauses to ensure full proprietorship guaranteed by comital authority to peasants who had legally cleared and settled the land (*aprisio*).[11] Addressed both to the inhabitants of Barcelona and Terrassa and to all the residents of the county, Charles the Bald's charter expressed a concern not only to defend his grandfather's gains but "to transform any desolate waste in the county into a cultivated bounty." The early capitularies erected a simple but sturdy Carolingian platform supporting a strong comital presence intended to defend both the city and the county of Barcelona, offer justice in public courts, and protect the rights of a free peasantry.

The consolidation of Carolingian institutions in the Spanish March had two major consequences for the subsequent development of Barcelona. First, it ensured that local counts held a virtual monopoly on public authority and provided military leadership for the fortress-city and its surrounding territory. Frankish military might had radically simplified the structures of power.

---

[10] Although no copy of the capitulary has survived, Ramon d'Abadal i de Vinyals carefully reconstructed it from later confirmations in *Catalunya carolíngia*, II. *Els diplomes carolingis a Catalunya* (Barcelona, 1926–52), 2nd part, 415–16. On the *Hispani*, see Roger J. H. Collins, "Charles the Bald and Wifrid the Hairy," in *Charles the Bald: court and kingdom*, eds. M. T. Gisbon and J. L. Nelson (2nd ed., London, 1990), 185–88.

[11] Ibid., 422–25.

Instead of a tangled web of immunities, private jurisdictions, and ancient loyalties to bishops and local churches, a minimal framework of civic life had to be constructed from the ground up. Second, the limits of the Carolingian advance in the *Marca Hispanica* raised Barcelona to the position of a dominant regional center. If Charlemagne's capitulary could boast of Barcelona's fame, its star shone all the more brightly because of the dark disappointments of Frankish defeats. The inability of the Franks to roll back the Muslim–Christian frontier beyond the Ebro, as they had intended, relieved Barcelona from having to compete with Zaragoza, Tortosa, Lleida, or Tarragona, whose venerable claim to ecclesiastical primacy delayed the erection of an archbishopric in eastern Iberia until the definitive Christian occupation of the old Roman provincial capital more than three centuries later. Muslim resistance to the Franks finally brought Barcelona out from under Tarragona's shadow. The Arab invasions had shattered the urban network inherited from the Romans;[12] the check to the Frankish advance at the Llobregat instead of the Ebro confirmed that the ancient urban order would not be reconstructed in the northeastern corner of the peninsula. Of all Iberian towns, none profited more from the dissolution of the Roman urban hierarchy than Barcelona.

In 878 Emperor Louis the Stammerer invested Guifré the Hairy, member of a powerful indigenous family, with the county of Barcelona: his descendants would continue to rule it for more than five centuries.[13] When Guifré divided the counties he had accumulated among his sons, Barcelona passed to his eldest, Guifré II (897–911), together with the adjacent counties, Osona and Girona. From this three-county nucleus, the House of Barcelona over many generations absorbed the other Pyrenean counties, pushed forward the frontier to the west, and, through a dynastic marriage in 1150, went on to acquire the kingdom of Aragon. Yet even with a growing list of territories patiently accumulated, the counts and the later count-kings always identified themselves with Barcelona, the linchpin of their Catalonian principality. When the

---

[12] José María Lacarra, "Panorama de la historia urbana en la península ibérica desde el siglo V al X," *La città nell'alto medioevo. Settimane di studio del centro italiano di studi sull'alto medioevo,* VI (Spoleto, 1959), 345–46.

[13] The identity of Guifré's ancestors has been the object of some dispute. His father was Sunifred, variously identified as the count of Osona or the count of Urgell–Cerdanya. On the controversy and the importance of Guifré's ancestry, see Collins, "Charles the Bald," 177–80.

sharp-tongued troubadour-baron Guillem de Berguedà let fly his acerbic verse calling Alfons I "king of Barcelona,"[14] he was in fact not far off the mark. Alfons, like others in his family, sought to rule his city firmly, but the turbulent past of his lands did not facilitate his rule. During the mid-eleventh century, a period of smoldering aristocratic revolts and endemic violence, comital lordship had faced a serious challenge, but, as we will soon see, opposition was eventually overcome. Urban authority remained remarkably unified. Firmly grounded in its Carolingian past and enjoying a hardy biological continuity, the comital dynasty tenaciously resisted alienating large blocks of regalian rights in the city and bitterly opposed anyone who tried to seize them from below. As a result, the power to command and mete out justice remained far more concentrated than was usual for medieval towns.

THE ROLE OF THE CHURCH

Not that the inhabitants of Barcelona lacked other lords. Throughout its early history, the city attracted powerful clans and religious institutions from throughout the territory directly subject to the House of Barcelona and beyond. The city's shops and the count's courts drew monks from upland religious foundations, members of military orders, and baronial families from their cold stone keeps looming over mountain valleys or perched on rocky hills overlooking their fields and peasants.[15] To attend the counts, accumulate supplies, purchase fineries, and, most importantly, make a showing at the hub of a coalescing Catalan culture, episcopal churches, powerful monasteries, and influential barons acquired town houses and bits of property in the intramural area and growing suburbs, but none accumulated large tracts of urban real estate nor established jurisdictional enclaves. The same was true of the older urban monasteries, Sant Pau del Camp, Santa

---

[14] *Guillem de Berguedà*, ed. M. de Riquer (Poblet, 1971), I, xx: 7, xxiii.

[15] For the early presence of rural nobles in the city, see Bonnassie, *La Catalogne*, I, 494. Urban residences were acquired by the churches of Vic (Arxiu Capitular de Vic, Liber donacionum, fols. 94v.–95r.) and Tarragona (ACB 3–38–4) and the monasteries of Sant Cugat del Vallès (*CSC*, II, no. 382), Santa Maria de Solsona (*Col·lecció diplomàtica del monestir de Santa Maria de Solsona, el Penedès i altres llocs del Comtat de Barcelona (segles X–XV)*, ed. A. Bach (Barcelona, 1987), no. 50), Sant Benet de Bages (Arxiu de Montserrat, perg. Sant Benet de Bages, 1318), Sant Llorenç del Munt (Arxiu de Montserrat, perg. Sant Llorenç del Munt, 37), and Valldaura (*Llib. bl.*, no. 137). Through donations, other Catalonian churches and monasteries also acquired bits of urban property.

Eulàlia del Camp, and Sant Pere de les Puel·les; in each case urban property remained clustered around the monasteries themselves.

Only the bishops of Barcelona, formidable castleholders in their own right, could have proven serious rivals to comital domination of the city. Under the Carolingians early privileges and the accumulation of substantial properties throughout the county created a strong foundation for the episcopal church.[16] Possibly to reinforce an attempt by Bishop Frodoin to impose the Roman rite on segments of the clergy still loyal to the Visigothic liturgy, in 878 Louis the Stammerer conceded to the church of Barcelona a customary third of the revenues from the city's market tolls, custom duties, and mint, complete judicial and fiscal immunity from comital control over all its property, its *domus* (cathedral and/or episcopal palace), and control over numerous religious houses in the diocese, including the well-endowed monastery of Sant Cugat del Vallès.[17] While this concession represents the most extensive alienation of public rights in the city's medieval history, subsequent bishops could not expand the breach opened in comital authority and stake out a compact, independent urban jurisdiction. The episcopal third in the mint and custom duties slipped from their grasp, although the third part of market tolls remained an episcopal possession until the early twelfth century;[18] it also proved impossible to make good on the direct control of regional churches granted by the emperor Louis. In Barcelona itself, episcopal administration swallowed nothing whole. The narrow slices of *regalia* carved from comital authority could not easily be administered separately, for they depended on the willingness of the count's men to hand over the episcopal share of revenues. A similar difficulty attended the concession made by Count Ramon Berenguer III, who granted the bishops tithes on all his rights and revenues in the city, including the mint and commercial duties.[19] Revenue collectors received frequent admonitions to turn over

---

[16] Gaspar Feliu i Montfort, "Els inicis del domini territorial de la Seu de Barcelona," *CHEC*, 11 (1976), 45–61, provides a solid basis for the early history of the episcopal holdings until 974. For later periods, one must still refer to the outdated sections in Sebastián Puig y Puig, *Episcopologio de la sede barcinonense* (Barcelona, 1929); *España sagrada*, eds., E. Flórez et al. (Madrid, 1787–1849), XXIX; and *VL*, XVII, XVIII, XIX. The most reliable general guide to the history of Barcelona's church is A. Lambert, "Barcelone (diocèse de)," *Dictionnaire d'histoire et de géographie ecclésiastique*, VI, cols. 671–715.

[17] Abadal i Vinyals, *Catalunya carolíngia*, II, 2nd part, 68–71.

[18] ACB LA IV, fol. 210, Mas X, no. 1275; ADB Mensa episcopalis, titulo V, no. 2.

[19] Puig y Puig, *Episcopologio*, ap. lviii; Capmany, II, no. 3.

the tithe to the church, an indication of dubious compliance with their obligation.[20] In addition, although the bishop and his canons were collectively the largest landowners in the city, their parcels of real estate lay scattered throughout the intramural and suburban areas. Without a dense nucleus of property and jurisdiction, bishops could not translate Carolingian immunities into an autonomous urban zone subject to a powerful episcopal court.

Although urban rents were far from negligible, the bishops and canons of Barcelona drew their income and influence principally from rural property, jurisdictions, and castles rather than from their rights in the city itself. The total military and financial resources available to the church, however, were considerable. Extending their hold on castles and peasants from a core of possessions in the eastern Vallès and the Pla de Barcelona into the frontier lands of the Penedès, the bishops ranked among the mightiest lords in Catalonia. At the siege of Valencia in 1238, Bishop Berenguer de Palau mustered a contingent of 80 knights with infantry; a decade earlier, he had commanded 112 knights during the conquest of Majorca. For his substantial contribution to the Catalan host during the latter campaign, he became the fourth largest landowner on the island, and the greatest among the princes of the Church.[21] Canons, bishops, and episcopal administrators formed a compact aristocratic cell within the city, haughtily proud, profoundly respected, but safely insulated from the bustling world of landlords, merchants, and artisans surrounding them. The canons rarely admitted wealthy burghers into their ranks, and of all the twelfth- and thirteenth-century bishops, only Arnau Ermengol (1138–43) possibly came from a high-ranking family with strong ties to the seat of his diocese.[22]

Enduring Carolingian traditions combined with common interests on the frontier to forge a close alliance between the comital dynasty and the bishops of its most prized town. Until the construction of a new, more spacious palace at Bishop's Gate

[20] E. g. ACA Reg. 43, fol. 39 v.; Reg. 57, fol. 176 v.; Reg. 63, fol. 87 v.; Reg. 74, fol. 9 v. The Templars, entitled to a tithe on royal revenues, also complained about delays in receiving their money from local officials: A. J. Forey, *The Templars in the Corona de Aragón* (London, 1973), 142–43.

[21] Puig y Puig, *Episcopologio*, ap. xcix; cf. Jaume I, *Llibre dels feits*, c. 53, in *Les quatre grans cròniques*, 31. On episcopal property on Majorca, *Historia social y económica de España y América*, ed. J. Vicens Vives (Barcelona, 1957–59), II, 26.

[22] He may be part of the Ermengol clan, a prominent Barcelona family of the early twelfth century. Bishop Arnau's will mentions numerous holdings in Provençals and houses in Barcelona, Puig y Puig, *Episcopologio*, ap. lxx.

completed by the 1160s,[23] the episcopal residence lay just across a narrow street from the comital palace, a physical proximity vividly expressing the intermingling of sacred and profane which formed the basis of Carolingian rule. The mutually reinforcing structures of episcopal and comital power proved stable enough to withstand the whirlwind of the Gregorian Reform, which in the late eleventh century swept away the long-standing framework of interdependence among lay and ecclesiastical princes in many parts of Europe. Although recent scholarship is slowly beginning to modify this neat picture, there is still a broad consensus that eleventh-century Church reformers cleared a path leading to distinctly separate spheres of religious and secular activity. In Catalonia, however, Bishop Bernat of Barcelona provided the leadership to rally support for the traditional order.

Resistance to the reformers stiffened on two fronts. First, Bernat sought to check the efforts of reforming monks from Saint-Pons de Thomières and Saint-Victor de Marseilles to spin a web of monastic affiliation across the Pyrenees by subjecting such renowned Catalan monasteries as Ripoll, Sant Benet de Bages, and Cuixà to their authority.[24] When Frotard, the abbot of Saint-Pons, expelled the monastic community from Sant Cugat del Vallès, the wealthy and venerable monastery in Barcelona's backyard, and tried to subject it together with nearby Sant Llorenç del Munt to his congregation, Bernat moved quickly and decisively. Allying himself with the archbishop of Narbonne, a dogged opponent of the reforming monks and the papacy, Bishop Bernat vigorously protested monastic colonization in his diocese directly to the pope. By initiating a protracted lawsuit, Bernat and his backers badly damaged the reputations of the aggressive monks from beyond the Pyrenees. Closer to home, Bernat attempted to deflate the pretensions of Berenguer de Lluçà, bishop of Vic.[25] An ardent supporter of Saint-Ruf d'Avignon

---

[23] For the date of construction, see Banks, "The topography," I, 292–94.

[24] Ultra-Pyrenean influences on Catalonian monasticism are well covered by Johannes Josef Bauer, "Rechtsverhältnisse der katalanischen Klöster in ihren Klosterverbände (9.–12. Jahrhundert)," *GAKS*, 23 (1967), 69–130; and Anscari M. Mundó, "Moissac, Cluny et les mouvements monastiques de l'est des Pyrénées," *AM*, 75 (1963), 551–70 ["Monastic movements in the East Pyrenees," in *Cluniac monasticism in the central Middle Ages*, ed. and trans. N. Hunt (London, 1971), 98–122].

[25] Paul Kehr, "Das Papstum und der katalanische Prinzipat bis zur Vereinigung mit Aragon," *Abhandlungen der preußischen Akademie der Wissenschaften (Philosophisch-historische Klasse)* (1926), 36–60 remains fundamental. On the setbacks incurred in reestablishing Tarragona, Lawrence J. McCrank, "Restauración canónica e intento de reconquista

and Saint-Pons, Berenguer de Lluçà had also encouraged papal intervention in the Catalonian church to an unprecedented degree while heading a regency council during the troubled minority of Count Ramon Berenguer III. An even more direct threat to the see of Barcelona, however, was Berenguer's attempt to reestablish the archbishopric of Tarragona under his authority. If he had succeeded, the archbishops of Tarragona–Vic would have asserted their primacy over the churches of eastern Iberia and surrounded the diocese of Barcelona. But Berenguer de Lluçà's plan proved premature, for he could not marshal the resources to secure a continuous occupation of Tarragona. Military setbacks on the frontier and the debacle of the Occitanian monastic reformers undermined the efforts of the bishop of Vic and his backers. Bishop Bernat of Barcelona had stood his ground. In Catalonia as in Languedoc, the Gregorian reform movement produced a momentary crisis, not a revolution.

The conservatism of Barcelona's church permitted the comital dynasty to intervene in its affairs without scandal. Only in 1207 did King Pere I finally agree to allow the cathedral chapter to elect a new bishop "without requiring any royal consent," although the bishop-elect still had to present himself immediately before his sovereign as a sign of fealty.[26] The church's help could also be counted upon on the frontier. To finance his ephemeral expedition to Majorca in 1114, Count Ramon Berenguer III received 100 mbts. from the canons and bishop; when hard pressed at the siege of Tortosa in 1148, Count Ramon Berenguer IV could count on an emergency loan of 50 lbs. of silver from the church of Barcelona, a sum sufficient to deplete the episcopal treasury.[27] Besides financial support, the bishops of Barcelona stood side by side with their lord on the field of battle against the Moors. Two bishops lost their lives during campaigns led by the counts, and during endless Valencian expeditions Berenguer de Palau was a boon companion of the greatest warrior of his dynasty, Jaume the Conqueror.[28]

One need not, however, characterize the military and financial aid extended by the bishops of Barcelona as a consistent pattern of

de la sede tarraconense, 1076–1108," *Cuadernos de historia de España*, 61–62 (1977), 237–39 and Paul H. Freedman, *The diocese of Vic: tradition and regeneration in medieval Catalonia* (New Brunswick, NJ, 1983), 29–37.

[26] Puig y Puig, *Episcopologio*, 179. [27] Ibid., aps. lx, lxxii.

[28] Bishop Aecia died on the Cordovan campaign of 1010, and Bishop Ramon Guillem on the Majorcan expedition in 1115, Puig y Puig, *Episcopologio*, 100–1, 139–40.

exploitation by the counts and count-kings. Episcopal loans were generally small, irregular, and secured through solid pledges on the fisc.[29] Only during the tense years surrounding the French invasion of Catalonia in 1285, when an episcopal vacancy (1285–88) overlapped with the crusade unleashed by the pro-Angevin pope, did the Crown dig deep into the coffers of the diocese of Barcelona.[30] The relative restraint demonstrated by the Aragonese monarchy in seeking financial support from local churches stands in stark contrast to the extortionate policies of Castilian kings, who at every opportunity used the excuse of crusades against the Moors to fleece their bishops.[31] Even though count-kings maintained a firm grip on the Catalan church, a durable balance emerged from the conservative resistance to Gregorian reformers and the opportunities and dangers of an expanding frontier.[32] For Barcelona, the stabilizing cooperation between its sovereign and bishop never permitted conflict between lay and ecclesiastical interests to shred the powers of command and judgment, which would have allowed local factions to pull out the tattered threads of lordship one by one. As Carolingian traditions dissolved in the politically fragmented world of northern Italy and Occitania, bishops often inherited the role of urban guardians and the protectors of the *res publica*.[33] Public rights and jurisdiction in Barcelona, however, remained of a piece and in lay hands.

[29] The largest recorded loan was for 10,000s. in 1258 (ACA Reg. 10, fol. 74 r.–v.). Others were 5,000s. (1265) (Reg. 14, fol. 76 v.); 7,000s. (1267) (Reg. 15, fol. 61 r.); 4,000s. and 400 mbts. (1269) (Reg. 37, fol. 1 v.); 450s. (1283) (Reg. 59, fol. 194 r.).

[30] After appointing Pere d'Espiells to act as interim head of Barcelona's church, King Pere II proceeded to purchase all episcopal and diocesan revenues for 60,000s., ACA Reg. 43, fol. 39 v.; Reg. 56, fol. 123 v.

[31] Peter Linehan, *The Spanish Church and the papacy in the thirteenth century* (Cambridge, 1971), 111–12, 123.

[32] For recent evaluations of the impact of the Gregorian movement on the Catalan church, see Bonnassie, *La Catalogne*, II, 701–5; Peter Linehan, "Religion and national identity in medieval Spain," *Studies in Church history*, 18 (1982), 181–84; Freedman, *The diocese of Vic*, 19–20. The reform movement also encountered serious difficulties in Languedoc, Elisabeth Magnou-Nortier, *La Société laïque et l'Eglise dans la province ecclésiastique de Narbonne (zone cispyrénéenne) de la fin du VIII° à la fin du XI° siècle* (Toulouse, 1974), 449–518, 550–63.

[33] Tabacco, *Egemonie*, 399–427; Gerhard Dilcher, *Die Entstehung der lombardischen Stadtkommune: eine rechtsgeschichtliche Untersuchung* (Aalen, 1967) 41–44, 88–89; Dupré-Theseider, "Vescovi e città," 80–91; André Chédeville, "De la cité à la ville, 1000–1150," in *Histoire de la France urbaine*, II, 146–48.

The city and its lord

THE CHALLENGE TO PUBLIC AUTHORITY

If the reassuring traditionalism of Catalonian bishops prevented a serious confrontation with their sovereign and a consequent dismemberment of urban rights, the men to whom the counts delegated their power felt the obligations to their lord did not prevent them from exploiting their offices as proprietary alienations. The most serious threat to public authority within the city came from those charged with its preservation. During the eleventh and the better part of the twelfth century, members of powerful castleholding families or ambitious, poorly endowed *castlans* (sergeants administering castles for their lords) served as local representatives of comital authority. They did not always prove reliable. Yet without the status and experience to command an armed following and exert force to back up a judgment, the formal delegation of authority mattered little; as a result, the rugged warriors who substituted for the counts aggressively exploited the rights they had acquired and sought to extend their power of coercion whenever possible for their own gain rather than for the fisc. Only the administrative reorganization inaugurated in the mid-twelfth century by Count Ramon Berenguer IV and advanced by his successor King Alfons I finally brought the activities of the count's men under control. As orderly management of fiscal resources and the mundane job of policing the community eventually took precedence over leading troops in battle and convoking grand but irregular courts, burghers for the first time participated in the administration of their own town. Font Rius and Jesús Lalinde Abadía, both experts in legal history, have carefully traced the basic institutional framework for Catalonian urban administration, yet by stressing normative practices rather than the social background and actions of local officials, their work has tended to identify the interests of those who held delegated authority too closely with those of their lords.[34] The men who first represented the counts in Barcelona were anything but bureaucrats.

The type of resources the counts possessed in Barcelona at first made the ability to command a more valued quality than efficient administration of property. Real estate formed a minor part of the

[34] Font Rius, "Orígenes del régimen," 368–76, 429–50; Jesús Lalinde Abadía, *La jurisdicción real inferior en Cataluña ("corts, veguers, batlles")* (Barcelona, 1966), 27–40, 53–55.

urban domain. If the Carolingians had inherited large blocks of land around the ancient forum and below the walls from the Roman and Visigothic fisc, these properties had largely been donated to the cathedral, parish churches, and urban monasteries before 1000.[35] The comital palace, a few adjacent houses and workshops, the street below Castellnou and a few suburban fiefs attached to it, plots in the northern suburb known as Cort Comtal, and a stretch of land on the shore, later the site of the merchants' compound (*alfóndec*) and the royal shipyards (*drassanes*), made up the bulk of urban land still in the hands of the eleventh-century counts.[36] Their twelfth- and thirteenth-century successors made no sustained attempt to acquire new properties or recover alienated land in the intramural or suburban areas.

On the other hand, great care was shown in preserving, defining, and cultivating rights pertaining to justice, the mint, the marketplace, trade, and public utilities, here broadly defined to include water rights, ovens, and, most importantly, mills. In the 1240s, when comparative figures first become available, revenues from royal mills in Barcelona constituted roughly half the income from the entire bailiwick, an area much larger than the city itself.[37] The construction and operation of grain mills on the Rec Comtal, the distribution of water to turn the mill wheels, and permission to draw water for irrigating valuable garden plots nearby gave rise to numerous disputes, all firmly adjudicated by the count or his representatives. Burghers could not grind their grain elsewhere, nor could flour be sold in private residences without authorization.[38] As in other parts of Catalonia, however, individuals who, through officeholding or brute force, had gained control of public authority attempted to appropriate it for themselves in order to coerce local residents into paying dues and to gain a monopoly over mills and ovens, the profitable points at which agricultural products were processed for consumption. From the mid-eleventh century banal lordship posed a serious challenge to sovereign authority and thereby redefined the dynamics of power in Bar-

---

[35] Mitjá Sagué, "Condado y ciudad," 279.

[36] A summary of the urban domain can be found in Bisson, *Fiscal accounts*, I, 166–68. Cf. *Els castells*, I, 500–48.

[37] The mills brought in 13,000s./yr. for 1247–48 (ACA perg. Jaume I, 1079) and 13,500s. for 1249 (ACA perg. Jaume I, 1156); the "bailiwick of Barcelona and others attached to it" brought in 24,136s. 3d. for 1239 and 25,641s. for 1240 (Huici-Cabanes, *Documentos*, II, no. 317).

[38] ACA Reg. 37, fol. 81 r.–v.

celona and throughout the Pyrenean region. This struggle affected towns as well as the countryside. Overlooking the growing market spreading out into the suburbs below the massive foundations of Castellvell, first the viscounts and then the early vicars of Barcelona tried to extend their powers of coercion at the expense of the privileges of the townspeople which the counts had guaranteed. The drawn-out struggle of the counts to hold their lieutenants in check largely defined the extent of authority to which the inhabitants of medieval Barcelona would be subject.

Carolingian viscounts and vicars possessed sweeping powers as general substitutes for the counts.[39] Although viscounts technically stood in for their lords throughout an entire county while vicars moved in more confined circuits, in fact no clear delineation of tasks or territorial boundaries existed. The earliest Carolingian charters of franchise for Barcelona refer indifferently to judgments made by the count or his representative (*comite aut ministro iudiciaria potestas*),[40] but a broad confirmation of the city's liberties by Count Berenguer Ramon I in 1025 established the right of the city's inhabitants to plead their causes before the count, the city's viscount (*vicecomes predicte civitatis*), or judges delegated by them.[41] By the end of the late tenth century, if not before, the viscounts had gained firm control of comital authority within the city. Attached to a single family by 985 at the latest, the office of the viscount of Barcelona helped raise its holders to the highest rungs of the aristocracy. In the city itself, the viscounts held the two comital castle-gates, Castellnou and Castellvell; the latter, the nucleus of their urban power, became known simply as Castellvell of the viscounts (*castrum vetus vicecomitalis*).[42] At its base the family privately owned some workshops and an oven, where one suspects a portion of the urban population were compelled to bake their bread.[43] If the privilege of 1025 attempted to check the encroachments of banal lordship on the rights of the urban community, as Bonnassie has suggested, it also confirmed the preeminence of the viscounts. The inability of Count Berenguer Ramon I to stand up to the bullying of violent, aggrandizing castleholders backed by their armed clienteles has given him the

---

[39] On Carolingian officials, see Lalinde Abadía, *La jurisdicción*, 25–49; Ramon d'Abadal i de Vinyals, "La institució comtal carolíngia en la pre-Catalunya del segle IX," *AEM*, 1 (1964), 64–67 [repr. in *Dels visigots als catalans* (Barcelona, 1969), 1, 215–18].

[40] José María Font Rius, *Cartas de población y franquicia de Cataluña* (Barcelona and Madrid, 1969–83), 1:1, nos. 1, 2.

[41] Ibid., 1, no. 15.   [42] *LFM*, 1, no. 237.   [43] *Santa Anna*, 11, no. 297.

reputation as one of the least effectual rulers of his dynasty. Appropriately, he has received the sobriquet *el corbat*, "the Bent."

By the 1040s the pressures building from the petty brutality of turbulent castleholders and their dependants erupted into a full-scale assault on public authority. For two decades the counts of Barcelona had to put down a series of insurrections by lords who refused to acknowledge comital sovereignty and subjected the free peasantry to new burdens. The most sustained and serious challenge was led by Mir Geribert, a member of the viscomital clan.[44] With his castles dominating the Penedès, the frontier territory west of Barcelona, this independent marcher lord in 1041 declared himself the prince of Olèrdola, after his principal castle, and directly challenged comital authority. His relatives did not hold back from the fray. Viscount Udalard II and his uncle Guisalbert, bishop of Barcelona, attacked the comital palace, causing the death of at least one of its defenders. The flood of violence unleashed by the viscomital family quickly eroded the foundations of public authority upon which comital power had rested. Public courts broke down, the procedures of Visigothic law were degraded, and castle-lords imposed new obligations on the free population within their grasp. In order to put out the glowing embers of revolt, which still flared up into flash fires until 1059, and reassert his rule over arrogant, ruthless aristocrats and avaricious, insecure *castlans* with their men-at-arms, Count Ramon Berenguer I turned to a new style of lordship. Oaths of fealty, private contracts of service with nobles and knights (*convenientiae*), and above all control of castles provided sturdy new buttresses for comital rule, stabilizing and in many instances covering over the cracked edifice of public authority. After Count Ramon Berenguer I had turned back the assault on Barcelona by the armed retainers of its viscount and bishop, the terms of submission dictated to the insurgents in 1044–46 include the earliest reference to a key element ensuring comital control of castles in Catalonia: the *castlà* installed by the bishop was required to open the castle to the count, his suzerain, even if the bishop, his immediate lord, refused.[45] The charter of judgment against Viscount Udalard II also contains an appended oath of fealty in which the viscount agreed to give the *potestas* over Castellvell to the count, i.e. to surrender it to him on demand. The

[44] On Mir Geribert's revolt, see Santiago Sobrequés i Vidal, *Els grans comtes de Barcelona* (Barcelona, 1961), 56–65; Bonnassie, *La Catalogne*, ii, 637–44.

[45] ACA perg. R.B. I, sense data, 3; Bonnassie, *La Catalogne*, ii, 698.

clause appears again in a viscomital oath in 1063, with the additional provision that the installation of the *castlà* required comital approval.[46] Ramon Berenguer I had managed to prevent the viscomital family from extending its banal lordship over the inhabitants of Barcelona by securing control of the principal castle-gate, the hub of local command. This check proved decisive, for the viscounts lost their influence in the city by the close of the eleventh century. Yet even though the control of castles, oaths of fealty, and private agreements had allowed the comital dynasty to thwart one of the proudest and most formidable baronial lineages in Catalonia, and prevent it from appropriating its authority in the city and, indeed, from challenging its sovereign power throughout the territories it controlled, the difficult questions of defining comital prerogatives and of holding local representatives of comital authority in check remained.

Count Ramon Berenguer I had successfully surmounted the crisis of 1040 to 1060 by appropriating and mastering private alliances and powers dependent upon castleholding, the very forces which had undermined traditional forms of authority. But precisely because personalized loyalty rather than obligations to an older system of legal procedures and customs bound the most powerful men in the principality to their lord, those who received delegated responsibilities looked upon their charge in blatantly exploitative terms. "Seigniorial terrorism," as Bonnassie described it,[47] continued well after the containment of the mid-eleventh-century crisis, and the count's men themselves were often the most feared offenders.

EXPLOITATIVE LORDSHIP AND ITS CONTROL

In Barcelona the prerogatives of comital lordship passed from the viscounts to the vicars, who first appear in 1094.[48] Their emergence can best be accounted for as a response to the bitter factionalism during the corule of Ramon Berenguer I's two sons, Ramon Berenguer II *Cap d'Estopes* (1076–82) and Berenguer Ramon II (1076–96). In 1079 the uneasy codominion resulted in accords partitioning Barcelona itself and other comital possessions within the county. The brothers planned to rotate their residence

---

[46] ACA perg. R.B. I, sense data, 39; *LFM*, I, nos. 337, 338.
[47] Bonnassie, *La Catalogne*, II, 598.
[48] ACB 1–1–250.

every six months between the comital palace and private houses; the split of comital rights probably provided the stimulus for the eventual construction of a second comital palace, the Palau Comtal Menor in the northern suburbs. Both urban inhabitants and urban property were treated as a treasure to be divided up among quarreling warlords: with this end in mind a list containing 54 Jewish heads of household (probably complete) was made and an incomplete tally of Christian residents begun, but the latter broke off after 143 names.[49] Not the slightest acknowledgment of a corporate urban identity exists, nor any recognition that its cooperation was required for effective rule. With his magnates "the lord Count Ramon made this division of all that is his in Barcelona": the town was literally split down the middle. Yet rights of justice, custom duties, market rights, and the mint were to be managed jointly. In other words the notion of urban unity which stubbornly persisted in these accords revolved around regalian rights and ancient legal procedures deemed indivisible; land, rents, buildings, jurisdiction, the town walls, Jews, and the community itself could be treated merely as patrimonial possessions and divided up at will, much in the manner of lords parcelling out their castellanies in smaller fiefs (*caballaria*). Older elements of public authority had survived rather uncomfortably together with the new private, patrimonial order.[50]

The violent death of Count Ramon Berenguer II under suspicious circumstances in 1082 forestalled the jurisdictional fission of medieval Barcelona, if its implementation had ever in fact begun. Suspected of plotting the crime, Berenguer Ramon II, remembered as the Fratricide, managed to retain the comital title on condition that it pass to the minor heir of his murdered brother, Ramon Berenguer III, when he came of age. Aristocratic polarization around the two courts therefore continued, and members of the viscomital family figured prominently in the opposition to the Fratricide's rule.[51] Involvement in the factional

---

[49] The central document of the partition, including the list of Jews, is edited in "Barcelona en 1079: su castillo del Puerto y su aljama hebrea. Documento inédito," ed., F. Fita, *Boletín de la Real Academia de la Historia*, 40 (1903), 361–68. For a summary of the provisions and general background, see Sobrequés i Vidal, *Els grans comtes*, 120–24 and Bonnassie, *La Catalogne*, ii, 851–53. ACA R.B. II, sense data, 71 contains the abbreviated list of Christian inhabitants.

[50] For the resilience of traditional forms of authority throughout Southern Europe after the eleventh century, see Bisson, "Some characteristics of Mediterranean territorial power," 143–50.

[51] Sobrequés i Vidal, *Els grans comtes*, 123, 131.

struggles among the Catalonian baronage further undermined the position of the viscounts in Barcelona. The family began to sell off its urban property during the reign of Berenguer Ramon II, a divestment completed in all essentials by the early twelfth century when the vicar, with the count's approval, purchased the remaining viscomital rights and properties (*de aquisicione vicecomitatus*).[52] By first advancing the patrimonial interests of their family in the city and then by linking their interests to a baronial faction, the viscounts fully embodied the new forces reshaping the structure of power throughout Catalonia in the mid-eleventh century. As a result, they had the most to lose from restored comital authority and proved the least dependable guardians of comital interests in Barcelona, particularly of those stubbornly indivisible rights of an older public order. By turning to vicars instead of viscounts, the counts attempted to tighten their grip on their dynastic headquarters.

Unlike the viscounts, members of a formidable and well-established aristocratic lineage, the early vicars had less exalted origins. The five vicars known to have held the office before 1150 came from the middling levels of the nobility, of *castlà* rank at best or underendowed branches of castellan families.[53] Their background, as far as it can be determined, suggests they had first gained experience of command in the countryside and possessed shallow roots in Barcelona itself. Arbert Bernat, mentioned as vicar in 1094 (with Berenguer Bernat, about whom we know little more than his name) and again in 1101, had strong ties with Lliçà in the Vallès,[54] while Guillem and Ramon Renart, brothers and covicars in 1113, belonged to a minor line of the Montcada, a

---

[52] *CODIN*, IV, no. cxiii. For the dating of this document, however, see Fritz (Yitzhak) Baer, *Die Juden im christlichen Spanien. Erster Teil: Urkunden und Regesten* (2nd ed., Holland, 1970), I, no. 18. For other alienations, see ACB LA I, fol. 236, Mas XII, no. 2674; LA I, fol. 96, Mas X, no. 1283; LA IV, fol. 36, Mas X, no. 1245; ACA perg. R.B. III, 269; R.B. IV, sense data 112; *CODIN*, IV, no. cxlii; *CSC*, III, no. 883; *Santa Anna*, II, nos. 297, 322; III, no. 566; "Documento del siglo XI relativo a Sant Andreu de Palomar (Barcelona) procedente del archivo de Sant Benet de Bages," ed. J. Sarrat i Arbós, *Revista de la asociación artístico-arqueológica barcelonesa*, 3 (1901–2), 634–36.

[53] Several individuals identified as early vicars by Carreras Candi, *La ciutat*, 295–96 do not in fact bear the title; he incorrectly connects the vicarial office with the command of Castellvell in the early twelfth century, but the individuals he cites appear to be *castlans*, not vicars. See the list of vicars in appendix 1.

[54] His will is found in ACB LA I, fol. 206, Mas X, no. 1167. His son, Arbert, became known as Arbert de Lliçà, presumably after his family's home, *Col·lecció diplomàtica de Solsona*, no. 57. The family also held tithes and the *sagraria* at Sant Cristòfol de Lliçà, ACB LA III, fol. 98, Mas XI, no. 1421.

powerful baronial family centered in Osona.[55] Berenguer Ramon de Castellet in all likelihood took his name from the castle of Castellet in Anoia, near the upper course of the Llobregat, for his son held the nearby castle of Freixa.[56] In the late eleventh century the counts gained control of a compact group of fortifications in the area once commanded by the viscounts, suggesting Berenguer's family may have held the castle to shore up comital power in the region.[57] By installing relatively obscure men without long-standing ties to Barcelona, the counts intended to secure control over the city and prevent their prerogatives from falling into the hands of threatening aristocratic houses.

This policy had unintended results. Ambitious, aggressive, and without a substantial patrimony, the early vicars viewed their office in blatantly proprietary terms, with an eye to extracting every possible obol from it even at the risk of incurring the count's wrath. The career of Berenguer Ramon typifies the ruthless exploitation characteristic of the early urban vicars. Shortly before 1113, the count had to use force to dispossess Berenguer Ramon of the office for failing to reach an agreement with the heirs of Arbert Bernat, the former vicar.[58] Yet in compensation Berenguer Ramon received in tenure the novel impositions (*novos usaticos*) on milling grain, taverns, the sale of grain, meat, and livestock at the market. The count ostensibly instituted these "new customs," but this may only reflect a confirmation of the ruthless efficiency of Berenguer Ramon, who retained the right to collect them. A later confrontation gives added weight to this supposition. Soon after succeeding his father, in 1132 Ramon Berenguer IV accused his vicar in Barcelona of levying extortionate dues (*sub umbra vicarie*) on bolts of cloth, saddles, yokes, iron implements, round cakes, bakers, fish, and dowries.[59] The vicar reluctantly agreed to repeal the levies only after a bitter argument laced with insults, which came within a hairsbreadth of ending in judicial combat. That the vicar retained his office and held the vicariate for a quarter century after two head-on collisions with his lord demonstrates that officeholders had strong proprietary claims on their charges and faced only sporadic attempts to place

---

[55] John C. Shideler, *A medieval Catalan noble family: the Montcadas (1000–1230)* (Berkeley and Los Angeles, 1983), 35–39.

[56] *Santa Anna*, III, no. 609   [57] *Els castells*, v, 294–306; infra 130–31.

[58] *LFM*, I, no. 382.

[59] *CODIN*, IV, no. cxiii; see n. 52 above for its date.

limits on their exploitation. During the early twelfth century the count's men themselves, bound to their sovereign by personal ties rather than shared habits of administration, proved the gravest threat to the privileges enjoyed by the urban community and to the traditions of public authority which stood behind them.

Toward the middle of the twelfth century, Count Ramon Berenguer IV resolved to tighten his control over his domain and regularize administrative procedures.[60] Spurred on by the excesses of his servants and the challenge of controlling the extensive new frontier territories secured by the conquests of Tortosa in 1148 and Lleida in 1149, the count in 1151 dispatched a group of auditors on an ambitious, if incomplete, survey of the fisc in Old Catalonia. This remarkable inventory formed a little Domesday Book for Catalonia, novel in its scope and form.

Yet signs of heightened comital interest in fiscal management actually appear a few years earlier in Barcelona, which, together with the urban fisc of Girona and Vic, are notably absent from the survey of 1151. The relevant documents reveal a concern to inscribe and fix obligations, a critical element in any initiative against officials whose actions often appeared arbitrary and unsupervised. Around 1150 Arnau de Font, bailiff of Berenguer de Barcelona, drew up a tariff list, the earliest known in Catalonia, in which the share of payments due the count and to his lord were itemized in order to reflect the appropriate division of revenues that was customary in the mid-1140s.[61] Since Berenguer de Barcelona had inherited his right to part of the tariffs from his father, the vicar Berenguer Ramon, the list fixes the amount owed the count, clarifying rights and preventing unauthorized charges. In order to counteract vicarial pressure, the count also began to turn toward different officials to manage his rights. In 1144 he granted the *amostolafia*, the ransom-right derived from the transport of Muslim captives from throughout Catalonia back to their homeland, to a prominent burgher, Arnau Pere d'Arcs, for the hefty sum of 150 mbts. and in the same year the first reference appears to a resident urban bailiff, the official responsible for the direct management of the urban fisc.[62] Although the details are

---

[60] These developments are now well known through the meticulous edition of the early records of account and introduction in Bisson, *Fiscal accounts*, I, 23–77.

[61] See appendix 4, no. 1.

[62] *CODIN*, IV, no. lxxxvi; ACA Reial Patrimoni, Batllia General, Classe 3ª, vol. 6, fol. 69 r.: "meus baiulus Barchinone."

obscure, the 1140s witnessed a series of significant innovations in fiscal administration.

Besides attempting to circumscribe vicarial rights, Count Ramon Berenguer IV also tried new means to tap the increasing wealth of the town. The most revealing, but at the same time perplexing, evidence of comital initiative in exploiting his urban domain is found in a list of townspeople drawn up in the hand of Ponç the Scribe, the count's principal notary, around 1145.[63] Individuals are noted in two columns on the recto and in a single, incomplete column on the verso; at the end of each line a number appears, generally indicating the number of names, but in several lines the scribe counted two individuals as a unit and in one instance counted three individuals as four. The unit tally adds up to 232, but three lines containing 7 individuals have no number by them. If they are included, the total is 239, but not all individual names are assessed as a single unit. As Banks has suggested, the scribe may well have intended to arrive at 240, the number of denars in a pound; if this is so, then the list surely represents an attempt to collect a tax on family heads or households, each having to contribute a penny for every pound demanded by the count.[64] A further clue about the nature of the document appears in an annotation, marked off by a square and placed toward the top of the list between the two columns on the recto: *molers*, millstone cutters. A privilege by King Pere I con-

---

[63] The document has recently been published and analyzed by Banks, "The inhabitants," 143–66, whose general lines of interpretation I fully endorse. Using a somewhat different means of dating the document, I place it in late 1145 or early 1146, for the first person whose death is indicated in other documentation is Pere Bofill (Pere Bonfi), referred to as deceased on March 29, 1146, the *terminus ante quem*: ACB LA I, fol. 318, Mas XI, no. 1597. Banks proposes a date between February, 1145 and June, 1146.

[64] Banks, "The inhabitants," 148–49, counts 240 individuals in the list, but under a different light, I arrive at 243. The difficulty arises in distinguishing names from units of assessment. Only 218 proper names appear; the other individuals on the list are referred to merely as relatives. In some cases, a man and his relatives are counted as a unit, in others they are counted separately: line 25 recto, "Renard, cum fratre suo, et cognato suo ⁲⁲⁲⁲" but line 27 recto, "Muza, Arnau Pere, et frater eius, Beren ⁲⁲," by which may be meant Muza, Arnau Pere and Beren his brother, or alternatively four different individuals. In addition, on two occasions the number of proper names on a line does not add up to the number at the end: line 5 verso, "Beren, Bosnia, Marti Petit ⁲⁲⁲⁲" but line 40 recto, "Ber, Rrover, Gid Mercader, Deusde ⁲⁲⁲." Banks attributes these discrepancies to scribal incompleteness or error, but they seem to reflect a conscious attempt to arrive at 240, even if this meant slightly different assessments for a few individuals, possibly based on unusually large or small holdings. In any case, the numbers at the end of each line provide a surer guide than individual names for arriving at the intended total. That the scribe seems more interested in units of assessment than in individual names in fact lends further weight to Banks' argument that the document is a fiscal survey.

firmed that his predecessors had granted a tax exemption to the *molers* of Montjuïc from any military obligations or general assessment, known as the *questia*.[65] The exemption helps explain the failure to tally three lines with seven individuals, two of whom have the same family name as a *moler* mentioned in the confirmation of exemptions made by King Jaume I in 1218.[66] The list therefore reveals the earliest attempt to assess a *questia*, an irregular tax which became an important source of income from the city, especially in times of military need; later it considerably exceeded the annual value of the entire urban domain. As Banks has shown by meticulously analyzing the propertyholding patterns of the individuals appearing on the list, the count's scribe made a systematic survey of non-ecclesiastical properties in the western and northern sectors of the town, grouping the community in a way to meet the needs of his master. In stark contrast to the planned partition of the city in 1079, in which no regard at all was shown for the integrity of the community, the tax list drawn up ca. 1145 sought to raise revenue for the count through a careful assessment of the urban population which respected and relied upon the local structures of residence and landholding. As administrative techniques slowly overshadowed coercion as a means of control, the outlines of the urban community began to stand out in the fiscal records.

Due to the initiatives of Count Ramon Berenguer IV, prominent burghers became increasingly involved with the management of the urban domain. Nowhere is this more evident than in the pledge by the count of his mills, tolls, and other rights in Barcelona to eleven townsmen for a loan of 7,700s. late in 1148, just as the last desperate push to take Tortosa was under way.[67] Long recognized as an early sign of cooperative action among local urban leaders, the document also demonstrates how the need

---

[65] Referred to in a confirmation of 1218: Huici-Cabanes, *Documentos*, 1, no. 6. The document does not explicitly include the exemption from the *questia* among the traditional liberties of the *molers*, but in a much later dispute involving the city councillors and the *molers* in 1283, Pere's privilege is taken to mean that the *molers* of Montjuïc were not required to contribute "in questiis exaccionibus seu collectis in dictis petitis a domino rege," in this case for arming galleys; AHCB Llibre vert, 1, fols. 257 v.–258 v.

[66] Banks, "The inhabitants," 158, line 37 of transcription: "Guillem dez Palad et Bernad de Palad"; Huici-Cabanes, *Documentos*, 1, no. 6: "Guillelmus Paleti."

[67] The document is now re-edited in Bisson, *Fiscal accounts*, 11, no. 143, but one should still take note of the older viewpoint of Francesc Carreras Candi, "Los ciutadans de Barcelona," *BRABLB*, 9 (1921), 137–40.

for credit encouraged the count to look upon his urban domain with a keen eye for assessing its value and getting at it quickly. With more territory to control and greater, or at least more attainable, ambitions, Ramon Berenguer IV could not remain content with handing over valuable urban rights and assets to officials who looked upon their charge as a license for unbridled exploitation. Townsmen themselves must have applauded the change, for it both helped rein in those who held power over them and, through their credit and managerial expertise, cracked open the door to local administration and allowed its profits to pour into the coffers of urban entrepreneurs.

TOWARD CIVIC ADMINISTRATION

The two basic movements evident in the initiatives of the 1140s, the limitation of arbitrary lordship and close supervision of the urban domain, both gained momentum in the second half of the twelfth century. Yet old habits of proprietary exploitation died hard. Two men who held the vicariate in the 1180s, Pere d'Alfou and Berenguer Bou, both prominent burghers, may have played on a patrimonial connection to secure the office because of their close association with the descendants of the petulant vicar Berenguer Ramon de Castellet, the former by fiefholding and the latter by marriage.[68] The tendency to regard fiscal resources as proprietary grants still was present in a dispute involving Pere Arnau the Knight (*miles*), in all probability the man who served as vicar during the 1150s.[69] Arnau demanded and received payment from a land sale near Cort Comtal, "in my fief, the count's allod" (*in meo fevo, in alodio comitis*) and demanded the purchaser recognize his wife, his descendants, and himself as lord, but not the count (*alium seniorem non proclames vel facias nisi tantum nos et successores nostros*). The fief (*fevum*), which in Catalan usage still designated public land held in tenure as compensation for service,

---

[68] Four generations of the d'Alfou family held fiefs dependent on the Regomir castle-gate from Berenguer Ramon and his son, ACB 1–5–34; Berenguer Bou married Berenguer Ramon's granddaughter, *CSC*, III, no. 1246.

[69] *Santa Anna*, II, no. 336. At least three Pere Arnaus can be identified by the names of their wives around 1160, but the association with the comital fief and his standing as a knight make a strong case for the indentification of the Pere Arnau mentioned here with the vicar. Pere Arnau the Knight does not appear elsewhere as an urban landholder, although a man by the same name subscribed to a comital charter in 1146, ACB 4–50–479.

is here hard to disentangle from notions of private ownership. The count-kings of the later twelfth century still turned to turbulent, aggrandizing men of *castlà* and knightly rank to fill the vicariate. Guillem Català, Joan de Cascai, Ermengol de Manresa, Guillem Tició, son of the *castlà* of Castelldefels in the Baix Llobregat, and probably Pere Arnau as well owed their promotions to service to the count and experience in commanding castles with their dependencies, not to urban propertyholding or local patronage.[70] As outsiders, they would have had few qualms about extracting as much from their offices as possible, without troubling themselves about the formalities of the tenure of public land, the community's traditional rights, or internal social balances. The only prominent townsmen to serve as vicar in the twelfth century were Pere d'Alfou, for the reasons mentioned above, and Pere Ricart, who, as we shall see later, ran afoul of the count because of a castle his family acquired. Since the vicar had to be familiar with military command to protect the count's peace and enforce judgments, recruitment to the office remained remarkably consistent throughout the twelfth century. The vicars themselves did not therefore become more compliant, but they did face stiffer resistance from the count and the community.

During the second half of the twelfth century, the bailiffs of Barcelona assumed a leading role in urban administration. This marked a critical turning point in the management of comital rights and authority, for the functions of the office proved an effective check on arbitrary lordship and permitted the count to grant the right to administer his revenues to individuals without fear of losing his prerogatives. Before the 1180s, however, the urban bailiff was a shadowy figure. In the early twelfth century he may have been little more than a rent collector of comital fees and dues, including mills and ovens, and possibly caretaker of the comital palace. Charters pertaining to the urban domain bear the subscription of the count, not his bailiff, who also fails to appear among witnesses in comital charters relating to the city. With the growth of population and the attendant revenues from urban utilities, the importance and responsibilities of the urban bailiffs surely increased, but only in the 1180s do their names and activities begin to emerge with regularity in the extant records.

[70] On the identity of the vicars, see appendix 1 and the lists in Bisson, *Fiscal accounts*, 1, 251–58. On Berenguer Tició's family, *CSC*, III, no. 1156; ACB 1–5–338, where they are associated with the countryside to the west of the city.

It was precisely during these years that King Alfons I began to improve his administrative techniques by organizing his archives and regularizing accounting procedures.[71] The heightened profile of bailiffs as fiscal managers left its mark on Barcelona. In a remarkably detailed memorial of account in 1186, the bailiff Llobell summarized his receipts not only from the bailiwick of Barcelona and the bailiwicks dependent upon it but from the vicariate as well.[72] Three items singled out in the account, the market oven at the foot of Castellvell, custom duties, and sale of meat at the butchers' market, had all either belonged to or had once been claimed by the vicar. The subjection of the vicar to the fiscal supervision of the urban bailiff, a person of substantially lower rank, must have occurred in the face of considerable opposition, for, as Bisson has shown, the institution of regularized accounting procedures by Alfons I throughout his domain from 1179 fixed the amount of profit officials could expect from their charges and thereby protected the community from extortionate demands.[73] Beneath the terse summation in charters of account one can sense a struggle not only between the urban vicar and bailiff for control over the city's resources, but also between two styles of lordship, one exploitative and patrimonial, the other administrative and supervisory.

As expertise in management, finance, and accounting vied with the martial qualities of command and coercion as desirable qualifications for local administrators, the social background of local officeholders changed. With the possible exception of Roig, all the documented twelfth-century bailiffs were Jews (see appendix 2). In addition, four of the five came from the same family, probably originating in the Penedès.[74] The count-kings turned repeatedly to proven and experienced fiscal specialists, a pattern which continued into the thirteenth century. Salamó Bonafos, Vital Salamó, and above all Benevist de Porta served as bailiffs for extensive periods until 1269, after which date Jews disappear from

---

[71] Bisson, *Fiscal accounts*, I, 86–101; Antonio Aragó Cabañas, "La institución 'baiulus regis' en Cataluña, en la época de Alfonso el Casto," *VII CHCA* (Barcelona, 1962), III, 137–42.

[72] Bisson, *Fiscal accounts*, II, no. 61; the bailiff again accounted for the vicariate in 1209, ibid., no. 125.

[73] Ibid., I, 106–8 and "Ramon de Caldes (c. 1135–99): dean of Barcelona and king's minister," in *Law, Church, and society: essays in honor of Stephan Kuttner*, ed. K. J. Pennington and R. Somerville (Philadelphia, 1977), 283–88 [repr. in *Medieval France*, 191–95].

[74] Bisson, *Fiscal accounts*, I, 269–71, and ACA Reial Patrimoni, Batllia General, Classe 3ª, vol. 6, fol. 96 v., where Vives and Perfet are referred to as nephews of Saltell.

the list of bailiffs. Significantly, prominent townsmen, especially members of the Durfort, d'Espiells, and Grony families beginning with the first decade of the thirteenth century often held the office for years at a time. The bailiff's relatively long tenure had less to do with patrimonial interests than with the nature of delegated financial authority and credit. Because payment not only for current operating costs but for non-related expenses incurred by the count-kings was assigned directly on revenues raised from all or part of the bailiwick, the bailiffs frequently had to extend credit to their sovereign in order for him to meet his expenses, debts which would then be recovered from the bailiwick's future income. In 1262, Benevist de Porta paid off a royal debt of 15,221s. 8d. and 126 mbts. to Guillem Grony, bailiff of Barcelona. Benevist, recently bailiff himself and an important royal financier, thereupon took over the post.[75] The intricate mingling of local administration and credit, so typical of early Catalonian government, made office-holding a lucrative entrepreneurial undertaking. Already dimly present in Count Ramon Berenguer IV's pledge of urban revenues to eleven burghers in 1148, the mercurial interplay between finance and political authority encouraged the leading figures of the town to pool their resources in order to play at the high-stakes game of royal finance. As we shall see in chapter 5, the funnelling of loans to the ambitious King Pere I and his courtiers in the early thirteenth century helped define and structure relationships among the emerging patriciate. By that time, the wealthiest burghers did not need to storm the gates of the old comital palace to assure themselves a leading role in town: they already held its key in pledge.

Under the watchful eye of the bailiff a lush undergrowth of revenue farming and credit covered over the urban fisc during the thirteenth century. By 1262 a subbailiff had emerged to assist with the increasing complexity of administration.[76] Throughout the twelfth century the day-to-day job of enforcing comital rights and operating a utility had either fallen under the direct supervision of the bailiff or had been assigned by the count to individuals, presumably for their lifetimes but in a few instances even passing to their heirs. In 1144 and 1145, for example, Count Ramon Berenguer IV granted the right to operate an urban mill to a group of individuals for two-thirds of the *multura*, pre-

---

[75] ACA Reg. 12, fols. 52 v.–53 r.   [76] ACA Reg. 12, fol. 5 r.

sumably the milling fee.[77] By 1238, however, the bailiff regularly sold the right to farm the mill revenues to investors for a fixed period, usually a year; because of the value of this resource, it sometimes was subject to an account separate from that of the rest of the bailiwick.[78] In a pledge of their tithe from urban revenues made by the Templars in 1253, ten separate offices directly related to the management of the urban fisc are mentioned, and six others were concerned with bailiwicks subject to Barcelona.[79] The sixteen offices referred to in the pledge represent a bare minimum. Because groups of investors would pool their funds to purchase the farm of important urban revenues and minor supervisory offices would now generally be held only for a short period, a significant number of burghers participated at some level of royal administration in the city. The proliferation of local offices and revenue farming therefore not only allowed townspeople themselves to manage important municipal utilities and fill supervisory roles but also made the bailiff an important focus of local patronage, dependent of course on the good will of the count-kings.

Even the prestigious post of vicar slowly opened in the thirteenth century to influential burghers, who alternated in office with nobles and knights. This testifies to the increased status of urban families such as the Durfort, Ombau, d'Espiells, de Vic, Mallol, Sunyer, and Ferrer since the vicar's function was identified with local military command, enforcing the peace, and passing judgment. Yet the office continued to attract members of prominent castellan and baronial families from the countryside, including the Plegamans, Centelles, and Peratallada. Fiscal responsibilities, on the other hand, were few. As a result of the struggle over urban lordship in the second half of the twelfth century, the vicars found their supervision over the urban economy and its revenues restricted, even though the precise jurisdictional limits between the vicar and bailiff were still a point of contention as late as 1266.[80] In the last decades of the thirteenth century, the urban bailiwick was worth at least six times as much as the vicariate, but the office of vicar continued to carry greater weight.

In contrast to the broad powers vicars held or usurped in the early twelfth century, their authority became increasingly con-

---

[77] ACA Reial Patrimoni, Batllia General, Classe 3ª, vol. 6, fols. 68 r.–69 v.
[78] ADB perg. Santa Anna, Carp. 8, 122; ACB 1–6–1249.
[79] ACA perg. Jaume I, 1332.
[80] ACA Reg. 15, fols. 31 v., 33 v. Cf. ACA perg. Jaume I, 1749.

fined to judicial and police functions in the thirteenth. By 1240, when a remarkable ledger permits a detailed investigation of the vicar's finances, 24 percent of his income derived from litigation brought before him and 64 percent from fines.[81] As early as the 1190s the vicar was closely associated with a regularly functioning court; we now hear of the "vicar of Barcelona's court," which sat at the "castle-gate of the court," previously known as "Castellvell of the viscounts."[82] The new name says much about the evolution of lordship. Once the hub of a powerful baronial clan determined to exploit the power delegated to it in violation of urban liberties and in blatant opposition to the comital dynasty itself, the old castle-gate around 1200 now served as the site where townspeople could come to receive justice from an officer of the sovereign.

By holding officials to account and gradually drawing prominent burghers into local administration, the count-kings tamed Barcelona's vicars and molded urban institutions to the outlines of local society. Public authority, although cast in a new form, forcefully reemerged by the end of the twelfth century through an administrative system built up by Ramon Berenguer IV, Alfons I, and their agents. Yet this represents only one response to the challenges created by the eleventh-century crisis. As a result of the direct assault on sovereign power and the encroachments of exploitative lordship, which continued well into the twelfth century, the public framework of urban life collapsed. During the obscure decades after 1100, however, townspeople faced with extortionate *novos usaticos*, instituted by the vicars with ferocious delight, slowly came to articulate common interests. By gradually learning to regulate internal disputes and resist, or profit from, seigniorial pressures, leading figures in local society began to exercise authority, an authority roughly fashioned from heterogeneous elements derived from local custom and the debris of a once thriving public culture rather than from a clearly defined body of delegated rights. The new form of urban leadership and its insertion into a new administrative framework can best be seen

---

[81] ACA Cartes Reials, caixa 2, extrasèrie, 65. The ledger covers a nine-month period in 1240 and 1241.

[82] The title "vicarius curie barchinonensis" appears in 1189, ACB 1–6–205; cf. ACA perg. Alfons I, 709 and perg. Pere I, 74. While "Castellvell of the court" becomes common usage in the thirteenth century, the earliest association of the site with the vicar's court refers to it as "ad portam civitatis curie barchinoensis ... ad portam castri de curia," ADB perg. Santa Anna, Carpeta de la creu, unnumb. parch. [21 v 1214].

in the settlement of disputes and in the workings of the vicarial court.

CONFLICTS, COURTS, AND THE URBAN COMMUNITY

In the early Middle Ages Catalonia clung tenaciously to the procedures and proscriptions set down in the Visigothic law code and, ultimately, to the Roman legal system which lay behind it. Frankish rule, always well disposed to fostering local customs, perpetuated and reinforced the native legal traditions in the *Marca Hispanica*. Professional judges, copies of the Visigothic code, evidentiary rules stressing written records, clear court procedures and summonses, and authoritative sentences backed by comital power continued to thrive in vibrant public courts well into the eleventh century, when in many parts of Europe great landlords and castle lords had already seized the rights to justice.[83] The challenge to comital power in the mid-eleventh century radically changed the nature of legal proceedings. As Bonnassie has shown, contemptuous aristocrats and *castlans* with their armed retainers defied attempts to haul them before public courts for their acts of violence; traditional legal procedures broke down as private agreements, negotiated compromises, and seigniorial pronouncements replaced sentences handed down by law-men at regularly convened courts. In some areas, such as Osona, conservative ecclesiastical influence and geographical isolation delayed the collapse of a traditional legal culture, but by 1100 familiarity with the precise provisions of the written law began to decline sharply.[84] What remained was a romantic invocation of the ancient force of Visigothic law, not a legal system founded as in the past on the scrupulous observance of its rules.

As ancient legal procedures were degraded and public courts crumbled, other means of settling disputes replaced them. Already in the tenth century the records produced by Catalonian courts

---

[83] On the survival of Visigothic law, see Walter Kienast, "La pervivencia del derecho godo en el sur de Francia y Cataluña," *BRABLB*, 35 (1973–74), 265–95; Aquilino Iglesia Ferreirós, "La creación del derecho en Cataluña," *AHDE*, 47 (1977), 99–423; Michel Zimmerman, "L'Usage du droit visigothique en Catalogne du IXe au XIIe siècle: approche d'une signification culturelle," *MCV*, 9 (1973), 233–81; and Bonnassie, *La Catalogne*, I, 136–44, 183–202. Cf. Yvonne Bongert, *Recherches sur les cours laïques du Xe au XIIIe siècle* (Paris, 1949), 57–78.

[84] Freedman, *The diocese of Vic*, 116–20; Zimmerman, "L'Usage," 277–81.

demonstrate a decline in quality and specificity of the procedures they record. During the ninth century the court itself produced documents to authenticate the individual stages of a suit, but this gave way to the production of private records by the winner, who memorialized the favorable judgment in a formal renunciation of further claims (*evacuatio*). Yet the use of professional judges, the frequent presence of counts or their delegates, and the citation of passages from the *Liber iudiciorum* still provided the foundations of public courts well into the early eleventh century. Catalonian judicial charters from the period in virtually all cases contain decisive adjudications for one party or the other.[85] The forms and procedures of settlement, however, changed as a result of the challenge to public authority. Private settlement among the parties themselves (*concordia, convenientia*), unilateral renunciation of rights by one side (*definitio, evacuatio*), and arbitration by means of judges selected by the litigants (*arbitratio*) offered ways of resolving conflict in the absence of any public authority to pass and enforce judgment. Because the available evidence usually reflects the outcome of a dispute rather than the process of resolution, the precise nature of the settlement in many cases remains hidden behind conservative legal terminology. The functional categories just mentioned, however, were far from clear cut. What might at first appear an unsolicited renunciation of rights or a voluntary accord often came about through collective pressure exerted by local notables, first known as the *boni homines* but later called *probi homines*, or *prohoms* in Catalan. At the session of a Carolingian court (*mallum*), a panel of "law-worthy men" (*boni homines*) often appeared to give evidence, act as signatories, or intervene as official mediators, but judges interrogated witnesses, determined procedures, and gave judgment. As a flexible system of compromise, which granted each party some of its claim, gradually replaced formal adjudication, which settled the dispute by exonerating one party and condemning the other, the role of the *prohoms* expanded significantly. A fluid group of prominent townsmen appear sporadically in the late tenth and eleventh century, attesting to documents, determining land values, setting property boundaries, and exercising an informal

---

[85] Roger J. H. Collins, "Visigothic law and regional custom in disputes in early medieval Spain," in *The settlement of disputes in early medieval Europe*, eds. W. Davies and P. Fouracre (Cambridge, 1986), 87–88, 99.

Table 2.1 *Dispute settlements in Barcelona, 1100–1290*

	Concordiae	Definitiones	Iudicia	Arbitrationes
1100–1139	1	5	3	0
1140–1179	8	12	1	0
1180–1219	17	4	9	3
1220–1290	7	2	65	32

authority based on a knowledge of local conditions.[86] With the breakdown of public courts presided over by representatives of the old Carolingian order, the *prohoms* became the leading force behind dispute settlements. The responsibility to ensure internal peace and stability made them increasingly self-conscious representatives of the urban community. But when the vicar emerged as the chief judicial officer in Barcelona and once again handed down normative justice from regular public courts, an alternative emerged both to the system of compromise settlement and to the role of the *prohoms*.

The nature of dispute settlements therefore offers a guide both to changes in the shifting nature of urban authority and an emerging sense of community. Table 2.1 summarizes the basic types of settlements reached among townsmen in Barcelona from 1100 to 1290; disputes among clerics or rare cases settled in ecclesiastical courts between laymen and clerics are excluded. The system of negotiated compromise appears most clearly in the concords (*concordiae*) and renunciations (*definitiones*), while normative justice is found in decisions reached by a representative of public authority (*iudicia*). Arbitrations (*arbitrationes*) represent a hybrid form in the present schema, for although the litigants themselves privately selected judges, the dispute usually ended in a complete exoneration of one party and the condemnation of the other.

Perhaps the most striking feature revealed by the table is the scarcity of records about dispute settlements of any kind during the early twelfth century, a particularly unsettled period in the

---

[86] On the early *prohoms*, called *boni homines* or *boni viri* before 1100, see above all Font Rius, "Orígenes del régimen," 415–50; K. Nehlsen-von Stryk, *Die* boni homines *des frühen Mittelalters. Freiburger rechtsgeschichtliche Abhandlungen*, new series 11 (Freiburg, 1981), 111–36.

city's history. While the extant documentation is in general poor for these decades, the clumsy, uncertain language of the extant records of dispute suggests that reasons other than the mere hazards of survival account for this dearth. Formality was, after all, greatly prized in judicial documents. From the variety of clauses employed in the charters, one senses that the scribe was searching for the exact word and the proper phrase. This hardly proved reassuring to the disputants and surely points to a fluid, transitional system of settling disputes. Even the three *iudicia* recorded before 1140 were unusual in their form and procedure. Two involved the count personally, who had to threaten military action and judicial combat to effect the condemnation of his feisty vicar, Berenguer Ramon.[87] In the other settlement tentatively classified as a *iudicium*, the vicar condemned the excesses of his predecessors and returned revenues to the bishop which they had unjustly appropriated.[88] These cases hardly reveal the survival of a smoothly run public court. Even negotiated agreements involved considerable variation in their formulas. While after 1140 charters routinely used the phrase "with the counsel of the *prohoms*," an uncomfortable mixture of formulas appears in the record of a *placitum* from 1139 in which the *prohoms* "judged and affirmed" the matter "without any doubt" (*iudicaverunt et affirmaverunt … absque ullo dubio*) even though the resolution of the dispute clearly involved a compromise.[89] In 1130, a concord was reached "with the counsel of the consuls and honorable men." Since no other reference to urban consuls appears anywhere else in Catalonia for another fifty years, this reference has justifiably been dismissed as the earliest indication of consular government,[90] yet it does reveal the fluidity in formulas which, in this case, may have been influenced by Catalonian contact with Provence and its consular regimes taking shape during this decade. Methods of resolving conflict thus appear tentative and experimental; records of compromise vary in form, while burghers shunned justice dispensed by the vicar, whose decisions must have appeared arbitrary and exploitative in the absence of established court procedures. The scanty evidence for the early twelfth century points to a judicial culture in disarray.

---

[87] *LFM*, I, no. 382; *CODIN*, IV, no. cxiii.   [88] ACB LA I, fol. 83, Mas x, no. 1275.
[89] *Llib. bl.*, no. 39.
[90] Font Rius, "Orígenes del régimen," 465–66, n. 761. For further discussion of the enigmatic reference to *consules* in 1130, infra, 182, n. 17.

The period from 1140 to 1180 was the age of the *prohoms* in Barcelona. During these decades, negotiated settlements arrived at with the aid of prominent burghers became common and the diplomatic form of the documents recording the resolution of conflict fixed. Even though the size and constitution of the mediating group varied, the absence of a solid institutional setting does not imply that the proceedings lacked formality or common points of reference. Through attempts to arbitrate disputes and pressure the parties to arrive at a solution, the *prohoms* established precedents and confirmed local customs in the absence of professional judges and reliable representatives of public authority to supervise courts. Although in practice the rules of justice under Visigothic law allowed for flexibility and the inclusion of local usages, its model of social stratification and the severity of its penalties became anachronistic by the end of the eleventh century together with the judicial procedures it assumed to be in operation. As the *boni homines* of the old Carolingian courts emerged as *prohoms* in the early twelfth century to assume the leading role in the resolution of disputes, they based their decisions on an evolving body of local customs, which slowly assumed sharper outlines. The *prohoms* themselves did not, however, intend to abrogate older laws but merely wished to supplement them. In the prologue to the *Usatges de Barcelona,* a code of regional custom that began to form in the mid-eleventh century, Count Ramon Berenguer I cited the authority of the *Lex Visigothorum* to justify his own legislation. At the local level, Barcelona's *prohoms* were also slowly solidifying their own legal traditions.[91] The charter of franchise to Agramunt in 1163 instituted the "usage of the city of Barcelona" (*usaticum Barcinonae civitatis ville*) and by the early thirteenth century explicit references appear to the customs of Barcelona in urban charters.[92]

Reliance on local custom and procedures assumed a prominent place in dispute settlement because of the degradation of public, authoritative justice. In a thesis widely accepted since its publication in 1940, Font Rius has shrewdly argued that in the twelfth century the *prohoms* of Catalonian towns gradually entered the

---

[91] On the flexibility of Visigothic law, see Roger J. H. Collins, " 'Sicut lex Gothorum continet': law and charters in ninth- and tenth-century León and Catalonia," *English historical review*, 100 (1985), 510–11.

[92] Font Rius, *Cartas de población*, I:1, no. 122; ACB 1–6–140 (1201): "secundum consuetudinem Barchinone." Cf. ACB 1–1–776; 1–6–1044, 2595, 3536; ACA perg. Jaume I, 274, 339.

curia of local officials, in Barcelona that of the vicar, a process leading to amicable cooperation between urban communities and sovereign authority.[93] Yet there is little to suggest that the vicar of Barcelona held public courts or dispensed normative justice in the mid-twelfth century. The *prohoms* were left to their own devices. The vicar appears in only two of twenty settlements before 1180 which mention the intervention of *prohoms*, and in these cases he did not possess special judicial prerogatives. Rather than a vicarial court drawing prominent townsmen into its orbit, the process seems precisely the reverse: the vicars occasionally participated with the *prohoms* in promoting compromises and in ensuring local customs. Because the vicars had posed a threat to their lords and to the rights of townspeople in the early twelfth century, their occasional inclusion among the *prohoms* before 1180 integrated them into the procedures of dispute resolution most commonly employed in the community and thereby held them in check. The prevalence of compromise over adjudication therefore strengthened the position of local leaders and provided a counterweight to the excesses of exploitative lordship.

After 1180, however, the vicar's court became the hub of justice in the city. The sudden change came about as a result of King Alfons I's determination to reform the Catalonian vicariate between 1173 and 1178. At the Cort of Fondarella in 1173, the king promulgated statutes intended to turn the old diocesan peace in Catalonia into an instrument of territorial, sovereign power; in the following years vicars and bishops were urged to raise local forces in their diocese to oppose peace-breakers.[94] As a result, the vicars assumed important new judicial and supervisory functions.

These initiatives had a swift and profound impact in Barcelona, not only in the formation of a regular vicarial court but also in the type of justice meted out there. The first sign of the change occurs in a dispute in 1180 between Sant Cugat del Vallès and Bernat de Tallada brought before the vicar Berenguer Bou. After "listening to the pleas of both parties and examining the documents," Berenguer Bou adjudicated the case by himself in favor of Sant Cugat.[95] In its procedure and resolution, the plea clearly reveals

[93] Font Rius, "Orígenes del régimen," 438–39.

[94] *Cortes*, I:1, 55–62. On these obscure events, see Thomas N. Bisson, *The medieval Crown of Aragon: a short history* (Oxford, 1986), 48–50.

[95] *Santa Anna*, III, no. 488; Berenguer Bou appears as vicar of Barcelona the same year in ACB 1–5–253. Cf. ACA Reial Patrimoni, Batllia General, Classe 3ᵃ, vol. 6, fol. 74 v.

the revival of normative justice dispensed at a secular urban court. The legal transformations behind the revival are multiple and intertwined: the promulgation of the complete *Usatges* with a markedly regalian tone by Count Ramon Berenguer IV, probably between 1149 and 1151; the infiltration of Roman and canon law into Catalonia in the late twelfth century; and a renewed interest in Visigothic law.[96] For the problem at hand, however, the distinctions among the various legal traditions are largely irrelevant, for they all reinforced the power of the vicar and promoted the use of documents, the summoning of witnesses, and the dispensation of authoritative judgment. All these features differ profoundly from those found in compromise settlements. Both systems coexisted and competed with each other from 1180 to 1220, but afterwards private compacts and evacuations lost ground. They customarily were employed for minor disputes, particularly over common walls and gutters between neighbors. To a large extent arbitration took the place of *concordiae* and *definitiones*, but the arbiters in many instances possessed legal training, followed evidentiary procedures, and reached decisions fully exonerating or condemning the litigants. The vicar's court, on the other hand, increased its efficiency and extended its jurisdiction. In 1208, a territorial competency is attested (*curie civitatis districtum*);[97] in 1227, a scribe became permanently attached to the court and an assistant, the subvicar, had been installed by 1234.[98] The transformation of the vicar from a ruggedly independent, often defiant delegate of comital authority to a dependable agent of justice presiding over regular courts reached its conclusion in the early thirteenth century, lending stability to local administration but also undermining the authority of the *prohoms* and the method of dispute resolution they promoted.

A FAILED CONSULAR MOVEMENT

The distinction between negotiated compromise and normative justice helps uncover the nature of power in the city and also sheds new light on a stubborn problem of Catalonian urban history: the

[96] See, in general, José María Font Rius, "El desarrollo general del derecho en los territorios de la Corona de Aragón (siglos XII–XIV)," *VII CHCA* (Barcelona, 1962), I, 290–306; Joan Bastardas i Parera, *Sobre la problemàtica dels Usatges de Barcelona* (Barcelona, 1977); José Rius Serra, "El derecho visigodo en Cataluña," *GAKS*, 8 (1940), 67–69 for late references to Visigothic law in renunciation clauses.
[97] ACB 1–6–202.   [98] ACB 1–1–1601, 1–6–1604.

late emergence and instability of autonomous municipal institutions. Elected urban representatives known as consuls first appear in Cervera (1182), Barcelona (1183), Perpinyà (1197), Lleida (1197), and at Vic (probably in 1185) – where the local bishop suppressed the movement for urban autonomy – long after consular regimes had been established in northern Italy and southern France.[99] These early references to urban consuls, however, tell us little about their function. Because the consulate remained moribund in Perpinyà for decades after its foundation, J. A. Brutails argued that the king had forced self-government on the town against its will for his administrative convenience.[100]

A similar problem exists for Barcelona. The handful of references to urban consuls fall between the years 1183 and 1219; yet from 1219 until 1249, when Jaume I set up a town council that, with some modification, remained until the Bourbon period, the sources grow silent about autonomous municipal institutions. Barcelona's consulate therefore reached its apogee precisely during the decades when the systems of negotiated settlement and normative justice were in competition and the vicar was organizing his court. The consuls came from the same group of eminent citizens who acted as *prohoms* and, like them, involved themselves in settling disputes but in a more formal manner than before. The most telling evidence comes from a plea held in the presence of a large assembly of townspeople in 1219 about a tax on flour (*leuda farine*) which residents were forced to pay, an imposition levied a century earlier by Berenguer Ramon de Castellet, whose heir alienated the right to a dependant, Pere d'Alfou.[101] With the vicar in attendance, four *consules* examined witnesses and adjudicated the suit in favor of the community, which henceforth did not have to pay the tax. Both the appearance of formal representatives (*agentes*) for the community and the emphasis on documentary evidence reveal traces of Roman law, a force which also made itself felt in the vicar's court. The consuls and the vicar were vying

[99] Font Rius, "Orígenes del régimen," 476–90; Paul Freedman, "An unsuccessful attempt at urban organization in medieval Catalonia," *Speculum*, 54 (1979), 479–91; Bisson, *Fiscal accounts*, II, no. 43.

[100] J. A. Brutails, *Etude sur la condition des populations rurales en Roussillon au Moyen Age* (Paris, 1891), 260.

[101] Font Rius, "Orígenes del régimen," ap. 7. The episcopal share in the *leuda farine* was unjustly seized by "certain vicars" before 1114, a veiled reference to Berenguer Ramon, ACB LA I, fol. 83, Mas x, no. 1275. In 1195 his son ceded fiefs "and much else" received from the bishop to the d'Alfou family, ACB 1–5–340.

to dispense normative justice.[102]

André Gouron has pointed out that the appearance of *consules* corresponded to the spread of Roman law in southern France,[103] an observation which also seems to apply to Catalonia. Yet in sharp contrast to conditions in Occitania, the count-kings reinforced sovereign rights and authority in Catalonia through fiscal initiatives and administrative reforms in the second half of the twelfth century. If vicars had continued to act as exploitative lords instead of agents of a sovereign, territorial order, the informal powers of the *prohoms* and the impulse to render normative justice provided by Roman law could well have converged to produce an aggressive municipal government determined to protect the rights of townspeople against extortion and usurpation. But as the vicar's court flourished, the consular regime withered. Even when the king established a permanent town council by fiat in 1249, he commanded his vicar to take an oath before it and to seek advice from the assembly for the principal royal official in the city was still the guardian of the community's will.[104]

CONCLUSION

The formation of early urban institutions in Barcelona and elsewhere in Catalonia did not come about through a dramatic, violent confrontation between townspeople and their lord, but the process was by no means as gradual and orderly as usually presented. A vibrant public culture dependent on written law and Carolingian offices had stubbornly persisted in Catalonia well into the eleventh century; by the thirteenth, sovereign authority stood firmly upon the foundations of supervised, dependable local administration and actively promoted the creation of municipal regimes. Because of this seeming continuity of sovereign authority, a linkage in large part created by the lack of careful studies on twelfth-century Catalonia and its vast, dispersed collections of parchments, the articulation of collective interests of the urban community gives the appearance of occurring gradually, quietly,

---

[102] An indication of the parallel jurisdiction can be found in a formula which appears in two charters from the same year (1214) in which a seller agrees to transfer property regardless of any "delays of the [vicar's] court or consuls" (*sine fatiga curie vel consulum vel alicuius persone non etiam aliqua iudiciali sentencia expectata*), ACB 3–29–242; ACA perg. Jaume I, 11. The clause subsequently disappears.

[103] Gouron, "Diffusion des consulats," 67–72.   [104] ACA Reg. 16, fol. 160 r.

and under the benevolent guidance of the count-kings. Yet below the surface, a tense, drawn-out struggle for power took place within the city.

The violent assault on the traditional order in the 1040s had a profound, long-term impact on urban organization. The consequences of this challenge to comital rule, however, took decades to resolve. Count Ramon Berenguer I had skillfully surmounted the immediate effects of the "feudal crisis" which confronted him by using forms of personal loyalty and private command to bolster his dynasty. But even though power in the city did not shatter into a myriad of private jurisdictions, his successors had to deal with the lingering threat exploitative lordship posed to sovereign, public authority by the very men to whom that authority was delegated. Only under Count Ramon Berenguer IV and King Alfons I did new fiscal and administrative initiatives begin to rein in their aggrandizing, defiant lieutenants. During this struggle, the urban community tentatively came to express its interests under the guidance of informal representatives who settled its disputes, established local customs, and supported the efforts of the count-kings to extend their control over local resources, which prominent burghers in turn obtained through credit or service to their lord. By the early thirteenth century the collective interest of leading townsmen and the assertion of sovereign power had converged to limit exploitative lordship in the city, a movement culminating in the formation of a stable vicarial court and the participation of burghers in local administration.

Because the categories of urban history have traditionally revolved around the polar opposition of "bourgeois" and "feudal" forms of organization, the communal movement has usually been treated as a novel, precocious, and uncharacteristic development in medieval Europe.[105] If, however, we consider it as part of a broad process of redefining the nature of power in the eleventh and twelfth centuries, urban communes and consular regimes no longer seem out of place. From the Lombard Plain to Catalonia, the traditional framework of public life had been swept away by the mid-eleventh century in both the countryside and the

---

[105] See the astute criticism of Reynolds, *Kingdoms and communities*, 155–58. Although I do not share her view that thirteenth-century municipal regimes are simply a formalized extension of a primitive urban collectivity, an *Urstadtgemeinschaft*, there is much to be said for her insistence on placing municipal governments in a broad framework of medieval lay communities.

towns.[106] In its place, new institutions were slowly forged from seigniorial, collective, customary, and public bonds in a bewildering variety of combinations. In northern Italy and Occitania, the largest, most aggressive urban communities experimented with different types of consular regimes and urban institutions; the tentative nature of autonomous urban regimes in Catalonia therefore does not in itself set it apart. What does distinguish Barcelona and other Catalan towns, however, is the degree to which the count-kings by the early thirteenth century succeeded in placing the collective interests of the urban community within the framework of public, sovereign authority, a feature Font Rius has forcefully and persuasively emphasized. Yet the House of Barcelona was not alone in this attempt. The counts of Provence and, most notoriously, the Emperor Frederick Barbarossa in northern Italy also tried to assert their power over towns in the late twelfth century by claiming public, sovereign rights, admittedly with little success. Yet in Italy Frederick's policies are remembered as high-handed and despotic interference by the *tyrannus teutonicus*, while the count-kings have earned the reputation as benevolent guardians of Barcelona and the Catalan towns. The difference derives from the confidence with which the leading members of north Italian towns, already firmly established, articulated their rights, with the help of local jurists and scribes. In Barcelona, however, many of the families which were later to dominate its public life emerged only in the 1140s and had not yet coalesced into a self-confident, independent urban leadership when the count-kings asserted their power in the city. To understand the forces which promoted the rise of these families, however, we must first examine the changes in the urban economy during the early twelfth century.

[106] Pierre Bonnassie, "Du Rhône à la Galice: genèse et modalité du régime féodal," *Structures féodales et féodalisme dans l'Occident méditerranéen (X^e–XIIIe siècles): bilan et perspectives* (Rome, 1980), 17–56 ["From the Rhône to Galicia: origins and modalities of the feudal order," *From slavery to feudalism in south-western Europe*, trans. J. Birrel (Cambridge, 1991), 104–31]; Fossier, *Enfance*, I, 454–61; Bisson, "Some characteristics of Mediterranean territorial power," 457–58; Tabacco, *Egemonie*, 226–40; Keller, *Adelsherrschaft*, 331–42.

Chapter 3

AN ABORTED TAKE-OFF: THE URBAN ECONOMY IN CRISIS, 1090–1140

The economic mechanisms triggering and sustaining the medieval urban revival have long fascinated historians and stimulated considerable debate. Few scholars, however, have managed to set the agenda for discussion in their field as decisively as the great Belgian historian, Henri Pirenne. After sweeping aside previous legal and institutional explanations on urban origins in a brilliant review article, he went on to present a classic and elegantly simple solution to the problem: the early growth of towns depended directly on the revival of long-distance trade, already evident in the tenth century.[1] The seductive power of his argument lay in its ability to account for the emergence of a commercial civilization, which he believed lay at the heart of medieval towns, without reference to the overwhelmingly agricultural, "feudal" world of the early Middle Ages. Because long-distance trade was supposedly generated in complete isolation from the villages, castles, and brutal lords that dominated the countryside, merchants injected a vital, totally new force into the moribund European economy. This explanation reassured advocates of nineteenth-century liberalism that the origins of the middle class had not been tainted with any unpleasant association with the aristocratic, privileged, and "feudal" values in early medieval society. Economically, Pirenne argued for an immaculate conception of the bourgeoisie.

The considerable body of literature that has arisen in response to these ideas has generally made the birth of medieval towns a painfully slow delivery. Criticism has proceeded along two basic lines. First, economic historians have expressed doubts that inter-

---

[1] His early critique of previous scholarly literature on urban origins, the point of departure for his later work, is Henri Pirenne, "L'Origine des constitutions urbaines au moyen âge," *Revue historique*, 53 (1893), 57–83 [repr. in *Les Villes et les institutions urbaines* (Paris and Brussels, 1939), I, 1–40]. The fullest expression of his mature ideas appears in his Princeton lectures, published as *Medieval towns*, trans. F. D. Halsey (Princeton, 1925).

regional trade by itself had the power to transform the European economy. By maintaining that commerce arose through a type of spontaneous generation, Pirenne ultimately failed to explain what needs it fulfilled in a supposedly static, agrarian society; while he traced the circulation of luxury goods, it remained unclear who purchased them and where they acquired the resources with which to buy them.[2] Second, advances in economic theory and medieval archaeology have encouraged a thorough reconsideration of the intensity, chronology, and, most importantly, the nature of trade. While the spade has unearthed considerably more evidence about early medieval commerce than was available from documentary sources,[3] a great deal of attention has also been focused on the social and political contexts within which exchange occurred in pre-market societies. Rather than reduce all systems of exchange to a modern market mechanism in which anonymous individuals buy and sell according to the dictates of supply and demand, early medieval historians under the influence of the substantivist school of economists have become convinced that the acquisition and redistribution of prestige items occurred according to quite different rules.[4] In order to secure and maintain a following in early medieval society, leaders rewarded their dependents with prestige items obtained through war or highly controlled trading emporia. This tributary system of exchange depended upon political and social controls, not market mechanisms. What Pirenne described as the rise of long-distance trade therefore corresponded to a much broader passage from a tributary to a market economy.

[2] For summaries of these criticisms, see A.B. Hibbert, "The origins of the medieval town patriciate," *Past and present*, 3 (1953), 15–27 [repr. in *Towns in societies: essays in economic history and historical sociology*, eds. P. Abrams and E.A. Wrigley (Cambridge, 1978), 91–104]; R. van Uytven, "Les Origines des villes dans les anciens Pays-Bas (jusque vers 1300)," in *La Fortune historiographique des thèses d'Henri Pirenne*, eds. G. Despy and A. Verhulst (Brussels, 1986), 13–26; David Nicholas, "Of poverty and primacy: demand, liquidity, and the Flemish economic miracle, 1050–1200," *American historical review*, 96 (1991), 19–28; Lopez, *Cambridge economic history*, II, 333–36.

[3] For recent attempts to evaluate the impact of archaeology on Pirenne's views of the expansion of towns, see Richard Hodges, *Dark Age economics* (London, 1982), 162–84; Adriaan Verhulst, "The origins of towns in the Low Countries and the Pirenne thesis," *Past and present*, 122 (1989), 3–35.

[4] Fundamental for the reevaluation of the early medieval economy is Karl Polanyi, "The economy as instituted process," in *Trade and markets in archaic societies*, eds. K. Polanyi, C. Arensbert, and H. Pearson (Glencoe, 1957), 243–69. Cf. Philip Grierson, "Commerce in the Dark Ages: a critique of the evidence," *Transactions of the Royal Historical Society*, 9 (1959), 123–40 and the useful summary of recent debates in Richard Hodges, *Primitive and peasant markets* (Cambridge, 1988), 1–34.

An aborted take-off

As a result of the productive research since the publication of Pirenne's work devoted to what Fossier has recently christened the "economic revolution" of Europe, the tables have been completely turned: rather than providing the generators for economic expansion, long-distance trade and the urban revival are now widely considered the result, even a secondary by-product, of a broad advance in material culture stimulated by increased agricultural production and a demographic surge beginning around 1000.[5] What seemed to Pirenne to be a rigid, stagnant agrarian world has turned out to be the most dynamic, expansive force in the medieval economy. Increasing profits from the land allowed lords to acquire more goods for consumption and display, while agricultural surpluses carted to newly established local markets provided an accumulation of capital for the entrepreneur.[6] Rather than offering an external stimulus to "kick-start" the economic engine, the intense long-distance trade networks of the twelfth and thirteenth century were built upon broad foundations from the bottom up. A convergence of forces led to the definitive transition, mental as well as material, from a tributary to a market system and culminated in an irresistible take-off of the Western economy.

Yet while broad agreement exists that an economic threshold had been irreversibly crossed at some point during the eleventh and twelfth century, the precise mechanisms of this transformation have been difficult to pinpoint given the scarcity of sources, especially regarding towns and exchange, before 1150. By that time, however, the most aggressive Mediterranean ports, including Venice, Genoa, Pisa, and Marseilles, had long become accustomed to the demands of long-distance trade. Because Barcelona emerged rather late as a commercial power and possesses a remarkably rich documentation, its early economic transformation can be studied in some detail. The passage from a tributary economy to a commercialized market system was by no means as continuous and relentless as is usually suggested, for the very forces which gave rise to Barcelona's early prosperity also inhibited its definitive transition to a center of long-distance trade.

---

[5] Fossier, *Enfance*, II, 644–799; Duby, *Early growth*, 181–210, 232–34.

[6] Robert S. Lopez, *The commercial revolution of the Middle Ages* (Englewood Cliffs, NJ, 1971), 56–60; Fossier, *Enfance*, II, 768–69; Hodges, *Primitive and peasant markets*, 88–95.

SIGNS OF CRISIS

In 985 Barcelona faced its darkest hour. In the final decades of the caliphate of Córdoba, al-Andalus produced a formidable military leader of exceptional energy and ability, al-Manṣūr. In a series of daring raids stretching from Galicia to the Pyrenees, the Umayyad general penetrated the heart of the Christian territories in the north. After a brief siege in the summer of 985, al-Manṣūr's army breached the Roman defenses of Barcelona, set fire to the city, "reduced to captivity those who had survived with their skins and took them away to Córdoba; from there they were dispersed to all the provinces."[7]

In spite of the drama of the event and its psychological repercussion on later generations, the physical damage to the city and the loss of population have probably been greatly exaggerated. The capture of Barcelona in fact ushered in an age of phenomenal economic and urban growth.[8] Bonnassie has even argued that the catastrophe had immediate beneficial effects, for by leaving a good deal of urban real estate without an owner it artificially created a lively land market.[9] Through the ransoming of captives and immigration, the small urban population had little difficulty replenishing itself. Just before 1000 we have our earliest evidence of suburban construction to the northeast of the defenses around Arcs Antics, below Castellvell, and to the southwest around the extramural church Santa Maria del Pi.[10] A comparable surge of human activity also began to transform Barcelona's hinterland just before the millennium. Mills were constructed, irrigation channels dug, fields planted with grapevines, olive and fruit trees, and a variety of garden crops. A clear indication of the intensity of growth can be found in the amount of labor and materials devoted to God: by the 1050s more than twenty churches stood within the narrow confines of the *territorium*.[11]

Bonnassie and Ruiz Doménec have carefully examined the

---

[7] The background and significance of the fall of Barcelona in Catalan historiography is considered by Ramon d'Abadal i de Vinyals, *Els primers comtes catalans* (Barcelona, 1958), 327–43, quotation at 330.

[8] An overview of Barcelona's eleventh-century growth can be found in *Història de Barcelona. De la prehistòria al segle XVI*, ed. A. Duran i Sanpere (Barcelona, 1975), 192–294; Carreras Candi, *La ciutat*, 213–50, 285–328; Bonnassie, *La Catalogne*, I, 487–95, II, 853–58.

[9] Bonnassie, *La Catalogne*, I, 343–47.

[10] ACB LA II, fol. 16, Mas IX, no. 89; 1–1–308; *Archivo condal*, no. 219; ACA perg. Ramon Borrell, 48.

[11] Bonnassie, *La Catalogne*, I, 491; Carreras Candi, *La ciutat*, 285–326.

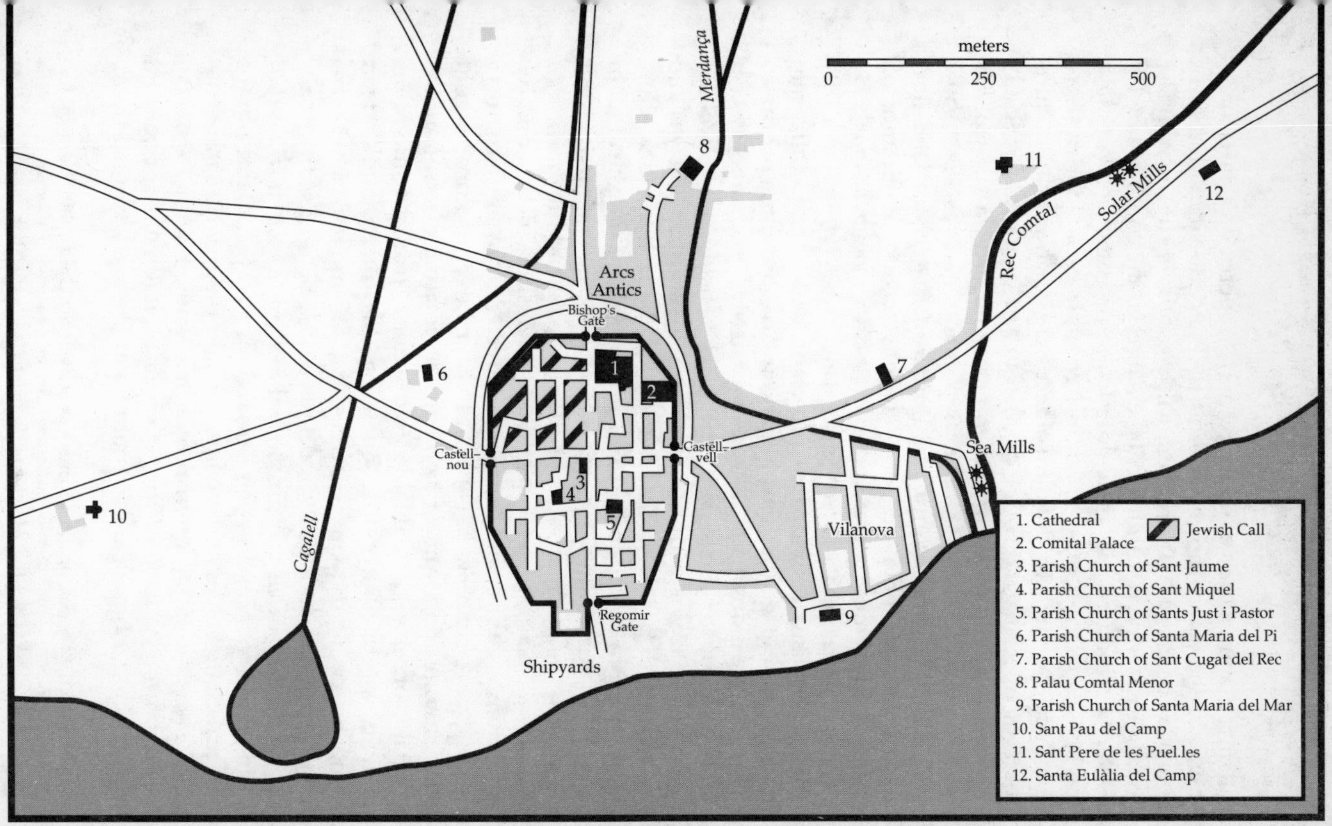
meters
0
250
500
Merdança
8
11
12
Solar Mills
Rec Comtal
Arcs
Antics
Bishop's
Gate
1
2
6
7
Castell-
nou
Castell-
vell
3
4
5
10
Cagalell
Vilanova
Sea Mills
9
Regomir
Gate
Shipyards
1. Cathedral
2. Comital Palace
Jewish Call
3. Parish Church of Sant Jaume
4. Parish Church of Sant Miquel
5. Parish Church of Sants Just i Pastor
6. Parish Church of Santa Maria del Pi
7. Parish Church of Sant Cugat del Rec
8. Palau Comtal Menor
9. Parish Church of Santa Maria del Mar
10. Sant Pau del Camp
11. Sant Pere de les Puel.les
12. Santa Eulàlia del Camp

Map 4 Barcelona in 1100

available documentation on the early impetus to Barcelona's growth in the eleventh century and the consequent evolution of the urban economy.[12] Both concur in attributing the initial phase of urban expansion to fundamental changes in the countryside. By the 980s a steady rise in agricultural output began, sustaining a growing population and providing enough basic foodstuffs to allow local peasants to devote some of their labor to the cultivation of specialized crops for the urban market. Especially important was the planting and care of vineyards, a particularly labor-intensive activity. Local entrepreneurs such as Pere Vivas and Ricart Guillem accumulated numerous parcels of land near the city and let them out on generous terms to peasants on condition that vines be planted (contracts *ad complantandum*). By 1100 Barcelona was ringed with vineyards. Its meticulously tended hinterland provided surpluses of wine, fruit, and grain which were sold at the urban marketplace, bringing profits to peasants and landowners alike. An extensive exchange system rapidly developed; focused on the market below Castellvell, it integrated the town with the surrounding suburban villages and attracted the dispersed freeholders in the Pla de Barcelona. Currency came into common use, greasing the wheels of exchange. In the wake of successful Catalan raids against the fragmented but still wealthy *taifa* principalities of Islamic Spain and the creation of tributary protectorates over neighboring Muslim rulers, a massive forced transfer of precious metals was effected from south to north in the eleventh century. In contrast to other areas of Europe, gold became a common means of payment. Percolating throughout the regional economy, the valuable gold mancus from Islamic mints found its way to Barcelona. But even this river of gold from al-Andalus could not quench the thirst for money; short-term credit, offered under openly usurious terms, became easily available. As a result of an energized local exchange system, the rapid spread of currency, and strong demand for every available plot of land, real estate values in the *territorium* and the city rose unrelentingly. The familiarity townspeople had gained with exchange, credit, and the creation of monetized capital from agricultural surpluses built a broad, stable foundation for extraregional trade,

---

[12] Bonnassie, *La Catalogne*, I, 488–96, and more extensively in "Une famille," 261–303. José E. Ruiz Doménec, "Introducción al estudio del crédito en la ciudad de Barcelona durante los siglos XI y XII," *Miscellanea barcinonensia*, 42 (1975), 17–33; "The urban origins," 265–86; "El origen," 55–86.

even though direct evidence for it is admittedly scarce. Commerce therefore supposedly represented the fruit of a maturing local urban market, not its seed.

The convergence of agricultural, market, and military factors around the year 1000 gave a powerful thrust to urban growth and thereby created the economic momentum that, according to this argument, would carry Barcelona into its great age of commercial expansion. The initial stages of an economic take-off which would transform virtually the entire West by the twelfth century can therefore be seen with remarkable clarity in and around Barcelona at the beginning of the new millennium. Because of the large amount of precious metal and especially gold in circulation, the city apparently had a head start on other small towns just beginning their revival. Once the mechanisms of growth had been triggered, however, historians have assumed that the ensuing take-off would encounter little resistance until faced with the structural crises of the late thirteenth and early fourteenth century, difficulties in large part produced by the very magnitude of previous growth. Of any period in medieval history, the twelfth century seems the most self-confidently expansive.

But this was not the case in Barcelona. Bonnassie and Ruiz Doménec ended their systematic documentary investigations just before 1100; both stopped at the edge of a precipice.[13] During the early twelfth century, the urban economy did not continue along its former trajectory but changed direction sharply and decisively. From 1090 to 1140 the city faced a deep, prolonged crisis. A number of indicators can be used to measure its intensity.

The clearest evidence for an extended period of economic difficulty comes from a sharp decrease in the activity of the real estate market in both the city and its hinterland. As long as urban wealth depended on the productivity of nearby fields and even garden plots just outside the ancient Roman walls, the average value of land sales offers a reliable guide to overall economic trends. When investors were anxious to acquire income-producing property near the city, they bought on a large scale and drove up real estate values. Prices for urban houses, shops, and lots also

---

[13] Bonnassie, *La Catalogne*, II, 835–36 noted a downturn in the use of gold coins in the city after 1080, but felt the system of exchange was not adversely affected. Ruiz Doménec also noted the sharp decline in the purchase of contiguous properties in "Urban origins," 270 but does not draw any conclusion from it. Cf. his later, less optimistic assessment, especially on Ricart Guillem, in "Génova y Barcelona en el siglo XII: la estructura básica de su realidad," *Saggi i documenti*, IV (1983), 54.

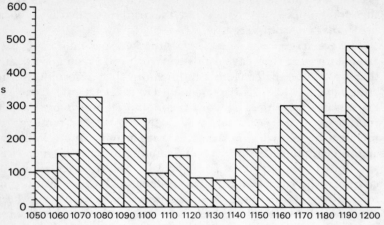

Figure 3.1 Average value of land sales in the *territorium*, 1050–1200

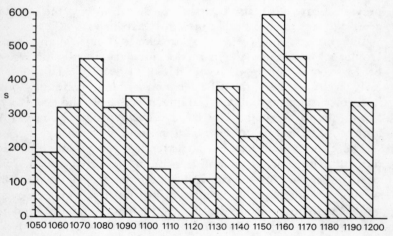

Figure 3.2 Average value of land sales in Barcelona and its suburbs, 1050–1200

increased when the town prospered, for well-heeled rural entrepreneurs and artisans felt its attraction. The average value of land
transactions in the urban area and the *territorium*, calculated from
602 contracts of sale, is presented in figures 3.1 and 3.2.[14] They

[14] For the intramural and suburban zones 234 sales are recorded; 368 for the *territorium*.
Because their unusually high value would produce a statistical distortion, sales in excess

reveal a consistent movement in the value of real estate investment in both the city and its hinterland.

Upon reaching unprecedented levels in the 1070s after almost a century of steady increases, the average value of land sales stabilized and then plummeted, falling to only a fifth of the earlier maximum during the opening decades of the twelfth century. A sustained recovery in both the city and the *territorium* occurred only after 1140, when the amount offered by buyers even exceeded previous highs. Not only did the average value of each transaction fall dramatically after 1100, but the total number of sales decreased significantly. Only forty-nine contracts recording the sale of urban property could be found for the period 1100–50, compared to ninety-one for 1050–1100 and ninety-four for 1151–1200. The documentation for the *territorium* presents a similar pattern.

Changes in the average value of land purchases provide a rough indicator of the scale of local investment and of demand for land, but to determine whether land values themselves fell accordingly we will have to turn to other evidence. Contracts of sale for urban property might include a house, workshop, cellar, garden plot, auxiliary buildings, a well, or even sections of the ancient Roman walls in a bewildering array of combinations; because of differences in the quality of construction, location, and the size of a lot, it is impossible to arrive at a standard unit with which to evaluate movements in the value of urban real estate. In Barcelona's *territorium*, however, charters of sale sometimes employed a standardized measurement called the *modiata*.[15] In keeping with the small scale of local viticulture and gardening, it represents a half hectare (4896 m²), a plot roughly 70 x 70 m. Standardized values for a *modiata* in Barcelona's hinterland from 1080 to 1200 are tabulated in table 3.1. Despite considerable variations among individual pieces of land, the available evidence shows a sharp drop in the price of a *modiata* after 1080; its value began to climb again only in the 1140s and soared in the latter third of the twelfth century. At 62 gold mancus of Barcelona (285s.) per *modiata*, the value for the vineyard recorded in 1080 provides an unusually high bench mark, yet it does accurately emphasize the peak that prices

of 1,500 quarternal solidi are excluded; eleven such sales are recorded in the *territorium* and eight in the city from 1050 to 1200.

[15] On the dimensions and background of the *modiata*, see Philip Banks, "Mensuration in early medieval Barcelona," *Medievalia*, 7 (1987), 46–49.

Table 3.1 *Price of a* modiata *in Barcelona's* territorium, *1080–1200*

Year	Number of *modiatae*	Reference	Total price	Standardized value per *modiata*
1080	1.5 (vineyard)	*Santa Anna*, II, no. 115	98 mancus of Barcelona	285s.
1085	1.5 (vineyard)	ACB LA II, fol. 79, Mas x, no. 1064	3 ounces of gold of Valencia	29s.
1092	3 (vineyard)	*Santa Anna*, II, no. 129	15 ounces of gold *rovalls* of Valencia	72s.
1093	0.5 (vineyard)	ACB LA IV, fol. 43, Mas x, no. 1115	14 mancus *rovalls* of Valencia	58s.
1102	2.5	ASPP, 60	60 mancus *rovalls*	50s.
1104	1.5 (vineyard)	*Santa Anna*, II, no. 155	108s. of good silver	83s.
1112	1.25	ACB LA I, fol. 381, Mas x, no. 1254	7 mbts.	39s.
1116	6 (land and vineyards)	*Santa Anna*, II, no. 175	12 mbts.	14s.
1118	4 (vineyard)	ACB 1–2–1365	25 mbts.	44s.
1124	1.5	*Santa Anna*, II, no. 196	2 mbts.	9s.
1126	3 (vineyard)	ACB LA I, fol. 186, Mas x, no. 1350	18 mbts.	42s.
1135	0.5 (vineyard, allod of Hospitallers)	ACB LA I, fol. 291, Mas XI, no. 1444	1.5 mbts.	21s.
1136	0.5 (vineyard, allod of Hospitallers)	ACB LA I, fol. 292, Max XI, no. 1452	1 mbt.	14s.
1138	2	*Santa Anna*, II, no. 224	5 mbts.	18s.
1145	2	ACB LA I, fol. 171, Mas XI, no. 1590	18 mbts.	63s.
1168	2 (vineyard)	ACB 4–43–507	55 mbts.	192s.

1169	6.75	ACB LA I, fol. 286, Mas XI, no. 1931	162 mbts.	168s.
1172	5.5	ACB LA I, fol. 378, Mas XI, no. 1960	170 mbts.	216s.
1177	1.75 (vineyard)	*Santa Anna*, III, no. 477	49 mbts.	196s.
1187	1 (vineyard, allod of canons)	ACB 1–5–286	30s. of Barcelona	30s.
1191	4 (allod of Sant Jaume)	ACB 1–5–391	700s. of Barcelona	175s.
1193	8	*Santa Anna*, III, no. 581	77 mbts.	67s.
1195	3	*Documents hebraics*, ed. Millás, no. 4	55 mbts.	128s.

for choice land near the city had reached. Between 1060 and 1080, the average value of a *modiata* of vineyard was 114s.[16] In stark contrast to these elevated prices, from 1090 to 1140 the average price of a *modiata* lost two-thirds its value, sinking to 39s., roughly the prevailing price around 1000. In other words, the rapid economic expansion which Barcelona had experienced after the millennium had stopped dead in its tracks by 1090.

Even though difficulties posed by monetary conversions and the variable nature of the property offered for sale makes quantitative indicators a very rough analytic tool, they nevertheless all point decisively in the same direction. From a maximum reached in the early 1080s, property values plummeted, sinking to somewhere between a third and a fifth of former levels by the early decades of the twelfth century. They remained depressed until roughly 1140 (despite the flukish surge in value of urban land sales in the 1130s),[17] when real estate prices recovered and then rose sharply

[16] This amount was obtained from the figures given by Bonnassie, *La Catalogne*, II, 925, who uses the traditional solidus as his money of account; the value is converted into quarternal solidi.

[17] The sharp rise in the average value of land sales in the 1130s in figure 3.2 derives from only six sales that decade, an unusually small statistical sample and indicative of a sluggish land market. Because the total numbers of sales is so small in comparison to the following decade, when it rises to thirteen, I tend to discount this sharp rise in average price since it

later in the century. As we shall see later in this chapter, the amount of credit, available liquidity, and the money supply became severely constricted by 1100 and began to increase on the same timetable as local property values. There can be little doubt about the severity and duration of the crisis afflicting the city and its hinterland, both of which displayed synchronized economic movements.

Other, more immediate indications of the difficulties faced by the city crept into the formulaic Latin of the charters. Several documents mention that private buildings had fallen into disrepair and required reconstruction by their tenants.[18] The most striking instance of urban decay was the suburban monastery of Sant Pau del Camp, which had fallen on such hard times (*valde est destituta*) that in 1127 a group of local *prohoms* handed it over to the abbot of Sant Cugat del Vallès to restore and reform.[19] The brief appearance of a raiding party from al-Andalus in 1115 was probably responsible for the physical damage to suburban areas and caused considerable suffering. In June, 1116 the grateful parents of Guifret ceded to him a substantial house with a stone stairway in appreciation for the support he had given them during the "frequent famines afflicting the region of Barcelona."[20] Although the damage done by the marauding army in 1115 was considerably less than that inflicted a century earlier by al-Manṣūr, the wounds took much longer to heal. The poor health of the local economy accounts for this slow recovery from the immediate damage caused by the soldiers of Islam, but the appearance of an army from al-Andalus was merely the symptom of a much more serious malaise affecting the prosperity of the city and its inhabitants. We will now try to determine its causes.

THE LOSS OF EL DORADO

Until the first decade of the new millennium, the tiny Christian communities in the north of the peninsula stood in the shadow of al-Andalus. Although the Muslim–Christian frontier did not neatly separate two hostile worlds but instead created a fragmented buffer zone made up of complex and shifting alliances,

---

fits in poorly with the other measures of the economy. The real recovery in the city began around 1140, not 1130.

[18] *CSC*, III, no. 833; ACB 1–1–1519; 1–2–784.   [19] *CSC*, III, no. 891.
[20] ACA perg. R.B. III, 191: "per plurimas famas qui fuerunt in patria Barchinone."

protectorates, and petty raiding, Christian rulers had basically been forced to assume a defensive posture toward the powerful caliphate of Córdoba. The devastating expeditions launched by the fearsome *caudillo* al-Manṣūr, in all over fifty, provided a grim reminder that well-equipped armies organized in the heartland of Spanish Islam could still overwhelm any force that stood in their way. His son ʿAbd al-Malīk (1002–8) continued to lead the armies of the caliph to new victories, but the deep-rooted factionalism that the splendors of the Cordovan court had so elegantly masked rapidly eroded the foundations of the caliphate at his death.[21] The military initiative quickly passed to Christian princes and warlords.

During the civil wars which engulfed al-Andalus after ʿAbd al-Malīk's death, Ramon Borrell, count of Barcelona, Ermengol, count of Urgell, and Sancho García, count of Castile, launched a daring raid on Córdoba in 1010 to place the leader of one faction, Muḥammad al-Mahdī, on the throne. For their efforts the counts are said to have received 100 gold pieces daily, each soldier two silver dinars, provisions, and all the booty they could seize from the opponents of the new caliph. The Cordovan expedition signaled not only a shift in military power but also in the balance between the two peninsular economies.[22] For generations after Ramon Borrell fought in Córdoba, not only did the frontiers of Catalonia remain free from attacks of massed Muslim armies, but gold and silver moved northward in massive quantities through tribute, plunder, and salaries paid to Christian mercenaries defending Muslim princes. Owing to the chaotic struggles during the death throes of the caliphate and incessant rivalries among the patchwork *taifa* kingdoms that replaced it by 1031, Christian warriors did not lack opportunities for employment and plunder. Even al-Manṣūr himself had employed Christian mercenaries. Intense competition therefore ensued among Christian leaders to control and direct the flow of precious metals to the north. By the middle of the eleventh century the counts of Barcelona had transformed irregular gifts from Islamic princes for temporary

---

[21] David Wasserstein, *The rise of the party kings* (Princeton, 1985), 41–46.
[22] On this turning point, see E. Lévi-Provençal, *Histoire de l'Espagne musulmane* (Leiden and Paris, 1950–53), II, 308–15; José María Lacarra, "Aspectos económicos de la sumisión de los reinos de taifas (1010–1102)," in *Homenaje a Jaime Vicens Vives* (Barcelona, 1965), I, 255–77 [repr. in *Colonización, parias, repoblación y otros estudios* (Zaragoza, 1981), 41–76]; Sobrequés i Vidal, *Els grans comtes*, 20–23, 43–46, 117–20; Bonnassie, *La Catalogne*, I, 343–55, 376–79.

alliances, truces, and military aid into a steady flow of "protection money" (*parias*). From 1050 to 1060 Count Ramon Berenguer I received 9,000 gold mancus annually from the neighboring Muslim rulers of Lleida, Tortosa, and Zaragoza.[23] His sons dreamt of extending their protection to Valencia, Murcia, Denia, and even Granada. Given the supremacy of the aggressive, well-armed fighters after 1010, remembered as the "year of the Catalans" in Arabic chronicles, the Muslim emirs found their most effective defense in a shield of gold.

The lucrative system of *parias* depended upon two basic factors: the political fragmentation of Islamic Spain and a rough parity among the Christian princes who sought to bring it under their protectorate. By the 1090s, however, the arrival of the Almoravids, a fierce, revivalist coalition of North African tribesmen, and the triumphs of El Cid Campeador had completely upset the delicate balances in eastern Iberia. As a result, the river of gold that had flowed to Catalonia was reduced to a trickle.

In a manner altogether in keeping with contemporary Christian *condotierri*, Rodrigo Díaz de Vivar, the heroic Castilian exile, sought his fortune across the frontier in the land of Islam. The *Poema del mío Cid* and the substantial literature which has grown up around him have made Rodrigo larger than life, but his impact on the tributary economy in eastern Spain still needs to be emphasized.[24] To the count of Barcelona and Catalonian barons, Rodrigo appeared an arrogant interloper. Just as the heirs of Ramon Berenguer I were laying the diplomatic and military groundwork to extend their protection over Valencia, Játiva, and Denia around 1077, El Cid and his troops began to intervene decisively in the political maneuvering of Christian and Muslim rulers. He first placed himself in the service of al-Muqtadir ibn Hūd of Zaragoza, once a tributary to the count of Barcelona. With a powerful new protector, al-Muqtadir not only successfully resisted paying *parias* but in 1082 even attacked the emir of Lleida-Tortosa, a regular tributary of the counts of Barcelona. El Cid's intervention in Lleida was only a forewarning of the serious setbacks he would inflict on Catalan aspirations. During the next eight years, the king of Castile, the count of Barcelona, and El Cid

[23] Bonnassie, *La Catalogne*, II, 666–69.

[24] The most penetrating discussion of El Cid's impact on eastern Spain remains Ramón Menéndez Pidal, *La España del Cid* (3rd ed., Madrid, 1947), I, 279–90, 309–91; see also Sobrequés i Vidal, *Els grans comtes*, 165–68, 179–80; Bonnassie, *La Catalogne*, II, 865–68.

competed to establish control over the kingdom of Valencia, racked by civil war, and its valuable connection to the gold route from North Africa. By 1088, Rodrigo had gained the upper hand in Valencia, but he soon had to defend his position against a formidable coalition assembled by Count Berenguer Ramon II. At the battle of Tévar in 1090, the Catalans suffered a humiliating defeat: the count and his magnates were captured and later released only upon payment of a hefty ransom. The dynasty of Barcelona was forced to abdicate its role as protector of Lleida, Tortosa, and Denia and surrender its main sources of tribute.[25]

For many Muslims, the luxurious courts maintained by *taifa* chieftains seemed just as intolerable as the extortion money paid to Christian warlords, but the alternative was hardly inviting. To stiffen Islamic resistance to Castilian advances, the governor of Seville, al-Mu'tamid, finally called upon the Almoravids. The results were a mixed blessing to Spanish Islam. While the militant, austere desert tribesmen turned back the Christian advance in the Meseta by 1086, their puritanical version of Islam clashed with the sophisticated *taifa* courts. The Almoravids quickly dispensed with local Muslim rulers and installed their own governors. The intricate system of alliances, intimidation, and tribute gave way to a much simpler, but bitterly antagonistic opposition between Christian and Muslim. For Catalonia, the Almoravid advance ensured that *parias* would not return even after El Cid had disappeared from the scene. Rodrigo's stubborn defense of Valencia blunted the first blow of a resurgent Islam in eastern Spain, but after his death in 1099 Christian and Muslim rulers alike were exposed to the full force of the invaders. Valencia and Tortosa capitulated in 1102; Lleida and Zaragoza in 1110. Having established advanced outposts on the frontier, the Almoravid governors launched raids into the Penedès in 1106–7, resulting in the sack of Olèrdola, once the rebel "capital" of Mir Geribert, and in 1114–15 sent a substantial army to seize Barcelona itself.[26] In pitched battles at Martorell and in the Pla de Barcelona, Catalan forces inflicted heavy losses on their enemies and stemmed the tide of Islamic victories. Yet even successful resistance to the Almora-

[25] According to the *Historia Roderici*, in Menéndez Pidal, *La España del Cid*, II, 948–49, Berenguer Ramon formally withdrew his protection over his Islamic dependencies.
[26] For discussion of the precise site of the battles, see Ferran Soldevila, *Història de Catalunya* (2nd ed., Barcelona, 1963), 179–80 and Sobrequés i Vidal, *Els grans comtes*, c. 3, n. 83 and 84.

vids did not herald a return to the earlier regime of *parias*.[27] Henceforth Catalan warriors would look upon the frontier as a source of land, recovered slowly and stubbornly, not as a marker on the road to a fabled realm overflowing with gold.

MONETARY CONSTRICTION

The loss of *parias* and booty from Islamic Spain had profound repercussions in Barcelona, for it disrupted the exchange mechanisms which had fostered eleventh-century expansion. Burghers and peasants alike in the Pla de Barcelona had both long grown accustomed to transact major business with the mancus, the gold coin minted in al-Andalus. By 1018 the quantity of gold in circulation even permitted the counts of Barcelona to mint their own mancus, of comparable weight to its Islamic counterpart and dutifully bearing Arabic inscriptions in praise of Allah and the commander of the faithful.[28] Use of traditional silver denars, minted throughout Catalonia since the Carolingian period, receded before the onslaught of Islamic gold by 1000. At 84 silver denars to the mancus, the scale of exchange occurring in Barcelona's lively land and credit market made the use of the traditional silver coinage cumbersome. A new silver coin, the *grosso* or *grosso de plata* set at three and a half times the value of the traditional solidus, was minted by the 1020s to keep up with rising prices and took its place along with the older denars.[29] But this did not stop the advance of the yellow metal. From 1060 to 1090, 98 percent of recorded monetary transfers in the city were made with the mancus. Townspeople had adopted a gold standard.

As the forced transfer of precious metals northward slowed after 1080, the amount of minted gold in circulation also fell, as indicated in figures 3.3 and 3.4. In contrast to the previous two decades, from 1080 to 1110 only 59 percent of recorded monetary transactions in the city were made by means of gold. Not only

---

[27] On this important point I agree with Sobrequés i Vidal, *Els grans comtes*, 190, who finds that the Almoravids effectively terminated *parias*. Bonnassie, *La Catalogne*, II, 869–70 considers this only an interruption in the collection of tribute.

[28] For an updated catalog of the numismatic evidence, including many splendid examples of the mancus, see Anna M. Balaguer and M. Crusafont i Sabater, "Els comtats catalans: les seves encunyacions i àrees d'influència," *Symposium numismático de Barcelona I* (Barcelona, 1979), 412–16. Still useful are the plates and discussion by Botet y Sisó, *Les monedes catalanes*, I, 25–47. On the rapid influx of gold, Bonnassie, *La Catalogne*, I, 363–413 is fundamental.

[29] Bonnassie, *La Catalogne*, I, 386–89 ; Botet y Sisó, *Les monedes catalanes*, I, 32, 38–39.

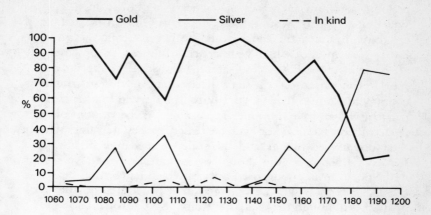

Figure 3.3 Percentage of payments in gold, silver, and in kind in Barcelona's
territorium, 1060–1200

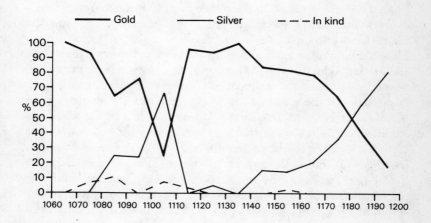

Figure 3.4 Percentage of payments in gold, silver, and in kind in the city and
suburbs, 1060–1200

were silver coins used more frequently, but payments in non-metallic mediums such as pepper and wax also begin to appear with some regularity after 1080. The disruption in the tributary economy founded on *parias* dealt the urban economy a major blow, the impact of which was particularly severe in the years just after 1100. As the figures indicate, the shock effect appears much more pronounced in the city itself than in the surrounding countryside, a sign that the highly charged urban market proved particularly sensitive to monetary changes. As the amount of gold in circulation stabilized or even decreased, real estate values started their downward plunge and the scale of exchange shrank. The sudden reduction in the supply of monetarized metal placed a brake on a century-long rise in prices which had set in as early as the 980s, precisely when the mancus first penetrated northeastern Spain. Even though the relative scarcity of gold from 1080 to 1110 was not the only factor retarding growth, townsmen long accustomed to dealing almost exclusively with the heavy gold mancus must have found the increasing reliance on silver deeply disturbing. It marked the end of an era of high prices and unbridled speculation in agricultural property.

Monetary confusion added to the difficulties overtaking the urban economy around 1100. In the early eleventh century, the mancus had provided a coinage of exceptionally high value and stability. After 1060, two smaller mancus were minted in Barcelona, one valued at 10 to the ounce of gold instead of 7 (*mancuso de decem in untia*) and a decade later another mancus at 14 to the ounce (also known as the *argenço*). These coins of lesser weight filled a demand for monetarized gold in even minor transactions and presented no inherent difficulty in equivalence since they were pegged to a standard ounce of gold (worth 49 traditional silver denars). The same cannot be said of a new, debased mancus from Valencia, referred to as *mancuso de Valencie* or *mancuso rovall*. Its value was only a fourth that of the old Islamic mancus.[30] First coined by al-Mu'tamid of Seville in 1077 to reduce a payment owed to Ramon Berenguer II by means of a scandalous debasement, the *mancuso rovall* soon entered Catalonia and displaced the other gold pieces during the 1080s and 1090s. The conquest of Valencian gold reflected the failure of the counts of

---

[30] Bonnassie, *La Catalogne*, II, 866–67, 898–99; Botet y Sisó, *Les monedes catalanes*, I, 52–53. Equivalences among the various coinages are summarized in appendix 3.

Barcelona to impose their protectorate over the Islamic chieftains of eastern Iberia. The count's moneyers consequently stopped striking gold coins in Catalonia.

Although the arrival of the *mancuso rovall* in Barcelona can only be firmly dated to 1085, it is likely that it had arrived in quantity early in 1082. Its appearance proved unnerving. A contract of sale from September of that year stipulated that payment be made in those mancus "which were circulating in March." Since two other land purchases made in March uncharacteristically used wax as the medium of exchange, there is a strong likelihood that the *mancuso rovall* forced Catalonian gold coins out of circulation at that time.[31] For those who had expected rents or the repayment of loans in the old currency, the sudden intrusion of a debased coinage of uncertain value must have entailed hardship or, at best, bitter haggling among the parties concerned. In 1098, another gold piece, which proved to be remarkably stable and of substantial weight, made its entrance into Barcelona: the morabetin minted by the Almoravids, after whom it took its name. Within a decade the morabetin replaced the *mancuso rovall* and remained the major gold piece in circulation well into the thirteenth century. It became such a widely used medium of payment throughout the peninsula that after the Almoravids stopped minting the coin King Alfonso VIII of Castile struck his own "good Alfonsine morabetin" or *maravedí*.

Because a resurgent Islam had stemmed the flow of precious metals into Catalonia, the new gold pieces from mints no longer under the control of the counts introduced further instability into an already shaken exchange system. Since the *mancuso rovall* and the morabetin were not set to the same standard as that of the earlier mancus, the relative value of the coins must have caused considerable confusion. Because morabetins came from a wide number of different mints in al-Andalus as well as North Africa, they consequently varied in weight; in the Islamic world the lack of mint controls often caused transactions to be concluded by weighing rather than counting coins. Might uncertainties in exchange rates help account for the curious hybrid term "mancus morabetin" (equivalent to "yen dollar" today) that appeared in charters during the decade immediately following the intro-

---

[31] Arxiu de Montserrat, perg. Sant Benet de Bages, 1574; ACA perg. R.B. II, 63; ACB LA I, fol. 41, Mas X, no. 1011.

duction of the Almoravid gold piece?[32] Botet y Sisó long ago noted that article 141 of the *Usatges*, "Solidus aureus," must surely date from the early twelfth century since it attempted to establish equivalences among the various coinages which circulated before 1100, when the morabetin was introduced.[33] While legal historians have assumed that "Solidus aureus" offered a means of updating the amount of fines imposed in different coinages by the code, it was also of current economic interest since rents continued to be cited in the mancus for generations after the actual coin had disappeared from circulation.[34] To landlords, setting rents in a traditional but increasingly scarce and, eventually, imaginary gold piece had the advantage of protecting them from the appearance of new coins of unknown value or mutations in the local coinages, a problem much on the minds of rulers and subjects alike in early twelfth-century Catalonia.[35] The introduction of new types of Islamic gold pieces therefore created considerable uncertainty about pecuniary obligations, particularly for future payments. Combined with a constriction in the gold supply, monetary insecurity hampered exchange and had its part to play in the economic difficulties facing Barcelona around 1100.

Yet a decade after the introduction of the morabetin, gold once again reigned supreme. Between 1110 and 1140, virtually all recorded land transfers in Barcelona and its hinterland were made by means of the morabetin. But how did the Almoravid coins come to Catalonia if *parias* had ceased and the counts themselves did not melt down mancus in order to mint their own morabetins?

This is indeed a thorny problem, one which has attracted surprisingly little attention among numismatists and economic historians alike. The answer probably lies in the reduced intensity of monetarized exchange and the divergent gold–silver ratios between Catalonia and al-Andalus. Despite the decline in tribute

---

[32] ACB 1–5–8, 61, 65; ACA perg. R.B. III, 111. Botet y Sisó, *Les monedes catalanes*, I, 57 discusses this curious expression in the document just cited (*mancusos .v. morabetinos*) and prudently assumes that it meant a gold coin of the type morabetin rather than an equivalence between mancus and morabetin.

[33] Botet y Sisó, *Les monedes catalanes*, I, 58; *Usatges de Barcelona i commemoracions de Pere Albert*, ed. J. Rovira i Emengol (Barcelona, 1933), art. 141, 245.

[34] From 1110 to 1150, all entry fees owed by leaseholders in the city were paid in morabetins, but twenty rents are given in mancus, nine in kind, and only four in morabetins. Rents in mancus continue to appear occasionally in the thirteenth century.

[35] Thomas N. Bisson, *Conservation of coinage: monetary exploitation and its restraint in France, Catalonia and Aragon c. A.D. 1000 – c. 1225* (Oxford, 1979), 50–64.

after 1080, a substantial quantity of minted and hoarded gold must surely have remained in the Pla de Barcelona and other regions in Catalonia during the early twelfth century. Gold clearly did not seep out through trade with Christian neighbors. Except for purchases of castles and rights made by the well-heeled counts of Barcelona, no gold payments are known in twelfth-century Languedoc, while in Castile morabetins came into general circulation only in the 1130s.[36] As the following section will attempt to demonstrate, neither maritime nor interregional commerce played a significant role in the urban economy until the 1140s. Once gold had arrived in Catalonia, it therefore remained within the self-contained parameters of an isolated regional economy during the early twelfth century. The exchange sector represented by the morabetin had shrunk to the available supply of gold. When the city once again expanded in the 1140s, silver grew steadily in importance since gold could not keep pace with the intensification of exchange. The retreat of the morabetin in fact heralded a new period of prosperity. The splendid façade of Barcelona's medieval economy would therefore be overlaid with silver, not gold.

The shrinkage of the exchange sector helps explain the dominance of gold in major land transactions for a generation after 1110 but it does not account for the swift substitution of the morabetin for the *mancuso rovall*. Did Muslim–Christian trade channel the Almoravid coins to Catalonia? While sporadic commercial contacts must have existed, Catalonia still had little to export to al-Andalus; the trickle of trade could not have produced the rapid introduction of the morabetin in large quantities. Sporadic raiding and the ransoming of captives, a permanent feature of the Iberian frontier, certainly accounted for some exchange of precious metals, but Christians did not necessarily enjoy a favorable "balance of trade" in the exchange of prisoners in the early twelfth century. The era of the great eleventh-century Catalan expeditions into the heart of al-Andalus had passed; Christian military dominance in the peninsula would return in a considerably altered context only after 1140.

One element which did carry over from those heady days when

[36] Mireille Castaing-Sicard, *Monnaies féodales et circulation monétaire en Languedoc (XIᵉ au XIIIᵉ siècles)* (Toulouse, 1961), 66–73; Jean Gautier-Dalché, "L'Histoire monétaire de l'Espagne septentrionale et centrale du IXᵉ au XIIᵉ siècles: quelques réflexions sur divers problèmes," *AEM*, 6 (1969), 60–64.

tribute steadily flowed north into Catalonia was a keen awareness of the relative values of gold and silver. Andrew Watson has pointed out that from the eleventh to the thirteenth century a "silver famine" gripped the Islamic world; rich in gold ore from sub-Saharan Africa, it was poor in silver.[37] The Almoravids in particular were awash in gold, for in the later eleventh century they gained direct control of African gold caravans passing from Sijilmāsa to Mediterranean ports from Tangiers to Tripoli, and from Ceuta to Spain.[38] Catalans, on the other hand, suddenly found that they could no longer satisfy the appetite they had acquired for the yellow metal. Theoretically, conditions were ideal for the transfer of precious metals across the frontier. A pair of documents mentioning exchange rates from the early 1130s makes it possible to calculate a minimum gold–silver ratio of 1:8.4.[39] This rate is only just below that prevailing at Genoa in 1159, which proved strong enough to attract gold from North Africa to the Ligurian republic. Around 1200 African gold brought six and a half times its weight in silver at Tunis, but in the

---

[37] Andrew Watson, "Back to gold – and silver," *Economic history review*, 2nd series, 20 (1967), 2–7.

[38] C. Vanacker, "Géographie économique de l'Afrique du Nord du IXe siècle au milieu du XIIe siècle," *AESC*, 28 (1973), 668–71.

[39] A document from 1134 gives the equivalence of 20 mbts. to 2 lbs. of silver, or 10 mbts. to a lb. of silver, ACA perg. R.B. IV, 28. The ambiguity of the reference relates to the type of morabetins involved. If they are morabetins in circulation, then, as other documents demonstrate, there would be 84s. to 1 lb. of gold; the gold–silver ratio would therefore be 1:8.4. Bòtet y Sisó, *Les monedes catalanes*, I, 67–70, believes, however, that the morabetins in question are in fact morabetins *mercaders*, a money of account valued at 120 to 1 lb. of gold; this would give a much higher ratio at 1:12. He attempts to confirm his assumption by using later sources which offer an equivalence of the morabetin in solidi. If 1 mbt. = 7s., the official rate of exchange under King Alfons I after c. 1174, there would be 70s. to the silver pound, or 46 to the silver mark (a mark is two-thirds of a lb.) at the rate quoted above. Botet y Sisó maintains that this would be excessive, for in the mid-eleventh century Ramon Berenguer I set a standard of 43s. to the silver lb.; this would mean a debasement from 43 to 70s. to the lb. in slightly over a century.

Based on an examination of the coins themselves, however, Anna M. Balaguer, "Statutes governing coinage in Iberian kingdoms during the Middle Ages," in *Medieval coinage and the Iberian area*, ed. M. Gomes Marques (Santarém, 1984–88), I, 125–27 marshals strong evidence to show that a debasement did occur under a second silver coinage issued by Count Ramon Berenguer I. In addition, a document from 1131, only three years earlier than the document cited above, provides the equivalence of 1 mbt. = 6.15s. (80s. for 13 mbts.). At 10 mbts. to the silver lb., the exchange rate indicates 61.5s. per lb. of silver, or 41s. in the silver mark. This is quite close to the reformed silver coinage, known as the quarternal solidus, later instituted by King Alfons I, at 44s. in the silver mark. The exchange rate from 1131 therefore strongly supports the assumption that the morabetins in question were not the morabetin *mercader*, but the morabetin in circulation, and that the gold–silver ratio was therefore 1:8.4.

thirteenth century the ratio at times sank below 1:5 in the Islamic world.[40] If one could set in motion the mechanisms for the exchange of gold and silver across the Muslim–Christian frontier, the potential profits were considerable.

Commerce offered one means of obtaining African gold for European silver in the twelfth-century Mediterranean; the complexities of this system, in which precious metals helped offset trade imbalances, have received careful attention, especially in relation to the booming ports of Genoa and Venice. But other avenues existed for the transfer of precious metals, including the export of bullion in the form of ingots. Catalonia had little to offer in terms of agricultural or artisanal products for export in exchange for Islamic gold, but it did possess silver, a legacy of its Carolingian past. Silver denars and obols had been used for small transactions even in the eleventh century, when parchments overwhelmingly record payments in gold. Here the written evidence is deceptive for it reflects only relatively large credit and real estate transactions.[41] Townspeople did not go before a scribe to memorialize the purchase of a bushel of grain, a handful of salt, or a barrel of wine; gold therefore traced the outlines of only the most privileged sector of exchange. The export of silver also did not leave any written evidence, but indirect references reveal that it did occur. In a dispute in 1101 over the delivery of 40 pounds of silver (*libra de plata*) pledged on the castle of Arraona, Ricart Guillem, a gentrified Barcelona real estate speculator, and his wife went to Zaragoza – still under Muslim control – with part of the silver they had obtained to change it for gold.[42] Others, including the first documented money changers (*cambiatores*) in Barcelona,[43] must also have known the road to Lleida, Tortosa, and Zaragoza to purchase Almoravid morabetins with silver. The larger the amount of silver involved, the more ingots were employed, for they provided an easy means of transporting precious metals. From roughly 1080 to 1140, large sums in silver are quoted in pounds of silver rather than in smaller units, a practice virtually

---

[40] Watson, "Back to gold," 25; Peter Spufford, *Money and its use in medieval Europe* (Cambridge, 1988), 184, 272.

[41] A point emphasized by M. Crusafont i Sabater, *Numismática de la Corona catalano-aragonesa medieval* (Madrid, 1982), 50.

[42] ACA perg. R.B. III, 74: "Ricardus et uxor eius aput Cesaraugustam in auro in ipso cambio auri pro plata superaverunt libre .ii. et media de plata."

[43] Two local *cambiatores* appear before 1140: Bonjudà (ACB LA I, fol. 302, Mas XI, no. 1496) and Pere (ACB LA I, fol. 170, Mas X , no. 1336).

unknown earlier, when gold mancus were abundant, and unusual later, when morabetins and solidi provided the primary units of monetary value.[44] Residents in the Pla de Barcelona came to imagine large sums in terms of silver bars as well as gold coins.

Small coins melted down into silver bars, ingots exchanged for Islamic gold coins of high value: the metamorphosis of precious metals from tarnished denars and obols into glistening bars of silver and, through exchange, heavy gold pieces curiously summarizes the blockage in the local economy. The monetary system was top-heavy, for it insisted on acquiring fifty-dollar bills in an economy that ran on quarters. Silver was pulled up from the bottom to make ingots; the small coins worn down as they passed through innumerable hands were transformed into gold morabetins carefully preserved for land acquisitions, loans, and pious donations. Prosperous burghers still tended to measure values on a grand scale even as the exchange sector was shrinking. By channeling substantial quantities of gold northward in the eleventh century, Catalan warriors had indirectly promoted speculation in land and agricultural markets in Barcelona, creating inflated values locally through a type of reflexive tributary economy. When the Almoravids dammed the flow of tribute, the urban exchange sector could no longer fill out the dimensions of its gilded frame.

THE INTROVERSION OF THE URBAN ECONOMY

The study of coinage can help explain the undulating movements of the economy and even perceptions of wealth, but monetary instability, however vexing in the short run, does not necessarily lead to the constriction of exchange; conversely, a stable and abundant coinage does not necessarily indicate prosperity. If local markets and interregional exchange are underdeveloped, the injection of precious metals will have little impact. In Castile and León, rulers and raiding parties were just as successful as their Catalan counterparts at extorting money from *taifa* chieftains. Yet in large parts of Asturias and Galicia barter did not give way to money payments, nor, in general, did the influx of gold deflect the

---

[44] ACB 1–2–486; ACA perg. R.B. III, 74, 160; Arxiu de Montserrat, perg. Sant Benet de Bages, 1574, and numerous citations in Botet y Sisó, *Les monedes catalanes*, I, 49, 55, 65. The pound was not used as a money of account until the second half of the twelfth century. On the frequent use of ingots as a basis of foreign exchange, see Spufford, *Money and its use*, 209–24.

direction of the Castilian economy before 1130.[45] Much of the liquid wealth was hoarded or offered in pious donations, including King Fernando I's famous gift of 1,000 gold mancus annually to Cluny, by far the largest single donation ever offered to Europe's premier monastery except for that granted by his son, Alfonso VI, who doubled the amount in 1077. Although the profits of war trickled into eleventh-century Barcelona through innumerable rivulets, their cumulative force swept the urban economy forward because the circuits of local exchange already existed to absorb the wealth of al-Andalus.

Wine, grain, olive oil, fruit, and garden crops provided the bulk of products available in the urban marketplace. As the urban population grew after the millennium, however, a modest craft and service sector took shape to meet its needs. Among early urban artisans shoemakers (*sabaters*) were by far the most prominent; they were the first craftsmen to achieve a sufficient degree of organization to require proof of professional expertise before one could join their ranks.[46] Before 1100 a handful of other craftsmen turn up in the abundant documentation: smiths, weapon-makers, bakers, millers, a tanner, and a weaver.[47] With the exception of armorers, however, urban craftsmen produced for local consumption and their numbers were too small to manufacture goods suitable for export. Barcelona's lively exchange sector therefore depended overwhelmingly on the sale of local agricultural surpluses at the market below Castellvell. Owing to the profitability of small, intensively cultivated plots in sight of the city walls, urban entrepreneurs feverishly bought up peasant allods, which they then exploited by hiring labor or by demanding a share of the produce. The prevalence of monetary exchange and rising prices encouraged landlords to seek rents in kind rather than in cash because of the possible gains from marketing their crops.

Wine was particularly coveted by thirsty Barcelonans. As Georges Duby has astutely pointed out, viticulture responds more directly to economic demand than to the exigencies of soil and climate.[48] The taste for wine grew with the size of urban money-

---

[45] Gautier-Dalché, "L'Histoire monétaire," 56–58.

[46] Philip Banks, "The origins of the 'Gremi de Sabaters' of Barcelona," *Quaderns d'arqueologia e història de la ciutat*, 18 (1980), 109–18.

[47] Bonnassie, *La Catalogne*, II, 855–56.

[48] Georges Duby, *L'Economie rurale et la vie des campagnes dans l'Occident médiéval* (Paris, 1962), II, 236–40. [*Rural economy and country life in the medieval West*, trans. C. Postan (Columbia, SC, 1968), 138–41].

pouches. Throughout the eleventh century townspeople with land outside the city and prosperous peasants with small parcels not needed for subsistence converted their fields to vineyards. To encourage specialization, landlords granted tenants favorable terms on condition that they plant vines. Arrangements set out in what is known as contracts *ad complantandum* characterize a new intensification of production: after granting a plot to a tenant, the owner generally required no dues for five to seven years, the time necessary for the vine to mature, and then ceded half the land and its produce to the peasant on condition that he continue to work the entire parcel.[49] For landlords, contracts *ad complantandum* demanded large investments in expectation of profits to be reaped many years in the future. Only a market-oriented agricultural economy as self-confidently optimistic as that of eleventh-century Barcelona could tempt urban entrepreneurs to buy up land for long-deferred profits with such relentless determination.

The spread of vineyards thus provides a good index of early urban investment. In the decades after 1000, tendrils began to envelop the monasteries, villages, but above all the towns of Catalonia; Bonnassie has shown that 42 percent of all land sales around Barcelona between 1001 and 1050 involved vineyards, a substantial increase from the 33 percent in the previous fifty years.[50] An analysis of vineyards in the twelfth century, however, reveals a substantially different pattern. From the proportion of land transfers (sales, donations, pledges, dowry payments) in the *territorium* presented in figure 3.5, it is clear that the vine stopped its advance after 1090. The percentage of transactions involving vineyards fell from a peak of 60 percent in the 1080s to 26 percent a century later. Since notarized land transactions in most instances indicate the owners of contiguous properties and specify whether the holdings are fields, vineyards, or orchards, this information provides a back-up gauge to measure the prevalence of vineyards. Both indicators reveal the same trend. After dropping substantially in the decades around 1100, the proportion of land given over to wine production stabilized for the next fifty years, then slowly receded until a spurt of expansion occurred at the close of the twelfth century. Even though viticulture clearly remained

[49] Roger Grand, "La 'complantatio' en el derecho medieval español," *AHDE*, 23 (1953), 754–59; Ruiz Doménec, "The urban origins," 273–76.
[50] Bonnassie, *La Catalogne*, I, 448–55.

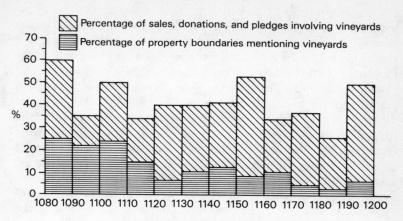

Figure 3.5 Vineyards in Barcelona's *territorium*, 1080–1200

important, the eleventh-century "wine boom" went flat after 1090.

Just as the advance of the vine was coming to a halt, land values plummeted and the scale of investment shrank. For urban investors with substantial rural property, these changes had a devastating impact. Having avidly bought up parcels of land when prices were high and immobilized liquid assets in the conversion of fields into vineyards that would not produce substantial profits for a decade, local entrepreneurs discovered that their assets had diminished substantially in value after 1090. Although there are no price figures available, profits from wine sales in all likelihood diminished as the exchange sector contracted. The engine that had driven eleventh-century growth had run out of steam.

Cramped between the sea and the rough Collserola range, the Pla de Barcelona did not provide adequate space for continuous agricultural expansion. In contrast to Northern Europe, there were no forests to clear and little land to be reclaimed by draining marshy areas; most of the available land had been tilled for centuries. Advances in production had come about through intensification of labor and the diversification of crops, largely stimulated by market demand. But by 1100 the demographic surge in and near the town showed signs of straining the productive capacities of the surrounding countryside; cultivators were approaching a limit to the amount of arable land which could be given over profitably to labor-intensive market crops. The planting of new grapevines virtually came to an end: of more than 300 sales and tenurial contracts from the *territorium* between 1150 and 1200, only 6 called for the conversion of fields into vineyards.[51] By 1160 one tenant even complained that he "upon bad advice had planted vines."[52] The marketplace pressured investors and peasants alike to extend vineyards to unsuitable soils and locations; the slight decline in viticulture after 1150 may well represent the adaptation of the rural economy to the limits imposed by the fertility of the land and climate. In comparison to the expansive eleventh century, the countryside near Barcelona appears lethargic in the twelfth. The general direction of the rural economy during the period is difficult to decipher in recent micro-histories of Provençana on the Baix Llobregat and in the Maresme just up the coast from Barcelona, particularly during the decades from 1100 to 1140.[53] The "agricultural revolution" could not sustain urban expansion indefinitely. Unless investments were diverted into other undertakings, the fields lying within the economic pull of the urban marketplace would continue to attract capital but return considerably fewer profits than before. When urban prosperity did return in the 1140s, inaugurating an even more powerful surge of economic expansion, significantly wine production did not increase and even declined slightly. The second stage of urban expansion would be built on quite different foundations from those of the first.

Yet in the early twelfth century, land continued to absorb liquid resources. Even though burghers made fewer and smaller purchases of allodial property than before, new credit mechanisms provided an alternative means for those with cash to obtain

---

[51] ACB 1–5–30, 136; 3–29–96; 4–43–507; *Santa Anna*, III, nos. 458, 640.

[52] ACA perg. extrainv., 3466.

[53] Jaume Codina, *Els pagesos de Provençana (984–1807): societat i economia a l'Hospitalet pre-industrial* (Barcelona, 1987), I, 59–62 describes the twelfth century as expansive. He admits that the signs are ambiguous and assumes that the general model of agricultural expansion in Europe must also apply to the area near Barcelona: "L'expansió local, doncs, és perceptible durant el segle malgrat les deficiències d'informació, i sintonitza amb el corrent general de l'època," 62. Only four of thirty-four recorded sales in twelfth-century Provençana occur before 1140. Coral Cuadrada, *El Maresme medieval: les jurisdiccions baronals de Mataró i Sant Vicenç/Vilassar (hàbitat, economia i societat, segles X–XIV)* (Barcelona, 1988), 181–23 also has difficulty characterizing the twelfth century. Land sales are no more abundant for the twelfth century than for the tenth and eleventh; further, only nine of twenty-five twelfth-century sales in the area occur between 1100 and 1140. Because of the narrow geographical focus of these studies, it is difficult to determine the evolution of the rural economy in the region before 1200.

control of agricultural production in the *territorium*. During the eleventh century, lending permeated all levels of rural and urban society in the Pla de Barcelona. It was an age of innocence for the profit economy: an abundance of gold and silver coins and the precocious spread of lending, here considerably in advance of many parts of Europe, had not yet attracted the disapproving attention of theologians and religious moralists. Anyone with ready cash, layman and cleric alike, offered credit to anxious borrowers under explicitly usurious terms. In most cases loan contracts required quick repayments, within a year or less; lenders could expect 50 percent annual interest, a sign of high demand for money.

Although eleventh-century credit in Barcelona has been the subject of several careful studies,[54] none have noted an important change in the loan contract itself. To secure credit, the borrower had to offer assets at least equal to the amount of the loan as security. Virtually all early loan contracts specify that if the borrower does not repay the debt when it falls due, the lender has the right to seize and dispose of the pledge. Interest usually took the form of cash or a fixed quantity of grain. Toward the end of the eleventh century, however, land offered in pledge became less of a surety than a source of interest. For a loan of 14 mancus in 1081, Guillem Bernat pledged a vineyard and two plots of land near the city to the priest Guillem Sendred, who "will have all the produce without fail that I might rightfully claim until I return the stipulated 14 mancus to you."[55] This is the earliest example to my knowledge of an open-ended pledge in Barcelona; it neither sets a date for repayment nor includes a clause permitting seizure of the land in case of default. But this would have been redundant, for the lender already possessed an indefinite right to the crops, the true profit from the land.

Contracts of this type evolved into the typical credit instruments of the twelfth century. In most instances, the contractual form was modified to include a repayment date after the harvest; if the borrower failed to redeem his pledge at that time, he would have to wait until the following year before he could claim it

[54] Bonnassie, *La Catalogne*, I, 399–409; Ruiz Doménec, "Introducción al estudio del crédito," 21–33.

[55] ACA LA IV, fol. 118, Mas X, no. 998: "habeas ipsos fructos fideliter quod inde exierint totum quod ego debui havere tantum usque dum reddam tibi suprascriptos mancusos .xiiii."

again. Through this device the creditor could gain control of the pledge for decades and even for generations while the debtor retained titular possession.[56] Thus, instead of offering quick liquidity, credit evolved into a tool of land control. From 1100 to 1150, 77 percent of loans involving townsmen were secured on rural property; this accounted for 80 percent of total credit in the city. Rather than stimulating circulation and turning the potential value of real estate into cash profits, credit operations had just the opposite effect after 1100: loans were used to obtain interest in the form of agricultural produce just at a time when the exchange sector was depressed.

The shift from short-term credit to the extended exploitation of agricultural pledges emerged in response to two elements that inhibited economic growth: uncertainty about the value of money and a psychological attachment to land as the primary form of wealth. For a lender repayment in coinage of uncertain value could easily erode his profits. The first credit contract with an open-ended period of redemption, cited above, takes great care to establish the specific coinage lent: "14 gold mancus of Barcelona money which circulates today, weighed *argenço* by *argenço*."[57] Because the debased *mancuso rovall* began to enter Catalonia around 1080, extraordinary caution had to be exercised to ensure the lender that time would bring gains instead of losses. Of all economic transactions in Barcelona, short-term loans depended most directly on confidence in the stable value of money, a confidence that was slipping away in the closing decades of the eleventh century.

Yet the retreat from employing money to turn quick profits through credit was symptomatic of an economy that still measured wealth in terms of land and its produce. Even though land values and, in all likelihood, agricultural prices had fallen, urban investors continued to plough money back into the land whether through direct purchases or, increasingly, through credit. By means of new contractual stipulations, creditors gained the

---

[56] The practice is clearly documented only in the early thirteenth century in charters recording the transfer of pledges, for which the dates of the original credit contract are recorded, but it had surely become common much earlier. E.g., ACB 1–6–1075, 1155, 2733.

[57] ACA LA IV, fol. 118, Mas X, no. 998: "mancusos .xiiii. auri monete Barchinone que hodie currit pensatos de argentio in argentio." The *argenço* is another name for the Barcelona mancus at 14 to the ounce of gold, half the value of the old Cordovan mancus.

right to exploit land offered in pledge, a movement in its effects similar to the conversion of allodial properties into leaseholds.[58]

Did the determination to look upon land as the primary source of wealth constitute a portentous lack of nerve on the part of enterprising Barcelonans? Investment analysts today would certainly have recommended broadening the portfolios of urban entrepreneurs, but few practical alternatives existed. While the failure to divert resources into non-agricultural endeavors did place a serious obstacle in the way of continued growth, it is nevertheless worth recalling that the city's prosperity in the eleventh century had come about through the convergence of two independent economic forces: a lively local market and the forced movement of liquid wealth from al-Andalus to Catalonia. Despite their beneficial convergence, these two systems did not fuse to create a new social group equally at home in both worlds. The Pla de Barcelona did not become saturated with Islamic gold because local investors hauled their wine barrels, jars of olive oil, and bushels of wheat to the market below Castellvell, nor did Catalonian knights set aside sword and hauberk to hawk the precious silks, furs, ivories, and slaves captured from the Moor in urban stalls. The profits from war and exchange were regulated by quite separate mechanisms. This situation contrasts sharply with the early development of the most dynamic Italian ports. In Genoa, Venice, Pisa, Amalfi, and Gaeta profit-making and pillaging remained indistinguishable for much longer than in the underdeveloped economies of the north.[59] On the dangerous and fiercely competitive seas of the Eastern Mediterranean, Muslims, Greeks, and Italians sought both profit and naval domination: the interests of warriors and entrepreneurs became inextricably intertwined. In Barcelona, these two social elements failed to fuse into an urban elite oriented toward the sea and keenly aware of the profits their resources could bring by pooling them for trade. Put briefly, what Barcelona's eleventh-century growth failed to produce was a group of prominent long-distance merchants.

If evidence for extraregional trade has been notoriously hard to come by even during the prosperous eleventh century, this is even more the case in the difficult decades after 1100. The role of trade

---

[58] Fossier, *Enfance*, II, 777–9; Duby, *Rural economy*, 252–54; Cinzio Violante, "Les Prêts sur gage foncier dans la vie économique et sociale de Milan au XIᵉ siècle," *Cahiers de civilisation médiévale*, 5 (1962), 167–68.

[59] Duby, *Early growth*, 260. Cf. Tabacco, *Egemonie*, 180–88.

in Barcelona's early growth has been greatly exaggerated. Both Bonnassie and Ruiz Doménec have argued that a steady expansion of the urban economy after 1000 culminated in the creation of commercial capital and the emergence of an important group of merchants in Barcelona by the end of the century.[60] The strongest support for this view comes from references to efforts to promote a Catalan navy. During the tenth and better part of the eleventh century, maritime traffic along both Christian and Islamic shores of eastern Spain was minimal. Neither organized navies nor corsairs played an important part in the complex military and political alignments that emerged after the Cordovan caliphate declined. Recognizing that his limited naval capabilities could pose a threat, Ramon Berenguer I began to build Catalonia's first fleet on Barcelona's shore below the Regomir Gate.[61] Yet when his son Berenguer Ramon II decided to attack Tortosa in 1092, he had to rely on a flotilla of 400 Genoese ships that King Alfonso VI of Castile had requested in order to counter El Cid; fortunately for the count, who apparently did not have his own ships for the contest, they had arrived too late to be of use in Valencia and were turned against Tortosa.[62] But by 1114, Catalan ships joined a Pisan and Occitanian flotilla to attack Majorca; during the 1120s, the count of Barcelona entered into treaties with the consuls of Genoa and the king of Norman Sicily. Even the fishermen and sailors with their tiny boats, the infrastructure to Catalonia's maritime expansion, living on the coastline near Barcelona were coming to the attention of their lords. When the inhabitants of Barcelona offered a tithe to the bishop in 1100, they agreed to pay it on the produce of the land and sea, and in 1104 the count offered his tenth on "everything due him on each ship large or small" to the church of Sant Adrià de Besòs.[63] The lords of maritime Catalonia began to turn their energies to the sea and to exploit the potential resources it had to offer.

While undeniable signs exist that a Catalan navy was gradually forming, its economic impact on Barcelona is far from clear. The initiative for naval expansion came from the counts and, possibly, from the Catalonian baronage, not from wealthy Barcelonans.

---

[60] Bonnassie, *La Catalogne*, ii, 856–59; Ruiz Doménec, "The urban origins," 285–86.

[61] ACA perg. R. B. II, sense data 48, 75.

[62] Sobrequés i Vidal, *Els grans comtes*, 140–41; Menéndez Pidal, *La España del Cid*, i, 416–18.

[63] Puig y Puig, *Episcopologio*, ap. lviii; *Marca Hispanica, sive Limes Hispanicus, hoc est, geographica et historica descriptio Cataloniae, Ruscionis, et circumjacentium populorum*, ed. P. de Marca (Paris, 1688), ap. cccv.

Except for four Jews given the privilege of transporting ransomed Saracens back to al-Andalus,[64] before the mid-twelfth century no one in the city is known to have owned a ship, surely a valuable commodity which would have turned up in local wills. As will be seen in chapter 5, the immediate impulse for naval construction came from a confrontation between the Genoese and the House of Barcelona. As the dynasty developed an ambitious political and dynastic program in Occitania, culminating in Count Ramon Berenguer III's marriage to Dolça, countess of Provence, in 1112, it inevitably ran up against the Genoese, who were attempting to dominate the markets along the coasts of Provence and Langue-doc. But did not Occitanian expansion and a new maritime aggressiveness merely offer partial replacement for opportunities once found in al-Andalus? In order to placate a turbulent nobility that had grown used to the wealth and luxuries seized from Muslims, the counts turned the restless energies of aristocrats and their armed clienteles in new directions, to political rewards in Occitania, to the settlement of the frontier zones of New Catalo-nia, and to the inviting waters of the Western Mediterranean. But like the earlier campaigns in al-Andalus, expansion in new direc-tions depended upon the pent-up aggressiveness of a highly mili-tarized society, barely held in check by its leaders, rather than upon the investments of urban entrepreneurs. It was precisely this separation, cultural as well as material, between profit-oriented burghers and nobles with their armed retainers seeking tribute, land, and office that caused Barcelona's early growth to grind to a halt.

This is not to deny that the naval buildup benefited some individuals in the city, nor that itinerant merchants stopped in Barcelona. But neither commerce nor maritime enterprise had yet attained the intensity, regularity, and complexity to reorient urban investment or engage the energies of prominent local families. Philippe Wolff detected the presence of a pedlar (*negocia-tor*) named Robert, possibly a native of Flanders, who fell ill and died at Barcelona in 1009, leaving the local canons fourteen cloths (*pallei*) of various colors.[65] Other adventurers must surely have traveled the same way, heading toward the fabled wealth of al-Andalus. Pirenne's "dusty-footed merchants" with their capital

---

[64] Baer, *Die Juden*, I, no. 13.
[65] Philippe Wolff, "Quidam homo nomine Roberto negociatore," *Le Moyen Âge*, 69 (1963), 129–39.

lashed to mules or even carried on their own backs must surely have passed through Barcelona on their way south, but they moved with ghostly anonymity, leaving only the faintest traces in local records. Although privileges and legal documents abstractly refer to merchants as a group, between the 1050s and the 1140s no townsman is known to have assumed the professional title of merchant. Resident foreigners, another barometer of commercial contacts, only begin to emerge in significant numbers during the 1130s.[66] To judge from testaments left by townspeople of the early twelfth century, Barcelonans hardly knew the world beyond Catalonia existed. Not a single testator left a pious offering for a church in Occitania, nor do bequests include accumulations of foreign cloth, spices, furs, or other luxuries, the staples of long-distance commerce. The amount of cash bequests shrank noticeably in the decades after 1100, leaving land and produce as the principal forms of inherited wealth. Thus, there is little to suggest that a significant amount of merchandise found its way to Barcelona through extraregional exchange, or that it provided an alternative to agricultural investment. Until local families invested in long-distance trade themselves and foreign merchants settled down in Barcelona, commerce existed only on the periphery of the urban economy.

CONCLUSION

The twelfth century has gained a reputation for irresistible expansion and effusive optimism. Yet if we are to judge the process by which demographic growth, increased production, the spread of money, and the articulation of new attitudes toward wealth led to the integrated, far-flung civilization of thirteenth-century Europe, the obstacles retarding, redirecting, and even temporarily reversing the powerful surge of material advance deserve no less attention than the forces driving this movement forward. Barriers to development, however, are difficult to detect. Usually by the time records become sufficiently concentrated to provide a serial history of economic trends, especially in early towns, the fundamental transformation in trade, local exchange, credit, and rural investment, in short the emergence of a profit-oriented economy, had already taken place. Catalonia, however, serves as a privileged

---

[66] Infra, 228–29.

laboratory where one can observe with remarkable clarity the developmental stages of what Fossier has called "Europe's infancy."[67] It was not an untroubled childhood. If during the eleventh century Barcelona had taken its first exhilarating steps toward becoming a major Mediterranean port, from 1090 to 1140 the city failed to find the confidence and initiative to venture beyond the secure, familiar confines of its well-tended hinterland.

But how should we characterize the economic difficulties that had set in by 1100? Did a twelfth-century depression overtake Barcelona? In the context of recent discussions about the European economic take-off, a twelfth-century depression is virtually an oxymoron. Did Barcelona therefore encounter its first cyclical downturn, a phenomenon familiar to those who have measured the movement of prices and wages during the next seven centuries in preindustrial Europe?[68] If by depression or cyclical downturn one means simply a decrease in the volume of economic activity, then the terms have little value in the present context for they do not convey the incomplete transformation of the urban economy toward a commercial foundation. The problem is not simply a matter of scholastic hairsplitting: the inability of Barcelona to continue its expansion simply does not fit into the prevailing models for the early growth of the European economy. It may be best to think in terms of a developmental blockage, since the term emphasizes an incomplete structural evolution rather than simply the contraction of a preexisting system. Because Barcelona failed to break out of the confined regional parameters that had contained its first phase of growth, it had not yet laid the social and economic foundations for its later prosperity.

Does Barcelona therefore constitute merely a curious exception, caused by its peripheral location on the Islamic–Christian frontier, to the rise of Mediterranean towns and in general to the West's economic take-off, or is it exceptional because of the fortuitous survival of its documentation? Milan and Piacenza

---

[67] See in particular Fossier, *Enfance*, II, 745–46, 794–97. This splendid synthesis is the first to incorporate fully the fruits of a generation of intensive labor in the archives of the Mediterranean, especially Bonnassie's work on Catalonia, into a broad view of Europe's early economic development.

[68] The methodological difficulties in establishing a quantitative, serial history even for thirteenth-century France are judiciously weighed by Gérard Sivéry, *L'Economie du royaume de France au siècle de Saint Louis* (Lille, 1983), 31–50. Attempts at establishing early economic cycles have been confined to the rural economy: Wilhelm Abel, *Agricultural fluctuations in Europe*, trans. O. Ordish (London, 1980), 17–37; D. L. Farmer, "Some price fluctuations in Angevin England," *Economic history review*, IX (1956), 34–43.

provide the best comparisons, for they both possess abundant early records and have been studied in close connection to their countrysides.[69] While both Lombard towns began a sustained expansion by the early tenth century, far earlier than Barcelona, their economic development seems at once more gradual and secure than that of the Catalonian capital. Even though Milan experienced a brief decline in land values during the 1030s and 1040s and Piacenza faced a slight dip in property prices in its hinterland from 1100 to 1140, there is nothing to compare with the collapse of real estate values that affected Barcelona for almost fifty years. While prominent urban families, both noble and non-noble, owned land around Milan and Piacenza and profited from agricultural expansion, merchants also played a significant part in the life of Lombard towns well before the year 1000, an indication of the close communications and relative prosperity of northern Italy in the post-Carolingian age. Trade and agriculture reinforced one another. Was it not the failure to link these two forces firmly through the formation of a new style of leadership that stifled Barcelona's early growth? Instead of trade, pillage and *parias* provided Catalonia with precious metals and luxuries. Townspeople, however, participated only secondhand in an archaic, yet splendidly successful, tributary economy, but once it collapsed commercialized exchange had not yet attained the volume and organization to replace it. Without the impetus of trade to spring it free from a narrow regional confinement, the urban economy turned in upon itself and stagnated.

Because of its ideological and romantic connections in modern historiography to such highly charged concepts as the bourgeoisie, democracy, and capitalism, early urban history has been prone to polemical, monocausal explanations. In opposition to an "externalist" explanation that considered long-distance trade as the *primum mobile* of the urban revival, an equally rigid "internalist" argument has countered that only agricultural surpluses and local exchange could provide the momentum necessary for the rise of urban economies. If several generations of scholars have cast in doubt Pirenne's immaculate conception of capitalism, in its place they have substituted an equally strong belief in the economic transubstantiation of bread and wine into spices, silks, cloth, and slaves. The difficulties faced by Barcelona in the early

[69] Violante, *La società milanese*, 108; Pierre Racine, *Plaisance du Xe à la fin du XIIIe siècle: essaie d'histoire urbaine* (Lille and Paris, 1980), I, 110–18, 126–63, 243–61, 347–50.

twelfth century, however, suggest that both a prosperous local market and extraregional exchange are required before the full potential of an urban economy can be realized. Neither "internal" nor "external" stimuli need logically precede one another, however, for both potentially drew strength from the freeing up of economic forces once the exchange function of towns, at both a local and an "international" level, superseded the political role that had allowed for their survival in the early Middle Ages.[70] Yet a firm connection between the two economic circuits, between local agricultural markets and long-distance trade, took time to achieve and depended upon local variations in the structure of each component. In Catalonia generally the agricultural sector proved the first to break through owing to the predominance of allodial property, the ease of real estate transfers, the creation of local markets, and the rapid penetration of coinage into the countryside, while external exchange remained encased within the circuits of an archaic, yet highly profitable war economy. In Barcelona a new group had not yet emerged to coordinate and link the "externalist" and "internalist" impulses for growth that would ensure the enduring prosperity of the urban economy. Because social and cultural factors could promote or retard such linkage, we must now consider how economic blockage changed the position of and relationships among the city's leading families.

[70] On the transition from the political to the economic function of towns, see Guy Bois, *La Mutation de l'an mil* (Paris, 1989), 125–32 [*The tranformation of the year one thousand: the village of Lournand from antiquity to feudalism*, trans. J. Birrell (Manchester and New York, 1992), 76–81].

Chapter 4

URBAN SOCIETY IN TRANSITION

The animation of urban life after the millennium strengthened the ties of Barcelona to the fields, vineyards, orchards, and gardens surrounding it and at the same time magnified its role as the nodal point of regional society. As the finely spun threads of economic and family interest became increasingly intertwined, more tightly woven, they created complex patterns in which any sharp contrast between rural and urban concerns dissolved. Rather than tearing the traditional social fabric, the early growth of Barcelona embellished the material, making it more sumptuous and enlarging its proportions to accommodate a broader framework of interchange.

Throughout the Mediterranean ancient Roman towns frequently retained distinctive administrative, military, and religious functions during the obscure, poorly documented centuries of the early Middle Ages. As they formed dense historical spaces or, in a rather clinical term, "central places,"[1] they attracted, concentrated, and coordinated diffuse networks of power through an intricate urban microcircuitry of social relationships. In historiographical terms, the revived towns of the medieval Mediterranean have increasingly assumed the appearance of compacted regions. Especially in recent reassessments of early urban growth in northern Italy, burghers have been stripped of much of the originality that earlier generations of historians had attributed to them. Summarizing recent tendencies in Italian urban studies, David Herlihy remarked that the city in itself can no longer be

---

[1] "Einleitung," to *Zentralität als Problem der mittelalterlichen Stadtgeschichtsforschung*, ed. E. Meynen (Cologne and Vienna, 1979), vii–xii; Alfred Haverkamp, "Die Städte im Herrschafts- und Sozialgefüge Reichsitaliens," *Stadt und Herrschaft: Römische Kaiserzeit und hohes Mittelalter. Historische Zeitschrift*. Beiheft 7 (Munich, 1982), 159–71, 178–201; Tabacco, *Egemonie*, 208–18.

regarded as an "independent unit of analysis."[2] Jacques Heers, Hagen Keller, Gabriella Rossetti, and Diane Owen Hughes have insisted on placing early urban populations squarely in the cultural, familial, and institutional settings of the rural-aristocratic worlds surrounding them;[3] the movement between expanding cities and their regions now seems so fluid as to make town walls porous. The direction of recent investigations points not merely to an "influence" of the countryside on towns or to an elucidation of "contact" between the two spheres, conceived as coherent and independent social spaces; rather, it seeks to demonstrate how feudal-aristocratic forms of organization shaped the contours of urban society from top to bottom. In the apt phrase of Renato Bordone, reflecting on the new perspective on urban life offered by the many investigations devoted to the Italian countryside, "in the past few years the *contado* at least in historiographical terms has conquered the city."[4]

If early towns are primarily conceived of as switchboards for the dispersed lines of social and cultural communication in the countryside, it becomes difficult to attribute a distinctively urban character to them in either political or social terms. Yet medieval writers clearly imagined towns as worlds unto themselves, prone to peculiar vices and deceptions but also arrogant and independent. Questions involving profit and the manipulation of money, typically urban activities, sent theologians and lawyers scurrying to their books in order to extrapolate new ethical standards for a disturbingly precocious urban environment, while the presence of merchants created an infraction in the rules imposed by the tripartite division of society into *ordines*. While social and

[2] David Herlihy, "Società e spazio nella città italiana del medioevo," *La storiografia urbanistica. Atti del 1.° convegno internazionale di storia urbanistica. Lucca 24–28 settembre 1975* (Lucca, 1976), 178.

[3] Heers, *Le Clan familial*, 21–55 and *Les Partis et la vie politique*, 106–18; Gabriella Rossetti, *Pisa nei secoli XI e XII: formazione e caratteri di una classe di governo* (Pisa, 1979) and "Histoire familiale et structures sociales et politiques à Pise aux XIᵉ et XIIᵉ siècles," in *Famille et parenté dans l'Occident médiéval*, eds. G. Duby and J. Le Goff (Rome, 1977), 159–80; Hagen Keller, "Die Enstehung der italienischen Stadtkommunen als Problem der Sozialgeschichte," *Frühmittelalterliche Studien*, 10 (1976), 169–211; Diane Owen Hughes, "Urban growth and family structure in medieval Genoa," *Past and present*, 66 (1975), 3–6 [repr. in *Towns in societies: essays in economic history and historical sociology*, ed. P. Abrams and E. A. Wrigley (Cambridge, 1978), 107–10].

[4] Renato Bordone, "Tema cittadino e 'ritorno alla terra' nella storiografia comunale recente," *Quaderni storici*, 52 (1983), 262.

economic historians have patiently been demolishing town walls, cultural historians have been diligently reinforcing them.[5] The vigorous and sustained reaction against the nineteenth-century equation of civic life with a merchant class has led to a scholarly fixation with aristocratic and rural perspectives on medieval urban growth, particularly in its initial stages. If meticulous local studies during the past generation have dispelled what Philip Jones refers to as the myth of the bourgeoisie even in Italy, the promised land of medieval urbanism, they have not had as much success in coming to grips with the emergence of aggressive, self-conscious civic polities.[6] It is often taken for granted that an initial surge of demographic and urban expansion created a mold that would determine the shape of urban societies for centuries to come. Yet only by examining how traditional loyalties and economic strategies became transformed in the compressed, pressurized environment of early towns can we arrive at a better understanding of medieval *civilitas*.

The parameters of a distinctively urban sphere took shape quite slowly in Barcelona. Carolingian privileges, directed to residents in both town and country, tended to treat the city not as an autonomous community but as a point of reference on an urban–rural continuum; Count Berenguer Ramon I followed this tradition by addressing his privilege of 1025 to the inhabitants of the city, its hinterland, and the entire county (*vobis omnibus habitantibus Barchinonam civitatem sive eius suburbium et omnem Barchinonensem comitatum*).[7] Since the liberties of townspeople hardly differed from those of villagers, there was little need to define an urban space with precision. Before the year 1000, the terms *comitatus*, *pagus*, and *territorium* were used interchangeably to designate the extent of Barcelona's jurisdiction throughout the county; *suburbium* could be applied to the countryside in the Pla de Barcelona and even to the monastery of Sant Cugat del Vallès beyond the Collserola range.[8] Only during the eleventh century did *suburbium*

---

[5] Jacques Le Goff, "Warriors and conquering bourgeois: the image of the city in twelfth-century French literature," *The medieval imagination*, trans. A. Goldhammer (Chicago, 1988), 151–76; Lester K. Little, *Religious poverty and the profit economy in medieval Europe* (London, 1978), 171–217; Georges Duby, *The three orders: feudal society imagined*, trans. A. Goldhammer (Chicago, 1980), 213–17; Fossier, *Enfance*, II, 980.

[6] Jones, "Economia e società," 188–89.   [7] Font Rius, *Cartas de población*, I:1, no. 15.

[8] Mitjá Sagué, "Condado y ciudad," 275–76. For examples of the elastic dimensions of Barcelona's *suburbium*, see *Archivo condal*, no. 224; *CSC*, I, no. 162; ACB LA II, fol. 93, Mas IX, no. 110. A similar fluidity between urban and rural jurisdictions also existed in Italy, Haverkamp, "Die Städte im Herrschafts- und Sozialgefüge," 166.

become restricted to settlements below the Roman defenses and the *territorium* to the city's immediate hinterland bounded by the Llobregat, Besòs, the mountains, and the sea, although neither zone as yet had rigid boundaries. Formal recognition of the common concerns shared by those residing within and below the town walls was also slow in coming. A well-known clause of the *Usatges* sets the fine for the death of a burgher on a par with that of a knight; those enjoying this elevated status are identified as *cives et burgenses*, residents of the intramural zone of Roman towns (*civitas*) and inhabitants of suburbs or new settlements (*burgum*).[9] While the inhabitants enjoyed the same status no matter on which side of the ancient ramparts they lived, the habit of describing the urban population as a collective whole took hold only as the various zones of settlement were acknowledged as forming a continuous urban space distinct from the fields around it. In a confirmation of privileges made by his predecessors, King Alfons I in 1162 granted his charter to "all the Christian inhabitants of Barcelona ... men and women alike," that is to the city as a whole with the apparent exception of Jews and Muslims.[10] The parameters of urban society were hardening. In 1218 the precentor of the cathedral won a suit against an alleged tenant who held property from the canons in the "garden" of Sant Pau del Camp, a zone on the fuzzy margins of the suburban area. Because the judges determined that the property had passed to a simple peasant (*simplex ortalanus*) rather than a burgher (*burgensis*), he did not enjoy the liberty granted to the urban inhabitants of bequeathing land without restriction.[11] Such a sharp legal border between rural and urban territory could only be erected once civic allegiance had loosened the bonds connecting the city to its region.

The economic and political difficulties of the early twelfth century undermined the moorings that had fixed Barcelona within the administrative and social configuration of the *Marca Hispanica*. Since the most complex web of familial and personal relationships which spread out from the city was spun by aristocrats and nobles, it is fitting that a discussion of Barcelona's relationship with its region begin with a consideration of noble houses.

---

[9] *Usatges*, art. 10, 210.
[10] Font Rius, *Cartas de población*, I:1, no. 120. The formula of address to "omnibus habitatoribus" became common in urban charters in the mid-twelfth century, ibid., II, 583.
[11] ACB 1–6–1298.

Owing to the threat of Muslim raids and the instability produced by the fragmentation of Carolingian power, during the ninth and tenth century rural aristocrats with their armed clienteles established residences in the largely empty stone shells of ancient Roman cities throughout the Mediterranean.[12] Small urban sites with easily defensible perimeters proved particularly suited to the reduced scale of occupation and the available military resources. Warriors entrenched themselves in towns. They built onto and on top of Roman walls, occupied stout defensive towers, and burrowed into the ruins of public buildings; to turn back the advances of demonic forces that imperiled their souls and those of their kinsmen and ancestors, nobles accustomed to violence made generous donations from the rural holdings they retained to ancient urban churches. Physical insecurity helped animate Mediterranean towns, which served a regional defensive role similar to that of rural fortresses in Northern Europe. With the economic expansion of the eleventh century, resident aristocrats, their dependents, petty nobles, and urban clerics all profited from the increased revenues in cash rents and produce they received from their rural property, part of which they could bring to urban markets. Historians have become used to treating aristocrats as familiar fixtures in the nascent civic worlds of the Latin Mediterranean.

While the presence of nobles and aristocrats in towns has been well documented from an early date, their place in the fundamental transformation in the structure of the nobility during the eleventh and twelfth century remains problematic. Dominated by models of family development from Germany and France,[13]

---

[12] Georges Duby, "Les Villes du sud-est de la Gaule du VIIIe au XIe siècle," *La città nell'alto medioevo. Settimane di studio del centro italiano di studi sull'alto medioevo,* VI (Spoleto, 1959), 232–41 [repr. in *Hommes et structures du moyen âge: recueil d'articles* (The Hague and Paris, 1973), 111–32]; Jean-Pierre Poly, *La Provence et la société féodale (879–1166)* (Paris, 1976), 286–300; Bryan Ward-Perkins, "The towns of northern Italy: rebirth or renewal?" in *The rebirth of towns in the West, A.D. 700–1050,* eds. R. Hodges and B. Hobley (Oxford, 1988), 16–27; Fossier, *Enfance,* II, 989–94.

[13] Fundamental articles by Tellenbach, Schmidt, and Genicot are now conveniently collected and translated in *The medieval nobility: studies on the ruling classes of France and Germany from the sixth to the twelfth century,* ed. and trans. T. Reuter (Amsterdam, London, and New York, 1979); see also Georges Duby, "Remarques sur la littérature généalogique en France aux XIe et XIIe siècle," *Académie des Inscriptions et Belles-lettres: comptes rendus des séances de l'année (avril–juin)* (Paris, 1967), 335–45 [repr. in *Hommes et structures,* 287–98; "French genealogical literature," *The chivalrous society,* trans C. Postan

investigations into the emergence of noble lineages in Southern Europe have tended to treat urban holdings and offices as an annex to rural estates and castles. The influential studies of Heers and Hughes have gone out of their way to emphasize that the establishment of aristocratic houses in Italian towns neither cut them off from their landed wealth and rural clienteles nor weakened corporate family bonds,[14] both important correctives to a traditional association of small, independent "middle class" households with urban societies. Aristocratic clans are often thought of as transplanting their way of life and internal organization from the countryside to the town. Yet for nobles with a long-standing association with cities either through officeholding or at least a temporary residence, the crystallization of family identity around a single male line of descent and a patrimonial core could present a dilemma. Hansmartin Schwarzmaier has found that in Lucca the tightening of family identity in the early eleventh century segmented the fluid clans of the early Middle Ages, thereby forming a relatively coherent urban leadership of officeholders from lesser nobles but also weakening their connections with their rural kin.[15] Even though a diffuse loyalty to distant relatives might provide the potential for common action, urban and rural branches of a noble family moved in different environments. Urban towers were not rural castles, despite recent attempts to make them so. The grating presence of rival families could not be easily avoided in a tiny urban world, nor could one ignore the ability of the city's lord to regulate internal balances by bestowing offices, fiefs, or patronage. Even if we can isolate common elements of aristocratic organization in urban and rural settings, the pressurized space of Mediterranean towns could fuse these social components into quite distinctive compounds.

(Berkeley and Los Angeles, 1980), 149–57]. For the contributions of recent investigations, see Thomas N. Bisson, "Nobility and family in medieval France: a review essay," *French historical studies*, 16 (1990), 597–613.

[14] Heers, *Les Partis et la vie politique*, 16–18; Hughes, "Urban growth," 105–11.

[15] Hansmartin Schwarzmaier, *Lucca und das Reich bis zum Ende des 11. Jahrhunderts* (Sigmaringen, 1972), 239–61. Carol Lansing, *The Florentine magnates: lineage and faction in a medieval commune* (Princeton, 1991), 34–35, 52, 64–83 has also emphasized that forms of association in towns, especially indivisible ecclesiastical rights, transformed families of petty nobles who emigrated to Florence into tightly organized lineages.

THE FALL OF THE VISCOUNTS OF BARCELONA

Aristocratic society in eleventh-century Barcelona revolved around its viscounts.[16] Firmly entrenched in both Castellvell, overlooking the market, and the castle of La Guàrdia, the linchpin of its rural patrimony perched on the rocky heights near Montserrat, this proud family stood astride two worlds, the small, bustling regional center of Barcelona and the turbulent uplands bristling with castles and men-at-arms. The viscounts moved easily in both, drawing strength from their personal properties and dependents centered on a network of castles around La Guàrdia, including Cabrera, Apiera, Castellet, Apierola, and Castellolí, and at the same time enjoying prerogatives of justice, military command, and the supervision of fiscal resources in Barcelona as representatives of the count. The combination of a private network of inland castles and the monopolization of urban public authority catapulted the viscomital house into the highest ranks of the Catalonian aristocracy by the late tenth century. Count Borrell II chose Viscount Guitard to participate in an embassy to the caliphal court at Córdoba in 974 and to head another delegation dispatched there two years later, missions that at once drew the Catalonian aristocracy toward the dense cultural and material weight in the south and made this group aware of its common interests and independence.[17] Adalbert, a younger son of Guitard, later followed the same road to Córdoba, but not to seek a truce; he died on the daring Catalan expedition into the heart of al-Andalus in 1010, a turning point in peninsular history that marked the ascendancy of the Christian north. Guitard's eldest son and heir to the viscomital title, Udalard I (985–1014), confirmed the military preeminence of his family by taking charge of Barcelona's defense against al-Manṣūr in 985. To consolidate its control of comital prerogatives in the city, the viscomital family arranged marriages with the ruling dynasty; the brothers Udalard and Geribert each married daughters of Count Borrell II, and the senior branch of the family reached the height of its power through the marriage of

---

[16] Pere Català i Roca, *Extinció del Vescomtat de Barcelona* (Barcelona, 1974) provides the most recent summary on the viscounts, but reference should be made to the views of Santiago Sobrequés i Vidal, *Els barons de Catalunya* (Barcelona, 1957), 29–32, Carreras Candi, *La ciutat*, 260–67, and Bonnassie, *La Catalogne*, I, 170–73; II, 783–85.

[17] Abadal i Vinyals, *Els primers comtes*, 320–21 sees these early missions as a *prise de conscience* by the nobility and a realization of their distance from the kingdom of the Franks.

Udalard II (1041–c. 1077) to Guisla, widow of Count Berenguer Ramon I and daughter of the count of Empúries, who in her will passed on the castles of Granera and Castellnou de Bages to her common descendants with Udalard. By function and by marriage, the viscomital clan thought of itself as a complementary annex of the House of Barcelona, for it possessed its own patrimonial power base with an independent family memory in the interior yet claimed an inherited right to act as the permanent representatives of comital authority at the nerve center of dynastic interests. To nobles and knights from throughout the county and beyond, the viscomital court at Castellvell acted like a magnet. How many warriors flocked to it in order to hear stories about Udalard's valiant but futile defense of the city against al-Manṣūr and his subsequent captivity, to learn of the fabled wealth of Córdoba, and to make plans for the next expedition to al-Andalus? It is perfectly appropriate that a viscomital charter from 1088 records the presence of a certain Guillem Pere *iocularis*, the earliest reference to a Catalan court entertainer.[18]

The decline of the viscomital house would have provided a wealth of material for any troubadour, for it involved family rivalry, treason, and knightly adventure in the land of the infidel. Through opportune marriages and an inherited right to exercise broad public powers, by the mid-eleventh century the viscounts and their relatives came to regard their prerogatives as patrimonial assets, governed by rules of inheritance and clannish interest. Claims of sovereignty by the count or legal tribunals in the distribution and management of lands and rights were increasingly resisted as unwarranted interference in family business. The tensions between Count Ramon Berenguer I and the leading figures of the viscomital house led to open revolt from 1040 to 1060; Viscount Udalard II and his uncle, Bishop Guisalbert of Barcelona, laid siege to the count in his urban palace and Udalard's cousin, Mir Geribert, led a prolonged insurrection from his frontier castles in the Penedès.[19]

In an intriguing article, Ruiz Doménec has recently attempted to interpret these disturbances not as a struggle between public and private authority but as the product of imbalances in the developing systems of descent and marital alliance, the foundation of what

---

[18] ACB 3–38–8(e).   [19] Supra, 60–61.

he considers the "feudal structure."[20] According to his model, as descent systems crystallized around patrilineages, a development observed among the nobility in Catalonia and in many other parts of Europe during the tenth and early eleventh centuries, the exchange of women through marriage regulated not only relationships among noble lineages but their relative status as well, for through hierarchical, asymmetrical exchange women were consistently passed down from a lineage of higher rank to one of lower status. Such an approach proves attractive in trying to account for the bitterness and desperation of Mir Geribert's resistance. In conformity with the role allotted to cadet branches of noble houses, his line of the viscomital house had been relegated to a subordinate position in the frontier zone of the Penedès and excluded from the possessions of his relatives around La Guàrdia and Barcelona. Unwilling to accept his marginalized role and to receive a wife from anyone but the counts, Mir Geribert entertained hopes of standing on equal footing with the main branch of his family and being recognized as such by the counts. His disappointments led to a violent confrontation, seen in this context as a rejection of his assigned function within the kin group.

Even though perceived snubs in his relationships with relatives and unmaterialized hopes of receiving a prestigious bride from his superiors may well have bruised the sensitive ego of this marcher lord and provoked him to dare bloody rebellion, his violence was turned against the count, not against his cousin the viscount or his uncle the bishop. Because Udalard II had established his proper matrimonial alliances with the counts, the attack he and his uncle Guisalbert led on the comital palace, according to Ruiz Doménec, had little connection with the stubborn defiance of his cousin, Mir Geribert; by his marriage to Guisla, the viscount could easily reconcile himself to Count Ramon Berenguer I and find a firm place in the grid of feudal marital alliances.

This approach, however, unduly underestimates the clannish cohesion of the viscomital house in its opposition to comital authority and fails to explain the count's attempt to circumscribe the power of the main branch of the viscomital family soon after its sedition had been put down. To reassert his control, the count

---

[20] José E. Ruiz Doménec, "La primera estructura feudal (consideraciones sobre la producción, el poder y el parentesco en Cataluña) (c.980–1060)," *Quaderni catanensi di studi classici e medievali*, 4 (1982), 301–68.

set out to subject castles in the core of the viscount's upland patrimony to his *potestas*; between 1058 and 1067, Ramon Berenguer and his wife Almodis purchased the castle of Cabrera, exchanged Apierola for Apiera and Castellet, and acquired property around the castle of Apiera.[21] Even though the viscounts had regained command of these castles again by 1139, they now held them, together with Castellolí, from the count.[22] Even the hub of viscomital power in Barcelona, Castellvell, was held on new terms. In a feudal convention of 1058, Viscount Udalard affirmed that he held the castle-gate from the count and renounced all new exactions he and his ancestors had imposed since the time of Count Ramon Borrell.[23] The tensions between the viscount and count of Barcelona certainly contain elements of family rivalry, but Count Ramon Berenguer I reined in his subordinate through his prerogatives as sovereign and lord, not as the senior member of his kin group. As Marc Bloch once observed, "The tie of kinship was one of the essential elements of feudal society; its relative weakness explains why there was feudalism at all."[24]

After its confrontation with Count Ramon Berenguer I, the viscomital house failed to maintain its position in Barcelona as its focus shifted toward its patrimonial assets around La Guàrdia and toward military exploits outside Catalonia. After 1060 the successive heads of the lineage gradually withdrew from urban life, ceding their urban property and utilities to minor branches of the family or to the Church. Udalard II kept a low profile once he had incurred the count's suspicion; he did not attempt to reverse the restrictions placed on his authority by the feudal convention of 1058 and kept aloof from urban affairs, at least to judge from his infrequent appearance as a subscriber to urban charters. If a cool distance mitigated potential conflict during the later years of Count Ramon Berenguer I, the corule of his sons brought factional rivalries within the Catalan aristocracy to the boiling point. Partisans of Ramon Berenguer II, the viscounts had to face the hostility of his rival Berenguer Ramon II, a conflict that prompted the viscounts to reorganize their urban property. Toward the end of his life Udalard II ceded a portion of the urban walls and towers adjacent to Bishop's Gate as well as substantial houses (*mansiones*) and workshops near the ancient Roman forum

[21] *LFM*, I, nos. 325, 326, 328, 330–32, 334–36.   [22] *LFM*, I, no. 341.
[23] ACA perg. R.B. I, 225; Bonnassie, *La Catalogne*, II, 650–51.
[24] Marc Bloch, *Feudal Society*, trans. L. A. Manyon (London, 1961), I, 142.

to clerics; his heir Viscount Gelabert Udalard (c. 1077–c. 1126) transferred a house by lease in 1083 and land by sale in 1088 at the heart of the city near the old forum to his daughter Erminiard and her husband Calví, later identified as one of the count's moneyers.[25]

These grants were part of an effort to strengthen viscomital influence secondhand by seeking allies within the Church and by using marriage to associate an important comital official with the family's interests. Not long before his death, Gelabert Udalard made similar arrangements in 1125 by granting urban houses to his daughter Ermessenda and his son-in-law Guillem Ramon, possibly the head of the Castellvell family, and bequeathing part of his urban oven to Sant Cugat.[26] Even command of Castellvell of Barcelona, the traditional hub of viscomital power, passed under the control of related families. After securing an oath of fealty from Gelabert for the castle-gate in 1110, in the following year the count installed Guillem Ramon de Castellvell (de Rosanes), the head of a prominent lineage intermarried with the viscounts; the son of Guillem Ramon also swore fealty for the post in 1126 and 1134.[27] Jordà de Sant Martí, related to the viscounts through his grandfather Mir Geribert and on good enough terms with the Castellvell to marry his son to a member of their clan, held Barcelona's principal castle-gate intermittently between 1112 and 1131.[28] The Castellvell and their clients had earned the trust of the counts in the early twelfth century, for both Guillem Ramon and his son Guillem Ramon II (1112–66) frequently attended the comital court and became intimates of the ruler; Count Ramon Berenguer III may have even given an illegitimate daughter named Mahalta to the latter in marriage.[29] Because the urban vicars had already appropriated prerogatives

---

25 ACB LA I, fol. 236, Mas XII, no. 2674; ACB 3–38–8(e and d); "Documento del siglo XI," 634–36.

26 ACA perg. R.B. III, 269; *CSC*, III, no. 883.

27 *LFM*, I, nos. 237–39, 339, 340. Blanca Garí, *El linaje de los Castellvell en los siglos XI y XII. Medievalia, monografías* 5 (Barcelona, 1985), 122, 131–32 speculates that a rift developed between the viscounts and the Castellvell in the early twelfth century despite their frequent marriage alliances. If this were the case, however, it is difficult to understand why Gelabert's grandson, Viscount Berenguer Reverter, later married a member of the Castellvell and the son of this couple, the last member of the lineage, left the bulk of his castles and properties to Albert de Castellvell.

28 *LFM*, I, no. 304. On the genealogical relationship of Jordà de Sant Martí to the viscounts and later to the Castellvell, see the chart in Sobrequés i Vidal, *Els grans comtes*, between 64 and 65 and Garí, *El linaje de los Castellvell*, 13.

29 Garí, *El linaje de los Castellvell*, 127–30, 183–95.

once exercised by the viscounts, the installation of independent
castlans from a trusted family closely allied with the viscomital
house provided Ramon Berenguer III with a discreet means of
easing the viscounts out of their seat of urban authority while at
the same time acknowledging an ancestral claim to the castle-gate
and providing a counterweight to unruly vicars. After 1145,
however, no further evidence of divided authority over the castle-
gate appears; henceforth it would remain in the firm grasp of the
vicars. In the intricate web of aristocratic kinship surrounding the
exercise of authority in Barcelona, the counts knew which strands
to pull in order to deprive a threatening but related rival of their
inherited rights of command at the hub of dynastic power.

If the viscounts had attempted to cover their retreat from the
city with a system of family alliances, the strategy failed miserably.
The property that Gelabert Udalard had ceded to Erminiard and
Calví the Moneyer had to be sold by their daughter Maria in 1155
because of "poverty," and although the Castellvell prospered in
the twelfth century they did not retain even a foothold in Barcelona. When Ramon de Castellvell, precentor of the cathedral,
donated a house on the Roman defenses which his ancestors had
held for over a century, the family surrendered its last piece of
urban property.[30] The principal successors to viscomital property
in the city failed to have any direct impact on urban affairs.

With Gelabert Udalard, the power of the viscounts in the city
had effectively come to an end. Squeezed out of Barcelona and
held in check in his upland patrimony by comital suzerainty,
Gelabert's son Reverter turned to the venerable traditions of his
forefathers and sought to restore the fame of his lineage through
war beyond the Christian frontier. Instead of leading expeditions
to al-Andalus, Reverter commanded Christian mercenaries in the
service of the emir of Morocco. Absorbed in his adventures in
North Africa, Reverter lost control of what remained of his
family's possessions in Barcelona. Formalizing the usurpation of
his valuable oven and stalls at the foot of Castellvell, the viscount
sold them to Bernat Marcús for 200 mbts. in 1155, thereby
liquidating his ancestral holdings in the city.[31] When Reverter's
son made out his testament in 1187 before returning to Morocco,
the last member of this proud lineage had nothing to bequeath

---

[30] ACB LA I, fol. 92, Mas XI, no. 1952; cf. LA I, fol. 227, Mas IX, no. 506.
[31] ACA perg. R. B. IV, sense data, 7; *Santa Anna*, II, no. 297.

from the city Udalard had once defended against al-Manṣūr.[32] Lacking direct descendants, he left the bulk of his upland castles and lands to the Castellvell. The nucleus of his patrimony centered on La Guàrdia had remained largely intact, even though it had become subject to comital *potestas*. Reflecting the durable connection of the family with its castle in Anoia, one of its members styled himself viscount of La Guàrdia, an appellation later adopted by the senior branch of the house. The title of viscount of Barcelona, now devoid of meaning, disappears once and for all from the charters in 1155.[33]

The change of toponyms provides elegant testimony to the new structure of aristocratic power and the difficulties that the viscomital lineage had in adjusting to it. Originally the viscounts held an office, not just a title. Like the handful of other Catalan aristocratic families that had emerged by the late tenth century, the viscomital house obtained its elevated status primarily from a close association with the count rather than from private family possessions or personal bonds with its clients. As representatives of public authority, the viscounts had provided a focus for regional society, drawing warriors to Barcelona to defend the city and the frontier it dominated from Muslim marauders, later leading embassies and armies to al-Andalus, and upholding ancient legal procedures and confirming inherited positions of subjects at their courts. Because the structures of authority integrated Barcelona with its county and region, the viscomital house could build up its power without any tension between its possessions in Anoia and its influence in the city.

Yet power to command and to render justice revolved around Castellvell de Barcelona, not La Guàrdia. After 1000, private, patrimonial interests began to overwhelm the traditional territorial order. In keeping with the movement to treat delegated authority as proprietary grants, older aristocratic houses attempted to subtract their delegated authority from comital supervision and treat it as a patrimonial asset, subject to the needs of the family. Here the tendency noted by Ruiz Doménec of aristocratic lineages to organize themselves according to privatized relationships of marriage alliances rather than officeholding or comital patronage reinforces rather than contradicts the challenge to public authority that, according to Bonnassie, culminated in the

---

[32] *LFM*, I, no. 347.   [33] *CSC*, III, no. 821; *Santa Anna*, II, no. 297.

violent crisis from 1040 to 1060. As a result of the new relations of dependence and authority emerging from this unsettled period, aristocratic power came to rest upon private control of castles and the peasants dependent upon them rather than on the exercise of territorial authority over free subjects. While the viscounts retained their ancestral castles and land under new terms, they were unable to recast their traditional rights in Barcelona into a patrimonial mold and pass them on to relatives. Urban power depended upon a complex matrix of converging family interests, not upon seigniorial lordship emanating from a castle controlled by a single lineage. As the counts reasserted their authority, they manipulated these forces to dislodge the viscounts from their traditional seat of urban power by the early twelfth century. Retreating to their upland castles or seeking their fortune in the North African desert far beyond the oppressive supervision of their lords, the last viscounts appeared much like other castellan lineages of the time except for their family memories and pride. Their past had been shaped equally by their mastery of the turbulent interior of Catalonia and their domination of local authority and aristocratic life concentrated in Barcelona, which echoed the values and organization of the regional society in which it was imbedded. Once the viscounts' ties to the city unraveled, Barcelona gradually loosened itself from the influence of the noble families that dominated the Catalonian countryside.

AN URBAN NOBILITY IN RETREAT

As the power of the viscounts of Barcelona was waning during the early twelfth century, no other aristocratic family moved forward to take their place. By that time, however, the great castleholders of Catalonia were poorly represented in the city. Given the interest of their ancestors a century earlier in maintaining town houses perched on the defenses or clustered around the old Roman forum at the heart of the intramural area, the nobility's subsequent aloofness during the drawn-out struggle between the comital dynasty and the viscounts represents a startling change in the composition of urban society. In the decades around 1000, a number of prominent and ascendant noble houses held urban property, including the Queralt, Alemany, Castellvell, Lluçà, Cervelló, Sant Martí, Rubí, Mediona, and three

viscomital lineages from elsewhere in Catalonia.[34] Attracted by the
grand ceremonial courts summoned intermittently by the count at
the Palau Comtal and by the martial leadership of the viscounts,
aristocrats confirmed their prominence in regional life by securing
a foothold in the city. If the evidence of propertyholding points
to an early *inurbaménto* by the ascendant houses of the upper
nobility just as Barcelona was beginning to expand, the process
soon reversed itself. After 1040 the rush from castle to town came
to an end. For the next hundred years no new aristocratic family
acquired urban property except through occasional marriage
transfers, while the older families one by one gave up their houses
through sale or donations to the Church.

By the early twelfth century, the barons of Catalonia were
represented by only a handful of families in Barcelona. Their
continued presence became a function of their command of the
castle-gates, which depended on the good will of the count.
Guillem Ramon I de Castellvell, his son, and Ramon Renart de La
Roca, second cousin of the seneschal Guillem Ramon de Montcada, all held Castellvell at different times between 1111 and 1134.
This provided an opportunity to strike new roots in urban soil.
Through marriage to the widow of Berenguer Bernat, an early
urban vicar, Ramon Renart de La Roca obtained rights to a house
near the intramural church of Sant Jaume. But his daughter, wife
of Pere Bertran de Bell-lloc, sold it in 1146.[35] It is also likely that
Guillem Ramon II de Castellvell reinforced his position in Barcelona by marrying Arsendis, daughter of Viscount Gelabert
Udalard, before 1125, thereby bringing her urban holdings into
the orbit of his family interests. Yet as we have seen, the Castellvell
had passed from the urban scene by 1171. Count Ramon
Berenguer III had involved both families in the restructuring of
authority dependent upon Castellvell of Barcelona, the command
of which proved a particularly delicate matter. After bolstering
the count's position, however, both the de La Roca and the
Castellvell quietly turned their attention away from Barcelona
and the counts made no effort to increase their influence in the
city. Their eminent standing in the regional nobility and influen-

[34] In addition to the references given by Bonnassie, *La Catalogne*, I, 494, see ACB 1–4–38;
LA I, fol. 157, Mas IX, no. 179; LA I, fol. 227, Mas IX, no. 506; Arxiu de Montserrat,
perg. Sant Benet de Bages, 1334; "Documents de juifs barcelonnais au XIᵉ siècle," eds. J.
Miret i Sans and M. Schwab, *Boletín de la Real Academia de la Historia*, 69 (1916), 569.
[35] ACA LA I, fol. 285, Mas X, no. 1230; LA I, fol. 288, Mas XI, no. 1609.

tial connections came in handy in the contest against insolent vicars to reassert comital power over the castle-gate, yet the danger also existed that new patrimonial claims would once again weaken comital authority over the city. Once the count had pried Castell-vell loose from the grip of the viscounts, he had no intention of handing it over to another aristocratic lineage.

Only two aristocratic houses, the Queralt and Bell-lloc, actively expanded their urban assets after 1140. Even though each family pursued different tactics to secure influence in Barcelona, both developed close ties with Castellnou, the city's western castle-gate. Less politically sensitive than Castellvell since it was not associated with powers of coercion, Castellnou nevertheless had more lucrative resources attached to it, including rural knights' fees, vineyards at Sarrià, revenues from the fish market (*piscateria*), and a valuable Jewish oven for the Call, whose Christian operators had to ensure that food baked there would be prepared according to Jewish custom.[36] Castellnou in itself was a lucrative prize, giving its holder a commanding position in the underdeveloped suburban zone to the west of the Roman walls. Berenguer de Queralt (d. c. 1135), successor to a line of powerful castleholders on the frontier of Old Catalonia, became one of the most influential barons at the court of Count Ramon Berenguer III, whom he served as seneschal.[37] In reward for his loyalty, Berenguer de Queralt received command of Castellnou and Castell del Port in 1121; both castles remained in the family for two generations. In a manner similar to that of other aristocrats of his time, however, shortly before his death Berenguer de Queralt donated a house near the cathedral, including part of the town wall and a tower, as a pious bequest to the Templars in 1134. Yet unlike any other member of the upper aristocracy, Berenguer's sole heir, Sibil·la, looked beyond her command over Castellnou to develop suburban land, for she devoted special attention to leasing out gardens and houses for improvement (*ad meliorandum*) in the sparsely settled zone near the Lepers' Hospital above the road leading to Castellnou during the 1180s. Later generations would remember the zone as Queralt's Garden even though it soon passed out of their control.[38] The use

[36] ACB 1–1–357, 1229; 1–2–1617; 1–6–2163; ACA Reial Patrimoni, Batllia General, Classe 3ª, vol. 6, fols. 100 v.–101 r.

[37] A brief outline of the family's background can be found in *Els castells*, v, 171–83.

[38] ACB 1–5–152, 283, 300; *Santa Anna*, III, nos. 574, 575; ADB perg. Santa Anna, Carp. 1a, 5–14.

of suburban land to obtain cash through loans or sale caused the fragmentation of these holdings, culminating with the pledge of Castellnou itself in 1218 to secure a loan.[39] When financially pressed, the Queralt sacrificed the property they had patiently developed and even their traditional association with Castellnou in order to preserve their power elsewhere. As other older aristocratic houses had done before them, they severed their ties to Barcelona.

The Bell–lloc, on the other hand, rose to the upper ranks of the aristocracy only in the twelfth century and were newcomers in the city, where they appear as property owners only in 1139 despite an earlier association with the suburban monastery of Sant Pau del Camp.[40] By marrying Sança, daughter of Ramon Renard de La Roca and Solstenda, widow of Berenguer Bernat the vicar, Pere Bertran de Bell–lloc assumed control of their property and influence in the intramural neighborhood below Castellnou. In a complex and obscure struggle during the 1150s with the descendants of Ricart Guillem over a section of the northwestern defenses, Pere Bertran's son and heir successfully maintained his control over the walls and eventually exchanged this strategic property with Count Ramon Berenguer IV. The count evidently relied upon the Bell–lloc as dependable allies in restructuring the alignment of influential local families in the area around Castellnou, later the site of the royal meat market and shops. Retaining their influence at court and the patronage of their sovereign, the heads of the lineage kept their properties between Castellnou and the intramural church of Sant Miquel in their hands and even gained control of the castle-gate itself in the early thirteenth century; they seemed the apparent successors to the Queralt. Inheritance, however, rapidly fragmented the family's urban holdings. After the death of Bernat de Bell–lloc, a division of the estate in 1232 left Castellnou split between two younger heirs, Ramon and Guillema, while the core of the patrimony, centered on the castle of Bell–lloc, passed to another son.[41] Now made peripheral to the family's power, the rights dependent on the castle-gate were partitioned or sold piecemeal.[42] Stripped of its

[39] ACB 1–1–1850; 1–5–326; ACA perg. Pere I, 64; Reial Patrimoni, Batllia General, Classe 3ª, vol. 6, fol. 101 r.–v.

[40] ACA perg. R.B. IV, 93; *Els castells*, II, 259–66; Bisson, *Fiscal accounts*, I, 64–65.

[41] ACB 1–1–357, 2163.

[42] ACA Reial Patrimoni, Batllia General, Classe 3ª, vol. 6, fols. 55 r., 101 r.–v.; ACB 1–2–1617.

fiefs and utilities, Castellnou, the last rallying point for aristocratic sentiment in the city, was used principally as a prison by the end of the thirteenth century. As Castellnou lost its importance, the Bell-lloc also disappeared from urban life and with them the last vestige of the great castleholding families of feudal Catalonia that had formed the backdrop to the first phase of urban growth.

Despite their early interest in Barcelona, the great aristocratic houses of the interior slowly disengaged themselves from urban society in order to focus their attention on rural castles, a dependent peasantry, and opportunities for land in New Catalonia. Because nobles withdrew gradually, almost imperceptibly from 1040 to 1140, this process has largely passed unnoticed.[43] The chronology of aristocratic flight from the city is connected to the profound restructuring of Catalan society in the wake of the "feudal crisis" of 1040–60, an unsettled period when nobles found the private control of castles, the maintenance of armed retainers, and creation of personal alliances a more effective means of securing power and status than the patronage of the count. The violent confrontation between Count Ramon Berenguer I and the viscomital house provided a dramatic climax to the disputed claims of authority, yet reverberations from the conflict could still be felt decades later. While the ruling dynasty did successfully reassert its command over Castellvell and obtained the allegiance of the great castleholders in the countryside, it also manipulated family loyalties to safeguard its power in Barcelona. Neither Ramon Berenguer I nor his descendants consciously pursued an urban anti-magnate policy, but they did play upon the multilayered, malleable alliances connecting noble houses to create a balance among them and, later, to counter the patrimonial claims on authority advanced by the early vicars and their descendants. The Queralt and Bell-lloc anachronistically retained their urban influence longer than their peers precisely because they served dynastic interests in the western zone of the city. Masters at the game of family politics, by playing off aristocratic factions one

---

[43] Banks, "The topography," II, 77–82 discusses patterns of aristocratic landholding. Noting a lack of interest in further acquisitions after 1040, he suggests that the count forced partisans of the viscount out of town, yet this does not account for the disappearance of families loyal to the dynasty. In a perceptive discussion, Federico Udina Martorell, "La expansión mediterránea catalano-aragonesa," in *Segundo congreso internacional de estudios sobre las culturas de Mediterráneo occidental* (Barcelona, 1978), 216–17 questions the applicability of the concept of "urban nobility," at least as employed by Italian historians, to Barcelona.

against the other the counts eventually rendered urban property peripheral to the interests of the barons of Catalonia.

The emergence of noble lineages in the eleventh century also made participation in urban life fit poorly into the family strategies of the castle-lords. As the focus of noble kin groups became fixed on an ancestral castle and its dependencies, the patrimonial core became reserved for a single line of male descendants, whenever possible the eldest son. The concentration of rural castles in the hands of a single lineage turned town houses into expendable appendages, passed on to younger heirs by testamentary bequest, granted to daughters in dowry, or donated to religious institutions to secure the entry of a relative. Since aristocratic power by the twelfth century rested on the exploitation of private estates rather than on the favors of the count or collective expeditions to al-Andalus organized by the viscounts, the transfer of urban residences to the Church or to allied families offered a residual association with the center of dynastic power as the actual exercise of authority was shifting to the countryside.

It is impossible to stress too strongly that Catalan aristocrats looked upon an urban residence as an access to patronage and a confirmation of their prominence on a regional stage, not as an economic investment. Alone among the high nobility, Sibil·la de Queralt showed an inclination to become an urban real estate developer, but this occurred quite late and the property was quickly sacrificed to meet other needs. Only the viscounts possessed substantial urban assets and originally took their family name from the city, but they too eventually adopted the toponym of an ancestral castle in the interior. Already by the mid-eleventh century, the viscounts had ceased to act as resident representatives of comital authority and territorial military commanders; they now appeared to behave as other castleholding families. As a result, the patronage network they commanded disintegrated. No other member of the high nobility proved able to fill the gap, for their influence was embedded in the countryside and they do not appear to have either maintained armed urban clienteles or provided a focus for neighborhood identity. Unless the count or viscount were in attendance, aristocrats very rarely subscribed to urban charters. Their presence in the city before 1040 illustrates the regional scope of diffuse family ties and a willing participation in a traditional territorial order; their withdrawal, for all practical purposes complete by 1140, was symptomatic of the strong pull of patrimonial castles, new opportunities on the frontier, and above all the streamlining of family structure around noble lineages. An exclusive club of Catalonian aristocrats would not dominate the history of medieval Barcelona.

THE PROFESSION OF ARMS IN URBAN SOCIETY

Below the level of the viscounts, the old aristocratic houses connected to the counts (*comtors*), and the aggressive lineages of castleholders stood a nebulous group of castle sergeants (*castlans*), knights (*milites*, *caballarii*), mercenaries, and prosperous free peasants with sword and hauberk. The social boundaries of the lesser nobility in the twelfth century is a particularly elusive topic, a problem that has hardly been broached in Catalonia. Even though warriors capable of maintaining a horse (*milites*) forced their way into the exclusive, grudging ranks of the old noble families by the second half of the eleventh century,[44] the lower limit of the nobility appears ill-defined and porous, permitting prosperous men-at-arms to rise in rank on the strokes of their swords and knights with scarce means to sink into the peasantry. According to the *Usatges*, if a man did not become a knight by the age of thirty, he would fall back into the peasantry; further, only those who could put white bread daily on their tables should be considered noble.[45] Knighthood does not yet appear to be securely heritable, nor is its threshold particularly elevated. One of the earliest articles of the same law code, dating from the mid-eleventh century, set the compensation for injuring a townsman at the same level as that for a knight; although usually cited to illustrate the respect enjoyed by burghers, it more likely reflects the less than savory pedigree of many knights. *Miles*, sporadically employed as a personal title and staunchly rebuffed by the aristocracy, retained a taint of low birth in twelfth-century Catalonia.[46]

In a society taking shape in the shadow of a violent frontier, the needs of defense and the profits of war drew a broad segment of the population into military operations. Rather than being monopolized by a class proficient in mounted combat, the profession of

[44] Bonnassie, *La Catalogne*, ii, 797–808.   [45] *Usatges*, art. 8, 210; art. 12, 210.

[46] Ibid., art. 10, 210. On the fluid boundaries of the lower nobility, see Thomas N. Bisson, "Feudalism in twelfth-century Catalonia," in *Structures féodales et féodalisme dans l'Occident méditerranéen (X^e–XIIIe siècles): bilan et perspectives* (Rome, 1980), 180 [repr. in *Medieval France*, 160–61].

arms provided opportunities to modest entrepreneurs of aggression, who hoped through combat to earn a horse and possibly noble status. *Caballeros villanos* (peasant knights) and efficient urban militias formed the backbone of the fighting forces in the vast, arid Meseta as the Christian frontier moved southward; *cabalers aloders*, modest freeholders able to maintain a horse and arms, formed a similar group in Catalonia, but it never attained the importance that the *caballeros villanos* held in the frontier zones of León, Castile, and Aragon.[47] Nonetheless, prosperous freeholders participating in the campaigns in New Catalonia and, later, in Valencia and Majorca were constantly pushing on the flimsy barrier separating *nobiles* from *ignobiles*. In the will of the widow Bonadona, we can catch a glimpse of a sturdy family of small farmers flirting with knightly rank in Barcelona's hinterland around 1100.[48] Forced to sell a *modiata* of land to raise the 4 mancus for her modest legacies to urban churches and monasteries, Bonadona nevertheless left her nephew and heir, Pere Balluvin, a hauberk, harness, and padding.[49] The charters do not reveal whether Pere ever received recognition as a knight, but the possibility certainly existed. Heavily weighted at the bottom with armed retainers and cavalrymen with a meagre patrimony, the lower level of the Catalonian nobility felt the constant pressure of prosperous, free peasants wishing to join its ranks by proving themselves in battle. As a result, the status ascribed to mounted warriors did not prove prestigious or durable enough to permit knights resident in Barcelona to form a cohesive, influential component of urban life.

Charters of land transfers and testaments contain passing mention of five knights who held property in early twelfth-century Barcelona: Abraham *caballarius* (d.c. 1112), Arnau Pere *miles* (d.c. 1143), Ramon Ponç *miles* (d. 1130), Guerau Bernat *miles* (d.c. 1144), and Pere Arnau *miles* (d.c. 1160). This certainly does not exhaust the list of those who might have boasted of knightly rank, for men possessing arms and capable of mounted combat or serving as *castlans* turn up sporadically in the local documentation,

---

[47] See in general Elena Lourie, "A society organized for war: medieval Spain," *Past and present*, 35 (1966), 54–76 [repr. in *Crusade and colonisation: Muslims, Christians and Jews in medieval Aragon* (London, 1990)]; James E. Powers, *A society organized for war: the Iberian municipal militias in the central Middle Ages, 1000–1284* (Berkeley and Los Angeles, 1988), 98–101. For Catalonia, Bonnassie, *La Catalogne*, ii, 797–808.

[48] ACA perg. R. B. III, 70. Cf. perg. R.B. III, 107; ACB 1–1–244.

[49] ACA perg. R. B. III, 70.

particularly before 1150. The title *miles* provides an inexact guide to locate the lower rungs of the nobility since scribes employed it inconsistently. Despite frequently being mentioned in local charters, Guerau Bernat appears with the title only three times and Ramon Ponç and Pere Arnau just once, a sign in itself that the attributes of knightly rank did not provide an all-inclusive label of social classification.

Blood and knightly status had not yet fused. Although researchers have tended to follow the lead of Georges Duby and assume that knights in Mediterranean Europe enjoyed both inherited status and a range of noble privileges formerly reserved for an older aristocracy by the twelfth century, doubts have recently been raised.[50] Barcelona admittedly offers a peculiar vantage point from which to investigate the question, yet it is nevertheless significant that none of the five men called *miles* can be shown to have received the title from their fathers or to have passed it on to their sons. With the exception of Pere Arnau, who served as the local vicar during the 1150s under Count Ramon Berenguer IV,[51] all owned substantial property in the city and the county, an indication that wealth as well as the ability to perform mounted combat was a necessary part of knightly status. In three instances, close relatives of the *milites* commanded castles, a function that placed them above mere soldiers on horseback. Ramon Ponç *miles* should probably be identified with the son of Berenguer Bernat, who held Castellnou and Castell del Port in 1119,[52] while Guerau Bernat's brother served as *castlà* of Font-Rubí and Bleda, both owned by Berenguer de Queralt in the early twelfth century.[53] Of all the identifiable urban knights, Arnau Pere had the deepest roots in urban society, for he was the grandson of Ricart Guillem, a wealthy Barcelona land speculator. Although we will consider the fate of this family in greater detail in the following section, in the

---

[50] While Duby's basic model was developed from his studies in the Mâconnais and northern France, he also attempted to apply it to the Mediterranean regions of Latin Christendom in "La Diffusion du titre chevaleresque sur le versant méditerranéen de la chrétienté latine," in *La Noblesse au moyen âge, XIe au XVe siècles: essais à la mémoire de Robert Boutrouche*, ed. P. Contamine (Paris, 1976), 39–70. Martin Aurell i Cardona, *Une famille de la noblesse provençale au moyen âge: les Porcelet* (Avignon, 1986), 31 notes a continuing distance between old aristocratic families and knights in the twelfth century. For Catalonia, see the remarks by Bisson, "Feudalism," 160–61.

[51] Supra, 68.

[52] ACB LA I, fol. 30, Mas x, no. 1304; LA I, fol. 43, Mas x, no. 1363.

[53] ACB LA I, fol. 292, Mas xi, no. 1479; *LFM*, I, no. 319; *Els castells*, III, 642–43, 841–42.

present context it is important to point out that Ricart's success in selling his wine and produce in the booming local market of the eleventh century gave him the resources to obtain the castle of Arraona late in life. The subsequent loss of the castle, however, did not prevent the family from establishing a connection with fortress command or from passing on martial qualities to a male descendant who styled himself *miles*. Without an established position of urban command, however, resident *milites* were accorded knightly rank almost as a residual honorific, acknowledging a family's association with castleholding but stopping short of validating any patrimonial claim to local power. For Arnau Pere, Ramon Ponç, and Guerau Bernat, the use of *miles* as a personal title seemingly offered a consolation prize for their lack of success in inheriting a castle command. Urban knights were clearly not an ascendant class but an ambiguous anachronism in early twelfth-century Barcelona, where aristocratic power and patronage were waning. The startling presence of a prominent local Jew, Abraham *caballarius*, among their ranks provides a vivid illustration that Catalan knighthood was a socially ill-defined category and as yet without a self-consciously Christianized code of conduct.

Inheritance patterns and the complexity of patronage networks converging on the city inhibited urban knights from establishing a firm patrimonial basis and a durable family identity. If aristocrats could anchor their kin group to an ancestral castle and its dependent territory that passed down a male lineage, the availability of adequate assets to provide for other children made this possible. Knights, however, possessed considerably fewer resources, while *castlans* could not firmly exercise an inherited right to castle command and control of the surrounding dependencies, since they served at the pleasure of their lords under the coolly contractual terms of written conventions. A tendency to attach enfeoffed knights directly to the castle or its overlord made it possible to replace the *castlà*, the castle sergeant who exercised command *in situ*, without disturbing the structure of the castellany.[54] When castles changed hands among related aristocratic lineages or were

---

[54] On the arrangements between castle-lord and *castlà*, set in the form of a treaty typical of feudal institutions in Catalonia, see Pierre Bonnassie, "Les Conventions féodales dans la Catalogne du XIᵉ siècle," in *Les Structures sociales de l'Aquitaine, du Languedoc et de l'Espagne au premier âge féodal* (Paris, 1969), 187–210 ["Feudal conventions in eleventh-century Catalonia," *From slavery to feudalism*, 170–94]; Bisson, "Feudalism," 155–57.

exchanged with outsiders, this allowed a new lord to establish one of his own clientele as *castlà* in his fortifications. Lesser nobles therefore had difficulty anchoring their kin group to castleholding. Instead, they tended to develop multiple and diffuse bonds with aristocrats, a feature no doubt accentuated in Barcelona because of its importance in regional life. The establishment of a patrimonial center for this group of insecure retainers therefore proved elusive.

In order to satisfy children's claims on their estates yet at the same time provide a stable center for a broader kin identity, urban knights imitated the great castleholding families by favoring a single male line whenever possible. Because actual family configurations could vary according to the number of surviving sons and daughters, the handful of extant wills from this group provides the surest evidence of their inheritance strategies. In 1138, Berenguer Bernat, brother of the knight Guerau Bernat, had to make provision for his relatively large family.[55] Berenguer, evidently his eldest son, received two castles held from Bernat de Barberà, Pere Bernat d'Oluja, and the count as well as the bequest of his father's armor; the second son Arnau gained control of a heterogeneous collection of properties, including a portion of the mills at Subirats in the Alt Penedès, a fief at Eramprunyà in the Baix Llobregat, and a substantial farm (*mans*) at Roca, possibly in the eastern Vallès; the third son, Arnau, was left the family's houses inside the walls of Barcelona so that he could join the "noble canons," who would acquire the property after his death. With his diverse holdings and allegiance to several lords, this prosperous *castlà* took great care to endow all his sons; while the will alludes to daughters as residual heirs, none are mentioned by name, probably the result of previous dowry arrangements. Yet each son played quite a distinct role in family organization. Berenguer Bernat passed on his military functions to a single male heir, while a second son was set up as a man of means in the countryside. Urban houses, however, did not figure prominently in the structuring of the family's future, but they did provide a means of raising its status through a connection with the prestigious canons serving Barcelona's cathedral. Berenguer Bernat therefore did not seem in the least squeamish about partitioning his estate in order to anchor family identity on rural castle command which passed to a single

---

[55] ACB LA I, fol. 292, Mas XI, no. 1479.

line; urban property, used to embellish family status through a donation to the cathedral, was never essential to the perpetuation of his lineage.

Even for knights with relatively concentrated properties in and near the city but without castle command, inheritance tended to favor a single line of descent even if it passed through females. Arnau Pere *miles*, for instance, left his urban houses, the bulk of his lands, and rights of supervision (*baiulia*) in the *territorium* to one of his two sons.[56] More revealing, however, is the disposition of Ramon Ponç, who, when confronted with the lack of sons, made careful provisions for his properties to pass to his daughter and after her to his only granddaughter.[57] In both these testaments of urban knights, the principal residence in Barcelona and the bulk of land in the adjacent hinterland were granted to the preferred descendant in entail, requiring that the estate pass down for another generation to a single heir. The lesser nobility connected to the city thus concentrated its property in a single line, preferably male but female in a pinch, rather than involve agnatic collaterals, i.e. brothers, nephews, and male cousins. In other words, lineal descent strongly outweighed the corporative interests of a wider kin group.

The promotion of a single line of descent through inheritance strategies produced the same effects among *castlans* and knights connected with Barcelona as among the great castleholding houses: it loosened their ties to the city. If a family of knightly rank possessed a patrimonial claim to fortress command, the prestige attached to a martial life passed through the eldest male line, which was strongly drawn toward rural castles; if its holdings became concentrated in a town house and properties integrated with the urban economy, it lost its military calling, still not a strictly inherited function, and found its patrimonial base narrowed, a process no doubt accelerated by the economic difficulties between 1090 and 1140. Whether pulled away from the city by the concentration of power in castles or lost among prosperous local landowners, urban knights did not emerge from the early twelfth century as a well-defined or assertive group in Barcelona.

It has long been a commonplace of Mediterranean history that aristocratic and knightly families thrived in the vigorous, expansive towns of the eleventh and twelfth century. Drawing off rents

---

[56] ACB LA I, fol. 103, Mas XI, no. 1545.   [57] ACB I–I–3565.

and agricultural surpluses from their estates, directing resources toward their urban strongholds, and rushing headlong into the tumultuous world of civic politics, rough, aggrandizing castle-lords, their relatives, and their armed clienteles are presented as staking out their sphere of lordship in the shadow of early medieval churches and ancient public buildings and seizing whatever authority had devolved to the occupants of those sites. The withering of Barcelona's urban nobility, however, fits this model poorly. Even though it did appear likely in the first decades of the new millennium that rural aristocrats and their men-at-arms would dominate early urban society, they lost interest in maintaining an urban foothold and gradually surrendered their town houses and sections of the old Roman wall between 1040 and 1140. To account for this slow but decisive turn in the city's history, one should first point to the stubborn resilience of the comital dynasty. By successfully resisting the challenge of the viscomital clan and gradually prying it loose from Castellvell, Count Ramon Berenguer I and his successors dislodged the keystone holding together the structure of aristocratic patronage and influence in the city. No other family again managed to concentrate such a wide array of powers. While aristocrats and lesser nobles did obtain command of urban castle-gates and rights to local utilities, the counts masterfully manipulated the complex network of family interests in order to prevent them from turning comital rights and assets into patrimonial possessions. As a result, the great castleholders from the interior as well as local *castlans* and knights were denied a solid urban mooring.

Elsewhere in the Mediterranean counts had generally surrendered their public powers over towns to bishops or acted as simply another aristocratic faction in the internecine struggles for urban power. Especially in northern Italy bishops had acquired comital functions over their episcopal seats and the territory dependent on them during the tenth and eleventh century;[58] as a result, territorial jurisdiction as well as control of ecclesiastical property became concentrated in the hands of the bishops, who possessed considerable resources to reward their aristocratic supporters. Nobles were rapidly drawn into the city, where they acquired residences, built towers, and established private chapels in an effort

[58] Dupré-Theseider, "Vescovi e città," 55–91; C. Manaresi, "Alle origini del potere dei vescovi sul territorio esterno delle città," *Bollettino dell'istituto storico italiano per il medioevo ed archivio muratoriano*, 88 (1944), 221–334.

to gain access to episcopal patronage. The *capitani* of Milan, powerful episcopal vassals, provide a famous illustration of the ability of bishops to draw rural aristocrats into their circle, but the pattern can be found elsewhere.[59] Once in control of ecclesiastical and public rights and properties, aristocratic families did not easily let them go. Because the city served as the hub of territorial power, urban towers offered a point of reference for noble interests and family identity throughout the region. They were owned collectively by consortial associations, also known as tower societies, which involved numerous kin groups.[60] Strongly agnatic in nature, the *consorteria* reserved shares in the tower for brothers, uncles, and male cousins at the expense of daughters. The corporate lineages or clans formed by consortial alliances were primarily, although not exclusively, an urban phenomenon in Italy, a manifestation of the interconnection between urban and rural spheres and testimony to the strong pull of cities both socially and jurisdictionally on their territory.

The contrast between the consortial organization of aristocratic clans in northern Italy and the pronounced patrilineal tendencies of early noble houses connected to Barcelona is striking and suggestive. The urban nobility in Southern Europe is usually thought of as a transplant. Maturing in harmony with castles and seigniorial lordship, aristocratic families supposedly were suddenly removed from their original environment and placed within a new, alien social body, the town. Their structure and function remained the same, even though they served a different end. Radical surgery, however, may not have been necessary, for throughout the early medieval Mediterranean the tiny communities of priests, judges, and officials attached to towns formed an integral part of regional life. Nobles did not suddenly discover "the town" in the tenth and eleventh century; rather, they adjusted to the evolving nature of urban lordship in the broader framework of territorial power. While in northern Italy the

---

59 Keller, *Adelsherrschaft*, 321–22, 386–92; Racine, *Plaisance*, 1, 193–98; George W. Dameron, *Episcopal power and Florentine society, 1000–1320* (Cambridge, MA, 1991), 22–37; Schwarzmaier, *Lucca*, 71–154; Tabacco, *Egemonie*, 213–16.

60 F. Niccolai "I consorzi nobiliari ed comune nell'alta e media Italia," *Rivista di storia del diritto italiano*, 13 (1940), 116–17, 292–342, 397–477 is the classic study; a useful summary is found in David Herlihy, *Medieval households* (Cambridge, MA, 1984), 88–92. Lansing, *Florentine magnates*, 89–97 points out that tower societies were not kin groups but societies of shareholders, yet they did work to consolidate the interests of the families involved.

collective but geographically diffuse interests of aristocratic families became focused on the public rights and ecclesiastical patronage condensed in episcopal cities, in Barcelona the counts stubbornly wrestled their prerogatives away from the powerful castleholding families, aggrandizing *castlans*, and ambitious knights they had installed as their representatives. As a result, noble power in Catalonia became anchored on rural districts dominated by private castles and patrimonial estates, not on towns.

Each of these settings promoted considerably different family structures, even though male descendants enjoyed preferential treatment in both cases. The emergence of tightly organized patrilineages helped preserve the nucleus of aristocratic power centered on castles and patrimonies in the Catalonian countryside, while the broad, agnatic clans in northern Italy demonstrated their effectiveness in the competitive arena of civic politics, the key to the control of the Italian countryside. The early communes in Lombardy, Tuscany, and Liguria emerged in an attempt to institutionalize and regulate aristocratic factionalism. In Barcelona, on the other hand, comital authority helped balance the competitive interests of local families that began to emerge after the nobles had withdrawn from town. In order to understand the multiple forms and social impact of aristocratic family organization, it is necessary to treat them as an integral part of the dynamics of regional power, which intimately involved ancient towns, rather than as an historically abstract model of kinship, a molecular compound of lines, circles, and triangles that kept its form in any setting. Aristocratic houses should therefore not be thought of simply as social transplants from countryside to town, which then accepted or rejected them; rather, they took shape in the profound restructuring of Mediterranean regional societies occurring during the eleventh century.

REACTIONS TO ECONOMIC BLOCKAGE

Because nobles with ties to the city withdrew slowly over generations rather than as a result of sudden, violent conflict, it is hardly surprising that their disappearance has not figured prominently in recent discussions about the first surge of growth in Barcelona. The most dynamic social elements clearly lay elsewhere. Local agricultural entrepreneurs have been singled out as the most innovative segment of urban society. By assembling small pieces of land with patient determination, they took advantage of the new prosperity derived from the vineyards, garden plots, and fields spreading out below the old Roman walls. Because their wealth depended upon the purchase and management of real estate, they have left a clear trail for historians to follow in the numerous records of land conveyance. Agricultural investors in Barcelona's hinterland formed a heterogeneous group, linked more by their attitudes to wealth than by their social background. In the Vivas family from the suburban village of Provençals, Bonnassie discovered a vivid example of social ascent in the fluid world of Barcelona's countryside around 1000.[61] By systematically purchasing valuable parcels of land near the city and carefully nurturing them as family assets over several generations, some members of the family rose from the ranks of the free, prosperous peasantry to move in the prestigious circle of cathedral canons and regional notables (*proceres*). Ricart Guillem, although connected with a prominent local family, provides an example of an investor who, according to Ruiz Doménec, surveyed the local land market with the cool calculation for profit of a cagey real estate developer, a "businessman" (*negociator*).[62] What makes the activities of these men remarkable was their ability to look upon land as a productive element in a vibrant system of exchange, as an asset to be exploited through the opportunities of the urban market.

The nature of local landholding facilitated their ascent. In contrast to the complex tenurial arrangements prevalent in Northern Europe, property rights in the Pla de Barcelona had not fragmented into a multiplicity of obligations weighing upon the land and its peasants to which various individuals might lay claim; rather, small allods were common throughout the eleventh century around the city. Money provided the tool with which to accumulate and concentrate pieces of suburban land, some of which were tiny slivers of soil measured in arm-lengths,[63] and to develop marketable crops for local consumption with relative ease and speed. The freedom with which land was transferred made possible the social mobility of the period. Because of Barcelona's economic precociousness after 1000, a glimmer of Weberian

[61] Bonnassie, "Une famille," esp. 270–77.
[62] Ruiz Doménec, "El origen," 75–86 and summarily in "The urban origins," 270–73.
[63] Banks, "Mensuration," 38–42.

rationalism has been detected in the systematic acquisitiveness of the leading agricultural entrepreneurs.

Whether this group of prosperous urban landowners was coalescing into a patriciate, however, is much less straightforward. Even though Batlle i Gallart has emphasized that the dominant families of thirteenth-century Barcelona were important landowners,[64] this is hardly an unusual feature of urban elites and need not be taken as their defining characteristic. The question is not so much whether urban notables held land and houses, but whether the exploitation of agricultural resources and the collection of urban rents created common political and economic objectives strong enough to fuse a heterogeneous assembly of proprietors into a cohesive group directing urban society.

Despite a widely held assumption about early European towns, the patriciate did not necessarily begin a steady ascent with the first signs of urban growth. In Barcelona the sharp downturn in land values and the constriction of exchange from 1090 to 1140 created a chasm between two distinct phases of urban expansion. While independent, small-scale farmers who continued to produce largely for household consumption may not have faced hardship as the result of the falling value of market crops grown on spare bits of land, agricultural entrepreneurs faced a significant reduction in income.

The following sections explore the responses of urban landowners to an era of economic constriction. The available documentation does not make the task easy, however, for in contrast to preceding decades the urban charters from 1090 to 1140 run particularly thin. More may be at work here, however, than the hazards of preservation. Ecclesiastical archives, the principal depository of charters for the period, usually received a bundle of parchments from a family's archive related to the title of property donated or sold to the Church. The scarcity of information in general during these decades and the absence of parchment series concentrated on an individual or his close kin reinforce the impression of retrenchment and stagnation. With few exceptions it is difficult to trace the activities of a single family over two or three generations during the early twelfth century. This in itself suggests that property conveyances occurred sporadically rather than systematically, possibly in reaction to critical stages in family

[64] Batlle i Gallart, "La burguesía," 8–13.

organization produced by death or marriage rather than through the pursuit of a consistent economic strategy. Financial difficulties rather than coordinated investments were therefore more likely to produce records of land transaction. Notoriety during these difficult decades should not be taken as a sign of success.

THE DESCENDANTS OF BERNAT RAMON THE RICH

The fate of one prominent family of landholders, however, can be traced in some detail as it stumbled across the sunken threshold of the twelfth century. Its members descended from a man who, soon after his death, was remembered simply as Bernat Ramon the Rich (*dives*).[65] That wealth provided a personal honorific says much about the new system of values emerging in Barcelona, where power increasingly derived not from noble blood and an inherited right to command but from money, real estate, and the access to comital patronage they brought. While surely no *parvenu*, few individuals in eleventh-century Barcelona took greater advantage of the fluid land market and the manipulation of cash to raise their standing than Bernat Ramon. Since his substantial intramural house between Castellnou and Sant Miquel bordered on a lot owned by his brother Guillem, the family must have been firmly established in the city for a generation or more since the property was at some point divided among heirs.[66] Between 1054 and 1079, however, Bernat purchased numerous properties in and around the city, especially in the *vilanova* near Sant Cugat del Rec, the first systematically developed suburban zone, and held land further away in the Vallès and Girona.[67] His substantial assets soon made him a figure of regional importance. As early as 1055 Count Ramon Berenguer I turned to him in order to acquit a debt of 7 ounces of gold.[68] That Bernat Ramon served his lord in a financial capacity is further suggested by his subscription to the oath required of the count's moneyers, one of the dozen comital charters in which he appears.[69] He had involved

---

[65] "Documents sur les juifs catalans aux XIᵉ, XIIᵉ, et XIIIᵉ siècles," eds. J. Miret i Sans and M. Schwab, *Revue des études juives*, 68 (1914). no. viii; ACB LA I, fol. 227, Mas x, no. 1198. *Història de Barcelona. De la prehistòria*, 224 is surely mistaken in claiming that Bernat Ramon was a younger brother of Ramon Berenguer I.

[66] ACA perg. R.B. I, 329.

[67] ACA perg. R.B. I, 229; perg. extrainv., 3466; ACB LA I, fol. 127, Mas x, no. 757; LA I, fol. 352, Mas x, no. 764; LA II, fol. 92, Mas x, no. 914; LA I, fol. 302, Mas x, no. 976.

[68] *LFM*, I, no. 398.   [69] Botet y Sisó, *Les monedes catalanes*, I, ap. vii.

himself so deeply in dynastic politics that his house had literally provided a base of operations for the counts: according to the planned partition of Barcelona in 1079 between Ramon Berenguer I's sons, while one brother occupied the Palau Comtal the other was supposed to reside in the house of Bernat Ramon.[70] While fraternal conflict was deeply dividing the leaders of Catalonian society, Bernat Ramon evidently compromised himself in the factional struggles that culminated in the murder of Count Ramon Berenguer II in 1082; he made no further acquisitions after 1079 and was even held prisoner for a time by the counts.[71] In spite of his extensive influence and wealth, Bernat Ramon nevertheless typifies the prosperous urban landlords who through agricultural investments and the manipulation of their liquid resources accumulated impressive fortunes in the speculative atmosphere of eleventh-century Barcelona. A prosperous burgher could easily employ his heavy purse to gain admittance to the company of aristocrats and counts. Because of the fluidity of Catalonian society, money easily forced open social barriers, but at the same time the tiny urban world of eleventh-century Barcelona moved to the rhythms set by the countryside. The most prosperous local entrepreneurs therefore felt irresistibly drawn from an urban to a regional stage.

Such a shift could cause family interests to diverge, particularly as the value and profitability of land in the green belt around the city declined sharply after 1090. In the activities of Bernat Ramon's heirs one can detect the tensions produced by economic and monetary contraction as well as the strategies adopted to preserve the integrity of family assets. Bernat left three adult children: Ramon Bernat, Pere Bernat, and Ermessenda. Neither of his sons sought to expand their inheritance by purchasing

70 ACA perg. R.B. II, sense data 39.
71 ACA perg. R.B. III, 178. The document (15 viii 1114) raises a number of problems, for it mentions only that Bernat Ramon was held captive by the counts (*condam captus a comitibus teneretur*) without alluding to which counts or the reason for their displeasure. It also mentions that Ricart Guillem and his wife Ermessenda made a loan to Ermengard, Ricart's mother-in-law (*socrui mee*) and, thus, the widow of Bernat Ramon, in order to pay for his release. Yet according to several documents Bernat Ramon's wife in the 1050s and 1060s was Ermessenda, the mother of Ermessenda, Ricart Guillem's wife, not Ermengard. The citation to Ricart Guillem's mother-in-law must therefore refer to the second wife of Bernat Ramon the Rich, the stepmother of Ermessenda. It is therefore unlikely that Ermengard was the mother of any of Bernat Ramon's children as José E. Ruiz Doménec indicates in "Système de parenté et théorie de l'alliance dans la société catalane (env. 1000–env. 1240)," *Revue historique*, 532 (1976), 318–19. The genealogical chart offered there should be used with caution.

additional agricultural land. Ramon Bernat entered the cathedral clergy and attained the rank of subdeacon, while Pere Bernat, although not easily identified, is probably the moneyer who bore that name.[72] Ermessenda, on the other hand, appears regularly in the many transactions she conducted with her husband, Ricart Guillem. The couple was extremely ambitious. While Ricart Guillem purchased a few bits of property as a young bachelor, his marriage to Ermessenda and the sizeable dowry she brought with her initiated a feverish spree of land purchases. Between May, 1065, when Ermessenda first appears with her husband, and October, 1066, 1,600 mancus were spent on numerous properties concentrated in the suburban zone around Santa Maria del Pi, not far from the section of the defenses held by Bernat Ramon.[73]

Like his father-in-law, Ricart Guillem possessed substantial resources to begin with and the astuteness to invest in agricultural specialization for Barcelona's market. He has been characterized as a *negociator*, a calculating businessman avid for technological improvements, wine exports, and profitable rural enterprises. There are, however, some difficulties with this assessment. No source identifies Ricart Guillem as a *negociator*, a title that disappears from the urban documentation in the late eleventh century; the plural *negociatores* also seems inappropriate for Barcelona's prosperous real estate developers. Its primary meaning is, of course, an itinerant merchant, the man according to the Lombard laws "who has no resources" (*qui non habet pecuniam*), *pecunia* used in this context not in the sense of coin but of land, flocks, or orchards, the forms of wealth *par excellence* in early medieval society.[74] This is not merely linguistic hair-splitting, for *negociator* fails to capture the allure that castleholding, campaigning in Islamic Spain, and aristocratic patronage presented to wealthy urban landlords. Probably compromised by the dynastic turmoil engulfing his father-in-law Bernat Ramon, Ricart Guillem turned his attention away from Barcelona after 1082 to

[72] Ramon Bernat appears as subdeacon in 1125 in a division with his nephew, Arnau Pere, concerning property of his parents Bernat Ramon and Ermengard, ACB LA II, fol. 125, Mas X, no. 1340. Pere Bernat *moneder* appears holding property in the *vilanova* near Sant Cugat del Rec, possibly the same as that once held by Bernat Ramon the Rich, *CSC*, III, nos. 833, 879; ACB LA I, fol. 127, Mas X, no. 757.

[73] The series of land conveyances involving Ricart Guillem is summarized in the chart presented by Ruiz Doménec, "El origen," 87–88.

[74] *Leges Langobardorum*, ed. F. Bluhme, in *Monumenta Germanica Historica, Leges*, IV (Hanover, 1869), Ahistulphi leges 2–3, 196.

purchase substantial farms in the county of Osona, acquire command of the castle of Cabrera from the viscount of Girona, hold fiefs from the powerful Montcada clan, and, in a complex series of credit transactions, gain allodial possession of the castle of Arraona in the western Vallès through a defaulted loan. Besides obtaining farms, fiefs, and castles in the interior, according to the *Historia Roderici*, Ricart Guillem fought among the Catalonian barons at the battle of Tévar against El Cid in 1090 and later found his way to Muslim Zaragoza to change silver bars for gold.[75] Close association with the great castleholders together with his extensive allodial property emboldened him to challenge Count Ramon Berenguer III's suzerainty over Arraona, a claim the count had to withdraw because he could not find the written oaths of its former castellans in his archive.[76] The dispute nevertheless soured relations between the count and Ricart Guillem, but it is surely not an issue that a man concerned exclusively with monetary profit and loss would press.

If seigniorial exploitation, castle command, and a taste for war and plunder fit poorly with the image of an industrious businessman, the reason lies in the assumption that urban and aristocratic society had disengaged and that the turn to a profit economy was sharp and decisive. But social fluidity and the crucial place of Barcelona in the broad regional framework of eleventh-century Catalonia blurred the boundaries of urban life, creating an ambivalent position for the city's wealthy landowners. They wavered between two attitudes toward wealth; on the one hand they looked upon their land as an economic asset to be acquired and developed with the intention of cornering the market on agricultural surpluses for the growing town, yet at the same time their liquidity brought them into the company of nobles, whose lands provided them with status, knights, and the power of military command. While Ricart Guillem may well have found castles, fiefs, and inland farms particularly attractive after 1082 because of

[75] Menéndez Pidal, *La España del Cid*, II, 946; ACA perg. R.B. III, 160, 162, 174. In the convention with his lord Ricart Guillem, Mir Riculf, *castlà* of Arraona, promises to follow his lord on campaigns to Muslim Spain (*ut quotiens idem Ricardus in hostem in Yspaniam perrexerit*), ACA perg. R.B. III, 169. Ruiz Doménec, "El origen," 82–83 discusses the new orientation of Ricart Guillem's interests, but comments only that his participation at Tévar was "curioso" and concludes he was not an important political figure.

[76] Bisson, "Feudalism," 168, 173 (the document appears as an addition in the reprint in *Medieval France*). The count, however, recovered his *potestas* over Arraona by 1129, ACA perg. R.B. III, 305.

the contraction of the urban economy, the alluring prestige and patronage connected with them should not be underestimated. The transition to a profit-oriented outlook was far from complete among well-to-do Barcelonans. For a man who had invested the fabulous sum of 10,000 gold mancus in his lifetime, Ricart Guillem oddly ignores any specific monetary bequests in his will but sets down with meticulous care the distribution of his farms, fiefs, and castles.

Under the pressure of a constricted urban market in the early twelfth century, the grandchildren of Bernat Ramon the Rich struggled to retain their property even as its value fell. No one in the family actively sought to extend their holdings, but neither did anyone sell off gardens, farms, or houses to meet their expenses. Rather than alienate their land, it was offered in pledge to secure loans. The indebtedness of Pere Ricart, the most prominent of Ricart Guillem's children, offers a vivid example of the financial squeeze facing urban landlords. In sharp contrast to his father, Pere made only a single recorded property purchase during his lifetime, but by the 1140s he had assumed eight loans totalling 578 mbts. and allusions exist to numerous others.[77] In 1142, he complained of his "great distress."[78] This certainly does not mean he was destitute, for an inventory of his possessions made about the same time includes forty-six *modiatae* of land, thirteen farms (*mansi*), eight gardens and vineyards, and the castle of Arraona, in other words virtually everything his father had bequeathed him.[79] Yet while Pere Ricart was rich in land, he was poor in cash. Liquid wealth had become immobilized in land, the surpluses from which could no longer provide the same level of profits in the urban market. Unfortunately we have no way of knowing whether the taste for fineries, largesse, and a noble way of life drained Pere's coffers or whether other obligations strained his resources, but he reacted with inflexibility to his budgetary imbalance. Instead of selling off parts of his holdings to increase liquidity, Pere Ricart stubbornly set out to defend all fronts at once by assuming a substantial burden of debt. Such a policy grew naturally from an attitude that looked upon land as a source of family prestige and security rather than as a business proposition.

Efforts to preserve the integrity of the family patrimony

[77] ACA perg. R.B. IV, 9, 60, 75, 100, 135, 196; perg. extrainv., 3466; ACB 1–5–120, 180.
[78] ACA perg. R.B. IV, 134: "in meis magnis necessitatibus."
[79] ACA perg. extrainv., 3466.

limited the possible responses to the difficult conditions of the early twelfth century. For three generations the core of Bernat Ramon's estate remained intact. Because the testament of Bernat Ramon has not survived, we do not know the precise terms he made in order to shape the future for his descendants. A good deal, however, can be inferred from the actions of his heirs. In addition, the will made by his son-in-law Ricart Guillem in 1114 offers a guide.[80] After dispensing quickly with pious donations by leaving a third of his moveables to be distributed as his executors saw fit, Ricart moved on to what concerned him most: providing for his three sons and two daughters. Only one more distant relative, a niece, received any bequest from his many properties, and even this acknowledgment of a larger kin group was written above the line, perhaps as an afterthought on the part of the testator. Each daughter received a piece of land in addition to what had been given her at marriage, and each son gained control of a fief or allod in his own right. But Ricart left his principal house on the town walls, the bulk of his lands in the *territorium*, and the fiefs at Gurb, Felgars, and Bag, as well as the castle of Arraona to his three sons in common with the proviso that his wife Ermessenda, who received the remaining two-thirds of his moveables but no land, would hold the entire estate until her death and if any of his sons died without a legitimate heir, his share would pass to the others. Ricart Guillem's heirs followed these terms to the letter. His widow Ermessenda still appeared acting in conjunction with her sons as late as 1132, and Pere Ricart secured the approval of his surviving brother Galceran for any transaction involving their inheritance. Managed as a unit by the male heirs, Ricart Guillem's estate passed essentially intact into the hands of Pere Ricart due to the early death of Bernat Ricart and the failure of Galceran to produce heirs. By delaying division, testamentary restrictions kept the patrimony concentrated during the succeeding generation and inhibited the individual alienation of property by any of Ricart Guillem's male heirs.

Even among a wider circle of relatives the provisions of a will could restrict the free disposition of family resources. In two cases nephews, uncles, and cousins had to agree to the division of lands inherited from Bernat Ramon. In a series of agreements from 1125 to 1130, Arnau Pere gradually separated his properties and

---

[80] ACB perg. R.B. III, 187. It is reproduced in the appendix to Ruiz Doménec, "El origen."

rights from those of his paternal uncle, the subdeacon Ramon Bernat.[81] The impulse to partition properties held in common probably came from Arnau's desire to act with greater independence due to the death of his father, yet the division was apparently resisted, for the actual evacuation of rights took five years to accomplish and Arnau was willing to pay the count the hefty sum of 100 mbts. to protect his claims.[82] Residual constraints on the disposition of Arnau Pere's property also came from another, more distant source: Pere Ricart, his second cousin. Even though one was related to his grandfather Bernat Ramon through his father and the other through his mother, both male and female lines of descent established some claim to a common inheritance, a link perhaps reinforced by an earlier settlement with their common uncle Bernat Ramon, a cleric with no known children.

The precise nature of the claims on the estate seem far from explicit, even for the parties involved. Because of the prevalence of informal compromises in which each side could expect some form of compensation, even dimly understood or partially remembered rights transferred by male or female descent had to be taken seriously. In a formal evacuation of mutual claims solemnly arranged with the counsel of the bishop of Girona, the vicar of Barcelona, and the sacristan Arnau, Pere Ricart and Arnau Pere c. 1139 meticulously defined their respective shares in numerous properties in the Pla de Barcelona, Vallès, and Osona; this extensive reordering and fission of common property was recorded later in a detailed inventory of their properties.[83] At this point common control of the inheritance was finally dissolved. Over three generations the tangled strands of kinship had been cut by death, multiplied by marriage, and intertwined by requirements that brothers hold an estate in common, yet inheritance

---

[81] ACB LA II, fol. 125, Mas x, no. 1340; LA II, fol. 125, Mas x, no. 1352; LA I, fol. 103, Mas x, no. 1376; ACA perg. R.B. III, 313 (another transcription is found in ACB 1-1-2060).

[82] ACB LA I, fol. 103, Mas XI, no. 1376. Since Arnau Pere begins to subscribe to charters in his own name in July, 1125 (ACB LA II, fol. 125, Mas x, no. 1340), this adds additional support to the identification of his father as Pere Bernat the Moneyer, who last appears in the sources in March, 1125 (*CSC*, III, no. 887); cf. supra, n. 72. In the composite genealogy offered by Ruiz Doménec, "Système de parenté," Arnau Pere is presented as the son-in-law of Guillem Bernat de Papiol, but this seems to be another, earlier Arnau Pere (de Papiol) who appears in *LFM*, I, no. 350. The descendants of Arnau Pere, son of Pere Bernat, are clearly identified as Pere de Barcelona and Bernat de Machiz, not Pere Arnau and Bernat Pere as indicated by the chart.

[83] ACA perg. R.B. IV, 93; perg. extrainv., 3466. The last, undated document is surely a product of the division and should therefore be placed c. 1139.

strategies had kept much of the assets of Bernat Ramon the Rich intact and in the hands of two grandsons fifty years after his death.

The descendants of Bernat Ramon had tenaciously kept their grip on the land passed down through inheritance, but to do so they had assumed considerable debts. The economic changes of the early twelfth century had gradually overtaken them. Strategies employed to prevent the fragmentation of agricultural property, the most secure source of wealth in eleventh-century Barcelona, placed collective restraints on its management. Reorganization of an estate in response to new economic situations was therefore discouraged. As the monetarized profits from agricultural surpluses declined after 1090, there was little attempt to sell off parts of the family inheritance in order to place resources in more productive areas or at least to avoid being strapped for cash. By concentrating property in too few hands, families also incurred the risk of biological extinction. When Pere Ricart died with neither a will nor children, Count Ramon Berenguer IV confiscated his property by right of *exorchia*, which allowed a lord to seize the property of an heirless, intestate dependent.[84] The other branch of the family fared no better. Arnau Pere had favored one of his sons, Pere de Barcelona, in his will;[85] since Pere in any case survived his brother, his father's property passed into his hands. In 1173 Pere de Barcelona, childless, joined the cathedral canons and made arrangements for them to receive most of his properties at his death.[86] Thus the substantial assets patiently accumulated by Bernat Ramon, quite possibly the richest individual in eleventh-century Barcelona, had passed to the control of the canons and the count in less than a century.

RENEWAL FROM BELOW

The difficulties confronting the heirs of Bernat Ramon the Rich were not unique; other wealthy urban families foundered in the early twelfth century. Having gained their wealth and influence in the booming agricultural economy of the eleventh century, prosperous landowners proved unable to transfer their economic

---

[84] *CODIN*, IV, no. cxvii. Since this appears as a banal charge on personal dependents, the count may well have claimed it because he had recovered the *potestas* over the castle of Arraona held by Pere Ricart. On the *exorchia* in general, see Bonnassie, *La Catalogne*, II, 826.

[85] ACB LA I, fol. 103, Mas XI, no. 1545.

[86] ACB LA I, fol. 36, Mas XI, no. 1985; LA I, fol. 103, Mas XI, no. 1986.

success to their descendants, who faced leaner times. The stagnation of the urban market and the absence of a developed trading structure rendered returns on agricultural investments minimal, yet land remained the basic source of wealth and prestige. Beyond declining profitability of agricultural investments, however, the collective identity of townspeople was not yet strong enough to integrate the well-to-do burghers into a cohesive, durable, and distinctively urban elite. As soon as a local landowner had accumulated substantial capital, his resources drew him into aristocratic circles and the networks of regional power. Political life in early twelfth-century Catalonia still played itself out on a regional level, not in the town or the castellany. The collective interests of burghers were still too inarticulate, the forms of urban authority too plastic to imprint agricultural entrepreneurs with a civic identity. Much like the early vicars of Barcelona, urban notables displayed ambivalent loyalties, with one eye turned to the complex allegiances entangled with urban authority and the other toward their patrimonial towers, farms, and family allies in the countryside. In contrast to later patricians, whose rents and properties were heavily concentrated in the Pla de Barcelona, one is struck by the wide dispersal of land owned by a number of prominent burghers as revealed in their wills. The judge Ramon Guitard is representative. Although not among the wealthiest burghers, in 1100 this respected local figure, a champion of the traditional legal order then in full retreat, owned land scattered throughout the counties of Barcelona and Girona yet maintained his principal residence in the city.[87] This pattern of landholding points to the persistence of a regional, territorial identity well into the early twelfth century. This broad context for the exercise of authority, later redefined by personal dependence and fiefholding, made an identification with the city tenuous. The civic allegiance of Barcelona's thriving entrepreneurs was constantly tested during the first phase of urban growth. They were not forced out of the city by pressure from below; rather they were drawn out into the aristocratic networks centered on rural castles and the cathedral canons or extinguished themselves by narrowing the channels through which they could pass down their property to future generations.

The early twelfth century did not mark a sharp rupture in the

[87] ACB 1–1–1844 and LA IV, fol. 28, Mas X, no. 1178. Cf. ACB 1–1–2543; LA IV, fol. 96, Mas X, no. 1283; LA I, fol. 30, Mas X, no. 1304; ACA perg. R.B. IV, 35.

city's history, yet the leading stratum of the urban community did undergo a slow, steady renewal. Because agricultural speculators no longer provided the impulse for continued expansion, their leadership slowly eroded. The reduced scale of exchange tended to promote individuals of modest means yet with access to a cash income. For artisans and purveyors to the counts, canons, and large landowners, the ability to accumulate even small amounts of liquid capital offered considerable leverage among landowners anxious for credit. Because local lending, exchange, and investment operated at a reduced level from 1090 to 1140, these transactions have left only faint traces in the sources, which overwhelmingly deal with real estate. The early twelfth century in Barcelona offers no spectacular success stories, the staples of an urban historiography still drawn to edifying accounts of the "rising bourgeoisie." Yet modest prosperity and anemic decline also have their place in the structuring of medieval towns. Beneath the level of the great agricultural speculators stood individuals who obtained cash through office, credit, or small-scale production. Through a gradual accumulation of liquidity they slowly gained access to urban utilities and suburban plots, assets that substantially rose in value as the city began to grow again after 1140.

This is not to deny that some prominent eleventh-century families did survive with considerable landed holdings, but to maintain their wealth and position they had to turn their investments away from agriculture. Very few made the transition successfully. The urban war bond of 1148 provides a useful marker to indicate the overall direction in which local society was moving.[88] Of the eleven burghers who lent Count Ramon Berenguer IV 7,700s. during the siege of Tortosa, only two belonged to families prominent before 1140: Bernat Marcús and Joan Martí.

Both their families had managed to maintain their economic viability in the stagnant urban economy for two reasons: they did not attempt to expand their agricultural investments in a depressed land market and each acquired a source of monetarized income. Of the two, Joan Martí possessed far fewer assets and had more modest beginnings than Bernat Marcús, for he descended from a family of local freeholders. His father, Martí Orúcia, did possess enough to provide Joan the substantial sum of 60 mbts.

[88] Bisson, *Fiscal accounts*, II, no. 143.

when he married in 1110,[89] a sizeable investment meant to secure an honorable marriage for his principal heir. Even though Joan Martí appears in 1139 among the local *prohoms*, his real estate holdings do not seem extensive, but he and his son did hold land in pledge for loans.[90] The picture of a small, prosperous landowner increasing his wealth through lending is confirmed by the testament of Joan's brother, Pere Bofill.[91] It provides an impressive balance sheet of outstanding credits and obligations. While possessing relatively little allodial property, most of which, including his home, he shared with his brother, Pere Bofill nevertheless possessed the rights to exploit several other assets, including mills on the Besòs owned by Sant Cugat del Vallès as interest on money the monastery owed him. Through numerous petty loans of no more than 12 mbts., he assured himself a modest profit; in eleven transactions he owed 34 mbts. to creditors but claimed outstanding debts of 62 mbts. Here we are far from the world of real estate speculators, sinking substantial sums into land purchases in hopes of obtaining large but delayed profits. Through the careful manipulation of small loans Joan Martí and his relatives could obtain agricultural surpluses as interest as well as the return of their capital: even the grandchildren of Bernat Ramon the Rich were in their debt.

Bernat Marcús, on the other hand, was heir to a long line of wealthy urban landowners who already appear in local sources by 1000. Unlike other urban notables, the family rode out the difficult decades of the early twelfth century with the properties it had inherited. Even though the Marcús were figures of regional stature, their properties were tightly concentrated in the Pla de Barcelona.[92] Once the urban population expanded again after 1140, Bernat Marcús turned his suburban land into valuable rental properties and added to his already considerable wealth. Yet unlike their peers in the eleventh century, the Marcús gained access to a valuable source of non-agricultural wealth: the mint of Barcelona. The association was long-standing and lucrative.

[89] ACB 1–5–67; cf. ACB LA I, fol. 308, Mas XI, no. 1614.

[90] ACB 1–1–286, 2060; ACA perg. extrainv, 3466; *Llib. bl.*, no. 39 and preceding note.

[91] *Santa Anna*, II, no. 202.

[92] A survey of the family's resources can be seen in the will of the last member of the male line, Bernat Marcús, son of the Bernat Marcús discussed here, *Santa Anna*, III, no. 609. Except for the castle of Freixa and the *villa de butarello* (Botarell?), inherited from Guillem and Berenguer de Barcelona, only two farms among his extensive properties lay outside Barcelona's immediate hinterland.

Marcús and Bofill (probably brothers) were granted contracts to operate the mint in 1056 and 1058; their descendants claimed an inherited right to a part of the house of coinage and a share of the strike, set at 4d. for 8s. of profit (4.2 percent) in the early 1180s.[93] In return for the continued privilege of exploiting this valuable right, it is hardly surprising that Bernat Marcús offered the count the largest amount in the collective loan in 1148 as well as acting as guarantor to extraordinary sums offered to Ramon Berenguer IV by Guillem Leteric, a Montpellier financier, in 1156 and 1160.[94] Comital patronage thus assured the Marcús a regular and substantial source of monetarized income, a resource many old landowning families must have envied in early twelfth-century Barcelona. While the assets available to Joan Martí would hardly have registered on a scale designed to measure the fortune of Bernat Marcús, both figures nevertheless emerged among the leading men in the city after 1140 because their families had managed to obtain sources of monetarized income without heavy additional investments in agriculture.

The relative rarefaction of specie after 1090 also accounts for the prominence of moneyers as a group in the early twelfth century.[95] Once the flow of Islamic gold had been reduced to a trickle, the craftsmen of coinage were among a handful of individuals assured of regular access to a cash income in a society that had grown used to the convenience of monetarized exchange. Six moneyers can be identified between 1100 and 1150: Calví, Pere Bernat, Bonmacip, Guillem Ramon, Moscio, and Guillem Bernat.[96] Only shoemakers (*sabaterii*) and smiths (*ferarii*) appear more often among craft names at this time than the *monetarii*. Barcelona's moneyers did not form an exclusive, hereditary guild, an "aristocracy of money" comparable to the *ministeria* of moneyers in northern and

---

[93] Botet y Sisó, *Les monedes catalanes*, I, aps. iv, v; Bisson, *Fiscal accounts*, II, no. 54. Ramon Marcús inherited rights in the building where money was minted, "quo fabricatur moneta," from his father before 1143 (ACB 3–29–230); the will of Bernat's son in 1195 speaks of his rights in proprietary terms: "omnem suum directum de ipsa sua moneta quod tenebat pro domino rege," *Santa Anna*, III, no. 609.

[94] *CODIN*, IV, nos. lxxxvi, cxxii.

[95] Robert S. Lopez, "An aristocracy of money in the early Middle Ages," *Speculum*, 28 (1953), 43 concludes from Italian evidence that the prominence of moneyers is a sign of monetary scarcity. In contrast to Italy, however, moneyers in Barcelona emerged rather suddenly as a group around 1100, another indication that monetary conditions in eleventh-century Catalonia were unusual.

[96] ACB LA II, fol. 18, Mas X, no. 1201; LA I, fol. 220, Mas XI, no. 1603; LA II, fol. 13, Mas X, no. 1375; ACB 1–5–115; *CSC*, II, no. 787; III, no. 883.

central Italy; the technical skills in mint operations, however, were highly regarded, for they provided continuity in the operation of a critical public institution. The Marcús' durable claim to a share of the coinage is quite unusual and points to an inherited right to supervise minting operations. Some *monetarii* belonged to prominent families; as already noted, Calví married the daughter of Viscount Gelabert Udalard, and Pere Bernat should probably be identified as the son of Bernat Ramon the Rich. Yet the other moneyers were not associated with aristocratic and landowning circles. Guillem Ramon, the moneyer most easily traced through the labyrinthine patterns created by subscriptions and attestations, appears frequently in charters not because of wealth but because he had gained a reputation for fairness and integrity among townspeople. He served as executor to four testaments and appears regularly among witnesses in urban charters from 1104 to 1123. Unlike urban notables of the eleventh century, Guillem Ramon owned little land, but he did obtain the right to operate two ovens and owned stalls and a workshop near the market.[97] Income from urban utilities and crafts attracted him more than heavy investments in vineyards and horticulture. Guillem Ramon's prestige derived from his association with the count, not from his personal property. As a reward for his services, Count Ramon Berenguer III allowed him (for a fee) to build arches and permanent structures on the ramparts near Castellvell, the first formal authorization recorded for construction between wall towers.[98] In the subdued conditions following an era of dizzying expansion, comital patronage and a source of ready cash provided moneyers with one of the few avenues of social ascent.

The seeming lethargy of urban society in the decades after 1100, however, conceals a gradual erosion of the wealth and influence of the old landowning families. Because they clung tenaciously to the vineyards, farms, and the fiefs they had once coveted, there were no spectacular failures, no sudden liquidations of their properties that would have left traces in contemporary land conveyances. Their decline was painfully slow. Debt and the obligation to provide their children with an honorable station gradually depleted the lands that were patiently assembled and carefully cultivated by earlier agricultural entrepreneurs. In this

[97] ACA perg. R.B. III, 179; perg. R.B. IV, 75; ACB LA I, fol. 63, Mas X, no. 1315; LA I, fol. 317, Mas XI, no. 1501; 1–5–14; *CSC*, II, no. 783.
[98] *Santa Anna*, II, no. 170.

stagnant economic environment the most dynamic individuals operated within relatively confined parameters, lending money cautiously in small amounts secured upon lucrative pledges, leasing ovens and mills, and patronizing craftsmen clustered around the market and comital palace.

This world of petty lenders, small-scale merchandisers, and shopkeepers largely escapes detection, but one can glimpse its potential in the activities of Martí Petit, i.e. Martin the Small (d.c. 1143). From the dowries of his two marriages, Martí acquired an oven at the center of town, workshops near the cathedral and the comital palace, and a considerable sum of cash.[99] He in fact stepped into the shoes of the father of his first wife, Udalard Bernat. Starting with the lease of a ramshackle building next to the cathedral, Udalard Bernat went on to construct several shops nearby to cater to the canons and noble visitors to the Palau Comtal.[100] First Udalard Bernat and then his son-in-law filled their purses with the gold coins their high-ranking clientele had to spend. Martí Petit in particular linked the world of artisans and suppliers with clerics, courtiers, and officials; while his name stands besides those of shoemakers, leather workers, and fishermen in local charters, his subscription is also found in the planned partition of Tarragona in 1118.[101]

Through lending and catering to aristocratic tastes, wealth was passing slowly, almost imperceptibly into new hands during the early twelfth century. Rather than providing the mortar to erect an urban oligarchy for the families that had dominated Barcelona's first phase of expansion, money undermined its very foundations.

CONCLUSION

The social transition of the early twelfth century represented more than the cumulative difficulties affecting individual families; it also encompassed a restructuring of the relationship between Barcelona and its region. Whereas upland castellans turned their attention away from the city, local landowning families experienced a gradual erosion of their wealth. Private lordship and the

---

[99] ACB LA I, fol. 45, Mas x, no. 1173; LA I, fol. 39, Mas x, no. 1290.
[100] For documentation and commentary about Bernat Udalard, see Balari Jovany, *Orígenes*, II, 699–71; Bonnassie, *La Catalogne*, II, 855–56.
[101] ACB LA I, fol. 186, Mas x, no. 1350; *LFM*, I, no. 245.

exploitation of outlying farms no longer integrated the dominant elements of urban society into a regional power structure. As a result, the urban community began to take on sharper outlines. At the same time, however, aristocratic families turned their attention away from the city. Through administration and investment, Barcelona thoroughly dominated its immediate hinterland within the narrow confines of the Pla de Barcelona, but it did not carve out an extensive *contado*. The aborted development of an urban aristocracy was crucial in setting the parameters and determining the nature of civic power. Barcelona would not provide a nerve center for collective aristocratic action.

The social changes analyzed in this chapter do not conform to generally held assumptions about the evolution of Mediterranean towns. Unlike the nascent communes of northern Italy and Occitania, Barcelona was not dominated in the early twelfth century by urbanized nobles and large landholders from its surrounding region. The city may well have been moving in such a direction during its first phase of growth, but economic difficulties and the stubborn resistance of the counts prevented aristocrats and agricultural entrepreneurs from fusing into a cohesive urban elite. The consequences of this change would leave a lasting mark on the city. The more sharply historians have turned away from characterizing early towns of Southern Europe as "commercial" or "bourgeois," the more importance they have attached to the role of resident aristocrats and large propertyholders in urban life. Presented as a social bridge between the potential of early towns and the expanding resources of the countryside, urban aristocracies elsewhere in the Mediterranean are credited with concentrating the resources of the hinterland in order to create the critical mass of capital required for commercial expansion.[102] Even if the relationship between a city and its *contado* is now characterized in terms of interdependence or complementarity rather than domination pure and simple, what Gioacchino Volpe once called "the blind egotism of the urban population,"[103] the nascent Italian communes nevertheless behaved as aristocratic leagues, limiting aggression among their members but also defending their rural

---

[102] Waley, *Italian city–republics*, 110–22; E. Fiumi, "Sui rapporti tra città e contado nell'età comunale," *Archivio storico italiano*, 114 (1956), 18–68.

[103] Gioacchino Volpe, *Medio evo italiano* (2nd ed., Florence, 1961), 252. Cf. recent characterizations by Racine, *Plaisance*, I, 291–92; Bordone, "Tema cittadino," 257–58.

seigniories from the advance of other lords or cities.[104] Communes acted in the manner of collective feudal lords, securing fealty and homage from rural castellans and villagers and extending their jurisdiction over the rural population whenever possible. From the early revival of towns in Italy, urban aristocrats provided continuity and promoted the expansion of urban jurisdiction into the *contado*. In Catalonia, on the other hand, the resilient conservatism of public authority allowed the House of Barcelona enough leverage to maintain a precarious balance among aristocratic factions in order to assert dynastic interests, a balance that would definitively tilt in favor of the counts after 1150. Urban jurisdiction would therefore form only a part of local administration, not a tool employed by the city's leading families to subject a wide territory to its interests. In Barcelona Count Ramon Berenguer I and his successors successfully countered the attempt of the viscounts to establish an independent banal lordship at the center of dynastic power, a victory later reaffirmed through a long struggle to keep the early urban vicars under control. As a result, noble families could not establish a firm patrimonial base within the town walls. Urban patronage in Barcelona would therefore not revolve around consortial towers of aristocratic clans but would focus on the comital palace.

The withdrawal of powerful aristocratic families was paralleled by the loss of influence of local landowners with heavy investments in nearby vineyards, gardens, and farms. Because agricultural entrepreneurs had played a major part in and profited from the surge of economic activity after the new millennium, their decline indicates that the urban economy was taking a new turn. Small-scale lending, supervision of the craft sector, and the operation of urban utilities provided alternatives to agricultural investments for individuals with modest but liquid assets and a keen eye for profit. The transition was subtle yet profound, for few of the prosperous landowners emerged after 1140 with their fortunes and status intact. The collective loan made by the burghers to Count Ramon Berenguer IV in 1148 provides eloquent testimony of a thorough turnover at the upper levels of urban society.

---

[104] Giovanni Tabacco, "Fief et seigneurie dans l'Italie communale: l'évolution d'un thème historiographique," *Le Moyen âge*, 75 (1969), 212–18; Haverkamp, "Die Städte," 198–202.

In an influential article published in 1914, Pirenne argued that patrician families lost their enterprising spirit after a generation or two; once an individual had accumulated his fortune through bold investments and trade, his heirs would inevitably become conservative rentiers.[105] It is tempting to apply this theory to Barcelona during the early twelfth century, but it is also deceptive. The Buddenbrooks complex Pirenne identified as an inherent cycle of capitalism was in its time a bold attempt to link economic and family history, what we might now fashionably call production and reproduction, but it fails to distinguish family biographies from the collective evolution of social groups. Despite the illustrative value of tracing the fate of individual family fortunes, in itself no simple task with the brittle information provided by twelfth-century land conveyances and testaments, the significance of the exercise lies in analyzing strategies employed to accumulate and preserve wealth and in determining to what extent members of the same group shared and perpetuated these strategies. Accidents of biological survival, individual aptitude, or abject incompetence could profoundly affect the fortunes of a single family, but not the reproduction of the collective strategies shared by leading urban houses to ensure their survival as a group in spite of the fate of its separate members. The agricultural investors of eleventh-century Barcelona failed to coalesce into a cohesive ruling body because they were simultaneously pulled in two directions, toward the urban market and toward the aggressive aristocratic world of the countryside.

To Pirenne, commerce provided the lifeblood of medieval urban communities; to invest in agricultural property was the antithesis of the entrepreneurial spirit, a betrayal of truly urban values. Barcelona's first phase of growth, however, depended on the combination of rural investment and the urban market, not their separation, and provided the basis for the accumulation of the first urban fortunes. But this did not lead directly to the unfolding of long-distance trading structures, for "foreign exchange" in eleventh-century Catalonia was essentially the product of war and tribute, not commerce. By concentrating agricultural surpluses for the local market, wealthy landowners in fact stood at a critical point of intersection between the monetarized wealth funneled from al-Andalus and the productive capaci-

---

[105] Henri Pirenne, "The stages in the social history of capitalism," *American historical review*, 19 (1914), 494–514.

ties of Barcelona's hinterland. Their very success encouraged them both to expand their landholdings and at the same time to become involved with castleholders and warlords, and even to participate in military campaigns themselves. As this structure of tributary entrepreneurship began to break down after 1090, Barcelona's wealthy urban landowners fell between two stools. If they clung to their land at all costs, a tendency promoted by their patterns of inheritance, the value of their assets declined and debts rose; if their wealth allowed them to become involved in fief- and castlehold-ing, they were drawn toward the upland world of castles and frontier expansion far removed from the city. The conjunction of economic forces and family strategies that had promoted the rise of agricultural entrepreneurs could not sustain economic growth in the early twelfth century.

The difficulties confronting Barcelona in the early twelfth century do not indicate a generational failure of entrepreneurial nerve; rather, they suggest that the first phase of growth did not culminate in a distinctive, independent, and self-confident urban community. During the early surge of economic expansion Barcelona had remained primarily a regional center, a reflection of the configuration of power throughout the lands subject to the comital dynasty. Only as the city began to pull apart from upland Catalonia in the early twelfth century did the urban community begin to take on sharp outlines and give rise to a coherent patriciate.

Chapter 5

THE PATRICIATE IN GESTATION,
1140–1220

The early twelfth century was a pivotal period in the history of Barcelona and of Catalonia generally. Often presented as a time of hesitation and uncertainty, these decades are squeezed uncomfortably between the internal reorganization of Catalan society in response to the "feudal crisis" of 1040–60 and the confident expansionism of the mid-twelfth century, culminating in the capture of Tortosa in 1148 and Lleida in 1149, the systematic settlement of New Catalonia, and the dynastic union with Aragon ensured by the marriage of Petronilla to Count Ramon Berenguer IV in 1150.[1] The early twelfth century represented, however, more than a pause in a single line of development. Counts, barons, and burghers alike were probing various directions of expansion, testing different forms of power, and exploiting new forms of wealth without yet fully establishing institutional structures and social gradations to stabilize the profound changes introduced in the eleventh century. A restive baronage, barely held in check by the comital dynasty, looked toward the slow territorial advance of the frontier, to Occitania, and, tentatively, to the Mediterranean in order to replace the lost revenues and prestige that raids on al-Andalus had once provided. Internally, the comital dynasty struggled to defend its prerogatives, still vaguely defined and loosely administered, against the aggrandizements of turbulent castellans, their armed clienteles, and especially those to whom it had delegated public authority. In the shifting balance among these forces, the families that had stood out among the relatively small population of Barcelona failed to establish a clear identity and a definite political role for themselves

---

[1] For general assessments of the period, particularly focused on the policies of Ramon Berenguer III, see Sobrequés i Vidal, *Els grans comtes*, 201–2; Soldevila, *Història de Catalunya*, 126, 145–46, who gives the most favorable account of the reign; and more recently Bisson, *The medieval Crown*, 26–29 and Josep Maria Salrach i Marés, *Història de Catalunya*, II. *El procés de feudalització* (Barcelona, 1987), 452–53.

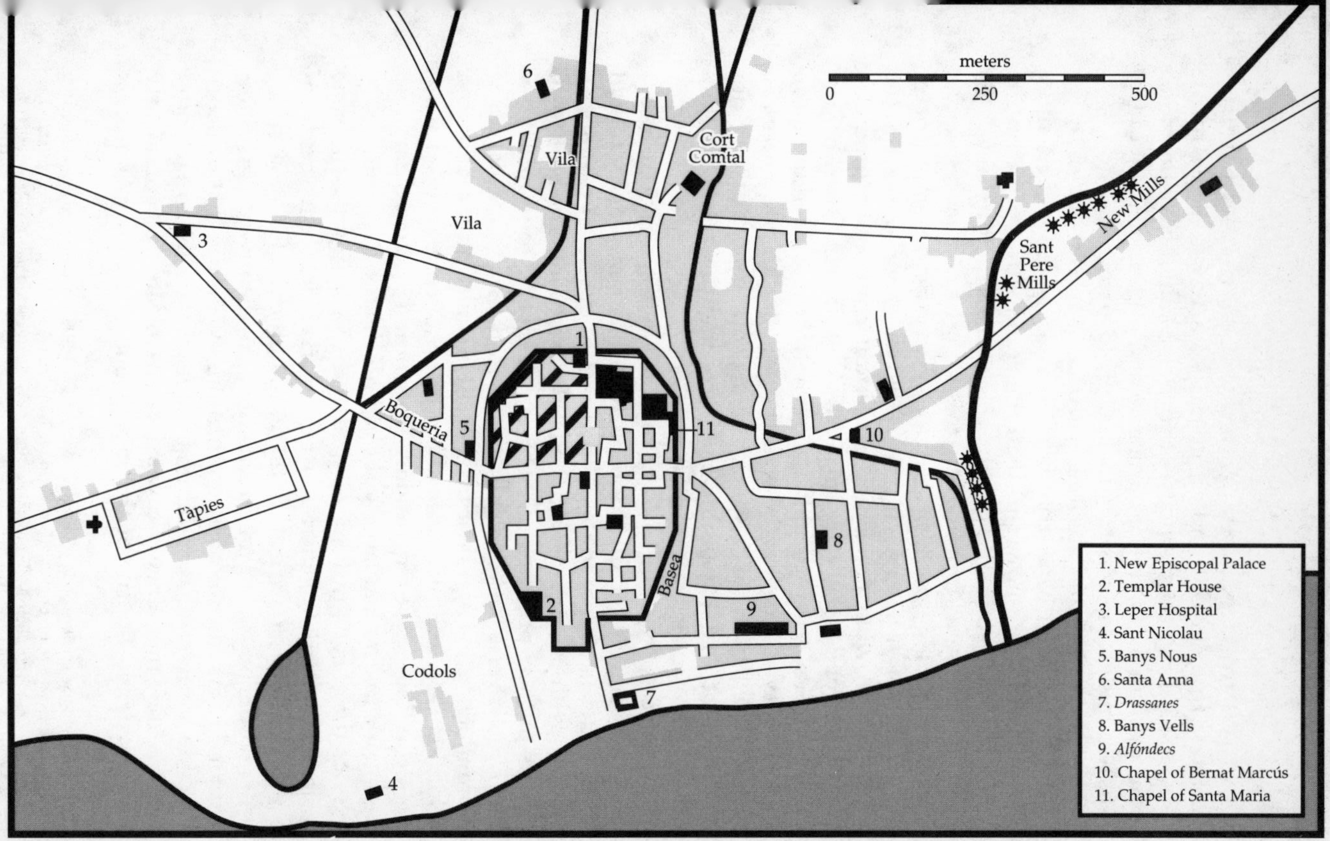

Map 5   Barcelona in 1200

Legend:
1. New Episcopal Palace
2. Templar House
3. Leper Hospital
4. Sant Nicolau
5. Banys Nous
6. Santa Anna
7. *Drassanes*
8. Banys Vells
9. *Alfóndecs*
10. Chapel of Bernat Marcús
11. Chapel of Santa Maria

New Mills

Sant Pere Mills

Cort Comtal

Basea

Vila

Vila

Vila

Boqueria

Codols

Tàpies

meters
500
250
0

and for the town. New elements within the city did not drive them out from below; rather, nobles with tentative ties to the town and large propertyholders had proven singularly unable to define a distinctively civic community and provide it with leadership. It is misleading to see in them a proto-patriciate.

The emergence of Barcelona's patriciate corresponded to the second surge of urban growth after 1140, a movement more sustained and more powerful than the reanimation of urban life around the millennium. The city was transformed by 1220. To accommodate new immigrants, the suburban zones expanded with breathtaking speed, in part by systematic development of large tracts of real estate in the *vilanovae*. To provide for the needs of a growing population, a vibrant craft sector produced specialized goods in greater quantities and varieties than before, and merchants began to link Barcelona to other Mediterranean markets. City streets already seemed charged with new energy in the mid-twelfth century. Who would profit by organizing this explosive internal expansion and directing the city's energies outward, however, remained unclear.

The process by which powerful new houses coalesced into a group which assumed direction of the urban community should not be reduced simply to the substitution of one set of families by another, as if these new arrivals had only to step into the broken-in slippers of their predecessors. The emergence of prominent new men from diverse backgrounds after 1140 and the perpetuation of their influence through their descendants entailed a reorganization of local power, itself determined by the productive forces driving the second surge of expansion. Agricultural entrepreneurs and rural castleholders had largely moved off the urban stage.

Since the alleged novelty of medieval towns in feudal Europe fascinated an earlier generation of historians, the emergence of town patriciates, regarded as the embodiment of a new civilization, took on an air of inevitability in their writings.[2] This attitude lingers in current interpretations. With the first evidence of resident merchants or burghers possessing substantial liquid wealth, the movement toward a patriciate is confidently announced, and the rise of this new group of wealthy families is

---

[2] Lestocquoy, *Aux origines de la bourgeoisie*, 65, 71; Carl Stephenson, *Borough and town: a study of urban origins in England* (Cambridge, MA, 1933), 170–73; Hans Planitz, "Zur Geschichte des städtischen Meliorats," *Zeitschrift der Savigny-Stiftung für Rechtsgeschichte. Germanistische Abteilung*, 75 (1950), 141–75.

charted in a steady trajectory that culminates in the formalization of economic control through the monopolization of political power. Even though allowances had to be made for the diverse backgrounds of early patricians as researchers probed into the pasts of more and more towns, the assumption remained that the first signs of urban renewal brought forth a dominant class characteristic of these new communities in formation.[3] Through the incorporation of *nouveaux riches* or the reorientation of older houses to new, more profitable investments, the original circle of wealthy families renewed itself and adapted to different circumstances while retaining its sense of cohesion. The alternating spasms of opening and closure of the patriciate are usually determined by an institutional test: the participation of leading families in municipal councils. This method, however, tells us little about the way in which the disparate elements within early towns first turned urban communities in a new direction before institutions emerged to define and perpetuate their power. Because of an assumed continuity in urban forms, the tendency still prevails to treat an abstract, synchronic "townness" as a concrete historical entity; as a consequence, the complex, highly differentiated structures of medieval towns at their apogee are often transposed onto the small, insecure populations of early towns. Only a conviction in the innate consistency of an "urban civilization" permits the telescoping of social organization over the centuries.

As the preceding chapters have argued, such a perspective distorts our image of the internal structure and the external relations of Barcelona during its initial phase of expansion. The patriciate taking shape after 1140 embodied a new civic identity. Even though a handful of prominent families did successfully pass through the narrow opening of the early twelfth century and previous features of political and social organization survived, these elements subsequently formed part of a community quite different in character from that which preceded it. Before exploring its salient features, it is first of all necessary to identify its leading element, the families that made up the patriciate.

[3] Hibbert, "The origins," 101–3. Ingrid Bátori, "Das Patriziat der deutschen Stadt. Zu den Forschungsergebnisse über das Patriziat besonders der süddeutschen Städte," *Zeitschrift für Stadtgeschichte, Stadtsoziologie und Denkmahlpflege*, 2 (1975), 13–14. Cf. the criticism on the coherence of early urban elites by C. H. Hauptmeyer, "Vor- und Frühformen des Patriziats mitteleuropäischer Städte: Theorien zur Patriziatsentstehung," *Die alte Stadt*, 1 (1979), 6–10.

PROHOMS AND PATRICIANS

Identifying medieval urban elites is a notoriously treacherous business. In spite of intense investigation into the social stratification of medieval towns, no satisfactory, generally accepted terminology has emerged to designate the leading members of these communities from the rest of the population.[4] Difficulties both theoretical and empirical have frustrated those who have put forward sweeping definitions. On the one hand, modern systems of classification largely depend on economic factors that fail to take into account medieval perceptions of status and order; on the other, the remarkable variety of social terminology used by medieval scribes and chroniclers as well as the bewildering array of urban institutions render direct comparisons among urban elites tentative. Instead of alluding to professional or economic activities, the terms most often used to refer to prominent burghers reflect moral qualities or lineage. Urban leaders were the "honest," "good," "tried and true," "senior," or "better" men (*honesti, boni, probi homines, seniores, meliores*) or, collectively, came from recognizable families or clans (*Geschlechter, parenteles, alberghi*). An experienced evenhandedness and moral probity, closely associated with inherited status, were the idealized qualities of urban rule.

The term patriciate most nearly conforms to these requirements. Even though Lucien Febvre and others following him have rejected it because it is not medieval in origin, the same criticism can be levelled against more scientifically fashionable expressions such as elite, ruling class, leading element, *couche dirigeante, Führungsschicht*, etc. Recent emphasis on "little communities" formed by clan, neighborhood, or confraternities embedded within an urban environment have caused patriciate to fall out of favor, yet problems of stratification within these smaller worlds remain.[5] Patriciate, however, retains an association in current usage with medieval urban culture; it evokes family ties, inherited status, and

[4] For recent debates about terminology, see Reynolds, *Kingdoms and communities*, 203–6; Bátori, "Das Patriziat," 1–5; Heers, *Les Partis et la vie politique*, 68–77.

[5] For recent criticism of purely vertical models of urban solidarity see Denis Romano, *Patricians and popolani: the social foundations of the Venetian Renaissance state* (Baltimore and London, 1987), 9–10; Thomas Brady, *Ruling class, regime, and Reformation at Strasbourg, 1520–55* (Leiden, 1978), 3–33; Brigitte Berthold, "Charakter und Entwicklung des Patriziats in mittelalterlichen deutschen Städten," *Jahrbuch für Geschichte des Feudalismus*, 6 (1982), 239–40.

political participation as well as wealth. Although the term *patricii* makes its first, tentative appearance only in the early fourteenth century, humanists later found its evocation of Roman and therefore civic nobility irresistible and promoted its use.[6] Already anachronistic by the time it became current, *patricii* nevertheless seemed an accurate description of politically influential urban families to the learned burghers familiar with towns not far removed from their medieval ancestry. If sixteenth-century humanists felt comfortable with the term, there is little advantage in rejecting it out of hand in favor of sociological terminology coined in the nineteenth and twentieth century.

But the use of patriciate is at best a halfhearted expedient. To define it too closely limits its value and reduces the advantages it offers for comparing groups of leading families in cities with quite different economic and social foundations. It provides an uneasy compromise to overcome an intractable lexical problem: the bewildering variety and frequent inconsistency in the vocabulary of status in medieval towns. Both the clergy and the nobility were better served by widely diffused Latin and vernacular titles of rank than townspeople. The problem is not just about word choice; it reflects a deeply felt ambivalence about the place of towns in the order of medieval society. Towns were, after all, an infraction in the rules of the tripartite division of society, a vexing anomaly in the divinely instituted three orders that took hold of the European imagination in the eleventh century.[7] Lords and intellectuals tended to treat towns as unified, undifferentiated collectivities, whose rights the entire population enjoyed, rather than as stratified communities. Precisely because of their concern to articulate civic values in reference to the urbanized culture of ancient Rome, humanists found in *patricii* a sweeping classification of political and familial distinction that suited their own urban world. The patriciate thus partially fills a conceptual void in medieval systems of classification. While artificial, it is nevertheless useful.

If patriciate is to be preferred to oligarchy, upper class, or elite when dealing with prominent urban families, its broad association with officeholding, inherited status, and wealth does not render

---

[6] *Patricii* are already documented for Brussels in 1303, F. von Klocke, *Das Patriziatsproblem und die Werler Erbsälzer* (Münster, 1965), 16, although the term gained currency only in the sixteenth century. On its spread, see Eberhard Isenmann, *Die deutsche Stadt im Spätmittelalter* (Stuttgart, 1988), 276.

[7] Fossier, *Enfance*, II, 980–81.

the task of determining its dimensions and character any easier. It is of critical importance, however, to distinguish between a group of families that monopolized municipal power and one that participated frequently in urban politics. Confusing the two distorts not only the size of patriciates but the significance of their actions.[8] If patrician families did indeed form an inbred caste, their marriage patterns, social relations, notions of patronage, and economic cohesiveness would be quite different than if they constantly had to renew and expand ties to a broader set of clients and relatives.

Participation in town councils or service within an inner circle of municipal magistrates provides a useful means of identifying prominent families, a gauge particularly appropriate for towns like Venice, Nuremberg, or Augsburg that formally closed their representative bodies to all but a closely defined number of families. Because the establishment of town councils is usually associated with the acquisition of municipal autonomy, some refuse to speak of a patriciate before the creation of collective representative institutions. For Barcelona at least, such an equation does not ring true. A permanent town council was established only in 1249 by King Jaume I, after a century of explosive population growth, increasing prosperity, and heightened civic pride. Many patrician families, as we shall soon see, had left their mark on urban politics long before they held the post of magistrate. A rudimentary municipal regime, as Font Rius aptly described it, already existed in the amorphous gatherings of *prohoms* and in the early, ill-defined consulate. As pointed out previously, however, both early forms of urban representation seemed to decline rather than gain in strength between 1220 and 1249. Without a strong degree of institutional continuity, the identification of a patriciate becomes particularly delicate, for the specific form patrician rule assumed provides only one facet of its character, not its entire identity.

To explore the degree of continuity and cohesion of Barcelona's patriciate, it is first of all necessary to determine to what extent families whose members had acted in the twelfth century as *prohoms* subsequently served as municipal magistrates in the thirteenth. We are much better informed about municipal magistrates than about the earlier *prohoms*. Because of the antiquarian interests

[8] Berthold, "Charakter und Entwicklung," 213–17; Reynolds, *Kingdoms and communities*, 204–5.

of Esteve Gilabert Bruniquer, a seventeenth-century municipal notary and director of civic ceremonies, numerous records about Barcelona's early institutions and public life have been preserved, including one notarial register, *un llibre antic excrit a mà privada*, which has since disappeared.[9] It contained lists of urban magistrates beginning with the very foundation of the municipal council by the king. Thanks largely to Bruniquer's diligence, despite occasional mistranscriptions, it is possible to identify every individual who served in the inner circle of civic government from 1249 until the municipal council was abolished in 1714. These lists have attracted very little attention to date, yet in them one can see a group portrait of Barcelona's patriciate. The *consellers*, as they came to be known, fluctuated between four and eight until a reform definitively fixed their number at five in 1274. Installed annually after 1265 by a group of twelve men appointed by the general assembly, the *consellers* served as a relatively small, prestigious executive committee in municipal affairs.

To create a rough index of those families most closely associated with the exercise of power, surnames that appear more than twice among the *consellers* between 1249 and 1291 have been tabulated and an attempt made to determine when these families first appear in urban charters (figure 5.1). This search yields twenty-four family names; together this group supplied roughly half the urban magistrates for the period (106 of 218).

One can hardly claim from these results that twenty-four patrician houses formed an exclusive clique monopolizing the magistracy. The executive council drew its members from a large pool of families, even if some appear more regularly than others. Over the fifty-two years of the *Consell de Cent* covered here, only seven times did the magistracy fail to include a *conseller* from a family that had not been previously represented; only once did it contain only members who had served on it before. While not democratic in the modern sense, the choice of magistrates did allow for broad representation of many eminent and some not so

[9] Esteve Gilabert Bruniquer, *Rúbriques del ceremonial dels mangífichs consellers y regiment de la ciutat de Barcelona*, ed. F. Carreras Candi and B. Gunyalons y Bou (Barcelona, 1912–16), I, 25–28. One of the first to appreciate the value of these lists, Agustí Duran i Sanpere, *Barcelona i la seva història* (Barcelona, 1973–75), II, 159, questions the accuracy of the oldest entries because their sources are anonymous. Even though there are orthographic peculiarities (Seria for Sarrià, La Cera for Lacera, etc.), the individuals in Bruniquer's lists regularly appear in contemporary charters and the royal registers; the reliability of his information seems beyond question.

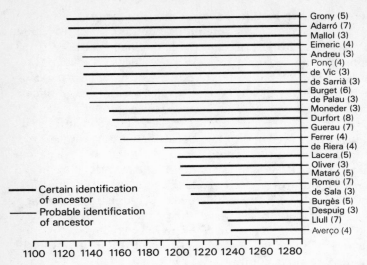

Figure 5.1 Earliest references to patrician families in Barcelona (the number of times the family name appears among the *consellers* is noted to the right)

distinguished families. On the other hand, members of eight families (Adarró, Burgès, Burget, Durfort, Grony, Guerau, Lacera, Llull) appear five times or more, holding almost a fourth of the available posts (50 of 218). While this small circle of prominent burghers repeatedly served as magistrates, they could hardly afford to ignore the interests of their peers. Moreover, sharing the same name does not necessarily mean sharing the same political objectives. Because some of the older families had formed separate branches over three or four generations by the time their members appear among the *consellers*, the degree of family cohesion needs to be clarified before one assumes third and fourth cousins form unified voting blocks. By identifying patricians through the repetition of names, prosopography tends to accentuate the continuity and cohesion of male descent groups. Yet even if the proposition that a patrician's name determines his actions is not called into question, political participation was not the preserve of a handful of wealthy families. Thirteenth-century Barcelona was not dominated by an oligarchy. A relative openness characterizes the early patriciate; because of its fuzzy institutional and juridical outlines, the leading families depended heavily on political and social skills that allowed them to engage the support of their fellow citizens. Until the divisive factionalism of the late fifteenth century, Barcelona maintained a remarkable institutional stability. It rested at least in part on the inclusiveness of its municipal government.[10]

If the durable municipal institutions established in 1249 provide a background against which an identifiable silhouette of the patriciate stands out, the malleable gathering of *prohoms* in earlier generations makes the contours of Barcelona's prominent families fainter. Often the *prohoms* are only referred to as an undifferentiated collectivity. True to ancient Frankish usage, *boni homines*, the older term for *probi homines*, do not appear among the subscribers to charters because they did not possess a clearly defined competency.[11] Scribes did, however, identify some members of the group by name in the body of the text, usually two to four, but followed with the formula "and other *prohoms*" (*et aliorum proborum hominum*). It is therefore impossible to determine the exact size and composition of assemblies of the "good men." Nonetheless between 1139 and 1220, urban notaries did refer to at least a few of the "multitude of *prohoms*" by name with some regularity.[12] Excluding clerics who participated by virtue of their office rather than their family connection, forty-two individual *prohoms* can be identified bearing thirty-two different family names during this crucial but obscure phase of urban development. While far from a complete census of prominent townspeople, these names do at least offer a rough index of the leading figures in twelfth-century Barcelona and a chronological framework for the emergence of patrician families.

A substantial genealogical continuity can be demonstrated between the twelfth-century *prohoms* and the late thirteenth-century magistrates. Of the twenty-four family names that appear more than twice among the magistrates, seven are found earlier among the *prohoms* (Adarró, Eimeric, Burget, Grony, Moneder,

---

[10] On the structure and composition of the fourteenth-century councils, see Charles-Emmanuel Dufourcq, " 'Honrats,' 'mercaders' et autres dans le Conseil des Cent au XIVᵉ siècle," in *La ciudad hispánica durante los siglos XIII al XVI* (Madrid, 1985), II, 1388–93 [repr. in *L'Ibérie chrétienne et le Maghreb XIIᵉ–XVᵉ* siècles (London, 1990)]; Mutgé Vives, *La ciudad de Barcelona*, 222–40.

[11] Nehlsen-von Stryk, *Die* boni homines, 115; Font Rius, "Orígenes del régimen," 420.

[12] From 1100 to 1139 and again from 1220 to 1249 *prohoms* are not usually named individually in charters. This may reflect more than a change in notarial style, for the presence of prominent individuals from 1139 to 1220 may have begun to overshadow their collective function. I have found fifty-two references to *prohoms* in urban sources between 1100 and 1249; all but twelve are concentrated between 1139 and 1220.

Ponç, de Sarrià). The overlap is even more striking if allowance is made for the earliest mention of magistrate families; twenty-one appear in urban charters before 1220, but only fourteen before 1180. Thus, half the oldest families whose descendants later served regularly in the urban magistracy appear in the fragmentary evidence for the *prohoms*. As figure 5.1 illustrates, around 1140 a group of families was emerging that would form the core of municipal government a century later. During the thirteenth century rapid commercial expansion eventually drew new houses into an orbit around the original patrician nucleus. While Barcelona's patriciate did not emerge as a monolithic block from a charmed circle of individuals who had experienced their first successes together and enjoyed the self-assured familiarity of an "old boys" club, nonetheless in the decades after 1140 a group of prominent burghers began to establish a style of urban leadership and a common set of economic interests that would determine the city's character for generations to come.

In the mid-twelfth century, however, the identity of the ascendant families was by no means assured. By taking the *consellers* between 1249 and 1291 as a point of reference and searching for their ancestors, the danger exists of making the line of progression too direct. Like a driver glancing in his rearview mirror, the road receding in the distance can appear straighter than it is since curves and exits tend to vanish on a distant horizon. Projecting family histories backward gives an unwarranted air of inevitability to their rise. If one tries to look ahead from, let us say, 1150, it is difficult to predict which families would assume a leading role in the city. Ancestors of some of the most prominent families among the *consellers*, including the Durfort, Mallol, and de Vic do not appear among the *prohoms* although they were all active in the later twelfth century. Moreover, not all *prohoms* established a male line of descent leading to the prominent magisterial families after 1250: Bernat Marcús, Berenguer Bou, and Martí Orúcia must have surely seemed solidly entrenched to their contemporaries around 1150, but their family names later died out.

That we lose track of the oldest families around 1140 is not due primarily to naming practices or to the quantity of surviving parchments. The ancestors of patrician families were for the most part not particularly wealthy or distinguished in 1140. Because of the economic constriction and social dislocation affecting Barcelona in the early twelfth century, family fortunes and categories of rank had largely to be built from the ground up.

Thus, the *prohoms* did not consist of a stable, homogeneous group of prominent burghers toward the mid-twelfth century. Both socially and institutionally, the composition of this group as well as its function were extremely fluid. The term *prohom* never served as an individual ascriptive distinction of rank; before 1200 the *prohoms* do not appear as part of an hierarchical ordering of the urban population. If an opposite exists to *probus*, which in this context means levelheaded, evenhanded, and fair-minded, it must be contentious, inequitable, or dishonest, not poor or undistinguished. The presence of *prohoms* in disputes, partitions, and transfers lent a collective moral force to the proceedings, a reassurance that through community pressure the required social obligations would be upheld. The *prohoms* originally did not so much stand apart from the community as enforce its will.

Gradually, however, the *prohoms* began to be distinguished from the rest of the urban population. While the counts and later the count-kings had commonly addressed their charters to the entire urban community, in 1203 King Pere I for the first time sent a privilege to the "*prohoms* and residents of Barcelona," a formulaic introduction amplified by Jaume I in an important commercial privilege of 1231 to "*prohoms*, citizens, and residents of Barcelona" (*probi homines, cives, et habitatores Barchinone*).[13] While the forms of address in the royal chancery varied, nevertheless they began to treat the *prohoms* as a discreet body within the town, a group with special responsibilities and social distinction. Yet as the status attached to the *prohoms* increased, their traditional functions as mediators in disputes and guarantors of a community-sanctioned order declined. The *prohoms* were therefore increasingly identified by who they were rather than by what they did; long after a municipal council was functioning and royal charters recognized its members as the representatives of the urban population, municipal privileges in their address still sometimes included the *prohoms* of Barcelona.[14] The evolution of the term from signifying a group informally enforcing communal stability

---

[13] AHCB, Llibre verd, I, fol. 206 r.–v.; Capmany, II, no. 6. Cf. ACA perg. Jaume I, extrainv., 2816; AHCB Llibre vermell, II, fol. 345 r.; Huici-Cabanes, *Documentos*, I, no. 60.

[14] ACA Reg. 12, fol. 149 r.; Reg. 42, fol. 157 r.; Reg. 66, fol. 144 r.; Reg. 74, fol. 14 v., etc. Unfortunately chancery formulas have received very little attention to date. See the comments by Burns, *Diplomatarium*, I, 141.

to identifying those citizens with elevated status within the urban population constitutes a critical turn toward the formation of the patriciate. In the early fourteenth century this movement reached its conclusion with the use of a new title to confirm the inherited status and social cohesion of patricians both individually and as a group. Henceforth Barcelona's elite would be known as *ciutadans honrats*, "honored citizens."[15]

The replacement of the old Frankish term for legal assessors and men of high repute, *boni homines*, by *probi homines* in the early twelfth century may already signal a change. While generally dismissed as an inconsequential substitution of one notarial formula for another,[16] the inherent conservatism of scribal culture does not give way easily to new terminology, especially in documents regarding disputes. There was indeed some equivocation in usage during the early twelfth century: in addition to *probi homines*, *honesti viri*, *nobiles viri*, *boni homines*, and even *consules* were used as titles for the same body,[17] a suggestive indication that these individuals were coalescing into a more cohesive, more aggressive group in the community than their predecessors even if their functions remained unchanged. In the mid-twelfth century the body of *prohoms* was certainly in full evolution. Composed of men for the most part without great wealth or entrenched status, this group of prominent burghers were slowly consolidating their leadership in the community and enjoying

---

[15] On the first use and significance of the term *ciutadans honrats* in the early fourteenth century, see Dufourcq, "'Honrats,'" 1362–63; J. M. de Palacio, "Contribución al estudio de los burgueses y ciudadanos honrados de Cataluña," *Hidalguía*, 5 (1957), 312.

[16] Font Rius, "Orígenes del régimen," 442–43; Balari Jovany, *Orígenes*, II, 534.

[17] ACB 1–5–5, 138; 1–2–1501; Font Rius, "Orígenes del régimen," 543, ap. iii. Even though some variation in scribal formulas does occur after 1150, forms of diplomatic address were considerably more consistent than in the early twelfth century. The variety of formulas used at the time adds further weight to the contention by Font Rius, "Orígenes del régimen," 465, n. 761, that the *consules* mentioned in 1130 were not part of a formal consular government but merely the *probi homines* dressed up with a term in vogue in Occitania. André Gouron, "Les Consuls de Barcelone en 1130: la plus ancienne organisation municipale à l'ouest des Alpes?" *AHDE*, 60 (1991), 205–13 places the early reference to *consules* in a more positive light, for he sees in it an indication that the community was experimenting with a better organized (but short-lived) municipal institution distinct from the *prohoms*. His strongest argument derives from the citation of four individuals as *consules*, a number which appears frequently in the earliest consulates in Occitania. Yet in the twelfth and early thirteenth century four individuals are occasionally named among the body of *prohoms*, although the number of men singled out by name vary considerably: e.g. ACB LA I, fol. 96, Mas XI, no. 2054; ACB Cartes Reials, C. 1–25, Oliveras Caminal, no. 8; ACB 1–6–2517. The mention of four *consules* in 1130 therefore probably indicates a transitional terminology rather than a new institution.

new prestige. "Good men" were turning into "distinguished citizens."

CRAFT PRODUCTION AND ITS CONTROL

The rise of new families around 1140 depended upon their ability to control, or at least organize and profit from, new sources of urban wealth. The evolution of the city's economy did not make the task simple, for the most dynamic new stimulus to production came from local artisans, often ruggedly independent and requiring little capital. Even though well-off burghers still were interested in acquiring small, productive agricultural plots below the walls, the innovative features of the local economy around 1150 no longer lay in the "green belt" surrounding the town but in the tiny stalls and workshops of craftsmen and merchants. Production and exchange, however, were dispersed and small-scale; to concentrate the growing wealth available in the city required patient accumulation of rents, attention to the supply of raw materials, prudent distribution of finished products, and, with access to royal patronage, control of local utilities. In its early stages the second surge of urban expansion beginning around 1140 offered the possibility of securing a modest prosperity for those who systematically developed their resources; it did not present opportunities for spectacular overnight fortunes in a speculative atmosphere of far-flung commercial networks.

In order to gain an overview of the urban economy's new contours, some light must first be shed on the structures of the poorly documented craft world. The partial census of townsmen made for the *questia* of c. 1145 provides a solid point of departure.[18] Of 218 proper names, 38 clearly refer to professional occupations: shoemaker (8), skinner (3), harnessmaker (3), woodworker (3), smith (3), taverner (2), physician (2), woolworker (2), merchant (2), baker (2), shieldmaker (1), moneyer (1), money changer (1), sailor (1), fisherman (1), shipwright (1), linen weaver (1), and butcher (1). The distribution of occupations overwhelmingly reflects trades to provide goods for local consumption, not export. The prominence of shoemakers (*sabaterii*) in the list is not accidental. Already firmly established in the eleventh century, shoemakers would later found the first craft confraternity in the

---

[18] On the nature of the document, supra, 66–67.

city in 1203.[19] The *sabaterii* fulfilled a basic need of the small urban population by producing not only shoes but other leather goods with simple tools and materials that demanded only modest cash outlays. Their shops were spread throughout the settled area and they generally held allods rather than leaseholds, with the more prosperous among them owning an occasional garden plot or vineyard.[20] The independence and modest prosperity of the shoemakers typify the rudimentary organization and limited capacity of the craft sector in early Barcelona; their prevalence in the *questia* list c. 1145 was more a reminder of the past than a signal for the future, for artisans would rapidly diversify into new occupations to appeal to a wider market and develop a more complex structure. Few far-flung commercial empires followed fast on the heels of cobblers.

The craft names attached to individuals that appear in the texts of land charters provide the surest means of identifying the contours of the city's craft sector. In the information gleaned from the parchments, one can observe the diversification and intensification of artisan production after 1140 in table 5.1, which gives the number of individuals active in a given trade in forty-year periods. Clearly trades devoted to the local market still predominated during the twelfth and thirteenth century. While shoemakers retained their importance, the service sector grew rapidly and came to include more specialized occupations in larger numbers, including carpenters, tailors, taverners, and butchers. Those occupations normally associated with thriving longdistance trade, such as weavers, merchants, sailors, and money changers, remained in the background, although there was a significant increase in this sector from 1140 onward. Yet animal skins, iron, and foodstuffs remained the basic materials of Barcelona's economy before 1220, not cloth, spices, or silver.

Artisans in the older, more established crafts tended to maintain a degree of ease and considerable independence throughout the twelfth century. This applies particularly to smiths and armorers. Throughout the early Middle Ages they were highly regarded for their power to transform ore into rare and valuable objects for war and agriculture, although the quasi-magical aura surrounding

---

[19] Banks, "The origins," 109–18. Shoemakers were relatively prosperous in towns where regional markets prevailed. Cf. Stouff, *Arles*, I, 282–83; Racine, *Plaisance*, II, 118–25.

[20] Numerous other streets were named after crafts before the first reference appears to the Cobblers Street (*vicus sabateriorum*) in 1253, ACB 1–6–1699; cf. ACB 1–6–1601.

Table 5.1 *Craftsmen active in Barcelona, 1100–1220*

Materials	1100–1140	1141–1180	1181–1220
Skins			
Cobblers	11	21	17
Skinners/Furriers	7	12	16
Blanchers	0	0	1
Totals	18	33	34
Metals			
Smiths	3	21	21
Catapultmakers	0	1	6
Knifemakers	0	1	1
Lancemakers	0	1	0
Bridlemakers	0	3	3
Shieldmakers	0	2	3
Coopers	0	3	1
Forgemaker (*fabricatus?*)	0	1	0
Totals	3	33	35
Money			
Moneyers	6	4	4
Money changers	2	5	3
Toll collectors	1	0	0
Totals	9	9	7
Food/Services			
Taverners	1	7	2
Bakers	1	1	5
Millers	0	0	3
Butchers	2	6	7
Painters	2	3	3
Fishermen	2	2	2
Troubadours	1	1	0
Carpenters	0	2	0
Tailors	0	1	3
Totals	9	23	25
Cloth			
Weavers	1	6	4
Carders	0	2	2
Fullers	1	0	0

Table 5.1 (*cont.*)

Materials	1100–1140	1141–1180	1181–1220
Dyers	0	1	1
Fustianmakers	0	0	1
Linenmakers	0	1	1
Totals	2	10	9
Trade			
Merchants	0	4	3
Sailors	0	1	1
Cloth merchants	0	1	3
Totals	0	6	7

the craft dissipated with the rapid diffusion of iron-working throughout the Catalan countryside after 1000.[21] By the mid-twelfth century Ferrer became a common family name even for those who no longer practiced the craft, a popularization complicating the identification of actual smiths and unduly inflating the presence of the craft in the figures above. Rich deposits of high quality ore lying near the surface in the Pyrenees and the prelittoral ranges promoted an active interest in metallurgy throughout Catalonia. A high manganese content produced a hardness close to steel, making Catalan longswords highly prized outside the region. From an early date lords were concerned about obtaining adequate supplies of iron for local smiths working in the Pla de Barcelona. In 945 the suburban nunnery of Sant Pere de les Puel·les received an iron mine near Terrassa in the Vallès, and iron appears near the top of Barcelona's earliest tariff list from c. 1150.[22] Rising demand for plowshares, hoes, nails, scythes, and other agricultural implements, the iron girders supporting the rise of agricultural production, turned smiths into kulaks in the sub-

[21] Attitudes toward metal workers in early medieval value systems are discussed by Jacques Le Goff, "Travail, techniques et artisans dans les systèmes de valeur du haut moyen âge (V^e au Xe siècle)," *Pour un autre moyen âge* (Paris, 1977), 108–30. On early Catalan metallurgy and the high reputation of Catalan arms, see Vilar, *La Catalogne*, I, 285–88; Bonnassie, *La Catalogne*, I, 472–75; Charles Singer, *A history of technology* (Oxford, 1954–84), II, 56, 71–73; Edouard Salin, *La Civilisation mérovingienne d'après les sépultures, les textes et le laboratoire* (Paris, 1949–57), III, 110.

[22] A. Pauli Meléndez, *El real monasterio de San Pedro de las Puellas de Barcelona* (Barcelona, 1945), ap. ii; appendix 4, no. 1.

urban villages of the Barcelonès, where they kept their forges because of the fire danger. With the basic equipment of their craft located some distance from the town walls, Barcelona's smiths provide a telling example of how deeply the roots of early urban artisans were plunged in the nearby countryside. When the smith Taià made his will in 1174, he left his houses and forge (*fabrica*) in Provençana, a brisk morning's walk from Barcelona, to his nephew, several small fields and a vineyard to his daughter, and a plot bordering on the road to the city to the monastery of Sant Cugat del Vallès for his burial; he also left obligations in Barcelona itself, including a small debt of 10s. to Arnau the bitmaker (*frenarius*) and the rent for houses held from the count below Castellnou, where he stored some wine barrels and grain bins (*bascule maiores et minores*).[23] A modest freeholder with a valued trade, Taià like other smiths was both a *coq du village* and a respected figure among urban artisans with whom he contracted debts and conducted his business. Although his own man by virtue of his allodial properties, he was also drawn toward the busy castle-gate commanding the western suburbs, soon to be the site of craft stalls and the royal meat market, and paid the rent for his urban houses to the count's bailiff.

The connection with the count, while not necessarily direct or personal, is nonetheless suggestive, for other smiths and, above all, armorers clustered in the streets below the comital palace. The counts sometimes sold them shops or houses in this zone, thereby creating a tiny core of shield smiths (*scutarii*), arrow smiths (*balistarii*), cutlers (*cutelarii*), and harnessmakers (*frenarii*) dependent on comital patronage and the aristocratic clientele concentrated in their courts.[24] Even though the armorers organized their shops on their own terms without a significant reliance on suppliers or independent retailers, the good will of the count and his aristocratic followers was required for the success of their business. Already in the twelfth century the resources of the count-kings were gradually causing this specialized craft sector to concentrate in one area; this is an early, telltale sign of the influence the Crown would exert on Barcelona's economy when it later embarked upon its adventurous Mediterranean expansion.

[23] *CSC*, III, no. 1094.
[24] *Poblet*, nos. 285, 287; ACA perg. varis, Marquès de Monistrol, 1; perg. R.B. III, 269; ACB LA I, fol. 97, Mas XII, no. 2137. A street below the comital palace was referred to as the *freneria* in 1224, ACB 1–6–1794.

While smiths, armorers, and shoemakers continued a tradition of autonomous craft production, which was kept in the hands of prosperous freeholders from the surrounding countryside and directed toward the local market, the fastest growing craft after 1140 involved the preparation of animal hides and furs. Producing items for export as well as for local consumption, tanners, skinners, and furriers came to depend on entrepreneurial investments from prosperous burghers and the intervention of specialized suppliers and distributors. The preparation of hides and pelts required considerable technical expertise, involving the use of chemicals and specialized tools for the removal of fatty tissues and putrefying residues, softening, cleaning, dyeing, cutting and mounting the pelts. Light, easily transportable, and, depending on type and quality, of considerable value, finished skins and furs have been unduly underrated as an article of long-distance commerce. The term usually conjures up silks, woolens, and spices rather than cat skins and cattle hides. Robert Delort has recently corrected this impression by uncovering the vast dimensions and complexity of the late medieval fur trade; for the most expensive and rarest furs such as ermine, mink, sable, lynx, marten, and leopard, proud trademarks of high rank, a far-flung distribution system connected the Baltic with the Sahara, and Iraq with England.[25] As a consequence of the successful raids into al-Andalus, Catalan warriors brought back not only gold and silver as plunder, but silks, fine linens, and expensive furs.[26] They quickly developed a taste for high fashion. According to Maurice Lombard, the Arabs introduced Europeans to many finer furs through constant raiding and the exaction of tribute in Spain.[27] Even more common skins, including wolf, squirrel, beaver, and cat as well as livestock hides, circulated widely and provided items of daily apparel, furnishings and utensils. Throughout the Pyrenees and its foothills roamed wild cats prized for their furs, including lynx, fox, and marten. Wolves, squirrels, genets, beavers, rabbits, and cats (black cat hides generally brought the highest prices) formed an integral part of the Pyrenean economy,

---

[25] Robert Delort, *Le Commerce des fourrures en Occident à la fin du moyen âge*, 2 vols. (Rome, 1978).

[26] Bonnassie, *La Catalogne*, I, 498. Cf. the vivid description of Muslim clothing and furs gathered as plunder by Castilian warriors in Claudio Sánchez Albornoz, *Una ciudad de la España cristiana hace mil años: estampas de la vida en León* (9th ed., Madrid, 1982), ap. 4.

[27] Maurice Lombard, "La Chasse et le produit de la chasse dans le monde musulman (VIIIe–XIe siècle)" *AESC*, 25 (1969), 572–93; cf. Delort, *Le Commerce*, I, 323–34.

while livestock grazed throughout the rugged hills and swampy lowlands of Catalonia.[28] The region's zoological diversity provided the skinners of Barcelona with abundant raw materials which its tanners and furriers turned into valuable items of export. Long-distance trade in pelts grew to considerable proportions during the second half of the twelfth century. Cat, genet, wolf, and sheep skins precede cloth in Barcelona's earliest tariff list, and Catalan ships sailed with large cargoes of skins. In a complaint registered against Genoa for an act of piracy committed by the republic's galleys during the late twelfth century, Guerau Estirat alleged losses of 840s. in sheep, wolf, and cat skins, and his companion Pere Estirat was robbed of 3,000s. in rabbit pelts.[29] Trade in furs and hides had by 1150 evolved far beyond local peasants swapping stiff pieces of leather at the urban market to one of the most profit-driven sectors of Barcelona's economy.

The available land charters and wills have little to say about the technical organization of this craft sector, for they refer generically to skinners (*pelliparii, pellicarii*), terms that cover a range of activities from simple tanning of sheepskin to finishing and trimming cloth with rare furs. Overall, however, the *pelliparii* seem notably less prosperous than shoemakers and smiths; they tended to hold leased property rather than allods, and their tenures consisted primarily of small plots on the fringes of the settled area, in part a function of the pollution caused by noxious chemicals and waste produced during the preparation of skins.[30] With relatively little capital of their own, the *pelliparii* relied on the investments and patronage of well-off burghers. In part the distant, dispersed, and intermittent sources of supply required the intervention of middlemen to gather unfinished skins from small upland suppliers and markets. Local butchers no doubt supplied their share of sheep skin and cow and goat hides, but this was only one dimension of the tanners' and furriers' trade. Pere Grony, the

[28] For the species prevalent in eastern Iberia, see Delort, *Le Commerce*, I, 167, 172–74, 205.

[29] Appendix 4, nos. 1, 2.

[30] Early *pelliparii* were most commonly found to the north around the Cort Comtal zone and to the east, near the Merdança stream: ACB 1–5–289, 1–6–1103; ACA perg. varis, Marquès de Monistrol, 15; ADB perg. Santa Anna, Carp. 2a, 63; Carp. de la creu, unnumb. parch. [8 xi 1216]; *Santa Anna*, II, no. 445; III, nos. 459, 491. Only 20 percent (2 of 10) of properties held by *pelliparii* in Barcelona from 1100–1220 were allods, compared to 84 percent (16 of 19) for smiths and armorers.

   A complaint was raised in 1270 against *pelliparii* fouling the waters of the Rec Comtal, just to the east of Skinners Street, ACB 1–6–1532: "se sustinere magnum dampnum . . . a lavatoribus pellium racione pilorum buquinorum et racione lanarum que mundabantur in reggo."

founder of one of the city's most illustrious patrician houses, appears in 1129 extending payment on credit of 10s. to a canon of Barcelona for a pelt (*pellicia*) and a half side of bacon.[31] As skins and furs grew into a significant export sector, a number of prosperous burghers became interested in renting shops to *pellipa-rii* and extending them credit. A system of economic clientage can be glimpsed in the will of Estefania, widow of Arnau the Tanner. Besides her husband's leased shops and the trade left to her son Arnau, Estefania had only a cape, some skins, and 20s. to leave her relatives and her church in 1216, yet she insisted her executors pay off a debt of 10s. by Easter to Bernat de Vic, a well-heeled patrician whose family name itself suggests a connection to the thriving tanning industry at Vic.[32] Bernat's father, Pere de Vic, held property in common with Berenguer *pelliparius* in the Cort Comtal area, and other well-off burghers, including Berenguer de Barcelona, son of the early vicar Berenguer Bernat, and Burget, rented shops to other skinners.[33] With its commercial potential and rapid growth after 1140, the craft of tanning and fur prepar- ation became integrated into an economic system dependent upon the resources of landlords, investors, and merchants. Lacking corporate organization and substantial assets, the *pelliparii* found the product of their labor profiting urban entrepreneurs, many of whom were members of the early patriciate.

As investors tightened their grip, a topographical concentration of the city's most expansive industry occurred to ensure its control. By 1214 a Skinners Street (*platea pelliparie*) is documen- ted, the first street in Barcelona to bear a craft name.[34] Located just to the east of Santa Maria del Mar and above the meat market (*macellus*), it lay within easy reach of the bustling commercial sector taking shape near the coastline just after 1200. A scramble for control of the area took place between 1212 and 1214. Origi- nally part of a large tract of suburban land owned by Bernat

[31] ACB LA I, fol. 49, Mas X, no. 1380. Although C. Batlle, A. Busquets, and I. Navarro, "Aproximació a l'estudi d'una família barcelonina els segles XIII i XIV: els Grony," *AEM*, 19 (1989), 285 maintain that the Grony had established themselves in the city only in 1138, Pere Grony already appears in 1126, ACB LA I, fol. 186, Mas X, no. 1350; cf. ACB LA II, fol. 155, Mas X, no. 1391; *VL*, XVII, ap. xlix. The article is considerably fuller for the thirteenth than the twelfth century.

[32] ADB perg. Santa Anna, Carp. de la creu, unnumb. parch. [8 xii 1216]; cf. ACB 1–6–16, which appears to refer to the same leased property.

[33] *Santa Anna*, II, no. 445; ACB 1–5–289; LA I, fol. 74, Mas XII, no. 2224; LA I, fol. 290, Mas XII, no. 2282.

[34] ACB 3–29–348.

Marcús, this area was already being developed by the time Bernat bequeathed it to his sister, Sança, in 1195.[35] Sometime before her death in 1202, Sança sold the property to her niece, Guillema, daughter of Bernat Marcús and wife of Guillem de Sant Vicenç, a noble in the Maresme region just up the coast from Barcelona. In a series of complex transfers between 1212 and 1214 related to both an internal reorganization of the Sant Vicenç family and to the need of urban financiers to provide massive loans to the king and his barons, Guillema technically sold the property to King Pere I for 10,500s., an amount put up by Pere's principal financier and accountant, Guillem Durfort, who then took possession of it as a royal grant "for his many favors and useful service."[36] Two years later, however, Guillem returned the property to Guillema de Sant Vicenç for "enough so that we are well satisfied"; a few days later Guillema then sold this precious piece of prime urban real estate for 11,000s. to Pere Moneder, a royal moneyer and an important urban financier in his own right.[37] The complexity and scale of these transactions are striking. No transfer of urban real estate before 1200 could compare with these amounts. The potential profit from the production and exchange of hides and furs had expanded to the extent that it drew the avid interest of kings, entrepreneurs, and urban developers, who tried to attract *pelliparii* to shops they owned in order to strengthen their position as economic middlemen. By 1256 a single block of over twenty shops on the Call de Born (*platea de boria*), just below Skinners Street, would bring the impressive sum of 2,437 mbts., or more than 17,000s. *dublenc*.[38] Economically integrated into regional and long-distance networks of exchange, the *pelliparii* were the first craft workers in Barcelona whose organization was shaped according to the needs of an export-oriented economy by the investments of Barcelona's leading families.

By the early thirteenth century the craft world in Barcelona

---

[35] *Santa Anna*, III, no. 609: "Concessit sorori sue Sancie domos suas novas cum operatoriis." This must refer to the property on Skinners Street since it is the only urban property Bernat specifically left to his sister, who later ceded it to her niece.

[36] ACB 3–29–248. In 1213 Guillem de Sant Vicenç was making arrangements for the future distribution of his estate among his sons, Cuadrada, *El Maresme*, 394–95. More significantly, however, the king was searching for credit from all his backers on the eve of the Battle of Muret. On the massive credit operations at the end of Pere I's reign, see Bisson, *Fiscal accounts*, I, 129–33, 149–50; II, no. 136.

[37] ACB 3–29–247, 248. On Pere Moneder's financial operations in these years, see Bisson, *Fiscal accounts*, II, nos. 135, 137, 138; ACB 1–6–2719.

[38] ACB 1–2–1711, 1712.

was flourishing, yet its internal organization revealed widening fissures. Older crafts producing primarily for local consumption, especially shoemakers, smiths, and armorers, consisted primarily of modestly prosperous shop masters, independent men who usually owned their own workshops and marketed their products directly to their customers. With most of their profits going into their own purses, the surge of urban growth after 1140 created a thriving sector of small craftsmen who avoided direct economic dependence on urban entrepreneurs and landlords. The most novel and dynamic elements of Barcelona's craft sector, the transformation of animal skins, and, although on much smaller scale, cloth manufacture and finishing, fell under the domination of land developers and investors.

In neither sector, however, did independent craft associations flourish. The *sabaters* (shoemakers) formed the earliest craft confraternity in 1203, but there is no reason to assume that at this early date its functions were professional and economic rather than social and charitable. First mentioned in the peace and truce statutes promulgated by King Pere I at the Cort of Barcelona in 1200, craft groups did not develop into cohesive corporate bodies in thirteenth-century Barcelona.[39] Significantly the *molers* (millstone hewers) at Montjuïc, pursuing an economic activity closely controlled by the Crown, were the first artisans known to possess formal representatives (*consules*) in order to promote their collective interests.[40] In general, however, the count-kings were suspicious of unauthorized lay collectivities and formally banned confraternities "due to the abuse of the brotherhoods."[41] Only in the fourteenth century did a lush undergrowth of craft associations and lay confraternities provide corporate and convivial settings which would thereafter figure so prominently in the city's social life.[42] In the city's early craft sectors diffuse personal ties of

---

[39] *Cortes*, I.1, 84.

[40] The consuls of the *molers* presented their grievances before the consuls of Barcelona in 1219, Font Rius, "Orígenes del régimen," 545–46, ap. vii.

[41] Mutgé Vives, *La ciudad de Barcelona*, 115. Carme Batlle i Gallart and Montserrat Casas i Nadal, "La caritat privada i les institucions benèfiques de Barcelona (segle XIII)," in *La probreza y la asistencia a los pobres en la Cataluña medieval*, ed. M. Riu (Barcelona, 1980–82), I, 158–59 note the absence of pious bequests to confraternities in thirteenth-century Barcelona and conclude that they were not well organized in the city at the time.

[42] The systematic study of Barcelona's confraternities and craft guilds has hardly begun, but Pierre Bonnassie, *La organización del trabajo en Barcelona a fines del siglo XV* (Bar-

economic and social dependence developed toward customers, landlords, investors, and even to the count-kings and their local officials and financial backers; these tended to stifle the formation of collective associations. As in the case of the armorers or the *pelliparii*, however, economic ties could produce topographic concentration and at least an informal recognition of a common identity among groups of artisans. Yet neither conflicts between artisans and entrepreneurs nor internecine struggles among tightly organized clans were to punctuate the city's thirteenth-century political history. Rather a scramble among leading families ensued to control dispersed resources and multiple, malleable forms of personal allegiance.

Competition for those points where both urban resources and loyalty were concentrated proved particularly intense. Lending provided one powerful instrument to gain access to them.

URBAN CREDIT AND ITS FUNCTION

While burghers had long resorted to credit in order to meet short-term needs and make their coins multiply, lending changed in scale and nature during the twelfth century. It came to promote longer, more complex relationships between creditors and debtors than during the first expansion of credit after the year 1000. Still under the spell of clerical moralists, economic and legal historians often see behind credit contracts ruthless usurers, preying on the desperation of peasants and the poor or, less reprehensibly, catering to the extravagant tastes of lay nobles and comfortably situated monks and canons. If loans did create, or at least exaggerate, economic imbalances among different social groups, this derived from the difficult adjustment to the rise of a money economy. To perpetuate their style of munificence and highly visible consumption, lords sought credit and offered their land in pledge; to help pay the money rents demanded by lords or simply to compensate for a bad harvest, peasants succumbed to financial dependence as well as personal servitude by using their land or labor to secure advances in cash or in produce from lenders.[43] These inequalities

<hr />

celona, 1975) provides a point of departure, although quite late. Some light on the subject has been shed by Mutgé Vives, *La ciudad de Barcelona*, 99–122.

[43] Georges Duby, "Le Budget de l'abbaye de Cluny, 1075–1155: économie domaniale et économie monétaire," *AESC*, 7 (1952), 155–71 [repr. in *Hommes et structures*, 61–82] and *Early growth*, 231–32 asserts that indebtedness among nobles and well-situated clergy represented a continuation of habits of generosity and display typical of the early

Table 5.2 *Credit in urban wills, 1100–1220 (Loans over 1,000s. are not included in the averages)*

	1100–1140	1141–1180	1181–1220
Total number of wills	20	22	47
Number of testators owing money (percent)	4 (20)	3 (14)	15 (32)
Average amount of each debt	32s.	105s.	176s.
Average total debt per will	91s.	176s.	318s.
Number of testators owed money (percent)	8 (40)	8 (36)	25 (53)
Average amount of each credit	68s.	328s.	205s.
Average total credit per will	112s.	697s.	867s.

intensified as money altered the relationships between lord and peasant, between suppliers and consumers. Such a picture of greed, desperation, and opportunity does not, however, adequately convey the role credit played in the burgeoning urban economy. Burghers had quickly learned to marshal credit for financial flexibility by converting rights over property into liquidity, cash which could then be invested in profitable real estate development, commerce, or political influence. Credit in twelfth-century Barcelona above all affected relationships among well-off burghers, not between rich and poor. Besides introducing new forms of economic dependence, credit could also create social interdependence.

Because the Pla de Barcelona was inundated with Islamic gold and silver in the eleventh century, modest freeholders and wealthy investors alike sought to make their coins multiply by renting them out for short periods, rarely for more than a year, at high rates of interest.[44] Credit was therefore widely diffused during the first phase of the city's growth among a broad segment of the urban population and freeholders in Barcelona's hinterland. In

medieval nobility. For the parallels between mortgage and tenure among the peasantry and the economic dependence promoted by credit, Violante, "Les Prêts," 146–68, 437–59; Toubert, *Les Structures*, 608–9; Philip Jones, "From manor to mezzadria: a Tuscan case-study in the medieval origins of modern agrarian society," in *Florentine studies*, ed. N. Rubinstein (Evanston, IL, 1968), 216–17.

[44] Supra, 112–15.

contrast to the specie-starved north, neither large religious houses nor Jews figure prominently in the early development of credit.[45] This pattern carried over, and even intensified, in the twelfth century. As the urban economy diversified and the pace of exchange quickened, townspeople resorted more than ever to credit to turn their resources into new areas of investment. The expansion of credit may best be illustrated through the mention of debts and credits in urban wills.

Two observations should be made in reference to the preceding data in table 5.2. First, the total proportion of wills mentioning loans remained high throughout the period under consideration, although slightly less than for Catalonia in general during the late eleventh century. A notable increase in both debtors and creditors, however, occurred after 1180. Because the testator could pass on outstanding credits to heirs, they tend to outnumber debts, which are frequently subsumed under a formulaic clause to the executor to meet all obligations of the deceased. Second, despite the relative stability of the number of debtors and creditors, the amounts involved jumped after 1140, both in terms of individual trans-actions and of the total level of indebtedness. An intensification of credit operations therefore accompanied the second phase of urban growth. Individuals began to assume multiple loans and were simultaneously creditors and debtors, a rarity in the early twelfth century. Only two of eight testators from 1100 to 1140 refer to holding more than a single instrument of credit, and only Pere Bofill can be shown to have died with more than two men in his debt.[46] By the early thirteenth century, however, prosperous burghers carefully calculated profit and loss in order to determine the moment to assume or cancel debts. With death approaching, Bernat Roig de Sant Cugat left a final earthly balance sheet in his will of 2,800s. of credits owed him and 1,290s. in debts; Guillem Rotger, in twenty-three separate transactions, left 7,730s. in

---

[45] Of eighty-three loan contracts from 1100 to 1180, only 2 percent record Jewish loans to Christians and 3 percent Jewish indebtedness to Christians. For the local clergy, the proportion rises to 8 percent of lenders and 6 percent of creditors, in fact probably a rather high figure since much of the documentation comes from ecclesiastical archives.

For the role of monasteries as credit institutions, the *locus classicus* remains R. Génestal, *Le Rôle des monastères comme établissements de crédit étudié en Normandie du XIe à la fin du XIIIe siècle* (Paris, 1901). For evaluations of clerics and Jews in the rise of credit, see Lopez, *Commercial revolution*, 60–62; Fossier, *Enfance*, II, 797–99; Spufford, *Money and its use*, 212–13.

[46] *Santa Anna*, II, no. 202.

credits and 2,944s. in debts.[47] Although neither man came from a particularly distinguished family, both nevertheless counted patricians among those involved in the lending operations that typify the intensity and dispersion the credit market had attained by 1200.

As the overall volume and amount of individual loans increased, credit mechanisms also underwent a pronounced change. While the amount of money lent and its recovery had constituted the critical elements in loan contracts in the early eleventh century, the exploitation of land offered in pledge came to stand at the heart of the loan around 1100.[48] Once mere collateral offered to secure credit, agricultural property became the source of interest. Visigothic law had sanctioned usury and sought only to limit the amount of interest. Continuing this tradition, Catalan scribes in the eleventh century did not hesitate to mention interest rates openly in terms of currency, usually in the range of 20 to 50 percent *per annum*.[49] After 1050, however, the terms of loan contracts changed. The lender, not the creditor, began to hold the pledge and receive its produce as interest. By 1100 loans generally assumed the form of *mort-gage*, in which the interest from the pledge did not go to extinguish the principal. Contracts did not equivocate about the right of the lender to "enjoy" (*exfructifere*) and "exploit" (*expletere*) his property.[50] While contracts set a minimum period for which the lenders were

---

[47] ACB 4–3–226, 4–8–16. ACB 1–5–35 offers an early example of credits and debts forming an addendum to a testament below the subscriptions, a "settling up" of accounts for the afterlife.

[48] J. de Malafosse, "Contribution à l'étude du crédit dans le Midi aux Xᵉ et XIᵉ siècles: les sûretés réelles," *AM*, 63 (1951), 126 argues that because of the breakdown of traditional legal structures, the lender commonly took possession of the pledge from the debtor in loan contracts in the tenth and early eleventh century in order to ensure repayment. Although the debtor in Catalonia generally kept control of his pledge in the early eleventh century according to Bonnassie, *La Catalogne*, I, 103, public courts could still enforce its surrender in case of non-payment. Even though the management of the pledged property differed somewhat, in both Catalonia and Languedoc the pledge was primarily a means of ensuring repayment in the early eleventh century, not a direct source of profit.

[49] On early Catalan credit, see Bonnassie, *La Catalogne*, I, 399–409; Ruiz Doménec, "Introducción al estudio del crédito," 17–33, who tends to underestimate the distinctive features of Barcelona's credit system by forcing it into models established for other areas.

[50] *Llib. bl.*, no. 45: "impignero tibi et vestris tali modo ut vos vel homo per vos in sana pace habeatis et teneatis et expletetis eandem parialatam terre secure et potenter." "Nouveaux documents des juifs barcelonnais au XIIᵉ siècle," eds. J. Miret i Sans and M. Schwab, *Boletín de la Real Academia de la Historia*, 68 (1916), no. 1: "de nostro iure in tuo tradimus dominio et potestate ut teneas et possideas cum fructibus que inde exierint ... interim tu teneas et possideas et exfructifices per tuum pignus."

entitled to hold their pledge, it became rare for them to demand the right to seize it in case of default: they simply continued to enjoy the use of the pledge.[51] This amounted to a virtual sale of the property offered in surety, while the debtor usually retained only the right to repurchase his gage.

In the late eleventh and early twelfth century credit forms in Barcelona were moving away from short-term, high-interest loans with fixed, monetarized profits to a system of long-term, perpetually renewable mortgages in which interest derived from the exploitation of agricultural land. In other words, the need for rapid liquidity declined as lenders tried to assume the management of their pledges. This hardly argues for a rapid commercialization of the urban economy. Despite their security, mortgages of agricultural property did not offer the lender a fixed term for repayment and a calculable rate of interest, a precision and predictability greatly valued in a thoroughly monetarized economy. Indeed, the abandonment of the creditor's claim to seize the pledge in case of default occurred during the monetary confusion of the late eleventh century.[52] Unless a lender could expect to receive his capital and interest in coins of comparable value to those he had lent, his investment was threatened. Owing to the uncertainties about coinage and equivalences in the decades around 1100, this calculation proved particularly uncertain, reflecting an uneasiness among investors about the abstract reckoning required to convert the value of land and agricultural surpluses into monetary sums. As a result credit moved toward a form of landlordship rather than evolving into a tool of rapid capital formation in the early twelfth century. This did not deny lending its profitability, merely its liquidity and flexibility.

Because the market value of property involved in credit transactions considerably exceeded its value in pledge, lending provided a cheaper means of acquiring rights to it than outright purchase.[53] But what precisely did the right to "exploit" and

---

[51] The most common date of redemption was the feast of Sant Miquel in September, late enough to allow for the crops to be harvested for the creditor's benefit.

[52] Supra, 102–4.

[53] The exact ratio between market and pledge value is difficult to determine for the period since it was very unusual for a debtor to sell the full title on property he had pledged. In 1135, however, houses near the cathedral, significantly urban not agricultural property, were pledged for 46 mbts. and sold three months later for 80 mbts., ACB 1–1–327, 1–5–97. This is in keeping with the ratio of two-thirds found at Saint-Riquier in Flanders by H. van Werveke, "Le Mort-gage et son rôle économique en Flandre et en Lotharingie," *Revue belge de philologie et d'histoire*, 8 (1929), 79 and in Normandy by

"enjoy" the property entail? In a few instances, the obligations of each party were clearly articulated. When Adalbert Donuç pledged a vineyard near Barcelona on February 28, 1106 to Ramon Domènec for a loan of 3 mbts., he agreed to cede half his rent (*directum*) to the lender until Christmas, when repayment was technically required, but after that they were to split the harvest (*fructus*), a shared division of profits that appears in another loan contract in 1139.[54] Most credit instruments, however, do not include such specific terms about the use of the pledge and allowed the creditor to work the land as he pleased at his own expense. In a late and unusually large loan, the royal seneschal Guillem Ramon de Montcada pledged half his ancestral castle with its domains to Berenguer de Soler, who received permission to employ or dismiss the seneschal's bailiff as he saw fit.[55] Despite its unusual nature, this last example nevertheless vividly illustrates that a pledge consisted of a cohesive unit of rights and dominion which even the seneschal had to transfer in order to satisfy his creditor. To make his loan productive, the pledgeholder generally had to secure labor to work the property if it were allodial, invest in seed or irrigation, arrange transport for the produce, and market it himself.[56] The investor had to do much more than watch his interest accrue in a passbook. Such a system clearly promoted a lengthy commitment of liquid capital and an enduring relationship between creditor and debtor. Even though the latter could, of course, repay the debt and recover his pledge, few chose to do so quickly in the early twelfth century. Clauses occasionally ensured that the creditor would be allowed to hold the pledge for a minimum period, sometimes for as long as ten years,[57] while the claim of redemption held by the debtor was extended indefinitely. Since virtually all burghers involved in credit operations possessed at least a modest amount of property, credit tended to link them in

---

Génestal, *Le Rôle des monastères*, 59–60; it is considerably higher than the ratio found in the Midi by Malafosse, "Contribution à l'étude du crédit," 112, n. 30.

[54] ACB 1–1–2249; ACA perg. R.B. IV, 100.

[55] AHCB perg., Carp. 1, unnumb. parch. [29 v 1212]: "Tali pacto ut hoc pignus teneas et expletes tu et quecumque persona velis accipiendo ibi omnia nostra iura et consuetudines donec leves inde .i. expletum grossum et integrum et deinde donec redimatur ... et fructus non computentur in sortem et baiulus qui ibi est sit ibi per te et sit tibi fidelis in omnibus tamen si tu volueris ibi mittere alium baiulum sit tibi licitum."

[56] An unusual contract in 1134 specified that creditor and lender were to split the revenues from the pledge, but if the debtor failed to work his plot he would lose title to it, ACB 1–5–96. Often the debtor was a landlord who had tenants or others work the plot.

[57] ACB 1–1–884, 1–5–313; ACA perg. R.B. IV, 100, 104; *Llib. bl.*, no. 55.

a long-term economic relationship that marked them off as the most dynamic element in urban society.

While mortgaging of agricultural property certainly continued after the early twelfth century, other forms of credit superseded it. As loan agreements began to change their nature, they made raising and transferring capital swifter and more flexible to meet the demands of an expanding exchange sector. The most significant modifications, although not technically novel, can be reduced to three elements: (a) pledging urban property with a fixed rent; (b) discounting and transferring credit instruments; and (c) spreading profits and obligations among a broader group of lenders and creditors. Whenever leaseholders of urban houses or properties paid a fixed annual rent (*census*), usually in cash but occasionally in grain, pepper or wax,[58] it provided a stable, easily calculable rate of return for the lender without requiring further direct investment to make the pledge profitable. Population pressures and increasing security for property owners, especially their insistence on profiting from the transfer of rights held by their tenants, significantly increased the profits of urban landlordship after 1140.[59] Land and buildings in the city and suburbs gradually became covered with layers of rights and obligations, each of which could serve as a pledge. To obtain two loans in 1201, Joan de Canals separately offered the *census* on his suburban property and then its *logerium*, apparently a subtle distinction between ground lease and building rental.[60] By taking out loans from several creditors and offering to each only a portion of the property's potential value in pledge, one could in effect divide up rights over land and buildings into smaller portions in order to obtain credit without losing title to the entire asset,[61] a system particularly suited to urban lots and buildings with their precise monetary rents. Unlike agricultural mortgages, urban property and rents did not have to be treated as a cohesive unit of exploitation since they did not require further investments in seed or labor to bring a profit. The debtor could therefore let others make use of his assets bit by bit.

Pledging urban properties and their rents made interest pre-

[58] Examples of non-monetary payments, rare after 1140, can be found in Arxiu de Montserrat, perg. Sant Benet de Bages, 1624; ACB LA I, fol. 112, Mas X, no. 1181; LA I, fol. 229, Mas XI, no. 1595.

[59] On the evolution of urban landlordship, infra 304–13.

[60] ACB I–6–2, 3 (another copy is found in I–6–407).

[61] E.g. ACB I–2–1007; I–5–234; ACA perg. Alfons I, 287.

dictable, but recovery of the principal, a substantial amount of capital, remained dependent on the initiative of the debtor, not the creditor. To release funds for other investments, lenders began to transfer their rights, memorialized in loan contracts, to third parties and to spread profits and risks among colenders and guarantors. Here we enter a murky netherworld of discounted, joint, and subsidiary loans. In these perplexing transactions, the parchment records of debt passing from hand to hand raise more questions than the terse legal clauses of the documents answer. Why, for instance, did Ermessenda sell her share of a brother's inheritance consisting of a pledge of 170 mbts. for only 10 mbts. in 1132?[62] How much did Guillem Genovès receive in 1228 after transferring six pledges, some over ten years old, to Ramon Boquer?[63] Precisely calculating the value of the parchment record of debt required some idea of when the debtor intended to redeem his or her rights; an evaluation of intent, involving the use of an intricate social calculus, entered into the economic equation in ways that escape detection in the abbreviated references to the transfer of credit instruments. In a similar fashion loans involving multiple lenders demanded a tacit understanding among the parties themselves about the degree of individual liability and the distribution of interest, critical elements in the transaction that lay concealed beneath notarial formulas. Occasionally one of the multiple lenders would formally transfer his or her rights to a partner by sale or pledge,[64] yet in most instances the precise arrangements took the form of a gentleman's agreement. The obligations of the debtor could also be spread among a wider circle through the involvement of guarantors, called *fideiussores* or *plevi datores*. In Roman law a *fideiussor* provided a personal surety to make the principal debtor meet his or her obligations.[65] While the addition of guarantors obviously provided added security to the lender, particularly when the loans were large, *fideiussores* in some instances repaid all or part of the loan even though the

[62] ACB 1–5–92.
[63] ACB 1–6–1155. The valuation of the transferred loans is here presented in quite uncertain terms: "Ante siquidem numeracionem dicte peccunie et dictorum instrumentorum redditionem feci tibi hanc concessionem et postea numerasti mihi dictam pecuniam."
[64] ACA perg. R.B. IV, 195; ACB 1–5–42; 1–6–408.
[65] *Corpus iuris civilis*, eds. T. Mommsen, P. Krüger, R. Schöll, and W. Kröll (4th ed., Berlin, 1912–20), Inst. 3, 20; Dig. 27, 7.

principal debtor remained solvent.[66] One suspects they did so for a profit. If arrangements among debtors and their backers extended beyond providing mere surety, *fideiussores* in effect acted as sublenders and provided another means of shifting obligations and assets among borrowers. As the pledging of urban rents, joint lending, and the use of *fideiussores* gained currency in the later twelfth century, lending operations moved away from long-term mortgages secured on rural property, in fact a form of lordship, and toward more flexible forms of raising, concentrating, and investing liquid assets. Many aspects of Barcelona's credit market, however, still depended upon rather informal arrangements and shared expectations among lenders, borrowers, and their backers. Loans circulated with increasing ease and rapidity among a wide circle of prosperous burghers; it was not an activity as yet dominated by professional moneylenders or merchant-bankers, who began to monopolize the credit markets of northern Italian towns by the late twelfth century. In Barcelona credit operations still retained the features of an insiders' game played by a group of wealthy families.

The Church's opposition to usury often bears the blame for the opacity of medieval loan contracts, but attitudes propagated by learned theologians and canonists had little effect on the entrenched, broadly supported credit operations in Barcelona until the anti-Albigensian crusaders from the North imposed a rigid orthodoxy on Occitania and the Fourth Lateran Council of 1215 launched an offensive against the profits from lending.[67] Before a full-scale clerical campaign against usury was unleashed, Catalan lenders did not display the slightest qualm about openly declaring interest, a testimony to the vigorous lay society of the South. The complexity of the operations outlined above suited the needs of entrepreneurs, not the minimum requirements of proper behavior established by canon law. Defying increasing clerical pressure, Arnau Adarró in 1214 boldly demanded his interest regardless of any papal prohibitions.[68]

---

[66] ACB 1–1–252: ".cxviii. s. quos persoluisti pro illis firmanciis quas tu Iohanna predicta fecisti per nos." Cf. ACB 1–6–2719.

[67] On early theological discussions about usury and the background to the Fourth Lateran's campaign, see John W. Baldwin, *Masters, princes, and merchants: the social views of Peter Chanter and his circle* (Princeton, 1970), I, 296–311; Jean Ibanès, *La Doctrine de l'Eglise et les réalités économiques au XIIIe siècle* (Paris, 1967), 14–20.

[68] ACB 1–6–1044: "Predictum itaque ortum ... tu et tui deinceps pro vestro proprio pignore teneatis habeatis possideatis et expletetis secure et potenter sine dimunitione non

Protest against the ecclesiastical crackdown on usury among Barcelona's entrepreneurs and patricians, however, quickly gave way to skilled concealment. By 1220 scribes had deleted from their formulas all open references to usury, unless Jews were involved, and to the lender's "enjoyment" or "use" of the pledge; yet they also inserted a new clause allowing the creditor to lay claim against all the debtor's assets in case of default. At least in the notarial formulas the pledge had reverted from a source of profit to a general security.

With the regular functioning of vicarial courts an efficient legal apparatus existed to enforce these general obligations, yet the formal requirements of the charters often obscured the true nature of the credit transaction. Interest was simply driven underground. Through fictitious sales, "improvements" to the lender's property, and outright deception, creditors still drew profits from the manipulation of property rights. Demand for money remained strong. In contracts openly mentioning interest before 1220, loans secured only by a risky general claim against the debtor's property could bring a 25 to 50 percent annual rate of return, whereas the mortgaging of rents and property brought in less than 15 percent because of the added security provided by the creditor's direct control of the pledge. Even if subterfuges occasionally allowed the usufruct from property to pass to the lender, the shift to a general pledge without requiring the debtor to give up the use of his or her property may have made lending less secure and more costly.[69] When King Jaume I in 1235 fixed the rate of interest for Jewish lenders at 20 percent and for Christian lenders at 12 percent, he may have tried to shore up confidence in a credit system disturbed by new forms of lending and soaring demand.[70] If the creditor no longer controlled the pledge, return of the principal (with whatever form of interest) at an agreed upon time again moved to the center of the loan agreement, an obligation dependent upon trust and personal guarantors, the *fideiussores*, as

---

in sorte debiti set in gaudita computando fructus istius pignoris non in hoc obstante iure vel precepto quod sit factum vel faciendum a domino papa et omni alio iure divino et humano."

[69] Ten loans secured on a general pledge openly mention interest rates between 1196 and 1215; six lenders were Jews, and four Christians: ACB 1–1–18; 1–5–371; 1–6–501, 788, 893, 2346, 3076, 3191, 3263, 3307, 7022. Two examples of interest on mortgages (1150, 1158) set rates at 13 percent and 15 percent, but one example from 1201 indicates a 23 percent return; ACB 1–1–2142; 1–6–2; LA I, fol. 374, Mas XI, no. 1786.

[70] *Cortes*, I.1, 126, 131.

well as on personal legal obligations. Although instituted at least partially in reaction to clerical hostility toward usury, the new contractual devices in fact reinforced the tendency already apparent to limit the length of the loan so that the creditor could quickly become liquid and invest in other activities. The campaign against usury did not disrupt credit mechanisms nor the many monetary transactions engaged in by patrician families, but it may well have increased the velocity of lending.

The demand for credit certainly did not slacken as a result of articulate and vehement clerical opposition to usury and the contractual alterations it provoked. In the opening decades of the thirteenth century there was a new urgency about raising capital through loans in order to meet the expanding scale of investments in commerce, suburban real estate, and royal and baronial finance. Even though lending was deeply ingrained among the city's leading families and still promoted economic cooperation, the bustling, speculative environment emerging around 1200 shifted the emphasis in credit operations to raising cash rapidly and efficiently, seeking out new financial ties, and liquidating obligations quickly in order to move on to other enterprises. The advantages of borrowing and lending were increasingly determined by immediate financial calculation rather than more subtle, slowly maturing investments in agriculture and social influence. This transformation depended on the function as well as the technical nature of loan contracts. It can best be summed up by the way in which one patrician family, the Adarró, adeptly managed credit over four generations.

Arnau Adarró (d. 1164), the founder of the house, first turns up holding a modest pledge of 6 mbts. from Pere Bofill in 1128.[71] During his lifetime Arnau judiciously employed his assets in credit transactions to secure not only the benefits of agricultural property but also the patronage of lords who could later reward him with offices and urban utilities. His will reveals a small but carefully managed patrimony consisting of a garden and houses at Torrent Profond, the well-irrigated zone just beyond the eastern suburbs, two vineyards, one jointly owned with his son-in-law, and his home, a solid building with a tower held from Sant Pere de les Puel·les, and other unspecified holdings, assets supplemented by a field at Albadon in the *territorium*, another property held in

---

[71] *Santa Anna*, II, no. 202.

pledge for 25 mbts., and a debt owed by the abbess of Sant Pere, secured on church ornaments.[72] Association with Barcelona's oldest nunnery, in part cultivated with a loan, proved valuable and enduring. Choosing Sant Pere as his final resting place, Arnau released the abbess from half her obligations on the loan immediately and promised the other half would be cancelled upon the death of his wife. But this bequest did not dissolve mutual obligations. Arnau held a valuable urban oven from the nunnery, which later granted Joan Mateu, Arnau's son-in-law, the right to operate it.[73] When Berenguer Adarró, great-great-grandson of Arnau Adarró, served as bailiff for Sant Pere's properties in the 1260s, his office reaffirmed a long-standing and lucrative association with the monastic community.[74] Credit had not only permitted an early patrician to round out his holdings and increase his profits, it also formed part of the ties his family would maintain with Sant Pere for generations.

Loans to the counts secured even more lucrative forms of patronage. In the emergency loan of 7,700s. to Ramon Berenguer IV during the siege of Tortosa in 1148, Arnau Adarró and his son-in-law together offered 660s.; seven years later Arnau offered to his lord 100 mbts., this time secured on tribute (*parias*) the count expected to receive from al-Andalus.[75] Credit in this context was actually speculation on the political and military success of the dynasty. Because of its loyalty and financial backing, the family gained control of the *amostolafia*, the right to transport redeemed Saracen captives back to their homeland. In 1184 King Alfons I confirmed this privilege, which extended over all his lands above Tarragona, to Bernat Marcús and Bernat Adarró, the grandson of Arnau who may himself have already held this right.[76] The partnership in this lucrative monopoly was strengthened when Bernat Adarró assumed four loans on behalf of Bernat Marcús just months after receiving the royal confirmation; since two of the loans involved the Islamic gold mazmudin, there can be little doubt that they constituted some form of commercial invest-

[72] ACB 4–1–70.
[73] ASPP, 98. Pere Adarró, Arnau Adarró's son, bought up property next to the oven, ACB 1–5–183; LA I, fol. 290, Mas x, no. 1855.
[74] ASPP, 317, 325.   [75] Bisson, *Fiscal accounts*, II, no. 143; ACB 1–5–150.
[76] ACB 1–2–140. Arnau Adarró's will in 1164 left any captives he held to his heirs, an indication of the family's activity in transporting captives long before receiving the privilege of 1184, ACB 4–1–70.

ment.[77] While the early members of the Adarró house employed
credit with skill and regularity, their profits derived as much from
the enduring economic involvement between lenders and creditors as from the quick, cold collection of interest. With its long-
term contractual obligations, credit helped stabilize economic
relationships in the mid-twelfth century and promoted interdependence among emerging patrician families.

In response to demands for larger loans and a rapid transfer of
capital, Arnau Adarró (d. c. 1244) employed credit quite differently
from his father, Bernat. A flurry of financial operations from
1214 to 1222 permitted Arnau to juggle assets and obligations to
play at the high stakes of baronial finance. During these years he
acted as guarantor to several credit transactions, sought release
from his obligation as *fideiussor* in others, sold property to pay off
debts inherited from his father, and assumed several new loans,
one of which he then offered to his business partner, Pere Grony.
In order to free himself from family encumbrances on his business
dealings, Arnau agreed to partition his father's estate with his
brother Bernat in 1217. The lion's share of the family holdings,
including an oven and the right to exploit the canons' Sea Mills,
passed to Arnau since he had redeemed them with his own money
from loans totalling 6,648s. and 712 mazmudins.[78] Even though
the property had technically belonged to the brothers jointly, for
Arnau, the more dynamic of the two, the need to move capital
swiftly among numerous enterprises took precedence over fraternal bonds. His most lucrative investments included loans to
Guillem de Cervelló, a prominent noble and financier to the king,
and to Guillem de Montcada. In 1218 Arnau provided 600s. to
Guillem de Cervelló, in part to refinance an earlier loan of 1,400s.
he had made together with Pere Grony.[79] The rewards compen-

[77] Arnau de Merola and Ponç d'Alest each lent Bernat Adarró 100 mazmudins, a double
morabetin, ACB 1-1-334. Several other references to mazmudins in the early thirteenth
century point to the family's heavy involvement in North African trade: ACB 1-1-328;
1-6-140, 2977, 3002, 3060; Maria Teresa Ferrer i Mallol and Arcardi Garcia i Sanz,
Assegurances i canvis marítims medievals a Barcelona (Barcelona, 1983), I, no. 6.
[78] ACB 1-6-4151: "Preterea est sciendum quod tu [Arnaldus] de tuo proprio redemisti
predictum honorem." Bernat received 1,000s. for renouncing his rights to the property.
[79] ACB 1-6-4159. According to Guillem de Cervelló's testament in 1226, the count-king
owed him 2,000 *auris* and 8,000s., while Guillem de Montcada owed him 2,000 mbts.,
Els Castells, I, 365-66. Cf. Thomas N. Bisson, "Las finanzas del joven Jaime I (1213-28),"
X CHCA (Zaragoza, 1980-82), I, 207-8 [repr. in English, "The finances of the young
James I (1213-28)," in *Medieval France*, 390-91, no. 12], which refers to an additional
8,000s. Guillem de Montcada owed to Guillem de Cervelló, who was to recover the
amount from royal property that he commanded.

sated him for the risks involved, for Arnau and his partner were to receive the revenues from the market of Granada in the Vallès until the principal was returned. Through credit aggressive urban entrepreneurs such as Arnau Adarró gained access to utilities and revenues from the exchange sector, rights still largely controlled by lords in the decades around 1200. Lending had not only changed its scale but also its function. Durable economic relationships created by long-term pledges of agricultural land gradually eroded in a new speculative environment promoted by economic expansion and baronial finance. Even though merchant-bankers and stable, large-scale companies still lay in the future, by the early thirteenth century the malleability of credit allowed Barcelona's wealthy investors to participate in financial and commercial operations on a scale hitherto unknown.

ROYAL FINANCE AND URBAN LORDSHIP

The most novel feature in the city's credit market, however, derived not from trade but from the demands of the count-king and his magnates.[80] In order to support dynastic ambitions in Occitania, Count Ramon Berenguer IV and King Alfons I resorted to loans from military orders, churches, barons, and Montpellier financiers, who received pledges primarily on tribute, tolls, and the domains of New Catalonia. What had been a means of meeting extraordinary expenses expanded under King Pere I into a form of administration. As long as the count-king and his baronial backers employed assets to secure credit with the expectation of quick repayment, the administrative and political repercussions were limited. When Ramon Berenguer IV pledged his principal urban resources in 1148 for an emergency war loan, the creditors evidently recovered their money quickly; consequently, they did not enjoy the right to exploit comital mills and assets for long if at all. The huge loans assumed by Pere I had quite different consequences. To support such heavy indebtedness, roughly 126 times as great after 1200 as during the early years of his reign, substantial portions of the fisc were ceded to creditors without

---

[80] For the impact of credit on administration, see Bisson, *Fiscal accounts*, I, 59, 79–86, 129–42 and "The finances of the young Jaume I," passim. General background to these reigns can be found in E. Bagué, J. Cabestany, and Percy E. Schramm, *Els primers comtes-reis* (Barcelona, 1960); Jordi Ventura, *Alfons el 'Cast'* (Barcelona, 1961) and *Pere el Catòlic i Simó de Montfort* (Barcelona, 1960); Ferran Soldevila, *Els primers temps de Jaume I* (Barcelona, 1968).

direct supervision. Pledges of royal lands and rights functioned in the manner of administrative appanages. An energetic, bold, and self-confident ruler, Pere seemed capable to contemporaries of pulling off his ambitious gamble of pawning assets at home to support political and military expansion abroad, an expectation seemingly confirmed after his prominent role in the victory against the Moors at Las Navas de Tolosa in 1212. But his ambitions and his life were soon cut short. At the Battle of Muret in 1213 the crusade unleashed against the Albigensian heretics thwarted his attempt to establish a Catalan protectorate over Languedoc, a dream his father and grandfather had shared, and left Pere dead on the battlefield. The military debacle placed a child of five on the throne and left royal finances in shambles. The commission of the Templars to act as general accountants for both Aragon and Catalonia in 1220 helped restore direct administrative control over the domain, and the young king under the guidance of his advisors slowly and painstakingly recovered the rights and revenues his father had ceded in pledge. For a generation, however, credit had provided the means to secure access to valuable elements of the domain for those able to play at the dizzying game of royal and baronial finance.

Over a dozen Barcelona families had the resources and the connections to provide the large sums needed by the king and his barons.[81] The period from 1190 to 1220 marked a new era in urban credit, for until then urban lending was a local operation, rarely involving aristocrats or the count-kings. The extraordinary collective loan in 1148 for the siege of Tortosa had no immediate sequel, and the amount seems paltry in comparison to the substantial credit transactions fifty years later.

As presented in table 5.3, the amounts of individual loans recorded in credit contracts grew slowly larger toward the mid-twelfth century, but the most notable feature is the number of extremely large loans contracted after 1180. Only 4.6 percent (4 of 87) of loan contracts between 1100 and 1180 involved amounts in excess of 1,000 ternal solidi, but between 1181 and 1200 the

---

[81] Alest (ACA perg. Alfons I, 644, 688); Bou (ACA perg. Alfons I, 691; perg. Pere I, 15); Dionís (ACA perg. Alfons I, 644); Durfort (ACB 1–6–3013; ACA perg. Pere I, 86, etc.); Ermengol (ACB LA II, fol. 108, Mas XII, no. 2287); d'Espiells (ACA perg. Alfons I, 643; ACB 1–5–354, etc.); Genovès (ACB 1–6–3013); Grony (ACB 1–5–350); Moneder (ACA perg. Pere I, 293); Roig (ACB 1–5–324, 4–3–226); Rotger (ACB 4–8–16); Soler (AHCB perg., Carp. 1, unnumb. parch. [25 v 1212]), Titó (ACA perg. Pere I, 73); Viladecols (Bisson, *Fiscal accounts*, II, no. 130).

Table 5.3 *Amounts of loans involving townsmen, 1100–1220*

	1100–1120	1121–1140	1141–1160	1161–1180	1181–1200	1201–1220
100s. or less	8	6	8	9	10	21
101s.–250s.	3	8	8	9	3	20
251s.–500s.	2	3	5	4	8	10
501s.–750s.	0	1	4	2	7	8
751s.–1000s.	0	0	2	1	3	4
over 1000s.	1	1	1	1	10	11
Totals	14	19	28	26	41	74

proportion jumped to 18.3 percent (21 of 115); virtually all large loans involved the count-king or leading nobles at his court.

The pressures created by such large credit operations galvanized Barcelona's financiers into a potent political force. For the first time urban lenders obtained the right to exploit castles and their dependencies offered in pledge by barons.[82] Anxious to gain access to aristocratic circles and the influence it could bring at the court of the count-king, Barcelona's notables strained their resources to the limit in order to satisfy the barons' demands. Not long after lending 4,000s. to Guillem de Cervelló and receiving the castle of Gelida in pledge, Berenguer Bou offered himself as *fideiussor* so that Guillem de Cervelló could secure two other loans of 6,000s. each; by 1200 Berenguer Bou had to pledge his property to secure a substantial loan for himself and his business partners.[83] In return for his financial backing, Berenguer Bou and his peers expected not only interest but access to local administration, prestigious association with baronial enterprises, and ultimately a share in the future of the ambitious count-kings. Even though few burghers lent directly to their sovereign, many urban notables did stand behind the barons at court, a testimony to the growing wealth and economic potential of Barcelona in the decades after 1200. Although we can only dimly perceive urban financiers maneuvering backstage at the court of Pere and the young Jaume, their money had no small part to play in orchestrating the exhilarating expansionism during both reigns.

[82] ACA perg. Alfons I, 643, 644, 688; perg. Pere I, 15, 77; ACB 4–8–16; AHCB perg., Carp. 1, unnumb. parch. [29 v 1212].
[83] ACA perg. Pere I, 15, 77, 86. Cf. ACA perg. Alfons I, 698.

Coordinating the complex financial operations of King Pere I was an astute entrepreneur from Barcelona, Guillem Durfort. Rising in the 1190s as a young man to supervise royal accounts during the last years of King Alfons I, Guillem Durfort became the court's chief auditor; assuming the title *procurator domini regis* by 1203, he was entrusted by King Pere I with the financial administration of Catalonia.[84] As the urgent need for credit overwhelmed the task of regular fiscal administration from 1204 to 1213, entire bailiwicks, vicariates, and castellanies were given out as personal benefices to creditors. Even though assigning future revenues to meet current expenses had long formed an integral part of administration in Catalonia, the vast new scale of credit encouraged the pledging of substantial portions of the domain for the foreseeable future to satisfy baronial financiers. Yet the evident dangers of this policy became fully apparent only after Pere's disastrous defeat at Muret. Under the regency council of the child-king Jaume, the barons cashed in their chips. For their outstanding loans Guillem de Montcada gained control of virtually all the lowland domains from Tortosa to Rosselló, Guillem de Cervera secured the revenues to Montpellier, and other nobles were assigned royal castles, public rights, and jurisdictional enclaves.[85] Because Catalan magnates cast such a long shadow over the early years of Jaume I's reign, the rule of his father appears reckless in retrospect. That the financial policies of Pere I did not seem unsound to his subjects before 1213 was largely the work of Guillem Durfort. Until his death, Guillem Durfort proved a financial wizard able to contain the damage from the Crown's huge deficit. Personally assigning bailiwicks, meticulously overseeing accounts, and skillfully employing extraordinary revenues, Pere's chief financier juggled available assets to keep royal credit viable and prevent the domain from falling under direct control of the magnates. Guillem Durfort often had to provide immediate credit from his own money chest: by 1212, the king admitted owing him debts totalling 60,000s.[86]

---

[84] For a discussion of Guillem Durfort's administrative work and the financial pressures that made it so valued, see Bisson, *Fiscal accounts*, I, 142–43, 148–50.

[85] Bisson, "The finances," 354–57; Soldevila, *Els primers temps*, 103–21; Shideler, *A medieval Catalan noble family*, 139–43, 147–50.

[86] ACB 4–82–60: "tamdiu donec de hiis que modo exierint et provenerint recuperaveris et habueris tu vel ille quem mandaveris verbo vel scripto .lx. milia s. de bona moneta barchinonensi bone legis quatuor denariorum et ponderis decem et octo solidorum que tibi debemus."

Speculation on the rosy future of ambitious, bold, and talented rulers brought substantial rewards in the form of access to urban utilities and the right to develop strategic elements of the domain. From King Alfons I Guillem Durfort received a substantial farm near the suburban village of Provençals and the opportunity to purchase 40 percent of the urban meat market; King Pere added a license to construct and operate two new suburban ovens, another oven and the fish market near the royal shipyards, and his two shares in the public baths, Banys Nous, after Guillem Durfort had purchased the third part from their Jewish proprietor.[87] Interest for such massive loans therefore took the form of the cession of bits of lordship, the right to demand payments from burghers or to operate urban utilities, which were critical points of control over the local economy. Like rural lords, Guillem Durfort and other Barcelona notables sought to tap the growing wealth of their society through banal exactions; in the end money lent the count-king proved a surer means of obtaining urban lordship than violent, arbitrary oppression of burghers or open defiance of the city's lord.

Yet Guillem Durfort did not restrict his interests to Barcelona. From as early as 1207 he held the royal castellany of Cotlliure, a valuable passage on both land and sea routes between Rosselló and the Catalan counties further south, already worth 2,000s. annually.[88] It can hardly be coincidental that in the same year King Pere granted a charter of franchise to the town's inhabitants, confirming its weekly market, instituting a fair, and ordering that the main road across the Pyrenees with its tolls be moved from Clusa in order to pass through Cotlliure and Banyuls.[89] While the charter of franchise speaks of promoting public order and instituting good customs (*multum expedit reipublice ... et bonis consuetudinibus invitare*), there can be little doubt that the new privileges worked for the benefit of Pere's finance minister since Guillem Durfort intended to exploit his pledge as a private lordship. In 1212 the king confirmed an earlier privilege allowing Guillem Durfort and his descendants to hold the castellany of Cotlliure, half its income on land and sea, half of Banyuls, and the sole right to construct baths, ovens, and windmills in Cotlliure until he had

[87] ACA perg. Alfons I, 641; Reial Patrimoni, Batllia General, Classe 3ª, vol. 6, fols. 100 r., 104 r.–v., 109 r.–110 r.; *Santa Anna*, III, no. 582; *VL*, XVIII, ap. vii.
[88] Bisson, *Fiscal accounts*, II, no. 120.   [89] Font Rius, *Cartas de población*, I:1, no. 223.

recovered his 60,000s. debt.[90] This amounted to a de facto alienation in all but word. Although Guillem Durfort's daughter
eventually sold the property in 1218 to Nunyo Sanç, count of
Rosselló, Conflent, and Cerdanya, through a complex agreement
with the purchaser she obtained the *vila* of Sant Feliu de Llobregat, itself part of the fisc, in pledge: this formed the basis of the
family's later claims to control a valuable estate in the Baix
Llobregat.[91] Through his financial leverage at court Guillem
Durfort sought not only to pry loose fragments of lordship in
Barcelona from the grasp of his sovereign but also to create a
small, cohesive seigniory at Cotlliure that would have tapped into
the riches flowing along the main commercial artery between
eastern Iberia and Occitania. Royal credit was gradually transferring lordship and administrative authority into new hands.

The slow, piecemeal, but marked shift in local power to Barcelona's financiers did not result from the corporate political
assertion of the *prohoms* as community representatives but from
the opportunistic appropriation of the right to control and exploit
ovens, mills, tolls, and taxes. Guillem Durfort catapulted to the
upper reaches of urban society, but he was no civic firebrand. His
interests in Rosselló reveal a man shrewdly diverting the general
movement of economic expansion for his own benefit whenever
the chance presented itself, not an urban leader patriotically intent
upon securing liberties for his town. He and his associates had too
much to gain from exercising powers conceded them by their
lord. Yet financial collaboration with the count-kings proved no
less effective in bringing about a transfer of rights and privileges to
urban notables than an open challenge to royal authority. Indeed,
the delegation of fiscal prerogatives to relieve financial pressures,
so typical of Mediterranean administrative traditions, allowed for
the creation of a new balance between urban wealth and political
authority in a manner quite different from the open antagonism

90 ACB 4-82-60: "confirmamus tibi et omnibus heredibus et successoribus tuis in perpe-
tuum donationem quam tibi fecimus de castalania castri et ville de Caucolibero et de
medietate omnium exitium reddituum proventuum expeletorum et obventionum
eiusdem castri et ville ac terminorum suorum de terra et de mari et de medietate etiam
totius ville de Baniuls et de eo scilicet quod tibi et tuis dedimus et concessimus licenciam
atque posse faciendi in Caucolibero balnea et furnos et molendina venti que omni nobis
non licet ibi facere ficti ullo modo."

91 ACB 4-82-109. Proprietary title to the estate passed to the Durfort through an
exchange with the king in 1243, ACB 4-82-1. For the subsequent history of the
property, see David Guasch i Dalmau, *Els Durforts, senyors de Baix Llobregat al segle XIII.
Quaderns d'estudis santjustencs,* 1 (Barcelona, 1984), 24-25.

pitting burghers against their lords in Northern Europe. In Barcelona the transfer of administrative authority and local privileges took place quietly and discreetly through credit negotiations at the houses of urban financiers rather than through seditious plots hatched in the dark corners of churches or tumultuous street demonstrations.

Guillem Durfort played such a pivotal role in fiscal administration and in reshaping urban power because he forged a link between an emerging group of wealthy Barcelona entrepreneurs and the royal court. Owing to his ability to funnel urban wealth to the count-kings and their magnates, Guillem pulled his kinsmen and associates into urban administration and gave them access to valuable urban resources. His family background may have already provided him with an introduction to baronial circles. Although a precise genealogical tree can not be recreated with any precision from the available documentation, its roots nevertheless appear extensive and tangled. The founder of the house may well be an individual named Durfort mentioned in the will of his father Guillem Ramon, *castlà* of Vacarisses.[92] Because the castle formed the linchpin of the Montcada estates in the western Vallès, it is tempting to posit an early association between one of the most powerful Catalan baronial houses, which supplied a line of seneschals to the counts of Barcelona, and an ambitious, talented, but underendowed line of petty nobles who served it. If the connection is valid, it would help explain in part why the Durfort had gained considerable prestige in Barcelona before

---

[92] ACA Monacals, perg. Sant Llorenç del Munt, Carp. 3, 264: "Et dimito ad Durfort et ad Arnaldus filiis meis ipsum nostrum alodium de Terracia que ibi abeo vel habere debeo simul cum ipso fevo de Bonastro et per supradictum fevum fiant homines de suprascriptus Raimundus et guadent ipsum kastrum de Vaccheriches sicut resonat in conveniencia Raimundi Guilelmi et Durfort et Arnallus." Durfort and Arnau de Vacarisses subscribed to a document involving the senescal Guillem Ramon de Montcada in 1147; ACA Monacals, perg. Sant Llorenç del Munt, Carp. 3, 281. On the importance of Vacarisses in the Montcada patrimony, see *Els castells*, II, 161–63; Shideler, *A medieval Catalan noble family*, 44–45, 52–56.

The name Durfort is unusual in Catalonia, and the family's early history has given rise to a number of theories. Guasch i Dalmau, *Els Durforts*, 21–22 associates the family with the castle of Durfort near the monastery of La Grasse in Languedoc, yet there is no documentary association of the Barcelona Durfort with the region. The place name also refers to a village in Anoia documented by 1130 (*Santa Maria de Solsona*, no. 43), which has led Batlle i Gallart, "La burguesía," 8, to conclude that the family came from the village. Ruiz Doménec, "Système de parenté," 318–19 schematically notes without reference that the father of Pere and Guillem Durfort was Pere de Terrassa, but I am unaware of the connection.

they became important urban propertyholders as well as their early interest in the Vallès and Montcada affairs generally.[93] An enigmatic reference exists to Ramon Durfort commanding two galleys at Barcelona for Guillem Ramon de Montcada in 1150, and in the 1160s Ponç Durfort served as the commander of the Hospitaller house in Barcelona, surely a respectable post for the member of a well-connected family without a substantial patrimony.[94] Whatever his precise ancestry, Guillem Durfort drew upon the influence and financial backing of his kinsmen, especially his nephew, Durfort d'Espiells. The d'Espiells can be traced to Bernat d'Espiells, who owned a house in the city as early as 1140 and had financial dealings with the hard-pressed Pere Ricart; Bernat later acquired rights to collect tithes on a rural district from Pere Ricart.[95] Like Guillem Durfort at the outset of his career, the d'Espiells owned little real estate but gained access to a number of choice properties through adroit manipulation of credit. When Guillem d'Espiells, the most enterprising family member of his generation, made out his will in 1195, he disposed of only two urban houses but held five pledges, as well as bequeathing 300 mbts. and 300 *quarterae* of barley for pious donations.[96] He and his relatives clearly knew how to make their coins multiply without relying on rents. By pooling his resources with kinsmen and associates, including Durfort, Berenguer Dionís, and Guillem de Viladecols, Guillem d'Espiells achieved a critical mass of capital allowing him to engage in baronial credit while diversifying his

[93] An individual named Durfort subscribed to numerous urban transactions, including one dispute involving local *prohoms*, between 1159 and 1185 (ACB 1–5–161; LA I, fol. 89, Mas XI, no. 2010; LA III, fol. 34, Mas XI, no. 2074; CSC, III, no. 1159) but does not appear as an urban property owner in the abundant land charters until 1184, when he purchased houses on the wall near the comital palace from his nephew Bartomeu (ACA Reial Patrimoni, Subsecció de la Batllia, Classe 2ª Aᶜ, vol. 9, fol. 187 r.). He did, however, hold two pledges in the Vallès, houses at Mollet from the bishop of Barcelona for 100 mbts. in 1180, and a mill at Rubí for 26 mbts. in 1170; ACB 1–6–213; LA III, fol. 34, Mas XI, no. 2074. His subscription stands next to that of Ramon de Montcada in a charter of 1177, and his relative Guillem d'Espiells in 1192 was involved in a loan of 600 mbts. to Guillem Ramon de Montcada pledged on the castle of Sant Marçal; CSC, III, no. 1112; perg. Alfons I, 643; cf. Shideler, *A medieval Catalan noble family*, 187–88.

[94] Andrés Pi y Arimón, *Barcelona antigua y moderna o descripción y historia de esta ciudad desde su fundación hasta nuestros días* (Barcelona, 1854), I, 258 transcribes the relevant document but does not cite its source; it appears authentic, but it has not been located since. For Ponç Durfort, see ACA Gran Priorato, armari 1, 11, 80.

[95] ACA perg. R. B. IV, 196; perg. extrainv., 3466 [c. 1139]; ACB LA I, fol. 211, Mas XI, no. 1913.

[96] *Santa Anna*, III, no. 610.

risks.[97] Whether through inherited connections or financial expertise alone, the Durfort and d'Espiells had caught the eye of King Alfons I before the career of Guillem Durfort took flight.[98] The broad ties to local society as well as a reputation for shrewd investments would serve the family well in the speculative euphoria of King Pere I's reign.

As financial pressures on the Crown mounted, Guillem Durfort played upon his connections with Barcelona's entrepreneurs to provide even greater sums to the king and his barons. In 1207 his nephew, Durfort d'Espiells, purchased the bailiwick of Barcelona "at the command of the lord king," a resource he would hold until the end of Pere's reign.[99] The installation of a close relative to supervise the urban domain bolstered Guillem Durfort's financial operations, for it allowed him to marshal the funds of urban investors with the assurance that local resources and patronage stood behind the loans. Besides debts shouldered by Guillem Durfort, by 1212 the king owed Durfort d'Espiells, Guillem de Viladecols, and Guillem Genovès 2,066 silver marks (90,904 alfonsine solidi), all but 250 marks supplied by Durfort d'Espiells himself.[100] In addition Durfort d'Espiells had extended 20,000s. to the archbishop of Tarragona in 1213 at the request of Guillem Durfort, who offered his own property held from the bishop of Barcelona as surety and promised compensation that same year "under the bond of kinship" (*sub vinculo parentele*) from the *monedatge* of Barcelona, Tarragona, and Vic for disbursements totalling 36,000s. made in his name by Durfort d'Espiells.[101] Finance on such a scale had no precedent in urban society, but the lucrative domain in Barcelona and the great promise of King Pere I kept confidence high.

But when the king lost his dream and his life at Muret in

---

[97] ACB 1–5–192, 213; 4–31–878, 879; ACA perg. Alfons I, 643. For other examples of collective investments by the family, see ACA perg. Pere I, 73; ACB LA I, fol. 211, Mas XI, no. 1913.

[98] Already in 1163 Bernat d'Espiells held property in the suburbs from the king, who then exchanged it with the bishop for houses next to the intramural church of Sant Jaume; ACB LA I, fol. 121, Mas XI, no. 1863; 1–1–310, 798. Later, in 1187, Alfons subscribed to the will of Dolça, sister of Durfort (not to be confused with Durfort d'Espiells) and mother of Pere and Guillem, possibly identical with Guillem Durfort; ACB 4–5–6. In 1192, early in Guillem Durfort's service, King Alfons I granted Guillem d'Espiells the valuable monopoly of constructing and operating an oven in the western suburbs; *Santa Anna*, III, nos. 574, 575.

[99] Bisson, *Fiscal accounts*, I, 264–65; II, no. 125.   [100] ACB 1–6–2013.

[101] ACB 1–5–2419; Bisson, *Fiscal accounts*, II, no. 136.

September, 1213, the bills suddenly fell due. Major lenders to the king were sent scurrying to meet their obligations. During the months following Pere's death, Durfort d'Espiells, now no longer bailiff, sold choice properties in and near Barcelona worth 7,400s. to the bishop (connected to the repayment of his 20,000 loan to the archbishop), pledged farms on the Baix Llobregat for 5,000s., and found it necessary to have Pere Moneder and Arnau de Merola pay an installment of 4,800s. in their capacity as *fideiussores* on the amount left outstanding from 40,000s. owed the courtier Bernat de Centelles.[102] The financial repercussions from the Crown's insolvency rapidly spread to a wide circle of Barcelona entrepreneurs, whose ties of blood or credit, and often both, implicated them in defaulted loans or the liquidation of pledges. As late as two weeks before Muret, Guillem Durfort was still offering his own urban property in pledge to ensure that Bernat de Granada, Ponç de Navarra, and Berenguer de Tarragona would fulfil their obligations as guarantors to Guillem de Montcada and acquit a 2,000s. debt in his name.[103]

With the debacle at Muret, Guillem Durfort had to ward off financial collapse for both himself and his new sovereign. As a result of such broad obligations, the demands of creditors immobilized assets, restricted further financial maneuvering, and exerted pressure for the dismemberment of rights and properties accumulated by the Durfort and their closest supporters. Berenguer d'Espiells, Durfort d'Espiells' brother and creditor to magnates in his own right, had to agree in 1215 to the extraordinary precaution of having twelve kinsmen (*parentes*) formally renounce all claims on a charter of transfer to Bernat Borotí, a major baronial financier from Vic, due to the conflicting claims that might arise from outstanding loans.[104] Even the purchase of land once owned by Durfort d'Espiells could engage the buyer in annoying and

---

[102] ACB LA I, fol. 370, Mas XII, no. 2543; LA I, fol. 373, Mas XII, no. 2544; LA I, fol. 373, Mas XII, no. 2545 and 1–1–2334; 1–6–2719, 3884.

[103] ACB 1–1–776.

[104] ACA perg. Jaume I, 49: "Quod ego Berengarius Despiels et filii mei Guilelmus et Petrus convenimus vobis Raimundo et Berengario de Meleu et Bernardo Barutini ut nos faciamus firmare cartas diffinitionis quas nos vobis fecimus omnibus parentibus nostris scilicet G. de Durfort et filiis suis P. et Romeo et Duroforti et G. et R. de Vila de Cols et R. et B. de Minorisa et Alamando Tizoni et fratribus suis G. et F. et B. de Terragona." On Berenguer d'Espiells' financial operations, see ACA perg. Pere I, 73; ACB 1–6–1448; AHCB, Carp. 1, unnumb. parch. [29 v 1212]. Cf. ACA perg. Jaume I, 134–36.

costly litigation in order to free it from the tangled web of credit obligations.[105]

When Guillem Durfort died in 1215 or 1216, a few years after the king he had served so well, it was necessary for the young King Jaume I to appoint Berenguer, bishop of Barcelona, to settle the complex matter of inheritance and cut through the Gordian knot of creditors' claims on the estate; the king himself had to extend a privilege to Guillem Durfort's principal heir, Pere Durfort, in order for him to alienate the property in Barcelona his father had held from the Crown.[106] This concession, however, did not come cheaply; it depended upon the return of all rights of hospitality (*albergae*) that Guillem Durfort had acquired from the fisc in Barcelona, the Vallès, and elsewhere. This formed part of the attempts at fiscal recovery promoted by Jaume's regency council, an effort advanced when Guillem Durfort by testamentary provision forgave half the 60,000s. the king owed him and his daughter, Guillema de Cervera.[107] The final disposition of Guillem Durfort's estate and the many claims against it resulted in a reorganization of family properties and rights. Unable to defend himself against a legal challenge to his father's claim to the Vila d'Alfou, a valuable suburban zone near the shore, Pere Durfort ceded any rights he possessed to Guillem de Mediona in 1219 and a few months later sold his share of Barcelona's meat market to Pere Grony.[108] Although the fiscal crisis that arose suddenly in 1213 showed signs of improvement by 1220, its impact could still be felt long afterwards among Barcelona's leading houses.

The short-term impact of Pere's disastrous defeat should not detract from the fundamental shift in urban power that had taken place in the early thirteenth century. Through the huge sums involved in royal and baronial finance, the right to exploit critical urban resources and develop expanding suburban zones changed hands. The transfers of property and prerogatives over urban utilities effected in these years would leave their imprint on the structure of local society for the rest of the century. Even though Guillem Durfort failed to pass on to his heirs all that he had acquired from the count-kings, this was largely due to a rapid,

[105] ACB 1-1-207.
[106] ACA perg. Jaume I, 131, 133; Huici-Cabanes, *Documentos*, I, no. 11.
[107] Bisson, "The finances," 360–62; no. 2. Guillem Durfort died by December 21, 1216, ACA perg. varis, Sentmenat, Indice 8, II, 27.
[108] ACB 1-1-1496; ACA perg. Jaume I, 131.

massive, and contested concentration of assets and privileges during a single generation. His descendants and relatives, however, retained large tracts of urban real estate and preserved their influence at court; this sufficed to ensure the family a preeminent position in Barcelona's patriciate.[109] Some rode the coattails of Guillem Durfort into administrative posts, including his kinsmen Durfort, Berenguer d'Espiells, Guillem de Viladecols, and Ramon de Manresa, who collected revenues in Cerdanya, Conflent, Rosselló, and Girona and accounted for shipbuilding expenses at Cotlliure, for a time Guillem Durfort's personal port. Others profited as well. The development and operation of local utilities would increasingly be conceded in the form of private grants to reward investors. Between 1192 and 1211, the count-kings are known to have made six grants ensuring their recipients the monopoly of operating ovens in different sections of the city.[110] This amounts to the fragmentary cession of banal lordship, which Duby considers the driving force in the internal growth of the European economy.[111] Whether through the appointment of creditor-administrators or the cession of milling and oven rights to reward lenders, the count-kings transferred essential elements of local lordship and authority into the hands of urban entre-preneurs. Without confrontation or communal agitation, Bar-celona's patricians obtained and profited from the exercise of local authority.

The massive loans to kings and barons also worked to reorganize control over suburban real estate ripe for development. As in the case of loans, the number of extremely large land transfers proliferated in the years around 1200. Entrepreneurs, as already noted, bought up large blocks of land on Skinners Street, a center of expansive craft activity. Yet the interplay of lordship, finance, and explosive growth was nowhere more evident than in the development of the shoreline and its adjacent commercial district. Since the abandonment of the *portus* below Montjuïc in the early eleventh century, ships were dragged ashore haphazardly on the beach below the Regomir Gate. King Pere I, however, began to organize and exploit the area's economic and naval

---

[109] Durfort d'Espiells again acquired the bailiwick of Barcelona in 1221 (ACB 1–1–145), and Bernat Durfort audited accounts as *scriptor racionis* at court in 1224 (Huici-Cabanes, *Documentos*, I, no. 75).

[110] *Santa Anna*, III, nos. 574, 575; ACB 1–1–141; ACA Reial Patrimoni, Batllia General, Classe 3ª, vol. 6, fols. 100 r., 102 v.–103 r., 104 r.–v., 109 r.–110 r.

[111] Duby, *Early growth*, 229.

potential. As a first step, the king acquired the *plaça* in front of Santa Maria del Mar through an exchange with the canons in 1201; two years later an *alfóndec*, a compound for foreign merchants, was standing next to the *plaça*, and by 1207 the walls of the *drassanes*, the royal naval yards, rose just to the east of the Regomir Gate.[112]

The economic potential of the shoreline, however, was left largely to royal financiers to develop. After 1200 Pere Moneder, who at his death still held outstanding debts of 72,000s. from the king, began to develop a *vilanova* near the shore to the east of Montjuïc, part of which he had acquired from the heirs of Bernat Marcús.[113] In 1207 Bernat Simó received a license to lease, sell, or pledge the coastal tract from the *drassanes* west to the Cagalell stream; the only obligations attached were that he leave room on the beach for ships to land and that he construct a street broad enough to allow a millstone to pass, no doubt hewn from the granite of Montjuïc, on its way to the port; today the street still bears the name Carrer Ample, "Broad Street."[114] This extensive grant resulted from his "many and gracious services to the king," for Bernat Simó had held the vicariate in 1203–4 and still claimed 300s. against it in his will almost twenty years later.[115]

More contentious and revealing, however, was the struggle over a coastal zone known as the Vila d'Alfou near the *alfóndec*, pitting Guillem Durfort and his heirs against Guillem de Mediona and the canons. Berenguer Ramon, the aggrandizing vicar of the early twelfth century, had once controlled the area for the canons, probably with the intention of securing command of the coastline below the wall and levying commercial tariffs there.[116] Control over the property, however, had been divided in the course of the twelfth century. Part passed to the d'Alfou family, which had for generations held a section of the *vila* in fief and in 1195 received broad protective powers referred to as the "hue and cry" (*de farra et de crida*) from Berenguer de Barcelona, Berenguer Ramon's

---

[112] ACB LA IV, fol. 12, Mas XII, no. 2322; 4–39–453; Bisson, *Fiscal accounts*, II, no. 107.

[113] ACB 1–1–2370; 1–2–1337; 4–15–213.

[114] ACB 4–39–453: "inter opus novum et plateam veterem per qua possit transire ample et spaciose unam molam cum sua pertica."

[115] ACB 1–6–40; app. 1.

[116] ACB 1–6–4073: "Que ville affrontatur sicuti in carta qua Berengarius Raimundi vicarius Barchinone qui fuit atavus mei Guilelmi de Mediona fecit Aimerico et uxori sui."

son.[117] The Durfort claim depended on alleged dowry arrangements between Guillem Durfort's daughter and Guillem d'Alfou, who evidently died without issue.[118] Other rights passed from Berenguer de Barcelona's daughter to her son, Guillem de Mediona, himself a creditor to the Crown.[119] The death of Guillem d'Alfou provided the stimulus for Guillem Durfort to extend his control over the coastal zone. After King Pere I had confirmed the canons' rights over the city's eastern shoreline in 1210, he granted Guillem Durfort "the honor you have acquired from the church of Barcelona in the suburbs of Barcelona from our *alfóndec* to the river."[120] Seeking to extend his jurisdiction over more of the coast, Guillem Durfort claimed through his daughter's dowry agreement that he held the Vila d'Alfou as an allod, part of which he then granted to his relatives, Guillem de Viladecols and Berenguer de Tarragona.[121] By 1213 Guillem de Mediona bolstered his position with a vaguely phrased royal confirmation of all the rights he held from the canons,[122] but when Guillem Durfort's heirs attempted to lay claim to the property by right of inheritance an open struggle for the *vila* ensued. After bitter litigation, Pere Durfort and his backers gave way. They admitted that the property was held by Guillem de Mediona in fief from the church, yet in what amounts to a compromise, the bishop purchased part of the contested property from Pere Durfort in 1218 and in 1220 repurchased his rights over the entire area from Guillem de Mediona.[123]

The entire drawn-out episode reveals how mounting financial and political pressures brought about a reorganization of land-holding in the burgeoning suburbs. In hopes of obtaining allodial possession of valuable real estate, Guillem Durfort challenged the traditional lordship of the local church and the descendants of a powerful vicar. Although this attempt was foiled, other prominent burghers used their wealth and political leverage to subtract choice suburban developments from the encumbrances main-

---

[117] ACB 1–2–1074; 1–5–340: "illud feudum ... quod proavus tuus Petrus Raimundi de Alfodio et avus tuus Guilelmus de Alfodio atque etiam pater tuus Guilelmus de Alfodio tenuerunt et habuerunt pro me et pro meos antecessores in Barchinona."

[118] ACB 1–1–793. Guillem d'Alfou had died by 1208, ACB 1–6–1933, 2316.

[119] On Guillem de Mediona, see Bisson, *Fiscal accounts*, I, 256; *Els castells*, III, 664.

[120] S. Sanpere y Miquel, *Topografía antigua de Barcelona* (Barcelona, 1890), II, iii–iv; ACA Reial Patrimoni, Batllia General, Classe 3ª, vol. 6, fol. 100 r.

[121] ACB 1–1–776, 842 [copy 3–38–19(c)]; 1–2–758.

[122] ACB LA I, fol. 193, Mas XII, no. 2534.

[123] ACB 1–1–2344; 1–2–758, 793; 1–6–4073.

tained by overlords. Barcelona's thirteenth-century patricians would not merely control suburban real estate, they would predominantly hold allods. In order to fend off the challenges posed by the rapid concentration of capital through credit and shifts in local power, the traditional owners of rights over land and real estate revenues had to define their prerogatives with ever greater precision. After the long battle over coastal development, in 1222 Guillem de Mediona set down in a splendidly detailed charter his inherited rights to collect Barcelona's port tolls and to claim rents on his shoreline property. The result was the extensive and justly famous tariffs of Mediona, an early monument to Iberian commercial expansion.[124]

But for Barcelona's wealthiest entrepreneurs, royal and baronial finance offered the most attractive form of "big business" available in the early thirteenth century. The sums involved far exceeded individual investments in commerce, agriculture, or urban real estate, and the rewards included the cession of urban lordship, utilities, and offices to financiers and creditor-administrators. Because the count-kings assigned control over fiscal resources so freely in order to satisfy their creditors, a significant transfer of local power to new hands took place once the need for royal credit had reached critical proportions and urban investors had secured the resources to satisfy it. Both conditions obtained in the opening decades of the thirteenth century, especially toward the end of King Pere's tense, exhilarating reign. For the first time Barcelona's financiers played a prominent role at court. Under the frantic pressure of royal and baronial credit, a group of urban families coalesced into a patriciate capable of commanding local resources and directing the collective energies of the town in new directions, but they did so through collaboration with their lord, not by spearheading communal opposition against him. The conjunction of royal and patrician interests emerging during these years would determine the basic framework of urban society until the civic conflicts at the close of the Middle Ages. Yet local notables gained such extensive influence only because Barcelona was growing wealthy, especially through commerce.

[124] Capmany, II, no. 3.

TRADE AND PROTECTION

The place of extraregional trade in Barcelona's early development has been the subject of lively polemics, all the more heated due to the scarcity of evidence. As long as historians assumed merchants provided the motor force for medieval urban growth, it proved easy enough to find evidence of extensive trading networks in every reference to a foreign coin or an exotic piece of cloth. In a bold hypothesis Vicens Vives once proposed that from as early as the Carolingian period Barcelona provided a commercial umbilical cord linking the rich, urbanized, and diversified economy of al-Andalus with the underdeveloped lands north of the Pyrenees.[125] A careful sifting of local archival material has not borne out his theory. The city's eleventh-century prosperity, as we have seen, depended upon a lively local market and the collective force of Catalan arms, not itinerant merchants. Agricultural surpluses did not easily turn into the capital necessary to ignite commercial expansion, for there is little evidence of Catalan trade in the early twelfth century.[126] Between 1054 and 1145, no Barcelona resident is known to have assumed the professional title of merchant (*negociator, mercator*).[127] That the stagnation of the urban economy lasted from 1090 to 1140 in itself reveals the inability of local elites to develop a viable long-distance trading structure.

Barcelona emerged from its regional isolation through the impulse provided by the political ambitions and naval sponsorship of the comital dynasty. While the role of the counts of Barcelona in initiating and stabilizing wider contacts between Catalonia and other regions in the Western Mediterranean has long been recognized,[128] the interplay of commercial development and military-

[125] Jaume Vicens Vives, *Manual de historia económica de España* (5th ed., Barcelona, 1967), 138–39 [*An economic history of Spain*, trans. F. M. López-Morillas (Princeton, 1969), 147–49]. In an earlier work Vicens Vives suggested that the gold of Albigensian heretics fleeing persecution in Occitania provided the initial accumulation of commercial capital in Barcelona, *Aproximación a la historia de España* (Barcelona, 1952), 85–87. His thesis was roundly criticized by Yves Renouard, "Les Principaux aspects économiques et sociaux de l'histoire des pays de la couronne d'Aragón au XIIᵉ, XIIIᵉ, et XIVᵉ siècles," *VII CHCA. Ponencias* (Barcelona, 1962), 260–61.

[126] *Supra*, 115–18.

[127] I have found no evidence of resident merchants between Guifret *negociator* (1054), ACB 1–4–185 and Joan *mercator* (1145), ACB 1–2–1194.

[128] See especially the debate on the background to this movement of expansion by Charles Higounet, "Un grand chapitre de l'histoire du XIIᵉ siècle: la rivalité des maisons de Toulouse et de Barcelone pour la prépondérance méridionale," in *Mélanges d'histoire du moyen âge dédiés à la mémoire de Louis Halphen* (Paris, 1951), 313–22; Ramon d'Abadal i

political strategy remains controversial. Scholars of Catalan maritime expansion have attempted in various ways to disentangle the objectives of the ruling dynasty and baronial factions from the interests of urban merchants in examining the forces that made the Crown of Aragon a major Mediterranean power, an exercise that in its essentials represents a sharp and abstract analytical distinction between feudal and capitalist components. The most extensive debates revolve around the correspondence in the later Middle Ages between the "island route" (*ruta de las islas*), i.e. the Crown's military hegemony over the Balearics, Sardinia, and Sicily, and the "spice route" (*ruta de las especias*), i.e. Catalan mercantile ties to the Levant,[129] but the problem is prefigured in the twelfth century. Ruiz Doménec has attempted to distinguish two sharply contrasting attitudes toward commerce in twelfth-century Barcelona: the exploitation of trade by taxing it, the policy of the counts and Barcelona's "urban nobility," and exploitation by trade through the price differential from buying and selling, the policy of actual merchants.[130] By treating profit- and power-oriented attitudes toward trade as antithetical, however, this approach fails to give sufficient weight to the effects, whether intentional or not, produced by protection offered in exchange for tariffs through the systematic application of force. The counts were not simply interfering heavy-handedly in the operation of a free market or oppressing Adam Smith's "system of natural liberty"; they offered a valuable product, protection and security within the areas where they possessed a monopoly on violence. As Frederic Lane pointed out long ago, protection has its cost and must figure in any consideration of

---

de Vinyals, "A propos de la domination de la maison comtale de Barcelone sur le Midi français," *AM*, 76 (1964), 315–45 [repr. in Catalan in *Dels visigots als catalans*, II, Barcelona 1969, 281–309]. Cf. Bonnassie, *La Catalogne*, II, 859–64 and Salrach I Marés, *Història*, II, 348–52.

129 For the main lines of debate, see Jaume Vicens Vives, *España: geopolítica del estado y del imperio* (Barcelona, 1940), 111; Mario del Treppo, "L'espansione catalano-aragonese nel Mediterraneo," in *Nuove questioni di storia medievale* (Milan, 1969), 259–300; Jocelyn N. Hillgarth, *The problem of a Catalan Mediterranean empire*. Supplement to the *English historical review*, 8 (London, 1975); Udina Martorell, "La expansión"; Vicente Salavert, "Nuevamente sobre la expansión mediterránea de la Corona de Aragón," in *Segundo congreso internacional de estudios sobre las culturas del Mediterráneo occidental* (Barcelona, 1978), 359–88.

130 José E. Ruiz Doménec, "Ruta de las especias / ruta de las islas: apuntes para una nueva periodización," *AEM*, 10 (1980), 689–97. His approach is taken from A. H. Hibbert, "The economic policy of towns," *Cambridge economic history*, III, 159–60.

exchange systems.[131] Especially in an area where incipient territorial powers were weak and violence among competing maritime communities common, the line between plunder and peaceful exchange, between extortion and competitive advantage remained fuzzy. By bringing their power to bear along the Occitanian coast, the counts of Barcelona provided a critical shield protecting and nurturing a fledgling Catalan commerce.

During the early twelfth century the republics of Genoa and Pisa and the counts of Toulouse and Barcelona all vied to dominate the coast between Liguria and Catalonia.[132] The Genoese, already active in the region by 1100, took an initial advantage. For naval support given to Raimond de Toulouse in the Holy Land, the most powerful lord in Languedoc bestowed extensive privileges on the Ligurian citizens at Saint-Gilles in 1109. But Pisa as well quickly secured favorable terms for trade at Narbonne, Montpellier, and possibly other ports. When Count Ramon Berenguer III turned his attention to Occitania, he had to deal with the opportunistic, aggressive Italian cities hoping to turn Provence and Languedoc into commercial satellites. Inheriting the suzerainty of Carcassonne and Razès from his grandfather, the count of Barcelona substantially extended his Mediterranean possessions through his marriage in 1112 to Dolça, countess of Provence; in the following year she formally granted her domains to her new husband. The marriage quickly propelled the count into an even wider set of Mediterranean alliances. In 1113 a pact was concluded with Pisa for a crusade against Majorca in order to eliminate the danger posed by Muslim pirates. Although the island had to be abandoned in 1115 or early 1116 after an initial success, by involving allied nobles from Provence and Languedoc

---

[131] See especially Frederic C. Lane, "The economic meaning of war and protection," *Journal of social philosophy and jurisprudence*, 7 (1942), 254–70 and "Economic consequences of organized violence," *Journal of economic history*, 18 (1958), 401–17 [repr. in *Venice and history: the collected papers of Frederic C. Lane* (Baltimore, 1970), 383–398, 412–28]. Surprisingly ignored by medievalists, Lane's ideas have been particularly influential in discussions of the rise of modern states and capitalism. A recent attempt to expand upon them is Niels Steensgaard, "Violence and the rise of capitalism: Frederic C. Lane's theory of protection and tribute," *Fernand Braudel center for the study of economics, historical systems, and civilizations. Review*, 2 (1981), 247–73.

[132] The best overview of the subject remains André Dupont, *Les Relations commerciales entre les cités maritimes de Languedoc et les cités méditerranéennes d'Espagne et d'Italie du Xᵉ au XIIIᵉ siècle* (Nîmes, 1943). See also Geo Pistarino, "Genova e l'Occitania nel secolo XII," *Actes du 1ᵉʳ congrès historique Provence-Ligurie* (Aix, Bordighera, and Marseilles, 1966), 64–129; Ruiz Doménec, "Génova y Barcelona," 25–86; Sobrequés i Vidal, *Els grans comtes*, 174–83, 188–90.

as well as Italians the expedition confirmed the new prestige of Ramon Berenguer. Returning to Provence in 1116 for the first time since his marriage, the count continued on a grand naval tour to Genoa, Pisa, and Rome, where he negotiated for a new crusade and the restoration of the archbishopric of Tarragona. The counts of Barcelona were now playing out their ambitions on a broad Mediterranean stage.

Yet when the count of Barcelona attempted to enforce his prerogatives in southern Frankland, his efforts provoked violent opposition. The lord of Baux led a faction of the Provençal nobility in revolt against their new lord on his return home in 1116; their stiff resistance was put down at the castle of Fos, a siege in which the "men of Barcelona" so distinguished themselves that they received their first commercial privilege, an exemption from a toll known as the *quinta*, the count's fifth of booty and captives.[133] An even wider and more dangerous conflict erupted in 1119 between Alphonse Jourdain, count of Toulouse, and Guillaume IX, duke of Aquitaine, backed by Count Ramon Berenguer III; a recent war between Pisa and Genoa added yet another dimension to this complex struggle. After years of intermittent warfare, the dispute was settled in 1125 by an agreement partitioning Provence with Ramon Berenguer retaining control over the maritime districts. The time had arrived for a general accord with Genoa, the traditional ally of Toulouse, for the count of Barcelona had made good his claim to command the waters off Provence. The point was brought home by the capture of a Genoese galley, whose passengers included the son of the consul and chronicler Caffaro.[134] Prompted by this seizure and the attacks on its ships during

---

133 Capmany, II, no. 1. The nature of the *quinta* has been in doubt, but references to it in the thirteenth century make clear that it refers to the comital share of booty on captives, not a general levy on all merchandise as maintained by Carreras Candi, *La ciutat*, 253–54. ACB 1-6-800 (1276): "Ego Anticus Titionis baiulus domini regis in Barchinona recepi et habui a te triginta solidos monete barchinonensis et ternalis ratione quinte domino rege pertinentis de quadam saracenna nomine Fatima et eius filia Zoffra et de quodam sarraceno nomine Iucef." Cf. ACA Reg. 58, fol. 96 v. On the resistance of Provençal nobles, Poly, *La Provence*, 325–29.

134 "Di due documenti che riguardano le relazioni di Genova con la Catalogna nel secolo XII," ed. L. Valle, *Il R. Liceo-Gionnasio 'C. Colombo' di Genova negli anni 1931–32, 1932–33, 1933–34* (Genoa, 1935), 31–35. Although José E. Ruiz Doménec, "En torno a un tratado comercial entre las ciudades de Génova y Barcelona en la primera mitad del siglo XII" *Atti di 1.° congresso storico Liguria–Catalogna* (Bordighera, 1974), 152 believes that the undated charter in which the Genoese negotiated for a reduction of the tariff paid to the count on each ship from 10 ounces of gold to 10 mbts. (1/7 the previous amount) dates from Ramon Berenguer's visit to Genoa in 1116, it was more likely

the conflict between the houses of Barcelona and Toulouse, the republic of Genoa wished to reach an accord. Through an intricate set of negotiations, the Genoese eventually acknowledged that they would have to pay 10 mbts. on each of their ships passing the coast from Nice to Tortosa to be "safe under the count's protection" (*secure in potestate comitis*). The treaty of 1127 concluded a successful act of resistance to Genoese commercial and naval hegemony over the Occitanian coast; it did not represent a balance struck between mutual trading partners.[135] The accord formed part of a broader set of agreements among the emerging maritime powers in Italy, Occitania, and Catalonia to carve out distinctive spheres of influence in the Western Mediterranean and stabilize mutual obligations. The treaty with Genoa alludes to an earlier accord on tariffs between the count and the inhabitants of Montpellier, and a year later Ramon Berenguer secured an alliance for a crusade against the Saracens with King Roger II of Sicily, who was himself attempting to strengthen relations with Pisa and Genoa.[136] By the third decade of the twelfth century naval expansion, dynastic ties, and commercial ambition had for the first time reached a stage where the rising powers of the Latin Mediterranean from Sicily to Catalonia had to find a balance among their competing interests over the waters once controlled by Islamic ships.

While the counts of Barcelona pursued familial and patrimonial

connected to negotiations after the cession of hostilities in Provence since it bears the subscription of Provençal notables. On its date, see Maria Teresa Ferrer i Mallol, "Els italians a terres catalanes (segles XII–XV)," *AEM*, 10 (1980), 429, n. 146 and Pistarino, "Genova e Occitania," 78–80. See also ACA perg. extrainv., 3137.

[135] Capmany, II, no. 2. I do not share the view that the treaty came about due to Barcelona's commercial advance as presented by Ruiz Doménec, "En torno," 155: "Génova le [Ramón Berenguer III] era necesaria: como ciudad que le ingresara en Europa, como ciudad que le comprara sus productos. No nos debe extrañar que Barcelona necesitando a Génova, la buscase." His opinions on the treaty are refined in "Génova y Barcelona," 41, where he argues that the Genoese "seduced" the count into the accord by pointing out that he could profit from their trade by levying tariffs. But the initiative in 1127 lay with the count, not the Genoese, and it seems unlikely that he was duped. The line of argument here rests on a caricature of clever merchant-capitalists outwitting a fumbling feudal lord, but this misrepresents the powers of coercion Ramon Berenguer III had attained over Mediterranean trade.

[136] Capmany, II, no. 2: "donent censum hominibus Barchinone sicut homines Montispessulani per consuetudinem iam dicti comitis donant." The Sicilian alliance is found in Michelle Amari, *Storia dei musulmani di Sicilia* (2nd ed., Catania, 1933–39), III, 396–98, n. 1. On the alliances of Roger of Sicily, see David Abulafia, *The two Italies: economic relations between the Norman Kingdom of Sicily and the northern communes* (Cambridge, 1977), 59–70.

interests across the Pyrenees, their objectives worked to the advantage of Barcelona. First and most obviously, they defended Catalan towns against aggressive competitors. Foreign merchants did not receive favored status or independent trading compounds in Catalan ports until Count Ramon Berenguer IV negotiated with the Ligurian republic for the use of its fleet in the conquest of Tortosa in 1148 at the price of ceding a third of the city to the Genoese, who soon found their enterprise less rewarding than expected and sold their share back to the count.[137] If the House of Barcelona had not been able to summon up far-flung military power and naval potential in southern Frankland and Catalonia, Italians would have turned their commercial superiority into a commanding position across the entire northern shore of the Western Mediterranean. While Genoese, Pisans, Sicilians, and Occitanians were not excluded from Barcelona, the counts and later the count-kings used their power to counterbalance the advantages enjoyed by competitors, in effect subsidizing the economy of the most prized town in Catalonia with force and political alliances. The early twelfth-century treaties foreshadowed later protectionist legislation, most notably the royal "navigation act" of 1227 prohibiting the loading of foreign ships in Barcelona when native vessels were on hand, and the expulsion of Italian bankers in 1267.[138]

In a pioneering article Charles Verlinden once postulated that Catalonian trade remained essentially passive well into the thirteenth century due to a lack of exports and the limited capacity of Catalonian shipping.[139] After fifty years of further investigation there is still some truth in his observation, but it nevertheless underestimates both the economic potential of redistributive trade and the ability of the Catalan sovereign to exert maritime power through his own warships or those of his allies in Occitania. The comital dynasty created the Catalonian navy. Until Count Ramon Berenguer I made provisions for the construction of a fleet in Barcelona below the Regomir gate, Catalonia could not be

---

[137] The abandonment of Tortosa marks a notable failure for the Genoese, possibly, as Schaube, *Handelsgeschichte*, 542 suggested, because the revenues from the city were less than expected. Cf. Abulafia, *Two Italies*, 232.

[138] The extensive history of later protectionist legislation in the Crown of Aragon is thoughtfully surveyed by Ferrer i Mallol, "Els italians," 394–428.

[139] Charles Verlinden, "La Place de la Catalogne dans l'histoire commerciale du monde méditeranéen médiéval," *Revue des cours et conférences* (1937–38), 586–605, 737–54 and "The rise of Spanish trade in the Middle Ages," *Economic history review*, 10 (1940), 49.

considered a naval power. The counts and barons remained the principal builders and owners of large ships and galleys well into the twelfth century; besides Bernat Marcús, only one other Barcelonan, Arnau Pere d'Arcs, is documented as a shipowner around 1150, and only after 1180 do references start to multiply.[140] Although the counts and barons of Catalonia constructed and commanded galleys, sailors and adventurers from the ports manned them on raids against Islamic ships and coasts, including the expedition to Majorca in 1114, and on trading voyages to foreign ports under armed protection. But the maritime privilege of 1117 and the reference to individuals from Barcelona selling slaves in Genoa's tariff list of 1128,[141] the first two official acts relating to the city's "foreign trade," are more concerned with the disposition of plunder than with the regulation of stable commercial networks. During the early phase of Catalan maritime expansion profits derived from violence, whether directly, through plunder, or indirectly, through tariffs, outweighed profits from commercial exchange, but both sources of wealth complemented one another and followed the dynastic and military trajectory of the counts of Barcelona. Because of their leadership in defining and securing the initial parameters within which Catalonian commerce could operate, in the thirteenth century the count-kings actively used their own ships to pursue maritime trade and, with the help of vessels owned by Barcelona's citizens, to carry on profitable raids against their enemies.[142] The dynamic interface of commercial profit and dynastic power initiated in the decades after 1100 would reach its full potential in the Mediterranean conquests of the Crown of Aragon during the thirteenth century.

---

[140] Ferrer-Garcia, *Assegurances i canvis*, II, no. 1. In 1150 Bernat Marcús claimed a "quinta ipsius galee" (*Llib. bl.*, no. 47) which probably refers to the galley itself but possibly only to the right to collect a share of the booty. No other references are known to me of a Barcelonan owning a ship before 1180.

[141] Capmany, II, no. 1; *Liber iurium reipublicae genuensis. Monumentae historiae patriae* (Turin, 1854), I, col. 32. Cf. the count's grant to Sant Adriá de Besòs of the tithe on all "booty and captives" (*tam de prediis et captivis*) from ships subject to him in 1104, *Marca hispanica*, ap. cccxxxv.

[142] Charles-Emmanuel Dufourcq, *L'Espagne catalane et le Maghrib aux XIIIᵉ et XIVᵉ siècles de la bataille de Las Navas de Tolosa (1212) à l'avènement du sultan mérinide Abou-l-Hasan (1331)* (Paris, 1966), 65–68; Robert I. Burns, "Piracy: Islamic-Christian interface in conquered Valencia," *Muslims, Christians, and Jews in the Crusader Kingdom of Valencia* (Cambridge, 1984), 113–14. See the revealing *societas* contracted in 1291 between citizens of Barcelona and Majorca to arm a royal ship for raiding, Arcadi Garcia i Sanz and Josep Maria Madurell i Marimon, *Societats mercantils medievals a Barcelona* (Barcelona, 1986), II, no. 12.

Once the counts had initiated and secured contacts with Occitania and the Italian republics, Barcelona gradually became integrated into the principal circuits of Mediterranean trade. The process, however, got under way in earnest only after 1140 and was largely set in motion by the commercial experience and trading contacts of resident foreigners. The local documentation contains references to twenty-six individuals bearing toponymic surnames from beyond the Pyrenees between 1100 and 1220: fourteen from Italy, especially Genoese and Lombards (a name here referring generally to individuals from northern Italy), eleven from Occitania, and one individual with the tantalizing name of Bernat Arabia.[143] Appearing in significant numbers just before 1140,[144] these immigrants appear to have melted quickly into the background; they married local families, owned properties scattered about the city, and settled down to the routines of Barcelona life. In contrast to Castile and Aragon, foreigners did not form separate *barrios*, distinguished by their language, custom, and occupation;[145] instead, they quickly developed close ties to local society, especially to entrepreneurs and craftsmen,[146] but some retained valuable links to their native cities and spread the commercial know-how of their countrymen to a previously isolated and commercially underdeveloped corner of the Mediterranean. Among the Italians who helped stimulate local trade and transfer new habits of thought and organization, Eimeric de Perugia (d. c. 1176) was perhaps the most successful. First mentioned in 1134, Eimeric appears repeatedly in the local documentation over the next four decades, lending and borrowing, buying houses and stalls at the marketplace and near Santa Maria del Mar, and arranging a marriage with a niece of Guillem Arbert, a local

---

143 The derivative place names are Lombardy (6), Genoa (4), Perugia (2), Pisa (1), Parma (1), Montpellier (4), Toulouse (3), Narbonne (2), Béziers (1), Monaco (1), and Arabia (1). For the Occitanian immigrants in the twelfth-century, see the study, based primarily on landholding patterns, by Philip Banks, "Alguns immigrants del Llenguadoc al Barcelona del segle XII," *Misel·lània d'homenatge a Enric Moreu-Rey* (Barcelona, 1989), i, 153–72.

144 Only six appear before 1140: Oliver Narbonne (1115), Pere de Béziers (1116); Oto Lombard (1120), Lambert the Pisan (1127), Eimeric de Perugia (1134), Ponç de Toulouse (1135).

145 Jean Gautier-Dalché, "Les Colonies étrangères en Castille," *AEM*, 10 (1980), 469–86; José María Lacarra, "Desarrollo urbano de Jaca en la edad media," *EEMCA*, 4 (1951), 139–55.

146 See in particular Ponç de Toulouse, who was associated with the armorers on the Call de Freneria, Banks, "Immigrants," 162–63.

notable.[147] Even though there is no explicit reference to his participation in commerce in the meager documentation, Eimeric's grandson, Arnau Pere Eimeric, operated a galley in 1198, and another descendant of the Perugian traded with Majorca in 1231 and served as King Jaume I's ambassador to Tunis.[148] Alone among Barcelona's patrician houses, the Eimeric sprang from foreign stock.

Much of the accumulated commercial experience from Italy and Occitania, however, was disseminated quietly and has left little trace. The will made by Saxio in 1184 offers a precious glimpse into the affairs of a businessman with strong ties to Montpellier.[149] In his shop inventory one can see the silhouette of a man devoted exclusively to trade: bolts of fine cloth, incense, gold rings, a sword, 130 leather hides, and precious metals valued at 146 gold mbts., 15 lbs. in silver coin, and 90 half marcs of silver (*mediae argenti*). The impressive array of merchandise and its obviously commercial nature are quite unlike anything in local Barcelona wills of the time, but Saxio maintained extensive credit and commercial dealings with local investors: Guillem Eimeric, Burget, Esteve Guitard, Berenguer Bou, Ramon and Bernat Ponç, Martí de Sant Cugat, and his nephew, Guillem d'Alest. Saxio's will also contains the first reference to two forms of contractual association crucial for the expansion of Catalonian trade in the following decades: a commercial partnership (*societas*) and a contract for joint ship armament.

Because of their familiarity with the contractual forms of association and their contacts with other commercial centers, immigrants from Occitania and northern Italy helped release the pent-up economic potential of Barcelona into maritime trade; their presence rapidly closed the gap in commercial techniques between Catalonia and its competitors.[150] Barcelona gradually

---

[147] ACB 1–5–20, 28, 159; 4–49–353; LA I, fol. 229, Mas XI, no. 1595.

[148] Ferrer-Garcia, *Asseguarances i canvis*, II, nos. 7, 9; Dufourcq, *L'Espagne catalane*, 81, 110–11.

[149] Appendix 4, no. 3. Besides his will, Saxio is otherwise known only in reference to a petty squabble with the canons over a piece of property after his death; ACB LA I, fol. 118, Mas XII, no. 2271; LA I, fol. 119, Mas XII, no. 2283.

[150] Recent archival investigations have corrected the view that thirteenth-century Barcelona lagged behind its competitors in terms of commercial techniques, a conclusion put forward by André Sayous, "Les Méthodes commerciales de Barcelone au XIIIᵉ siècle, d'après des documents inédits des archives de sa cathédrale," *Estudis universitaris catalans*, 16 (1931), 155–98. For a rectification of Sayous' ideas, see the useful intro-

emerged as a maritime emporium by drawing on the collective trading experience and shipping capacity of the entire Western Mediterranean. While the use of foreign vessels for trade was still necessary, new forms of collective ownership defrayed the cost of private naval construction and armament. In late twelfth-century Catalonia it became possible to own a half, a third, or a fourth of a ship; by 1236 one could invest as little as 36s. in arming a galley.[151] Besides commercial partnerships, *comanda* contracts, fusing capital and labor for short-term trading ventures in the tradition of the Venetian *colleganza* and Genoese *societas maris*, were in use by 1206.[152] With increasing access to maritime routes and better organization, more and different types of merchandise became available. The best proof lies in a comparison between Barcelona's earliest tariff list (c. 1150) and the tariffs of Mediona (1222). Not only does the number of items included rise from fifty-six to ninety-seven, but foreign cloth and spices replace furs, skins, and livestock at the top of the list. That Catalonian trade evolved from the exchange of animal products and raw materials to trafficking in luxury items during the course of the twelfth century receives further confirmation in a complaint made by two Catalan merchants whose merchandise was seized by Genoese galleys near Narbonne during the reign of King Alfons I. This unusually detailed record of piracy allows us to peer into the ship's hold and examine its cargo: it consisted principally of cat and rabbit skins, leather, wax, dye, light cloth (*fuag*), and two precious bolts of cloth from Chartres.[153] Raw materials and furs are much in evidence, but this early indication of access to the fine cloth of Northern Europe points to the future. Cloth from Bruges appears in Barcelona in 1180, and fine dyed Stamfort cloth (*capapels de Stamfort de grana*) in 1203:[154] the city had now come of age as a commercial hub, connected to the great axis linking Northern Europe and the Mediterranean. A cloth hall stood near the market by 1194, and in the following decade a new merchant elite first

duction to the Catalan translation of his works by Garcia i Sanz and Feliu i Montfort, *Els mètodes comercials*, 9–44.

[151] *Llib. bl.*, nos. 157, 173; ACB Cartes Reials, C. 1–28, Olivares Caminal, no. 8; ACA perg. varis, Sentmenat, Indice 8, III, 8.

[152] Noted in Batlle i Gallart, "La burgesía," 16, n. 23.

[153] Appendix 4, no. 2. Although the two merchants do not appear to be from Barcelona, they did carry wax from a prominent Barcelonan, Guillem d'Alfou, the father-in-law of Guillem Durfort.

[154] ACB 1–1–1763; 1–6–256; ADB perg. Santa Anna, Carp. de la creu, unnumb. parch. [29 iv 1203].

makes its appearance: the *draperii*, professional cloth merchants.[155] Thus, even though Barcelona's merchant marine was still struggling to expand in 1220 and local industries for mass exports, particularly cloth, were lacking, the city nevertheless prospered by drawing upon the collective naval and commercial resources from Occitania and Italy which dynastic expansion had first made available. Immigrants and foreign ships helped launch Barcelona onto the main currents of Mediterranean trade.

Once the volume of international trade had expanded significantly and profits from commercial exchange began to exceed those derived directly from plunder and protection, the count-kings sought new ways to draw revenues from maritime commerce. This helps explain the extensive reorganization of the city's waterfront just after 1200. Rather than simply exacting a price for protection through a monopoly of force, the count-kings actively sought to promote trade. Always strapped for money, King Pere I concentrated visiting merchants in the *alfóndec*, surrounded, like the cloth hall at the market, by workshops he owned, and a July fair was instituted there to attract business;[156] he also rewarded his major urban financiers with the right to build up the Ribera and profit from rents. It would be misleading, however, to conclude that the financiers and entrepreneurs who gained control of the coastal zone merely drew off commercial wealth through rents, credit, and administration. Berenguer d'Espiells, the bailiff's brother, had entered into several commercial partnerships before 1208, while Pere Arnau Grony, whose kinsmen were important landlords in the Ribera, was exporting wheat from Empúries in his own ship (*galiote*) in 1194.[157] Rather than stifling profit-driven exchange, access to the administration of trade allowed the commercial interests of those who controlled it to take flight; both the d'Alfou, associated with the coastal district and possibly the tariffs

---

[155] *Llib. bl.*, no. 372. A woman, Romana *draperia*, first used the title in 1206, ACB 1–6–447; subsequently many of the wealthiest thirteenth-century merchants came to use the appellation. For an example of their extensive investments and commercial operations, see Batlle i Gallart, "La família i la casa d'un draper de Barcelona," 69–91.

[156] Bisson, *Fiscal accounts*, II, no. 107; ACB 4–33–74. The lease of property next to the *alfóndec* in 1223 mentions the additional income derived from renting space to fair goers, ACB 4–33–748: "Ita scilicet quod de logerio quod inde provenerit tempore Barchinone nundinarum habeamus ego et mei medietatem et tu et tui aliam medietatem." For scattered later information about the fair, see Carme Batlle i Gallart, "En torn de la fira de Barcelona," *Cuadernos de arqueología e historia de la ciudad*, 18 (1977), 129–39.

[157] Garcia-Madurell, *Societats mercantils*, II, no. 2; ACB 1–5–330.

controlled by Berenguer de Barcelona, and the Adarró, granted a monopoly for the exchange of prisoners with Muslim Spain, invested in commercial operations at an early date.[158] Even as Barcelona's merchants were exploring more distant routes to North Africa, Sicily, and the Levant, far beyond the reach of the Crown's protective mantle, the main interests of urban entrepreneurs became ever more closely entwined with the naval and political resources of the count-kings. This concurrence helped define the character of Barcelona's thirteenth-century patriciate and provided a constant source of strength for a seemingly impoverished monarchy.

CONCLUSION

From 1140 to 1220 a small group of families emerged to dominate Barcelona's growing economic potential and assume authority within the city. They would remain the core of the city's thirteenth-century patriciate. Because the creation of autonomous municipal institutions, the formal "emancipation" of bourgeois communities from feudal control, has traditionally dominated medieval urban historiography, the patriciate has frequently been identified with an ability to provide community leadership and display its power through representative municipal institutions. In this vein the creation of a town council in 1249 is usually presented as the culmination of a slow process of community solidification and the confirmation of a new civic leadership by the wealthiest, most influential, and often the most commercially successful families. Yet the emergence of Barcelona's patriciate, the formation of a distinctive style of rule that would reproduce itself for generations to come, took place long before King Jaume I's decree and under quite different circumstances.

The critical phase in its formation occurred during the opening decades of the thirteenth century and had little to do with an assertion of corporate rights or communal representation. The field of collective action by urban notables, the *prohoms*, in fact became restricted as local authority passed to influential creditor-administrators, whose financial leverage with the count-kings allowed them to gain extensive control over local offices, valuable utilities, and prime suburban real estate. Yet they were not *minis-*

[158] On the d'Alfou, ACB 1–6–2682; ACA perg. extrainv., 3308; on the Adarró, ACB 1–2–140; 1–6–140, 328, 3002.

teriales, men who had emerged from the *familia* of their lord, remained personally bound to him, and envied the nobility's cultural arrogance and swaggering style of command. They had emerged in an expansive urban economy as independent entrepreneurs. By gradually concentrating the small-scale, dispersed resources available in the urban economy after 1140 through credit, patronage of the craft sector, real estate development, and commercial investment, a few burghers had accumulated substantial amounts of capital and had gained experience at shrewdly manipulating their assets; their success attracted the attention of the count-kings and his barons. By underwriting the expansionist policies of an ambitious monarchy and a restive baronage, a small group of urban financiers emerged around 1200 to invest on a scale hitherto unknown; they thereby gained access to new resources within the city and exercised authority that distinguished them from other burghers. Barcelona's patriciate coalesced under the intense financial and political pressures created by dynastic expansion. This concurrence of patrician and royalist interests would remain a trademark of Barcelona's elite throughout the later Middle Ages. The city's leading families did not spearhead a movement for municipal autonomy and urban democracy; they attained power through a leveraged buyout of lordship.

Chapter 6

FAMILY STRUCTURE AND THE
DEVOLUTION OF PROPERTY

The attainment of power by a new group of Barcelonans involved not just the cumulative acts of individual entrepreneurs but the collective strategies of patrician families. While the importance of family organization and blood ties in structuring and perpetuating the power of medieval elites has long been acknowledged, early urban patriciates have in fact received little attention in the growing literature on domestic life and kinship.[1] The dearth of materials for many towns before 1250 in part explains this neglect, but so too does the assumption that precocious social climbers, particularly wealthy burghers, the *enfants terribles* of medieval society, took their cue from the nobility. The high profile of aristocratic clans in the early city–republics of northern Italy, where a rich and carefully exploited documentation does exist, has accentuated the tendency to deny a distinctive pattern of family organization to early townspeople.[2] Somewhat defensively medievalists have had to counter the charge that towns in themselves dissolved traditional family bonds, a theme dear to early sociologists and social reformers such as Weber and Le Play, who looked upon medieval towns as the avatars, for better or worse, of modern life.[3] Yet the insistence on accentuating features that early

---

[1] An important recent addition to the sparse literature on early urban families outside Italy is John H. Mundy, *Men and women of Toulouse in the age of the Cathars* (Toronto, 1990). For an orientation to the burgeoning literature on medieval family and kinship from the tenth to the thirteenth century, three useful syntheses, each from quite different perspectives, are now available: Herlihy, *Medieval households*, 79–111; Jack Goody, *The development of the family and marriage in Europe* (Cambridge, 1983), 103–56, 222–61; Fossier, *Enfance*, II, 905–50. Significantly early urban societies outside Italy receive little attention in these works.

[2] Heers, *Le Clan familial*, 43–56; Paolo Cammarosano, "Structures familiales dans les villes de l'Italie communale," in *Famille et parenté dans l'Occident médiéval*, eds. G. Duby and J. Le Goff (Rome, 1977), 180–83; Rossetti, "Histoire familiale," 166–67, 174–78.

[3] For the strong influence that early theorists on the social consequences of modern industrial cities have exerted on assessments of pre-industrial urban families, see Hughes, "Urban growth," 105–6; James Casey, *The history of the family* (Oxford, 1989), 11–14;

urban communities held in common with other segments of medieval society has come at the price of denying them an autonomous evolution, especially in terms of family structure. In Barcelona, however, the economic blockage of the early twelfth century, the decline of agricultural entrepreneurs, the withering of an urban nobility, and the consolidation of ascendant families into an early patriciate at the beginning of the thirteenth century suggest that the forces reshaping a distinctively urban milieu encouraged a rearrangement of patrimonies and a restructuring of family bonds.

During the invigorating period of European expansion after the year 1000, the most far-reaching reformulation of kinship structures and domestic institutions came in response to an accentuation of agnatic filiation, particularly pronounced among the nobility, and the success of the Church in imposing a model of strict monogamy on the laity, to the disadvantage of children from "illicit" unions. Both factors worked to sharpen the focus of kin identity and streamline family structures. In contrast to the diffuse, loosely defined kin groupings characteristic of the early Middle Ages, in which women added as much as men to the complex circuitry of blood ties that spread out horizontally, agnatic lines of descent began to predominate. Property and family memory among European elites became increasingly attached to males, who either collectively exploited their inherited rights over land, offices, castles, and privileges in consortial associations or deferred to the preeminence of a single male heir in a *lignage*. The Church too had its part to play in enforcing a new ethic that sharpened an awareness of descent. Gregorian reformers had insisted on the sacramental force and the indissolubility of marriage, which ensured paternity and legitimacy of heirs, and at the same time imposed an extended incest taboo, which technically could only be determined by knowledge of seven generations of ancestors. The most widely accepted social causes for these changes, most notable in aristocratic societies from the tenth to the twelfth century, are basically two: the need for protection in an expanding, competitive, and violent feudal world and a desire to preserve the integrity of the patrimony. The weakening of traditional public order in the tenth and eleventh centuries encouraged families to tighten their ranks in a defensive retrenchment; the

Stefan Breuer, "Blockierte Rationalisierung: Max Weber und die italienische Stadt des Mittelalters," *Archiv für Kulturgeschichte*, 66 (1984), 47–85.

well-known tower societies of northern Italy, owned exclusively by male members of powerful families, afforded protection and a sense of cohesion amid the incessant civic feuds that shaped Italian civic life.[4] Competition over new sources of wealth also encouraged tighter control over patrimonies. As the exploitation of land, peasants, and banal rights eclipsed war and plunder as the basic means of securing wealth, measures were taken against the harmful effects produced by the partition of estates, particularly offices, castles, and fiefs that could not easily be divided without threatening their integrity. Patrimonies were therefore concentrated around a single heir, usually the eldest son, or kept undivided and exploited jointly by brothers. A sharpened genealogical awareness took precedence over dimly understood cognatic relationships as *antecessores* replaced *propinqui* in determining a family's prestige and power.[5] Although the precise chronology and extent of these changes is still debated, a broad consensus has developed that noble houses stressed agnatic over cognatic filiation, adopted strategies to preserve estates intact, and offered a family model that penetrated ever more deeply into European society.

Whether the conditions promoting these transformations existed in nascent towns, however, has received surprisingly little consideration outside Italy. The fluidity of property transactions produced by rapid expansion of a monetary economy, the relative security offered by many urban lords, and the importance of contractual as well as familial forms of association all suggest that prominent burghers may have employed inheritance strategies

---

[4] The general thesis relating an extended family solidarity to political disorder is most clearly articulated by Fossier, *La Terre*, I, 262–73 and by Georges Duby, *La Société aux XIᵉ et XIIᵉ siècles dans la région mâconnaise* (2nd ed., Paris, 1982), 215–27, 366–68 and "Lignage, noblesse et chevalerie au XIIᵉ siècle dans la région mâconnaise: une révision," *AESC*, 27 (1972), 802–23 [repr. in *Hommes et structures*, 395–422; "Lineage, nobility and knighthood," *Chivalrous society*, 59–80]. Bonnassie applies the thesis to the Catalonian nobility in *La Catalogne*, I, 281–82; II, 547–49. On Italian tower societies and questions of corporate ownership see Niccolai, "I consorzi," 116–17, 292–342, 397–477; David Herlihy, "Family solidarity in medieval Italian history," in *Economy, society and government in medieval Italy*, eds. D. Herlihy, R. S. Lopez, and V. Slessarev (Kent, OH, 1969), 173–84; Manlio Bellomo, *Profili della famiglia italiana nell'età dei comuni* (Catania, 1966), 107–41; Lansing, *Florentine magnates*, 84–105.

[5] On the rise of genealogical literature, see Duby, "Remarques sur la littérature généalogique," 335–45; and Karl Hauk, "Haus- und sippengebundene Literatur mittelalterlichen Adelsgeschlechter von Adelssatiren des 11. und 12. Jahrhunderts her erläutert," *Mitteilungen des Instituts für österreichische Geschichte*, 62 (1954), 121–45 ["The literature of house and kindred associated with medieval noble families, illustrated from eleventh- and twelfth-century satires on the nobility," in *Medieval nobility*, 61–86].

and blood ties in quite different ways from the nobility. Barcelona provides a fresh vantage point from which to consider the problem because of its sharp change of direction in the twelfth century and the rather late emergence of its leading families. Should we follow Lestocquoy and refer to them as "patrician dynasties"?

THE LANGUAGE OF KINSHIP

Our own ability to identify the bonds of kinship and attempt to uncover family organization depends upon the terms of relationship and naming patterns recorded by medieval scribes. The vocabulary of kinship in medieval Catalonia was relatively poor in comparison to the complex terminology available in Germanic and Celtic languages during the early Middle Ages, and even in comparison to early Latin.[6] With the lexical precision capable of denoting cousins to the fifth degree lost in late antiquity, the Latin available to the scribes of twelfth- and thirteenth-century Barcelona provided rather meager tools with which to construct a complex framework of possible blood relationships among the men and women who transacted business before them. The terminology of the charters remained conservative, with little influence from vernacular forms. Beyond the immediate ego-centered family of father (*pater*), mother (*mater*), brother (*frater*), sister (*soror*), son (*filius*), daughter (*filia*), paternal aunt (*amita*), paternal and maternal uncle (*avunculus, patruus*), brother- and sister-in-law (*cognatus, cognata*), son-in-law (*genus*), stepbrother (*filius consanguinius*), and niece, nephew, or grandchild (*nepos*), precise relationships among relatives were left up in the air, and the information in individual charters provides little help in clarifying connections by reference to a common ancestor. Besides revealing a restricted lateral range, kinship designations also had a restricted depth perception. Scribes rarely mentioned grand-parents, and only two references to a great-grandparent (*proavus, atavus*),[7] both patrilineal, are known to me among the thousands

---

[6] Donald Bullough, "Early medieval social groupings: the terminology of kinship," *Past and present*, 45 (1969), 3–18; T. M. Charles Edwards, "Some Celtic kinship terms," *Bulletin of Celtic studies*, 24 (1971), 105–22; Goody, *Development of the family*, 262–78; E. Beneviste, "Termes de parenté dans les langues indo-européennes," *L'Homme*, 5 (1965), 5–16; Toubert, *Les Structures*, II, 693–711.

[7] ACA perg. Jaume I, 168; ACB I–5–34. Significantly both involve grants made by the early vicar Berenguer Ramon to the founders of the Grony and d'Alfou houses;

of charters examined for this study. The grammar of kinship was therefore rudimentary and suited to a system centered on a compact set of relationships anchored on the married couple and their children.

Two lexical features, however, placed the conjugal unit in a broader context. First, a keen awareness of immediate maternal and paternal kin was maintained. The burghers of Barcelona kept the distinction between *avunculus*, the mother's brother, and *patruus*, the father's brother, quite clear; further, *amita*, though rare, retained its classical meaning of paternal aunt. In contrast to Latium, where notaries artificially revived these classical terms in preference to the vulgar forms of aunt and uncle (*thia*, *thius*) but without an awareness of their original matri- and patrilineal connotations, Catalan scribes clearly distinguished between two sets of close collateral relatives.[8] On the other hand, terms for wider kinship networks did not separate maternal and paternal kin into distinct groups, nor do they give a clear idea of the relative closeness of the blood tie. *Consanguinii*, *propinqui*, *parentes*, and *amici* could all encompass broadly defined bilateral relationships, ranging from parents, wife, and brother to vaguely identified relatives, shading into non-related family allies in the case of *amici*.[9] Even though no specific vocabulary existed to sort out the longer strands of maternal and paternal bonds, scribes were able to make this broad distinction when the need arose. In a disputed case about the appointment of a tutor over minor children, an issue that could easily lead to competition between the child's two sets of relatives, a royal judge found it necessary to summon both

association with this powerful figure in the early twelfth century formed a point of reference for the family memory of these two patrician houses.

[8] Cf. Toubert, *Les Structures*, I, 706.

[9] The most flexible term appears to be *amici*. It could, for instance, include a wife and brother, as in one will from 1160, *CSC*, III, no. 1029: "eligo manumissores meis amicis, id sunt: Ramon de Montemenedi et Mir Guilelmum, fratrem meum et mulier mea; precor vos amicis meis..." The term often encompassed close relatives and family supporters, particularly in judicial disputes, cf. ACA Reg. 38, fol. 45 v.–46 r. The vocabulary of kinship and friendship overlapped in this case, although the linkage of the two categories does not seem so complete as in the phrase *amici carnales*, indicating vast kin groups dear to Marc Bloch, *Feudal society*, I, 123–35. I do not find evidence that *consanguinii* refer to a close group of in-laws, while *propinqui* represent more distant relationships, as suggested by Ruiz Doménec in the context of categories of asymmetrical exchange, "Système de parenté," 312. *Propinqui* appear regularly in marriage contracts as the group to which property passes in case the couple fails to produce a legitimate heir, ACB 1-1-1520 (1136): "propinqui mei quibus iure succedent predictas domos." Cf. ACB 1-5-24, 44, 237.

maternal and paternal kin (*convocatis cognatis et necessaris personis tam ex parte patris*); a female testator also took care to ensure that in case her children died her property would not pass to her husband's relatives but to her own (*propinquioribus eorum ex parte matris*).[10] Even though relationships among more distant kin were often obscure, the retention of a bifurcating kinship vocabulary for immediate collaterals promoted an awareness of broad divisions between maternal and paternal relatives.

A second significant feature is the lexical ambivalence in relation to the family household. *Familia*, a rare and learned word in thirteenth-century charters, had various dimensions. True to its classical meaning, it often implied a unit larger than that of the nuclear family. In a lawsuit initiated because of the delayed payment of a dowry, rancorous as only domestic disputes can be, Berenguer Durfort refused to support his wife's wet nurses and slave because by his restricted definition they did not form part of her *familia*; a judge found otherwise and upheld a conception of the family that included dependents.[11] The notion of authority could even take precedence over close biological ties and coresidence; Felipe d'Espiells insisted that his daughter and son-in-law live under his roof, but spoke of "your family and mine" (*familia mea et vestra*) since his daughter would technically be under her husband's authority.[12] Yet supervision over dependents and household members as well as inherited rights became increasingly connected to an awareness of descent, which embedded the *familia* within a wider kin group. When a childless widow, for instance, wished to ensure that her property would not pass from her "line or family" (*non exeat de genere sive familia mea*), she clearly had in mind something other than a nuclear family or her immediate household.[13] During the thirteenth century terms for descent groups (*parentela*, *genus*) began to overlay the constricted but precise ties among individuals, linked like molecules by scribes who noted the relationship among men and women by the tie of father, mother, brother, sister, nephew or niece. It even became possible to speak of a "line of descent."[14] This did not indicate, however, that families became strictly organized around a single

[10] ACB 1–6–1015; 4–12–65.   [11] ACB 1–6–4106.
[12] ACA perg. varis, Marquès de Monistrol, 168.
[13] ACB 4–3–140.
[14] ACB 1–6–1554: "ratione sanguinis et linee parentele." Cf. ACA perg. varis, Marquès de Monistrol, 101, 162.

line of heirs, the *lignage* of French aristocratic society, but that they acknowledged certain rights and obligations transmitted from a common, dimly remembered ancestor. This broad concept of lineal descent, here best described as a "house," created large, murky pools of relatives. In his will of 1284 Joan de Banyeres made donations to twenty-five "needy souls from my house" (*pauperes de parentela mea*), if that many could be found; this hardly argues for intimate terms of familiarity among kin.[15] In their use of kin terms Barcelona's thirteenth-century scribes reveal a heightened awareness of descent, but it still represented an abstract, fluid concept within which the cohesive, conjugal family could be placed.

Local usage in Barcelona thus appears to have put up a considerable amount of resistance to the general European shift in kinship terminology from what Jack Goody calls a bifurcating collateral system (which distinguishes between maternal and paternal lines) to a lineal structure (which does not); townsmen in Barcelona continued to think in terms of the mother's brother and father's brother rather than uncles. Although Goody argues that this lexical leveling came about through the Church's prohibitions on consanguineous marriages, a strategy that gives equal structural weight to relatives on both sides, the persistence of a bifurcating terminology in Barcelona suggests something quite different: substantial influence if not outright interference of both maternal and paternal kin in the conjugal family. This is not to argue, however, for the preponderance of an "extended" over a "nuclear" family, a contrast that Toubert has characterized as a false dilemma.[16] Quite clearly the precise semantic field of kinship had contracted since late antiquity to the confined parameters set by the husband and wife and rarely extending beyond aunts, uncles, nephews, nieces, and grandchildren. Married couples with their offspring certainly formed the nucleus of family identity, but they did not exist in complete independence from more distant

---

15 ACB 4–10–1. Cf. ACB 4–17–6, 1–6–402: "ad presens plenam memoriam non habeo de pluribus consanguineis meis pauperibus."

16 Toubert, *Les Structures*, I, 710–11. Bloch, *Feudal society*, I, 137–41, challenged medievalists to determine whether families of the European past were large, patriarchal agglomerations, or small, conjugal units. Recent discussions of family and kinship have tried to give a nuanced answer by considering in which social contexts large kin groups were operative. See especially Stephen White, *Custom, kinship, and gifts to saints* (Chapel Hill and London, 1988), 125–29, 197–200; Goody, *Development of the family*, 222–27; David Nicholas, *The domestic life of a medieval city: women, children, and the family in fourteenth century Ghent* (Lincoln, NE, 1985), 1–12, 175–208.

relatives. Surrounding this basic core was a nebulous conglomeration of kin, who could exert varying degrees of pressure horizontally, through maternal or paternal groupings, or, increasingly in the thirteenth century, vertically, by appealing to rights and loyalties based on lineal descent. The problem therefore does not lie in uncovering an uninterrupted movement from a large to a small family, but in determining the degree and form of influence exerted by kin on married couples and specifying the contexts in which it occurred.

In addition to the systematization imposed by kinship terminology, onomastic evidence provides access to the study of medieval families. While much remains to be done in the study of the variety of names and the stabilization of naming patterns in medieval Catalonia, Balari Jovany established their general evolution at the turn of the century.[17] Even though it is no longer possible to share his belief, widely held at the time, that names can provide an index of the ethnic composition of a given population, his general periodization for the stages in naming patterns still holds. The early Middle Ages marked a sharp break with classical Roman practices that had established through a lengthy series of names an individual's precise position within a kin group. In the ninth and tenth century, single names, without a clear indication of filiation, were the norm among all levels of the population. Because this change was well under way in the late empire, there is no need to attribute the dislocation of previous patterns to Visigothic influence, although Germanic names enjoyed a great deal of popularity. Balari Jovany went too far, however, in asserting that the use of single personal names existed in complete independence from wider family connections, for the repetition of a given name among close kin may have encouraged a broad clannish identity.[18] A name pool larger and more varied than that of later centuries helped avoid the confusion caused by several individuals bearing the same name in the small-scale societies of the early Middle Ages.[19] Yet the use of highly individualized names failed to provide an onomastic connection to kin. Lineal identity was

[17] Balari Jovany, *Orígenes*, I, 565–601.
[18] Note, for example, the preference for Guislabert and Udalard among the family of the viscounts of Barcelona, Sobrequés i Vidal, *Els grans comtes*, genealogical chart after 64.
[19] The rarity of shared names in the ninth and tenth century can be most easily seen in the index to *Archivo condal*. See also Federico Udina Martorell, "Noms catalans de persona als documents dels segles X–XI," *Miscelánea fiológica dedicada a Mons. A. Greiera* (Barcelona, 1962), II, 387–402.

truncated, and names in themselves failed to provide an indication of collateral relationships.

A firm connection between names and filiation began to form in the early eleventh century. Especially in land charters, where title usually depended on inheritance, the notation "child of" (*filius, filia, prolis*) was added to personal names of men and occasionally of women during the eleventh century; gradually the reference to child became redundant and disappeared, leaving a personal name attached to that of the father. Thus Pere Ricart was the son of Ricart Guillem, and Ponç Arbert the son of Arbert Berenguer, a pattern that allows sons and paternal uncles to bear the same name, but not nephews or grandchildren. The original link between multiple names depended upon the relationship between father and child, a two generational family, rather than on membership in a large kinship network. In order to distinguish individuals in a growing population, after the year 1000 qualitative or professional titles would occasionally be joined to a personal name (e.g. Martí Petit = Martin the Short; Bernat Ferrer = Bernard the Smith) or places of origin added (Guillem de Vic). The human density of urban life seems to have accelerated the use of multiple names in Barcelona; in the partial list of urban inhabitants from c. 1079, more than eight out of ten burghers were cited by more than a single name, a proportion roughly the same as in the tax list c. 1145.[20]

Even though the use of multiple names had already become common by the late eleventh century, a profound shift nevertheless took place in the time between the compilation of the two lists: by the mid-twelfth century the patronymic family name had imposed itself as the dominant, most enduring element of the naming system. A few urban families, most notably the Marcús and Vivas, had passed on their distinctive patronymic from generation to generation before 1100, but the practice became common only around 1110. It is tempting to connect the emergence of the family name with the reorganization of urban wealth and property taking place during the period of renewed urban growth under way after 1140; an eponymous ancestor who established himself in an expansive urban economy could indeed offer a solid point of reference for later family identity. While the intensity of

[20] ACA perg. R. B. II, sense data, 71; Banks, "The inhabitants," 157–58. The list from c. 1145 records 53 single names among 217 total individuals identified; 34 consist of a craft appellation attached to a personal name.

urban growth could have affected the precise chronology in the history of names, the general impoverishment in the number of personal names during the eleventh and twelfth century encouraged townspeople to establish their identity by reference to a family past rather than the new juxtaposition of names at every generation.[21] Unusual appellations such as Revellus, Leopardus, Floridius, Godimir, Ermovigia, Babilonia, and Elegancia gave way to the ubiquitous Pere, Bernat, Guillem, Berenguer, Ermessenda, Agnès, and Guillema; more than half the 217 individuals surveyed c. 1145 shared one of the 7 most popular names.[22] As Toubert has suggested, the need to avoid confusion and a scribal scrupulousness in a society increasingly familiar with notarial instruments also worked to expand the use of patronymics.[23] Whatever the precise relationship among economic, onomastic, and notarial factors, the stabilization of patronymics around 1140 made individuals conscious of forming part of a kin group larger than their immediate family and ensured that it would endure over generations, far longer than the bond between parent and child.

The long-term movement from individualized personal names to stable family patronymics attached to a limited range of first names was certainly not unique to Catalonia, but the chronology indicated here, particularly the rapid spread of the *nomen paternum* around the middle of the twelfth century, does suggest that a new conception of family identity was taking shape at the time. The language of kinship and naming practices began to articulate new dimensions to blood ties, lineal in nature, yet without seriously impinging on the cohesion of the marital couple. But the balance among these different elements is difficult to determine from language alone. While the family patronymic began to stabilize around 1140, in the early thirteenth century land charters frequently established identity by reference not only to the father but the mother as well. Did this represent resistance to the rise of the family patronym, a confirmation of the independence of the

---

[21] The thinning out of personal names in Tuscany after 1200 has been connected to the strengthening of lineal ties by David Herlihy, "Tuscan names, 1200–1530," *Renaissance quarterly*, 41 (1988), 576–77.

[22] Banks, "The inhabitants," 155. The prevalence of a handful of names can be quickly confirmed in the *index nominum* of *CSC* and *Santa Anna*, both of which are concentrated in the eleventh and twelfth century. For a later period, see Enric Moreu-Rey, "Antropònims a Barcelona als segles XIV i XV," *Estudis d'història medieval*, 3 (1970), 113–20.

[23] Toubert, *Les Structures*, I, 700.

conjugal family in the face of emerging patrilineal structures, or did it merely reflect the growing formality and expansive precision of notarial instruments? And, more generally, how closely did the learned Latin of Barcelona's scribes correspond to vernacular usage and lay perceptions of the family? Any attempt to answer these questions demands an awareness of the grammar of kinship, both its structure and limitations, in order to grasp the contours of historical families among medieval townspeople.

INHERITANCE AND STRATEGIES OF HEIRSHIP

The most detailed extant information about familial relationships in medieval Barcelona relates to the transmission of property, especially between the living and the dead. Even though recent concentration on kinship has tended to disengage the lines created by descent and marriage from the social and economic background on which they are etched and to examine them in isolation, once European societies settled down after the millennium, they tended not to develop extensive kin networks in the absence of property.[24] The regulated distribution of land and liquid assets from one generation to the next not only largely determined the economic survival and structural balances within patrician houses, it also affected the personal relationships among heirs. This section, however, will concentrate on the mechanisms and strategies of heirship and leave consideration of intrafamilial relationships for chapter 8. While it would be presumptuous to assume that all ties of blood were knotted with property, practices to determine succession nevertheless do provide a blueprint of family organization. The large number of extant urban wills in Barcelona present in considerable detail how individual burghers intended to pass on their estate, but to understand the inheritance strategies employed one must first turn to the legal and customary restraints on testators.

Medieval Catalonia clung tenaciously to the contractual forms and language of Visigothic law. This legal and notarial conservatism was particularly evident in the extensive use of oral and written testaments, which, in the phrase of Jean Bastier, consti-

---

24 David Sabean, "Aspects of kinship behaviour and property in rural Western Europe before 1800," in *Family and inheritance*, eds. J. Goody, J. Thirsk, and E. P. Thompson (Cambridge, 1976), 97–101; Hughes, "Urban growth," 123–24; David Herlihy and Christiane Klapisch-Zuber, *Les Toscans et leurs familles* (Paris, 1978), 506–11.

tuted *une survivance wisigothique*.[25] While in neighboring Languedoc the use of wills was rare in the tenth and eleventh century and
testamentum signified a written act in general, in Catalonia the
word at an early date assumed the specific meaning of testamentary dispositions distinct from other acts of donation.[26] The traditionalism of legal and scribal culture also preserved a knowledge
of the inheritance provisions of Visigothic law that carried over to
influence the compilations of local customary codes. Even after
King Jaume I had formally prohibited the use of Visigothic,
Roman, and canon law in secular cases at the Cort of Barcelona
in 1251,[27] a judge settling an inheritance dispute at Martorell, a
village at the entrance to the Pla de Barcelona, could boldly
declare in 1277 that, "It is known that in this region judgments are
rendered according to Gothic, not Roman law."[28]

The rules regarding succession in the Code of Ervig (681), the
final redaction of Visigothic law that formed the point of reference for subsequent generations, stress three main elements in
succession: (i) the obligation of the testator to pass on the bulk of
his property to his descendants; (ii) the preeminence of direct lineal
claims, first descendant then ascendant; and (iii) the right of all
children, whether sons or daughters, to share equally in the
inheritance. A testator could dispose freely of only a fifth of his
property (*legitima*) if he left children behind; without a will
everything would go to them. In the absence of children, the
inheritance would pass, in order, to grandchildren, great-grand-
children, parents, and grandparents.[29] Without direct descendants,

---

[25] Jean Bastier, "Le Testament en Catalogne du IXᵉ au XIIᵉ siècle: une survivance
wisigothique," *Revue historique de droit français et étranger*, 51 (1973), 372–417. See also
Zimmerman, "L'Usage du droit visigothique," passim and Bonnassie, *La Catalogne*, I,
262–65. On Visigothic testamentary practices, see Manuel de Pérez de Benavides, *El
testamento visigótico: una contribución al estudio del derecho romano vulgar* (Granada, 1975);
P.D. King, *Law and society in the Visigothic kingdom* (Cambridge, 1972), 108–10, 239–50;
R. Aubenas, *Cours d'histoire du droit privé*, III. *Testaments et successions dans les anciens pays
de droit écrit au moyen âge et sous l'ancien régime* (Aix-en-Provence, 1954), 16–17. Surviving
Catalan wills to 1025 (137 in number) have now been meticulously edited and carefully
studied, particularly in regard to their legal and diplomatic aspects, by Antoni M. Udina
i Abelló, *La successió testada a la Catalunya altomedieval* (Barcelona, 1984).

[26] Bastier, "Le Testament," 380–81; Udina i Abelló, *La successió*, 48–49.

[27] *Cortes*, I:1, 38.

[28] ACB 1–6–4056: "Sciendum est quod iudicatur in partibus istis secundum gothicam et
non secundam legem romanam ... debet fieri divisio a patre inter filios equaliter et sic
debet pater ex necessitate testari secundum gothicam." The decision accurately reckoned
the share of inheritance according to ancient Visigothic practice.

[29] *Lex Wisigothorum*, ed. K. Zeumer, in *Monumenta Germaniae Historica, Leges*, I (Hanover
and Leipzig, 1902), IV. 5. 1; IV. 2. 1 and 2.

however, men and women could dispose of their property with complete liberty; collaterals possessed no formal claims to the estate. Finally, "a woman should come into the inheritance equally with her brothers,"[30] an unequivocal affirmation that daughters enjoyed equal claims along with sons to their parents' estate. Visigothic law granted only one exception to the iron rule of equal inheritance among direct descendants: the right to favor a single heir with an "improvement" (*melioratio*, Catalan *millora*) to his or her share, eventually fixed at a third the portion due all direct descendants (or four-fifteenths of the entire estate).[31] Although testaments executed in accordance with Visigothic forms distinguished Catalonia from other Mediterranean regions because of their conservatism, early appearance, and wide use, they nevertheless did not give an individual a free hand to pass down property to future generations. The revival of Roman law, which began to make itself felt in Catalonia by the late twelfth century, is widely held to have brought greater testamentary freedom than in the past, and with it the power to reshape family organization.[32] *Recognoverunt proceres*, the royal privilege setting forth the customs of Barcelona in 1284, eased the requirements for oral wills and increased the part of the estate a testator could dispose of freely from one-fifth to seven-fifteenths, in fact the amount allowed under Visigothic law plus the *melioratio*. [33] Yet it remains unclear whether legal changes actually corresponded to shifts in inheritance practices. Even within the traditions of direct lineal legacies and equality among heirs, ambiguities in legal requirements and custom could allow for different strategies of heirship.

Wills themselves provide the surest guide to detect variations in the way individuals tried to shape their estates. Admittedly they tell us only how Barcelonans intended to organize the material and spiritual well-being of their family rather than the actual

[30] Ibid., IV. 2. 9.
[31] For its continuing importance in Iberian inheritance practice, see A. Otero, "La mejora," *AHDE*, 32 (1963), 5–131.
[32] Font Rius, "El desarrollo," 291, 296; Bastier, "Le Testament," 416. On the supposed testamentary freedom brought by Roman law, an idea long ago promoted by Maine, see the comments of Diane Owen Hughes, "Struttura familiare e sistemi di successione ereditaria nei testamenti dell'Europa medievale," *Quaderni storici*, 33 (1976), 930–34.
[33] *CODIN*, IV, nos. viii, x; Jesús Lalinde Abadía, "El derecho sucesoria en el 'Recognoverunt proceres'," *Revista jurídica catalana*, 62 (1963), 651–64; Guillermo María de Brocá y Montagut and Juan Arnell y Llopis, *Instituciones de derecho civil catalan vigente* (2nd ed., Barcelona, 1886), I, 42.

postmortem arrangements, but when examined as a whole they can reveal the direction of customary practices. Fortunately Barcelona's local archives have preserved a large number of urban testaments, constituting, when assembled, one of the richest collections for the early history of any European city at the time.[34]

The following analysis will be based on 263 testaments made by lay people from 1100 to 1290. They do not, however, represent an even cross-section of the urban population. Men constituted 68 percent (179) of the testators, a disproportion more pronounced for the twelfth century, when slightly less than one testament in five (9 of 47) were made by women, than for the thirteenth, when the proportion rises to slightly more than one in three (75 of 216). The most notable change in the legal condition of women who left wills relates to marital status; only one of the ten female wills in the twelfth century was made by a married woman, while in the thirteenth century almost as many wives as widows recorded their final wishes in regard to the distribution of their property. As we shall see in the following section, the testamentary freedom enjoyed by married women after 1200 indicates a significant increase in their claims over conjugal property.

Besides differences based on sex and marital status, the surviving collection of testaments does not accurately reflect the distribution of urban wealth. The more resources an individual possessed, the greater the need to make arrangements for their division at death. While examples of burghers of quite modest means are not lacking, wealthier citizens are nevertheless most heavily represented in both the twelfth- and thirteenth-century wills, but it is impossible to draw even an approximate quantitative line to distinguish the most affluent since real estate, not easily converted into monetary standards, constituted a substantial portion of the inheritance.

The form in which the testaments have come down to us also heavily weights them in favor of the rich. They all survive on parchment, either as originals or copies made within a generation or two after the death of the testator. In contrast to wills found only in notarial registers, which usually encompass a broad cross-section of the population, those recorded on parchment were

---

[34] 283 lay and ecclesiastical thirteenth-century wills from the Diversorum and Pia Almoina series of the ACB have been cataloged and used to investigate patterns of pious and charitable donations by Batlle and Casas, "Caritat privada." Scattered Barcelona wills, however, exist in other series within the ACB and in other local archives.

expensive and preserved and copied for specific reasons; they found their way into local archives, chiefly ecclesiastical, because they either constituted key elements to land title or provided evidence of large contributions for pious purposes. The selective survival of parchment testaments, increasingly a notarial instrument de luxe, therefore strongly accentuates information about succession among Barcelona's wealthy and influential families. Since the outlines of the patriciate can only be made out in the early thirteenth century and it remained an open group for generations afterwards, reference to the entire corpus of extant wills in addition to the chance survival of a handful of testaments from a single family provides the surest method to determine strategies of heirship.

The distribution of property depended first of all on the number of surviving children. Despite the concentration in the historical literature on the partitioning of estates among multiple heirs, this occurred in only a minority of cases: 37 percent of testators (98) left no legitimate children, 29 percent (77) had only one, and another 11 percent (28) had children of the same sex.[35] Biological continuity therefore had a considerable influence in determining the available options.

A single surviving heir obviously presented the simplest situation, leaving the person confronting death with only pious legacies and minor personal bequests to friends and relatives to consider. Complications could arise, however, if the heir was female. Even though a daughter clearly received preference over collateral males, family property was sometimes distributed more widely when the only heir was female, especially in the early twelfth century. With only one surviving daughter Ponç Ellmar in 1131 granted the bulk of his property, including his residence, to the canons of Barcelona and the monks of Sant Cugat del Vallès, while his daughter received only two *modiatae* near the shore and half a vat; a generation later Guillem Sunyer left his only daughter, already married and capable of producing heirs, two-thirds of his possessions while giving the rest to the Church.[36] In both instances the amount given for pious donations clearly exceeded the limit

35 A comparable proportion of childless testators (255 of 632, or 40 percent) has been noted in wills recorded primarily in the Genoese registers, although this includes ecclesiastical testaments as well; Steven Epstein, *Wills and wealth in medieval Genoa, 1150–1250* (Cambridge, MA, 1984), 73.

36 ACB 1–1–295 (copy in LA 1, fol. 72, Mas XI, no. 1413); 1–1–359. Cf. ACB 1–1–356 (copy in LA 1, fol. 50, Mas XI, no. 1414).

set by Ervig's Code. Even though instances of individual piety exceeding the letter of the law are known in eleventh-century Catalonia,[37] in Barcelona this practice often occurred at the expense of a sole surviving daughter, but gradually this practice died out by the late twelfth century. The desire of a father to memorialize his kin through gifts to churches and earn his personal salvation could outweigh his concern to secure the integrity of family property passed through a female line; while a sole surviving daughter could clearly not be excluded from an inheritance, the cohesion of an estate was not paramount in family strategy at this early stage of urban development.

A related problem arose when all surviving children were daughters. In two notable cases, the absence of a male heir encouraged men from prominent families, Bernat Marcús and Pere d'Espiells, to persuade a son-in-law either to assume their family name or to give it to a future male heir in order to perpetuate the line, an act that in fact constituted an informal adoption.[38] Here the issue did not concern inheritance rights and the integrity of the estate, since the daughters all received substantial legacies, but the lineal continuity of the family through a patronymic. The question, however, could only arise once family names, with their emphasis on agnatic descent, had stabilized. While the existence of female heirs in both cases presented a weak link in family organization, their place in inheritance strategies had changed significantly. Until the mid-twelfth century female heiresses could not completely secure the integrity of the family patrimony, which remained the collective concern of males; as a result, the claims of daughters tended to give way to the corporate memorialization of the kin through alienations to the Church. By the late twelfth century, however, heiresses threatened to break the lineal identity of their house by failing to perpetuate its name. Thus, even in what at first appears a relatively straightforward matter of direct succession, subtle variations reveal different attitudes toward family structure and its perpetuation through the generations.

If nuanced strategies existed when only a single direct

---

[37] Udina i Abelló, *La successió*, 79; Bonnassie, *La Catalogne*, I, 263, notes that inheritance practices diverged most sharply from Visigothic law in regard to legacies to churches; several of his examples of extremely generous pious donations involved testators who were left with daughters as their only heirs.

[38] *Santa Anna*, III, no. 609 (1195); ACA perg. varis, Marquès de Monistrol, 168.

descendant survived, the possibilities multiplied substantially in the absence of children. In contrast to societies which promoted concubinage or adoption in order for a family to produce a direct descendant, the insistence of the Church on strict monogamy and the discouragement of adoption did not allow childless individuals to employ fictive kinship in order to perpetuate their name. As already noted, Visigothic law made no clear provisions for the settlement of an estate in the absence of lineal descendants or ascendants; given the unlikelihood that grandchildren would be on hand to inherit in the absence of surviving children, parents were the most likely residual heirs. Yet this occurred only rarely, for there would be little need for men or women to make a will unless they had already established a separate household and left their parents' authority, especially paternal authority. Only a single will was made when the father was still alive, and mothers turn up in only ten instances to share in the estate with brothers and sisters or to hold the inheritance in usufruct until their deaths, when the inheritance would be divided among siblings.[39] In most cases, therefore, childless adults were at liberty to dispose of their goods, yet actual practice strongly favored male lateral succession; brothers and nephews were usually given preference over sisters and even spouses.

As table 6.1 illustrates, childless individuals, whether male or female, possessed a great deal of latitude in disposing of their estates. The variety of close relatives favored as principal heirs and the large number of testators who distributed their goods widely among their kin group demonstrate that family property neither devolved consistently to the surviving spouse nor passed through a clear circuitry of kinship. Statistical analysis, however, unduly simplifies the family situation, for the absence of spouses, brothers, sisters, or nephews, as well as the emotional bonds within these kinship categories could affect individual choices. Still, the rarity with which childless testators left their property to spouses is striking. Of the thirty-four individuals who identified living spouses, only twelve favored them, a neglect as common among women (four of eleven) as men (eight of twenty-three). Even though a substantial portion of the marriage gift technically had to return to the close relatives of the husband or wife, a portion could

---

[39] E.g. *Santa Anna*, III, no. 610; ACB 4–3–26; 4–10–51; 4–15–68. In contrast to legacies made directly to siblings, when the estate reverted to the mother before distribution all the brothers and sisters were usually enjoined to share the property equally.

Table 6.1 *Principal heirs among childless testators*[40]

	Men (59)		Women (39)	
	%	N	%	N
Spouses	14	(8)	10	(4)
Brothers	17	(10)	13	(5)
Sisters	7	(4)	8	(3)
Nepotes[41]	15	(9)	21	(8)
Other relatives	8	(5)	15	(6)
No clear preference	39	(23)	33	(13)

nevertheless be disposed of freely in addition to common property acquired during the marriage. This happened in only a few cases, however, and for the most part involved people of modest means.[42] For those with substantial assets, it was common for spouses to receive only confirmation of their marriage gift and a few moveables, often personal items such as clothes, bedding, or jewelry; sometimes they were not mentioned at all. The rarity with which both wives and husbands made their spouses principal heirs in Barcelona contrasts sharply with the situation in contemporary Genoa, where childless heirs seldom left the main portion of their estate to their kin despite similar legal prescriptions to do so.[43] The strength of Genoese lineal ties defined by males helps to explain the difference. In order for a couple to retain its material independence against the broad claims of collateral lines in the Genoese clans, it would have to reinforce itself when faced with the dangerous prospect of a barren marriage by one spouse granting inheritance rights to the survivor, sometimes, as Steven Epstein suggests, under the pretext that by an undiscovered pregnancy a widow could still produce a legitimate heir.

[40] For the purposes of the table, a principal heir is the person to whom the testator left the bulk of his or her property or was formally designated as *heres*, a practice that began in the early thirteenth century. In many cases, a clear preference can not be demonstrated.

[41] *Nepos* can be a nephew, niece, or grandchild, but in virtually all instances it indicates nephew. The presence of grandchildren is shown by scribes naming their parents; nieces never became main heirs.

[42] For examples of simple testamentary arrangements among individuals with few goods, including the grant of assets to the spouse, see ADB perg. Santa Anna, Carp. 9, 51; ACB 1–2–81; 1–6–2323; APR, 227.

[43] Epstein, *Wills*, 99–103.

On the other hand, the range of kin with claims on the conjugal fund in Barcelona was much more confined: the integrity of the conjugal fund depended upon a relative balance between two kin groups of limited dimensions. The independence of the married couple therefore did not require internal reinforcement to maintain itself, nor was the threat from male collaterals so pressing that property would be reabsorbed by a vast, branching kinship structure.

Childless marriages in Barcelona usually resulted in the return of land, houses, and rents to close natal kin. Brothers and nephews, however, were strongly favored over spouses, sisters, and nieces in the distribution of the estate. Only in a single instance was a sister preferred to a brother, while nieces never figured prominently in inheritance strategies.[44]

Especially during the early twelfth century, a loose notion, certainly not a conscious rule, obtained that brothers had a corporate claim to the inheritance. Not only were brothers and – in case they predeceased the testator – fraternal nephews given equal shares, but they were enjoined to hold them together. When Bernat Arbert died in 1140, he simply noted that, after his pious and personal donations, the rest of his property, including his residence, should pass to his two brothers, Pere and Ramon; a generation earlier, Mir Ramon not only left his main properties to his two brothers but insisted that one look after the other's share (*in baiulo*) for seven years and took care to ensure that if one brother died, his share would pass to the other.[45] By the early thirteenth century, however, joint legacies had decreased significantly and one among the brothers or brother's sons was sometimes given special importance.[46] When Bernat Ponç divided the bulk of his property between his nephews Pere Ponç and Bernat Ponç in 1223, he nevertheless favored one by adding the houses and shops where he lived; three years later Maria, daughter of Bernat Roig, parcelled out her lands and honors to her three brothers and one of their sons, yet Maria proclaimed that she should love her brother Guillem, presumably the eldest, above all

44 Only Ramon Ferrer, who made his will in Montpellier, favored a sister at the expense of his brothers, ADB perg. Santa Anna, Carp. de la creu, unnumb. parch [25 v 1274].
45 ACB 1–1–2534; LA I, fol. 326, Mas XI, no. 1506. For similar divisions and restrictions on alienations outside male collateral branches, see ACB LA IV, fol. 96, Mas X, no. 1283; LA I, fol. 30, Mas X, no. 1304.
46 Sisters' sons, when distinguished among the *nepotes*, received small legacies; see ACB 4–15–68.

others.[47] Thus, despite the technical freedom allowed childless testators, male siblings and their descendants were generally accorded the strongest claim on the inheritance, outweighing even the bonds between husband and wife. While family continuity clearly did not involve unilineal descent groups, nevertheless, during the thirteenth century a movement can be detected away from collective management of an estate by male descendants to the elevation of a single line of descent. This new strategy of heirship made itself apparent not only when a person had to confront the difficult choices posed by the lack of children, but also by their abundance.

According to the injunctions of Visigothic law, all children had an equal right to the estate of their parents. But to what extent was this practice followed in an expansive urban setting more than five centuries after it had been formalized in Ervig's Code? To answer this question, it is first of all necessary to determine what contemporaries understood by an "equal share" of inherited property. All children mentioned in wills received some form of legacy, but in most cases it is impossible to determine the value of real estate, clearly the most important consideration. By comparing the number of sons and daughters who received land, houses, and rents rather than cash settlements, however, it is possible to provide a rough indicator of the preference of testators over time. The following chart analyzes the legacies left to a total of 514 legitimate children, 276 sons and 238 daughters. As in other statistical studies of medieval populations, daughters are consistently underrepresented, an imbalance just slightly more pronounced among male testators, 46 percent of whose children were daughters, than females, among whom the proportion rises to 48 percent. Explanations for the low numbers of women in medieval data have ranged from childhood neglect or even infanticide to their subordinate status in fiscal or administrative surveys,[48] but in testaments inheritance strategies mattered most. After an examination of Genoese wills, Epstein concluded that the low number of daughters should be attributed to their exclusion from further inheritance claims after they had received their dowry.[49] This

---

[47] ACB 4–3–179; 4–12–43. Cf. ACB 4–15–68; 4–10–61; 4–6–27.

[48] For a penetrating analysis of the traps posed by medieval statistical data on sex ratios, see Herlihy, *Medieval households*, 64–68 and the much more detailed discussion in Herlihy and Klapisch-Zuber, *Les Toscans*, 326–49.

[49] Epstein, *Wills*, 82.

Table 6.2 *Legacies made by male and female testators*

	No. of sons	Land	Money	No. of daughters	Land	Money	Other bequests
Legacies by male testators							
1100–1150	15	15	0	12	8	1	1
1151–1200	24	22	1	26	14	10	1
1201–1250	66	55	11	50	18	30	2
1251–1290	95	69	26	81	17	62	2
Legacies by female testators							
1100–1150	6	6	0	4	1	0	1
1151–1200	8	8	0	7	4	0	1
1201–1250	14	11	3	10	5	4	1
1251–1290	48	30	18	48	20	22	6

explanation does not apply to Barcelona, however, for daughters frequently received supplemental legacies to their dowries, which their parents consistently mention as constituting their daughter's *legitima*, their rightful share of the inheritance. Because of the integrated part married daughters played in family organization, it is more likely either that very young daughters were sometimes lumped together with the "remaining children," who received minor residual legacies, or that men failed to mention daughters who had taken the veil as regularly as other women. Despite Visigothic tradition, discrimination against daughters did exist either by failing to include them among heirs or, as the statistics in table 6.2 indicate, by offering them less valuable parts of the estate for their "fair share."

The numbers in table 6.2 reveal two general trends: first, a movement from a wide dispersal of real property in the early twelfth century to its restriction for favored heirs, particularly sons; second, a tendency for women to distribute their property more equitably among their children than men. Overall boys were twice as likely to receive land, houses, or shops as girls, yet women left real estate to 43 percent of their daughters, while men limited the amount to 34 percent. The interaction between these two contradictory tendencies would determine family organization as economic expansion reshaped medieval Barcelona.

Within Visigothic tradition two possibilities existed in order to prevent the fragmentation of the estate among multiple heirs:

impartible inheritance and preferential treatment of a single heir.
While Visigothic law did contain provisions for granting a limited
amount of additional property to one child through the *melioratio*,
its provisions did not address the question of impartibility. During
the early twelfth century testators preferred the solution offered
by impartibility, either by granting property jointly to their
children or through stipulations requiring that they not divide
their inheritance for a fixed period, usually from twelve to fifteen
years after the death of the parent.[50] But not all descendants were
included. When an individual had numerous children to provide
for, the shares granted to sons and to daughters formed separate
sets of legacies; in reversionary clauses, the shares granted one son
would pass to his brothers in case he died childless, and similar
provisions existed for daughters. Testators were most concerned
that sons rather than daughters retain property in common, an
institution called *frarisca* in Catalan.[51] This did not necessarily
mean that all sons received equal treatment, nor that the brothers
of necessity resided together, although this may have been desirable. In 1124 Arbert Berenguer left half his home, an oven, and
allods in Barcelona to his son, Guillem Arbert, and the other half
to another son, Ponç Arbert, yet a third son, Arbert, and his only
daughter, Erminard, each received separate outlying properties.[52]
In order to encourage two of his three sons to live together,
Arbert Berenguer further stipulated that their mother should hold
their inheritance for her lifetime, but if his sons could not get
along with her (*vivere in pace*), she would receive a separate
property and presumably leave the house. In the absence of sons, a
daughter could even be used to perpetuate a *frarisca*. Pere Bofill in
1128 left half the house he shared with his brother, Martí Orúcia,
to one of his two daughters,[53] an unusual measure but nonetheless
indicative of the compelling force that shared inheritances exerted
over strategies of heirship during the early twelfth century. While
the *frarisca* certainly did not disappear, it nevertheless gave way

---

[50] For provisions prohibiting division, see ACA perg. varis, Marquès de Monistrol, 6;
perg. R. B. III, 107; ACB LA I, fol. 103, Mas XI, no. 1545.

[51] Impartible inheritance among brothers has received little attention in medieval Spain but
has been carefully studied elsewhere. See Jean Gaudemet, *Les Communautés familiales*
(Paris, 1963), 100–20; R. Aubenas, "Réflexions sur les 'fraternités artificielles' au moyen
âge," in *Etudes historiques à la mémoire de Noël Didier* (Paris, 1960), 1–10; Herlihy, "Land,
family, and women," 104–10; Toubert, *Les Structures*, I, 716–34; Monique Bourin,
Villages médiévaux en Bas-Languedoc: genèse d'une sociabilité (Paris, 1987), II, 57–61.

[52] ACB 1-1-2233 and ACB LA III, fol. 1, Mas X, no. 1317.

[53] *Santa Anna*, II, no. 202.

gradually to individualized bequests by the late twelfth century. Testators came to specify precisely what each heir should receive rather than make joint bequests, particularly in regard to real estate. With widely dispersed properties and investments, Bonet de Manresa in 1160 left his house near Santa Maria del Mar to his son Pere, but his shop and his land in Montpellier to another son Joan and 200 mbts., a shop, and other property at Tortosa to Almandine, one of his two daughters.[54] Even though Bonet granted other unspecified goods in Barcelona equally to all his children, by the division of key elements in his estate he hoped that the family bonds among his descendants would help coordinate disparate economic interests rather than form the basis of corporative exploitation of the patrimony. Thus, even though the raw figures presented above point to a rapid dispersal of property by the early thirteenth century rather than joint heirship and delayed division, terms more exact in the present context than impartibility, restricting major legacies to a limited number of children offered a means of stabilizing and perpetuating family wealth.

Yet another alternative began making headway by 1200: the promotion of a single heir. This did not, however, take the form prescribed in the *Liber iudiciorum*. Despite the widely held opinion that Catalonia remained more closely tied to early medieval legal habits than other areas of the peninsula, testators in twelfth- and thirteenth-century Barcelona generally had a poor grasp of the Visigothic *melioratio*, an institution still current in Old Castile at the time.[55] Only a single will associates an "improvement" with the *tercia*, the ancient third of all property due the children that could go to a favored heir, while through a conflation of legal language Pere Grony intended to leave separate *maioria* to both his eldest son and his eldest daughter, thereby increasing their share of the inheritance.[56] Eventually virtually all heirs who had received a premortem transfer through a marriage gift or other donation could expect a small supplement, sometimes called a *melioramen-*

---

[54] ADB, perg. Santa Anna, Carp. de la creu, unnumb. parch. [6 ii 1160].

[55] The precise quantity of the *melioratio* had already been forgotten by the eleventh century, Udina i Abelló, *La successió*, 80–81. Cf. Otero, "La mejora," 73–88.

[56] ACB 4–1–35 (1236): "iure institutionis terciam partem omnium bonorum meorum." The testament of Pere Grony is now published in Batlle-Busquest-Navarro, "Aproximació a l'estudi," no. 3: "Stacia filia mea maior aliqua habeat maioriam ... dictus filius meus maior possit habere per maioriam dictas domos."

tum.[57] Even though the specifics of the Visigothic *melioratio* had long been forgotten, the practice of reserving central portions of the estate, particularly the family house or urban real estate, for a single male heir gained currency toward the end of the twelfth century. Berenguer d'Arcs, founder of an early patrician house, in 1173 left his home, gardens, and property in the city and territory of Barcelona to his son Ramon, but his daughter was only to have a share with her brother in the profits from the *amostolafia*, the right to transport and ransom Muslim prisoners.[58] When confronted with providing for a much larger brood in 1203, Guillem Ombau the Younger left important legacies to each of his three sons and two daughters, yet he clearly favored one son named Guillem by the bequest of his own houses and properties near the city, while the others received a substantial portion of their legacies in money.[59] The core of the patrimony was slowly gravitating toward a single line of descent.

The tendency to favor a single child has usually been attributed to the infiltration of Roman law in Catalonia, but the movement was already under way by the time Justinianic legal language penetrated notarial formulas. It is certainly true that the tendency to promote a single heir at the expense of other children received additional impetus through the institution of the Roman *heres* (Catalan *hereu*), who assumed all legal responsibilities and liabilities incumbent upon the deceased. Yet the *hereu* makes its first appearance in local wills only in 1227,[60] and it met resistance from the older traditions promoting an equality of heirs; in blatant violation of Roman legal precepts, testators began to name several, or even all children *heredes*, an inflation of legal vocabulary that culminated in the employment of a redundantly grandiloquent phrase, *heres universalis* or *heres generalis*.[61] Thus, while a realignment of inheritance around a single male line of descent can be detected by the late twelfth century and gained momentum thereafter, it neither came about primarily through changes in legal form nor did it completely overcome the claims of all children to a substantial portion of the estate.

[57] ACB 4–3–207. The additional legacy is also referred to as *pro complimento* or *pro suplemento hereditatis*.
[58] ACB 4–3–242.
[59] ADB perg. Santa Anna, Carp. de la creu, unnumb. parch. [29 iv 1203].
[60] ACB 4–17–71.
[61] *Heres generalis* first appears in 1259, ACB 4–3–129; *heres universalis* in 1264, ACB 4–2–29.

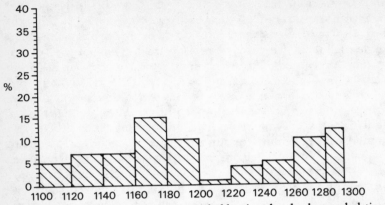

Figure 6.1   Percentage of joint propertyholders in urban land perambulations, 1100–1290

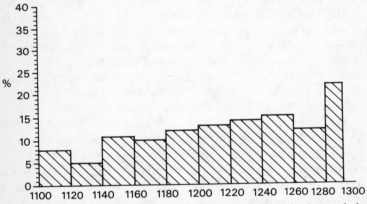

Figure 6.2   Percentage of female propertyholders in urban land perambulations, 1100–1290

Succession in twelfth- and thirteenth-century Barcelona was therefore not the product of rigid rules taken either from Visigothic or Roman law. Yet even if one looks in vain for unambiguous mechanisms regulating the transfer of property at death, the evidence from testamentary provisions uncovers a reorientation from a corporative to a lineal strategy of succession. To evaluate the impact of this shift on local propertyholding, however, other types of evidence need to be considered. Heirs often found ways of subverting inheritance customs or contravening the intention of the testator through informal arrangements with other family members; Zvi Razi has gone so far as to deny a clear correlation between inheritance customs and family structure in the English countryside during the late Middle Ages.[62]

Fortunately notarial traditions in the Mediterranean have preserved a means of evaluating landholding patterns, for in land transfers scribes routinely noted down the owners of adjacent property. By analyzing the percentage of joint landowners – in Barcelona usually denoted as *filii* of the deceased – in perambulations, the surveys of neighboring properties, it is possible to create a rough index of the proportion of burghers who held land jointly and of women who held property in their own name.[63]

Variation in the proportion of joint holdings did not move in a single direction during the 190 years surveyed: there was clearly no simple, unidirectional trend toward the breakup of common property, somewhat romantically related to "extended families" in older historical literature, and an "individualization" of landholding under the impact of urbanization. The evidence from perambulations indicates that impartible inheritances retained and even increased their popularity among burghers during the difficult decades of the early twelfth century and into the early phase of renewed economic expansion, then suddenly fell off in the decades around 1200. Joint heirships thereafter did not simply disappear, but slowly regained ground from the middle of the thirteenth century. The chronology presented here places the pivotal point in the reorganization of family property in the decades around 1200, precisely when prominent local families were fusing into a patriciate. Under the financial and economic pressure created by an expansive urban economy and the empty pockets of the king and his barons, the city's most assertive families attempted to free their resources from collective restraints in order to put them to use through credit or sale in the restructuring of wealth and power taking place within the city. The most valued family resources tended to concentrate in the hands of a single male heir, a strategy promoting the rapid movement of

---

[62] Zvi Razi, *Life, marriage, and death in a medieval parish: economy, society and demography in Halesowen, 1270–1400* (Cambridge, 1980), 56–57.

[63] The figures come from a survey of 4,289 property boundaries, 40 percent of which refer to streets, ecclesiastical property without mention of a lay tenant, public buildings, or other natural features and have been excluded from the calculations. When emphyteutic property is involved, the allodial holder or, in the case of Church property, the first lay tenant is counted.

assets into new investments. During the stagnant decades after
1100, families had employed joint and impartible inheritances to
conserve the agricultural properties accumulated in a more prosperous period, but this tactic prevented inherited wealth from
moving in new directions in the increasingly diversified urban
economy emerging in the mid-twelfth century. Promotion of a
single heir facilitated a rapid deployment of resources in an
exhilarating period of economic diversification. While the accentuation of a single male line of descent hardly represents a novelty
in medieval society, the circumstances and chronology of this
trend in Barcelona do not conform to the reasons usually put
forward in order to explain the emergence of noble patrilineages.
For the European aristocracy, the creation of what Herlihy has
termed a "dynastic model" of family structure centered on a
single line of male descent has been seen basically as a defensive
reaction, intended to preserve fiefs and estates from the harmful
effects of division; in Barcelona, however, the material favoritism
shown to a single male heir offered an aggressive response to a
burgeoning economy and the restructuring of urban property
and power.

If Barcelona's emerging patriciate seemed to toy with the
creation of *lignages* in the early thirteenth century, other forces
resisted preferential treatment of a single male heir. Established
habits of equal division did not completely give way, but, more
importantly, the nature of the conjugal fund gave women a
vigorous role in family organization. As figure 6.2 clearly shows,
women increased their control over property as patrician houses
were consolidating. To understand the role exercised by women,
however, it is necessary to examine the nature of marital assigns.

MARITAL ASSIGNS AND WIDOWS' RIGHTS

Once God, the universal creator, had in the beginning of the world
created everything from nothing, he shaped the form of woman from
the bone of a sleeping man: making one from two, He showed that two
should be one. On good authority a man leaves his father and mother
and cleaves to his wife, and they will be two in one flesh. Accordingly I,
Pere Adarró, for the sake of procreating children, choose to take for my
wife Guillema, and I grant her a dower (*dos*), namely the gift of the tenth
part of all my possessions, moveable or immoveable, that I have at
present or, God willing, will acquire in the future wherever they may be.
If anyone tries to impinge upon her dower or gift, may he not succeed,

Family structure and devolution of property

but for the presumption alone let him atone with ten pounds of pure gold. Further, may this dower or gift remain secure and firm for all time.[64]

The marriage contract between Pere Adarró and Guillema in 1162 fuses religious injunctions with the transfer of property. In moral terms marriage fulfilled the natural order, it continued a divine imperative already prepared by God's final act of creation; in secular life the joining of man and woman in one flesh reworked the bonds of kinship, producing a new social cell nourished from the creation of a conjugal fund that the couple had to defend against unwarranted outside interference. By the mid-twelfth century at the latest, the ritualistic language in the charter just cited had already become customary in Barcelona. Other documents would contain the specific arrangements for the amount of the marriage gift between husband and wife, yet the pious solemnity of the above act, whether recorded separately or added to the bottom of the detailed dower contract, concluded marriage negotiations. Notably absent is any reference to the ancient Visigothic ceremony of the exchange of bronze rings (*anuli arrarum*), a purely secular ritual which had marked the culmination of the long process of the marriage suit, betrothal, and, finally, wedding (*nuptiae*).[65] In its place stand moral injunctions about the Christian order. In his examination of the formation of medieval marital practices during the eleventh and twelfth century, Duby has pointed to the tension between lay and ecclesiastical models of marriage, especially at odds over questions of polygamy, the ease of divorce, and the return of marital assigns. By the twelfth century, this tension had been resolved in Barcelona; religious

---

[64] ACB 1–5–181: "Conditor omnium deus cum in mundi inicio cuncta creasset ex nichilo ex osse viri dormientis formam fecit mulieris ex uno duos faciens duos unum esse debere monstravit. Ipso testante. Relinquit homo patrem suum et matrem et adherebit uxori sue et erint duo in carne una. Qua propter in dei nomine ego Petrus Adarronis procreandorum filiorum amore elegi mihi sponsam occurrere nomine Guilelmam et facio ei dotem vel donationem decime partis omnium rerum mearum mobilium sive immobilium quas in presenti habeo vel in antea deo largiente ubique locorum adquisiero. Si quis contra hanc dotem ad infringendum venire temptaverit nullatenus facere possit sed per sola presumptione libras .x. auri puri componat et insuper hec dos seu donatio firma et stabilis omni tempore permaneat."

[65] On the intricacies of the various stages in Visigothic marriage, see King, *Law and society*, 223–35. Reference to the ceremony of ring-giving lingered on into the eleventh century in Catalonia, and much longer in Castile; Bonnassie, *La Catalogne*, 1, 258–59; Heath Dillard, *Daughters of the Reconquest: women in Castilian town society, 1100–1300* (Cambridge, 1984), 46–47.

precepts reinforced secular practice to ensure the stability of marriage and regulate the transfer of property to children. Older traditions, however, had not been completely effaced, for the marriage gift granted by Pere Adarró consisted of the ancient Visigothic tenth (*decimum*). Yet when Pere Adarró wedded Guillema, a reciprocal marital transfer, the dowry which the wife brought with her into the marriage, was already transforming the marital system in medieval Barcelona.

The rise of dowry in the medieval Mediterranean has recently drawn the attention of social historians and anthropologists, for the endowment of a woman by her own family with assets played a critical role in the restructuring of kinship after the millennium. In a sweeping and suggestive article, Hughes has placed the fundamental shift from "brideprice" (what I refer to as dower) to dowry in the Latin Mediterranean between the eleventh and thirteenth century.[66] In the early Middle Ages the dowry (*dos*) familiar to the Roman world had disappeared. Although the precise chronology and form varied from region to region, Hughes associates the reemergence of the ancient Roman dowry, which soon considerably exceeded the amount of dower, with the consolidation of agnatic kinship and the marginalization of daughters from the inheritance strategies of their own kin group. Because, according to Hughes, families generally chose to grant the dowry in cash, an act which precluded wedded daughters from making any further claims on the estate, the core properties of the patrimony were reserved for one or several sons. In what amounts to a preemptive strike on female heirs, parents granted daughters dowries in order to pass the essential elements of their property intact to sons.

[66] Diane Owen Hughes, "From brideprice to dowry in Mediterranean Europe," *Journal of family history*, 3 (1978), 262–96. English terminology in regard to marital assigns has produced considerable confusion in both historical and anthropological literature, since current usage tends to blur the distinction between the marital assign passing from husband to wife and that passing from the control of the wife's family to her husband. Goody, *Development of the family*, 240–43 attempts to dispel the fog surrounding the technical terminology; he objects to the use of "brideprice" during the high Middle Ages since the husband's contribution was not primarily intended to compensate his in-laws for the transfer of their daughter but rather to support the wife herself and their future children. Although Goody prefers the terms "indirect dowry" instead of "bride-wealth" or "brideprice" and "direct dowry" for dowry, I find the terms too artificial to express such a common and fundamental element of social life. Although somewhat archaic, "dower" and "dowry" seem preferable in the present context to "indirect" and "direct dowry," although they conform to his definitions.

While broad agreement exists about the overall movement toward dowry and its critical role in the reorganization of kinship structures in the high Middle Ages, considerable uncertainty remains about its function in regulating relationships between kin groups and especially its impact on the bride's family. Objecting to the view that dowry disinherited women, Jack Goody insists that it formed part of a pattern of "diverging devolution" in which both sons and daughters receive property, although at different times in their lives.[67] From a considerably different perspective, Christiane Klapisch-Zuber includes ceremonial aspects of marriage transactions in her calculus of kinship and concludes that elegant nuptial gifts and elaborate weddings, a prominent feature of marriage in Renaissance Italy, paid for by the groom's family balanced the high value of the dowry payment.[68] While a great deal of analysis has been devoted to the role of dowry in determining the place of daughters within their natal families and in regulating the alliance between the kin of the bride and groom, its implications for the management of the conjugal fund and the independence of the new couple has received considerably less attention. Family status depended not just upon the amount of dowry bestowed upon a daughter and the splendor of her wedding, but on the fate of the couple. Rights gained by daughters through dowry played a critical part in family organization and in the on-going, multilayered relationships among wives, husbands, and their respective sets of in-laws. Let us now turn to see precisely what rights husband and wife in Barcelona enjoyed through each of their marital assigns.

In his formulaic marriage contract to Guillema in 1162, Pere Adarró promised a tenth (*decimum*) of his property to the bride in accordance with the language of the *Liber iudiciorum*. Visigothic law includes detailed provisions for dower, the martial assign

---

[67] Goody, *Development of the family*, 255–61. For more extensive discussions of his insistence that dowry be considered within a broad context of property transfers between generations, see "Inheritance, property and women," in *Family and inheritance*, eds. J. Goody, J. Thirsk, and E. P. Thompson (Cambridge, 1976), 10–36 and *The oriental, the ancient and the primitive: systems of marriage and the family in the pre-industrial societies of Eurasia* (Cambridge, 1990), 13–16.

[68] Christiane Klapisch-Zuber, "Le Complexe de Griselda," *Mélanges de l'Ecole française de Rome*, 94 (1982), 7–43 ["The Griselda complex," in *Women, family, and ritual in Renaissance Florence*, trans. L. G. Cochrane (Chicago, 1985), 213–46]. She is particularly critical of analyzing the amount of dowry in terms of the supply and demand for brides, a perspective considered by David Herlihy, "The medieval marriage market," *Medieval and Renaissance studies*, 6 (1976), 1–27.

from groom to bride, but makes no reference to a counter-gift which the family of the bride would grant to her at the time of marriage. Conforming to traditional legal usage, the charter still calls the gift offered by Pere the *dos*, a sign in itself that the system of marital assigns had been completely reversed in the early Middle Ages since the word means dowry in classical Latin, while for the Visigoths it designated precisely the opposite gift. Except in the archaic language of the marriage formulary, however, Barcelona's scribes referred to the dower as the *sponsalicium*. By the twelfth century, its value bore little relationship to the ancient Visigothic tenth.[69] In detailed dower contracts the groom offered his wife a sum of money secured upon a pledge of his property; it was usual in the twelfth century to specify precisely which pieces of property would provide surety for the transfer of the cash dower, probably in an effort to avoid disputes with children from a widow's claim over a portion of the entire estate. The *sponsalicium* therefore constituted a security, or more precisely a promise of future support to the bride from a portion of her husband's property. In an early example of this practice, Bernat Udalard in 1100 promised his wife Eg 400 gold mancus for her *sponsalicium*, but until she had actually received the sum, she was to hold half of certain houses in Barcelona owned by her husband.[70] Did Eg ever receive her gold? If later practices are any indication, it is likely that she did not, at least not until her husband died and even then it was unclear precisely what portion she might actually claim from the estate of Bernat Udalard.

Rather than a clear transfer of designated property or money from groom to bride, the *sponsalicium* moved toward a broad grant of rights to the wife over all her husband's property. By the early thirteenth century a general pledge involving all the husband's property, present and future, rather than specific portions thereof backed up the amount of dower promised in the marriage contract. During her husband's lifetime, a wife consequently had to consent to all property transfers made by her husband since they

<hr>

[69] Bonnassie, *La Catalogne*, 1, 259–60 believes the *decimum* still accurately reflected the amount of the dower in the early eleventh century; cf. Udina i Abelló, *La successió*, 83–84 and Jesús Lalinde Abadía, "Los pactos matrimoniales catalanes (esquema histórico)," *AHDE*, 33 (1963), 165, 167. Neither early dowry contracts nor wills after 1100 mention a tenth except in formulaic documents like the one cited in n. 64 above; reference to the *decimum* finally disappears from the formula in the 1270s, ACB 1–6–1205, 3493, 3845, 4172, 4194.

[70] Lalinde Abadía, "Los pactos," no. 3.

affected the dower; further, when widowed, she had to receive the amount of the dower before a division among other heirs could occur. The more general the pledge of dower, the more difficult the later division of the husband's estate. The shift in dower from the assignment of specific assets for the widow's support to a general entitlement of the widow over the deceased's estate can most clearly be seen in testamentary provisions husbands made for their wives. Until the 1170s, married men, following a long-standing tradition, usually specified in their wills precisely what wives were to receive for their dower in order to prevent any further claims by their spouses on the inheritance. In an oral testament published in 1013 upon the altar of Sant Pancraç in the church of Santa Maria del Pi, the executor of the deceased Cristià made quite clear what his wife should receive for her dower but allowed nothing more: "And I [the deceased's executor] order a charter drawn up for his wife Lobeta for the allod of Orta...and the houses which he owned in Barcelona...with the condition that she may not otherwise demand her dower (*decimum*) from him [the deceased] or her children nor seek any of his possessions, moveable or real, of any kind whatsoever."[71] In the last quarter of the twelfth century, however, male testators begin their wills with a general confirmation of the *sponsalicium* rather than a specific list of what it should consist.[72] The actual portion of the estate a widow received was a matter of private negotiation, sometimes fraught with anger, between the widow and her children in order to free up their inheritance. Private agreements with the widow began to appear at the same time. In 1171 Guillema, the widow of Arnau Adarró, signed a charter declaring to her son Bernat that she had received compensation for 500 mbts. "from the dower (*sponsalicium*) your father made to me" and renounced any further claim on the estate; in the following year Bernat Adarró himself contracted a marriage and promised 600 mbts. to his wife.[73] In order for heirs to take off on

---

[71] Udina i Abelló, *La successió*, no. 96: "Et iubeo cartam facere ad uxori sua Lobeta de ipso suo aluade de Orta ... et de ipsos domos que abebat in Barchinona ... in tale captione ut non requirat ipsum suum decimum nec ullam aliam rem in facultatibus suis, nec ad ipsum, nec ad filiis suis, de mobile vel inmobile, de omnia et de omnibus." Cf. ibid., no. 105; *Santa Anna*, II, no. 271.

[72] *Santa Anna*, III, no. 478; ACB 4–9–132; LA I, fol. 277, Mas XII, no. 2225.

[73] ACB 1–5–44, 217. For other examples of private accords between children and their widowed mothers, see ACB 1–5–253; 1–6–940, 1070; ADB perg. Santa Anna, Carp. de la creu, unnumb. parch. [13 i 1193].

their own, it became increasingly necessary to seek the approval of their father's widow.

The power women gained over their husbands' property through dower also depended upon their ability to dispose of it as they saw fit. Visigothic law allowed a widow to dispose freely of a quarter of her dower (*dos*), with the remainder going to her children; if the marriage lacked legitimate issue, however, she could dispose of her entire dower unless she failed to make a will, in which case it reverted to her husband and his kin.[74] While allowing for somewhat more latitude in the disposition of dower than for inheritance, Visigothic rules nevertheless left widows relatively little freedom to alienate the property of their deceased husbands. Practices in Barcelona diverged considerably from these restrictions. While a widow naturally enjoyed the entire *sponsalicium* for her lifetime, dower contracts allowed her at death free disposition of at least half the marital assign from her deceased husband even if she died intestate, yet it was not uncommon for the proportion to be as high as two-thirds.[75] The remainder would pass to her children or, if none survived her, would return to her husband, his kin, or whomever he designated. By granting women the right to distribute a substantial portion of property assigned them by their husbands regardless of whether the marriage ended with or without children, customary dower practices in Barcelona made the widow a formidable figure with broad discretionary powers over property received from her husband's kin. Even though women tended to pass on most of the property they controlled to their sons and daughters, they nevertheless possessed considerable latitude in distributing it among heirs. A son dared to antagonize his widowed mother only at great risk to his inheritance. The evolution of dower therefore reinforced wives' claims over the joint management of their husbands' property and made widows a potent force in maintaining the cohesion of the conjugal fund and in determining the ultimate distribution of inheritance.

In addition to the *sponsalicium* granted by their husbands, women also brought into the marriage property from their own family, the dowry, usually called by its vernacular name *exovar*,

---

[74] King, *Law and society*, 236–37.

[75] For examples of wives receiving the right to dispose of more than half their *sponsalicium*, see ACB 1–5–44, 254, 469; 1–6–2010, 2189, 3453, 3763, 3821, 3986, 4299; 3–29–185; ADB perg. Santa Anna, Carp. 1a, 5, 12.

but sometimes given its classical Latin name *dos* in the thirteenth century.[76] Visigothic law does not mention such assigns, a clear indication that the Roman dowry had disappeared in the early Middle Ages. Dowry had reasserted itself in Catalonia, however, by the eleventh century, long before the revival of Roman law. Recently restored, the dowry seemed less stable in its diplomatic form than the well-established *sponsalicium* and fewer examples survive. The transfer was first expressed in terms of an interfamilial donation at the time of marriage (*donatio ad diem nuptiarum*) and was directly linked to the amount a daughter could expect for her inheritance (*damus tibi per tuam hereditatem*).[77] Other than mentioning that the bride was being handed over (*tradere*) with the dowry to her husband, charters do not specify precisely how the property should be treated after the marriage. During the twelfth century the dowry consisted primarily of real estate and clearly constituted a form of premortem settlement between a daughter and her parents; additional stipulations or even separate charters occasionally added further conditions, specifying that parents would continue to reside in or enjoy usufruct from property given their daughter in dowry until they died and even to receive rent from her and her husband until that time.[78] Only in a single instance (evidently a transitory experiment) did the dowry contract imitate the form of the *sponsalicium* in which the bride granted her husband a marriage gift with a monetary value secured upon a general pledge of her property.[79] Intended for the maintenance of the bride based upon her own claims to her natal family's property, the earliest dowry contracts in Barcelona therefore stressed the relationship between the bride and her own parents and kin in respect to inheritance, not the place of dowry as a constituent part of the new conjugal fund.

During the thirteenth century, however, the emphasis of

76 On the linguistic change, see Lalinde Abadía, "Los pactos matrimoniales," 182–83. The term *dos* is first recorded in 1194 with the meaning of dowry at Barcelona, ACB 1–5–52: "ego Bernardus Adarronis et uxor mea Berengaria damus tibi Joanne filie nostre ad diem nuptiarum in dotem et per tuam hereditatem ..."
77 ACB 1–5–21 (1139). Cf. ACB 1–5–24, 133, 1525; ACA Gran Priorat, armari 1, 67 and preceding note.
78 ASPP, 92; ACB 1–6–323.
79 Fortunately both the dowry and the dower contracts survive for the marriage between Pere Arnau and Guillema in 1174, ACB 1–6–236, 237. Executed on the same day, they are virtually identical in language, conditions, the number of witnesses, and the amounts involved; even though the two charters contain distinct marital assigns, both dowry and dower are called *sponsalicia*.

dowry contracts shifted to the mutual obligations created by gift and counter-gift between bride and groom. By 1250 the amount of dowry, the *exovar*, began to exceed that of the dower by two to one, a proportion officially sanctioned in *Recognoverunt proceres* as the custom in Barcelona. Although information about the comparative value of the two marital assigns is far from abundant since contracts for the *exovar* and *sponsalicium* were redacted separately, the proportional amount brought by husband and wife into the marriage at first demonstrated considerable flexibility: of six known sets of marital assigns before 1250, two were equal, three were larger on the part of the husband, and one indicated that the wife made the largest contribution.[80] As dowry established its quantitative superiority, it also changed the entire system of marital assigns. While the *sponsalicium*, once the most significant marital transfer, had constituted an independent promise of support by a husband to his wife, it was now thought of in terms of a counter-gift to the amount the wife brought with her in dowry. Not only was the dower pegged at half the amount of the *exovar*, its very name changed to reflect this dependence: the dower was no longer called the *sponsalicium*, the marriage gift, but the "addition" to the dowry (Latin *augmentum*, Catalan *excreix*).[81] Because the donation of the *excreix* now took the form of a reflexive transfer dependent on the amount of the *exovar*, diplomatically the two marital assigns fused into one document, signifying they had become integrated parts of a single, interrelated, and standardized transaction. In a formula acknowledging the primacy of the dowry in the conjugal fund, the groom recognized that he had received a certain amount in dowry from his bride, to whom he consequently granted an *excreix*; he would then pledge his property not only for the amount of the marital gift he had assigned to her but also for the amount of dowry she had brought into the marriage.[82] Even though the new marital contracts combining *exovar* with *excreix* now rarely permitted wives the free disposition at death of any portion of the martial assign from their

[80] ACB 1–5–16 and LA I, fol. 39, Mas X, no. 1290; 1–5–236, 237; 1–6–397, 3973, 3986; 3–29–256; ARM perg. Pascual, XIII, 9.

[81] The phrase first appears at Barcelona in a marriage contract between Pere Boquer and Geralde, daughter of Martí de Montcada, in 1234, ACB 3–28–256: "Addo seu adcresco tibi .ccc. morabetinos."

[82] E.g. ACB 1–6–854, 3845, 4172, 4194; ADB perg. Santa Anna, Carp. 1a, 70; ACA perg. varis, Marquès de Monistrol, 113. On similar changes elsewhere in Catalonia, see Lalinde Abadía, "Los pactos," 194–97.

husbands, women nevertheless retained full rights over their own dowries and in fact tightened their hold over their husbands' property, which now was pledged to maintain the entire marital fund. While technically distinct, the portions contributed by bride and groom created overlapping rights, for the husband managed the dowry brought by his wife, who in turn possessed rights over his property. The new conjugal fund therefore represented a complex intermingling of rights controlled by both husband and wife; further, it promoted a balancing of influence between the respective kin groups which had contributed the property to set up the new couple.

While changes in the system of marital assigns and the eventual emergence of dowry as its dominant element have been noted before in Catalonia, previous scholarship has ignored their impact on family organization. Attributing these developments simply to a revival of ancient Roman practices skirts the issue, for certain elements began to emerge already in the eleventh century.[83] Two features, however, are striking in the overall movement of marital assigns during the twelfth and thirteenth century: the maintenance and even the strengthening of the wife's rights over the conjugal fund and, second, the heavy involvement of her kin in the marriage owing to the rise of dowry.

Bonnassie has pointed to the remarkable degree of material independence enjoyed by women in eleventh-century Catalonia; they could buy, sell, and pledge land independently of their husbands, and donations or sales *inter vivos* between husband and wife, or between mother and son, were common.[84] He attributes this latitude to a strict separation of goods; women had a strong claim to equal shares of their parents' estate, while they retained exclusive power over their personal property (*parafernalia*) and dowry after marriage and even obtained through the *sponsalicium* claims over their husbands' goods. Wives in twelfth- and thirteenth-century Barcelona by and large continued to exercise substantial authority over property during marriage, but the growing interconnection of dower and dowry tended to cloud over the separation of goods. Real estate or funds brought with the bride in

---

[83] Legal historians have to date dominated discussions about Catalan marital assigns and strongly emphasize Roman influence, Lalinde Abadía, "Los pactos," 195, 198; Brocá, *Derecho civil catalan*, I, 236. For criticism of such an explanation in medieval Latium, see Toubert, *Les Structures*, I, 752–56.

[84] Bonnassie, *La Catalogne*, I, 274–75.

dowry were clearly to be used for her support, but husbands usually assumed the responsibility of managing them. Estàcia, for instance, pledged to repay her husband for improvements and repairs he had made to the house she had received for her dowry, and in a transaction on a grander scale Pere de Blanes admitted holding 4,000s. from his wife Guillema, who had just arrived at a settlement with her brothers concerning the inheritance from her father, Pere de Viladecols, in addition to what he already held from her dowry.[85] Even if an informal supervision of dowry may have restricted independent transactions by wives, a supposition strengthened by the rarity of *inter vivos* donations between spouses in the thirteenth century, women extended their right to be consulted in the transactions made by their husbands. Emboldened by new legal sophistry and the revival of a Roman constitution known as the *senatus consultus Velleyani*, which permitted wives to annul any contract made by their spouses without their permission if it involved dotal property, some widows in Barcelona and Rosselló refused to honor the debts of their deceased husbands because they had not explicitly renounced this ancient privilege. King Jaume I had to issue decrees in 1241 and 1261 to put an end to the subterfuge.[86] Even though this ruse failed, it nevertheless points to the considerable authority women exercised over their husbands' property by right of dowry. In order to avoid any challenge to their actions, men began to seek formal appointments as procurators from their wives.[87] Representative of the different relationship developing within the conjugal fund, charters of procuration tended to replace donations *inter vivos* between husband and wife in the later thirteenth century. While a complex intermingling of rights and assets within the conjugal fund may have diminished the independence of wives in managing their property, it worked to heighten their influence within the family.

The rise of dowry helped secure a substantial degree of authority for wives in Barcelona since it heavily involved their natal kin

[85] ACB 1–6–488, 1942. Even *parafernalia*, goods owned in complete independence by women, came under the management of husbands, ACB 4–15–85, 180; 1–6–3853.

[86] ACA Cartes Reials, Jaume I, Caixa 1, 71, noted in Sara Cunchillos Plano, "Breves extractos de los documentos contenidos en la caja primera de Jaime I, de 'Cartas reales', conservadas en el Archivo de la Corona de Aragón," *X CHCA* (Zaragoza, 1980–82), II, 494, no. 71; Huici-Cabanes, *Documentos*, II, no. 331. Yet in 1271 a widow still refused to honor her deceased husband's debts because she had not formally renounced the clause, ACA perg. Pere II, 177. On the spread of this clause in Iberia, see Jesús Lalinde Abadía, "La recepción española del senadoconsulto Velleyano," *AHDE*, 41 (1971), 335–72.

[87] ACB 4–39–442; 4–40–493; 4–50–419.

in the marriage. To clarify this point, it is necessary to consider dowry as part of an overall system of transfers by which women obtained property.[88] In contrast to the dotal regimes in northern Italy, the grant of the dowry to *barcelonines* did not exclude them from making further claims on their parents' estates. Even though dowry contracts between parents and daughters couched the transfer in terms of an early receipt of inheritance, women could later make further demands if they thought their portion was either inequitable or the division of property had changed because of the death of a sibling after the original agreement had been struck. Agnès, the youngest daughter of Pere Grony, successfully sued her brothers for an addition to her dowry once her father had died, asking for her fair share of the inheritance (*legitima*); in a comparable dispute in 1257, the judge Arnau Barbot allowed a married woman to demand compensation from the estate of her deceased father under the broad principle, "that the full portion of the inheritance (*legitima*) is not due to children until after the death of their parents."[89] Here the devolution of property to women forms a continuum extending from the grant of a dowry to later claims against the parents' estates. Whereas contemporary Genoese wills tended to ignore married daughters, Barcelona's testators regularly included them among heirs, stated how much they had received at marriage, and in many instances made small additional bequests (*pro complimento hereditatis*) to even up the daughters' portion and express an enduring bond of affection. In Barcelona the dowry clearly did not exclude a married woman from further rights of succession, nor did her kin grant it to compensate the husband for "taking her off their hands"; rather than serving to disinherit a daughter, dowry formed part of a system of property transfers to women extended over time. The system of marital assigns in Barcelona therefore did not encourage patricians to cast off their daughters like family jetsam in order to guarantee the prominence of a patrilineage; instead, it kept husbands acutely aware of the continuing interference of their in-laws during the marriage.

Delays in transfer of the dowry also worked to reinforce ties between a wife and her natal family. Although a handful of dowry

---

[88] On this approach, see Goody, *Development of the family*, 257–61; Casey, *History of the family*, 74–79.

[89] ACB 1–6–3981; ADB perg. Santa Anna, Carp. 1a, 2–16: "quod legitima non debetur filiis nisi post mortem parentum."

contracts contain specific timetables for delivery, usually spaced over a year, tacit understandings between the groom and his wife's family must have been even more common. In one revealing document Arnau de Torrelles declared that even though his son-in-law admitted in a charter that he had received the full 750 mbts. dowry promised to Arnau's daughter, only 500 mbts. had actually been delivered.[90] The longer the dowry was delayed, the more delicate the relationship between the husband and his in-laws. In case the husband maltreated his wife or failed to use the dowry for her support, judges were not loath to return the dowry to the wife's natal kin.[91] Even an extended separation could temporarily break up the conjugal fund and place the dowry under the control of the wife's relatives. When Jaume de Vic prepared for a long absence from Barcelona in 1260, probably on a commercial voyage, he entered into a contract in which his wife was returned to her parents' house, where she would live on the dowry that had not yet been transferred to him.[92] Through the slow devolution of property through dowry and a continuing claim on inheritance from her parents, a wife could employ the leverage provided by her natal kin to ensure that her rights within the marriage were protected.

Yet as the dotal regime began to dominate the system of marital assigns, a triumph manifested by the conversion of the *sponsalicium* into the *excreix*, widows lost some power to manage family assets. No longer did they have a right to dispose of a portion of their husbands' property at death as they had once done under the older terms of dower; while a widow of course enjoyed the use of her dower as long as she lived, at her death the entire *excreix* with rare exception passed either to her children or, if none survived, returned to her husband's kin. Further, because the *excreix* constituted a substantially smaller portion of the marriage fund than the *exovar* contributed by her own relatives, a separation of assets at the death of her husband could be achieved with greater ease than before. By making a woman increasingly dependent on material support from her own natal kin, dowry prevented her from being fully integrated into the inheritance strategies of her husband's relatives. As a result, beginning around 1250 (see table 6.3) it became less common for male testators with children to designate their wives as administrators of the entire estate for their lifetimes

[90] ACB 1–6–3990. For examples of delayed payments specified in the dowry contract itself, see ACB 1–6–434, 4117, 4181; ACA perg. varis, Marquès de Monistrol, 169.
[91] ACA Reg. 41, fol. 76 v.; Reg. 56, fol. 52 v.   [92] ACB 1–6–1147.

Table 6.3 *Testamentary appointment of widows to manage estates*

	1100–1150	1151–1200	1201–1250	1251–1290
Male testators with wife and children	6	11	27	35
No. of above who appointed widows to direct the estate	2 (33%)	6 (55%)	11 (41%)	6 (17%)

provided they did not remarry, or, in the language of the charters, to make them *dominae et potentissimae*.[93]

Even though widows fulfiled an important supervisory function over minor children in their role as guardians, after 1250 their prerogatives rarely extended beyond the time when their children came of age. The abrupt decline in the number of widows granted broad powers to direct their deceased husbands' estates corresponded to two changes in the way property devolved on succeeding generations: the spread of the *excreix* and the institution of the *heres*. The principal heir, generally the eldest son, came to replace the widow at the head of the family as she came to rely for her support on the *exovar* rather than the *excreix*.[94] While the separation of goods at the death of her husband partially relaxed the earlier tension between the widow and her children, anxious to receive their individual portions of the inheritance, it also promoted a rapid division of the estate. Agreements between sons and their widowed mothers no longer provided the key for the rearrangement of family property. With widows free to dispose of their dowries and daughters rapidly receiving their inheritances, it is hardly surprising that a growing amount of property fell into the hands of women toward the latter half of the thirteenth century.[95] Earlier the extensive power of the widow had served to keep the entire conjugal fund intact; once her authority had diminished due to changes in the system of marital

[93] The phrase first appears in 1192, ACB LA I, fol. 277, Mas XII, no. 2225: "domina et potens tocius sui honoris et omnium rerum suarum"; the appointment of widows to manage the entire estate, however, is much older.

[94] The tense transition is vividly expressed in the will of Arnau Coll in 1250, ACB 4–1–35: "set volo quod Arnalete uxor mea teneat et possidat omnia bona mea et sit inde domina et potens simul cum dicto filio meo toto tempore vite sue...quem insituto heredem post obitum dicte matris sue." Cf. ACB 4–10–44.

[95] Supra, figure 6.2.

assigns, inheritance strategies shifted toward placing more resources and authority in the hands of a single male heir.

The evolution of marital assigns in Barcelona during the twelfth and thirteenth century does not, however, admit to an unambiguous decline in the role of married women. Although dowry indisputably emerged as the dominant element in the system of marital transfers, the implication of this shift for the position of women as wives and widows is complex and, at times, contradictory. While historians most familiar with northern Italian cities have argued that the rise of dowry produced a progressive deterioration in the material position of women from the twelfth century onward and their marginalization within the increasingly agnatic orientation of kinship structures,[96] this judgment can not be generalized to the entire Latin Mediterranean. When considered in conjunction with an overall movement of property from generation to generation through both inheritance and marital assigns, the rise of dowry seems to have strengthened the economic viability and independence of the new couple in some regions by granting additional rights to the wife and a degree of control over her husband's property. In Latium, where a similar marital regime emerged in the eleventh and twelfth century, Toubert speaks of an *apogée féministe*.[97] In Barcelona the intricate interface of rights and property created by the transfer of marital assigns caused women to surrender a degree of independence in disposing of their property as they wished, but it increased their authority over and management of the conjugal fund. The change is particularly evident in the late twelfth and early thirteenth century, when the amount of dowry and dower were more balanced and flexible than later; because of the considerable control wives gained over the distribution of their dower, they were drawn toward their husbands' relatives and, as widows, enjoyed remarkably broad powers in managing the estates of their husbands. Once the proportional amount of the dower was reduced through the *excreix* and a wife's rights to distribute her husband's property restricted, the dominance of dowry gave the wife's natal kin greater weight within the marriage yet at the same time somewhat reduced the prerogatives of widows in the management of the entire conjugal fund. These

---

[96] Herlihy, *Medieval households*, 98–103; Hughes, "From brideprice," 276–87; Cammarosano, "Structures familiales," 182–85.

[97] Toubert, *Les Structures*, I, 761.

rather subtle shifts in balance between the influence exerted by husband and wife and their respective sets of in-laws, the most direct consequence of changes in the system of marital assigns, should not obscure the influence marriage gifts had in promoting the fundamental economic cohesion and independence of the married couple in Barcelona. True to the moral injunctions in the marriage contract, Pere Adarró and his bride Guillema did indeed leave their respective mother and father, even if they did not stop listening to their parents' advice.

CONCLUSION

In surveying the subtle transformations in the linguistic and structural outlines of family and kinship organization that occurred over two centuries of rapid economic change and urban expansion, one can not help but be struck by the remarkable strength of Visigothic tradition. Even though customary practices had long deviated from the precise rules of the *Liber iudiciorum*, burghers at all levels of society sought to provide reasonably equivalent shares of their property to all their children, male and female. It is within this context that one must evaluate the role of marital assigns, for dowry clearly did not constitute a form of female disinheritance in Barcelona.

Diverging devolution coupled with cognatic filiation provided considerable resistance to emergent agnatic tendencies that came to dominate the kinship structures in the city–republics of northern Italy. In one of the first systematic analyses of notarial material for the study of family history, Herlihy noted the prominent economic role of women in Spain and southern France from the eighth to the twelfth century in comparison to other areas of Europe and attributed it to favorable provisions in Burgundian and, above all, Visigothic law.[98] His general conclusion still stands and can even be extended for another century, when the formal aspects of Visigothic legal culture withered as customary usages and Roman law overlay older traditions. Yet the authority women held over property manifested itself in quite different forms as family organization changed. Because of the early independence of wives over their own assets, the material continuity of the family depended upon delayed partition and joint management of inheritances among brothers. This corporative form of patrimonial stability manifested by the *frarisca* conformed

[98] Herlihy, "Land, family, and women," 204–9.

to a conservative economic regime dependent upon the accumulation and exploitation of land in order to profit from the urban market. As Barcelona emerged from its economic torpor, new forms of wealth encouraged a weakening of corporate ties on property; the decline of joint heirship, evident from the 1170s, was paralleled by the consolidation of dotal marriage, which accorded wives prerogatives over the distribution of their husbands' estates, and the grant of extensive powers to widows, who perpetuated the fusion achieved in marriage of two sets of family resources. Finally, around 1250, the preeminence of dowry and the consequent diminution of the dower heightened the influence of the wife and her natal kin in the marriage but left the future direction of the family to the principal male heir. The chronology traced here represents tendencies rather than sudden breaks in family organization, yet the considerable authority vested in women, even though manifested in different forms, remained an enduring and defining feature of social organization in Barcelona.

In contrast to what is often rather casually assumed about the emergence of Mediterranean urban elites, Barcelona's patriciate did not assume a pronounced agnatic structure comparable to the patrilineal organization of the aristocracy or the segmented, branching clans characteristic of Italian noble families. The thwarted development of an urban nobility was critical in the subsequent structuring of patrician houses. Rather than adopt pronounced agnatic structures, the city's leading families employed inheritance strategies and marital assigns to create bonds of alliance among themselves rather than reinforce lines of direct descent. Barcelona offered a fluid, expansive, contractual world in which the system of marital assigns provided an effective mechanism to lessen any divergence between wealth and status.[99] In the highly competitive and potentially volatile environment taking shape in the early thirteenth century, relatively truncated lines of descent and a system of marital assigns fostering cooperation among in-laws promoted social equilibrium. Yet this balance among patrician houses proved difficult to maintain in the wake of the maritime and commercial expansion that finally turned Barcelona into a major Mediterranean power.

---

[99] On the use of dowry for "social climbing" in highly monetarized societies, see Sara A. Dickey and Steven Harrell, "Dowry systems in complex societies," *Ethnology*, 24 (1985), 111–19; Goody, *The oriental, the ancient and the primitive*, 111–12, 191–92; Casey, *History of the family*, 84–85.

Chapter 7

CONSOLIDATION AND CONFLICT: PATRICIAN POWER AND MEDITERRANEAN EXPANSION, 1220–91

In late December, 1228, King Jaume I, now a tested and self-confident ruler at age twenty, convoked a plenary court at Barcelona, where he confirmed the peace and truce throughout Catalonia and finalized his plans for the conquest of Majorca. After speeches from ecclesiastical dignitaries and barons, Pere Grony rose to address the assembly:

"My lord, we, the entire city of Barcelona, give thanks to God for the good fortune He has granted you, and we trust in Our Lord that you will accomplish what you set out to do. Let us be the first in offering you the galleys, ships, and boats which stand ready in Barcelona to serve you in this honorable host, for the honor of God. And we shall act in such a manner that we will forever earn your favor for the service we will now perform for you."

I [King Jaume] did not wish to consult the other towns since none present carried greater weight than Barcelona. Tarragona and Tortosa agreed with the words that the *prohoms* of Barcelona had spoken.[1]

As recounted in the king's own *Book of Deeds*, the speech by a patrician representing the entire populace of Barcelona concluded the deliberations of this fateful assembly, the planning committee for Catalan colonialism.

Ambiguities streak the seeming transparency of this offer of support. Besides revealing a probable lapse in the king's memory of the event since Pere Grony had in fact died a year before the gathering,[2] the text presents a jumbled mixture of motives in

---

[1] Jaume I, *Llibre dels feits*, c. 54. King Jaume's remarks here are particularly difficult to unravel: "E per ço no hi volem pus metre de les ciutats, e car no n'hi ha plus sinó Barcelona. E Tarragona et Tortosa acordaren-se a la paraula que els prohòmens de Barcelona dixeren." Soldevila notes in his edition that the first sentence appears to mean only representatives from Barcelona attended the Cort, but what follows clearly contradicts this reading. Cf. ibid., c. 49.

[2] Pere Grony, clearly the spokesman for his house in the early thirteenth century, made his will in May, 1227, and later in the year his widow was appointed tutor of his children, as noted in Batlle-Busquets-Navarro, "Aproximació a l'estudi," 287; they believe another member of the family was present. A minor son Pere survived, but it seems unlikely that

explaining the city's rush to aid the venture: municipal pride, loyalty to the Crown, material and political self-interest, and the wish to serve God. While historians have tried to isolate the various components embedded in these words and assign different weight to the religious, commercial, and dynastic factors behind Catalan Mediterranean expansion, forced arguments to advance monocausal explanations have often resulted in what Vicente Salavert has judiciously labelled a "simplifying intellectualism."[3] What an abstract, analytical dissection of the various individual motives tends to overlook is the collective impact of their convergence. That each element, especially military, fiscal, and commercial, provided reinforcement for expansion is too often taken for granted. Yet only in the reign of Jaumes I's father did urban deputies regularly attend the Corts,[4] and, as we have seen, Barcelona's entrepreneurs did not become major financiers to the count-king and his barons until around 1200. Urban and dynastic interests therefore became tightly interlocked, or at least assumed a vibrant new form, only in the generation before the conquest of Majorca. From Jaume's own account of the assembly, however, there can be little doubt that Barcelona spoke for the other cities of Catalonia in ceremonial support of the king's designs.

The conquest of Majorca brutally completed in 1229 opened a new chapter in the maritime and commercial history of the Crown of Aragon. Primarily a Catalan undertaking, it directed the restless energies of barons and their men-at-arms in new directions and drew upon the collective naval potential of Catalonia and Occitania. Besides reaffirming the peace and truce statutes, at the urging of the independently minded baron Nunyo Sanç,

he would have acted as spokesman for the entire community at such a solemn gathering. It is much more likely that Jaume remembered Pere Grony as a prominent figure in the city and mistakenly associated his name with the proceedings.

[3] Salavert, "Nuevamente sobre l'expansión," 373–76 points out that the rhetorical polarization between those who see the expansion in purely economic terms and those who stress political and military strategies actually obscures the common ground both schools hold. For the essential lines of debate, see supra, 221–23 and the recent summary by Felipe Fernández-Armesto, *Before Columbus: exploration and colonisation from the Mediterranean to the Atlantic, 1229–1492* (Philadelphia, 1987), 13–18, who stresses dynastic and chivalrous elements.

[4] On the early Corts, still in need of careful study, see the comments of Evelyn Proctor, "The development of the Catalan Corts in the thirteenth century," in *Homenatge a Rubió i Lluch* (Barcelona, 1935), III, 535, and Thomas N. Bisson, "Prelude to power: kingship and constitution in the realms of Aragon, 1175–1250," in *The worlds of Alfonso the Learned and James the Conqueror: intellect and force in the Middle Ages*, ed. R. I. Burns (Princeton, 1985), 37–40.

count of Rosselló and kinsman of the king, the Cort at Barcelona made the unusual provision of allowing the king to collect the *bovatge*, customarily levied only at royal accessions, throughout Catalonia; what had once been a tax to secure the "peace of beasts" (*pax bestiarum*) had become an invasion subsidy, later granted as well in 1236, 1264, and 1286 for the conquests of Valencia, Murcia, and Menorca.[5] Following time-honored precedents of previous Catalan rulers, King Jaume I helped secure internal peace by directing violence toward Muslim princes. But he also turned to subject and allied towns for backing. In addition to the ships available in Catalan ports, the king commanded the naval resources of Marseilles, Montpellier, Narbonne, and other ports of Languedoc and Provence. The entire adventure provides a clear sign of growing independence, for Jaume was the first count-king able to undertake a major naval operation without the support of an Italian fleet. If the subsequent subdivision and distribution of houses in Palma and farms in the interior according to the *repartiment* provide an accurate measure of the forces contributed by the various towns, it appears that Tarragona and Marseilles sent more ships and men into battle than did Barcelona. Whatever the city's level of participation, Barcelona did not hesitate to seek special commercial advantages. A privilege in 1231 exempted its inhabitants from commercial tolls on Majorca, and another grant in the following year freed them from all royal tariffs throughout the entire Crown of Aragon, a trading subsidy far more valuable than the small fields and houses its citizens received on the island.[6] Owing to the limited range of medieval galleys, this advanced island base provided a key to commanding the vital trunk route, the artery of trade along the northern Mediterranean coast, and oriented Barcelona's maritime aggressiveness toward the south;[7] the occupation of Majorca confirmed the city's maritime destiny and made the island a focal point for the imperial designs of its rulers. With the occupation of Sicily in 1282, Catalans not only gained access to new resources but forced themselves center stage in Mediterranean politics. The material advantages Barcelonans gained from these adventures can only be understood within the

---

[5] Bisson, *Conservation*, 60–61, 88–91; Ferran Soldevila, "A pròposit del servei del bovatge," *AEM*, 1 (1964), 580–83.

[6] Capmany, II, nos. 8, 9.

[7] On the technical factors restricting the range of medieval galleys, especially limited supplies of fresh water, see Pryor, *Geography, technology, and war*, 71–86, 99–100, 158–59.

context of the new military and political patterns established by King Jaume I and his successors.

While the basic stages of the Crown's military and diplomatic expansion in the Mediterranean are well known, relatively little attention has been devoted to their effects on Catalonia itself. Commercial wealth increased dramatically in the thirteenth century, and there is little doubt that among Catalonian towns Barcelona stood to profit the most. The city experienced a feverish period of growth in the two or three generations following the conquest of Majorca, a demographic upsurge unmatched in the city's pre-industrial history. Whether the creation of new commercial fortunes destabilized the patriciate, which had only recently consolidated its power, remains an open question.

A new categorization, first appearing in charters assessing taxes and fines, divided the urban population into *maiores*, *mediocres*, and *minores*, what became known in the vernacular as the city's three "hands" (*mans*) and was later reflected in the organization of Barcelona's municipal council.[8] Yet did these categories accurately depict a new social stratification based on wealth and occupation, or were they merely clumsy expressions drawn from the well-worn vocabulary of Mediterranean urban politics? The trifold division of the urban populace into "greater," "middling," and "lesser" groupings already had a long history in Italian and Occitanian towns, where it expressed not so much differences in wealth, occupation, or political influence as inherited status and its attendant privileges.[9] The "reordering" of Barcelona's population did not, however, efface the older distinctions between *prohoms* and *cives*, a contrast based on prestige and informal authority rather than on wealth or inherited privilege and long maintained in the formulas of royal charters. In numerous articles on thirteenth-century Barcelona, Batlle i Gallart, one of the first to make use of the archives of Barcelona's cathedral in order to explore social history, has tried, with admitted difficulty, to identify the "greater" and "middling" categories with oligarchs and merchants. After accumulating fortunes through maritime trade and naval armament, Barcelona's "first oligarchy" in her view became

---

[8] The earliest reference to this division appears in the assessment of a local tax in 1226; the second in the levying of a general fine on the entire urban population in 1258 for the murder of Bernat Marquet, Huici-Cabanes, *Documentos*, I, no. 81; IV, no. 929.

[9] Keller, *Adelsherrschaft*, 41–61; W. Goetz, *Die Entstehung der italienischen Kommunen im Frühen Mittelalter* (Munich, 1944), 53; Rösch, *Der venezianische Adel*, 61–64.

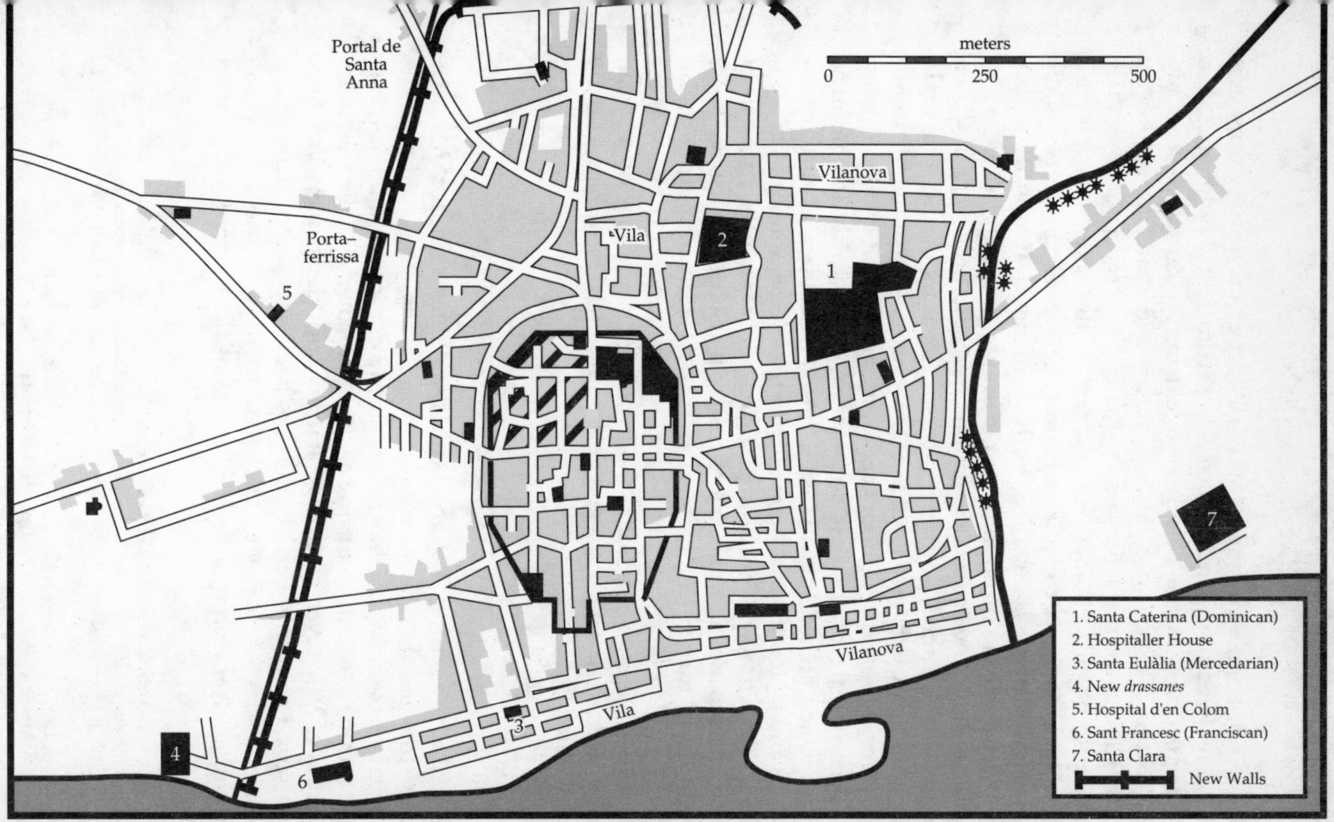
meters
0
250
500
Portal de Santa Anna
Porta-ferrissa
Vilanova
Vila
Vilanova
Vila
1
2
3
4
5
6
7
1. Santa Caterina (Dominican)
2. Hospitaller House
3. Santa Eulàlia (Mercedarian)
4. New drassanes
5. Hospital d'en Colom
6. Sant Francesc (Franciscan)
7. Santa Clara
New Walls

Map 6 Barcelona in 1290

more conservative by the second half of the thirteenth century as it monopolized municipal offices, lived from rents, and engaged in "speculation," while commercial expansion produced a group of *nouveaux riches*, who came to resent and challenge its power. The rigid distinction between aggrandizing traders and wealthy rentiers and officeholders emphasized in this interpretation thus foreshadows the late medieval conflict between merchants and the *ciutadans honrats*.[10] Whether the lines of political conflict within medieval urban communities were drawn primarily according to distinctions in wealth, occupation, or class, however, has been openly challenged in recent years.[11] In response to the rapid demographic expansion and economic prosperity of the thirteenth century, towns throughout the West experienced growing pains. There is little doubt that competition for wealth and political power heightened social tensions in communities whose institutions and styles of social deference were only beginning to crystallize, yet what was once often taken for a popular struggle of artisans and aspiring merchants against patrician rule has on closer inspection turned out to be merely a struggle among patrician factions. The problem merits further attention in Barcelona, for patrician lines were quite short at the beginning of Catalan Mediterranean conquests, and new commercial wealth potentially destabilizing.

THE TECHNIQUES OF TRADE

By the time King Jaume I sailed with his fleet for Majorca, investors and merchants in Barcelona already employed the basic forms of commercial association that would provide the contractual framework for maritime exchange throughout the thirteenth century. Whatever advantage Italians and Occitanians had once possessed in commercial techniques had evaporated. Among the major ports of the Mediterranean there were no longer any technological secrets, at least in terms of the notarial instruments

---

[10] This approach is most fully articulated in Carme Batlle i Gallart, "La vida y las actividades de los mercaderes de Barcelona dedicados al comercio marítimo (siglo XIII)," in *Le genti del mare mediterraneo* (Naples, 1981), 1, 292–94. Cf. Batlle i Gallart, *La Crisis*, 1, 36–44.

[11] Heers, *Les Partis et la vie politique*, 64–76; Guy Fourquin, *The anatomy of popular rebellion in the Middle Ages*, trans. A. Chester (Amsterdam, New York, and Oxford, 1978), 27–83; Reynolds, *Kingdoms and communities*, 203–18.

employed to associate capital and labor for overseas trade.[12] Differences among the great trading centers emerged not so much from technical forms of doing business, but from the organization of foreign markets and the place of commerce within urban society.

The *comanda* provided the backbone of maritime commerce in thirteenth-century Barcelona.[13] Like the Genoese *societas maris* and the Venetian *colleganza*, it consisted of a fiduciary contract combining elements of command and deposit. The investor (*stans*), usually sedentary, transferred at his own risk either money or merchandise, occasionally both, to a merchant (*gestor, comandatarius*) who promised to sell or exchange the goods overseas and return with money or other merchandise. The division of profits, always clearly spelled out, was to occur immediately upon the ship's return: in Barcelona, as in most other areas, three-fourths went to the capitalist, who had placed a part of his assets at risk, and one-fourth to the merchant for his labor and the dangers he faced *en route*. Since the contract was valid for only a single voyage, *comandas* encouraged a wide diffusion and rapid turnover in investments. Merchants wished to receive goods and money from numerous individuals for their voyage, while investors tried to spread their risks by entrusting coins and goods to several different merchants. Only rarely did two or more people pool their resources in the form of a commercial company (Latin *societas*; Catalan *companyia*) in order to speculate in maritime trade.[14] In contrast to the *comanda*, a *societas* required its participants to contribute both capital and labor, usually for the conduct of overland trade, the operation of a shop or, toward the close of the century, the establishment of banking tables; profits and risks were divided according to the proportional contribution of each member and settled at the dissolution of the *societas*, usually several years after the contract was concluded.[15] Sea loans (*cambium maris*),

---

[12] On the similarity in contractual forms of commercial association and their diffusion, see Yves Renouard, *Les Hommes d'affaires italiens* (3rd ed., Paris, 1968), 62–84; Dufourcq, *L'Espagne catalane*, 58–62; supra, 228–30.

[13] Most, but not all, thirteenth-century *comanda* contracts from the ACB have been edited and thoughtfully introduced by Arcadi Garcia i Sanz and Josep Madurell i Marimon, *Comandas comerciales barcelonesas de la baja edad media* (Barcelona, 1973), nos. 1–71.

[14] Only two examples of investment from a *tabula societatis* appear among the surviving *comandas*, Garcia-Madurell, *Comandas comerciales*, nos. 29, 31.

[15] Garcia-Madurell, *Societats mercantils*, I, 225–33, 236 divide a "developmental" from a "mature" stage in the evolution of Barcelona companies at c. 1250; while the *societas* was evolving from an association serving the needs of overland trade to providing a new

Table 7.1. *Loan contracts involving burghers, 1221–1290*
(loans of more than 1,000s. not included)

	Total number	Total amount	Average amount	Number of Jewish loans	Amount of Jewish loans (% of total)
1221–1230	28	6,551s.	234s.	5	10
1231–1240	51	9,284s.	182s.	14	16
1241–1250	48	9,096s.	190s.	17	18
1251–1260	26	4,463s.	172s.	15	86
1261–1270	37	6,724s.	182s.	20	55
1271–1280	66	16,184s.	245s.	36	70
1281–1290	67	19,778s.	295s.	38	68

which spread risks between investor-lender and merchant-borrower, had also appeared in Barcelona's mercantile sector; although this contract would eventually evolve into a popular form of maritime insurance by the fourteenth century, it was not widely used before 1300.

Commercial expansion brought with it a change in the credit market. In the early thirteenth century credit was widely diffused throughout the urban economy. Although wealthy entrepreneurs found it advantageous to extend large amounts to kings, barons, and each other, they were not professional moneylenders; neither were money changers, foreigners, and Jews, who appear rarely in local credit operations before 1220. Through their legal stipulations loan contracts had evolved increasingly into instruments to provide rapid liquidity rather than to secure long-term profits from the usufruct of land or rents offered in pledge. Owing to increased demand for money to fuel overseas trade during the thirteenth century, the earlier dispersion of available capital in individual hands gave way to concentrated banking associations and Jews began to play a prominent role in providing short-term loans. Once again loan contracts provide a means of measuring these changes.

Two features stand out from the figures in table 7.1. First, the average amount of recorded loans remained relatively small over

structure for maritime commerce, the authors admit that only in the 1290s did the amounts involved in commercial *companyies* become substantial.

seventy years of intense commercial development. Second, the proportion of credit extended by Jews to Christians rose dramatically after 1250, when the surge of prosperity produced by North African trade was reaching its peak. Did the Jews of Barcelona provide the money to drive Catalan Mediterranean expansion forward?

Here caution must be exercised because of the nature of the surviving evidence. Careful research into the thirteenth-century Jewish communities of Catalonia has emphasized that Christians from all walks of life turned to Jews frequently for cash loans but that Jewish moneylending remained for the most part a small-scale yet highly appreciated operation.[16] The records of debt in Barcelona also show that Jewish loans were for the most part modest and offered on an occasional basis by a large number of non-professional lenders within the city's *aljama* (Jewish community). Yet some Jewish notables did became important lenders. Concentrating on all credit contracts involving Barcelona Jews in the thirteenth century, Leila Berner has demonstrated that three families of notables, the Adret, Cap, and Gracià, appear as creditors in 29 percent of the documents (98 of 336), while a large number of petty lenders supplied the rest of the loans; the emergence of these wealthy lenders illustrates how the city's prosperity promoted new Jewish families which challenged the authority of the older aristocrats (*nesi'im*) in Barcelona's *aljama* by 1241.[17] Yet even loans made by the wealthiest Jewish notables were usually not large.

The figures leave the impression that Christians slowly ceded the credit market to Jews beginning in the 1230s and virtually abandoned the field in the 1250s, just as overseas trade was booming. But here the nature of the documentation proves deceptive. Because the loan contracts survive only on parchment

[16] Richard W. Emery, *The Jews of Perpignan in the thirteenth century: an economic study based on notarial records* (New York, 1959), 26–66; Mathias Delcor, "Les Juifs de Puigcerdà au XIIIᵉ siècle," *Sefarad*, 26 (1966), 32–37; Immaculada Ollich i Castanyer, "Aspects econòmics de l'activitat dels jueus de Vic, segon els 'Libri judeorum' (1266–1278)," *Miscel·lànea de textos medievals*, 3 (1985), 7–118; and the recent synthesis by Joseph Shatzmiller, *Shylock reconsidered: Jews, moneylending, and medieval society* (Berkeley and Los Angeles, 1990), 71–103.

[17] Leila Berner, "A modest enterprise: Jewish moneylenders in thirteenth-century Barcelona," paper presented to 100th Meeting of the American Historical Association, December 27–30, 1985; Bernard Septimus, "Piety and power in thirteenth-century Catalonia," in *Studies in medieval Jewish history*, ed. I. Twersky (Cambridge, MA, 1979), I, 197–230.

and not in notarial registers for this period, they overemphasize Jewish lenders, who would wish an expensive parchment copy for added security in case their claim against an insolvent or recalcitrant Christian debtor would be challenged. Moreover, the aggressive stance taken against usury by the Church after the Fourth Lateran Council in 1215 gradually forced Christians to conceal their profits on lending through fictitious real estate transfers, sales on credit, and outright deception. As the hostility of clerical moralists drove interest underground, the growing importance of banks allowed clients to settle accounts through a stroke of the pen in private ledgers, which have since disappeared.[18] The parchment loan contracts therefore seriously underrepresent the relative importance of Christian lending. While a few charters register complaints of religious institutions against burdensome debts owed on the Call, neither wills nor court proceedings leave the impression that heavy indebtedness to Jews was common. This is not to deny, however, the important role Jewish credit played in the thirteenth century. Rather than burdening artisans with debt or bankrolling major commercial investments, Jewish lenders in Barcelona provided modest, short-term loans to merchants and entrepreneurs who had sunk their resources into administration, trade, ship building, or real estate development. Christian borrowers in more than half the instances promised to repay in six months or less, and 70 percent of the charters indicate full and timely repayment.[19] In addition, those seeking loans from Jews were rarely destitute or bankrupt. Joan de Banyeres, one of the most dynamic and successful cloth merchants of his generation, is known to have contracted eleven loans ranging from 200s. to 3,151s. from six different Jews between 1274 and 1282, while members of such wealthy and established patrician houses as the Adarró, Durfort, Grony, and de Sanaüja had to seek loans for quick cash of 200s. or less.[20] The high degree of investment in commerce and real estate produced substantial profits for Barcelona's patricians, but it also left a place for short-term credit. Even if Jewish coffers did not provide the capital to power the city's economic engine, they did offer liquidity to keep the gears turning smoothly and at high speed.

[18] Stephen P. Bensch, "La primera crisis bancaria de Barcelona," *AEM*, 19 (1989), 315–19.

[19] Berner, "A modest enterprise," notes that 18.7 percent of borrowers promised to repay in less than six months and 35.4 percent in six months.

[20] ACB 1–6–63, 174, 257, 387, 398, 866, 994, 1548, 1734, 2089, 2330, 2444, 2718, 2771.

COMMERCIAL ZONES AND PATRICIAN INVESTMENT

Comanda contracts, short-term, individualistic, and specific instruments of investment, best fulfilled the needs of Barcelona's overseas trade in the thirteenth century. The recent publication and meticulous study of samples from Barcelona's business contracts has laid bare the technical framework for Catalan trade in the late Middle Ages, yet it has in some sense exaggerated the complexity of commercial transactions in the thirteenth century. Even though every component of the early *comanda*, *societas*, and *cambium maris* shows subtle variations that point to the complex trading associations prevailing when Catalan Mediterranean trade was at its height, merchants and investors in the thirteenth century preferred relatively simple and direct contractual arrangements. This conformed to an individualistic, fluid commercial environment. In its early stage of maritime expansion Barcelona had not yet produced large family companies dominated by merchant-bankers, pooling substantial reserves of capital and establishing branches in foreign cities. Even though large banking associations were beginning to form in the last quarter of the thirteenth century in Barcelona, none of its patrician houses could boast of extensive trading and financial connections comparable to the Leccacorvi of Genoa, the Bonsignori of Siena, or the Scotti of Piacenza.[21] In Barcelona *societates* rarely involved more than two investors, the sums involved were modest, and their duration short; commercial capital moved rapidly among a wide variety of merchants and investors, who incessantly redefined old business contacts and looked for new partners. Rather than relying upon strong corporate or familial structures to order their commercial undertakings, Barcelonans opportunistically cooperated in exploiting the trade routes their ships and arms had opened.

The fragmentary survival of individual commercial contracts does not allow for even a rough estimate of the overall volume of trade, but collectively these documents can at least point out its general direction. Table 7.2 summarizes the number of voyages recorded in commercial contracts and provides the average

---

[21] Bensch, "La primera crisis," 320–27. For points of comparison, see Edward D. English, *Enterprise and liability in Sienese banking, 1230–1350* (Cambridge, MA, 1988), 41–51; Robert S. Lopez, *La primera crisi della banca di Genova (1250–59)* (Milan, 1956); Racine, *Plaisance*, II, 965, 975; III, 1110–15.

Table 7.2 *No. of recorded voyages overseas and average amount of contract,*
1200–1290

	North Africa		Ultramar		Romania	
	Voy.	Av. Amt.	Voy.	Av. Amt.	Voy.	Av. Amt.
to 1250	3	187s.	2	962s.	0	0
1250–1269	8	723s.	5	784s.	2	451s.
1270–1290	14	303s.	3	290s.	9	509s.
Totals	25	431s.	10	663s.	11	606s.

	Christian Spain		Sicily		Southern France	
	Voy.	Av. Amt.	Voy.	Av. Amt.	Voy.	Av. Amt.
to 1250	3	287s.	2(?)	208s.	2	365s.
1250–1269	3	420s.	2	823s.	1	80s.
1270–1290	10	354s.	5	193s.	1	150s.
Totals	16	279s.	9	270s.	4	240s.

	Genoa	
	Voy.	Av. Amt.
to 1250	0	0
1250–1269	0	0
1270–1290	1	150s.
Totals	1	150s.

amount of each contract to 1290. The data are taken from seventy-seven *comanda* contracts, eight maritime loans, and twelve references to outstanding *comandas* in wills or charters recording their settlement.[22]

[22] The documents used are as follows: Garcia-Madurell, *Comandas comerciales*, nos. 1–11, 14–16, 18, 19, 23–26, 28–38, 40–49, 51–54; Ferrer-Garcia *Assegurances i canvis*, II, nos. 2, 4–6, 9–11, 15, 16; ACB 1–1–30, 328; 1–6–61, 110, 182, 485, 746, 842, 975, 989, 1263, 1583, 1813, 1990, 2126, 2537, 2728, 2870, 2905, 2916, 2990, 3001, 3014, 3175, 3207, 3274, 3297, 3338, 3543, 4275; 4–6–27; 4–51–720, 722, 736; ACA perg. varis, Sentmenat, Indice 8, III, 24, 29, 76, 81; ARM Cod. 342, fols. 9 v., 13 r.; Rafael Conde y Delgado de Molina, "Los Llull: una familia de la burguesía barcelonesa del siglo XIII," *XI CHCA* (Montpellier, 1983), II, 371–408, nos. 1, 7–10; Carme Batlle, Joan J. Busqueta, and Coral Cuadrada, "Notes sobre l'eix comercial Barcelona–Mallorca–Barbaria, a la segona meitat del s. XIII," *XIII CHCA* (Palma, 1987–89), ap., 40. The number of voyages is less than the total number of *comandas* since several contracts refer to the same journey.

These figures first of all draw attention to North Africa. Recorded voyages involving commercial contracts to the southern shores of the Mediterranean substantially exceed those to any other trade zone; even if the Eastern Mediterranean basin is counted as a whole, the number of voyages to North Africa is still somewhat larger than those to the Levant and the Byzantine Empire, but surely trade with Majorca and Sicily should be connected to that with the Maghrib in any reshuffling of commercial systems. Transfixed by the sheen of oriental silks and the aroma of spices, historians of early Catalonian trade have traditionally been drawn to the Eastern Mediterranean in the wake of crusader ships along the *ruta de las especias*.[23] Yet Catalans elbowed their way rather late into the trading circuits of Egypt and the Levant that the Venetians, Genoese, and Occitanians had already opened up by the early twelfth century; but in Ifrīqiya (the Arabic term fusing the old Roman territories of Africa Vetera and Africa Nova, stretching from Tripoli to eastern Algeria) and especially in Morocco, they were pioneers.

As early as the tenth century, North Africa constituted the terminus for the gold and slaves transported on the Saharan caravan routes, fanning out from Sijilmāsa to towns dotting the coast from Morocco to Mauritania. Indirectly Catalan warriors had tapped this route in the eleventh century by seizing gold from al-Andalus through raids, *parias*, and service to *taifa* princes. Attached to an Islamic commercial corridor to Egypt and the Levant, the cities of Tunis, Bougie, and al-Mahdiyya each formed an early hinge of Mediterranean trade, where products from the East could be turned toward Latin ports from Italy to Iberia.[24] With the collapse of Islamic control in Sicily, Norman rulers quickly learned to look upon North Africa as the southern flank of their military and political activities during the early twelfth century, while Genoese, Pisan, and Marseillais merchants estab-

---

[23] Vicens Vives, *España: geopolítica del estado*, 105, 111; Lluís Nicolau d'Olwer, *L'expansió de Catalunya en la Mediterrània oriental* (3rd ed., Barcelona, 1974), 13–24. Despite the evidence in their own collection, Garcia-Madurell, *Comandas comericales*, 20, still remark that Barcelona's trade depended upon "una larga ruta primordial, constituida por la ruta comercial del Mediterráneo Oriental, la ruta de las especias, y una serie de rutas derivadas."

[24] Goitein, *A Mediterranean society*, I, 211–14; Michael Brett, "Ifriqiya as a market for Saharan trade from the tenth to the twelfth century AD," *Journal of African history*, 10 (1969), 347–64; David Abulafia, "Asia, Africa and the trade of medieval Europe," *Cambridge economic history*, II, 466–68.

lished regular trading contacts there.[25] Catalan ships and merchants arrived later on the African side of the Sicilian Channel than the Normans or Italians, although their presence is attested before 1229.[26] The conquest of Majorca, however, provided a base that brought Catalan galleys within easy range of the North African coast and assured them naval dominance; it allowed Jaume I and his successors to become the principal foreign political and military force in Ifrīqiya and mirrored in many respects the influence the Norman Roger II of Sicily had wielded through a temporary occupation of al-Mahdiyya, Tripoli, and Jirba in the mid-twelfth century. With their militias, commercial compounds, client emirs, and missionaries, the Catalans after the conquest of Majorca established an enduring yet flexible protectorate over the Maghrib, encouraging trade, hiring out their ships and soldiers to quarrelling Islamic princes, and receiving tribute in exchange for peace.[27] Picking up where the Normans had left off, Aragonese monarchs and merchants found their African interests frequently touching the affairs of Sicily. In 1262 the marriage of the Infant Pere, heir apparent to King Jaume I, to Constance of Hohenstaufen, daughter of King Manfred of Sicily and granddaughter of Emperor Frederick II, solidified the anti-Angevin position of his dynasty and laid the foundation for the acquisition of a new kingdom for the House of Barcelona. Yet Desclot, official chronicler to King Pere II, presents the Sicilian Vespers as a ripe plum falling into the king's lap while he was abroad on a well-prepared but disappointing expedition to Tunis.[28]

While the Crown's policy in Ifrīqiya amplified and restructured the commercial and military contacts initiated by Normans and Italians, the momentum of Iberian expansion carried over to

25 Abulafia, *Two Italies*, 49–53 and "The Norman kingdom of Africa and the Norman expeditions to Majorca and the Muslim Mediterranean," *Anglo-Norman studies*, 7 (1985), 26–49 [repr. in *Italy, Sicily and the Mediterranean, 1100–1400* (London, 1987)].

26 Bernat Desclot, *Llibre del rei en Pere*, c. 14, in *Les quatre grans cròniques*, 421; Ferrer-Madurell, *Assegurances i canvis*, II, nos. 5, 6.

27 Dufourcq, *L'Espagne catalane* will long remain the classic work on the subject, although he did not have access to the important materials regarding Barcelona in the ACB at the time of his study.

28 Ferrer-Madurell, *Assegurances i canvis*, II, nos. 2, 3; Desclot, *Llibre*, c. 88. While many have argued that Tunis merely provided a feint for the Sicilian adventure, the primacy of Pere's ambitious North African policy is emphasized by Hans Schadek, "Tunis oder Sizilien? Die Ziele der aragonishen Mittelmeerspolitik unter Pere III. von Aragon," *GAKS*, 28 (1975), 335–49; cf. Dufourcq, *L'Espagne catalane*, 238–59.

Catalan penetration into the western rim of the Mediterranean.[29] Even though Ceuta, the Mediterranean gateway to Morocco, is cited as the western limit to Barcelona's "navigation act" of 1227, piracy and political considerations played a greater role here than in the central and eastern Maghrib. In an obscure episode, Catalans evidently launched a crusade against Ceuta in 1234, and Jaume later sent troops to support one faction in an internal Moroccan struggle, but only two Barcelona *comanda* contracts mention either Morocco or Ceuta as their destinations.[30] With the Treaty of Monteagudo in 1291, the kings of Aragon and Castile formally divided their North African spheres of influence; the Catalans ceded their political ambitions in Morocco to Castile in order to pursue commercial and military interests in Ifrīqiya.

Barcelona quickly assumed a leading role in Catalan trade with North Africa, but the Crown did not intend for the city to monopolize it. To the contrary, Catalan trading centers in the Maghrib were part of a royal "open door" policy, encouraging merchants from throughout the mainland and Majorca to do business with each other under the supervision of the Crown. Business arrangements could be made independently in the trading compounds of Ifrīqiya as well as at the command of Barcelona's investors at home; Catalan agents in North Africa received deposits, closed commercial contracts, and arranged shipping to destinations throughout the Mediterranean.[31] A Catalan *funduq*, a foreign trading compound authorized by Islamic rulers, existed by 1253 in Tunis and another by 1258 in Bougie; each was subject to a consul appointed by the king, not by the municipal council of Barcelona as would be the case in Alexandria and Constantinople.[32] Fierce competition ensued for the right to hold the two consulates, usually purchased for a year or two; entrepreneurs from throughout the Crown held the post, although

---

[29] On the Moroccan ambitions of the Catalans, see above all Dufourcq, *L'Espagne catalane*, 157–68, where he tends to overestimate commercial contacts. Cf. his later remarks, which place the greatest weight on political and military motives, "Vers la Méditerranée orientale et l'Afrique," *X CHCA. Ponencias* (Zaragoza, 1980–82), 13–24 [repr. in *L'Ibérie chrétienne*].

[30] ARM Cod. 342, fol. 13 r.; ACB 1–6–1553.

[31] ACB 1–6–39, 846, 1303, 2648, 2928; ADB perg. Santa Anna, Carp. 1a, 5–23.

[32] Once again reference should be made to Charles-Emmanuel Dufourcq, "Les Consulats catalans de Tunis et de Bougie au temps de Jacques le Conquérant," *AEM*, 3 (1966), 469–79 [repr. in *L'Ibérie chrétienne*]. A slightly earlier reference to the existence of a Catalan *funduq* in Bougie than that offered by Dufourcq appears in a Barcelona will from 1258, ACB 4–10–15: "Sanctae Mariae alfondeci catalanorum."

prominent figures in Barcelona showed a special interest. Ramon Ricart, whose son married the daughter of Berenguer Durfort, twice maneuvered himself into the position of consul of Tunis and, in at least one term, managed it at a distance from Barcelona by subfarming his office to two others.[33] Commerce mixed with military adventure, which included growing numbers of Catalan mercenaries fighting for Islamic princes, drew the attention of the city's patricians to the sun-baked compounds of Tunis and Bougie, sometimes in an official capacity. King Jaume I turned to Guillem Grony, Arnau Eimeric, and Jaume de Montjuïc to find early ambassadors in order to represent the Crown's interest before the "king of Tunis," while Felipe d'Espiells supplied armor and war-horses to Catalans in the service of a local emir.[34] Drawn in part by his family's traditional association with the *amostolafia*, the office of prisoner exchange between Christian and Muslim, Berenguer Adarró was heavily involved in North African trade as was his brother-in-law, Arnau de Ribes; Berenguer was also the son-in-law of the nobleman Marimon de Plegamans, who during his service as vicar of Barcelona conducted the first known diplomatic mission from the Aragonese monarch to the Ḥafṣid rulers of Tunis around 1235.[35] The combination of dynastic designs, military and naval expansion, and commercial self-interest encouraged the direct participation of Barcelona's established patrician houses in North African affairs. Although the penetration of Ifrīqiya

---

[33] Dufourcq, "Les Consulats," 474–78. Ramon Ricart already had business interests in North Africa before his appointment as consul. Just before setting out for Tunis in August, 1274, he transferred three commercial *comandas* totalling 500 lbs. to his son, Ramon Ricart, who had received the amount in dowry from his wife Maria, daughter of Berenguer Durfort, ACB 1–6–1158.

[34] On patricians employed as royal ambassadors, Dufourcq, *L'Espagne catalane*, 115–17, 129. APR, 152 (1261): "nos Berengarius Aymerici presbiter et Berengarius de Mogia uterque nostrum insolidum confitemur et recognoscimus nos debere tibi Filipo de Spiellis et tuis ratione trium guarnimentorum corporis et equi et ratione duorum equorum et ratione alterius aricu et aliarum rerum ... quadringentos et sexagintos bisancios argenti ... promitimus paccare tibi et tuis ... in prima solucione quam ab hoc die in antea recipiamus a domino Miramcimulino vel ab eius alcayto." The priest Berenguer Eimeric should be identified with the rector of Sant Pere de Pinet in the diocese of Girona, one of the first Catalan chaplains in the Maghrib, Dufourcq, *L'Espagne catalane*, 106. On the arms trade to Christian knights in the Maghrib, see Garcia-Madurell, *Comandas comerciales*, no. 18.

[35] ACB 1–6–1173, 1379, 1720, 2851. Dufourcq, *L'Espagne catalane*, 93–94 mistakenly considers Marimon de Plegamans a citizen of Barcelona and part of a "dynastie bourgeoise," but he and his descendants are always referred to as *nobiles*, not *cives*, and never served on the *Consell de Cent*. For the family's elevated, and resented, place in urban society, see infra, 321–23, 335–38.

proved to be a collective undertaking by the growing Catalan towns, Barcelona's leading figures were not content to remain merely overseas investors and absentee overseers manipulating from a distance this dynamic sphere of Catalan expansion on the southern shores of the Mediterranean.

Trade itself consisted principally in the export of northern woolens obtained in Languedoc, fustians and linens acquired from local sources, followed by cereals, olive oil, figs, wine, and hides; a flourishing black market was also developing in weapons, naval supplies, and (in times of official embargo) grain in spite of fulminations by popes and kings.[36] Catalan ships also transported sugar, cotton, and rice from Valencia, Granada, and southern Italy to destinations along the North African coast.[37] On return voyages merchants imported not only local products, such as wax, cumin, goatskins, fruits, and figs, but also obtained ginger, cinnamon, pepper, and dye (*oricha*), products demonstrating that the Maghrib could provide a convenient short-cut on the spice routes to the East.[38] Tlemcen became an important supplier of alum, a sulfate critical for cloth production and tanning. In an impressive transaction involving more than 28 tons (571 1/2 quintals) of alum shipped through Castile, Ramon de Banyeres arranged for the delivery of his substantial cargo with an envoy of Yaghmurāsan, emir of Tlemcen; a third of the 4,000 bezant purchase price was to be provided by Ramon Ricart, future consul of Tunis and Alexandria.[39] In the decades following the conquest of Majorca, the Crown's formidable naval position allowed North African trade to thrive; more than Sicily or the Levant, the Maghrib provided the trade link that transformed Barcelona into a major Mediterranean emporium. The city's commercial tolls from North

---

[36] Garcia-Madurell, *Comandas comerciales*, nos. 4, 7, 18, 26, 28, 31–34, 38, 40; ACB 1–6–2990, 3001, 3274, 3338; 4–10–15; ARM Cod. 342, fols. 9 v., 13 r.; ACA perg. varis, Sentmenat, Indice 8, III, 76. On the obscure forbidden trade with the Muslims, see the remarkable evidence brought to light by José Trenchs Odena, " 'De Alexandriis' (el comercio prohibido con los musulmanes y el Papado de Aviñón durante la primera mitad del siglo XIV)," *AEM*, 10 (1980), 237–320.

[37] Garcia-Madurell, *Comandas comerciales*, nos. 9, 42; ACB 1–6–2916, 2990.

[38] Garcia-Madurell, *Comandas comerciales*, nos. 4, 6; ACB 1–6–39, 1303; ACA Reg. 42, fol. 144 r.

[39] The negotiations are known through two documents, the first dated June 30, 1250, published without reference to its source (which I have been unable to locate) by Joaquím Miret i Sans, "Un missatge de Yarmoraced de Tremecen a Jaume I," *BRABLB*, 9 (1915), 48–51, and a second, dated July 27, 1250, ACB 1–6–3695. On the political context within which the negotiations occurred, see Dufourcq, *L'Espagne catalane*, 145–46.

African trade were worth 6,130s. per annum in 1248 and 1249; if these were included in the total farm of all commercial tolls in 1253 for 9,400s., as appears likely,[40] then trade with the "Saracen shore" represented two-thirds of Barcelona's foreign exchange at the time.

Trade with Ifrīqiya, however, should not be seen in terms of a rigid north–south axis anchored at Barcelona and Tunis; rather, it formed part of the complex currents of exchange moving along the Italian, Occitanian, and Iberian coasts. The diffusion of trade routes toward the south and west appear clearly in an extensive investigation concluded in 1302 by the bailiff of Barcelona in order to fine merchants and captains who failed to pay tariffs at Tortosa.[41] The confessions of eighty-five individuals indicate the destinations of their ships in voyages undertaken between 1242 and 1292. Because merchants passing through Tortosa were usually headed for the western Maghrib rather. that Tunis or Bougie, this unusual record reveals the multiple destinations of the ships as they passed through Palma de Majorca or Eivissa and then, fanning out into the "Mediterranean Channel" separating Barbary from southern Iberia, made their way to Oran, Alcudia, Togo, Ceuta, Seville, Málaga, Almeria, Alicante, and Valencia. Trade with Barbary, Granada, and Andalusia followed a finely spun web of intersecting routes rather than a well-defined shipping lane. Catalans trading in Ifrīqiya also looked toward Sicily. Taking advantage of the punitive measures instituted by Emperor Frederick II against Genoa in 1238, Barcelona's merchants during the 1240s intensified their trading contacts with Sicily, where they came in search of grain and cotton.[42] Following trading patterns

---

[40] The bailiff of Barcelona sold the "leudas cum littore sarracenorum" in 1248 for 12,260s. for two years, ACA perg. Jaume I, 1120. The document is unusual in that it represents the first extant contract for the farm of Barcelona's commercial tolls and the only one known to me which indicates the specific trade zone involved. In 1253 Pere de Lissac farmed the "leuda domini regis Barchinone et quintario," for 9,400s., ACA perg. Jaume I, 1332, 1336. All subsequent farms of the tolls are referred to as the "leuda et quintalis."

[41] AHCB, Processos, sèrie XXIII-2, noted in Dufourcq, *L'Espagne catalane*, 42 and now analyzed more closely by Batlle, Busqueta, and Cuadrada, "Notes sobre l'eix comercial," 33–47, who perhaps mislabel this complex circuitry of routes an axis.

[42] On the break between Genoa and Frederick, see Schaube, *Handelsgeschichte*, 488. Erich Maschke, "Die Wirtschaftspolitik Kaiser Friedrichs II. im Königreich Sizilien," *Vierteljahrschrift für Sozial- und Wirtschaftsgeschichte*, 53 (1966), 310–11 notes, however, that some clandestine trade with Genoa continued. The presence of resident Catalan merchants is documented by Carme Batlle i Gallart, "Les relacions entre Barcelona i Sicília a la segona meitat del segle XIII," *XI CHCA* (Palermo, 1983), II, 156–60, yet whether

developed by Italians, Catalan ships laden with Sicilian grain sometimes headed for North Africa rather than their homeland; in 1286 King Alfons II pointedly demanded that Berenguer de Conques account for his actions, since he had been given a license to ship grain from Sicily to Barcelona but ended up selling his cargo in Bougie.[43] Jean-Pierre Cuvillier has uncovered a "triangular trade" already in existence in 1260 organized by a Catalan entrepreneur, Guillem de Peralada, who from Barcelona financed grain shipments carried on a Marseillais ship from Sicily to Genoa. Four other Catalan financiers, including the Barcelona banker Ramon Fiveller, may have had similar designs in 1285, for they lent King Pere II substantial sums in Genoa, for which they received the right to export 2,348 *salme* of Sicilian grain, but in this case to Catalonia because of the dearth produced by the impending French invasion.[44] Even after members of the Aragonese royal house ruled the Sicilian kingdom, Catalan merchants formed only one component, and by no means the dominant element among Lombard, Ligurian, and Occitanian shippers, in the complex business of Sicilian wheat export, a staple of Mediterranean trade.[45] In Palermo and Trapani as well as in Tunis and Bougie, merchants from Barcelona did not engage in commercial operations directed exclusively toward their home port, nor did sedentary capitalists in the Ribera supervise every aspect of their business; instead, Catalans profited by integrating themselves into a broad network of exchange linking the principal ports of the Western Mediterranean. Independence and a cosmopolitan opportunism would long be features of Catalan traders overseas.

Because of its strategic location, Majorca provided an important advanced outpost for Barcelona's merchants. To the chronicler Pere Marsili, the island was the *cap de creus*, the crossroads of the Western Mediterranean sea lanes.[46] Long before Jaume's

they formed a "colony" at this early date, as she asserts, or were quickly absorbed into the host community remains unclear.

[43] ACA Reg. 65, fol. 125 v. Cf. Reg. 58, fol. 44 v. and Abulafia, "Norman kingdom," 29, 33; Maschke, "Wirtschaftspolitik," 304–5.

[44] Jean-Pierre Cuvillier, "Barcelone, Gênes et le commerce du blé de Sicile vers le milieu du XIIIᵉ siècle," *Atti del I.° congresso storico Liguria-Catalogna* (Bordighera, 1974), 220–34; *Codice diplomatico dei re aragonesi di Sicilia*, ed. G. La Mantia (Palermo, 1917–56), I, no. xciv.

[45] Henri Bresc, *Un monde méditerranéen: économie et société en Sicile, 1300–1450* (Rome, 1986), I, 545–52.

[46] On Majorca's importance as a point of intersection on several trade routes in the late thirteenth and early fourteenth century, see David Abulafia, "The problem of the

troops brutally seized the island and divided up its land and towns among themselves, it had served as a rendezvous for Christian mariners from northern Italy, Occitania, and Catalonia.[47] While Barcelonans played a prominent role in the conquest of the island, its patrician houses were not keen on building up their rural holdings; only the Durfort demonstrated an interest in strengthening their position as landlords on the island systematically, in part a consequence of their early role as royal bailiffs in Majorca and a marriage with the Tornamira family, old allies of the Montcada and an important conquest family. The island's farmland and rich olive groves for the most part fell into the hands of smallholders; after the turbulent first decade of settlement, the notarial registers at Palma reveal that citizens of Barcelona were more likely to sell their small *alqueries* than obtain new land.[48] Houses and shops in Palma, however, were quite a different matter. Soon after the original participants in the invasion had received their allotments, fierce competition ensued to obtain trading stations in Majorca's bustling port. Barcelona's inhabitants found Count Nunyo Sanç especially accommodating; the enterprising lord of Rosselló had a strong interest in promoting trade since he controlled part of Barcelona's *alfóndec* and commercial tolls.[49] Prominent Barcelona families took care to see that these choice properties in the island's main port remained in the right hands. After purchasing two shops in Palma in 1242, Bernat Despuig rented them to his brother, while Tomàs de Vic, a member of one of the oldest patrician houses, became a citizen of Palma.[50] Marriage could also help cement ties to the mainland. After years of doing business together, Bernat Sesfonts of Barcelona and Joan Homdedeu of Majorca arranged a match between their children: the dowry consisted in part of shared capital invested in trade.[51]

While not all commercial dealings between Barcelona and

Kingdom of Majorca (1229/1276–1343). 2. Economic identity," *Mediterranean historical review*, 6 (1991), 42–48.

47 Francisco Sevillano Colom, *Historia del Puerto de Palma de Mallorca* (Palma, 1974), 176. Barcelona's earliest sea loan involves a merchant bound for Majorca, Ferrer-Madurell, *Assegurances i canvis*, II, no. 1.

48 See, for example, ARM Cod. 345, fols. 237 v.–238 r.; Cod. 342, fols. 2 v., 8 r., 29 v.; Cod. 349, fol. 61 r.–v.; Notarios, P-1, fols. 11 v.–12 r.

49 ARM, Cod. 341, fols. 4 v., 16 r., 20 r., 35 v., 56 r., 95 r. Nunyo Sanç received the right to use his property on the shore for a "statica vel alfondica" in 1222, ACB 4–32–479.

50 ARM Cod. 342, fol. 14 r.; ACA perg. varis, Marquès de Monsitrol, 140.

51 ACB 1–6–2787; Garcia-Madurell, *Comandas comerciales*, nos. 14, 15.

Palma attained such a degree of intimacy, the island nevertheless provided a critical nexus of investment. In the commercial contracts concluded in Barcelona itself, very few non-residents took part, a sign of the city's domination of and protection over its local market.[52] Palma, on the other hand, provided a clearing-house for investments, focusing commercial capital from throughout Catalonia and beyond on the island hub of maritime exchange; from there it could be directed elsewhere. Catalan merchants from different cities on the mainland not only made trading arrangements among themselves on the island, but with Italians as well and even Muslims.[53] Barcelona's patricians were not slow to take advantage of the possibilities. Little more than a decade after the conquest, Berenguer Burget entered into an agreement in Palma with Berenguer de Montcada, Ramon, bishop of Majorca, and other investors for a voyage to Islamic Spain expected to bring in 10,000 bezants, probably from raiding;[54] Arnau Eimeric, Pere Genovès, Pere Mallol, Bernat Sesfonts, Guillem de Banyeres, and Jaume Ferrer also invested heavily in trade and ship construction in the Balearics.[55] Because of such strong ties created by an incessant movement of men and capital, Majorca acted not so much as a trading partner with Barcelona as a springboard to propel its investors and traders further into the Mediterranean.

As a result of their commercial and naval expansion in the Western Mediterranean, Barcelona's merchants established closer contacts with markets in Egypt, the Levant, and the Greek world. Although Benjamin of Tudela reported the presence of merchants of *'Arangon*, presumably Catalans, among the Western trading communities in Alexandria and Tyre by the mid-twelfth century, only after 1250 do subjects of the Crown of Aragon emerge as a distinct mercantile group. A consulate over all Catalan merchants in the East (Ultramar) was established at Alexandria in 1262; six years later the king authorized Barcelona's municipal council to select the Alexandrine consuls, a privilege the *Consell de Cent* retained for four and a half centuries. With increased trade to the restored Greek Empire, a separate consul was also installed in

---

[52] In eighty-five commercial contracts concluded in Barcelona, only four non-residents can be clearly identified, and only a single knight and one Jew appear as investors, Garcia-Madurell, *Comandas comerciales*, nos. 8, 10, 14, 16; ACB 1–1–30; 1–6–1513.

[53] ACB 1–6–764, 2008, 2808; ARM Cod. 342, fol. 115 r.; Novells (1290–1313), fol. 1 r.

[54] ARM Cod. 342, fols. 102 v., 113 v., 118 r., 136 r.

[55] ACB 1–6–726, 2579, 2785; Ferrer-Madurell, *Assegurances i canvis*, II, no. 9; Garcia-Madurell, *Comandas comerciales*, no. 30.

Constantinople in 1281; later the Palaeologue emperor Androni-
cus II granted Catalans a tariff reduction.[56] The delegation of
supervisory responsibilities over subjects of the Crown in the East
to Barcelona secured its commanding position in this important
sector of exchange, which would later be the main source of the
city's commercial prosperity.

Yet by exporting Northern cloth, hides, and arms, the standard
items of European trade with the Levant, Barcelona merchants did
not possess any particular advantage over the Venetians, Genoese,
Pisans, and Occitanians who had already marked off their zones of
commercial influence; Catalans only managed to establish a solid
foothold in the highly competitive eastern markets in the late
thirteenth century. With the fall of Acre in 1291 and the dislocation of traditional trade routes in the Levant, Catalan trade with
Egypt became sporadic; this suggests that it had not yet attained
the intensity and regularity to surmount this momentary crisis in
East–West exchange.[57] Indeed, more evidence exists for trade
with the Byzantine Empire than Egypt and the Levant in the
1280s, confirming Vicens Vives' suspicion that Romania provided
an important early opening in the Eastern Mediterranean for
Barcelona.[58] Further, the average amount of commercial investments in trade to Ultramar, as presented in table 7.2, does not
substantially exceed that for North Africa and is roughly the
same from 1250 to 1290, although the evidence is admittedly far
from abundant. Thus, neither Levantine nor Byzantine trade
appears to have formed a privileged area of exchange whose high
profits created a trading elite within the merchant community, as
was the case in Genoa and Venice, where the wealthiest families
had the resources to dominate trade with the Levant and Byzantium.[59] Clearly this trade involved some of Barcelona's most

[56] Olwer, *L'expansió*, 32–35, 41–44; del Treppo, *Mercaders catalans*, 21–25. On the
installation of a Catalan consul in Constantinople, see Stephen P. Bensch, "Early Catalan
contacts with Byzantium," in *Iberia and the Mediterranean world of the Middle Ages: essays
in honor of Robert I. Burns* (forthcoming).

[57] To date the best indication of the volume of Egyptian trade in the early fourteenth
century comes from royal fines for illicit trade, assembled by Francesco Giunta,
Aragonesi e catalani nel Mediterraneo (Palermo, 1956–59), II, 119. The wild gyrations in the
figures he presents do not support his claim for the regularity of trade, as pointed out
by Ashtor, *Levant trade*, 36–37 and del Treppo, *Mercaders catalans*, 24.

[58] Vicens Vives, *Manual de historia económica*, 191.

[59] Although Garcia-Madurell, *Comandas comerciales*, 22 argue that amounts invested in
thirteenth-century *comandas* to Egypt and the Levant were substantially higher than
those for other areas, the authors mistakenly cite documents transcribed in their own
edition or incorrectly identify the destination of the voyages, e.g. nos. 4, 7, 14, 15. Cf.

aggressive merchants, Pere de Bosc, Bernat Sesfonts, Pere de Malla, but members of patrician houses occasionally participated as investors, including Berenguer Adarró, Bernat de Vic, and Bernat Sesfonts' son-in-law, Berenguer Mallol, whose relatives had served as vicar of Barcelona and consul of Tunis.[60] Yet all these individuals had commercial ties stretching from Murcia to Constantinople; the intensification of trade in the Eastern Mediterranean basin in the late thirteenth century therefore must be kept in perspective, for it had not yet attained the volume to create a commercial hierarchy in Barcelona, or to separate *nouveaux riches* from established patrician houses. Although Egypt, the Levant, and Byzantium have long been considered an area of limitless fortunes and the source of Barcelona's commercial wealth, until the closing two decades of the thirteenth century the Eastern Mediterranean remained a valuable adjunct to the trading zone marked off by the maritime power of the Crown of Aragon from Sicily to Valencia, and from the Maghrib to Occitania. As Barcelona was emerging as a major Mediterranean emporium in the mid-thirteenth century, however, its merchants and investors looked primarily to the south, not the east.

Critical to the success of long-distance trade was the export of cloth, especially the fine woolens of northern France and the Low Countries. By the fourteenth century Barcelona had developed its own cloth industry, particularly devoted to light fustians, its characteristic export in the late Middle Ages. Although the first cloth mill on the city's outskirts was constructed at the Clot complex as early as 1244 and the Durfort were operating cloth mills in the nearby countryside at Matoses in 1228 and on the Llobregat in 1265, the number of industrial mills in spite of these pioneering efforts began to increase significantly only around 1300.[61]

Erik Bach, *La cité de Gênes au XIIe siècle* (Copenhagen, 1955), 46–60; Rösch, *Der venezianishe Adel*, 88, 111; Michel Balard, *La Romanie génoise (XIIe–début du XVe siècle)* (Rome, 1978), I, 236–37; II, 694–700.

60 Garcia-Madurell, *Comandas comerciales*, nos. 5, 19, 41, 44, 45; ACB 1–6–182, 183, 485, 1263; ADB perg. Santa Anna, Carp. 1a, 2–62, 63. On the Mallol family see ACB 3–38–181(e); ACA Reg. 58, fol. 104 v.; Reg. 37, fol. 80 v. Useful comments on Barcelona trading families investing in the East can be found in Batlle i Gallart, "La vida y las actividades," 334–35; David Abulafia, "Catalan merchants and the western Mediterranean, 1236–1300: studies in the notarial acts of Barcelona and Sicily," *Viator*, 16 (1985), 216–23 [repr. in *Italy, Sicily and the Mediterranean*].

61 ACB 4–51–579: "super molendinum draperium de Cloto." A later reference to the cloth mill on the Clot is found in ACA Reg. 74, fol. 86 v. For the Durfort mills, Huici-Cabanes, *Documentos*, I, no. 103; ACA perg. Jaume I, 1864. On the development of Barcelona's cloth industry at the end of the thirteenth century, see J. Reglà Campistol,

Barcelona's merchants obtained their woolens principally from Montpellier, Perpinyà, Narbonne, and Carcassonne, the terminus of cloth merchants from the north.[62] A royal privilege first attests to Catalans visiting the Champagne fairs only in 1259, just on the eve of the first economic downturn that heralded the decline of these great centers of international trade. Significantly, the privilege, allowing the election of Catalan consuls in Champagne, was addressed to leather dealers, not cloth merchants, from both Barcelona and Montpellier.[63] Occitanian middlemen would supply the bulk of northern woolens to Barcelona's drapers.

Because of the close political and cultural bonds linking the coastal regions of Catalonia, Rosselló, and Languedoc as well as the intensity of exchange, trade was organized on different lines from overseas traffic. *Comanda* contracts to Occitania or Perpinyà are rare and, with the exception of two early investments, involve relatively small amounts; instead of concluding their business operations after each voyage, Barcelona's drapers regularly purchased cloth from suppliers in Rosselló and Languedoc on credit. Joan de Banyeres, one of Barcelona's most successful merchants, bought cloth totalling 3,158s. 10d. from Guillem de Borday of Perpinyà, a debt repaid over the course of two years; when Ramon Oliver, another Barcelona merchant, declared bankruptcy in 1264, two merchants appeared from Carcassonne to recover an outstanding loan of 125 lbs.[64] Perpinyà sometimes served as a convenient meeting place for Barcelona's drapers to conclude purchases with exporters from Montpellier, a city subject to the Aragonese monarch where some Catalans owned their own shops.[65] Suddenly taken ill in 1274 at his *operatorium* in Montpellier, where he was surrounded by his bolts of cloth,

---

"El comercio entre Francia y la Corona de Aragón en los siglos XIII y XIV y sus relaciones con el desenvolvimiento de la industria textil catalana," *Actas del primer congreso internacional de pireneístas*, 1 (1950), 3–25.

[62] On cloth trade and production in these towns, see Richard W. Emery, "Flemish cloth and Flemish merchants in Perpignan in the thirteenth century," in *Essays in medieval life and thought in honor of A.P. Evans* (New York, 1955), 153–66; Kathryn L. Reyerson, "Le Rôle de Montpellier dans le commerce des draps de laine avant 1350," *AM*, 94 (1982), 26; Sivéry, *L'Economie*, 214–19.

[63] Capmany, II, no. 15. Two loan contracts from 1261 refer to two Barcelona merchants bringing hides to the fair, presumably to exchange for cloth, Maria Teresa Ferrer i Mallol, "Nous documents sobre els catalans a les fires de la Xampanya," *X CHCA* (Zaragoza, 1980–82), II, 151–59. No other references to direct contacts with Champagne are known. On the decline of the fairs, Sivéry, *L'Economie*, 220–45.

[64] ACB 1–6–257, 2488, 4005.

[65] ADPO série E, Reg. 10, fols. 9 v.– 10 r.; Reg. 13, fols. 32 r., 43 r.; Reg. 15, fol. 33 v.

books, and cash, Ramon Ferrer of Barcelona made out his will witnessed by two Catalan associates, Ramon de Mesurata, a Barcelona canon, and Ramon Llull.[66] Because of their ability to fuel overseas trade with cloth purchased on credit in Languedoc and Rosselló, Barcelona's drapers formed the most dynamic element in the thirteenth-century merchant community. Several made their way into the patriciate in the thirteenth century, and even an older house such as the Burget could boast of a cloth merchant in its midst.[67]

The surge of commercial activity that followed in the wake of the conquest of Majorca profited established patrician houses as well as the most dynamic merchant families. Yet new opportunities did not create a social cleavage within the city between "old" and "new" money, between rentiers and merchants. Of the twenty-four families who most frequently held the magistracy in the late thirteenth century, fourteen can be shown to have participated in the relatively small number of recorded maritime *comanda* contracts; further, members of patrician houses established before 1200 are slightly better represented than newer houses.[68] Yet even the most venerable patrician families had relatively short pedigrees when Catalan troops first disembarked at Palma in 1229; most had distinguished themselves only in the previous generation. They were therefore still closely tied to the world of finance, shipping, and trade growing up in the expansive Ribera district as commercial profits soared, already reaching new heights toward mid-century. Spotty evidence from the purchase price of Barcelona's tolls suggests that although the volume of exchange did increase

---

66 ACB 1–2–1022 and ADB perg. Santa Anna, Carp. de la creu, unnumb. parch. [25 iv 1274].

67 The following individuals belonged to the twenty-four families who regularly supplied urban magistrates: Berenguer Burget draper (ACB 1–6–1798); Pere Despuig draper (ACA perg. Pere I, 1629); Guillem Guerau draper (ACB 1–6–267); Berenguer de Sarrià draper (ACB 3–29–153). In addition Guillem Oliver *mercader* (ACB 1–1–1405) and Arnau and Pere de Riera *cotoners* (Conde, "Los Llull," no. 9) were magistrates.

68 Nine of fourteen families established before 1200 appear in the thirteenth-century *comanda* contracts and sea loans before 1290: Adarró (ACB 1–1–328; Garcia-Madurell, *Comandas comerciales*, no. 19; Ferrer-Garcia, *Assegurances i canvis*, II, no. 7); Eimeric (ibid., nos. 7, 11; Garcia-Madurell, *Comandas comerciales*, nos. 30, 49); Mallol (ibid., nos. 20, 38); Mataró (ACB 1–6–2916); Palau (Ferrer-Garcia, *Assegurances i canvis*, II, nos. 5, 6; ARM, Cod. 342, fol. 13 r.; Garcia-Madurell, *Comandas comericales*, nos. 4, 45); Riera (?) (Conde, "Los Llull," no. 10); Sarrià (Garcia-Madurell, *Comandas comerciales*, nos. 29, 32); de Vic (ACB 1–6–1263). Only four of nine families established after 1200 appear in commercial contracts: Despuig (ARM, Cod. 342, fol. 13 r.; Garcia-Madurell, *Comandas comerciales*, nos. 10, 38); Llull (Conde, "Los Llull," nos. 4, 5, 8, 9, 10; ACB 1–6–2724); Oliver (ACB 1–6–2126, 2757); Sala (Garcia-Madurell, *Comandas comerciales*, no. 44; ACB 1–6–1900).

Table 7.3 *Value of the farm of commercial
tolls in Barcelona before 1290 (in ternal solidi)*

1253	6,266s.
1258	5,559s.
1260	7,200s.
1262	5,500s.
1271–73	8,000s./yr.

somewhat in the two decades for which information is available, commercial activity was not rising rapidly during the 1250s and 1260s.[69]

Owing to the relative stability of the figures in table 7.3, it appears that the volume of commerce experienced the most rapid rise in the generation after the Majorcan expedition; seizure of this vital port provided the impetus for organizing the control of trade through the consulates of Tunis, Bougie, Constantinople, and Alexandria in the second half of the thirteenth century. The relative stability of North African trade toward mid-century may well have caused Barcelona's merchants to look for new markets further east, particularly in the Byzantine Empire which found in the Crown of Aragon a natural ally against the Angevins. The War of the Sicilian Vespers accentuated the probing of new trade connections, for the alignment of the sovereign king of Majorca with the French and the papacy harmed direct commercial relations with Catalonia.[70] Thus, the older patrician houses were just beginning to assert themselves when Barcelona's commercial potential was unfolding through North African trade. It is hardly surprising that they felt comfortable in the world of merchants and did not hesitate to invest in trade themselves. While the intensification of commercial relations with Romania and the Levant toward the end of the century promoted newer, more

[69] The figures in table 7.3 are taken from ACA perg. Jaume I, 1332, 1334, 1615, 1682; Reg. 19, fols. 1 v.–3 v. The figure for 1258, taken from ACA perg. Jaume I, 28, is problematic since it refers to the tenth due the Templars from the commercial tolls, worth 840s. Since the account refers to the revenues for the entire year, it is difficult to determine whether the amount is given in the solidus *dublenc* or the solidus *de tern*, instituted in June, 1258. I assume the amount refers to what the revenue farmer paid before the year began, and thus represents 8,400s. *dublenc*, or 5,559s. *de tern*.

[70] Abulafia, "The problem of the Kingdom of Majorca," 43–44; Bensch, "Early Catalan contacts."

daring merchant and entrepreneurial families, the volume of trade in the East was not sufficient to overturn the wealth and prestige of the older houses, which vied among themselves to enlist new families as their allies and supporters rather than exclude them. Investments in overseas trade had evolved into a sensible, even a prosaic undertaking rather than a gamble made by ambitious social climbers. To pay for her pious bequests, Agnès, daughter of Pere Grony, made provisions in her will in 1289 assigning "all the money I have at my death in gold and silver coin or other moneys, in merchandise, or in [whatever else] I hold or others retain for me in commercial societies and *comandas*."[71] Throughout the thirteenth century Barcelona's patricians never lost their taste for commercial profits even if they did not always board ships themselves to sail to North Africa, Sicily, and the East.

Because the weight of Barcelona's trade at first lay in the Maghrib rather than the Levant, its successful expansion involved not only sedentary investors and overseas traders, but also nobles, sailors, and adventurers from throughout the Crown of Aragon attracted by the potential of a Catalan maritime empire. Shielded from commercial and naval competition by protectionist measures at home, Barcelona directed its maritime investments toward Majorca and the Catalan outposts in North Africa; these were rough and loosely structured colonial worlds, still fearing Muslim attack yet open to trading populations from throughout the Western Mediterranean. It was the edge of its sphere of commercial interest that set the tone for Barcelona's trading community, for capital exported from Barcelona often fused with resources contributed by investors from other towns and was turned in new directions at Palma, Tunis, or Bougie. Commerce, piracy, war, and diplomacy converged in these outposts created by the tense, unstable balance among Christian and Islamic powers. Barcelona's trading network would not be closely supervised by large family companies with extensive assets from their shops and warehouses on the Ribera; rather it would fall under the control of individual merchants who received the use of capital for short periods and acted with a large degree of independence overseas. Considerable silent wealth was slowly accumulated in Barcelona by relatively modest investors involved in numerous, diverse, and small-scale enterprises. The diversity and fluidity of

---

[71] ACB 4-1-62. Cf. 4-8-98, in which a testator encourages the tutors of his children to invest their funds in trade.

the city's commercial community partly explains the reticence to employ ascriptive professional titles indicative of specialized commodity trading. The absence of merchant or craft guilds thus hardly seems remarkable. Although the city possessed only weak confraternal organizations, patricians and petty merchants were nevertheless united in encouraging the development of trade.

A HIERARCHY OF RENTS

Growing commercial prosperity also increased the value of urban property as artisans, shopkeepers, and laborers immigrated to the developing suburban zones. Revenues drawn from rights over urban houses and undeveloped lots had not been a major source of wealth during the first phase of urban growth, for through the mid-twelfth century most land and buildings were either allodial or leased on relatively simple terms from the canons or local churches. To profit from the city's explosive demographic growth, patricians who had acquired substantial tracts of suburban land began to develop them systematically through subdivisions and drew revenues from new sets of rights that covered urban soil with multiple layers of obligations and payments. What came to distinguish many patrician families was not merely that they owned substantial amounts of urban real estate, but that they held allods or Church property; this placed them in a privileged position within the hierarchy of rents.

Revenues from urban landlordship offered a substantial new area of potential profit, which may well have seemed more attractive to thirteenth-century investors than rural property. While patricians and well-off burghers certainly maintained their interest in the carefully tended orchards, vineyards, and fields in the Pla de Barcelona and extended their holdings along the narrow coastal strip to the northeast, it is unclear whether the densely settled and heavily worked lands around the city could be made to yield substantially higher returns. From close study of the peasantry of the Baix Llobregat and the Maresme, it is clear that rents remained relatively stable in the thirteenth century, usually fixed at a fifth or fourth of the produce, while only marginal land was available to extend the area under cultivation; the suburban village of Provençana seems to have faced economic hardship in the early thirteenth century, and Berenguer Durfort complained about damage to his mills at Molins de Rei and Sant Baudili in the Baix Llobregat at the hands of marauding nobles.[72] During the thirteenth century burghers sought to insert themselves between the rent-paying tenant and the allodial proprietor, often a church, in order to obtain part of the profits from the *territorium*; some of the most promient patricians also began to consolidate compact units of exploitation centered on a tower or *mas*.[73] Yet the most dynamic sector of landlordship lay not in the countryside but in the city itself.

While a ceiling to agricultural output was being reached in the limited amount of arable land surrounding the city, suburban real estate was booming. Land, houses, and shops in the Ribera district or in the eastern suburbs near the Call de Boria were in great demand; a workshop on the thriving Skinners Street purchased in 1225 for 120 mbts. (1600s. *dublenc*) was sold in 1228 for 3,200s., double the previous price.[74] Large tracts of land that had remained sparsely settled or given over to garden agriculture were divided into small parcels and leased to tenants on condition they undertake construction on the property. A splendid series of parchments documents the parcelling out of lots one by one along the western shoreline from 1245 to 1255 by Guillem de Vic and his wife, sister of Bernat Simó, who had inherited the property, and others built up city streets that bore the names of their thirteenth-century patrician developers: Bernat de Vic, Berenguer Durfort, Jaume Gerard, Jaume Eimeric, Guillem Moneder, and Martí de Montcada.[75] Because urban historiography still conjures up the image of indolent, sated oligarchs living off rents in order to create a contrast with cunning, industrious merchants in constant pursuit of new profit, the urban real estate market in the expansive thirteenth-century economy rarely receives its due. Patricians participated in commercial investment and moved easily in the world of merchants, yet they did not feel any contradiction in turning their resources to the development of residential urban

---

[72] Codina, *Els pagesos*, I, 73–124, esp. 78–79, 110–11; Cuadrada, *El Maresme*, 267–72; ACA perg. varis, Marquès de Monistrol, 145.

[73] Coral Cuadrada, "Sobre les relacions camp–ciutat a la Baixa Edat Mitjana: Barcelona i les comarques de l'entorn," *Acta mediaevalia*, 11–12 (1990–91), 162–65, 169–70; Joan J. Busqueta i Riu, *Una vila del Territori de Barcelona: Sant Andreu de Palomar als segles XIII–XIV* (Barcelona, 1991), 175–216, 231–35.

[74] ACB 4–32–511, 513.

[75] On the development of the western coastline, see ACB 4–39–447, 452, 465, 468, 476, 481, etc. On street names, ACB 1–6–883; 4–32–58(b); ACA Reg. 63, fol. 65 v.; perg. varis, Marquès de Monistrol, 100, 121; ADB perg. Santa Anna, Carp. de la creu, unnumb. parch. [21 viii 1271].

property. It is also difficult to find a successful merchant who did not own some houses or shops in the city or purchase a garden plot or vineyard outside its walls. If pressures created by economic growth were heightening social tensions in Barcelona, then one should not look for the point of conflict in an abstract distinction between patrician rentiers and ambitious entrepreneurs but within the structures of landholding itself.

By 1200 most leased land in the city was granted according to the terms of emphyteutic tenure. Emphyteusis originated as a landholding contract in the late Roman Empire and was consequently memorialized in Roman legal texts. It granted the resident a perpetual lease on property in return for a small rent (*census*); the tenant could freely pledge, sell, sublet, and bequeath to his heirs the land or buildings he held, but the landlord retained dominion and the right to approve and profit from the transfer of the leased property. The spread of emphyteusis has been studied almost exclusively in relation to Catalan rural society, where it is usually regarded as an advantageous form of perpetual lease for peasants and often compared to a fief.[76] Its impact on urban landlordship, however, has received little attention.

The rise of emphyteutic tenure in Catalonia has usually been discussed in relation to the reception of Roman law during the closing decades of the twelfth century. In Barcelona the word emphyteusis first appears in a charter from 1196, one of the earliest references to the institution in Catalonia, but its constituent elements had appeared much earlier.[77] In addition to the annual rent and the ability of the tenant to alienate his rights, the characteristic features of the lease in Barcelona consisted of three prerogatives retained by the landlord: the right of first refusal (Latin *fatica*; Catalan *fadiga*), an entry fee (Latin *introitum*; Catalan *entrada*), and a transfer fee (Latin *laudesimum* or *laudimium*; Catalan

---

[76] J. M. Pons i Guri, "Entre l'emfeuteusi i el feudalisme (els reculls de dret gironins)," in *La formació i expansió del feudalisme català. Actes del col·loqui organitzat pel Col·legi Universitari de Girona (8–11 de gener de 1985) [Estudi General. Revista del Col·legi Universitari de Girona, 5–6]* (Girona, 1986), 411–18; Paul Freedman, *The origins of peasant servitude in medieval Catalonia* (Cambridge, 1991), 145–49; Francesc Carreras Candi, "Notes sobre los origens de la enfitiusis en lo territori de Barcelona," *Revista jurídica de Catalunya*, 15 (1909), 1–92. A useful beginning to the study of Barcelona's rents in the late Middle Ages is offered by Manuel Riu Riu, "La financión de la vivienda, propiedad horizontal y pisos de alquiler en la Barcelona del siglo XIV," in *La ciudad hispánica durante los siglos XIII al XVI* (Barcelona, 1985), II, 1397–405.

[77] ACB LA I, fol. 116, Mas XII, no. 2269. Cf. Freedman *Origins of peasant servitude*, 147, n. 117.

lluïsme). The oldest and most basic of the three was the *fadiga*, for it ensured the owner's *dominium*. If a tenant had made arrangements to alienate his or her rights to a third party, the *fadiga* allowed the owner to repurchase them at the price contracted by the tenant within a stipulated period, customarily set at thirty days in Barcelona. Already in use in the late eleventh century, the right of first refusal allowed landowners to let out their property without fear of losing control of it through the actions of their tenants.[78] Since early leases were often granted with the expectation that tenants would improve the property they received by building houses or other structures at their own expense, the amount of improvements could far exceed the value of an empty lot. Unless a landlord held the right to the *fadiga*, as property passed to succeeding generations of tenants the danger existed that the owner's rights would erode. Although a landlord received no monetary compensation from declining to exercise the right of repurchase, the ability to restrict the alienation of property provided the basis for the *lluïsme*, the fee owed by the tenant on the transfer of the rights he or she possessed to a third party. The charge appeared soon after 1200 in urban land transactions, and its value was substantial: the nunnery of Sant Pere de les Puel·les customarily charged a fourth of the sale price, but it often reached as high as a third.[79] The *lluïsme* thus constituted the most novel element in the mature form of emphyteutic tenure and brought substantial profits to landlords. The *entrada*, a one-time payment by the new tenant, provided another important source of income for the individual who held dominion over the land; although it was an old fee, only in the late twelfth century did it become common. Thus, the profits landlords derived from their multiple rights over property consisted not only of an annual rent, but also charges exacted upon the transfer of rights by the tenant. While emphyteusis provided stability for peasant cultivators and contained no taint of servitude, in the volatile markets of Barcelona it allowed landlords to reap substantial benefits from charges on alienating rights over real estate and encouraged other investors to gain a share of those charges.

[78] The earliest example of the thirty-day clause in Barcelona known to me is found in ACB 3–38–8(d) (1083). Cf. Carreras Candi, "Notes," 21, n. 2 (1094).

[79] The earliest explicit mention of the fee in urban land charters appears in 1210, ACB 1–6–1470. Carreras Candi, "Notes," 55 believes the fee consisted of a third of the sale value of the property, but this seems to be the maximum; cf. ASPP, 145, 153; ACB 1–6–1470, 3698; ADB perg. Santa Anna, Carp. 1a, 34; Carp. 2a, 93, 573.

Table 7.4 *Property transfers and rents, 1200–1290*
(Sales in excess of 1,500s. not included)

	Average amount of property sale	Average cost for 1s. rent	Average amount of entry fee per 1s. of rent
1201–1210	522s.	14.3s.	8.9s.
1211–1220	319s.	16.6s.	9.5s.
1221–1230	329s.	21.2s.	22.1s.
1231–1240	441s.	21.0s.	18.8s.
1241–1250	268s.	17.4s.	9.2s.
1251–1260	305s.	22.8s.	5.6s.
1261–1270	498s.	65.3s.	9.4s.
1271–1280	303s.	41.3s.	4.7s.
1281–1290	395s.	36.0s.	7.8s.

Because emphyteutic leases in their mature form reinforced the *dominium* of the allodial owner, the economic value of urban property shifted from the rents themselves to the charges levied on transfer and entry. The *entrada* encouraged tenants to sublease their rights; in turn, a tenant would profit from the increased value of the property by receiving a share of the *lluïsme* along with the owner whenever a subtenant alienated his or her rights. As a result, during the thirteenth century emphyteusis forged a chain of landlordship between the allodial owner and the individual who actually resided on the property, paid rent, and was responsible for the various fees connected with the property. By the late thirteenth century layers of property rights covered urban soil, creating a hierarchy of landlords.

The urban real estate market changed radically as allodial property became burdened with rents and obligations. Its contours can best be seen in the evolution of average sale prices and the value of rents in table 7.4.

The city's economic vitality in the thirteenth century did not produce a rapid transfer of urban land and rents to new owners. The average value of individual real estate sales actually declined after 1210, reversing a tendency that had set in during the 1140s. Great care must be shown in interpreting the data, however, for the figures surely do not correspond to a period of falling land values. Rather, they point to the increasing scarcity of allodial land in the city, its subdivision into small parcels, and the fragmentation of property rights in the hands of multiple landlords. In contrast to the open, fluid land market of the twelfth century, when large blocks of relatively undeveloped and allodial urban real estate were still available, the weight of landlordship slowed down the transfer of urban property in the thirteenth century, when patrician houses retained and developed the suburban land they had acquired during their rise.

Profits for those who held rights over real estate clearly grew in relation to the expansion of the urban population. Townspeople were willing to pay more than ever before for rents and the rights of lordship over urban land, even if they could not gain full proprietorship. The average cost of purchasing 1s. of rent trebled between 1200 and 1280 and reveals an intense demand by the 1260s. The rent itself, however, was often insignificant in comparison to the purchase price during that decade: it brought on average only a paltry 1.5 percent annual return on the purchase price but in reality much less since the investor often bought a rent paid by a subtenant or even a sub-subtenant and therefore owed rent to those below him or her on the chain of emphyteutic landlords. In such situations, profits came principally from the *lluïsme* and the *entrada*. The entry fee fluctuated wildly in relation to the amount of rent; the relationship between the two reveals no clear statistical trend. For small garden plots at the edge of urban development, the allodial owner either charged a nominal *entrada* or even none at all; for valuable workshops or houses in the bustling Ribera or expanding artisan quarter to the east of the market, it could soar to as much as fifty times the amount of annual rent or more.[80] Especially for valuable suburban shops and houses, the *entrada* thus more closely corresponded to the actual value of the property than its rent, thereby allowing the proprietors an immediate and substantial gain from the increased value of their property. Together with the *lluïsme*, the entry fee offered windfalls to real estate developers. The period from 1260 to 1284 was a golden age for Barcelona's landlords.

Yet the fees levied for transfers and the partitioning of property rights among multiple landlords through emphyteusis also produced friction. Once tenants began to pay *lluïsme* on alienations,

---

[80] For examples of unusually high entry fees worth fifty times or more the amount of annual rent, see ACB 1–6–1305, 1291, 1608, 3409; 1–1–454; ACA perg. varis, Marquès de Monistrol, 66, 177; ADB perg. Santa Anna, Carp. 2b, 434; Carp. 8, 140.

landlords tried to impose the transfer fee on all types of conveyances. But did the *lluïsme* apply when property was given in
dowry, divided among heirs, or offered in pledge? Did the allodial
owner have the power to restrict the alienation of rights by a
subtenant once the transfer fee was paid or break the lease if the
property were not maintained?[81] On these questions tenants
quickly put up such stiff resistance to the new levies that King
Pere I in 1211 found it necessary to impose a penalty on any tenant
selling, leasing, pledging, or renting land without the landlord's
permission.[82] In general, tenants with emphyteutic leases in Barcelona successfully opposed attempts to restrict the alienability of
their property rights or impose charges on leases kept within the
family; *Recognoverunt proceres* later confirmed the customary
privileges ensuring that Barcelona's citizens would not be charged
the *lluïsme* on dowry transfers and that division among heirs did
not require the landlord's consent.[83] Its provisions marked a
significant clarification in the nature of emphyteusis, which came
to represent a privileged form of free tenure throughout
Catalonia.

In addition to raising questions about the fees owed by tenants,
emphyteutic tenure created the delicate problem of determining
the rights enjoyed by multiple landlords. If through a series of
leases three or even four landlords possessed rights through
emphyteusis, what share of the *lluïsme* and *entrada* should each
party receive? Unfortunately we are poorly informed about the
distribution of profits from landlordship, but the issue was hotly
contested by the 1280s. With real estate and rents bringing high
prices, the amount that the third or fourth landlord received from
the transfer or entry fee proved burdensome for those actually
paying rents and occupying the property. To quell discontent,
King Pere II mandated a reduction of these fees; in *Recognoverunt
proceres*, the king cut the *lluïsme* on royal property by half and in
1285 decreed that throughout Barcelona and the *ort i vinyet* it
should not exceed a tenth of the sale price. The decision raised a
storm of protest, particularly from local churches since they still
held substantial portions of the urban real estate by allodial right.

[81] For disputes involving these questions, see ACB 1–6–1470; 3–29–264; ACA Reg. 59, fol.
117 v.; ADB perg. Santa Anna, Carp. 2a, 203.
[82] *Cortes* 1:1, 89.
[83] On the salient features of the code in regard to landlordship, Careras Candi, "Notes,"
53–54; Freedman, *Origins of peasant servitude*, 148–49.

Because ecclesiastical complaints were the loudest and the most sustained, Carreras Candi argued that the *lluïsme* had benefited mainly the clergy, which as "petty feudal lords" had restricted laymen from buying and selling property and "harmed the free development of the city."[84]

The anticlericalism evident in Carreras Candi's pioneering study, however, caused him to pass over the fact that many lay landlords, especially patrician families, also found their revenues from urban real estate reduced. Since early land charters tell us so little about the way emphyteutic landlords split their income, it is difficult to know who suffered most from the reduction. In an enactment of 1285, the king sought to clear up the matter. The decree contained detailed regulations which established precisely how much each party claiming emphyteutic rights should receive; it also distinguished between lay and ecclesiastical claims and considered the portion due to as many as four landlords.[85] The landlord closest to the rent-paying tenant, not the allodial owner, profited the most from a conveyance, for he received half the *lluïsme* or *entrada* while the remainder was divided up among others lower down on the ladder of landlordship, with slightly less due a cleric than a layman. If, for instance, there were three landlords (*domini*), two lay and one clerical (the regulations always consider clerics the allodial holders), the "first" (lay) lord received 50 percent of the *lluïsme*, the "second" (lay) lord 25 percent, and the "third" (ecclesiastical) lord 21 percent, with the remaining 4 percent returned to the seller. The church had good grounds for complaint, for it may have earlier received the lion's share of the transfer fee. The church of Santa Anna, for instance, began a lawsuit against one tenant who sublet his land and paid only a fourth of the *lluïsme* on the entry fee to his landlord; the prior succeeded in pressing his claim for a half.[86] Those who had most recently acquired rights over property therefore appear to have gained the most by the reforms, at the expense not only of ecclesiastical institutions but also of the older patrician houses, whose ancestors had acquired allodial property or leased land from

---

[84] On the bitter and sustained complaints by Barcelona's clergy, see Carreras Candi, "Notes," 50–71, esp. 51; ACA Reg. 71, fols. 9 v., 13 r., 91 r.

[85] Transcribed in Carreras Candi, "Notes," 57, n. 1. Cf. the decision rendered by arbitrators on *lluïsmes* at Sant Celoni in 1280, J. M. Pons i Guri, "Sentència arbitral sobre lluïsmes, subestabliments i altres drets emfitèutics a Sant Celoni," *Recull d'estudis d'història jurídica catalana* (Barcelona, 1989), I, 235–47.

[86] ADB perg. Santa Anna, Carp. 2a, 203; cf. Carp. 2b, 573.

the canons on easy terms in the late twelfth and early thirteenth century. The reduction in conveyance and entry fees made the rights over land held in emphyteusis somewhat less valuable, a decrease reflected in the falling purchase price of rents in the 1280s (see table 7.4). Disputes over the *lluïsme* in the 1280s involved not only a growing resentment of tenants against urban landlords, whether ecclesiastical or patrician, but also a debate about the profits from the property rights at various levels in the hierarchy of leaseholders during the expansive thirteenth century.

Although the reforms instituted by King Pere II released some of the tension building between allodial lords and their tenants and made it easier for tenants to retain larger profits from alienating or developing their holdings, the layering of rents made the occupants of leased houses and shops aware of the status of their landlords through rents they paid and the rituals of property transfer. While extant land charters and legal texts present cold figures about real estate values and abstract notions of *dominium*, relationships between landlords and tenants were nevertheless personal, for they encompassed notions of social standing as well as economic advantage. Even nominal rents for small parcels enforced some formal contact between many urban residents and patricians, whose permission also had to be obtained before a tenant could enter into a major property transaction. The transfer to new landlords of rents and power over the disposition of urban lots and buildings did not entail merely the strokes of a notary's pen but a ceremonial introduction of the new proprietor to his tenants. After the former owner took the buyer by the hand across the threshold of the building, the latter surveyed the property "from door to door," accepted keys to the entrance which were then used ritually to lock and unlock the door, and received an acknowledgment from the assembled tenants that they now owed their new landlord all appropriate rents and obligations. As the chain of emphyteutic leases lengthened, by the 1270s purchasers found it worthwhile to have the ceremonial transfer witnessed and recorded by scribes in a separate charter to confirm their rights; the elderly widow of Bernat Marquet insisted on being propped up in bed to perform the customary rituals of introducing a new landlord to the tenants.[87] The possession of urban land thus brought with it authority and status as well as revenues.

[87] For examples of the ceremony, see ACB 1–6–991; 4–32–57(c); 4–39–388; 4–40–503; 4–42–305.

Emphyteutic leases artificially expanded the amount of urban real estate for investors. It did so not by enlarging the zone of intense settlement (although the expansion of the suburbs was occurring as well) but by vertically extending legal rights, which permitted several landlords to benefit from the same piece of property in the city's most profitable quarters. Thriving artisans and small-scale merchants could therefore invest in rental income and its attendant rights, but allodial holders, especially patricians and the local clergy, still formed the foundation for the construction of multistoried parchment profits from emphyteusis. Typically the king took action to deflate the pressures built up on rents by the weight of multiple landlords and the social friction it produced; the privileges contained in *Recognoverunt proceres* and the reduction of the *lluïsme* established a new balance in the structure of urban real estate and allowed those who had recently accumulated sufficient resources to take their place on the ladder of landlordship. Yet Barcelona's patricians still occupied the first rungs; even if less money passed down from those higher on the ladder of landlordship than during the golden age of rents, one still had to seek their permission before beginning the climb.

The structure of urban rents did create friction within the urban community, for, like sedimentary deposits, rights over land, shops, and houses built up in layers over time. Whether these economic interests were pronounced enough to determine the basic pattern of urban society, however, must be judged in light of the evolving political structure of the community.

MUNICIPAL REPRESENTATION AND URBAN POWER

The institutional framework of urban government assumed new and durable forms during the last half of the thirteenth century, as Font Rius has so clearly demonstrated in his numerous studies.[88] What effect these changes produced on the distribution of power within the city, however, remains unclear. With disarming optimism nineteenth-century historians were fond of associating early municipal regimes with a primitive urban democracy intended to counteract "feudal oppression" or "oligarchic domination."

[88] Still fundamental is Font Rius, "Orígenes del régimen," 491–95. Cf. his later reflections on the theme, José María Font Rius, "Jaume I i la municipalitat de Barcelona," *Discurs inaugural de l'any 1977–78 de la Universitat de Barcelona* (Barcelona, 1977) [repr. in *Estudis sobre els drets*, 676–83].

Revisionist work in a more cynical age has arrived at rather different conclusions.[89] Even though municipal institutions exhibited remarkable variety in organization and often changed in form and procedure, the influence of patricians and factions of leading families did not necessarily diminish. Further, urban lords in many cases promoted rather than resisted the creation of municipal regimes and found many collaborators among urban notables. Given the close association of the count-kings with Barcelona, it is useful to consider the formation of its municipal institutions not merely as a direct expression of community identity but also as a recasting of patrician and royal power.

The most fundamental innovation in Barcelona was the creation through royal enactments of municipal magistrates and a town council. Between 1249 and 1274 the municipal government of Barcelona assumed the basic form it would retain until its abolition in 1714. On April 7, 1249, King Jaume I issued a brief edict from Valencia appointing four "peace men" (Latin *paciarii*; Catalan *paers*) to look after the good of the city; three months later he issued a more detailed charter, which mandated the *paers* to select an assembly to aid them and advise in choosing salaried successors to their offices each year. The two edicts of 1249 formed the cornerstone of Barcelona's municipal constitution, but later enactments altered and embellished its provisions in 1258, 1260, 1265, and 1274. The king set the size of the general assembly at 200 in 1258, but later reduced it to 100; the number of magistrates, whose title changed from *paer* to *conseller*, eventually was set at 5. These adjustments eventually produced a stable municipal government consisting of an executive committee of 5 magistrates (*consellers*), chosen by a delegation of 12 assemblymen, and the general council of 100, or *Consell de Cent* (although the actual number of representatives increased over the years), appointed by the magistrates.

The king crafted Barcelona's municipal institutions with care and deliberation over a quarter of a century; they did not represent a hasty concession to the forceful demand for autonomy on the part of the urban population or factions within it. Because of the considerable degree of experimentation as well as the late emergence of an autonomous regime, interpretations have varied in explaining its significance and the motives behind its creation. At

---

[89] For recent revisionist approaches, see Heers, *Les Partis et la vie politique*, 41–63, 192–97; Reynolds, *Kingdoms and communities*, 168–98.

the first Congrés d'història de la Corona d'Aragó in 1909, Josep Pella i Forgas considered the royal charters of 1249 a "reform" of earlier, informal institutions; with various modifications, his position has found a strong echo in later studies.[90] Augustí Duran i Sanpere maintained that the decrees merely provided an "official declaration" of a municipal regime that had already taken shape through other grants and privileges from the king, whose officials had kept close control of urban government, while Font Rius places the edicts in the context of a "maturation" of Catalan urban institutions, the crystallization of a slowly unfolding community identity.[91] Elements of the new constitution were without doubt present much earlier; the local *prohoms* had acted as informal representatives of the city, and the Cort of Barcelona in 1214 amplified legatine statutes introduced from Occitania by ordering that two "peace men" be elected in each city to aid the vicars. Yet, as already noted in chapter 2, these precedents did not lead smoothly and inevitably to the creation of municipal magistrates and a town council. As the vicarial court became a stable source of territorial authority and patrician families assumed a prominent place in royal administration in the city, the role of *prohoms* diminished and the early consular regime withered; Barcelona's patricians found that collaborating with royal authority rather than spearheading a drive for communal independence provided the surest means to secure their influence. As a result community identity remained amorphous in Barcelona, for its leaders spoke as much for the count-king as for the urban population. The formation of municipal institutions therefore must be treated from a royalist as much as from an urban perspective.

Barcelona's privileges of 1249 formed part of a broad program of municipal reorganization undertaken by King Jaume I throughout the Crown of Aragon. New constitutions were granted to Tàrrega (1242), Valencia (1245), Montpellier (1246), and Palma de Majorca (1249) as well as to Barcelona; they provided the underpinnings of an administrative and fiscal framework undergoing rapid renovation to encompass the vastly expanded realms. The early charters for Valencia, Barcelona, and

---

[90] Josep Pella y Forgas, "Establement per Jaume I del Concell de Cent de Barcelona," *CHCA* (Barcelona, 1909), I, 42–43.
[91] Duran i Sanpere, *Barcelona i la seva història*, II, 87; Font Rius, "Orígenes del régimen," 490–503.

Palma de Majorca resemble one another closely in diplomatic form and institutional content.[92] They concentrate on the selection of a small group of magistrates endowed with a vaguely formulated directive to supervise urban affairs and protect royal interests, not upon the prerogatives of a larger accessory assembly, which from a modern perspective might seem the true foundation of representative government. Through the system of co-option and non-renewable annual terms, a large number of patricians and prominent townsmen served as magistrates. As we have seen, in Barcelona members of twenty-four patrician families held slightly less than half the available positions of *paers* or *consellers* from 1249 to 1291, while the rest were distributed widely. While not democratic in a modern sense, the magistracy was nevertheless representative in medieval terms, for it effectively spread the responsibility of guarding urban privileges and the obligation to support the Crown among the wealthiest and most influential families, those which burghers expected to rule. With formal representation, it also became easier for the Crown to expect and organize aid from the entire urban populace. None of the urban communities, it must be remembered, is known to have clamored for the independent regimes they received from the king in the 1240s, for with autonomy came added responsibilities, as King Jaume I and his successor would frequently remind the city.

The early municipal regime acted timidly. Little evidence exists to show that Barcelona's magistrates and council rapidly carved out a clearly delimited sphere of judicial and regulatory competence. The privilege of 1249 granted a broad mandate to the *paers* to "govern, administer, and rule the city in fidelity to us and for the common utility of the community," yet magistrates were to limit themselves to communal matters and not interfere with the justice dispensed by the vicar, who was, however, enjoined to seek their advice.[93] Only the cumulative, practical experience of day-to-day government clarified these provisions. The magistrates promulgated regulations (*ordinacions*) in 1260 controlling meat and poultry prices, and possibly others concerning innkeepers and wholesalers (*corredors*) as early as 1251, yet, except for

---

[92] Alvaro Santamaría, "Los consells municipales de la Corona de Aragón mediado el siglo XIII. El sistema de cooptación," *AHDE*, 51 (1981), 291–364; José María Font Rius, "Valencia y Barcelona en los orígenes de su régimen municipal," in *Estudios jurídicos en homenaje al Profesor Santa Cruz Teijeiro* (Barcelona, 1974), 291–315 [repr. in *Estudis sobre els drets*, 639–57]; Ferran Soldevila, *Jaume I, Pere el Gran* (Barcelona, 1955), 60–61.

[93] Font Rius, "Orígenes del régimen," ap. ix.

scattered initiatives related to food supplies and the quality of craft production, municipal authorities do not appear to have pursued new legislation aggressively; city leaders seemed content to rely on the vicar and bailiff for public order and the regulation of civic affairs, at least until the 1280s.[94] Despite incessant complaints about the pollution caused by dyers and fustian weavers, for instance, the magistrates and council did not take action themselves but finally prodded the recalcitrant bailiff into setting down the city's first industrial zoning regulation in 1255.[95] The judicial competence of the magistrates was also fuzzy. The only known intervention of the *paers* occurred in 1250, when the king appointed them in conjunction with royal judges to settle a complaint about property development brought by Guillem Burgès and Bernat Pagan against Berenguera, wife of Guillem de Vic. The case revealed that the *paers* were entering uncharted territory for they were unclear "whether they should proceed in the manner of peace men and undertake an investigation to get at the truth or act in the manner of regular judges and observe the procedure and order of the law."[96] The procedural insecurity voiced during the case laid bare the novelty of the institution. Rather than leaping at the chance to assert their jurisdiction, the magistrates remained content to limit their judicial intervention to exceptional or particularly sensitive proceedings; when in an act of municipal self-assertion the magistrates condemned noblemen for acts of violence, the king still had to issue charters in order to validate their decision.[97] Even though *Recognoverunt proceres* in 1284 confirmed that the city had jurisdiction in criminal cases, the *prohoms* assisted the vicar and did not press for an independent municipal court. Barcelona's magistrates were therefore slow to take full advantage of the administrative and judicial autonomy offered them in the charter of 1249.

As a financial and fiscal organ of the Crown, however, the municipality quickly found its footing. The very establishment of the magistracy entailed the formation of a communal fund. The

[94] Font Rius, "Jaume I i la municipalitat," 678–80.   [95] Capmany, II, no. 12.

[96] ACB 4–40–456: "Cum vero contenderetur et in dubium verteretur super processu cause presentis utrum debebat procedere tamquam paciarii et veritatem inquirentes vel tamquam meri iudices sollempnitate et iuris ordine observato habita deliberacione super forma litterarum domini Regis dixerunt paciarii et iudices se debere procedere tamquam paciarii et veritatem inquirentes super iure utriusque partis tam per testes quam per instrumenta."

[97] AHCB Llibre verd, fols. 227 v.–228 r.; ACA Reg. 95, fol. 52 r.

paers were required to account for their office upon the installation of their successors, and, in contrast to the early Valencian regime, provision was made for the payment of a salary (*salarium quod de comuni fuerit statutum*). From this modest beginning, Barcelona's magistrates soon used their communal resources to gain influence with the king. An overlooked account from 1251 notes that the city's *prohoms* held the rights to the bailiwick of Barcelona for that year.[98] Did the city receive royal revenues from the bailiff in compensation for a loan, possibly the price of urban autonomy, or did the purchase represent a bold attempt by the municipality to manage the urban domain? Whatever the answer, Jaume soon found it profitable to negotiate with Barcelona's magistrates for extraordinary revenues and loans. During the troubled final years of his reign, the king relied increasingly on irregular subsidies to finance the suppression of Muslim resistance in Valencia, the defeat of rebellious Catalonian nobles at home, the expedition to Murcia, and his promised crusade to the Holy Land. The city of Barcelona proved one of his greatest treasures. Even though a tallage (*questia*) had been assessed on the city as early as 1145, only financial emergencies justified its collection; in the later thirteenth century, however, the *questia* formed part of a vaguely formulated package of general levies connected with exemptions from military service, loans, and "general services."[99] The amounts from these irregular contributions, whatever their specific justification, were substantial. While the *questia* brought in 26,000s. in 1209 and 20,000s. in 1222, the municipality routinely contributed 80,000 to 100,000s. in the later thirteenth century.[100] Further, the magistrates were willing to offer generous loans or "favors" to the Crown in exchange for short-term exemptions in what amounts

---

[98] ACA perg. Jaume I, 1255: "faciamus tradi et deliberari domui milicie Templi decimum sibi pertinentem in redditibus quibuslibet tocius baiulie Barchinone et baiulorum ad ipsam spectantibus ut actenus accipere consuevit non obstante scilicet vendicione a domino rege probis hominibus Barchinone de dictis redditibus facta nec obstante etiam aliqua promissione vel obligacione eisdem facta ab illis qui dictos redditus a predictis probis hominibus Barchinone emerunt."

[99] In 1269 the king granted the city a four-year exemption, no doubt for a generous contribution, from "questiis, donis, mutuis, generalibus serviciis, et adimprivis, et ab exercitibus, et cavalcatis, et ab redemcionibus exercitum et cavalcatarum," ACA Reg. 16, fol. 144 r. Cf. Reg. 14, fol. 82 v.; Reg. 20, fol. 248 v.

[100] Bisson, *Fiscal accounts*, II, no. 125 (1209); ACA perg. Jaume I, 186 (1222); 80,000s. (1257) Reg. 10, fols. 29 v., 31 v.–32 r., 72 r.; 100,000s. (1273) Reg. 14, fol. 52 r.; 80,000s. (1276) Reg. 20, fol. 350 v.; 100,000s. (1284) Reg. 62, fol. 61 r.

to taxation with a velvet glove.[101] Already in Jaume's later years the Crown was turning toward irregular general levies rather than income from the domain in order to meet its needs; this expanded to become the primary means of royal finance by the early fourteenth century.[102] Although the extant evidence does not permit an accurate evaluation of the total fiscal burden shouldered by the citizens of Barcelona, it leaves little doubt that it was substantial. If the king had not formed a municipal regime to legitimate and participate in raising revenues on such a scale, he could not have depended so heavily on his Catalan capital for financial backing.

Thus, rather than resulting in financial independence, the formation of an autonomous municipal government at first created even closer ties between prominent citizens and the monarchy. As both magistrates and royal financiers, Barcelona's patricians found the system much to their liking, for it provided substantial revenues to please the king, ensure his patronage, and secure rapid repayment and profits on their own loans. A large portion of extraordinary revenues quickly went into patrician purses. Of 60,000s. collected from the city in 1266, 30,000s. went to repay a debt owed Ramon Ricart, a citizen of Barcelona and royal consul in Tunis, and Romeu Gerard, who served among the first group of municipal magistrates; of 100,000s. raised in 1273, 22,351s. went to Guillem Durfort, 2,400 mbts. (21,600s.) to Berenguer de Lacera, and 8,881s. to Guillem Grony.[103] What to modern eyes might well appear a blatant conflict of interest seemed a natural coordination of power, resources, and status to the townspeople of Barcelona during the early years of its municipal regime.

While a formal distinction between revenues for royal and civic purposes existed, it proved difficult to separate the two in practice. Burghers certainly raised complaints against inequitable assessments, but there is little to indicate resentment against the way in which magistrates put the funds to use. Responding to protests

---

[101] In exchange for a 60,000s. loan in 1266, the Crown agreed not to tax the city until it was repaid, ACA Reg. 14, fols. 82 v., 83 r.; after receiving an aid of 80,000s. for his planned crusade, the king granted a four-year tax exemption to the city in 1269, ACA Reg. 16, fols. 144 v., 159 v. Cf. Reg. 15, fol. 107 v.; Reg. 19, fol. 187 v.

[102] On the Crown's heavy reliance on subsidies in the early fourteenth century, see Christian Guilleré, "Les Finances royales à la fin du regne d'Alfonso IV el Benigno (1335–36)," *MCV*, 18 (1982), 51.

[103] ACA Reg. 14, fol. 83 r.; Reg. 18, fol. 52 v.

raised by townspeople, the king in 1226 established that any future levies in the city be apportioned according to the assets of each contributor (*per solidum et libram*) no matter whether the funds were destined for the king or the community (*vel propter nos vel propter aliquod comune vicinitatis*). A unitary method of assessment therefore existed at an early date, although representatives of the major, middling, and minor "hands" had to work out the details; the earliest expression of the "ordering" of the urban population therefore had to do with tax brackets, not social classes.[104]

Not surprisingly the valuation of tax liability remained a sensitive issue. In 1277, the city's patricians (*maiores richi homines Barchinone*) complained about the assessment of the *bovatge* to King Pere, who issued detailed instructions as to how to treat such items as freed slaves, the *lluïsme*, stored provisions, and pledges; other more modest citizens found their privilege of tax exemptions challenged, especially, as in the case of the *molers*, when their claim rested on a hairsplitting distinction over their liability for royal or communal taxes.[105] Yet while bickering about tax liability persisted, no hint exists that the citizenry felt their magistrates had misused the funds collected, even though a large portion of the revenues went to the Crown and, ultimately, to the very patricians who had first raised the revenue. The creation of a municipal regime therefore was not primarily a means of defusing civic factionalism or reducing the control of patrician families through representative assemblies; rather it provided a means of coordinating the energies and resources of citizens, patricians, and the monarchy under the pressures and possibilities presented by a vibrant period of economic and political expansion.

Significantly, the emergence of municipal institutions at first did not seriously infringe on the powers of the urban vicar and bailiff. While the series of charters that gradually fashioned the urban constitution progressively insisted on the obligation of local royal officials to consult with the magistrates and municipal assembly and execute their pronouncements, an obligation ritually confirmed through an oath taken by the vicar and a promise of

---

[104] Huici-Cabanes, *Documentos*, I, no. 81; cf. ibid., IV, no. 929. For an overview of Catalan municipal taxation and methods of assessment, see José María Font Rius, "La administración en los municipios catalanes medievales," in *Historia de la hacienda española (épocas antigua y medieval): homenaje al Profesor García de Valdeavellano* (Madrid, 1982), 202–16 [repr. in *Estudis sobre els drets*, 617–26].

[105] On the assessment of the *bovatge*, ACA Reg. 40, fols. 2 v., 67 r.–v.; on exemptions, ACA Reg. 20, fol. 248 v.; Reg. 38, fol. 31 v.; Reg. 42, fol. 196 v.; supra, 67, n. 65.

fealty offered by the bailiff before the municipal assembly, justice, military command, and urban utilities remained in their hands. No evidence exists of serious jurisdictional disputes between the magistrates and royal officials during the period when municipal institutions were emerging.

The easy cooperation among magistrates and royal officials has been considered a result of careful constitutional craftsmanship, but social and financial considerations also facilitated this institutional synthesis. Both King Jaume I and his son King Pere II generally turned to local patricians to fill the posts of urban vicar and bailiff; of twenty-one known vicars from 1220 to 1285, thirteen were burghers, and of the twenty-two bailiffs, fifteen came from the city.[106] Even though a handful of patricians, including Romeu Durfort, Guillem Grony, Ferrer Mallol, and Antic Titó held at various times both the vicariate and the bailiwick, the pattern of recruitment differed for each office.

Associated primarily with judicial and military functions over a broad territory, the vicariate still proved the more prestigious post. In addition to patricians, it attracted knights and lesser nobles, especially from the nearby Vallès, a region eventually incorporated into the vicariate of Barcelona. Vicars tended to hold their office for shorter periods than bailiffs; although the king did not allow a single patrician house to monopolize the vicariate, the prominent townsmen who did hold the position exercised authority comparable to that of the nobility.

The vicariate, however, did not extend a bridge for rural nobles to enter Barcelona's patriciate. Here the exception proves the rule. The most prominent vicarial family in thirteenth-century Barcelona was the Plegamans, descendants from a younger branch of a castellan family in the Vallès.[107] Three generations distinguished themselves through their extended tenure as urban vicars and their

---

[106] For a list of vicars and bailiffs, see appendices 1 and 2. Further, eight of the twenty-one vicars came from those families identified as providing the largest number of magistrates in figure 5.1; ten of the twenty-two vicars also came from the same category. I have not included Marimon de Plegamans and his son Romeu de Marimon, both considered noble, among the burghers.

[107] Ramon de Plegamans, founder of the Barcelona branch of the family, was evidently a younger son, for he ceded the ancestral castle of Plegamans to his brother Bernat in 1217, ACB 1–6–1208. Some information on the family can be gleaned from *Els castells*, II, 95–96; Bisson, *Fiscal accounts*, I, 258; Vilar, *La Catalogne*, I, 407, 443, 445–46; and Josep Maria Madurell i Marimon, "Romeo de Marimón de Plegamans y de Montoliu (1256–1309), señor de Sant Marçal," *Hidalguía*, 99 (1970), 251–88 and "Marimón de Plegamans y de Montoliu (1256–1295)," *Hidalguía*, 103 (1970), 941–50.

service to the king: Ramon de Plegamans (vicar in 1202, 1209–10, 1218–19), his son Marimon de Plegamans (1230–31, 1235–37, 1240–41), and his grandson Romeu de Marimon de Plegamans (1275, 1285–87, 1291, 1293–96, 1298–99). Beginning his career as a financier to King Pere I and urban vicar, Ramon eventually served as "bailiff and vicar of Catalonia" while King Jaume I was campaigning in Majorca; later, during the Valencian conquests, Jaume installed Marimon as general procurator in Catalonia and employed him on critical diplomatic missions, including the first Catalan embassy to North Africa around 1235;[108] finally, Romeu found favor with four successive monarchs, who dispatched him as royal envoy to Morocco, Egypt, and Sicily and placed him in command of several military campaigns. During the thirteenth century, the Plegamans were assimilated into the baronage. Yet they remained firmly ensconced in Barcelona's commercial heart. Taking advantage of his position as vicar during the early development of the Ribera district, Ramon de Plegamans obtained a solid house facing the cemetery in front of Santa Maria del Mar and the neighboring royal *alfóndec*. From this commanding site, the Plegamans maintained a high profile in the port area and the marketplace throughout the thirteenth century. They owned valuable shops and stalls around the *alfóndec* and below Castellvell, operated an oven at the *drassanes*, held part of the *quartera* (supervision of grain measurement), and customarily kept a cask used for a public measurement standard (*mensuraticum casca*) in their own stall.[109] Yet while the family conducted business with merchants and patricians on the Ribera, it kept an air of aloofness; scribes regularly refer to the Plegamans as *nobiles*, a title denied patricians even after intermarriage with members of the nobility, and no member of the family held the post of magistrate in the thirteenth century. A powerful aristocratic house implanted late in the city through the vicarial office, the Plegamans carried great weight in urban government and at the royal court, yet patricians also resented their presence. It is therefore difficult to concur with Charles-Emmmanuel Dufourcq's characterization of the family as a "dynastie bourgeoise."[110]

[108] ACB 1–6–1604; this document was referred to from a secondary source by Dufourcq, "Vers la Méditerranée orientale," no. 9, who did not have the original available.

[109] ACB 1–6–225, 3973; 4–30–158, 163; 4–33–740, 759; ADB perg. Santa Anna, Carp. 1a, 141; Carp. 2a, 141; ACA Reg. 19, fol. 59 v.

[110] Dufourcq, *L'Espagne catalane*, 94.

No other noble house associated with the vicariate established itself in thirteenth-century Barcelona. Indeed, the Plegamans often seem disdainful of patrician circles, whose social habits and political forms they did not fully share. The monarchy employed the office to distribute power and prestige among a number of the most eminent patrician houses and reward nobles who firmly backed their sovereign, but, with the exception of the Plegamans, this did not permit any family to use the office as an entrenched urban political base. Much like the magistracy, the vicariate allowed for the acknowledged leadership, even political domination, by a group of patricians, but not the monopolization of power by a single family or clique.

The recruitment and tenure of urban bailiffs followed a rather different pattern. The office often remained in the same hands for several years at a time, while Jews rather than rural nobles tended to hold the post in addition to patricians. After the financial crisis of his early years had been surmounted, King Jaume I found in his new conquests a means to reward his creditors and relieve financial pressures. Yet even though the king in 1228 prohibited the sale of vicariates and bailiwicks, the bailiffs of Barcelona still largely owed their position to their ability to offer credit to the Crown. Administration of the urban domain remained substantially unchanged; the king assigned payment to creditors on his future revenues under the supervision of the bailiff, who was expected to make advances from his own resources to meet current expenses. This explains the long tenure of finanicier-administrators, especially Guillem d'Espiells (1278–81, 1283–84), Pere de Castellasol (1252–55), Vital Salamó (1247–50), and above all Guillem Grony (1260–62, 1265–68, 1270–74) and Benevist de Porta (1257–60, 1262–64, 1267), who together dominated Barcelona's fiscal economy during the growing financial and political difficulties at the end of Jaume's reign.

The period proved decisive, for it marked the end of a strong Jewish presence in urban fiscal administration and the assertion of firm patrician control over the urban domain. Born to a prominent Jewish family in Vilafranca del Penedès, Benevist de Porta emerged as a major royal financier in the 1250s. With recorded loans totalling more than 240,000s. to the Crown, he gained the right to administer a number of important revenues and bailiwicks, including Girona, Cotlliure, Vilafranca del Penedès, Lleida, Majorca, and Barcelona.[111] Excessive royal indebtedness explains the prominent role of Guillem Grony, whom the Crown employed as a counterweight to Benevist. It is difficult to decide, however, whether the two considered themselves competitors or allies, for they passed the bailiwick between them and from 1264 to 1267 held the office jointly, exploiting it according to the terms of a private business contract (*societas*).[112] Jaume went to extraordinary lengths to satisfy both: he authorized them to sell on their own initiative all or part of the bailiwick and took the unprecedented step of appointing Guillem Grony to hold both the vicariate and bailiwick concurrently in 1264 and 1265.[113] Because urban bailiffs were by the nature of Catalonian administration heavily involved in royal finance, the danger remained that the urban domain, of critical importance to burghers as well as the king, would be treated as a patrimonial asset by its administrator, especially during times of financial pressure. The consequences may have been less menacing to patricians and the municipality when one of their own held the post; after Benevist de Porta, no other Jew held the bailiwick of Barcelona. Yet pledging the royal patrimony remained a concern to townspeople and monarch alike. Upon his accession in 1276, King Pere II ordered the urban bailiwick seized to determine what resources the Crown retained and what had been pledged to creditors; soon, however, Guillem d'Espiells held the bailiwick as firmly as Guillem Grony once had. Under Pere's successor, King Alfons II, a "house cleaning" was attempted, with outsiders being appointed to both the vicariate and bailiwick, while a central fiscal officer, the *mestre racional*, began to oversee fiscal administration of the entire Crown with new efficiency. For the city itself, however, these reforms were merely half-measures. Only in the 1330s did the municipality gain true fiscal autonomy by buying up royal and ecclesiastical rights,

---

111 Benevist has received brief treatment by Francesc Bofarull i Sans, "Jaime I y los judíos," *CHCA* (Barcelona, 1909), II, 886; Fritz (Yitzhak) Baer, *A history of the Jews of Christian Spain*, trans. L. Schoffman (Philadelphia, 1961), I, 146; J. Lee Shneidman, *The rise of the Aragonese-Catalan empire, 1200–1350* (London and New York, 1970), II, 440. Baer, *Die Juden*, I, no. 96; ACA Reg. 10, fols. 84 r.–v., 109 v.; 117 r., 168 r.; Reg. 13, fols. 139 v., 226 r.; Reg. 14, fols. 18 v., 44 v., 47 r., 74 r., 170 v.; Reg. 15, fols. 17 v., 52 v., 131 v., 140 r., 144 r.

112 ACA perg. Jaume I, 1903.

113 ACA Reg. 10, fol. 32 r.; Reg. 13, fols. 237 v., 289 r.; Reg. 16, fol. 167 v.

decreeing their abolition, and replacing them with new impositions.[114]

The formation of municipal institutions thus did not produce a radical break in the political orientation, fiscal responsibilities, or social composition of urban leadership. Barcelona continued to function after 1249 much as it had done before, as a political organ within the enlarged body of the Crown of Aragon, not an independent merchant-republic. Yet the count-kings had always found their richest and most dynamic city difficult to rule effectively and exploit efficiently. Through the creation of municipal institutions and especially the magistracy, it became possible to engage a large component of the city's wealthiest, most politically active houses not only in the cooperative exercise of power but also in the collection of revenues for the Crown. Because patricians had much to gain by supporting their sovereign with money and service, Barcelona's municipal regime remained firmly embedded in a grid of dynastic interest. During the decades after 1249, the greatest change was the increased fiscal burden borne by the citizens of Barcelona, not their political independence in municipal or political affairs. In the short term urban autonomy therefore heightened the royalist orientation of Barcelona's patriciate, not its independence. It is therefore hardly surprising that three of the city's first four magistrates, Berenguer Durfort, Arnau de Sanaüja, and Guillem de Lacera, had already learned to govern as vicars or bailiffs.

ROYAL PATRONAGE AND THE PROFITS OF EXPANSION

Enriched by commercial investments, urban utilities, lending, and landlordship, the patrician houses at the summit of urban society exercised power cooperatively through municipal institutions and individually through local royal administration. The balance maintained through this system, however, could easily be tipped, particularly by the resources gained from the Crown's territorial acquisitions and its command over critical aspects of Mediterranean exchange. To support dynastic ambitions extending from Murcia to Sicily and bolster the strategic position won in the Balearics and North Africa, King Jaume I and his successors

[114] Jean Broussolle, "Les Impositions municipales de Barcelone de 1328 à 1462," *Estudios de historia moderna*, 5 (1955), 3–19.

looked for financial and naval support from aristocrats and urban notables throughout Catalonia, but especially from Barcelona. Because the count-kings assumed an increasingly active role in controlling maritime exchange through protectionist legislation, export licences, the regulation of privateering, and the supervision of the North African *fanādiq*, they helped determine the place of Barcelona's patrician houses within the dynamics of Catalan Mediterranean expansion.

The close connection established between the royal court and Barcelona's leading entrepreneurs under Pere I and Jaume I's regency council carried over into the period following the seizure of Majorca. The Durfort, by then old hands at royal finance, continued to hold high offices at court and in the Catalan colonies. According to the king's autobiography, Berenguer Durfort was the first person appointed bailiff of Majorca, only recently subdued, while Bernat Durfort, who supervised royal accounts in 1225 as *scriptor racionis*, later served as bailiff of the island in 1242.[115] Guillem Durfort, grandson of King Pere I's chief accountant, was chamberlain (*repositarius*) from 1269 to 1273 for Jaume I, ambassador to England for Pere II and Alfons II, and treasurer to Queen Blanche, wife of Jaume II.[116] By marrying Guillemona, daughter of Berenguer de Tornamira, a prominent Majorcan noble, Guillem Durfort strengthened his family's ties to the island, where they held a mill in Palma, fiefs, gardens, and numerous farms.[117] Berenguer Burget, descendant of a Barcelona financier and a major cloth supplier for King Jaume I and his court, held the post of vicar of Majorca in 1234 and 1236.[118] To reward a tradition of loyal service and generous credit, King Jaume I allowed the Durfort and Burget to administer an incipient colonial society; both families extended their influence on the island, which served the Burget as an outpost for their far-flung commercial ventures and the Durfort as a point of political leverage beyond the mainland. The king occasionally compen-

---

115 Jaume I, *Llibre dels feits*, c. 71; Huici-Cabanes, *Documentos*, II, no. 75; ACB 1–6–4093, 4181, 4197.
116 ACA Reg. 14, fol. 46 r.; Reg. 16, fol. 46 r.; Reg. 19, fol. 77 v.; Reg. 64, fol. 198 v.; Reg. 72, fol. 11 r.; Reg. 105, fols. 127 v.–128 v.; Soldevila, *Jaume I, Pere el Gran*, 40–41.
117 ACB 1–6–3458, 4181; on the Majorcan possessions of the Durfort, ACB 1–6–4093, 4099.
118 On cloth sales on credit to the court, ACA Reg. 10, fols. 29 v., 72 r. Berenguer Burget is recorded as vicar of Majorca in ADB perg. Santa Anna, Carp. de la creu, unnumb. parch. [13 xii 1234]; Carp. 8, 106.

sated Barcelona's patrician houses, including the de Vic, Lacera, and Grony with urban utilities and scattered farms in the realm of Valencia, yet such assets remained peripheral to these families' main concerns and not an invitation to establish independent branches in the newly conquered realm to the south.[119] Neither in Majorca nor Valencia did the Crown attempt to set up its principal backers in Barcelona as frontier lords with cohesive blocks of land and coercive power, nor did the city's patriciate provide a primary recruiting ground for colonial administrators. The count-kings, however, did not hesitate to assign fiscal resources in the newly acquired kingdoms to major Barcelona lenders,[120] yet royal control remained firm. In order to enjoy the new resources available to an expansionist monarchy, Barcelona's leading citizens would have to keep their money chests open.

Command of the sea provided another delicate interface between royal power and patrician interests. We know relatively little about the ships owned and operated by the king himself until the early fourteenth century; although allusions to royal galleys and smaller craft exist for both Jaume I and his successors and the Crown did insist on retaining direct control of Barcelona's ship-yard, the *drassanes*, naval power deployed by the kings of Aragon depended largely upon franchised entrepreneurs rather than a state navy.[121] The Crown of Aragon exercised its maritime power not by clearing the sea lanes with its own ships but by compelling captains and sailors who were its subjects to submit to its rules and offer it aid.

The independence of captains and shipowners as well as the dangerous waters contested among various Christian and Muslim powers did not make the task easy. Schaube argued that the Catalan victory in Majorca depended upon the ability of King Jaume I to focus the dispersed forces of Catalan pirates on a common enemy, whose island base was itself, according to the English chronicler Matthew Paris, "teeming with pirates and

---

[119] ACB 1–6–153, 2215; ACA Reg. 16, fol. 197 r.–v.; Reg. 19, fol. 172 r.; Reg. 37, fol. 38 r.; Huici-Cabanes, *Documentos*, III, no. 898.

[120] Ramon Ricart, for example, was granted revenues of Murviedro in 1274 and Majorca in 1275 for large loans to the king, ACA Reg. 19, fol. 188 v.; Reg. 20, fols. 214 v., 227 r., 263 r. Later King Jaume II assigned the revenues of Majorca to a Barcelona banker, whom he installed as bailiff, Bensch, "La primera crisis," 322–23.

[121] On the royal navy, Dufourcq, *L'Espagne catalane*, 66–67, 296; Arcadi Garcia i Sanz, *Història de la marina catalana* (Barcelona, 1977), 75–90, 189–227; King Pere II appointed Bartomeu Novellet custodian of the *drassanes* in 1285 for a salary of 1,000s./yr., ACA Reg. 58, fol. 107 v.

thieves." Privateering remained a viable enterprise, contracted
with the same cool formality as any commercial undertaking. It
tapped the collective resources and energies of a society just
finding its sea legs. In 1238 Domènec Llull, Ramon de Caldes, and
Guillem Bosa invested as little as 36s. in arming a small ship
(*barcha*) sent to raid Islamic Spain, while at Majorca four years later
Berenguer Burget of Barcelona in partnership with the bishop of
Majorca and others collected a total of 10,000 bezants with the
same objective in mind.[122] A buccaneering fever, infecting clerics
as well as urban entrepreneurs and shipowners, spread after
Majorca had fallen and Valencia lay prone before Jaume's crusaders. In 1250, however, the king forbade his subjects from
undertaking any naval raids without royal permission. As Burns
has convincingly argued, the decree did not intend to prohibit
privateering but to license it.[123] The regulation marks an important turning point in royal control over Catalan naval forces, for
attacking Islamic shipping and launching coastal raids would
henceforth take the form of a privilege, granted in accordance
with the ebb and flow of diplomatic relations with North Africa,
not a right of aggressive towns and aristocratic privateers. What
had been independent, unsupervised initiatives by corsairs became
an instrument of dynastic policy. Apparently disappointed with
the results of an embassy to the Ḥafṣid emir in 1264, the king
authorized Guillem Grony, who had headed the mission, to arm
his ship in order to inflict as much harm as possible on the subjects
of the "sultan of Tunis." Guillem Grony, at the time bailiff and
vicar of Barcelona, in fact served as the corsair-commander of
Barcelona's contingent to the Catalan fleet deployed in an escalating war against Islamic North Africa; the municipality itself
contributed two galleys, the canons of Barcelona in the name of
the archbishop of Tarragona another, Berenguer Spanyol and
Pere de Vilar, two local shipowners, armed their *leny*, christened
the *Falconet*, with other shareholders in order to join in the naval
engagement.[124] The king did not let such services go unrewarded:

122 Conde, "Los Lull," no. 1; ARM Cod. 342, fols. 102 r., 136 r. Cf. ACB 1–6–786; ARM
    Cod. 342, fol. 98 r.
123 Huici-Cabanes, *Documentos*, III, no. 538; Burns, "Piracy," 116–17. Burns, however,
    underestimates the novelty of the decree by arguing that seigniorial and municipal
    authorities had previously authorized privateering, which was not the case. Cf.
    Dufourcq, *L'Espagne catalane*, 89–91.
124 ACA Reg. 12, fol. 126 r.; ACB 1–6–393; Capmany, II, no. 16; Johannes Vincke,
    "Königtum und Sklaverei im aragonischen Staatenbund während des 14. Jahrhun-

he granted Guillem Grony and his crews a moratorium from all claims by creditors or business partners for a full year; the canons and city would not have to pay taxes on any of the booty seized by their galleys; and, most revealing of all, Barcelonans were promised a two-year open season for attacking Islamic shipping regardless of any subsequent truce. Through royal control privateering had turned not only into a potent weapon of Mediterranean politics but also into a means to reward shipowners and armorers for their services.

Yet in order to contend effectively with the Genoese, Pisans, Angevins, and other competitors on the sea, the Crown needed not only to license marauders but to command a fleet to accomplish its bold maritime initiatives. In the latter half of the thirteenth century the kings of Aragon took an increasingly active and direct role in naval procurement, which brought naval outfitters in Barcelona to new prominence. The two most notable beneficiaries of the escalating naval arms race set in motion by the business of Sicily were Berenguer Mallol and Ramon Marquet; appointed co-admirals of the home fleet in 1285, they gained fame by successfully repelling the French navy sent to attack Barcelona.[125] The backgrounds of the two families parallel one another and underscore how royal patronage could translate far-flung Mediterranean contacts and administrative experience into a commanding position in Barcelona's patriciate.

The early history of the Mallol and Marquet is obscure, and their prominence in Barcelona can not be pushed back much beyond 1200.[126] Both families were tied to the sea and prospered on the rising tide of commerce. Berenguer Mallol's kinsmen thrived in the vastly expanded Mediterranean world opening to Catalan traders, shippers, and administrators. Pere Mallol served as bailiff in Majorca for the viscount of Béarn, a major landowner on the island, to whom he and four other Barcelona investors rented their ship under construction at Eivissa for 39,000s. in 1270; Ferrer

---

derts," *GAKS*, 25 (1970), no. 3. On others involved in the war, see Dufourcq, *L'Espagne catalane*, 114–17, Burns, "Piracy," 113–14.

[125] Their exploits are vividly portrayed by Desclot, *Llibre*, c. 157–58 and especially by Muntaner, *Crònica*, c. 129–41. A well informed popular account, based on the royal registers as well as the chronicles, is offered by Ferran Soldevila, *El amirall Ramon Marquet* (Barcelona, 1953).

[126] A Bernat Mallol appears among prominent burghers by 1211, ACB LA I, fol. 372, Mas XII, no. 2497; LA IV, fol. 29, Mas XII, no. 2505; in 1183 King Alfons I granted Bernat Marquet one of the Clot mills, which Ramon Marquet still held in 1275, ACA Reial Patrimoni, Batllia General, Classe 3ª, vol. 6, fols. 52 v., 54 r.–v.

Mallol was a trading associate of Guillem de Banyeres, one of Barcelona's most successful cloth merchants, and also held the bailiwick and vicariate of Barcelona for several years, including a term as vicar in 1275 for a loan of 35,000s. to the king.[127] Building on his family's trading and shipping connections, Berenguer Mallol early in his career invested in Levantine commerce, married the daughter of Bernat Sesfonts, a Barcelona entrepreneur with strong ties to Majorca, and in 1270 rented a fully armed ship, which carried horses on board, at Aigues-Mortes for the impressive sum of 2,500 lbs. *tournois*, but we do not know whether for privateering or for the king's service.[128] In the 1240s and 1250s, the Marquet were also heavily involved in overseas trade. Of Ramon Marquet's two brothers, Bernat owned part of a ship trading with Jaén, and Pere left pious donations in his will to the church at Acre and to pilgrims traveling to the Holy Land. Ramon Marquet himself is known to have commanded two vessels on trading voyages to the Levant, shipped grain from Catalonia to the Templars at Acre, and served as royal ambassador to the sultan of Egypt in 1261.[129] Trade had already caused the far-flung affairs of the two families to intersect in 1265, when Berenguer Mallol sailed with his bolts of cloth from Châlons, Arras, and Lleida on the ship of Ramon Marquet to the eastern rim of the Mediterranean, but the needs of King Pere II during the perilous years following the Sicilian Vespers would fuse their common interests and backgrounds into a single destiny.

With their proven seamanship and close ties to administration and trade, Ramon Marquet and Berenguer Mallol became specialists in naval procurement for the king. Already in 1280 King Pere II had paid for ships under the command of Ramon Marquet, who later captained a vessel in the expedition against Tunis in 1282.[130] Yet this merely offered a prelude to the feverish work undertaken by Ramon and Berenguer Mallol in the shipyards of Barcelona in 1284 and 1285. Together they organized the outfitting of twelve galleys and four armed *lenys*; three other new galleys had to be constructed and others armed for a minimum of

[127] ACA perg. Jaume I, 1017, 2016; Reg. 37, fol. 80 v.; Reg. 58, fol. 114 r.; ACB 1–6–2994, 3676.

[128] ACB 1–6–1270; 3–38–181(e); Garcia-Madurell, *Comandas comerciales*, no. 19.

[129] ACA perg. Alfons II, 264, 292; Reg. 11, fol. 194 r.; perg. varis, Sentmenat, Indice 8, III, 8; ACB 1–6–4275; 4–15–3 and ADB perg. Santa Anna, Carp. 9, 488; Garcia-Madurell, *Comandas comerciales*, no. 19.

[130] ACB 1–6–2295; Desclot, *Llibre*, c. 79.

60,000s., but more was later required, including an additional 60,000s. subsidy contributed directly by the municipality.[131] Naval armament on such a scale was as much a work of finance as marine engineering and naval command. It involved considerable outlays by its organizers but also brought substantial rewards. Even though it is impossible to estimate the direct financial benefit to the contractors and what "admirals and captains are accustomed to have by right," Berenguer Mallol and Ramon Marquet gained access to royal resources within the city, including the supervision of cloth standards (*roudaria*), and assumed a commanding position in Barcelona's shipyards, essential to the defense of the city and the Crown.[132] Even when a measure of calm had returned once the French fleet turned back and Roger de Lluria inflicted a series of humiliating defeats on Charles of Anjou, the need for substantial naval forces remained. King Alfons II in 1289 authorized the construction of two new galleys at royal expense in Barcelona and another four galleys from the city's contribution of 40,000s.; in a concession to collective defense, he devoted half the profits from raiding to the completion of the city's new wall and allowed Berenguer Marquet and Berenguer Mallol to name the admiral, captains, and supervisor of naval armaments (*scriptor armatae*) from among the citizenry.[133] Other merchants and shipowners felt threatened, however, for they feared that naval armorers for the Crown with their political weight and added resources would gain undue influence in a highly competitive commercial environment. To allay those fears, in 1288 Alfons II ordered that royal officials should not form commercial societies with naval armorers or corsairs, but in fact no clear separation of commercial, military, and administrative functions could be maintained.[134] Because of the new scale of Mediterranean naval operations, royal support turned two talented and well-connected patricians into Barcelona's shipyard bosses.

Owing to the convergence of royal and municipal interests in maritime expansion, Barcelona was well on its way to establishing itself as the center of naval armaments for the entire Crown of Aragon, a position it would continue to enjoy during the fourteenth and fifteenth century.[135] Although Berenguer Mallol and

---

[131] ACA Reg. 56, fol. 7 r.; Reg. 65, fols. 127 v., 134 v., 161 r.; Muntaner, *Crònica*, c. 129.
[132] ACB 1–6–4046; ACA Reg. 65, fol. 8 r.   [133] Capmany, II, no. 44.
[134] Ibid., no. 43; cf. Dufourcq, *L'Espagne catalane*, 66.
[135] Bresc, *Un monde méditerranéen*, I, 309–15; del Treppo, *Mercaders catalans*, 433–36.

Ramon Marquet wielded exceptional power in the Ribera during the 1280s, it was nevertheless symptomatic of a new concentration of resources and patronage building up within urban society as the city and the Crown tried to absorb and control new commercial and territorial gains.

Neither social rigidity nor patrician exclusiveness produced these interlocking interests; rather, they grew spontaneously from the new demands of commercial and political success. Particularly significant in this regard was the rise of merchant-bankers in the last quarter of the thirteenth century.[136] Earlier banking in Barcelona had been limited in scope; it had not attracted the interest of patricians, nor did its practitioners expand their operations beyond money changing, holding deposits, and extending small loans into the areas of royal finance and trade. During the final third of the thirteenth century, the range and intensity of banking activities suddenly increased. In 1270 and 1271, Jaume Ferran made two investments of 25 lbs. each from a joint banking table he operated (*de societate tue tabule*) on two separate commercial voyages, one to Sicily and Tunis, the other to Barbary; these represent the first documented instances of a banking consortium investing its funds in overseas commerce. Banking associations still tended to be small and short-term; in the twelve months intervening between the two *comanda* investments just cited, Jaume Ferran dissolved his original partnership with Bernat Sesfonts and split up the deposits and profits, which totalled 1,476 lbs.[137] Even though Barcelona banks could not compare with those of the Italians in the amount of capital raised or the range and complexity of their operations, they nevertheless began to enlarge their field of activities abroad while enjoying protection from foreign competition at home. Realizing the importance of Barcelona's bankers for his own finances, King Jaume I in 1268 prohibited foreigners from setting up changing tables in the city.[138] As a result of protectionist legislation, local bankers began to establish a foothold in trading operations. Guillem Pere Dusay, a Barcelona banker, was involved in commerce and shipping along the Catalan coast from Tortosa to Cotlliure; at Perpinyà a merchant of Lucca even appointed him to collect all the debts owed the Italians throughout

---

[136] Bensch, "La primera crisis," 317–27.
[137] Garcia-Madurell, *Comandas comerciales*, nos. 29, 31; ACB 1–6–108.
[138] Capmany, II, no. 22.

Aragon and Catalonia.[139] Without the limitations placed on foreign competition, the Lucchese merchant would have deposited his profits at the table of one of his own countrymen in Barcelona.

The money changer's art gained an air of respectability. It attracted not only ambitious merchants anxious to expand their capital base but also members of established patrician families; de Vic, Romeu, Sarrià, Llull, Burgès, and d'Espiells appear prominently among the *campsores* during the last quarter of the thirteenth century.[140] In addition to facilitating commercial investment and increasing their profits with interest-bearing loans, bankers also drew the attention of the king, who found them willing financiers and tax collectors. The Crown was already using Barcelona bankers to disburse revenues collected from the *questia* of 1276 and the *bovatge* of 1280, and it became increasingly reliant upon them for loans.[141] Simó de Vic, member of one of Barcelona's oldest patrician houses, used the capital of his bank to finance his way into the royal court. By 1292 the new king of Aragon, Jaume II, admitted that his predecessors had accumulated substantial debts with Simó de Vic; the "banker and merchant to our court," as the king called him, was ordered at that time to redeem the royal table service from the Templars, assist in distributing 50,000s. left in the will of Alfons II, and provide 13,000s. to ransom the archbishop of Tarragona.[142] For his many services, the king granted Simó de Vic in that same year the right to supervise all grain shipments from Sicily to Barcelona and other parts of the realm.[143]

The right to export Sicilian grain, literally Barcelona's daily bread by the late thirteenth century, offered one of the surest ways for the Crown to reward Barcelona's financiers. Dynastic expansion culminated in the occupation of Sicily in 1282 and with it control of the island's highly centralized system of grain exports.

---

[139] ACA Reg. 56, fol. 64 v.; Reg. 66, fol. 165 r.; perg. varis, Marquès de Monistrol, 167; ADPO série E, Reg. 13, fol. 38 r.

[140] ACB 1–6–920, 4–33–74(b); ADB perg. Santa Anna, Carp. 1a, 5–25; Carp. 8, 20; ACA perg. varis, Marquès de Monistrol, 162.

[141] ACA Reg. 38, fol. 31 v.; ACB 1–6–920.

[142] ACA Reg. 92, fols. 23 r.–v., 141 r.–v., ; Reg. 95, fols. 50 r., 98 r.–v. Cf. ACA perg. Alfons II, 229, 231; Reg. 58, fol. 96 v.

[143] ACA Reg. 192, fols. 110 v. –111 r.: "officium recipiendi per vos vel alium vel alios locum vestri in civitate Barchinone et in aliis locis existentibus in rippariis vel maritimiis Catalonie, Maiorice, Valencie, vel aliorum locorum iurisdicione nostra frumentum et alia victualia ... de partibus Sicilie vel de aliis quibuscumque partibus."

Yet the king had already begun regulating the distribution of grain within the Crown of Aragon by granting export licenses in the mid-1270s, in part to allay concerns about adequate supplies in Barcelona. In 1278 King Pere II formally prohibited the export of grain anywhere within his realms without royal permission; in 1280 he reassured the *prohoms* of Barcelona that grain exported from Tortosa would be sent to the city rather than elsewhere.[144] These measures have usually been interpreted as a natural progression of state control over the economy, yet it is more likely that they were taken in reaction to a reduction in grain supplies from Sicily. Barcelona's merchants had been trading vigorously with Sicily since the 1240s at the latest and a small Catalan community had taken shape at Palermo and elsewhere on the island, but after 1272 there is no evidence of direct exchange with Sicily until the revolt of 1282. The Angevin position had hardened, leading to sporadic suspensions of grain exports to Genoa, Pisa, and Byzantium during the 1270s. These restrictive policies evidently discouraged Catalan merchants, whose monarch now championed the Hohenstaufen claim to the Sicilian throne.[145] Although Catalans could no doubt obtain Sicilian grain indirectly at other markets, growing political tensions with Charles of Anjou compelled King Pere II to supervise grain shipments within his own realms. The grain trade throughout the Western Mediterranean was coalescing into a coherent, interdependent system sensitive to political as well as economic balances; from an Aragonese perspective, the Catalan occupation of Sicily therefore restored an earlier pattern of exchange and amplified, rather than created, royal control over the export of foodstuffs. With his new granary, the king of Aragon could afford to satisfy his creditors. For their loans Simó de Vic, Arnau Sabastida, Berenguer de Fenestres, Berenguer Fiveller, and other Barcelona bankers and financiers received licenses to export Sicilian grain. This took precedence over rewarding the entire city for its support during

---

[144] ACA Reg. fol. 40, 165 v.; Reg. 48, fols. 37 r., 79 r.

[145] Besides the absence of direct information about Catalan-Sicilian trade after 1272, news of the accidental death of a Barcelona sailor who settled in Palermo took four to five years to reach Barcelona, where his estate was settled in 1280, Batlle i Gallart, "Les relacions," no. 3. This hardly argues for close communication between Barcelona and Palermo at the time. Cf. Cuvillier, "Barcelone, Gênes et le commerce du blé de Sicile," 165; Bresc, *Un monde méditerranéen*, I, 553.

the Sicilian Vespers, for only in 1288 did the king grant tariff reductions to all Barcelona merchants trafficking on the island.[146]

As expansion began to increase the pressure on banking, financial, and trade systems during the closing decades of the thirteenth century, the House of Aragon began to feel the fiscal strains of supporting a dispersed empire. As a result, the king employed his control over grain and other resources as a means to retain the support of his underwriters in Barcelona. Both the monarchy and Barcelona's patriciate began to play for higher stakes than ever before. In 1300 the strain became too great. Burdened by massive deficits, the king could no longer satisfy Barcelona's most aggressive investors, a failure which set off the city's first major bank collapse.[147] Yet during the daring reign of Pere the Great, who seized Sicily and made his claims stand up against the armies of France, and the stabilizing rule of his successor, Alfons II, the Crown's future seemed bright, and Barcelona's patricians sought royal patronage and willingly invested massive sums to obtain it. Together with new sources of wealth, however, the commercial and political successes the city enjoyed after 1250 produced heightened competition within the patriciate itself.

FACTIONALISM AND CIVIC VIOLENCE

In the second half of the thirteenth century outbursts of violence jarred the apparent social calm of the city and deeply disturbed the king. The causes and scale of the disturbances are often obscure, ranging from personal vendettas to assault, arson, and murder committed by angry mobs, but they are usually associated with patrician houses. Bernat de Plegamans, Jaume Ferrer, Guillem Eimeric, Bernat de Rovira, Jaume Titó, Bernat de Sanaüja, Pere de Montjuïc, Bartomeu Romeu, and Berenguer Riera, virtually a roll-call of representatives from the most powerful patrician families, were all accused of individual assaults or murders, and many others were implicated in mob violence, either as victims or perpetrators.[148] The sustained administrative record provided by

---

[146] ACA Reg. 58, fols. 48 v., 66 r.; Reg. 66, fols. 43 r., 59 v., 80 v.–81 r.; Reg. 72, fol. 48 v., etc.

[147] Bensch, "La primera crisis," 321–27.

[148] ACA Reg. 16, fol. 222 v.; Reg. 19, fols. 59 v., 176 r.–v.; Reg. 20, fols. 212 r.–v., 261 v.; Reg. 40, fols. 5 r., 55 r.; Reg. 58, fol. 178 v.

the royal registers from 1257 onward allows us to peel away the placid, formal veneer of private notarial contracts and examine the festering tensions that led to acts of individual and mob violence. The better-known conflicts have often been presented as symptomatic of class antagonism between patricians and the "middling hand" of merchants and artisans or as a reaction to the resented monopolization of power by a closed "oligarchy."[149] Even though popular resentment against landlords and municipal officers provides part of the background to these disturbances, what this perspective overlooks is the competitive intensity among patrician houses to exploit new resources and gain access to the king. The edifice of patrician power was not shaken by mobs storming its gates, but by rumblings from within.

One of the earliest royal registers contains a pardon granted by King Jaume I on January 15, 1258 to "all the citizens of Barcelona, greater, middling, and lesser" for the murder of Bernat Marquet during a riot in which the victim of the crowd's fury was stoned to death and his houses and goods burnt.[150] The attack infuriated the king. He quickly instituted a special inquest to determine the complicity of such notables as Berenguer Adarró, Bernat Eimeric, Arnau d'Arlet, Guillem de Montjuïc, Berenguer Ponç, Berenguer Suau, Arnau and Bernat Pelegrí, Pere de Viladecols, and Bernat d'Olzina. The price of royal mercy was also high: 10,000 mbts. Even though the collective fine implies that the entire citizenry was involved, in fact the extent of the disturbance was relatively limited and its causes stemmed from intense competition in the booming Ribera district.

Bernat Marquet, brother of the admiral-to-be Ramon Marquet, had developed close ties to the area and its dominant families. While a young man he owned a galley with seven others, worth 7,500 bezants when it was captured after putting out from Jaén in 1242, and his brother Pere Marquet was coproprietor of a ship with Guillem de Lacera and Marimon de Plegamans. In 1236 Bernat Marquet married Elisenda, daughter of a prosperous entrepreneur and landowner named Joan de Roig; through her dowry, set at the substantial sum of 650 mbts., he gained control of

[149] Batlle i Gallart, *La crisis social*, I, 70–74; Vicens Vives, *Historia social y económica*, II, 206; Soldevila, *Jaume I, Pere el Gran*, 124–25; Font Rius, "Jaume I i la municipalitat," 672–73; Philippe Wolff, "L'Episode de Berenguer Oller à Barcelone en 1285: essai d'interprétation sociale," *AEM*, 5 (1968), 207–22.
[150] Huici-Cabanes, *Documentos*, IV, no. 929.

valuable properties in the western suburbs at Cogoll, just above the shoreline, and further north at the old Vila de Queralt, which he held by emphyteutic tenure from Felipe d'Espiells. During the 1250s Bernat Marquet began to sublease his properties and encouraged construction in both zones, which were affected by the coastal real estate boom occurring in the adjacent honor of Guillem de Vic and his wife Berenguera. He also held property on the Ribera itself, including a lot next to Bernat Durfort and a house and shops adjoining the home of Marimon de Plegamans, close to the royal *alfóndec*; it is likely that his substantial house at the center of the maritime district was the site of the riot that cost Bernat Marquet his life shortly before July, 1257.[151] The attack threatened more than a single patrician family; it also menaced the social peace of the city and royal control of the Ribera.

The Marquet were making their mark in urban society as real estate developers and merchants during the 1240s and 1250s, just as the city was absorbing the first surge of prosperity from Mediterranean expansion and experimenting with new institutions. Patrician investment focused on the coast spreading out below Santa Maria del Mar. Land was subdivided into small parcels; houses, stalls, and workshops were feverishly being constructed; and patricians such as the Plegamans, Marquet, and Durfort made the Ribera and its adjacent districts their home. As economic rivalry for control of shops and rents intensified, disputes about property rights and boundaries became more frequent and acrimonious.[152]

As patricians sought to exploit their rights to the fullest over every bit of the coastline, rapid development brought tensions and resentment against those forcing their way into the area. Blocks of allied families emerged to defend their interests. It is significant that none of the distinguished citizens suspected of inciting the riot of 1257 had business dealings with the Marquet or subscribed to their charters in the two decades preceding the attack, while business associates and allies of the Marquet such as the de Roig, Burgès, d'Espiells, Durfort, Plegamans, and Llull are absent from

---

[151] Despite the importance of Bernat Marquet's death, information about his life remains in unpublished and little-known parchments: ACB 1–1–846; 1–2–1304; 4–15–3 (Pere Marquet's will, a copy of which is found in ADB perg. Santa Anna, Carp. 9, 46); 4–32–714; 4–33–781; 4–37–65(a); 4–38–327; 4–42–328, 347, 348; ACA perg. varis, Sentmenat, Indice 8, III, 8. Testamentary executors were implementing the provisions of his will on July 26, 1257, the *terminus ad quem* for the riot, ACB 4–33–781.

[152] For disputes about coastal property in the mid–thirteenth century, ACB 4–32–709, 711; 4–39–419, 420; 4–40–456; 4–42–456; 4–39–52, 408.

the complaint. In addition, many of the conspirators were linked by crisscrossing ties of blood, business, or friendship. Bernat Suau and Berenguer Adarró, uncle of Esclaramonda, the daughter of Ferrer d'Olzina, subscribed to the marriage contract of Bernat d'Olzina, whose first wife was a member of the Ponç family; Bernat d'Olzina also served as executor to the will of Arnau Pelegrí. Bernat Eimeric, who owned a substantial house with a tower on the main artery of the Ribera, the Carrer del Mar, Berenguer Adarró, Guillem de Montjuïc, and members of the Arlet family transacted business with one another.[153] Although the scattered fragments of information available in the sources do not allow for a satisfactory recreation of the dense social patterning created by ties of neighborhood, family, friendship, and business, one can nevertheless perceive loosely organized alliances taking shape among patrician families acting to protect their spheres of interest. Bernat Marquet and his brothers had perhaps grown too successful as land developers and Levant traders; they had provoked the irritation and envy of competitors who found their presence next to the Plegamans house at the *alfóndec*, and the royal patronage it could bring, unnerving. When the king granted Ramon Marquet the use of a royal galley to trade with Alexandria and transport royal envoys, these concerns were confirmed.[154] In the spring or summer of 1257, because of incitements that our sources stubbornly refuse to reveal, these latent tensions polarized the Ribera, inflaming latent suspicions that turned two patrician cliques into hostile camps. Not class hatred, but factional jealously within the patriciate claimed the life of Bernat Marquet.

The row on the Ribera left the community shaken, for it threatened to turn patrician rivalries into deeply ingrained civic dissension. The king took quick and decisive action. His main concern was not merely to punish offenders but to restore balances. In July and August of 1258 he granted individual pardons to a number of minor figures who had admitted their guilt.[155] More important still, he took initiatives to reorganize the Ribera and Barcelona's municipal government. On the very day the king imposed a collective fine of 10,000 mbts. on the citizenry, he freed Barcelonans from all commercial tolls throughout the Balearics and undertook a reform of the municipal council, which was now to have 8 magistrates and a general assembly of 200. A week earlier

[153] ACB 1–1–30, 2452; 1–6–135, 300, 755; 4–33–749.   [154] ACA Reg. 11, fol. 194 r.
[155] Huici-Cabanes, *Documentos*, IV, nos. 1031, 1032, 1037, 1057

he had instituted a new regime for the Ribera, "because there are no regulations and grave events and serious harm have taken place there."[156] Withdrawn from the jurisdiction of the vicar and bailiff, the coastal district was placed under the authority of an individual chosen by the *prohoms* of the Ribera with the responsibility of looking after naval defense, collecting taxes, and supervising urban development. The decree created an experimental regime, authorized for only a year and renewable at the pleasure of the king and the district's *prohoms*; it was followed by the hasty promulgation of a set of twenty-one regulations (*ordinacions*) devoted to commercial and maritime matters in August, 1258, partially drawing upon provisions that would later appear in the *Llibre del Consolat de Mar*, the first systematic collection of Western maritime law. These measures tightened control over the Ribera and gave it a set of rules to regulate disputes about commercial and naval matters that arose in the maritime community.

While the connection between the riot culminating in Bernat Marquet's death and municipal reforms has been noted before, its social context has largely been misunderstood.[157] Once the notion that the agitation in 1257 represented a popular revolt against oligarchic domination is put to rest, both the municipal reorganization and the close control of the Ribera can be cast in a different light. By enlarging the magistracy, the king hoped to enfranchise more of Barcelona's families in order to defuse tensions by striking a balance among patrician factions. The first members of the enlarged magistracy included Berenguer Adarró and Pere de Viladecols, both of whom were under investigation for complicity in the assault; but Ramon Romeu and Bernat Burgès, once business partners of Bernat Marquet, also held seats.[158] With detached equanimity the king attempted through his reforms to work out a new political calculus that would stabilize an explosive situation.

Part of his efforts were also directed toward closer control of

---

[156] Capmany, II, nos. 13, 14; Huici-Cabanes, *Documentos*, IV, nos. 930, 932. On the maritime ordinances, see especially José María Font Rius, "La universidad de prohombres de Ribera de Barcelona y sus ordenanzas marítimas (1258)," in *Estudios de derecho mercantil en homenaje al Profesor Antonio Polo* (Madrid, 1981), 199–240 [repr. in *Estudis sobre els drets*, 685–711]; G. Colon and A. Garcia i Sanz, *Llibre del Consolat de Mar* (Barcelona, 1981–87), III, 183–95, 256–57.

[157] Batlle i Gallart, *La crisis social*, 71–3; Font Rius, "Jaume I i la municipalitat," 672–73.

[158] Bruniquer, *Rúbriques*, I, 26; ACA perg. varis, Sentmenat, Indice 8, III, 8.

the Ribera. Because traditional categories of urban historiography have depended upon a supposed contrast between an oppressive patrician oligarchy and a rising merchant class, the creation of a separate jurisdiction for the *prohoms* of the Ribera and the promulgation of a maritime code have been interpreted as an instance of mercantile secession from oligarchic control. Nothing could be more deceptive. Barcelona's patriciate maintained a strong presence in the Ribera, and its members were heavily involved in trade. The first *prohom* chosen to supervise the coastal district was Guillem Grony, who had also led the inquiry into Bernat Marquet's death and soon thereafter held the bailiwick and vicariate of Barcelona. The special jurisdictional enclave created on the shoreline therefore did not arise from a separatist movement by the "merchant class"; rather it fulfilled a need to control the district closely with the active cooperation of the resident patrician families after a traumatic outburst of violence and to create regulations for settling divisive issues in the conduct of overseas trade. Patricians supported rather than opposed efforts to reduce the volatile tensions on the shore. It is therefore hardly surprising that once calm had returned, the *prohoms* of the Ribera did not attempt to press for greater autonomy from the municipal council, for socially the two groups overlapped. Even though the *Consolat de Mar*, a separate court devoted to the settlement of maritime disputes, had formed by 1284, the coastal district did not become an independent mercantile enclave. After the institutional experiment of 1258, the powers of the *prohoms* of the Ribera were limited to settling conflicts over property boundaries, approving local construction projects, and supervising the discharge of ships anchored offshore.[159] The municipal council and the royal vicar and bailiff soon resumed their authority over the shoreline once a degree of calm had returned and maritime ordinances had been established, but this could only be expected since commerce was the patriciate's business.

Yet rivalries among patrician families continued to smolder, flaring up into angry assaults and murders. With its bustling exchange sector and its feverish pace of new construction, the Ribera was still prone to sudden mêlées. While passing in front

[159] On the ephemeral nature of the reorganization of the coastline, see Font Rius, "La universidad," 707–11 and Carme Batlle i Gallart, "Els prohoms de la Ribera de Barcelona i llurs atribucions en matèria d'urbanisme (segona meitat del segle XIII)," in *El Pla de Barcelona i la seva història* (Barcelona, 1984), II, 155–60.

of the massive house of Marimon de Plegamans, adjacent to the Marquet home, Guillem and Jaume de Mar began to taunt Berenguer Pascal, calling him a good-for-nothing crony (*baccalarus non vaga*); a shouting match erupted, a rock was thrown, knives were drawn, and a free-for-all erupted. At the end of the imbroglio Berenguer Pascal lay dead.[160] Was the incident merely a senseless rampage by restless urban youth gangs? Because the king himself, the bishop of Barcelona, and the archdeacon of Vic heard the case in early 1271, it obviously was treated as a matter of some consequence. The veiled connection with the Plegamans is suggestive, for only a few months earlier a pardon was granted to Romeu and Bonanat Plegamans for their involvement in a feud (*rixa*) that resulted in the deaths of Berenguer de Plegamans and Jaume Ferrer in one faction and Guillem and Ferrer Saletes in the other.[161] It is difficult to piece together a coherent pattern of motives and family alliances behind these outbursts, yet taken together they present a backdrop of factional conflict and family blocks motivated neither by ideology nor clearly defined economic interests, but by kinship, neighborhood, and patronage.

Heavy penalties for those involved in Barcelona's feuds are sprinkled throughout the royal registers. To cite only a few of the more infamous cases, Berenguer de Sanaüja, relative of one of the municipality's first four "peace men" of 1249, received a pardon for the murder of Pere de Montjuïc for the price of 5,500s.; Berenguer de Lacera was fined 1,000 mbts. for his part in a brawl near the market; and Guillem Eimeric, whose father Bernat had been implicated in Bernat Marquet's death, was exiled for two years for his part in an assault.[162] The evidence of simmering factional violence and family vendettas has been consistently overlooked by local historians intent upon demonstrating the gradual and peaceful emergence of the city's representative institutions or the formation of a coherent, closed oligarchic class. Yet the crafting of early municipal institutions must be seen at least in part as a mechanism to release the pent up pressures from the festering feuds among patrician families in order to maintain civic stability.

The most unsettling agitation in thirteenth-century Barcelona occurred during the tense weeks before Easter, 1285, as the French army and fleet were massing to launch their crusade against the Crown of Aragon. According to a hostile witness, the chronicler

---

[160] ACA Reg. 16, fol. 221 r.–v. [161] ACA Reg. 19, fol. 19 v.
[162] ACA Reg. 20, fols. 212 r.–v., 261 v.; Reg. 40, fol. 4 r.

Desclot, Berenguer Oller, a man of low birth (*de vils gents*), organized the lesser folk (*poble menut*) in opposition to the city's leadership.[163] After having done great harm to the church, the bishop, and the *prohoms* by despoiling them of their dues (*rendes*) and rents (*sensals*), Berenguer Oller allegedly hatched a plot to massacre the clergy, Jews, and wealthy burghers and deliver the city into French hands. After Berenguer Oller naively went out to receive the king of Aragon, who had come to Barcelona for the Easter celebration, he was seized and taken to the comital palace; along with seven of his companions, Berenguer Oller was summarily hanged and 600 of his supporters fled the city in confusion.

Because of the obvious disdain Desclot displayed toward Berenguer Oller and his supporters, it is difficult to give full credence to his judgments, but there can be little doubt that the disturbance posed a serious threat to urban leaders. To Philippe Wolff, the *poble menut* consisted not of the impoverished rabble but of small artisans and merchants who resented the heavy weight of rents and usurious loans they had to pay the city's well-to-do, including clerics and Jews as well as patricians.[164] Desclot refers ominously to popular discontent about rents and an array of payments due landlords, and these complaints surely form part of the background to the heated dispute over the reform of the *lluïsme* set in motion in 1284 and 1285. Resentment against gouging landlords and the pressures placed on artisans and the poor, who held up the tiered system of rents and property rights, clearly made Berenguer Oller a popular figure in the city, but other factors need to be examined before concluding that the agitation in Barcelona during the spring of 1285 was a clear reflection of class antagonism.

The community was under immense strain in the early months

---

[163] Desclot, *Llibre*, c.133. Wolff, "L'Episode," 210–14 offers a thoughtful commentary and analysis of Desclot's famous text.

[164] While Wolff, "L'Episode," 210–13, quite rightly stresses the resentment provoked by landlords' excessive charges, he believes that Desclot is referring specifically to the introduction of lifetime and perpetual annuities (*violaris* and *censals morts*). Although the term *vivolarium* appears as early as 1114 in Barcelona, it seems at first to refer to a long-term lease and only slowly takes on the form of an annuity. See, for example, ACB LA fol. 96, Mas x, no. 1283; 1–1–356; 1–6–3984; ACA perg. varis, Marquès de Monistrol, 118; ADB perg. Santa Anna, Carp. 1a, 1–63; Carp. 2, 233; ASPP, 143. Before 1290 annuities were rare and limited to the lifetime of the purchaser (*violaris*); *censals morts* spread afterwards. On later practices, Yvan Roustit, "La Consolidation de la dette publique à Barcelone au milieu du XIVᵉ siècle," *Estudios de historia moderna*, 4 (1954), 39–47. On the structural reforms of the *lluïsme*, supra, 310–13.

of 1285. Because of the danger of imminent invasion by King Philip the Bold of France, the city was being turned into an armed camp and a supply center for defense; the royal registers contain frantic orders to ensure grain imports, and peasants subject to the command of the urban vicar were soon ordered to bring their stores to the city.[165] Sailors, soldiers, armorers, and shipwrights from throughout the Crown were pouring into the city in order to prepare its defense; in short, Barcelona was turned into a social tinderbox, ready to explode with the slightest spark.

The frantic concentration of supplies in the Catalan capital together with a destabilizing influx of outsiders also caused old enmities and distrust to surface among factions within the patriciate, made all the more touchy by pointed complaints against rents. Because of the royal licensing of grain exports, suspicions of hoarding and profiteering came to the surface. Rumblings could already be heard in 1283, when at a session of the *Consell de Cent* one representative accused Guillem de Roca, Arnau Sabastida, Berenguer de Fenestres, and Cervera de Riera, custodian of the *drassanes*, of causing a grain shortage in the city to line their own pockets; these individuals, all wealthy burghers involved in royal finance, appear again among importers of Sicilian grain in 1285, and further charges against unauthorized exports were leveled against other prominent citizens.[166] Many in the city felt that influential patricians and financiers with access to the king were taking undue advantage of their position in a time of common danger. Swelling resentment against factional control of grain imports and restricted access to urban resources seems to be behind the fall of Guillem d'Espiells, a member of one of the oldest and most influential patrician houses and the urban bailiff during the troubled spring of 1285. When Guillem d'Espiells fled the city in disgrace that summer, the king ordered his seizure and arrest for defaulting on money owed the Crown.[167]

In the persecution that followed Berenguer Oller's execution, the king's arrest orders contained the names of numerous individuals involved in the sedition. While most were artisans or individuals of modest means, condemnations extended to several

---

[165] ACA Reg. 43, fol. 123 r.; Reg. 56, fols. 70 v., 105 r., 118 r.; Reg. 57, fols. 141 v., 150 v.; Reg. 58, fol. 56 r., etc.

[166] ACA Reg. 60, fols. 1 r., 34 v.; Reg. 58, fols. 48 v., 66 r., 102 v.; Reg. 66, fols. 43 r., 59 v., 80 v.–81 r.

[167] ACA Reg. 57, fol. 150 r.; Reg. 66, fols. 21 r.–v.: "fisicalem et publicum debitorem."

patricians and their kinsmen: Berenguer de Riera, son-in-law of Bernat Eimeric, Pere d'Olm, son-in-law of Bernat Grony, and Simó de Vic, who, as we have seen, would later become court banker and purveyor to King Jaume II.[168] Further, five of the twenty-one individuals contained in the longest arrest list would subsequently serve as town councillors.[169] Patrician factionalism played its part in promoting Berenguer Oller's cause. Perhaps the most revealing figure in this regard was Simó de Vic. Already engaged in the grain trade in 1278, when his ship was seized at Marseilles, he later found royal favor restored after the revolt and began to finance the import of Sicilian wheat in 1287.[170] His family, among the oldest patrician houses in the city, had earned a highly visible place among the city's distinguished citizens, but it also created formidable enemies. In the late 1270s Simó's kinsman, Bernat de Vic, was involved in a particularly bitter feud with two other influential houses, the Ricart and Palau. In an act of intimidation, Guillem and Romeu Ricart blocked the doorway of Bernat de Vic's house with a cart and added insult to injury by stuffing a libelous note in the mouth of the ass that drew the cart; these same vandals later attacked the house of Guillem de Noguera and moved on to commit further outrages against two other families. When the feud culminated in the arson of Bernat de Vic's home, the king imposed a stiff 20,000s. fine on the culprits and sent them into exile for five years.[171] Unfortunately, the condemnations and fines handed down by the king and his urban officials in this festering rivalry permit us only to identify individuals and gauge the intensity of a conflict, not the personal grievances or the immediate source of contention. Yet the feud involving the de Vic, and others like it, opened a series of fissures in urban society, which engulfed clients and allies as well as kinsmen; these splits grew wider from the intense competition for grain export licenses pitting Barcelona's bankers and financiers against one another for royal favor, from the resentment against the profiteering landlordship of large real estate developers, and from the tense uncertainties of waiting for an enemy attack in an armed camp. Thus, while Berenguer Oller's attempt to form a counter-government did draw strength from a growing dissatisfaction with the

[168] Reg. 56, fols. 56 v., 106 v., 122 v.; ACB 1–6–1539, 3820; 4–9–134.
[169] Batlle i Gallart, *La Crisis social*, I, 41.
[170] ACA Reg. 40, fol. 9 r.; Reg. 72, fol. 48 v.
[171] ACA Reg. 40, fol. 74 v.; Reg. 42, fol. 218 v.; Reg. 44, fol. 183 r.

rents and fees paid by artisans and petty merchants to the city's old and established lords of the land, the cracks in Barcelona's social edifice did not follow straight, horizontal class fissures but, in the manner of fine lines in aging porcelain, spread like a spider's web in all directions.

CONCLUSION

Rivalries within the patriciate did not create clear divisions that can be excavated through a type of social archeology, which uncovers clearly distinguished layers of older and newer families, of rentiers and merchants. Instead patrician houses were incessantly renewed, reorganized, and reoriented in a scramble for royal offices, access to trading networks and business associates, and urban utilities and real estate. The growing contentiousness within thirteenth-century Barcelona resulted from its remarkable commercial success within the framework of an expansive Mediterranean territorial power. Yet in contrast to Italian cities, which experienced comparable growth, Barcelona's patrician cliques did not polarize into two opposing parties, each attempting to monopolize municipal power, nor did they take the form of vast kinship groups integrating neighborhoods and clienteles into cohesive, inward-looking blocks.[172] Because urban power did not manifest itself exclusively through municipal institutions but intersected dynastic politics as well, its monopolization proved elusive. Influence gained by one patrician family did not result in the exile of its rivals, for the king himself assumed the role of a sovereign *podestà*. Quarreling patricians welcomed his intervention as peacemaker and judge in their quarrels, but they could not dispense with him at their pleasure. The king possessed too many resources; he distributed offices, rewarded his financial backers with revenues from his dispersed Mediterranean holdings, and provided a political and naval framework which prominent Barcelonans could not afford to ignore. As a result, Barcelona's patriciate remained open and flexible; no single house or patrician clique proved capable of securing all the complex mechanisms needed to exclude its rivals from municipal power. The patriciate was not a closed oligarchy stiffened by a rigid internal hierarchy, but a shifting constellation of prominent families formed and reformed through

[172] Cf. Heers, *Les Partis et la vie politique*, 41–63, 77–82, 101–5.

wealth, royal patronage, and ties to allies and associates throughout the Western Mediterranean.

Even though no formal legal or political privileges marked the patriciate off from the rest of the urban population, nevertheless it did develop a sense of cohesion and continuity. This was not only a function of the accumulation and preservation of wealth, but of the reproduction of a cultural identity.

Chapter 8

PATRICIAN CONTINUITY AND FAMILY IDENTITY

The character of Barcelona's patriciate can not be explained solely in terms of wealth and the exercise of power. Even if detailed tax registers had survived to reveal the precise amount of income and property every burgher possessed and municipal and royal rolls listed every bailiff, town councillor, revenue farmer, and mill owner, this would not in fact significantly sharpen the resolution on the silhouette of the patriciate projected in the preceding chapters. The humbler ranks of the urban population did not recognize the city's distinguished citizens by reviewing their tax returns or scrutinizing their diplomas, laborious tasks whose relevance mercifully remains a trade secret of modern investigators. Artisans, petty merchants, and laborers came to identify and associate patricians with certain family names, the circle of individuals whom they could marry, the churches and charitable institutions they supported, and a type of public display and comportment that gave them a mark of distinction. Only through the perpetuation of a cultural style and a family identity could the patriciate as a group retain its coherence as individual *parentelae* joined it and established houses became extinct.

Not until the patriciate began to take shape after the mid-twelfth century did a distinctively bourgeois culture assert its character and independence in Barcelona. Previously wealthy, influential families connected with the town had largely shared the aspirations of the provincial nobility, which itself had close relationships with Barcelona and its lords. As we have already seen, the most conspicuous families of the eleventh and early twelfth century felt irresistibly drawn toward rural castles and fiefs. Ricart Guillem, sometimes portrayed as Barcelona's eleventh-century Horatio Alger, found his family's fate revolving around the castle of Arraona, not his residence in town. A provincial notable such as Berenguer Bernat left his substantial intramural house to a younger son destined for the clergy but reserved his castle and fiefs in Anoia and the Baix Llobregat for his principal heirs.[1] By the second half of the twelfth century, however, emerging patrician houses looked upon castles as objects to exploit in pledge, not as envied rungs on a social ladder. Unlike rural nobles who continued to wander among their fortresses and farms, Barcelona's distinguished citizens lived firmly ensconced in their solid stone houses cramped in by stalls and workshops along the Ribera or above Santa Maria del Mar; they looked warily upon the rough world of swaggering castellans and hardened, poor men-at-arms just beyond the Collserola. Because aristocratic society left such a strong imprint on the nascent Italian communes and, although to a lesser degree, on the towns of Languedoc and Provence, it has become a commonplace to present patricians as aping the manners of blue bloods.[2] Yet the social fission between aristocratic networks in the interior and urban entrepreneurs, in all essentials complete by the mid-twelfth century, had permitted urban society to take shape with nobles at arm's length but always looking over its shoulder. Ties between patricians and petty nobles would be established once again in the thirteenth century, but under terms dictated by the adeptness burghers displayed in handling money and commanding maritime expansion. By then, however, patricians had established a self-conscious identity of their own.

MARRIAGE ALLIANCES

Bonds of matrimony lashed Barcelona's patriciate together. But the material these ties were made of, the strength and independence of the conjugal pair, and the relationship among individuals and their kin groups all changed in the course of the twelfth and thirteenth century. The affirmation of dowry as the leading element in the system of marital assigns tended to prevent the full integration of wives into their husbands' families, since women brought not only property but the interests of their natal kin into the match. The choice of marriage partners therefore became an

---

[1] ACB LA i, fol. 292, Mas xi, no. 1479.

[2] Georges Duby, "La Vulgarisation des modèles culturels dans la société féodale," in *Niveaux de culture et groupes sociaux: actes du colloque réuni du 7 au 9 mai 1966 à l'Ecole normale supériure* (The Hague and Paris, 1967), 33–41 [repr. in *Hommes et structures, 299–308*]; Michelle Luzzati, "Familles nobles et familles marchandes à Pise et en Toscane dans le bas moyen âge," in *Famille et parenté dans l'Occident médiéval* (Rome, 1977), 275–96; Waley, *Italian city-republics*, 165–67.

increasingly important element in promoting cooperative undertakings among patrician houses and in manifesting their status.

Recent discussions about marriage have unfortunately tended
to divorce the nature of marital assigns from the system of marital
alliances. Because it has become fashionable to stress the primi-
tiveness of medieval and other preindustrial societies, an abstract
matrix of kinship has tended to impose itself upon and even
obliterate other types of social organization and patterning.[3] If one
boils down the complex elements of marriage to their most basic
component, an exchange of women between two social groups,
then the "elementary structures" of kinship take precedence over
transfers of wealth, status, and patronage. In acephalous tribal
settings, the systematic exchange of women may well provide one
of the few tools of social interaction and "diplomacy" among
isolated and carefully circumscribed groups, but the danger exists
of oversimplifying relationships created through marriage in
complex societies, especially in the volatile economic environment
of expansive towns. Barcelona's patricians had more to exchange
than their daughters.

Ruiz Doménec has found in Lévi-Strauss' model of asymmetrical exchange theory a useful tool to analyze relationships among
the upper levels of the Catalan aristocracy in the eleventh and
twelfth century.[4] By dividing well-defined ranks within the
nobility into "wife-givers" and "wife-takers," he has shown that
over several generations the counts tended to seek matches for
their daughters with the sons of the viscounts, and the daughters
of viscounts with the sons of the great castellan families; women
were handed down by their relatives to men of lower social status
and personal dependents, thereby ordering the relationships
among the leading aristocratic families and underscoring social
divisions with blood lines. The attempt to impose this model on
large, less cohesive social groupings, particularly on urban society,

---

[3] See, for instance, the thoughtful discussion in Casey, *History of the family*, 74–85, who is,
however, misled into concluding that the early Catalan aristocracy organized itself
exclusively through an exchange of women and did not provide dowries for its brides.
For recent criticism of the alliance theory of marriage, championed by Lévi-Strauss, see
Goody, *The oriental, the ancient and the primitive*, 8–13, 68; Adam Kuper, "Lineage theory:
a critical retrospect," *Annual review of anthropology*, 11 (1982), 71–95.

[4] Ruiz Doménec, "Système de parenté." 305–8. His ideas on the early nobility, where
exchangist models do prove helpful, are expanded in *L'estructura feudal: sistema de parentiu
i teoria de l'aliança en la societat catalana (c. 980–c. 1220)* (Barcelona, 1985). Garí, *El linaje de
los Castellvell*, employs the same method on a castellan family and also minimizes the role
of marital assigns.

is, however, methodologically and empirically flawed.[5] The number of families counted among the ranks of counts, viscounts, and castellans in the territory subject to the counts of Barcelona was relatively restricted, and their status was already defined in terms of office, castleholding, and lineage. Barcelona's population, however, had still not separated itself into clearly defined ranks in the late twelfth and early thirteenth century; indeed, intermarriage among its leading families helped consolidate their common interests and status. The fluid outlines of the patriciate therefore offered a wide choice of marital alliances; the more open the patriciate, the greater the number of acceptable marriage partners. Moreover, the size of dowry payments and previous cooperation in business or administration between the families involved could easily outweigh earlier marital alliances, especially in the calculating world of urban entrepreneurs and merchants. It would be precisely a new, subtle calculus of money and kinship, not an exclusive preoccupation with lineage and rank, that defined marital strategies in the upper levels of urban society.

To solidify their influence, individual patrician houses generally encouraged matches with a wide array of families rather than concentrating resources on one heir or marrying repeatedly into a single kin group. Owing to the slow emergence and flexible dimensions of Barcelona's patriciate, it is difficult to think in terms of endogamy until the leading houses became well established. Patrician houses were still relatively young in 1250, and their number was growing. It therefore took several generations of intermarriage before the ban on consanguineous matches became a serious impediment to the selection of marital partners. Yet the preference for seeking brides and grooms from a relatively large group of ascendant urban houses and occasionally from the lesser nobility may have more to do with the need to integrate successful newcomers together with their resources into established houses than the taboos of incest as defined by the Church. For at least two or three generations after 1200, marriage alliances did not reveal a coherent system of ranking within the patriciate, but by the end of the thirteenth century an intricate web of affinity and consanguinity enmeshed all the major patrician houses.

To examine the patterns of marriage more closely and explore

---

[5] Ruiz Doménec, "Système de parenté," 320 is forced to divide the urban population artificially into *ministeriales, negociatores,* and *cives* to make his model work; a number of his genealogies are also suspect, supra, 153, n. 71; 158, n. 82; 212, n. 92.

how the individual ties worked to reshape the productive resources of the households involved, reference will be made to five families whose genealogies are presented in appendix 5: the Durfort, Grony, Adarró, Eimeric, and Lacera. The first three are among the oldest and most prominent patrician houses, whose rise can be traced to the mid-twelfth century; the Eimeric, as noted earlier, also date from the same period but were founded by an Italian immigrant and retained a strong interest in trade; finally, the Lacera were relative newcomers and represent the ascendant families that made their mark around 1200.

Even though many other genealogies have been compiled for this study, the chance survival of wills, dowries, and property divisions among heirs makes the outlines of the five families chosen here somewhat more continuous and detailed than most, but the available documentation does not permit the reconstruction of every branch and twig of any family tree. The very attempt to recreate family genealogies is in itself an historical distortion both empirical and functional. Empirically, because women with rare exception did not perpetuate a family name. Genealogical trees consistently cover over affinal ties; it would be instructive, for instance, to analyze descent independently through daughters and sons, but the sources simply do not permit such a method at this early date. Functionally, because early patricians did not yet share the aristocratic passion for genealogy. Even in rather detailed court proceedings about conflicting title to property, urban notables did not present long family titles or betray a strong identification with ancestors. Family memory was truncated. Although a lineage consciousness was developing by the late thirteenth century, contemporaries did not imagine their own blood relationships in terms of horizontal and vertical lines; beyond their immediate family, burghers categorized their kinsmen into ill defined blocks of *consanguinii* and *propinqui* loosely placed on the father's and mother's side. Paradoxically, in the zeal to reconstruct meticulous and extended genealogies, one runs the risk of distorting contemporary perceptions and lived experiences of kinship.

Intermarriage among the most powerful thirteenth-century patrician houses came about slowly. Among the most striking features in the early history of the Adarró, Durfort, Grony, and Eimeric (i.e. some of the oldest and most powerful families) is the rarity of direct marriages among their members. The match arranged in 1275 between Berenguer Adarró and Margarida, daughter of Pere Grony, represented the first marital alliance between two families that had become prominent over a century earlier;[6] this is the only clearly documented marriage known to me before 1290 among four of the most distinguished patrician houses examined here, roughly a century and a half after they can first be detected in the sources.

Even though a significant proportion of notable houses began their rise at roughly the same time, Barcelona's patriciate nevertheless did not emerge in the early thirteenth century as a cohesive block of related families fused by kinship and marriage. It is all too easy to find links among any number of the most politically active and economically privileged families and rush to the conclusion that the patriciate consisted of a closed circle of relatives.[7] At first, however, many of the dominant houses in Barcelona tended to keep their biological distance from one another. When the opportunity presented itself, matches with prosperous but not socially threatening families were preferred. The brother of Ponça, the first wife of Eimeric de Perugia, was Guillem Arbert the Physician (*medicus*), and Eimeric and Ponça's son Guillem wedded Guília, sister of Pere Arnau and Guillem Ponç, each solidly established burghers but not among the ranks of royal officials, major entrepreneurs, or royal financiers; in the late twelfth century the three daughters of Pere Grony, the founder of his house, married Esteve Gerard, Ramon Sunyer, and Guillem Burget, all prosperous burghers but again not among the most dynamic figures of their generation.

The most attractive marriages of all involved members of wealthy families which appeared to be on the verge of extinction. Toward the mid-twelfth century Arnau Adarró contracted a marriage with Berenguera, sister of Berenguer Donuç, whose relatives were substantial agricultural entrepreneurs around 1100; by 1200 the Donuç disappear from view, but the descendants of Arnau Adarró formed the most prominent branch of his family, nourished at least in part with the resources of his first wife. Yet the greatest prizes in twelfth-century Barcelona were the four daughters of Bernat Marcús, the last male of his eminent line.

---

[6] ACB 1–6–4172.

[7] Reynolds, *Kingdoms and communities*, 204–5; Brigette Berthold, "Zur Heiratspolitik des mittelalterlichen Städteburgertums," *Magdeburger Beiträge zur Stadtgeschichte*, 3 (1981), 3–19.

Because his sons-in-law or their kinsmen appear in the will of Bernat Marcús redacted in 1195, it appears that all four had already taken husbands by the time of his death: Ramona and Berenguera went to two brothers, Ramon and Pere de Ferran; Guillema (also called Guília) to Bernat de Sant Vicenç, a minor noble from the Maresme, and Sanceta to Pere Grony.[8] The partition of Bernat Marcús' estate was of capital importance, for it involved control of substantial tracts of land in the developing eastern suburbs between Santa Maria del Mar and the chapel of Bernat Marcús (probably established by the grandfather of the four sisters). Sizeable portions of the property had already been offered as pledges for loans from Guillem Durfort and his kinsman Joan de Montjuïc, who together with other burghers competed for these valuable tracts.[9] While the two daughters married to the brothers Ferran received outlying properties, Sanceta and Berenguera together received virtually all the urban real estate accumulated by their ancestors. The need to protect the property encouraged an enduring marital alliance between the Grony and Sant Vicenç, particularly since Sanceta, wife of Pere Grony, had died by 1202. Over the course of three generations three Grony women married into the main branch of the Sant Vicenç. Given the value of the tracts involved and the restructuring of urban property taking place in the early thirteenth century, powerful allies could prove useful. Yet marriage did not always triumph over money and political influence. By 1214 Guillem Durfort employed his leverage with the king to compel Guillem de Sant Vicenç to sell a substantial portion of what was once Marcús property to him for the hefty sum of 10,500s., although it was quickly sold again in an obscure and contested transaction to Pere Moneder for 11,000s. Might this affair have left bitter memories that contributed to an attack in 1259 by Berenguer de

---

[8] *Santa Anna*, III, no. 609; ACB 1–6–667; ADB perg. Santa Anna, Carp. 1a, 4–1, where Sanceta is clearly the wife of Pere Grony, not Pere Arnau Grony, who also subscribes. Cf. the genealogical chart in Batlle, Busquets, Navarro, "Aproximació a l'estudi," after 300. A useful account of the relations between the Grony and Sant Vicenç family is found in Cuadrada, *El Maresme*, 391–402.

[9] According to Bernat Marcús' will, *Santa Anna*, III, no. 609, Guillem Durfort held property at Torrent Profond, near the mouth of the Rec, and possibly more in pledge, while Joan de Montjuïc was owed 1,000s.; three years later Joan de Montjuïc purchased property at Torrent Profond for that amount, possibly from an arranged settlement, ACB 4–50–550. For other references to the division of Marcús property, ACB 1–1–365, 2370; 1–6–23, 2899; 4–3–226; ACA perg. varis, Marquès de Monistrol, 16, 18; Gran Priorat, armari 1, 26.

Sant Vicenç' retainers (*satallites*) on the Llobregat mills held by the Durfort?[10]

The breakup of the Marcús properties, however, was only the most spectacular case in the competition among ascendant families to amass property and control urban utilities in the city in the decades after 1200. Given the incentive to strengthen new patrician houses with the resources of older families of urban notables in decline or faced with extinction, it is hardly surprising that the ancestors of Barcelona's thirteenth-century patriciate usually preferred not to marry each other but to look opportunistically for profitable matches where they could find them in what amounts to a process of family recycling. This attitude discouraged direct marital alliances among its most successful practitioners and left substantial social space between them. Barcelona's patriciate therefore did not take shape as a well-defined "economic tribe" whose internal relations and external boundaries were originally traced by kinship and marriage; rather, during the late twelfth and early thirteenth century it consisted of a set of ascendant and relatively independent houses competing to concentrate resources and power spread among many hands.

As the earliest and most successful houses settled down, the social space between them was gradually filled by intermarriage and, more typically, by the absorption of new families. The Lacera provide a good example of this process. While the family name appears in urban records just after 1200, Guillem de Lacera provided the stable point of reference for later generations. By the early 1220s he was heavily involved in royal and baronial finance, served briefly as urban bailiff in 1231, owned a ship with Marimon de Plegamans and Pere Marquet, and maintained interests in Majorca.[11] Through timely involvement in finance, trade, and administration, Guillem de Lacera rode the crest of the first wave of Mediterranean expansion to gain quick notoriety in Barcelona. His descendants married well, allying themselves with older patrician houses shortly after mid-century and reaffirming older business associations. Of his three grandchildren, two contracted

---

[10] ACB 3–29–242, 248, 265; ACA perg. varis, Marquès de Monistrol, 122. The amount of the sale exceeded the value of the dowry (1,000 mbts. = 7,000 quaternal solidi) that Guillema, daughter of Bernat Marcús, brought into her marriage to Bernat de Sant Vicenç, ACB 1–5–50(a) and (b); in effect, Bernat de Sant Vicenç as a widower converted the dowry into cash in order to merge it with his own possessions.

[11] ACA perg. Jaume I, 173, 846; ADB perg. Santa Anna, Carp. 1a, 1–53; ARM Cod. 42, fol. 28 r.; for later loans to the king, see ACA Reg. 10, fols. 24 v.–25 r., 71 r.

matches with leading patricians: Berenguer de Lacera married the daughter of Jaume Grony; Elisenda, Guillem de Lacera's granddaughter, wedded Bernat Durfort; and his great-grandson Guillem de Lacera became the son-in-law of the admiral Ramon Marquet. Anxious to solidify their position, newer families quite understandably hoped for matches with the most influential houses; this ambition was hardly remarkable, but the ease with which it was accomplished does merit attention. Although not unknown, it was nevertheless quite unusual for patricians to reserve their sons and daughters for intermarriage with a restricted number of houses maintaining a comparable status; they preferred to leave room for the incorporation of new families, which brought with them tangible assets rather than a recognized, inherited status. Instead of forming a closed oligarchy marked off by bloodlines, Barcelona's patriciate remained remarkably open and flexible throughout the thirteenth century. Indeed, new families in the thirteenth century provided the social mortar for the older patrician houses, filling in the biological space between them and gradually setting them in a recognizable pattern. Marriage strategies among patricians therefore differed markedly from those preferred by the nobility, which through a systematic and sequential exchange of brides passed down from lords to retainers reproduced an internal hierarchy and ordered relationships among lineages. In town, money could thicken or thin the bloodline.

As emerging patrician families began to secure their standing in the decades after 1200, their ability to provide substantial dowries to their daughters displayed their new status and social pretensions. While dowry had already emerged as a significant element in the system of marital assigns by the twelfth century, the amounts involved grew substantially after 1200. The figures tabulated in table 8.1 illustrate the point.[12] Drawn from 120 marriage contracts involving individuals from diverse social categories, they are nevertheless surely weighted in favor of larger exchanges which would be more carefully recorded and preserved.

Even though surviving marital contracts before 1200 are far from abundant, extremely large dowries clearly became common

---

[12] The figures have been taken from marital endowments to both brides and grooms. Whenever the amount of a dower (*excreix*) was included in the same contract as the dowry (*dos*), I have excluded the former, since it became fixed at one-half the dowry, in order to avoid doubling the statistical weight of a single document. All figures are converted to quaternal solidi.

Table 8.1 *Amounts of urban marital assigns, 1100–1290*

Amount	1100–1200		1201–1250		1251–1290		Totals
	Dower	Dowry	Dower	Dowry	Dower	Dowry	N %
Over 7,500s.	0	0	1	2	0	6	9 (8)
5,001–7,500s.	0	1	0	7	0	6	14 (12)
2,501–5,000s.	2	0	0	12	0	5	19 (16)
1,001–2,500s.	1	6	0	8	0	7	22 (18)
500–1,000s.	1	4	0	9	1	6	21 (18)
Under 500s.	1	3	1	19	2	9	35 (29)
Totals	5	14	2	57	3	39	120 (100)

among the most distinguished patrician houses only in the course of the thirteenth century. This does not correspond, however, to a general inflationary trend in marital assigns. The proportion of small marital gifts of 1,000s. or less, almost half the total, remained relatively stable. Artisans and small property owners could afford to offer their daughters only small endowments, usually ranging from 300s. to 700s. This was far from adequate to secure widows a comfortable pension. In order to provide for their livelihood, widows with modest resources therefore sought remarriage and were valued as much for their labor as for the property they brought into the match. Daughters of patrician houses, however, received substantial resources to ensure their upkeep without depending upon their husbands' families. As a result the remarriage of widows was actively discouraged among the well-to-do; Bernat Durfort went so far as to deny his wife Berenguera custody of their children if she took another husband or entered a religious house.[13] Through their large marital assigns patrician widows with children could afford to remain unmarried, thereby avoiding the rivalries produced by the claims of children from *le second lit* and maintaining control over the management of their deceased husbands' estates. The independence of widows was a mark of patrician distinction.

By transferring substantial rights to women at the time of

[13] ACB 4–3–115. With the same goal in mind, Romeu Durfort added a yearly pension of 1,000s. to the 1,000 mbts. his wife Guillema could freely dispose of on condition that she not remarry, ACB 1–6–513. Cf. 4–17–59.

marriage, parents through dowry secured the material independence of a daughter within her husband's house and encouraged the active interests of brothers and uncles in its management. High dowries thus confirmed the interests of the entire male-centered family; it provided not only a lure to bring in a "good catch" but more importantly a means for a patrician house to extend and reinforce its standing among its peers. Although the size of individual dowries was a matter of careful negotiation, letting one daughter go more cheaply than another was not commensurate with maintaining family status. When testaments occasionally mention the amounts granted to several daughters, they fall within a comparable range. Bernat de Sanaüja, for instance, gave his three daughters 300, 350, and 400 mbts. at the time of their marriage, while Joan de Mans, faced with the unenviable task of providing for five daughters, managed to provide dowries of 300, 380, 500, and two of 450 mbts.[14]

Of all the factors ordering relationships within Barcelona's patriciate, the size of the dowry was perhaps the most revealing. The ability to provide a daughter with 1,000 gold mbts. or more in a dowry marked a threshold, for it demonstrated that a family had moved into the leading circle of patrician houses. During the thirteenth century the Durfort and Grony routinely provided their daughters with 1,000 mbts. at marriage, yet elder males could also expect as much or more from their own spouses.[15] In the three successive marriages contracted by Bernat Durfort between 1254 and 1274, Elisenda, daughter of Guillem de Lacera, brought 1,500 mbts. in dowry, Brunisenda, daughter of Bernat Burget, 1,400 mbts., and Berenguera, daughter of Ramon de La Granada, 1,300 mbts.[16] It must be remembered that while dowries were lost to a patrician house through daughters, they were gained through wives and daughters-in-law. Over several generations the economic losses or gains would tend to balance out. Only in those cases in which wives and daughters-in-law with large dowries were "collected" by one family while sons with a smaller marital portion were "distributed" to other families would marriage turn into a profitable business. Because Bernat Durfort, the *dominus* of

---

[14] ACB 4–15–148; 4–10–44. Cf. ACB 1–6–4094; 4–17–25; 4–3–219; 4–15–180; 4–9–104.

[15] All known dowries granted to daughters of the Durfort family before 1290 were 1,000 mbts., ACB 1–6–264, 1756, 4194; 4–3–115; ACA perg. varis, Marquès de Monistrol, 144, 145.

[16] ACB 1–6–122, 3762, 3845.

his house, held such a prominent and established place in Barcelona's patriciate, he could attract the daughters of his peers with consistently larger dowries than those customarily provided for his own daughters. The Durfort, however, married both their sons and daughters to a wide array of patrician families. Because wealth made ranking within the city's leading families so fluid, it is impossible to establish cohesive groups of "wife-givers" and "wife-takers" over several generations. One of the functions of high dowries was to regroup wealth among patrician houses, which could afford to bestow substantial resources on daughters as well as sons. Over time this accentuated the cohesion of those houses able to provide large dowries and obscured the internal differentiation within the patriciate.

Large dowries, however, could add to a woman's "honor" in order to make her an attractive match for sons of the nobility. During the thirteenth century marriages between regional nobles and patricians were still rare, but they usually involved the marriage of daughters with substantial dowries from older patrician houses to the sons of noblemen. These were spectacular matches involving a substantial reorganization of family property. When Guillem Durfort, King Pere I's trusted accountant, married his daughter Guillema to the nobleman Berenguer de Cervera, she received in dower from her husband 2,000 mbts., pledged on the castles of Guàrdia Pilosa and Granyanella. Although no record of the accompanying dowry has survived, it surely must have included claims to the coastal town of Cotlliure; through a series of sales and exchanges involving this valuable port in Empúries, Guillema, widowed and without issue, eventually obtained through her dowry and inheritance the *vila* of Sant Feliu de Llobregat. This profitable and cohesive seigniory in the Baix Llobregat, acquired at least in part as a consequence of the large dowry needed to contract a match with the nobility, would become one of the foundations of the continued prosperity and influence of the Durfort family.[17] The series of matches between women of the Grony house and the Sant Vicenç also involved extremely large marital assigns, including 2,000 mbts. in dowry brought by Sança, daughter of Jaume Grony, into her marriage with Berenguer de Sant Vicenç.[18] As we have seen, this led to a

---

[17] ACB 1–6–1223; 4–82–1; Bisson, "Finances," no. 2.
[18] ACB 1–5–50(a); 1–6–907, 3474. Cf. Batlle, Busquets, Navarro, "Aproximació a l'estudi," 295; Cuadrada, *El Maresme*, 394.

reorganization of property in the expanding suburban zone above Santa Maria del Mar. The significance of these matches lies in the ability of large dowries to alter previous patterns of marital alliance. Among the aristocracy, women were handed down from lords to their dependents; with large marital assigns, however, it became possible to pass women up from the patriciate into the nobility.

This constituted not merely a variation on the marital patterns followed by the nobility, but their subversion. Nineteenth-century novels have perhaps made us too familiar with the figure of the impoverished aristocrat compromising his honor but filling his purse by taking the daughter of a wealthy bourgeois to the altar. Such *mésalliances*, however, were still unusual and no doubt disturbing in thirteenth-century Barcelona, for the rise in dowries among well-to-do burghers threatened to turn "good breeding" on its head.[19] Only the wealthiest and most influential patrician houses, especially the Durfort and Grony, whose men were no strangers at the royal court, found in their daughters a means of increasing family honor through a noble marriage. The rather limited extent of this movement of social ascent into the nobility testifies to its disruptive potential. As Barcelona's patriciate settled down, aspiring families must have envied the most privileged houses, which could marry their daughters to noblemen, and would offer more to enter into marital alliances with them. The Durfort and Grony confirmed their elevated status by contracting marriages with influential families outside Barcelona, not by creating an internal urban hierarchy through matches with the same set of patrician families and their allies.

Because of the growing value of marital assigns, which affected both dowry and *excreix*, the mandatory and proportional counter-gift from the groom, marriage alliances tended to be opportunistic rather than clearly circumscribed by family tradition, neighborhood, or economic ties. With the exception of those rare alliances with noble lineages, whose pronounced patrilineal structure promoted strict rules for the exchange of women between lords and dependents, patricians tried to enlarge their

---

[19] Reactions to the inflation of dowries are considered by Casey, *History of the family*, 84–85; Hughes, "From brideprice to dowry," 43–44; Stanley Chojnacki, "Marriage legislation and patrician society in Venice," in *Law, custom, and the social fabric in medieval Europe: essays in honor of Bryce Lyon*, eds. B. S. Bachrach and D. Nicholas (Kalamazoo, 1990) 163–86.

circle of kinsmen rather than restrict it or define its social parameters too closely. Their choice of spouses lacked the conscious
exclusivity typical of late medieval Florence or Genoa, where
partners were sought to reinforce family ties within cohesive
neighborhoods or among sets of allied kin groups. The relative
weakness of lineage identity in Barcelona is largely responsible
for the difference, but dowry also played its part. As family
property and identity increasingly centered on male lines of
descent in northern Italy, women together with the property
they brought could be sacrificed to maintain an abstract notion
of family honor without seriously threatening the material core
of the estate. They were pushed to the margins of family
identity; indeed, they often helped establish its parameters. As
Duby has shown, noble lineages in France frequently married
their daughters to extend territorial or political influence, while
in Italian cities wracked by feuds the exchange of women could
bring an end to violence; in such instances wives served virtually
as hostages to make peace with hostile kin groups.[20] While
staking out the limits of family prestige, women and their
dowries were nevertheless largely expendable in terms of lineage
continuity. During the formative period of Barcelona's patriciate, however, marital alliance depended more on the amount of
dowry than on lineal pedigree. With property and liquid assets
distributed relatively equitably on daughters as well as sons, each
new match redistributed assets and status. In an era of expansive
growth, the high value of marital assigns contributed by both
bride and groom to the conjugal fund in general promoted social
cohesion and stability, for, unlike venerable family titles, it
allowed status rapidly to adjust to wealth. What distinguished
patricians in Barcelona from the rest of the population was therefore not so much who but how they married. If a new family
could afford to grant its daughters 1,000 gold pieces for their
dowries, it could easily find its way into high society. While
artisans and petty traders concluded their marital contracts with
silver coins, patricians insisted on speaking of their marriages as
being made of gold.

---

[20] Christiane Klapisch-Zuber, "Women and the family," in *Medieval callings*, ed. J. Le
Goff, trans. L. Cochrane (Chicago, 1990), 287–88; Georges Duby, *Le chevalier, la femme
et le prêtre: le mariage dans la France féodale* (Paris, 1981), 113–15, 250–60, 281–88.

DOMESTIC CONTROL

Wealth and status affected not only the choice of marriage partners but also the organization of households. Through a careful
sifting of tax registers of late medieval towns, especially the
Florentine *catasto* of 1427, we now know that patrician households
possessed distinctive demographic contours and followed a characteristic family cycle.[21] It has become possible to peer through a
statistical keyhole into Tuscan households and see the inner workings of the most privileged families. Not only did Florence's
richest houses contain more residents than their poorer neighbors,
they also manifested more complex generational patterns. In order
for the household head to maintain key elements of family property intact, it proved advantageous to keep children, especially
sons, from "leaving the nest" too early in order to marry. Young
men were therefore kept under the roof and the authority of their
father, while the wife of the male heir would be expected to move
into her father-in-law's house. The relatively large size and inter-
generational complexity of Italian patrician houses thus were not a
function of excessive births, but of a strategy to retain the cohesion
of family property and the lineage. Patrician paternalism offered
an effective form of social birth control, or at least limited the
procreation of legitimate heirs. Even though no other early urban
source can match the thoroughness and detail of the Florentine
catasto, which alone of medieval tax records consistently furnishes
the ages of household members, the model it presents of patrician
households parallels the less complete picture of other Italian
urban elites and displays marked similarities with the dynastic
organization of rural aristocratic households. Because of the similarity, it is often assumed that, at least in Italian towns, the *grande
maison* grew from the inherited habits of an urbanized nobility
already imbued with a strong sense of patrilineage.

Barcelona offers the opportunity to hold up these assumptions
to close scrutiny, for historically its early patriciate had a distant
relationship with the rural aristocracy and did not organize itself
around a single male line. While the stacks of assorted thirteenth-
century parchments accumulating in Barcelona's churches and the
royal archives can not compare with the extensive fiscal records of

---

[21] Herlihy and Klapisch-Zuber, *Les Toscans*, 491–522.

late medieval Italy, they nevertheless can be made to reveal the extent of domestic control within patrician households. Because random sets of wills and private contracts among family members fail to provide a sufficient basis for even a rough demographic profile, attention will have to be focused on formal elements in the structure of the domestic domain.

To this point, we have spoken rather abstractly about patrician houses, but they were firmly rooted in a physical residence, the *domus*. Centuries of subsequent urban development have destroyed, covered over, or radically altered the homes of Barcelona's early patricians, but documentary references indicate that they were ample, solid stone structures typical of private dwellings throughout the medieval Mediterranean.[22] Even though the *domus* could refer not to a single building but to a main house and its ancillary structures in the adjacent yard or occasionally even to individual rooms within the main building, the word nevertheless expressed a shared residential identity. As elsewhere in the Mediterranean, the principal residence provided at the same time a living space, storage area, bureau, and economic center. The main building consisted of two or, for the wealthiest families, even three stories. The ground floor of a substantial patrician house usually contained a storage area (*cellarium*) for wine and grain, workshops, and rooms for servants or slaves, while the top floor was divided into a large central living space (*solarium*), a kitchen, and smaller individual chambers. The ample home of Berenguer Durfort had twelve rooms and a kitchen on the second floor and the *solarium* on the third. A squat attached tower (*pignaculum*, *turris*), rare in the twelfth century, enjoyed a vogue in the substantial new houses built in the thirteenth, probably in imitation of the old houses attached to the Roman wall-towers rather than for any military value. Pere Adarró's stout *domus* at Cort Comtal could be referred to simply as his "tower."[23] A reflection of growing prosperity, patrician houses constructed in the suburbs

---

[22] The documentary evidence on private houses is carefully surveyed by Banks, "The topography," II, 663–87. Carme Batlle i Gallart, "La casa i les béns de Bernat Durfort, ciutadà de Barcelona, a la fi del segle XIII," *Acta mediaevalia*, 9 (1988), 9–51 has published a valuable and lengthy inventory of the household goods of the Durfort residence near Santa Maria del Mar; see also her comments in "La casa burguesa en la Barcelona del siglo XIII," in *La societat barcelonina a la baixa edat mitjana. Annexos d'història medieval*, I (Barcelona, 1983), 9–51.

[23] ASPP, 143; cf. ACB 1–5–338. For examples of towered houses in the Ribera district, ACB 1–1–2452; 1–6–4288; ADB perg. Santa Anna, Carp. 8, 118.

assumed grander dimensions and, with their height, towers, and attached workshops, outshone the older residences in the intramural area and along the Roman defenses. By the 1250s scribes began to speak of suburban "palaces" (*palatia*), a word formerly reserved for the residences of counts and bishops.[24]

The compact, sturdy houses with their *cellaria* and work spaces provided both an emotional and economic anchor for patricians. As a result, great care was shown in handing down to future generations their residence and attached properties. Yet turning the ancestral home into a control center for the affairs of the entire family took time to achieve. In the early twelfth century a house provided the focus of fraternal cooperation; testators often enjoined their sons to hold the house together and manage substantial parts of the estate jointly. That eldest sons would reside together harmoniously may well have been the ideal rather than a common occurrence, yet household heads rarely made elaborate provisions assigning parts of their estates to specific heirs. The continuity of a house and its family identity was considered a cooperative responsibility of its male members, not the duty of a single heir.

Typical of this system were the many private agreements among heirs partitioning their inheritance after their fathers' death. When Eimeric de Perugia died shortly before 1180, Guillem Eimeric, surely his eldest son, came to an agreement through the mediation of the vicar and other *prohoms* with his mother Alexandra and his three brothers, Pere, Bernat, and Pere Arnau; Alexandra, evidently still in charge of his younger brothers, received a house just to the west of Santa Maria del Mar, near the site of the future *alfóndec*, together with other properties, while Guillem Eimeric struck out on his own and set up a new household nearby. Twelve years later Guillem's two brothers Pere and Bernat effected another division of the remaining property between themselves, evidently after the deaths of their mother and brother Pere Arnau; they split their Barcelona residence in two and separated their lands and rights outside the city according to their own wishes except, the scribe added parenthetically above the line, "for the restrictions of our father's testa-

---

[24] ADB perg. Santa Anna, Carp. 1a, 5–6; ACB 1–1–2439; 1–2–1711 (1256): "De quator enim operatoriis que sunt versus dictam plateam de boria et construuntur subtus voltam palacii Berenguerii [Pelegrii] fratris mei."

ment.''[25] Whatever plan Eimeric de Perugia entertained for his estate and the future of his family, his heirs hammered out its specific design among themselves. While still alive the father entered into contracts alone, without the explicit participation of his children, and made no premortem arrangements to lay out the path his descendants would have to follow. The continuation of the Eimeric house depended upon the willing cooperation of its sons, not upon the strict discipline of the father reaching beyond his grave through limitations placed upon the actions and resources of his descendants. Under these conditions it is hardly surprising that each heir moved in a separate direction and eventually established a different household.

The fission of early patrician houses into separate branches in the late twelfth and early thirteenth century can also be seen in the early history of the Adarró family. In his testament of 1164, Arnau Adarró, the family's founder, left his own residence at Cort Comtal and other properties to his son Pere, but he also bequeathed another house and garden to a second son Arnau; even though the elder Arnau Adarró intended that his sons establish separate residences, Arnau Adarró nevertheless granted the rest of his assets (after deducting an adequate inheritance for his only daughter) to both his sons in common and further specified that his wife hold all his property for her lifetime. In the next three generations separate accords among the descendants of Arnau Adarró would sort out conflicting claims and carve out distinct spheres of interest, but the most dynamic branch of the family eventually settled into the house near Sant Cugat del Rec, not the ancestral residence at Cort Comtal.[26] Without a clear physical center, the focus of the descent group appears weak. Heirs were guided more by a desire to secure their own independence, often regulated by the death of a widow with her claims upon dowry or the need to provide funds for the marriage of descendants, rather than by an overarching concern to preserve the common interests and physical integrity of the *domus*. Further, settlements among heirs frequently involved non-kin in order to strengthen the implementation of the agreement. These critical moments in the

---

[25] ACB Cartes Reials, C. 1–2, Oliveras Caminal, no. 4; 1–5–23, 325: "habeat ad suam voluntatem faciendam salve tamen vinculo testamenti patris nostri." On Guillem Eimeric's residence, ACB LA I, fol. 118, Mas XII, no. 2244; LA I, fol. 119, Mas XII, no. 2235.

[26] ACB 1–5–226, 338; 1–6–1541.

cycle of a patrician house were therefore worked out in public before other *prohoms* and more distant relatives rather than in private behind the closed doors of the ancestral home. In a division among the male heirs of Pere Grony a decade after his death, Marimon de Plegamans, vicar of Barcelona, appointed eleven distinguished townsmen "prudent and discreet" to attend to the matter. Proverbial wisdom provided a justification for splitting what their father had left undivided: "Understanding that it is a natural vice to neglect what is held in common ... they expect that each with his share will strive to look after his own property with loving care."[27] Not only does the charter reject any sentimental attachment to the ancestral home and lineage solidarity, it also directly contravenes the testamentary stipulations of the father. Branches of patrician families were slowly grafted to durable residences during the late twelfth and early thirteenth century, but this was the result of incessant negotiation, compromise, and private accords among descendants at every generation rather than a conscious crafting of family patterns by elder males of the line. With the strengthening of paternal control, however, a more cohesive structure emerged in the course of the thirteenth century to ensure the continuity of patrician houses.

While both private accords dividing the estate among heirs and hortatory expressions of cooperation characterize the ordering of prominent Barcelona families in the late twelfth and early thirteenth century, premortem settlements and increasingly elaborate testamentary provisions gradually allowed the household head to tighten his grip over those living under his roof. The heavy hand of paternal authority reshaped patrician houses. The greater the responsibilities placed in the hands of the father and his principal heir, the more elaborate the stratagems to ensure the direct line of descent.

The change can best be seen in the great care the Durfort displayed in arranging their future. Strategies for family continuity clearly moved away from a loosely organized, unstable exploitation of common rights and generally formulated claims among descendants to a streamlined, careful management of assets by the head of the house. Although the testament of Guillem Durfort has not survived, the meticulous accountant to King Pere I

---

[27] ACB 1–2–1656: "Attendentes etiam quod naturale vicium est negligare quod commune est ... denique attendentes quod quilibet pro iuribus intendet circa rem propriam diligentem curam adhibere." Cf. ACB 1–6–3981.

clearly left a will when he died sometime between 1214 and 1216. Yet his final wishes could not be fulfiled without the intervention of outside parties. The tremendous debts carried by Guillem Durfort on behalf of the Crown certainly added pressure to clarify claims on the estate, yet vagueness about the individual portions due heirs characterized the testamentary provisions made by patricians at the time. Cooperation between his two sons carried over briefly after the death of their father, but King Jaume I himself had to appoint the bishop of Barcelona to sort through the claims of creditors and arrive at an equitable separation of goods, which left Pere Durfort with 10,000s.[28] Even though Guillem Durfort had evidently transferred the share of property due to his only daughter Guillema at the time of her marriage to Guillem de Cervera, the brothers found it prudent to acknowledge the marital gift in exchange for their sister's renunciation of any further claims to the estate in 1220, just as the family was tying up the loose ends of their father's bequests.[29] The complex series of accords among heirs temporarily gave rise to three distinct branches through two sons and one daughter (when Guillema died childless her brother Romeu Durfort acquired her properties), but the contours of the family took shape as much by arrangements among descendants and the pressures of creditors, kinsmen, and public authority as by the will of the father.

As patrician houses stabilized their holdings, family heads laid out more detailed plans for succeeding generations. In contrast to the flurry of accords and litigation occurring after the death of Guillem Durfort, the will made by his son Romeu Durfort in 1266 left little room for maneuvering among heirs.[30] All bequests to his three sons and one daughter were spelled out in the clearest possible terms; each descendant received specific properties and rents, and each bore a clear obligation in paying for the testator's bequests to his wife and religious institutions. In case one of the children died heirless, reversionary clauses determined how the

---

[28] ACB 4–51–564 and ACA perg. varis, Sentmenat, Indice 8, II, 27 record Pere and Romeu Durfort disposing of property jointly in 1216, the *terminus ad quem* of their father's death. Cf. ACA perg. Jaume I, 77, in which Pere and Romeu have rights in the same *mans* in 1217. For the intervention of the king and bishop, ACA perg. Jaume I, 131, 133; Huici-Cabanes, *Documentos*, I, no. 11.

[29] ACB 1–5–732. Soon thereafter Guillema's husband formally made out his dower contract; he evidently could not be sure of the value of his wife's dowry until the death of her father and the recognition of any further claims to inheritance, ACB 1–6–4072.

[30] Romeu Durfort's testament survives in three copies, ADB perg. Santa Anna, Carp. 9, 52; ACB 1–1–1463; 4–17–59.

shares would be distributed among the survivors. Ensuring the continuity of the male line was foremost in the mind of Romeu Durfort. Jaume, apparently the youngest son, was encouraged to study in order to become a cleric, but in case his two brothers died without legitimate issue he was instructed not to enter an order but to take up their inheritances. Besides making provisions for living heirs, Romeu Durfort even considered the unborn; if he left his wife with child at the time of his death, his children were to place their future sibling in a religious order and provide 200 mbts. for his or her livelihood. Typical of the ballooning clauses in late thirteenth-century wills, elaborate provisions dealt with every conceivable contingency and firmly established the ranking of descendants; an intricate maze of provisions, now enforced by authoritative, evidentiary courts, provided the testator a powerful instrument to guide the course of his house even from the grave.

What is most striking about the carefully considered estate planning of Romeu Durfort, however, are the arrangements to set in motion the distribution of property even before his death. Having administered his patrimony for roughly fifty years after the death of his own father, Romeu Durfort made sure his children had already established themselves in their intended position within his house. His daughter, Margarida, had obtained her portion of the estate through her dowry of 1,000 mbts., granted at the time of marriage twenty years earlier; Romeu Durfort remembered her with an additional bequest of 20 mbts. in his will.[31] Romeu, his third son, was to remain under his mother's control until he turned twenty and then claim his inheritance, but Guillem and Jaume had already received their shares in what the will refers to as an "inheritance charter" (*instrumentum hereditatis*). A record of this premortem transfer (*donatio inter vivos*), executed in 1260, has survived. It forms part of the arrangements made for the marriage of Guillem, the family's main heir, to Guillemona de Tornamira but includes stipulations about obligations and the exercise of power within the family.[32] Guillem Durfort agreed that he and his bride would reside in his father's house and attend to the needs of his parents; provisions were added about the support of Guillem's mother in widowhood and of his brother, Jaume, whose inheritance the principal heir would ensure. In return Guillem Durfort received control of the family house and

[31] ACB 1–6–264.
[32] ACB 4–82–4. The *dos* was received from Guillemona a year later, ACB 1–6–4181.

shops at the Vilanova de Mar owned by the family, Banys Nous (the city baths near Castellnou), and the *vila* of Sant Feliu de Llobregat, returned to the main branch of the family after Guillema de Cervera's death. To seal the pact, Romeu Durfort received homage from his son according to the *Usatges de Barcelona*. The formal and ritual acts leading to the transfer of rights to the descendants of Romeu Durfort were carefully crafted over decades according to the designs of the family patriarch. A strict sense of authority within the house was maintained and crowned with the act of homage made by the son to his father, a ritual of subordination but also of lineal continuity from the household head to his heir. The restructuring of patrician households in the mid-thirteenth century therefore did not come about due to a new awareness of blood ties or a redefinition of the kin group but through the use of new legal forms to ensure paternal authority and its transfer to a male heir, who firmly ruled his *domus*. The consolidation of patrician houses represents a consummate act of conscious family planning by their patriarchs.

Within the household itself, fathers kept a closer eye on their sons, daughters, and daughters-in-law than in the past. Although private charters do not offer consistent, detailed information about the age at which sons could gain control over property and inheritances, a critical moment in the family development cycle, indirect indications suggest that their material independence was delayed for those in the households of the well-to-do. Testaments and marital contracts in the thirteenth century were increasingly age conscious. According to Visigothic law, children could testify in court, make contracts, and record their testaments when they reached majority, set at fourteen, but they could assume full control of their portion of family property only at age twenty. In the ninth and tenth century, Bonnassie has found evidence of children younger than fourteen acting with full legal capacity, which encouraged an *émancipation hâtive*, giving youths considerable independence from parental control.[33] Barcelona's patricians, however, took measures to clamp down on their sons. While testators usually set twenty as the age their heirs could gain control of their inheritances, some insisted that the grants not be made until their children reached twenty-four or twenty-five. Further restrictions were placed on the right to bequeath property

[33] King, *Law and society*, 243–45; Bonnassie, *La Catalogne*, I, 271–72.

before age twenty if the heir died childless; reversionary clauses also recirculated family assets according to the wishes of the family head, not sons who had failed to perpetuate the house.[34] While fathers attempted to delay young men from striking out on their own, they also sought matches for their daughters at a young age in order to develop family alliances. The executors of Bernat de Banyeres' will conceded a dowry, considered a charitable act by the testator, to Constança at age twelve, when she had reached puberty (*plena puberitas*), while the daughter of Arnau Adarró successfully broke her engagement to Arnau Ombau because it had been made before she had turned twelve, the age of puberty (*annus nubilis*).[35] During the course of the thirteenth century, patricians manifested their control over the future of their house by delaying the material independence of their sons and marrying their daughters at an early age. Although clear and direct evidence is not available to document the methods fathers employed to adjust the timing of the family development cycle, the growing number of precise stipulations about age in testaments, marital contracts, and disputes in the thirteenth century suggests this was a relatively new development. As paternal control gradually over-shadowed cooperation among the elder males of the house, it limited the options for children and restricted their independence.

The fleeting glimpses offered by private charters into the domestic life of Barcelona's thirteenth-century patriciate conforms to a distinctive model of medieval family formation posited by Herlihy: strict controls on the independence of sons, who married late, and the young age of brides.[36] It differs from both early medieval patterns, in which domestic control was weak and men and women usually married at the same age, and a later system described by J. Hajnal as the "European model of marriage," in which both women and men married late during the early modern and modern period.[37] Why the system of early marriages for daughters and late marriages for sons proved so attractive to patricians and other medieval elites, however, remains unclear.

---

[34] For clauses delaying emancipation past age twenty, a restriction enjoying considerable popularity after 1250, see ACB 1–6–132, 2709; 4–9–221; 4–15–180; ACA perg. varis, Marquès de Monistrol, 162.

[35] ACB 1–6–1422, 4180.

[36] Herlihy, *Medieval households*, 103–11; Herlihy and Klapisch-Zuber, *Les Toscans*, 393–419. Cf. Mundy, *Men and women of Toulouse*, 81–82.

[37] J. Hajnal, "European marriage patterns in perspective," in *Population in history*, eds. D. V. Glass and E. C. Eversely (London, 1965), 101–43.

Because patrilineal tendencies were so pronounced among the great houses of Italian towns, those most carefully tended gardens of early family history, control over young men provided the most important variable. By keeping sons under the paternal roof, critical family assets, it is often argued, could remain under the control of a single male line.

The young age of brides, however, has attracted less attention. If the preservation of family assets was the primary goal for delaying the marriage or emancipation of sons, the same should apply to daughters. Other factors, however, clearly outweighed the maintenance of common resources and induced a father to "give away" a young bride. When a young woman moved into the home of an older husband, she established an alliance with her marital kin group that would often outlast her marriage. Accommodation within the new set of personal relationships was essential. Adjustments in the behavior of the wife and among members of the two allied families may have come about more easily when the bride was young. The transfer of the wife to a new house initiated a time of testing. When Sança, sister of Berenguer Adarró, went to the house of her new husband, Guillem de Torrelles, he agreed to acknowledge receipt of her dowry of 1,500 mbts. only after he had lived with his bride for two months. The delayed payment of dowry, occasionally by contractual agreement, also served to encourage a gradual habituation of the new couple to the influence of their respective sets of in-laws.[38] By contracting marriage for daughters at a young age, even before puberty, a father exerted strong control over the choice of marriage partners and ensured the virginity of the bride and the honor of his house. Parental authority gained added legal force through a royal decree in 1244; since concern was voiced about the seduction of maidens and the daughters of distinguished citizens, the king declared that any woman contracting marriage or eloping without the consent of her parents or guardian would lose all claim to parental property and her lover would face perpetual exile.[39]

The tensions of bringing a new wife under the authority of her father-in-law led to a drawn-out dispute between the Durfort and Lacera families. In 1254 Berenguer Durfort contracted a

[38] ACB 1–6–2377. For examples of prearranged dowry payments over time, ACB 1–6–4117, 4181.
[39] Huici-Cabanes, *Documentos*, II, no. 392.

promising match for his son Bernat with Elisenda, daughter of Guillem de Lacera. Significantly in this instance the fathers of the bride and groom had the charters for the marital assigns drawn up, not the future husband and wife as was customary. All did not go well, however, when Bernat Durfort took his bride to live with him in his father's house. A bitter dispute arose between the two families, which ended up before six judges appointed by the vicar in 1259. Berenguer Durfort and his son claimed that 119 mbts. of Elisenda's 1,500 mbts. dowry had yet to be paid, while Guillem de Lacera complained that his son-in-law failed to support his wife's female slave and attendants. At the heart of the discord lay Elisenda's honor, status, and position within her new household, which her father felt responsible to protect and may, as Batlle i Gallart has suggested, have been threatened by her father-in-law's remarriage.[40] The slow payment of the dowry allowed Elisenda's father to intervene directly in the affairs of the Durfort family; indeed, he literally forced Berenguer Durfort to divide his house. The judges insisted that Elisenda and Bernat be given a separate, walled-off flat above the *cellarium*. In addition, she was to have one female slave and a wet nurse for any child born to her (three years for a boy but only two for a girl) and receive fine clothes from the fair at Vilafranca del Penedès. But the patriarch's authority was maintained: Elisenda would have to eat at the table of Berenguer Durfort and his new wife.[41]

The dispute revolved around the conflicting claims for status and control of a father over his daughter, whom he had given to another kin group, and those of a household head over his daughter-in-law. In a manner altogether in keeping with the legal formalism of the thirteenth century, the smoldering dispute was, if not put out, at least temporarily smothered by judges in court, not by the participants themselves, their close relatives, and more distant kin; the affair revealed the building pressures created by patriarchal control in the privacy of the *domus* and the possibility of legal intervention owing to the heightened formality of that control. The judicial decision preserved the obligation of a husband to maintain his wife honorably with her dowry, according to the terms of the marital contract, but at the same time it confirmed paternal authority; the need to find a compromise

[40] Carme Batlle i Gallart, "La casa barcelonina en el segle XIII: l'exemple de la família Durfort," in *La ciudad hispánica durante los siglos XIII al XVI* (Madrid, 1985), II, 1350.
[41] ACB 1–6–3762, 4106.

demonstrates that women were valued standard-bearers for their natal families and retained close ties with them. Paternal authority and an emerging sense of lineage still had to accommodate a system of marital assigns and honor that accorded wives and widows considerable domestic influence and status. A widow might even take her sons back to the house of her own natal kin and use her dower, in fact the assets of her husband's relatives, to support them; in a strictly patrilineal system, such a situation would constitute an act of family treason against the male line.[42] By using the material leverage provided through dowry and the involvement of their own kin in its maintenance, patrician women carved out their own sphere of influence within their husbands' households. As the case involving Elisenda demonstrates, women often controlled their own domestic slaves by the late thirteenth century, while earlier the disposition of household domestics had largely been in the hands of men.[43] Thus, even though formally subordinate to a father's or a husband's control, wives and widows could in a sense balance the interests of the two male-dominated houses they represented. The creation of a new couple and the establishment of a new conjugal fund certainly did not grant women independence, but the substantial assets vested in them and the honor of their natal kin allowed them to counter agnatic tendencies and gain a formidable role in shaping the future of their children.

By the late thirteenth century, Barcelona's patrician houses at first sight resembled those of Italian urban elites in their age structure and patriarchal control. Sons long remained under their fathers' roofs, daughters married early, eldest sons received preferential inheritances, and household heads attempted to exercise strict control over their children, resident daughter-in-laws, and dependants. Based on the historical experience of northern Italy, this form of domestic organization and control is usually considered an extension of the patrilineal organization of noble families that settled in towns at the very outset of the urban revival. Indeed, the persistence of aristocratic traditions, particularly the strength of aristocratic patrilineages, is often felt to lie at the heart of the "Mediterranean town." Yet they could, of course, not be

---

[42] Estefania, widow of Guillem Eimeric, reimbursed her brother Arnau Ombau for food and shelter for herself and her son Guillem from her dower, ACB 1–6–109.

[43] Stephen P. Bensch, "From prizes of war to domestic merchandise: the changing face of slavery in Catalonia and Aragon, 1000–1300," *Viator*, 25 (1994) (forthcoming).

reproduced without women. The formal elements of domestic control and lineal descent through males depended upon the degree to which women were excluded from property rights, but women could not be completely neglected or "given away" without threatening the honor of their male relatives. The different needs of patrilineages and individual couples, the tension between what Goody calls the unilineality of descent and the bilaterality of devolution, created delicate balances within individual houses that the formal elements of domestic control often masked.[44] While the structural design and exercise of authority of patrician houses in the medieval Mediterranean may resemble one another from the outside, the dynamics of family relations behind closed doors could vary considerably.

In Barcelona the habits of the nobility had little direct bearing on the degree of lineage consciousness and the strength of paternal authority within the patriciate. Lineage did not constitute a carefully designed, cohesive, and autonomous institution that patricians borrowed from the aristocracy in order to consolidate their power and organize their households. Rather, it emerged contingent upon the control of patrimonies and the efforts of elder males to tighten their grip over the members of their houses. Without precise instruments to enforce his will, however, a patrician patriarch could not shape the contours of his house for future generations. The proliferating clauses and detailed provisions of testaments, premortem transfers, and marital assigns, so typical of the elaborate charters drafted in the thirteenth century, provided the necessary tools, while functioning public courts, staffed by legal experts, ensured that they would operate effectively. Earlier informal compromises, accords, and divisions worked out among heirs largely determined the fate of the family; in the thirteenth century it was dictated by the household head. The "textualization" of domestic life did more than merely formalize conventional arrangements: it allowed fathers to heighten the importance of the male line. As Barcelona's charters lengthened after 1200, the bloodline thickened.

LITERACY, LAW, AND PATRICIAN CULTURE

In their detail, complexity, and concise legal stipulations, the thirteenth-century family charters of Barcelona's distinguished

---

[44] Goody, *The oriental, the ancient and the primitive*, 478–82.

citizens reveal a society that felt itself at ease with the technical formality and precision of notarial instruments. In this they were expanding upon a traditional concern for the use of charters among the laity. Visigothic law had instilled a deep respect for written evidence, court citations, and strict procedures among at least those immediately involved as judges and possibly a broader segment of the population which found security in decisions rendered "by the book." Lay judges demonstrated a familiarity with precise provisions of the *Liber iudiciorum* well into the eleventh century, and the surviving copies of the code, with a single exception, are small, simple, and worn manuscripts, not luxury codices. Influential laymen associated with the courts certainly recognized the value of presenting charters in formal proceedings, and one can infer that the secular judges themselves had attained a sufficient degree of literacy to read the code itself. The judge Ramon Guitart, who owned houses in Barcelona, left a bequest in 1100 to the priest Ramon Guillem including not only his law book (*liber suus iudicesalis*) but also a psalter and an "ethics book" (*liber eticus*), possibly containing the prologue, consisting of maxims, composed in 1012 by another Barcelona judge, Bonhom, as an introduction to his *liber iudicum popularis*.[45] Deeply conservative in nature, the judicial culture anchored on Visigothic law promoted the utility of a literate mode of communication in lay society and encouraged those involved in rendering judgment to have direct access to the written provisions of the law books. Even though the ability to read the learned Latin of the laws remained the domain of a privileged few in the early Middle Ages, this proved sufficient to establish the place of charters in the conduct of important business among laymen and gave literate traditions a distinctly legalistic cast. While a growing number of laymen demonstrated an ability to manipulate at least a rudimentary Latin and, in some instances, to attain scholarly training from the eleventh century onward, even in early medieval society the laity had already become

---

[45] ACB 1–1–1844 and LA iv, fol. 28, Mas x, no. 1178. On the literacy of lay judges in other areas of the peninsula, see Roger Collins, "Literacy and the laity in early mediaeval Spain," in *The uses of literacy in early mediaeval Europe*, ed. R. McKitterick (Cambridge, 1990), 127–32 and F. Valls Taberner, "El *liber iudicum popularis* de Homobonus de Barcelona," *AHDE*, 2 (1925), 200–12; for a discussion of the extant manuscripts of Visigothic law, M. C. Díaz, "La *Lex Visigothorum* y sus manuscritos – un ensayo de reinterpretación," *AHDE*, 46 (1976), 163–223.

accustomed to employ written documents as tools of social order.[46]

In order to understand the implications of the expanding use of literacy, one must first of all attempt to distinguish among different levels of reading and writing. An educated cleric wishing to familiarize himself with the liturgy, elements of canon law, and some patristic texts would require broader training in Latin than a real estate developer or financier interested in securing title or rights through a charter. The more extensive Latin training of the higher clergy and their closeness to the sacred page endowed their learning with a special gravity and prestige. As late as 1255 a local canon still could let slip his age-old clerical pride in being a master of the written word for, when senility prevented him from subscribing to a charter, he had to authenticate it with a mark in the manner of an unlettered laymen, *signum laycale*. Yet "illiteracy" did not necessarily imply complete unfamiliarity with writing. In medieval usage *literatus* simply referred to someone with competence in Latin, while an *illiteratus* indicated a man without Latin training but who might be quite educated and even able to write in the vernacular. Thus the biographer of Ramon Llull in the early fourteenth century did not consider it demeaning to describe his hero as an *illiteratus* in his youth, when he was fond of composing in his native tongue and singing troubadour verse but had only a smattering of Latin grammar. From the eleventh century onward, however, the gap between *literatus* and *illiteratus* was gradually being bridged by "practical literacy," to use the term of M. T. Clanchy.[47] This need not require extensive training in Latin but does imply a rough understanding of the provisions of a charter and, most important of all, a deep commitment to the utilitarian employment of documents. More than merely a personal skill, literacy provides a mode of communication that allows for the dissemination of texts beyond the realm of the spoken voice.[48] In eleventh- and twelfth-century Barcelona, charters were

---

[46] The assumption that early medieval society, and especially the laity, operated in an overwhlemingly oral context has been forcefully challenged by Rosamund McKitter-ick, *The Carolingians and the written word* (Cambridge, 1989), esp. 77–134 and 211–70.

[47] ACB 4–37–65(a). On the weakening of the cultural divide between *literati* and *illiterati*, Herbert Grundmann, "Litteratus–Illitteratus," *Archiv für Kulturgeschichte*, 40 (1958), 1–65; M. T. Clanchy, *From memory to written record, England, 1066–1307* (Cambridge, MA, 1979), 175–201.

[48] Brian Stock, *The implications of literacy: written language and models of interpretation in the eleventh and twelfth century* (Princeton, 1983), 6–10 explores the formation of "textual

not merely an inscription of transactions but a commemoration of rights and obligations. Transfers through sale, donation, or pledge therefore demanded bestowal of all relevant charters pertaining to the history of the property involved. In 1152, before the assembled *prohoms* of Barcelona, Eimeric de Perguia "redeemed the land and rights as they are contained in the charters which Martí Petit possesses and recovered his pledge together with the charters."[49] Whether or not the parties involved could comprehend every word contained in the texts, they clearly understood that the cession of claims depended directly upon the formal transfer of charters. In 1207, one donor was forced to declare that no document relating to the property in question remained in her possession, and later in the century documents were drawn up to record the transfer of charters kept in a box from one party to another for safekeeping.[50] Even for those with the most rudimentary understanding of Latin, the manipulation of written texts already played a critical role in the business activities and judicial system of Barcelona in the eleventh and twelfth century. The appearance of autographs by lay people, some of quite modest means, may tell us relatively little about their literary skills at the time beyond a familiarity with the alphabet, but it clearly demonstrates their close engagement with a world framed by the precision and clarity of Latin charters.[51]

While we are accustomed to think of the Latin Mediterranean as a bastion of the written word, the defensive posture was more pronounced in some regions than others. Conservative adherence to scribal formulas and legal procedures may have caused Catalan scribes to lag behind their counterparts in Italy and southern France in adopting Roman legal formulas; notarial culture, while solidly entrenched, expanded slowly.[52] The type of acts thought

communities," in which writing even affects the illiterate or quasi-literate through the recitation of texts and helps structure oral communication.

[49] ACB 1–5–138: "Quem honorem sicut in ipsis scripturis quas inde habebat Martinus Petith continetur redemit predictus Aimericus de Perusia et recuperavit cum scripturis pignorem." Cf. ACB 1–5–256.

[50] ACB 1–6–1181, 3002.

[51] On the appearance of lay autographs on Catalan charters by the early eleventh century, Bonnassie, *La Catalogne*, I, 505.

[52] J.M. Pons i Guri, "Característiques paleogràfiques dels llibres notarials catalans fins el 1351," *VII CHCA* (Barcelona, 1962), III, 228–30. For the general evolution of the Catalan notariate, José Bono, *Historia del derecho notarial español* (Madrid, 1979–), I.1, 118–22; I.2, 28, 128–39 and Francesc Carreras Candi, "Desentrollament de la institució notarial a Catalunya en lo segle XIII," *Miscelánea histórica catalana* (Barcelona, 1905–6), I, 323–60.

worthy enough to be inscribed on parchment did not increase substantially before 1200. The impressive number of surviving twelfth-century charters can leave the erroneous impression that townspeople scurried to the scribe's table to record every detail of their lives, but this was clearly not the case. Barcelona retained a relaxed atmosphere of small-town familiarity before 1200. Day-to-day business, including commercial transactions and trade associations, were conducted orally, while charters were reserved for acts that would require authentication years in the future, particularly land conveyances, pledges, wills, and dispute settlements. Until the 1140s members of the local clergy had drafted the charters needed by townspeople to secure their rights and direct their affairs. Clerics connected to the cathedral, especially the subdeacon Ponç and the levite Guillem, also in charge of the cathedral school (*capud scole*), were particularly active, but a relatively large pool of clergy participated in setting down the town's affairs on parchment during the early twelfth century. Burghers thus had recourse to any one of several clerics when they needed the service of a writer; scribal culture was therefore loosely organized and completely in the hands of the Church. This state of affairs changed rapidly with the emergence of Pere de Corró, a lay scribe. From the time he first appeared in local charters in 1143 until his death c. 1194, Pere de Corró composed the overwhelming majority of extant parchments involving the laity in Barcelona. He quickly replaced clerical scribes and became the dominant agent of the written word in the city, the first lay "professional writer" documented since late antiquity.[53] Pere de Corró came from a local Barcelona family. With his solid house located near the *miraculum*, a brief walk from the cathedral or the comital palace, he sat at the very heart of the old *civitas*. In 1151 Ponç, the principal scribe to Count Ramon Berenguer IV, obtained the adjacent house.[54] Together Pere de Corró and Ponç

---

[53] By the 1150s Pere de Corró had already overwhelmed the competition; of thirty-six urban land conveyances in that decade, he composed thirty. By way of contrast, six different clerical scribes were involved in the seventeen urban land conveyances extant for the first decade of the twelfth century; except for Ponç the subdeacon, who drafted six charters, none of the others drafted more than three. Pere de Corró's importance can quickly be seen from the list of scribes culled from the charters of the ADB by Alturo i Pujol, *Santa Anna*, I, 63–70. On the remarkable duration of Pere de Corró's career as *scriptor*, see ACB 1–5–110; LA I, fol. 287, Mas XII, no. 2280.

[54] ACB I, fol. 220, Mas XI, nos. 1675 and 1676; 1–5–161. Pere de Corró's parents held property in the suburbs near Santa Anna, indicating that he was not a new arrival, *Santa Anna*, II, no. 323. On Ponç, see Bisson, *Fiscal accounts*, I, 246–47; II, no. 145.

had their fingers on the pulse of power within the city. The close connection of Pere de Corró to his neighbor Ponç, *scriptor comitis*, suggests that contact with the count may have helped Pere dominate the drafting of urban charters, but he also embodied the need of an assertive community to have a competent lay scribe, whose primary responsibilities lay with the burghers rather than the Church, at the center of its affairs. Still, the emergence of Pere de Corró as the city's principal scribe did not create a rapid expansion in the use of charters, for he could provide most of the writing services required by the town personally, although in the last twenty years of his life he was aided by his son, Pere de Corró Junior. By way of comparison, the citizens of Toulouse provided enough work to keep thirty public notaries occupied around 1200. During the twelfth century Roman traditions alone did not in themselves ensure every Mediterranean town an equal start in the race to achieve the "literate mentality." Barcelonans were lifted rather late on the rising tide of pragmatic literacy.[55]

The number of notaries, however, multiplied with breathtaking speed during the long reign of King Jaume I, who regulated their appointments and oversaw scribes installed by local communities. By the 1280s, more than forty public notaries were active in Barcelona. They produced an increasing variety of documents. After 1200, for instance, scribes not only drafted more wills but also composed charters acknowledging that an individual or institution had actually received a bequest. Greater care was taken to record the renunciation of rights by all possible parties, no matter how distant their claim, involved in a land conveyance. By the late twelfth century royal administrators kept informal, updated inventories of domains assigned to them, and in 1240 a merchant referred to the books he kept in his shop.[56] Commercial contracts also quickly crystallized into standardized forms. That new types of commercial association remained in notarial Latin rather than in Catalan provides yet another hint that merchants and entrepreneurs easily grasped the contents of these documents.

The proliferation of charters and notarial instruments in

[55] John H. Mundy, "Urban society and culture: Toulouse and its region," in *Renaissance and renewal in the twelfth century*, eds. G. Constable and R. Benson (Cambridge, MA, 1982), 234. Based on his mastery of the thirteenth-century royal registers, Burns, *Diplomatarium*, I, 112–15 tends to exaggerate the "literacy gap" between the Mediterranean and a backward feudal North by assuming that the literate mentality was already firmly established by Jaume's reign; it was in fact just starting to expand in Barcelona.
[56] Bisson, *Fiscal accounts*, I, 100–1; ACB 1–6–2997: "prout in libro operatorii continetur."

business, administration, and family matters alike required at least a rudimentary Latin to make use of them fully, for vernacular charters were still rare. Of more than 8,000 documents swelling the registers of Jaume I, only thirty-nine are in Catalan, mostly concerning lists or portions of judicial testimony.[57] The emergence of Romance languages and their perceived distance from Latin has recently been subject to a radical reevaluation. According to Roger Wright, Latin and vernacular Romance languages were not developing along separate paths in the early Middle Ages; rather, before the Carolingian period in Francia and the eleventh century in Spain, Latin was simply regarded as the written form of the spoken vernacular in each locale and a reader would simply give Latin words a vernacular pronunciation. Only with the revival of neoclassical pronunciation norms did an awareness emerge that vernacular was distinct from Romance dialects as Latin yielded to diglossia. Yet the Latin of the charters did not fossilize into an archaic language increasingly distant from spoken Romance but continued to assimilate vernacular forms and vocabulary, perhaps, as Thomas Walsh has suggested, because the study of Latin was largely oral, consisting of the rote repetition of paradigms and the memorization of word lists which allowed for the influence of vernacular phonology on Latin orthography.[58] Catalan notarial Latin was thus hardly a dead language but a freestanding construct that responded to the growing weight placed on the written word. We should therefore not assume that a complete chasm existed between the written language of the charters and the spoken language of the marketplace, shops, and shipyards.

Beneath the stiff formulas of the charters very little direct evidence exists about the ability of well-to-do burghers to read the documents or how precisely they would have obtained a basic knowledge of Latin. No diocesan statutes were enacted to supervise elementary schools or masters in Barcelona, as they were in the struggling municipal schools of frontier Valencia, but the lack

[57] Josefina Font Bayell, "Documents escrits en català durant el regnat de Jaume I," *X CHCA* (Zaragoza, 1980–82), II, 521–23; Burns, *Diplomatarium*, I, 119.

[58] Roger Wright, *Late Latin and early Romance in Spain and Carolingian France* (Liverpool, 1982), 104–46; Thomas J. Walsh, "Spelling lapses in early medieval Latin documents and the reconstruction of primitive Romance phonology," in *Latin and Romance languages in the early Middle Ages*, ed. R. Wright (London and New York, 1991), 206–18. On the penetration of Catalan words and forms into the charter evidence, Bonnassie, *La Catalogne*, I, 504–5; Bisson, *Fiscal accounts*, I, 11–12; Burns, *Diplomatarium*, 134–7.

of formal regulation may well indicate that local clerics and later university graduates regularly offered instruction to young students, as the *Decretals* of Gregory IX urged them to do.[59] Without the ability to understand the terms of a pledge, the amounts invested in a *comanda* contract, the commands of a royal missive, or the legal clauses planted like landmines to maim the unwary before the formal closure of a document, patricians would have been at a distinct disadvantage in a world increasingly shaped by the technicalities of the written word. The care with which they preserved, inventoried, copied, and even recorded the transfer of parchments as well as the incessant use of documents in legal pleas provides an indirect indication that patricians fully understood their value and many could manage to decipher them. Secular latinity would not rest upon the rhetorical training provided in the literary primers, the *ars dictandi*, but upon an ability to deal with ways of thought and expression spread through notarial formularies, the *ars notariae*.

Some patricians, however, did not remain content with a rough grasp of notarial Latin and sought a formal training for their sons, particularly in the law. Catalans began to stream into the schools of Bologna soon after 1200, six or seven decades behind the Italian and Provençal students who flocked to the masters expounding the text of the revived Roman law. Among the earliest was a local canon, Master Albert, who with the sharp acumen of a Catalan tradesman extended loans to students from his homeland, a type of remunerative financial aid package. The study of Roman and canon law flourished in Barcelona's cathedral chapter, which provided an early stepping stone for the renowned decretalist Ramon de Penyafort, the foremost canonist of his day.[60] Legal training was also prized in patrician houses as well as in the cathedral. Often a younger son was encouraged to pursue his studies as a means of limiting the number of heirs and delaying marriage; the classroom could provide as effective a means of birth

[59] Robert I. Burns, *The crusader kingdom of Valencia: reconstruction on a thirteenth century frontier* (Cambridge, MA, 1967), I, 106–8.

[60] Joaquím Miret i Sans, "Escolars catalans al estudi de Bolonia en la XIIIª centuria," *BRABLB*, 8 (1915), 137–55; Hastings Rashdall, *The universities of Europe in the Middle Ages*, eds. F. M. Powicke and A. B. Emden (2nd ed., Oxford, 1936), I, 156; II, 121. On Ramon's legal interests at the time, Stephan Kuttner, "Zur Entstehungsgeschichte der 'Summa de casibus poenitentiae' des hl. Raymund von Penyafort," *Zeitschrift der Savigny-Stiftung für Rechtsgeschichte. Kanonistische Abteilung*, 39 (1953), 419–34 [repr. in *Studies in the history of medieval canon law* (London, 1990)].

control (at least of legitimate children) as the monastic cell. In 1221 Pere de Sanaüja, relative of one of Barcelona's first four magistrates, made provisions in his will guaranteeing his son Arnau a generous annual pension of 25 mbts. as long as he remained *in scolis*. The investment certainly paid off, for King Jaume I frequently appointed Arnau de Sanaüja to serve as a royal judge to settle disputes in Barcelona. His father was the first Barcelona testator to offer support for the advanced studies of his son, but others followed.[61] Since no durable university existed in the Crown's Iberian realms until King Jaume II founded one at Lleida in 1300, students traveled to Montpellier, Paris, and above all Bologna for higher studies. Law held the strongest attraction.

A small group of lawyers, the *iurisperiti*, make their appearance just after 1250. Over the next forty years, thirteen individuals appear with the title of *iurisperitus* in Barcelona charters, but the number of civil lawyers surely exceeded that number since those trained in law did not employ the title consistently. The professionalization of the law lagged a generation or two behind the consolidation of the vicarial court, with its insistence on documentary evidence, authoritative judgment, and Romanizing formulas. Even with the shift in legal systems toward the end of the twelfth century, vicars for decades continued to appoint judges to settle individual cases from among prominent burghers reputedly knowledgeable in the law and learned canons, who flaunted their education by attaching *magister* to their names. A new group of upstart and avaricious lawyers therefore did not suddenly displace the judicial weight of older patrician houses; instead, patrician culture gradually absorbed the new legalism rather than resisting it. Guillem Eimeric, who in 1251 was the first Barcelonan to bear the title *iurisperitus*, came from a prestigious patrician house, as did some of his colleagues.[62] For families heavily involved in administration with its attendant judicial responsibilities, some familiarity with the law was essential. Berenguer Durfort possessed a copy of the *Decretals*, and Arbert de Banyeres, member of an aspiring merchant family, happily purchased two books of Roman law from a priest for the hefty sum of 13 lbs., roughly half

---

[61] ACB 4–15–148. Arnau de Sanaüja appears as a royal judge in ACA perg. varis, Marquès de Monistrol, 88; Reial Patrimoni, Batllia General, Classe 3ª, vol. 6, fol. 74 v. Cf. ACB 4–1–20; 4–8–86.

[62] Guillem Eimeric *iurisperitus* first appears in ACA perg. varis, Marquès de Monistrol, 101. The *iurisperiti* Guillem Ombau, Ramon de Noguera, Berenguer de Riera, and Bernat Ponç were also members of prominent families.

the amount of a substantial commercial *comanda*.[63] The expansion of legal training, or at least some knowledge of Roman and even canon law, reinforced rather than challenged the dominance of patrician houses. The impact of the new legal science on Mediterranean urban societies varied considerably. John Mundy has found that Toulouse's leading families sternly resisted the professionalization of law since it reduced their role in informal arbitrations and allowed the centralizing power of the king and the Church to erode municipal self-government.[64] In Barcelona, on the other hand, knowledge of canon and civil law tied patricians ever more closely to the king and kept the doors to local administration open. Royalist rather than republican sympathies gave a distinctive legalistic coloring to Barcelona's patriciate.

The technical cast of mind connected to scribal and legalistic culture carried over from Latin to the vernacular. Catalan took shape in close connection to charters and juridical texts, which rapidly raised it to the level of a literary language.[65] While Catalan translations of saints' lives and legal codes, including portions of the *Liber iudiciorum*, the compendium of maritime law known as the *Llibre del Consolat de Mar*, and possibly the *Usatges*, existed in the thirteenth century, the formidable Majorcan polymath Ramon Llull, descendant of a Barcelona patrician house, is credited with creating the first "authentic" Catalan literature a decade or two before 1300. Local wills and inventories mention family charters and occasionally legal texts, but they have scant evidence of vernacular books or "literature." Catalan, however, did creep onto parchment and onto its replacement, the paper that became increasingly accessible after the conquest of the mills of Játiva. The vernacular left its clearest mark not on intimate expressions of the heart, but upon accounts and laws. The vernacular elocutions one can hear beneath the brittle Latin of the early accounts of Catalonia eventually break through to be heard on their own. Already in the list of burghers drawn up for the *questia* c. 1145, personal names assume their Catalan form. The language of surveying, reckoning, and accounting for both business and administration

---

63 ACB 4–3–162; 1–6–564: "duos libros legales vidilicet codicem in uno volumine et institutiones cum auctentico in alio volumine."

64 Mundy, "Urban society and culture," 234–35.

65 On "preliterary" Catalan and its close connection to notarial and legal styles, Manuel Sanches Guarni, *Aproximació a la història de la llengua catalana: creixença i esplendor* (Barcelona, 1980), 162; Josep Nadal and Modest Prats, *Història de la llengua catalana* (Barcelona, 1982–88), I, 163–86; Burns, *Diplomatarium*, I, 116–24.

was the first to abandon the forced Latin of notarial formulas and assume the ease and flexibility of the vernacular. Dorsal notations on *comanda* contracts occasionally reveal merchants settling accounts and exchanging merchandise with the swift strokes of their pens in Catalan, quite in contrast to the standardized notarial Latin on the front of the document.[66] Bankers quickly learned to reckon in the vernacular. A parchment copy made from the ledger of a Barcelona banker c. 1296, the earliest extant banking record in Iberia, also reveals a highly evolved business language in Catalan.[67] Alexander Murray has pointed out that the emergence of an arithmetic mentality was closely connected not only to trade but also to the growing efficiency of government in the thirteenth century;[68] in Catalonia one should add that thinking in numbers and accountability was closely related to the emergence of the vernacular. For Barcelona's patricians, counting men and money was indeed their native tongue.

While patricians may have felt at ease when they went to the notary's table and the vicar's court, they did not necessarily hold up the scribe and the lawyer as ideals to emulate. The wealthiest and most influential citizens were certainly no strangers at the royal courts of the thirteenth century and to some extent imitated the aristocratic culture and comportment displayed there. Around 1200 urban wills begin to reveal a new concern for fashion. Expensive furs, dyed woolens from Northern Europe, and exotic Islamic silks indicated not only the material prosperity of townspeople but a love of display, for which aristocrats set the style. The noble life also found its expression in courtly poetry of love and knightly adventure, which local troubadours sang in Provençal, the linguistic sister of Catalan. *Ioculatores* occasionally turn up as subscribers in urban charters from both the twelfth and thirteenth centuries and appear, like the troubadours of Toulouse, to have blended unobtrusively into their urban setting.[69] The appeal of courtly entertainers was not limited to the aristocracy. Owing to

---

[66] ACB 1–6–199, 512, 3176, which correspond to Garcia-Mardurell, *Comandas comerciales*, nos. 27, 37, 40; the authors unfortunately chose to ignore dorsal notations in their otherwise careful edition.

[67] Bensch, "La primera crisis," 319–20 and appendix.

[68] Alexander Murray, *Reason and society in the Middle Ages* (Oxford, 1978), 188–210.

[69] Mundy, "Urban society and culture," 235–38, 244–47 concisely deals with the documentary evidence for urban troubadours in Toulouse. On the importance of Catalans in Provençal poetry, de Riquer, *Història de la literatura*, I, 21–39. Three entertainers can be identified before 1220 in Barcelona, but little is known about them except for their name. Their relative anonymity suggests a modest social position.

the perils of overseas trade and the collaborative effort of towns-men and nobles in Catalan maritime expansion, Barcelonans would not have felt in the least out of place listening to stories of knightly adventure, feats of arms, and *fin' amors*, or in enjoying the pointed invectives aimed against feckless vassals. On overseas expeditions patricians frequently engaged pages (*scutiferi*), while the swords and helmets included in their wills demonstrate that they knew how to wield arms.[70] Horses, however, were alto-gether exceptional in the thirteenth century even for the wealthiest burgher. The sea created a new balance between the cultural traits clumsily labelled "feudal" and "urban," between the swaggering pride of the castellan and the calculating aggressi-vity of the maritime adventurer. Barcelona's patriciate moved easily in both traditions, without considering them in any way forced or contradictory. What is surely the most famous secular painting in thirteenth-century Catalan art comes from the Palau Aguilar, a solid patrician house on the fashionable Carrer de Montcada: it depicts Jaume the Conqueror sitting in his field tent, surrounded by his barons and knights, as he makes his battle plans for the siege of Majorca.

Even though Barcelona's patricians could put on aristocratic airs, command galleys, serve as ambassadors to kings and princes, fight shoulder to shoulder with knights throughout the Mediter-ranean, and marry their daughters to the sons of nobles, it was nevertheless their raw latinity and respect for the forms of written law that secured their place and perpetuated their identity as a ruling group in urban society. Neither the militaristic bravado nor the oral culture of the baronage that aspiring urban notables envied could completely compensate for a foreshortened lineal memory and the lack of ancestral castles. The ability to cope with, if not always command, the written word did, however, provide a new means for memorialization, for it allowed patricians closer ties to the local church. Because of some familiarity with Latin, men such as Pere d'Espiells or Guillem Eimeric could finish their lives as cathedral canons. Without some training in Latin received in their youth, such a move would not have been possible. Religious patronage and a need to strengthen ties between the living and the dead were crucial in perpetuating the identity of patrician houses.

[70] ACB 1-1-1463; 4-1-8; 4-9-221.

RELIGIOUS PATRONAGE AND THE CULT OF ANCESTORS

During the thirteenth century prominent citizens of Barcelona forged new links with local churches and demonstrated a heightened concern for the memorialization of ancestors through the foundation of family tombs and chantries. Recalling kin was molded into a pious act. While the connection between religious patronage and family identity is a recurrent theme in the Middle Ages, burghers struggled to maintain a viable balance between laying up stores in heaven and keeping the family *cellarium* well stocked on earth. Historians have arrived at quite different conclusions about the effect urban life produced on personal piety and family continuity. Studying patterns of testamentary donations and funerary display, Jacques Chiffoleau has argued that in Avignon during the fourteenth and fifteenth century economic mobility and the disruption of traditional patterns of sociability led to flamboyant funerals and highly idiosyncratic donations to clergy and the poor, all expressions of a progressive movement of religious self-expression and individualism; sifting through Sienese wills for the same period, Samuel Cohn has arrived at just the opposite conclusion: the demands of lineage and family severely limited individual planning for the afterlife.[71] The correlation between pious intentions and the need for material and genealogical continuity defies a simple, unidirectional movement from medieval to modern. Because patrician houses had such shallow foundations in early thirteenth-century Barcelona, the commemoration of ancestors through masses, chapels, and family tombs had a critical role to play in stabilizing family identity. By connecting family names and ancestors to the traditions of local churches, a spiritual pedigree could anchor and reinforce a thin, wavering bloodline.

The proliferation of new orders, the consolidation of patrician houses, and the changing social composition of traditional religious communities in an expansive urban environment all created new demands on both the urban clergy and their patrons after 1200. Yet the most notable change in pious legacies from the twelfth to the thirteenth century was an ever sharper focus on the

---

[71] Jacques Chiffoleau, *La Comptabilité de l'au-delà: les hommes, la mort et la religion dans la région d'Avignon à la fin du Moyen Age, vers 1320–vers 1480* (Paris, 1980), 153–208; Samuel K. Cohn, *Death and property in Siena, 1205–1800: strategies for the afterlife* (Baltimore, 1988), 97–155.

town itself. Although neither the average number nor amount of *pro anima* legacies changed significantly until the end of the twelfth century, around 1140 Barcelona testators gradually lost interest in upland religious institutions. From 1100 to 1140, 69 percent of urban wills directed legacies toward monasteries and churches outside Barcelona and its *territorium*, but the proportion fell to 36 percent during the next sixty years and continued to decline to a mere 7 percent in thirteenth century. The bishop and canons, who embodied an older territorial identity, also received substantially fewer donations; while 52 percent of testators remembered those serving in the cathedral in the twelfth century, the proportion fell to 23 percent from 1200 to 1290. The parameters of sacred space dramatically tightened around the city itself.

Even the most prosperous families found it difficult to work their way into the cathedral. For earlier generations the canons and urban monastic communities had constituted foreign enclaves in urban society, for they were made up of aristocrats and, increasingly in the twelfth century, lesser nobles from the county of Barcelona. Emerging urban families found it difficult to crack their ranks. Some twelfth-century canons did come from older families residing in the city, but the dispersed inland properties and castles of these early families make it difficult to label them urban. Of the dynamic new houses that asserted themselves after 1140, only the d'Arcs managed to place their sons among the exclusive group of canons before 1200.[72] In the thirteenth century several patrician houses succeeded in effecting the entry of their children into the canonate, including the Grony, Banyeres, and d'Espiells; Berenguer d'Espiells even rose to the rank of chanter (*precantor*).[73] Yet the cathedral chapter remained a focus of provincial society, anchored on families of aristocratic and noble background but permitting a handful of patrician houses to confirm their ascent by having their sons serve its ancient altars. Townspeople in general did not appear particularly anxious to place their

---

[72] Because Arnau Pere d'Arcs, the house's founder, received the right to supervise the ransoming of captives, he established a close relationship with the counts and the aristocratic world represented in the local cathedral; *CODIN*, IV, no. lxxxvi. Berenguer and Ramon d'Arcs, probably uncle and nephew rather than brothers, were canons by the 1170s, and another relative Berenguer d'Arcs became a levite in the cathedral during the same decade. The family seems to have paid dearly for the privilege, for they donated substantial amounts of land to the canons and appear to have lost some of their importance after 1200. On their donations, ACB 1–1–2524; LA I, fol. 167, Mas XI, no. 2006; LA I, fol. 108, Mas XI, no. 2004.

[73] ACB 4–43–553.

children in religious orders. Among 508 children appearing in urban wills, only 13 (7 daughters and 6 sons) had either already entered the religious life or were clearly expected to do so by their parents. Since the proportion of the clerical population was surely in excess of the 2.5 percent of children destined for the Church, one can not assume that patricians looked upon local monasteries and churches simply as a dumping ground for unwanted sons and daughters.[74]

As elsewhere in Europe, new religious orders and local nunneries proved more attractive to urban society than the cathedral and the older Benedictine houses. Even before the arrival of the friars in the early thirteenth century, two new canonical orders rapidly gained popularity in the city: the Order of the Holy Sepulcher, which had established the convent of Santa Anna in the northern suburbs by 1145, and the Augustinian canons, established in 1155 through a reform of the old Benedictine monastery Santa Eulàlia del Camp.[75] While both orders were frequently mentioned in local wills from their foundation, Santa Anna, which possesses a richer documentation than Santa Eulàlia, drew individuals from a number of patrician houses into its ranks, including Berenguer d'Espiells and Ramon de Vic, while Pere Grony, Guillem Ombau, and Berenguer de Lacera established chapels there.[76] By incorporating service to neighbor and the edification of the community into their cloistered vocation, the new canonical orders responded to the needs of the urban populace and looked forward to the friars. Once they arrived in Barcelona, both Franciscan and Dominican communities quickly attracted donations from and provided confessors to Barcelona's patricians, whose consciences were pricked by the sin of usury and the friars' sermons. Already in 1223, only two years after Dominic's death, the Preaching Friars, the city's most popular new religious order in the thirteenth century, received their first bequest from a prominent townswoman, but the Franciscans lagged only slightly behind. Berenguer de Roig, in close contact with the mendicants, made provisions for

---

[74] The political and economic motives for monastic oblation and donations by the French nobility have been questioned by Constance B. Bouchard, *Sword, miter, and cloister: nobility and the Church in Burgundy, 980–1198* (Ithaca, 1987), 225–46.

[75] On the early history of these houses to 1200, see the detailed presentation, based on the archives of these communities that came into the possession of the ADB, by Alturo i Perucho, *Santa Anna*, I, 41–180.

[76] ADB perg. Santa Anna, Carp. 2a, 96, 116; Carp. 8, 209; Carp. de la creu, unnumb. parch. [24 xi 1285].

his wife to enter the Franciscan order in 1236, while one son of Bernat Oliver entered a generation later. In a characteristic intersection of new religious ideals and the needs of urban society, Pere Ferrer de Vic, whose kinsmen had close ties to banking, oversaw local Franciscan finances as their *procurator*.[77]

But the orders of canons and friars in Barcelona did not push aside monks and local clergy. The most striking feature of thirteenth-century wills is not the popularity of new religious institutions but the proliferation of bequests to all local churches and monasteries. Support of these older religious establishments most fully embodied an emerging civic self-consciousness. Testators began to leave bequests to several parish churches or monasteries. In 1173 Berenguer d'Arcs, member of an ascendant patrician house, became the first Barcelonan to leave donations to all six parish churches, a bequest that would become customary for the city's well-to-do in later decades.[78] Final donations were also offered to every urban hospital, even if one or two were singled out for special generosity. At the same time that the totality of pious institutions in the city received recognition, ties to individual parish churches also became stronger and more articulate; in 1232, Maria, daughter of Bernat Roig, was the first urban testator to mention the parish in which she resided.[79] While nine new monasteries, including the popular Franciscan and Dominican friaries, and four new hospitals attracted pious bequests in the thirteenth century, parish churches and older Benedictine houses also flourished. Indeed, the proportion of testators specifying their final resting place in parish churches rose from 30 percent in the twelfth century to 53 percent in the thirteenth, mostly at the expense of the cathedral. As parish allegiances intensified, disputes arose among local churches, monasteries, and the canons regarding parish boundaries and the right of a burgher to be buried in the church of his or her choice.[80] Thus a new, concrete religious topography was being worked out with considerable detail during the early thirteenth century, as townspeople acknowledge the cohesiveness of the town as a collective religious community and at the same time reinforced their own attachment

[77] ACA perg. varis, Marquès de Monistrol, 31; Reg. 43, fol. 129 r.; Reg. 62, fol. 147 v.; ACB 4–2–54; 4–3–130.
[78] ACB 4–3–242.   [79] ACB 1–2–602.
[80] See, for instance, the dispute over burial between Santa Anna and Sant Eulàlia del Camp in 1267, ADB, perg. Santa Anna, Carp. 2b, 541, or that between the canons and Santa Eulàlia del Camp in 1195, ACB LA I, fol. 123, Mas XII, no. 2262.

to the local parish. The religious allegiances taking shape around 1200 therefore were not carry-overs of ancient parish loyalties but expressions of a new civic identity.

As charitable institutions and religious houses proliferated after 1200, testators fragmented their bequests in order to support pious works of the urban clergy as a whole, even though larger donations sometimes went to favored institutions. In response to these multiple obligations, the number of individual pious legacies mushroomed and the total amount of money left for *pro anima* bequests increased sharply. On average testators made only four donations to churches in the first half of the twelfth century, but from 1220 to 1290 the number rose to ten. During the same period the value of donations more than doubled. By splitting their legacies into a myriad of pious donations, the residents of Barcelona confirmed the religious unity of the city through their shotgun aim at salvation. The dispersal of pious legacies so characteristic of thirteenth-century wills expressed a new sense of place, an interest in projecting good works throughout the urban community rather than concentrating upon two or three favored churches or monasteries as burghers had done in the past. The vision of an extended, diffuse but distinctively urban spiritual space seems less a symptom of religious indifference on the part of hard-headed entrepreneurs and merchants or a perceived inability of specific donations to direct the soul's journey through the afterlife (suggestions recently put forward to explain patterns of pious donations in Siena[81]) than an expression of the unity of civic life. Yet just as testators both rich and poor acknowledged the devotional life of Barcelona as a whole, patricians became increasingly concerned with marking off a place of distinction among the dead for their ancestors and kin.

The well-to-do became obsessed with the disposition of their final remains and funerary rites. During the twelfth century, only slightly more than half the testators specified their place of burial; after 1200, virtually every will included the place of interment at the head of the list of arrangements for the afterlife and contained detailed provisions for the church that accepted the corpse to receive the largest donations. While artisans and modest shopkeepers might be content with leaving their bodies along with a few solidi to Santa Maria del Pi, the parish church in the poor

---

[81] Cohn, *Death and property*, 67–68.

western suburbs, patricians preferred distinctive tombs placed beneath a vault (*volta*) at the cathedral, the Franciscan or Dominican house, Santa Anna of the Order of the Holy Sepulcher, or Santa Maria del Mar, the suddenly fashionable church near the bustling Ribera. Some wished to join parents or children in the tomb. Guillem Dionís, the last of a prominent twelfth-century family, was the first Barcelonan to request burial among his relatives in 1197, but the practice soon spread.[82] Provisions were even made for disinterring relatives at considerable expense in order to bring them to the city. Although choosing her own burial place with the nuns of Sant Pere de les Puel·les, the sister of Arnau Bou arranged to have her father's bones brought from Olot to the Hospitaller house in Barcelona for 100s. *dublenc* from money her deceased husband had left her; Joan de Ponç was willing to spend 200s. *de tern* to have the remains of his son disentombed and translated from Girona.[83] The anonymity of the grave thus rapidly gave way after 1200 to a conscious effort to cluster kin around family tombs and urbanize the dead.

Together with clear instructions about the site of burial, during the thirteenth century the dying also sought to perpetuate the memory of themselves and their kin by connecting it to specific altars within local churches and monasteries. Perhaps the most personalized touch was the disposition of the burial shroud. Usually made from expensive purple cloth, after the funeral it would be left to cover the altar dedicated to the saint who would intervene for the deceased and his or her relatives. In a visible display linking the corpse in the tomb with the cleric steering the soul through the afterlife, Berenguer de Vic left two luxurious cloths (*purpurae*) to Sant Jaume, the parish church where he would be buried, one in which to wrap his body in the tomb and the other for the priest's robes.[84] Specific instructions for family masses and donations for perpetual altar lamps, pious acts virtually unknown before 1200, further anchored patrician houses to specific sacred spaces within local churches. By the middle decades of the thirteenth century prominent patrician houses such as the Durfort, Lacera, Adarró, Marquet and Sunyer are known to have established private chantries. Through their *ius patronatus* the

---

[82] ACB LA i, fol. 46, Mas xii, no. 2293: "iuxta parentes meos sepleiar." Cf. ACB 4-1-62; 4-6-25; 4-8-29.

[83] ACA perg. varis, Marquès de Monistrol, 31; ACB 4-10-46.

[84] ADB perg. Santa Anna, Carp. de la creu, unnumb. parch. [13 xii 1277].

founders and their descendants retained the right to install the priests their donations supported in order to say masses for "the entire line" (*de genere suo*).[85] Because these centers of family devotion and commemoration required descendants to protect and maintain endowments, they engaged family members in a common, ongoing undertaking that reinforced links to ancestors. It is precisely in regard to the preservation of pious endowments that concern for the *parentela*, the descent group, weighed most heavily upon the minds of Barcelona's patricians. An awareness of lineage therefore grew up in close connection with new forms of thirteenth-century devotion and intervention for the dead. Just as control within patrician houses was slowly concentrating in the hands of a single male line, close kin began giving lavish support to the tombs of their ancestors.

Yet in their concern for perpetuating family identity in the afterlife and ensuring material continuity on earth, patricians did not isolate their own bloodlines from a more general identification with urban life. Even though an emerging sense of lineage found expression in the construction and endowment of chantries, family tombs, and donations to individual altars, wealthy Barcelonans continued to make bequests to virtually all urban religious institutions. Urban religion did not become fragmented into an agglomeration of private chapels and neighborhood churches as patrician houses stabilized their power in the thirteenth century, for devotional patterns acknowledged the religious identity of the city as a whole as well as the special role of a larger kin group. In the few cases for which a series of testaments survive for the same house, preference for a single family burial site did not constrain distinguished citizens from selecting their final resting place in other urban churches. The Durfort and Grony established close ties with the cathedral and left large donations to its altars, but the remains of their members were as likely to be scattered among local churches and monasteries as found in the family tomb. While civic and lineage strategies for the afterlife are often seen as opposing forces in factious Italian towns, in Barcelona they complemented rather than divided the pious obligations of the dying.

---

[85] The earliest charter in which a patrician formally established a chantry dates from 1259, when Guillem de Lacera left a substantial donation for a new altar in the cathedral and for the priest attached to it, ADB perg. Santa Anna, Carp. 1a, 18. Indirect references, however, reveal other patricians who had founded chantries earlier, ADB perg. Santa Anna, Carp. 2a, 198, 268; ACB 1–1–498; 4–6–45.

Self-centered concerns for the fate of kin failed to push aside a general obligation to support all of the city's churches, monasteries, and hospitals. Indeed, the need to ensure family continuity together with the growing awareness of lineal descent through males seemed to radiate from the tombs of relatives into every corner of the city. As patrician houses secured their place in Barcelona, their devotion expressed itself not in a clannish aloofness but in the full integration of their lineages into the material and religious life of the city.

CONCLUSION

Traditional interpretations of the culture and social life of Mediterranean towns have stressed a deeply imbedded factionalism based on political parties or, more recently, agnatic clans. Civic values, centered on a jealous community patriotism, and pride in lineage, an inheritance of aristocratic life, supposedly stood in blatant opposition to one another. The emergence of Barcelona's patriciate, however, suggests a different pattern. As the city's distinguished citizens began to solidify their influence over the urban economy and exercise local authority with confidence in the thirteenth century, they did not carve the city up into clannish enclaves. Because patricians as a group lacked formal juridical definition and possessed only a short pedigree, they willingly received new members among their ranks through marital alliances. While toying with links to lesser nobles, the city's leading families rarely resorted to an injection of noble blood to mark them off from other wealthy and ambitious urban entrepreneurs, whose culture and background they shared. The most powerful houses were still expansive and outward-looking; they did not seal themselves into a closed network of relatives and dependents. An increased awareness of lineal descent, expressed in both the internal control of patrician households and in religious patronage, had to accommodate the devolution of family resources to both men and women. While exhibiting greater respect for male ancestors, patricians also connected the status of their houses with daughters, to whom they granted larger dowries than ever before. A heightened lineage awareness overlay older, deeply imbedded cognatic structures but did eliminate them. Rather than hardening into rigid institutions, both kinship and marriage systems reacted to changes brought about through economic growth and the consolidation of patrician houses in the thirteenth century by fostering a heightened self-awareness of individual families yet promoting the cooperation and stability of the patriciate.[86] Ties of blood and marriage could operate at different levels simultaneously, often resisting and even undercutting each other, for they permitted a cultural identification with patrilineages but at the same time spread wealth among a broad array of influential houses to ensure the continuity of the patriciate as a whole. This pattern was reproduced for generations to come: it helped ensure that Barcelona's patriciate would not face extinction as a result of cultural or political ossification.[87]

Lineage identity therefore appears weak and uncertain in Barcelona, but patricians came to share a culture oriented toward law, a practical latinity, and a threatening, dynamic maritime world. Barcelona's patricians did not come to dominate the Catalan Mediterranean by imperiously commanding its maritime resources from their comfortable houses on the Ribera. Rather, they plunged willingly into the vibrant, competitive colonial societies and merchant outposts that dotted the sea. Urban and aristocratic tastes intersected not so much in the delicate, controlled environment of royal courts but on the docks at Palma de Majorca, Montpellier, and Palermo, or in the sun-bathed *fanādiq* at Tunis and Bougie. The great families of Barcelona learned to command ships and resources, not castles and courts. Yet this would eventually provide enough status to demand a form of recognition until then reserved for the nobility. Even though Barcelona's distinguished families lacked a distinctive honorific attached to their name, by the mid-thirteenth century it became common to address their members as lord and lady, *dominus* and *domina*.

---

[86] Lansing, *Florentine magnates*, 35–37 has recently stressed the structural relativity and reactive nature of lineage organization in thirteenth-century Florence.

[87] James S. Amelang, *Honored citizens of Barcelona: patrician culture and class relations, 1490–1714* (Princeton, 1986), 85–101 has also emphasized the fluid outlines of the patriciate in the early modern period.

CONCLUSION

The early growth of Barcelona and the formation of its patriciate form a small part of a much larger theme: the economic take-off of the West. While there can be little doubt that towns prospered and expanded in conjunction with a spectacular long-term rise in agricultural productivity after the millennium, situating urban communities within the broad advance of material culture has proven a particularly elusive problem in recent historiography. Once regarded as economic innovators dominated by a commercial bourgeoisie, medieval towns now have assumed many of the social characteristics of the rural world that surrounded them and supplied their food, revenues, and capital. As what to earlier generations appeared a gaping chasm separating feudal and bourgeois has narrowed, the distinctiveness of early urban societies has diminished. To speak of the "birth" of medieval towns, or in the Mediterranean, a region of ancient civic life, of their "rebirth" has an anachronistic ring, since the metaphor implies the emergence of an autonomous, clearly distinguished social and political entity.[1] If abstract definitions of the town have been put to rest, alongside them lies the stark town–country dichotomy so central to classical theories of political economy from Adam Smith to Karl Marx. As a result, recent scholarship has emphasized the rural dimensions apparent in medieval urban economies and societies to such an extent that it threatens to obliterate the distinction between town and country. With its splendid documentation Barcelona has offered the opportunity to reconsider problems connected to the emergence of early urban communities and the formation of a leading group within the town as it assumed a self-conscious urban identity.

The preceding study has sought to present the emergence of Barcelona not in terms of a radical break with the dominant forms

[1] Ward-Perkins, "Towns of northern Italy," 16–17.

of power within Catalan society but as an appropriation of lordship by a new group of families in the city. The particular form this transfer assumed defined the character of the city's medieval patriciate. This does not imply, however, that the leading urban houses merely adopted styles of command and authority from the aristocratic world around them, nor that Barcelona as a community was assimilated into the rural, seigniorial structures which encased it.[2] Because traditional historiography has made medieval urban identity contingent upon a categorical rejection of feudal society, it has chosen to dismiss as inconsequential ongoing relationships between bourgeois families and urban lords since the latter are deemed to be external to the independent world of the town. Yet the collaboration of Barcelona's ascendant families with the count-kings through finance, officeholding, and naval ventures proved critical in establishing the identity of the patriciate, which thereby provided the community as a whole with leadership to promote its interests. Through a series of choices relating to economic concerns, the cooperative exercise of local power, and the degree of participation in larger territorial enterprises, patricians traced out a common set of strategies that gradually made the town an autonomous unit within a feudal regime but at the same time a close ally of that regime.[3] Although not a revolutionary group, Barcelona's patrician houses nevertheless articulated a new form of leadership that would reproduce their power and thereby establish a coherent, assertive role for the city within the framework of the Crown of Aragon.

Part of the difficulty in traditional accounts of early urban growth derives from a simplistic identification of a city's mature patriciate with the social elements that stood in the forefront of the early phase of development. By uncovering the first references to merchants, agricultural entrepreneurs, shipowners, and artisans, historians have often contented themselves with isolating individual families based on their economic activity and tracing their rise, usually presented as a triumph over the resistance offered by

[2] Hilton, *English and French towns*, 152 sensibly challenges recent interpretations that overemphasize the rural nature of medieval towns, even in respect to the small market towns he stresses.

[3] For views about the collaboration of towns with feudal regimes, see Barel, *Ville médiévale*, 155–62; Jacques Le Goff, "Ludwig IX. und der Ursprung der feudalen Monarchie in Frankreich," *Jahrbuch für Geschichte des Feudalismus*, 14 (1990), 112–13; Hilton, *English and French towns*, 32–52.

threatened secular or ecclesiastical lords. The internal relationships among the leading families of urban notables and the place of towns in a wider struggle for lordship have received considerably less attention. In Barcelona, the first phase of urban expansion that began just before the year 1000 did not lead directly to the formation of an urban patriciate. During the eleventh century the city not only remained closely tied to its immediate hinterland but also formed part of a much wider, regional society focused on the counts and bishops of Barcelona. Its prosperity depended on the conjunction of a local market-oriented agriculture and a tributary, frontier economy driven by the success of Catalan arms in extending an extortionate protectorate over the petty princes of al-Andalus. Urban agricultural entrepreneurs and upland aristocrats therefore mixed easily in the small, thriving community growing up within the ancient Roman ramparts and slowly spreading out below the walls. In a study of two mountain valleys near Lucca and Arezzo, Chris Wickham has argued that rural aristocracies were already oriented toward their regional towns as early as the eighth century; long before urban economies in Tuscany began to expand to dominate their *contadi*, the social and political role of towns fostered territorial cohesion.[4] Because the raid of al-Manṣūr destroyed Barcelona's records before 985, it is impossible to see quite so far back in the history of the Catalan capital, but a similar relationship between the town and its region existed in the eleventh century. But the interests of local notables were not exclusively urban. As a result, a compact, coherent group of leading burghers did not emerge to create a corporate identity promoting municipal autonomy and projecting the city's influence into the interior. Eleventh-century Barcelona therefore shared a typical Mediterranean legacy from the early Middle Ages as the focus of a broad territorial identity.

The question of continuity between Roman and medieval towns has long intrigued historians and provided one of the foundations for constructing the model of the Mediterranean town. Because towns had such deep and strong roots in the South, Ennen argued that the old *civitates* retained their unity, attracted elites from the countryside, and went on to govern substantial territories around them. The Italian city-state thereby becomes the bench mark of a distinctively Mediterranean urban experience

[4] C. J. Wickham, *The mountains and the city: the Tuscan Appennines in the early Middle Ages* (Oxford, 1988), 129–36, 334–35, 353–57.

which drew its strength from the ancient Roman subsoil, while towns in the North had to carve out autonomous spheres of influence within territorial states or principalities.[5] While administrative, religious, and public functions may have lingered to varying degrees in the towns of Italy and southern Frankland during the early Middle Ages, the demographic and material transformation of the West after 1000 and the attendant struggle over power and lordship reworked whatever ancient traditions that remained into distinctively new forms.

The reanimation of urban life in the Latin Mediterranean must be set in the context of a broad restructuring of power that created feudal society. Old Roman towns, after all, possessed a dominantly political function. Their economies had depended upon a drain of revenues and surpluses from the surrounding territories and a restricted craft sector to cater to the needs of counts, clerics, and aristocrats; trade was encased within a tributary system of exchange determined by political organization.[6] The collapse of an older territorial order in the eleventh century set in motion a struggle for power at every level of European society and at the same time unleashed competition to control the new wealth that increased agricultural production, markets, and monetarized exchange offered; the urban revival was therefore not a rejection of feudal society but part of its emergence. The very dynamism of the urban economy made it an attractive prize, but neither lords nor ascendant groups within towns found it easy to control and exploit. During the eleventh and twelfth century counts, viscounts, bishops, abbots, magnates, knights, and wealthy burghers vied to tax, judge, and defend the urban population, which gradually assumed a sense of community in the course of these struggles. The strength of local aristocracies, the extent of episcopal authority, the collaboration of prominent burghers with their lords, and the ability of sovereign authority to resist and restructure the challenges to public order all shaped the vibrant towns that grew up in the ruins of ancient Roman monuments. These social elements fused in a myriad of combinations once urban institutions and social structures began to crystallize and provide solid foundations for Mediterranean towns as they gained self-confidence in the thirteenth century. Even if one can point abstractly to Roman precedents for individual elements within

[5] Ennen, "Les Différents types" 398–402.
[6] Bois, *Transformation of the year 1000*, 78–80.

the maturing urban societies of the eleventh and twelfth century, the global transformations of power and economic organization both rural and urban created completely new contexts for towns in the South. Struggles over lordship and autonomy did not have a single outcome, however, but varied according to region and local social structures. In Provence and Languedoc, knights and petty nobles tended to fragment towns into separate zones of authority until the brutal imposition of sovereign power by the Capetians; in Tuscany and Lombardy, towns attracted aristocratic clans and thereby increased their influence over the surrounding territory; in Aragon and Castile, civic militias helped control a threatening frontier with the monarchy's support, and in Catalonia, urban notables through finance and administration strongly identified themselves with the interests of their sovereign.[7] Each of these solutions created quite distinct styles of urban societies. When placed within a comparative framework, this study suggests that an ideal type of Mediterranean town drastically oversimplifies the revival of urban life in the Latin Mediterranean and the social structures that grew from it. Rather than judge renascent towns of the South according to a single model, which emerged to illustrate why Northern European towns supposedly represented the "purest" form of medieval urbanism, it may be best to locate them on a scale calibrated to measure a number of factors: the degree of social cohesion, ranging from the cooperation of urban notables in Barcelona or Venice to their polarization at Genoa; relationships of the town to sovereign, public authority, which gained strength over time in Catalonia but disappeared in Lombardy and Tuscany; and the influence and style of urban aristocracies, which could set the pattern of public life in Pisa or Florence but lost ground in Barcelona. Whatever might have survived from a common Roman heritage in the tenth century, it was the forces unleashed during the next two centuries of economic expansion, demographic growth, and institutional transformation that left their imprint on the revived and expansive towns of the Latin Mediterranean.

Throughout Catalonia, the surge of economic productivity

---

[7] For recent comparative assessments of the urban revival in the Mediterranean, see Fossier, *Enfance*, II, 980–1010; Barel, *Ville médiévale*, 32–40; Hilton, *English and French towns*, 87–90; José Maria Font Rius, "Un problème de rapports: gouvernements urbains en France et en Catalogne (XIIe et XIIIe siècles)," *AM*, 66 (1957), 293–306 [repr. in *Estudis sobre els drets*, 599–610]; Wolff, "Barcelone et Toulouse," 586–92.

beginning to build even before the new millennium eventually overwhelmed the stability of the traditional territorial order. Competition to control new forms of wealth created profound social tensions, which erupted into violence during the "feudal crisis" from 1040 to 1060. While there can be little doubt about the gravity of the crisis, it required generations to determine its long-term impact. Based on Duby's influential work on the Mâconnais, French regional studies have stressed the rapid formation of small seigniorial cells controlled by aristocratic houses in response to the collapse of early medieval societies and their Carolingian foundations; this rapid, even revolutionary transformation created feudal Europe. The eleventh century has gained a reputation for innovation and imagination; the twelfth for normalization and secure growth.[8] Following this model, Bonnassie has proposed that Catalan society quickly regained its stability after 1060 by organizing itself around a self-confident and expanded nobility, castleholding, and banal lordship; the region would advance on a steady institutional and economic trajectory during the twelfth century.[9] In Barcelona, however, this did not come to pass. The reassertion of comital power, based on the reinforcement of effective public authority and administration, and the reversal of frontier successes brought about a gradual restructuring of local lordship. Once the comital dynasty had quelled the insurrection touched off by the viscount of Barcelona and his kin in the early 1040s, another century was required to dislodge this powerful aristocratic family from the city and exert control over the comital administrators who replaced the viscounts. As a result, the ties of the rural aristocracy to Barcelona were severed. The crucial stage in the structuring of urban society therefore came about not as a direct result of the first phase of urban growth but in a broad, drawn-out crisis of territorial lordship.

Further, the early surge of the urban economy clearly under way by 1000 did not prove sufficient to sustain growth or to trigger the creation of a vigorous commercial sector, the mainstay of the city's late medieval prosperity. From 1090 to 1140 burghers faced a period of severe economic contraction. The market-oriented agriculture promoted by urban entrepreneurs failed to

---

[8] R. I. Moore, "Duby's eleventh century," *History*, 69 (1984), 36–49; Fossier, *Enfance*, I, 289–300, 595–601; Chédeville, *Chartres*, 527–29.

[9] Bonnassie, *La Catalogne*, II, 866–70.

expand beyond the tiny urban hinterland, while aristocrats turned their attention and resources away from the city to their upland estates. At the same time a resurgent Islam stemmed the flow of Islamic gold from the dependent princes of al-Andalus into Christian coffers, sending a shock wave through the local economy. Rather than fusing to lay the foundations for a "commercial revolution," the local real estate market and the tributary economy created by war and extortion collapsed. A second phase of growth, dependent upon urban real estate development, finance, artisanal production, dynastic expansion, and commerce, began to unfold after 1140. It presented burghers with economic and social possibilities quite distinct from those of the eleventh century. Through the systematic and repeated selection of strategies in order to concentrate and exploit resources, a new group of families were emerging by the mid-twelfth century to form Barcelona's early patriciate. This new urban elite was neither simply the formalization of an older lay collectivity already in existence nor was it the inevitable product of the first surge of urban revival; rather, it embodied a new and distinctly urban identity fashioned in response to the conditions of the twelfth century. Only with the new opportunities presented by the second phase of growth would the patriciate consolidate and reproduce its power.

The struggle over lordship and the blockage of the early urban economy had two other important consequences: first, Barcelona and its leaders emerged with a weak sense of corporate identity; second, aristocratic families did not serve as the models for the organization of patrician houses. Both factors would profoundly affect the nature of the emerging patriciate.

The most spectacular manifestations of urban collective solidarity occurred when medieval towns demanded privileges or a degree of autonomy from their lords, occasionally in an armed insurrection against seigniorial authority. The emergence of an autonomous community in Barcelona, however, was painfully slow and uncertain. Although the counts of Barcelona successfully surmounted their feudal crisis, they found the task of securing their power and exploiting their resources in Barcelona, the richest part of the domain, an especially delicate matter. The truculent vicars installed in the early twelfth century to protect comital interests proved no less aggrandizing and insolent than the viscounts they replaced. Financially pressed and striving to hold their administrators to account, the early count-kings turned for support to wealthy urban financiers, who in return for their loans gained offices, valuable suburban land, and the right to exploit mills and ovens. Because the movement of power and urban resources to influential burghers occurred through a slow seepage rather than a dramatic flashflood, it did not lead to a confrontation with the town's lord. But this also meant that the early patrician houses originally did not exercise power collectively; consequently, the town did not quickly form cohesive corporate institutions nor act in the manner of a *seigneurie collective*. Instead, the count-kings intervened through patronage and financial necessity to establish internal balances among the city's leading families. In terms of autonomy and corporate identity, which to earlier generations of urban historians embodied the essence of medieval towns, Barcelona seems underdeveloped, but its patriciate nevertheless adopted a consistent strategy of cooperation within its own ranks and with its lord in order to perpetuate itself. Individual collaboration with the count-kings rather than collective defiance or factional polarization would become a trademark of Barcelona's medieval urban elite.

The difficulties of the early twelfth century also thwarted the development of an urban aristocracy, frequently considered the defining feature of Mediterranean towns. Great clannish, agnatic kin groups, whether organized as *consorterie* or patrilineages, both semi-rural and semi-urban in nature, would not dominate the social landscape of Barcelona as they did in northern Italy. As a result, Barcelona notables turned their attention away from extensive agricultural investments and inland castles toward royal finance, suburban real estate, and trade. The tiny *territorium*, not a large *contado*, would therefore provide the stage on which Barcelona's patricians would perform.

Not only did the social links to upland Catalonia dissolve with the withdrawal of noble families, but noble patrilineages did not provide the model for the internal organization of patrician houses. The history of medieval families in the twelfth and thirteenth century has concentrated almost exclusively on aristocratic households with their pronounced patrilineal organization. In Barcelona, however, older cognatic traditions and the legacy of Visigothic law in a conservative society put up strong resistance to the rise of agnatic lineages. Because all heirs continued to receive substantial portions of an inheritance, patrician houses could not ignore the interests of women and younger sons to the advantage of a single male heir. As patrician houses consolidated their position in the early thirteenth century, preference was shown to the eldest son, but this took the form of strengthening his control over the household in order to establish family identity rather than excluding his brothers and sisters from common family property. With the bulk of a woman's inheritance passing to her at the time of marriage in the form of dowry, she and her relatives exerted considerable influence over the actions of her husband. Rather than presenting an unwanted burden in a kinship system centered on males, women from Barcelona's patriciate provided a means of stabilizing relations among major houses and, through their large dowries, allowing wealth to adjust to status. Although competition among patricians houses could be intense, the flexibility encouraged by a system of diverging devolution and resilient cognatic structures prevented the bitter, simmering rivalries so typical of northern Italian towns. Thus, the family structure of Barcelona's patriciate more closely resembles the loose, bilateral organization of Ghent's leading citizens than the tightly knit lineages of Florentine magnates.[10]

By the time King Jaume I embarked on his ambitious Mediterranean conquests in 1229, Barcelona's patriciate had already gained its footing. The vast new opportunities of commerce and colonial enterprise reinforced the interlocking interests of the Crown and the leaders of the dynasty's largest, most active city. Through new resources from territorial acquisitions, commercial privilege, trade protectionism, and, after the Sicilian Vespers, special access to Sicilian grain, the count-kings rewarded patricians individually and the city as a whole for their financial and naval contributions to the expanding confederation of the Crown of Aragon. Yet Barcelona did not monopolize the commercial or the naval potential encompassed within the Crown. In contrast to Genoa or Venice, it did not intend to carve out a seaborne empire in the Western Mediterranean nor did it aspire to be a city-state within Catalonia. Instead Barcelona took a place, albeit a prominent place, within the Mediterranean federation established by the Aragonese monarchs. What is sometimes referred to as the Catalan Mediterranean empire in fact resembled a Mediterranean Hansa, based on the cooperative interdependence of cities throughout Catalonia,

[10] Nicholas, *Domestic life*, 17–32, 70–108, 181–86.

Valencia, Occitania, and the Balearics, but presided over by a dynastic umpire to regulate disputes and discourage rivalries. Barcelona offered leadership but not economic domination over the financial and commercial potential of the Crown of Aragon. As a result, its patriciate showed broad interests in naval armament and royal finance as well as in colonial administration and trade. This diversity of interests helped keep the patriciate open and flexible during Catalonia's golden age of maritime expansion. The sea itself forged a balance among aggressive barons, merchant adventurers, and urban entrepreneurs, all under the watchful eye of the House of Barcelona.

Even though medieval Barcelona did not form the center of an independent city–republic, it was as much an embodiment of Mediterranean urban life as Genoa or Venice, Milan or Florence. It drew its strength from common cultural elements found throughout the region: a deeply imbedded respect for the written word, the material remnants of a Roman civic past, and the revival of dowry as the center of its marital system. Yet all these elements fused in the twelfth and thirteenth century to create and perpetuate a distinctive style of urban life and leadership. Barcelona's patrician houses may have lacked the flamboyant wealth of their Italian counterparts, but they also knew how to make good use of the resources and opportunities they did possess. Although they lacked a firm corporate identity, this fluidity and openness allowed them to attain a remarkable degree of stability and to reach a viable balance between wealth and inherited status. Even the most ambitious and powerful patrician houses learned to exercise restraint; as a result, factional rivalries would not overwhelm municipal politics. With the exception of the fifteenth-century crisis, stability and openness would remain enduring characteristics of Barcelona's patriciate through the *ancien régime*.[11]

The Renaissance historian Francesco Guicciardini, hardly a man generous with praise for cities other than his own beloved Florence, seemed to concur with this assessment. With images of Florentine palaces in the back of his mind, Guicciardini made the following observation when he visited Barcelona in 1512: "While there do not seem to be any particularly notable or grand private residences, houses throughout the entire city are quite attractive.

[11] Amelang, *Honored citizens*, 221–22.

Its people have a saying, 'it is a city for everyone.' "[12] Yet three hundred and fifty years earlier another intrepid traveler also noted the modest but vibrant prosperity of the Catalan capital. Benjamin of Tudela, with whom we began our journey into Barcelona's medieval past, had already identified the essential character of this society in its formative period.

[12] Francesco Guicciardini, *Diario del viaggio in Spagna*, in *Ricordi, diari, memorie*, ed. M. Spinella (Rome, 1981), 132: "Non vi si vede edifici particulari molto notabili né molto eccellenti, ma universalmente le case sono belle e belle in ogni luogo della città, in modo che come dicono loro veramente, è città per tutto."

VICARS OF BARCELONA

(Complete references are given until 1260, when the royal registers begin to provide abundant information about royal officials.)

Date	Name	Reference
1094	Arbert Bernat	ACB 1–1–250.
	Berenguer Bernat	Ibid.
1101	Arbert Bernat	ACA perg. R. B. III, 67.
Before 1113	Berenguer Ramon de Castellet	*LMF*, I, no. 382.
1113	Guillem Renart	*Santa Anna*, II, no. 170; *LFM*, I, no. 382.
	Ramon Renart de La Roca	Ibid.
1114	Guillem Renart	ACB LA IV, fol. 210, Mas X, no. 1275.
1125	Berenguer Ramon	ACA perg. R. B. III, 267, 269.
1129	Berenguer Ramon	ACB LA I, fol. 103, Mas X, no. 1376.
1131	Berenguer Ramon	*CSC*, II, no. 909.
1132	Berenguer Ramon	*CSC*, II, no. 920.
1135	Berenguer Ramon	ACB 1–1–327; 1–5–97.
1137	Berenguer Ramon	ACB 1–1–368; LA I, fol. 285, Mas XI, no. 1467.
1138	Berenguer Ramon	ACB LA I, fol. 7, Mas XI, no. 1477.
1139	Berenguer Ramon	ACA perg. R. B. IV, 93; Reg. 1, fol. 6 r.; *Santa Anna*, II, no. 226; ACB LA III, fol. 196, Mas XI, no. 1494; *VL*, XVII, ap. xlix; *Llib. bl.*, no. 938; *CODIN*, IV, no. xxx.
1151	Guillem Arbert	ACA Reg. 1, fol. 6 r.
Before 1152	Pere Ricart	ACB 1–5–138.
1152	Berenguer Bernat	ACB LA I, fol. 326, Mas XI, no. 1686.
1154	Pere Arnau	Bisson, *Fiscal accounts*, I, 256.
1155	Pere Arnau	*Santa Anna*, II, no. 297.
1156	Pere Arnau	Bisson, *Fiscal accounts*, I, 256.
1157	Pere Arnau	Ibid.
1160	Guillem Català	Ibid., I, 255.
1161	Guillem Català	Ibid.
1168	Guillem Català	ACB 1–5–205.

1170	Guillem Català	Bisson, *Fiscal accounts*, I, 255.
1180	Berenguer Ramon	Ibid., I, 252.
	Berenguer Bou	Ibid., I, 251–52; ACA Reial Patrimoni, Batllia General, Classe 3ª, vol. 6, fol. 74 v.; *Santa Anna*, III, nos. 487, 488, 490.
1181	Berenguer Bou(?)	Bisson, *Fiscal accounts*, I, 251–52.
1182	Berenguer Bou(?)	Ibid.
1189	Pere d'Alfou	Ibid., I, 256.
1190	Pere d'Alfou	ADB perg. Santa Anna, Carp. de la creu, unnumb. parch. [8 vi 1190].
1191	Joan de Cascai	Bisson, *Fiscal accounts*, I, 251–52.
1193	Ermengol de Manresa (?)	Ibid., I, 254.
1194	Ermengol de Manresa (?)	ACB 1–5–353.
1195	Berenguer Bou(?)	Bisson, *Fiscal accounts*, I, 251–52.
1196	Joan de Cascai(?)	Ibid., I, 256.
	Berenguer Tició(?)	Ibid., I, 252.
1199	Pere de Medina	Ibid., I, 257.
1201	Pere de Medina	Ibid.
1202	Pere de Medina	Ibid.
	Ramon de Plegamans(?)	Ibid., I, 258.
1203	Bernat Simó	Ibid., I, 253.
1204	Bernat Simó	ACB 1–2–1614(b).
1205	Pere de Medina	Bisson, *Fiscal accounts*, I, 257.
	Guillem de Mediona(?)	Ibid., I, 256.
1208	Berenguer Sunyer	Ibid., I, 252.
1209	Ramon de Plegamans	Ibid., I, 258.
1210	Ramon de Plegamans	Ibid.; ACB 4–1–76.
1211	Berenguer Sunyer(?)	Bisson, *Fiscal accounts*, I, 252.
1212	Berenguer Sunyer	Ibid.; ADB perg. Santa Anna, Carp. de la creu, unnumb. parch. [1 x 1211].
1213	Berenguer Sunyer	ACB LA III, fol. 68, Mas XII, no. 2509.
1214	Arnau Ombau	ACB LA III, fol. 68, Mas XII, no. 2559.
1215	Arnau Ombau	ACB 1–6–2595; 4–43–52; LA IV, fol. 214, Mas XII, no. 2579; ADB perg. Santa Anna, Carp. 8, 63.
1217	Arnau Ombau	ACB 3–32–15.
Before 1218	Guillem Sunyer	ACB 1–6–859.
1218	Ramon de Plegamans	Ibid.
1219	Berenguer Sunyer	ACB 1–6–1219.
	Ramon de Plegamans	Bisson, *Fiscal accounts*, I, 258.
1220	Bernat Borotí	Bisson, "Las finanzas," no. 5.
1221	Bernat Borotí	ACA perg. Jaume I, 175.
1223	Bernat Eimeric	ACA perg. Jaume I, 209.
1224	Pere de Vic	ACB LA I, fol. 385, Mas XII, no. 2610.
1225	Berenguer Burget	ADB perg. Santa Anna, Carp. 1a, 4–12; ACA perg. Jaume I, 260; *CSC* III, no. 1300.

1227	Berenguer Burget	ACB 1–6–1694; ACA perg. varis, Marquès de Monistrol, 42.
1228	Berenguer Burget	ACB 1–6–463, 3823; ADB perg. Santa Anna, Carp. 2a, 115; ACA perg. varis, Marquès de Monistrol, 42.
1230	Marimon de Plegamans	ACB 4–50–544.
1231	Marimon de Plegamans	ACB 1–6–262; 4–29–39; ACA perg. Jaume I, 428; ADB perg. Santa Anna, Carp. 2a, 133.
	Romeu Durfort	ADB perg. Santa Anna, Carp. 2a, 115.
Before 1232	Arnau de Sanaüja	ACA perg. varis, Marquès de Monistrol, 57.
1232	Romeu Durfort	ACB 1–1–1489.
1234	Romeu Durfort	ACB 1–6–2268; ACA perg. Jaume I, 520; *CSC*, III, no. 1327.
1235	Marimon de Plegamans	ACA perg. Jaume I, 648; ACB 4–43–521.
1236	Marimon de Plegamans	ACB 1–6–1283, 1604.
1237	Marimon de Plegamans	ACB 1–1–1425.
1239	Marimon de Plegamans	ACB 1–2–1656.
1240	Marimon de Plegamans	ACB 1–6–3725; 4–43–482; *CSC*, III, no. 1263.
	Pere Ferrer	ACA Cartes Reials, caixa 2, extrasèrie, 65.
1241	Pere Ferrer	Ibid.; ADB perg. Santa Anna, Carp. 1a, 1–57.
	Marimon de Plegamans	ACB 1–6–3725.
1242	Joan de Centelles	ACB 1–6–2165; ACA perg. varis, Sentmenat, Indice 8, III, 7.
1244	Joan de Centelles	ACB 1–6–2524; 4–50–515.
1245	Joan de Centelles	ACB 1–6–1466, 3750; 4–42–378.
	Romeu de Marimon	ACB 1–6–1411.
1246	Joan de Centelles	ACB 4–42–378.
1247	Pere de Castellasol	ACB 1–6–1473.
1251	Pere de Castellasol	ACB 1–6–243, 2379; 4–42–3476. ACA perg. varis, Marquès de Monistrol, 102.
	Romeu de Marimon	ACA perg. varis, Marquès de Monistrol, 101.
1252	Jaume Grony	ADB perg. Santa Anna, Carp. de la creu, unnumb. parch. (transcription of document dated 19 xii 1225).
	Ferrer Guerau	ACB 4–30–158.
1257	Guillem Grony	ADB perg. Santa Anna, Carp. 1a, 2–16.
	Pere de Castellasol	ACB 4–43–524.
1258	Pere de Castellasol	ACA Reg. 10, fol. 32 r.; ACB 4–42–348, 4–43–525.

1259	Pere de Castellasol	ACB 1–6–2379, 4106. ADB perg.
		Santa Anna, Carp. 1a, 2–20.
1260	Pere de Castellasol	ACB 1–6–1173; 3–29–216.
	Jaume Grony	ACA Reg. 11, fol. 186 r.
1262	Guillem de Torrelles	ACA perg. Jaume I, 1722.
	Jaume Grony	ACB 1–6–4032.
	Benvenist de Castellasol	ACB 1–6–2677.
1263	Guillem de Torrelles	ACB 4–51–710.
1264	Guillem de Torrelles	ACA Reg. 13, fol. 155 r.
	Guillem Grony	ACA Reg. 14, 17 v.
1265	Guillem Grony	ACA Reg. 13, fol. 289 r.
1266	Ferrer Mallol	ACB 1–6–3875.
1267	Ferrer Mallol	ACA Reg. 15, fol. 25 v.
1269	Ferrer Mallol	ACA Reg. 35, fol. 1 v.
1270	Guillem Durfort	ACA Reg. 37, fol. 3 v.
1271	Guillem Durfort	ACA Reg. 14, fol. 117 v.
1272	Guillem Durfort	ACA Reg. 21, fol. 54 v.
1273	Guillem Durfort	ACA Reg. 19, fol. 50 r.
1274	Guillem Durfort	ACA Reg. 22, fol. 7 r.
	Ferrer Mallol	ACA Reg. 20, fol. 199 r.
1275	Ferrer Mallol	ACA Reg. 37, fol. 80 v.
	Romeu de Marimon	*CODIN*, vi, no. liii.
1276	Ferrer Mallol	ACA Reg. 38, fol. 61 r.
1277	Ferrer Mallol	ACA Reg. 39, fol. 183 r.
1278	Ferrer Mallol	ACA Reg. 40, fol. 72 r.
1279	Ferrer Mallol	ACA Reg. 41, fol. 38 r.
	Gombau de Benvenist	ACA Reg. 41, fol. 96 r.
1280	Ferrer Mallol	ACA Reg. 42, fol. 205 v.
	Gombau de Benvenist	ACB 1–6–2712.
1281	Gombau de Benvenist	ACA Reg. 49, fol. 19 r.
1282	Gombau de Benvenist	ACA Reg. 50, fol. 243 v.
1283	Gombau de Benvenist	ACA Reg. 60, fol. 32 r.
	Bernat de Riera	ACA Reg. 44, fol. 241 v.
1284	Bernat de Riera	ACB 4–32–625.
	Bernat de Peratallada	ACA Reg. 62, fol. 102 v.
1285	Bernat de Peratallada	ACA Reg. 62, fol. 113 r.
	Antic Titó	ACB 1–6–4099.
	Romeu de Marimon	ACA Reg. 65, fol. 2 v.
1286	Romeu de Marimon	ACA Reg. 66, fol. 24 v.
	Bernat de Peratallada	ACA Reg. 66, fols. 25 v.–26 r.
	Antic Titó	ACA Reg. 74, fol. 26 v.
1287	Guillem de Calders	ACA Reg. 75, fol. 40 r.
	Romeu de Marimon	ACA Reg. 74, fol. 26 v.
1288	Guillem de Calders	ACA Reg. 79, fol. 11 r.
	Berenguer de Claperes	ADB perg. Santa Anna, Carp. 2a, 282.
1289	Guillem de Calders	ACB 1–6–4046.
1290	Guillem de Cort	ACB 1–6–3789.
1291	Romeu de Marimon	ACA Reg. 86, fol. 15 v.

Appendix 2

BAILIFFS OF BARCELONA

(Complete references are given until 1260, when the royal registers begin to provide abundant information about royal officials.)

Date	Name	Reference
1179	Vives	Bisson, *Fiscal accounts*, I, 277.
	Perfet	Ibid., I, 270–71.
1180	Perfet	Ibid.
1181	Llobell	Ibid., I, 269.
1183	Llobell	Ibid.
1184	Llobell	Ibid.
1185	Llobell	Ibid.
1188	Llobell	Ibid.
1190	Roig	Ibid., I, 276.
1191	Roig	Ibid.
1192	Roig	Ibid.; *Santa Anna*, III, no. 574.
1193	Roig	Bisson, *Fiscal Accounts*, I, 276.
1199	Perfet	Ibid., I, 270–71.
1200	Perfet	Ibid.
1203	Perfet	Ibid.
1204	Perfet	Ibid.
1205	Perfet	Ibid.
1207	Perfet	Ibid.
	Durfort d'Espiells	Ibid., I, 264–65.
1208	Durfort d'Espiells	Ibid.
1209	Durfort d'Espiells	Ibid.
1211	Durfort d'Espiells	Ibid.
	Perfet	Ibid., I, 270–71.
1213	Perfet	Ibid.
	Durfort d'Espiells	Ibid., I, 264–65.
1215	Perfet	Ibid., I, 270–71.
	Roig(?)	Ibid., I, 276.
1216	Ramon de Font(?)	ACB 1–6–2249.
	Perfet	ACB 3–35–53.
1217	Perfet	Bisson, *Fiscal accounts*, I, 270–71.
1218	Perfet	Ibid.
1222	Durfort d'Espiells	Ibid., I, 264–65. ACB 4–33–240.

1223	Durfort d'Espiells	ACB 1–6–332; ACA perg. varis, Marquès de Monistrol, 30.
1224	Perfet	Bisson, *Fiscal accounts*, I, 270–71.
1225	Perfet	Ibid.
1226	Perfet	Ibid.
	Durfort d'Espiells(?)	Ibid., I, 264–65.
1227	Bernat Durfort	Bofarull i Sans, "Jaime I y los judíos," no. ii.
1228	Bernat Durfort	ACB 1–1–1763, 1601.
1229	Berenguer Durfort	ACA perg. varis, Marquès de Monistrol, 48.
1231	Guillem de Lacera	ACA perg. Jaume I, 442; perg. extrainv., 3688.
1233	Salamó Bonafos	ACA perg. Jaume I, 499.
1234	Salamó Bonafos	ACA perg. Jaume I, 520, 522; ADB perg. Santa Anna, Carp. 2a, 154.
1236	Guillem Ferrer	ACB 4–33–759.
1237	Romeu Durfort	ACA perg. Jaume I, 711.
1240	Romeu Durfort	Huici–Cabanes, *Documentos*, II, no. 317.
1243	Salamó Bonafos	Bofarull i Sans, "Jaime I y los judíos," no. iv.
1244	Ferrer Alemany	ACB 1–6–1617; ADB perg. Santa Anna, Carp. 1, 85.
1246	Joan Dorca	Arxiu de Santa Maria del Pi, perg. vells, 56; ACB 4–42–578.
1247	Vital Salamó	ACA perg. Jaume I, 1079, 1090.
1248	Vital Salamó	ACA perg. Jaume I, 1120.
1249	Vital Salamó	ACA perg. Jaume I, 1155, 1156.
1250	Vital Salamó	ACA perg. Jaume I, 1186, 1190.
1252	Pere de Castellasol	ACA perg. Jaume I, 1292.
1253	Pere de Castellasol	ACA perg. Jaume I, 1322, 1340.
1254	Pere de Castellasol	ACA perg. Jaume I, 1367; ACB 1–6–3339.
1255	Pere de Castellasol	ACB 1–6–2193; ACA Reial Patrimoni, Batllia General, Classe 3ª, vol. 6, fol. 74 v.; Capmany, II, doc. 12.
1257	Benevist de Porta	ACA Reg. 10, fol. 16 r.
1258	Benevist de Porta	ACA perg. Jaume I, 1525; Reg. 10, fol. 84 r.–v.
1259	Benevist de Porta	ACA perg. Jaume I, 1563; ACB 4–51–711.
1260	Benevist de Porta	ACA perg. Jaume I, 1605.
	Guillem Grony	Garcia-Madurell, *Comandas comerciales*, no. 12.
1261	Guillem Grony	ACB 1–6–1353.

1262	Benevist de Porta	ACA Reg. 12, fol. 53 r.
	Guillem Grony	Ibid.
1263	Benevist de Porta	ACA Reg. 12, fol. 29 v.
	Guillem Grony	ACA Reg. 14, fol. 44 v.
1264	Benevist de Porta	ACA Reg. 13, fol. 237 v.
	Guillem Grony	Ibid.
1265	Guillem Grony	ACA Reg. 13, fol. 289 r.
1266	Guillem Grony	ACA Reg. 15, fol. 10 v.
1267	Benevist de Porta	ACA Reg. 15, fol. 73 r.
	Guillem Grony	ACA Reg. 15, fol. 53 r.
1268	Guillem Grony	ACA Reg. 28, fol. 32 r.
1269	Guillem Grony	ACA Reg. 16, fol. 164 v.
	Ferrer Mallol	ACA Reg. 35, fol. 1 v.
1270	Guillem Grony	ACA perg. Jaume I, 2015.
1271	Guillem Grony	ACA Reg. 35, fol. 60 r.
1272	Guillem Grony	ACA Reg. 21, fol. 54 v.
1273	Guillem Grony	ACA Reg. 19, fols. 1 v.–3 v.
1274	Guillem Grony	ACA Reg. 19, fol. 177 v.
	Esteve de Cardona	ACB 1–6–4139.
1275	Esteve de Cardona	ACA Reg. 20, fol. 196 r.
	Antic Titó	ACA Reg. 20, fol. 214 r.
	Pere Carbonell	ACB 3–29–249.
1276	Antic Titó	ACA Reg. 20, fol. 339 v.
	Ramon Romeu	ACA Reg. 39, fol. 186 v.
1278	Guillem d'Espiells	ACA Reg. 40, fol. 85 r.
1279	Guillem d'Espiells	ACA Reg. 41, fol. 71 v.
1280	Guillem d'Espiells	ACA Reg. 44, fol. 177 r.
1281	Guillem d'Espiells	ACA Reg. 50, fol. 152 r.
1282	Guillem d'Espiells	ACB 4–30–178.
1283	Guillem d'Espiells	ACA Reg. 59, fol. 191 r.
1284	Guillem d'Espiells	ACA Reg. 43, fol. 52 r.
1285	R. Alemany	ACA Reg. 58, fol. 17 v.
1287	Berenguer de Conques	ACA Reg. 75, fol. 1 r.
1288	Galceran de Noguera	ACA Reg. 78, fol. 2 v.
1289	Pere de Sant Clement	ACA Reg. 78, fol. 27 r.
1291	Bartomeu de Vilafranca	ACA Reg. 86, fol. 2 v.

Appendix 3

COINAGES AND EXCHANGE VALUES

Monetary conversions during the twelfth and thirteenth century in Catalonia raise special problems since both gold and silver coins were in circulation. Characteristic of Catalonia was the use of the solidus as a money of account rather than the pound (1 lb. = 20s.). Originally the solidus of Barcelona was both a coin and a money of account, but by the eleventh century only denars and obols were actually minted. Both the silver content and the weight of the denar fell in the tenth and early eleventh century, but from the reign of Ramon Berenguer I (1035–76) until the institution of a slightly debased quaternal coinage (four parts fine, 44s. to the mark) c. 1174, the denar remained relatively stable in value.[1] King Alfons I's quaternal coinage was cited at 1 mbt. = 7s., while the older coinage was valued at 1 mbt. = 6.1s., although sometimes slightly higher equivalences are given. Since no new coinage was issued between the mid–eleventh century and Alfons' reformed coinage, the conversion used is 1 old s. = 1.15 quaternal s. Except for a brief and unsuccessful attempt to institute a debased coin known as the *bossonaya* by King Pere I in 1209 and 1213, the quaternal coinage remained in circulation until 1222, when King Jaume I issued a new denar known as the *dublenc* (2 parts fine, 88s. to the mark). In 1258 the king issued a stronger ternal coinage (three parts fine), which remained the stable money of Barcelona in the later Middle Ages. The equivalences are therefore 1 quaternal s. = 2 *dublenc* s. = 1.33 ternal s. Unless otherwise noted, figures presented in charts or graphs are converted to the quaternal solidus of Alfons I.

Of Islamic origin, gold coins are cited by dinars and ounces of gold, but their wide use in Catalonia quickly made the population familiar with their exchange value for silver. Charters therefore often mention an equivalence in silver coinage. Until 1056, the mancus from Islamic Spain and its imitation minted in Barcelona were the equivalent of the classical dinar at 7 to the ounce of gold.[2] In 1056 a new mancus at 10 to the ounce (*de decem in untia*) was struck at Barcelona, and from 1070 an even lighter mancus at 14 to the ounce (*de quatrodecem in untia*). A highly debased mancus from Valencia, sometimes referred to as the *mancuso rovall*, entered Barcelona c. 1082; 4 ounces of Valencian gold were equal to 1 old ounce of Cordovan gold. Thus, by the late

---

[1] A useful summary of the changes in weight and silver content based on an extensive examination of the surviving coins is found in Balaguer, "Statutes," 126. On the quarternal coinage, see Bisson, *Conservation*, 76–77.

[2] On the chronology of the different issues of gold coinage, Bonnassie, *La Catalogne*, II, 898–99; Botet y Sisó, *Les monedes catalanes*, I, 25–70.

Ounces of Cordovan gold	Ounces of Valencian gold	Mancus of Cordova	Mancus of Barcelona (*ad decem*)	Mancus of Barcelona (*ad quatrodecem*)	Mancus of Valencia	Morabetin	Solidus de plata	Solidus
1	4	7	10	14	28	8	14	49
	1	1.75	2.5	3.5	7	2	3.5	12.5
		1	1.4	2	4	1.1	2	7.0
			1	1.4	2.8	0.8	1.4	5.0
				1	2	0.55	1	3.5
					1	0.28	.5	1.8
						1	1.75	6.1
							1	3.5

eleventh century, four different types of mancus had been struck, but the charters usually distinguish among them. According to article 141 of the *Usatges*, "Solidus aureus," which must certainly date from the early twelfth century because of its concern for the morabetin, 100 ounces of Valencian gold was worth 200 mbts., or 1 mbt. = 3.5 mancus *rovall*. Despite the normative nature of the text, charter evidence confirms its accuracy. Placing the morabetin in the conversion chart above gives it a value of 6.1s.; a rare early reference in a charter from 1131 citing the direct equivalence of the morabetin to silver coinage sets its value at 6.15s., thereby offering independent corroboration from the exchange value established in the *Usatges*.[3] The equivalences of the various types of gold coinage in circulation are summarized in the above table.

In addition to silver coinages of Barcelona, the mancus, and the morabetin, several other currencies occasionally appear in the sources, although they are of minor importance in statistical analysis. A morabetin of account, or morabetin *mercader*, was sometimes used in the twelfth century; its value was set at 5 old s. The mazmudina, a double dinar originally issued by the Almohads, contined to be minted in Granada and was copied by Castilian kings from Fernando III (1217–52) onward. Ḥafṣid bezants appear sporadically in commercial contracts with North Africa and are valued at 4.9 ternal s. in 1263;[4] the old bezant of Alexandria was cited at 14.3 s. in 1277.[5] A rare equivalence between the silver coinages of Melgueil and Barcelona appears in 1257, when 1 s. Melgueil = 1.7s. *dublenc*.[6]

---

[3] ACB 1–5–71: ".l.xxx. s. denarii Barchinone et si ipsa moneta mutaverit vel minuerit .x.iii. mbts. bonos."

[4] ACB 1–6–308, 2382. On equivalences with North African gold coinages, see Peter Spufford, *Handbook of medieval exchange* (London, 1986), 309–12.

[5] Garcia-Madurell, *Comandas comerciales*, no. 41. Cf. Spufford, *Handbook*, 307.

[6] ACA Reg. 10, fol. 29 v.

Appendix 4

SELECT DOCUMENTS

Doc. 1
[c. 1150][1]

Arnau de Font, bailiff of Berenguer de Barcelona, commands a list to be made up specifying the share of Barcelona's commercial tolls owed to him and to Bonjudà, Saltell, Bonfe, and Rancaios and the share owed to the king.

    A. Original parchment. 265 x 303 mm. AHCB perg., Carp. 1, unnumb. parch.[2]

    a. Published by Jaume Sobrequés i Callicó and Sebastià Riera i Viader, "La lleuda de Barcelona del segle XII," *Misel·lània Aramon i Serra. Estudis de llengua i literatura catalana offerts a R. Aramon i Serra en el seu setantè aniversari* (Barcelona, 1984), IV, 340–41.

    Ego Arnallus de ipsa Fonte baiulus Berengarii de Barchinona feci scribi eximenta ville et partiones sicut vidi per duos annos in vita Boniiude deinde in vita*ᵃ* et Saltelli et Bonefidei et Rancaiosi. Primum mercator qui exit de Yspania donat de*ᵇ* .xl. unum de qualicumque avere aportat et si intrat illuc de Barchinona cum sua mercada assecurat vel in*ᶜ* Barchinonam aplicet et redeat. Quod cum sua mercada assecurat ut in Barchinonam aplicet et redeat. Quod nisi fecerit debet dare de .xl. unum et passaticum de qualibuscumque avers illuc portet preter auri*ᵈ* et hoc totum est domini excepto passatico in quo habet Berengarius de Barchinona tercium et excepto blancho et piscis et clede et anizon et vidre et classe et ferri et papiro hec datur de .xx. unum et de .xl. unum qui ibi ponitur ad iniuriam et pecatum. Capit Berengarius vigesimum et potestas quadragesimum. De sarraceno et hebreo et mostarau donat de .xxx. unum et habet ibi dominus rex duas partes et Berengarius terciam partem. Corium bovis .ii. d. et libra site .ii. d.

---

[1] Bonjudà died not long before June, 1146 (ACB LA I, fol. 49, Mas XI, no. 1608); the tariff list was therefore probably made not long after his death since the scribe added *deinde in vita* as an afterthought above the line. Saltell purchased an allod held in pledge by the children of Bonjudà in 1147, ACB LA I, fol. 217, Mas XI, no. 1620. Because the count-kings employed the title *dominus rex* only after 1150, there is a strong case for dating the document very early in the reign of Ramon Berenguer IV as king of Aragon.

[2] Dorse: De leudea. *De exitis domini Regis et Berengarii.* In late twelfth-century hand.

ᵃ *deinde in vita*, above line. The phrase is attached to Saltell according to the transcription of Sobrequés and Riera, who fail to indicate that it is placed above the line. According to my reading, however, it refers to Bonjudà, not Saltell, which makes a precise dating possible.

ᵇ *denarios*, Sobrequés and Riera (in all sections).   *ᶜ* *litore*, crossed out.

ᵈ *preter auri*, above line; *precium auri*, Sobrequés and Riera. *nec inde que habet*, crossed out.

Documents

et duodena de murilegis .ii. d. et illa de ianetes .ii. d. et de vulpis .ii. d. et centum
de agnines .ii. d. et pena facta de anines .ii. d. et est unum numerum de leuda et
alium usatici et est leuda Berengarii et usaticum domini regis. Centum de
buchinis .ii. s. et centum de cunillis .iii. d. et duodena cordovani .iii. d. et de
badanis .iii. d. et centum de cabrids .iii. medaies et pena facta eorum .iii. medaies.
De hoc levat potestas terciam partem per usatico et in duobus que remanent habet
Berengarius terciam partem. Corda de teles scilicet .vii. canas et media dat .ii. d.
unde levat postat .i. d. per usaticum et in alio habet Berengarius tercium. Pecia
fustanni .ii. d. quanticumque sint et est unus denarius potestatis[e] et in alio habet
Berengarius tercium. Cana totius[f] panni de lana donat .i. d. de unaquaque cana
optimo et avol postquam habuerit .iiii. palmos de amplo unde levat postat
septimam partem et in alio quod remanet habet Berengarius tercium. Pena
cirogrillorum .iii. d. et de gats .iii. d. et de vulpis .iii. d. Copertorium gats vel de
vulpis .iii. d. et levat potestas de unaquaque .i. d. per usaticum et in alio habet
Berengarius tercium. Equus venditus .xvi. d. et mulus et runcinus .xvi. d. et equa
.xvi. d. sarracenus .xvi. d. purpura .xii. d. cindatus de valore .xii. d. et pannus de
Hosca .xii. d. et de subtilibus .vi. d. tapeta .xii. d. almuzelies .vi. d. bagatels .ii. d.
et in his levat rex medietatem per usaticum et Berengarius aliam medietatem.
Trossellus .viii. d. de passatico et si vadit per terram .vii. d. et obolum et habet ibi
potestas duas partes et Berengarius terciam partem de qualicumque avere sit.
Quintale piperis .xx. d. et anyx .xx. d. et encenz .xx. d. canela .xx. d. masticus
.xx. d. cera .viii. d. gala .viii. d. alum .viii. d. cuminus .viii. d. linus .xviii. d.
cotonus .viii. d. falleta .xx. d. De his capit dominus duas partes et Berengarius
tercium. Coure .viii. d. estain .viii. d. que dividentur eadem ratione de illis quibus
est usaticum domini regis et leuda Berengarii quicquid inde mercator emit de illis
qui per mediunt partiuntur. Si ibi habet aliquid de usatico levat potestas usaticum
illi et aliud dividunt per medium baiuli domini regis et Berengarii. Lana vendita
de .xx. unum et de passatico .viii. d. la carga unde capit rex meditatem et
Berengarius aliam medietatem.

Doc. 2
[1162–1196]

List of damages caused by Genoese to merchants of Catalonia.
A. Original parchment. 194 x 223 mm. ACA perg. extrainv., 3308.

Memoria de pecunia et rebus quas Ianuenses abstulerunt hominibus domini
regis aragonensis.

Nichola Arrozal abstulit Berengario de Cavalleria et suis in mense augusti .ii.
cargas de grana pulcra de marcha et .ii. pennas bonas de cunillis et .lx. lb. de cera.

Rotulinus et Augerius de Castello abstulerunt Gerallo Eschasseti cunillos et
gatos et lanetas et costabant .xlii. lb. denariorum barchinonensis monete exceptis
missionibus que constaverunt .clx. s. de dampno et hoc iuravit G. Escassetus esse
suum in eorum potestate in gradu de Magalona et alia vice in Barchinona.

Bocha Danel abstulit Pineto ad gradum Narbone .d. bechunas que ei costabant
.cxx. mbts. et ad suum nepotem .ii. tressellos panni de Xartres unde ivit Ianuam et

---

[e] posostatis, Sobrequés and Riera.   [f] totius, above live.

non potuit inde habere directum et costavit inter capitale et missionem .l. lb. barchinonensis monete et de Petro Estirati .iii. miliaria et media de cunillis.

Petrus clerico in galea que exiebat de Almaria abstulit et cepit in ligno Arnalli de Sancto Paulo .xiii. chintars de cera de Guilelmo de Alfacio.

Papa Rancaios in galea de comune Ianue habuit .xxxii. pannos de fuag de Raimundo pellicerio genero de Patx et costabant .lxiiii. lb. milgorienses et Gerallus de Someres de Barchinona perdidit ibi .xiiii. pannos de fuac.

Doc. 3
NOVEMBER 18, 1182

The will of Saxio.

B. *Translatum* dated May 10, 1194, from A.
ACB LA i, fol. 47.
Ind.: Mas, XII, no. 2110.

Hoc est translatum iudicii de testamento Saxii. Ultime voluntatis cuiusdam viri defuncti nomine Saxii cuius ordo infra .vi. menses coram sacerdote et Petro de Corrone barchinonensi scriptore vicario Mironis iudicis legaliter actus est. Nos scilicet Stephanus Gerardi et Guilelmus de Podio testes et iuratores sumus. Testificamur namque iurando per deum vivum et verum super altare Sancti Felicis maritiris quod est constructum in ecclesia beatorum martirum Iusti et Pastoris infra menia urbis Barchinone supra cuius sacrosancto altare has condiciones manibus nostris iurando contingimus quam vidimus et audivimus et presentes eramus ea hora quando iamdictus testator gravi egritudine detentus fecit suum testamentum in quo elegit manumissores Guilelmum Aimerici et nos Stephanum Gitardi et Guilelmum de Podio quibus precepit ut si eum mori contigerit antequam aliud testamentum faceret ita distribuerent res suas et honorem suum sicut hic ordinavit. Primum habebat in domo Petri de Levo .cxxx. coria bobum sua propria et preterea debebat ei Petrus de Levo .li. s. et Stephanus Gitardi .vi. lb. et .vi. s. de quibus fuerunt .lx. s. de illa societate quam habuerat cum Petro de Levo et debabat ei Burgetus .viii. mbts. et Berengarius Bovis .xx. s. et Raimundus Poncii .xv. s. et Bernardus Poncii .viii. s. Martinus de Sancto Poncio .xxx. s. super una espada et ex alia parte .x. mbts. quos ei dederat ad armandum mediam octavam in sagitia et debebat ei Guilelmus Aimerici .xliii. s. super uno scindato rubeo et uno anulo auri cum maragdine et habet .cxxii. macemutinas in archa sua de quibus erant .xv. de nepote suo Guilelmo de Alesto et habebat .xc. medias argenti et .xxiiii. mbts. et .xv. lb. in denariis minus .xii. d. et peciam unam de ranciano et .iii. anulos auri et unum curatorem auri. Et habebat Guilelmus de Carcassona .iiii. quintales incensi suos et .xxv. s. in denariis et habebat .vi. cannas inter fuag et gordonem et .ii. cannas de sallia rubea et habebat in domo .ii. quintales de in-/ᵛcenso preterea. Et accepit pro anima sua .dcc. s. de suis rebus de quibus dimisit Sancte Eulalie de Campo .cxl. s. et suum corpus et barchinonensi canonice .xxx. s. et Sancto Petro Puellarum .xx. s. et Sancto Paulo de Campo .x. s. et Sepulcro Domini .x. s. et infirmis .xxx. s. et Sancto Iusto .x. s. et Sancte Marie Maris et presbitero .x. s. et Sancto Michaeli .x. s. et Sancto Yacobo .x. s. et Sancto Cucuphati .x. s. et Hospitali Ierusulemi .x. s.

et Sancto Vicencio de Petra Bona .x. s. et Sanctis Crucibus .xx. s. et pauperibus et viduis .xxx. s. et alios .xxx. per helemonsinam et domino regi .lxx. s. et hoc quod inde superaret distribuerent manumissores nomine sui in suam sepulturam in quo melius viderent pro anima sua. Dimisit nepotibus suis Guilelmo de Alesto et Petro de Salceto .c. macemutinas et si aliquis eorum in ipsa captivitate obiret porcio sua remaneret alteri. Concessit nepoti suo Stephano Aicardi medietatem tocius sui orti et tenedonum eius de Barchinona salvo censu canonice. Concessit consanguinee sue Guilelme omne debitum quod de ipsa et vir suus Martinus de Sancto Poncio ei debebant. Concessit Guilelmo Aimerici omne debitum quod ei debebat. Concessit Burgeto omne quod ei debebat. Concessit Stephano Gitardi .xlvi. s. de debito quod ei debebat. Concessit Guilelmo de Podio suam caxam novam. Concessit suam capam meliorem suis parentibus de Calidis sicut sui manumissores distribuerent. Concessit nepoti suo Bernardo Pelegrini aliam medietatem tocius sui orti et tenedonum eius de Barchinona salvo censu canonice. Concessit nepotibus suis Bernardo de Fontanis et Guilelmo de Fontanis mansiones suas de Monte Pessulano. Concessit Petro de Levo .xx. s. de debito quod ei debebat. Omnia vero que remanerent ubicumque habebat et habere debebat de suis rebus dividant et donarent sui manumissores in quo melius vidissent pro anima sua ad eorum voluntatem sine vinculo ullius hominis vel femine. Hoc totum ita ordinavit iamdictus testator in suo testamento .ii. kalendas novembris anno domini .m.c.lxxx.ii. et post obitum suum sic stare mandavit. Deinde ingravescente langore quo detinebatur discessit ab hoc seculo kalendas novembris et eodem anno. Hanc igitur ultimam voluntatem predicti testatoris. Nos predicti testes sicut vidimus et audivimus et ab ipso conditore rogati extitimus in prescripto altari manibus nostris iurando coram sacerdote, et prescripto Petro de Corrone vicario iudicis et alii testibus presentibus veram esse fideliter corroboramus. Atque ex hoc aliter suam voluntatem non mutavit nobis scientibus. Late condiciones .xiiii. kalendas decembris et anno prefato.

Sig. Stephani Gitardi. Sig. Guilelmi de Podio. Nos huius rei testes et iuratores sumus.

Sig. Mironis iudicis. Sig. Burgetus. Sig. Guilelmi Aimerici. Sig. Iohannis de Maurimon. Sig. Ramundi de Mari. Sig. Geralli de Ulmo. Bertrandi de Marimo. Bernardus del Podio. Iohannis de Salis. Petri Suniarii. Petri Bruni. Guilelmi Veiagerra. Arnalli Mathei. Guilelmi Aimerici pueri. Geralli sacerdotis. Nos qui huic sacramento presentes adfuimus.

Signum Petri de Corroni scriptoris prenominati qui hoc scripsit cum litteris suprapositis in linea .vi.ª et emendatis in .viiii.ª et .xiii.ª et .xx.ª et in ista eadem linea. Die et anno quo supra.

Sig. Guilelmi Decimarii. Sig. Petri Poncii. Sig. Raimundi presbiteri. Sig. Raimundi presbiteri. Sig. Berengarii de Vilafrer. Nos qui huic translationi presentes adfuimus.

Sig. Petri de Corron scriptoris qui hoc translatum scripsit .vi. idus madii. Anno domini .m.c.xc.iiii. cum litteris dampnatis et suprapositis in linea .xv.ª et .xvi.ª

Appendix 5

SELECT PATRICIAN GENEALOGIES

ADARRÓ

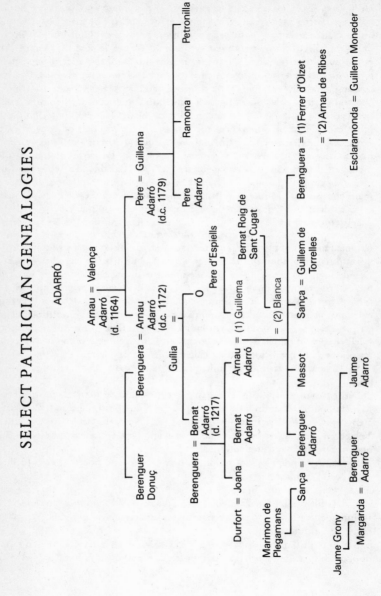

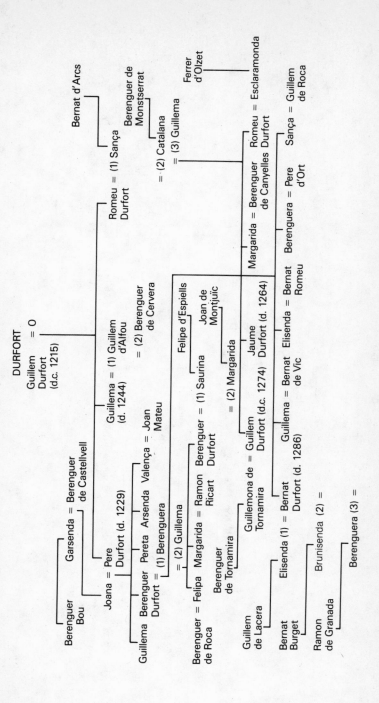

DURFORT

EIMERIC

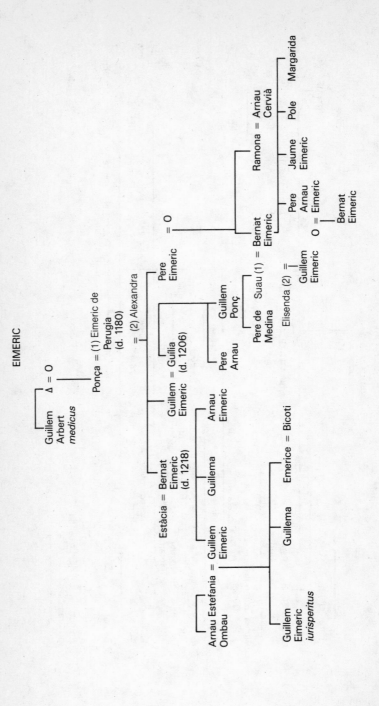

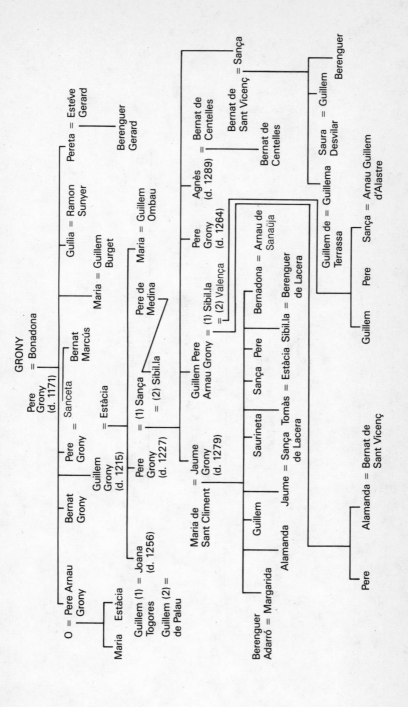

GRONY

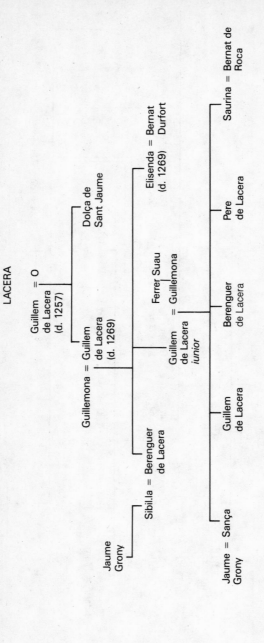

LACERA

BIBLIOGRAPHY

UNPUBLISHED SOURCES

Barcelona

ACA: Cancelleria Reial: Pergamins (including extrainventaris and sense data): Ramon Berenguer II, Berenguer Ramon II, Ramon Berenguer III, Ramon Berenguer IV, Alfons I, Pere I, Jaume I, Pere II, Alfons II.

Cancelleria Reial: Registres Reials for the reigns of Jaume I, Pere II, Alfons II; Reg. 1, 6, 8–25, 27, 28, 35, 37–44, 46–51, 56–60, 62–66, 74–82.

Cancelleria Reial: Cartes Reials, caixes 1, 11.

Monacals: Pergamins Sant Benet de Bages, Sant Llorenç del Munt.

Reial Patrimoni: Batllia General, Classe 3ª, vol. 6; Subsecció de la Batllia, Classe 2ª Aᶜ, vol. 9.

Gran Priorat de Catalunya (Orde Sant Joan de Jerusalem): Pergamins, armari 1.

Pergamins varis: Marquès de Monistrol; Sentmenat, Indice 8, 11 and 111.

ACB: Cartes Reials.

Cartularis: Libri antiquitatum, 4 vols.

Pergamins: Diversorum A (1–1), B (1–2), C (1–4 for 11th cent.; 1–5 for 12th cent.; 1–6 for 13th cent.).

Aniversaris: Morabatins (2–9 to 2–32).

Caritat: Privilegis Reials (3–3).

Morabatins (3–9).

Pabordies, gener a desembre (3–27 to 3–39).

Pia Almoina: Testaments (4–1 to 4–20).

Morabatins (4–30 to 4–56).

Baix Llobregat (4–59).

Majorca (4–159).

ADB: Mensa episcopalis.

Pergamins Santa Anna (including Documents Reials, or Carpeta de la creu).

AHCB: Cartularis: Llibre vermell, 3 vols.; Llibre verd, 3 vols.

Pergamins.

Processos, sèrie XXIII-2.

Santa Maria del Pi: Pergamins.

Sant Pere de les Puel·les: Pergamins.

Bibliography

Montserrat

Arxiu del monestir de Monsterrat: Pergamins, Sant Benet de Bages.

Palma de Majorca

ARM: Pergamins Pascual.
  Reial Patrimoni: Codis Reials, 341, 342, 345, 346, 349, 350.
  Reial Patrimoni: Pergamins, XIII.

Perpinyà

ADPO: Notarial registers, série E, Reg. 1–17.

Puigcerdà

Arxiu Històric Comarcal de Puigcerdà: Protocols, Reg. 1.

Sant Cugat del Vallès

ARP: Pergamins.

Vic

ACV: Liber dotationum antiquarum.

PRINTED SOURCES

Abadal i de Vinyals, Ramon d'. *Catalunya carolíngia*, 3 vols. Barcelona, 1926–52.
El archivo condal de Barcelona en los siglos IX–X, ed. F. Udina Martorell. Barcelona, 1951.
L'arxiu antic de Santa Anna de Barcelona del 942 al 1200 (Aproximació històrico-lingüística), ed. J. Alturo i Parucho, 3 vols. Barcelona, 1985.
Baer, Fritz (Yitzhak). *Die Juden im christlichen Spanien. Erster Teil: Urkunden und Regesten*, 2 vols. 2nd ed., Holland, 1970.
"Barcelona en 1079: su castillo del Puerto y su aljama hebrea. Documento inédito," ed. F. Fita, *Boletín de la Real Academia de la Historia*, 40 (1903), 361–68.
Benjamin of Tudela. *The travels of Benjamin of Tudela*, in *Early travels in Palestine*, ed. and trans. T. Wright. London, 1848.
Bisson, Thomas N. *Fiscal accounts of Catalonia under the early count-kings (1151–1213)*, 2 vols. Berkeley and Los Angeles, 1984.
Burns, Robert I. *Diplomatarium of the Crusader Kingdom of Valencia. The registered charters of its conquerer Jaume I, 1257–1276*, 2 vols. to date. Princeton, 1985– .
Capmany y de Monpalau, Antonio de. *Memorias históricas sobre la marina, comercio y artes de la antigua ciudad de Barcelona*, 2nd ed., revised and introduced by E. Giralt i Raventós and C. Batlle i Gallart, 3 vols. Barcelona, 1961–63.
Cartulari de Poblet, ed. J. Pons i Marquès. Barcelona, 1938.

Bibliography

Cartulario de "Sant Cugat" del Vallés, ed. J. Rius Serra, 3 vols. Barcelona, 1945–47.

Cervantes, Miguel. *El ingenioso hidalgo Don Quijote de la Mancha*. Madrid, 1976.

Codice diplomatico dei re aragonesi di Sicilia, ed. G. La Mantia, 2 vols. Palermo, 1917–56.

Colección de documentos inéditos del archivo general de la Corona de Aragón, eds. P. de Bofarull y Mascaró et al., 42 vols. Barcelona, 1847–1973.

Coll i Alentorn, M. "El Llibre de les nobleses dels reys," *Estudis universitaris catalans*, 13 (1928), 485–524.

Col·lecció diplomàtica del monestir de Santa Maria de Solsona, el Penedès i altres llocs del Comtat de Barcelona (segles X–XV), ed. A. Bach. Barcelona, 1987.

Colon, G. and Garcia i Sanz, A. *Llibre del Consolat de Mar*, 4 vols. Barcelona, 1981–87.

Corpus iuris civilis, eds. T. Mommsen, P. Krüger, R. Schöll, and W. Kröll, 3 vols., 4th ed., Berlin, 1912–20.

Cortes de los antiguos reinos de Aragón y de Valencia y principado de Cataluña, 26 vols. Madrid, 1896–1922.

Desclot, Bernat. *Llibre del rei en Pere*, in *Les quatre grans cròniques*, ed. F. Soldevila. Barcelona, 1971.

"Di due documenti che riguardano le relazioni di Genova con la Catalogna nel secolo XII," ed. L. Valle, *Il R. Liceo-Gionnasio 'C. Colombo' di Genova negli anni 1931–32, 1932–33, 1933–34*. Genoa, 1933, 31–35.

"Documento del siglo XI relativo a Sant Andreu de Palomar (Barcelona) procedente del archivo de Sant Benet de Bages," ed. J. Sarrat i Arbós, *Revista de la asociación artístico-arqueológica barcelonesa*, 3 (1901–2), 634–36.

Documentos de Jaime I de Aragón, eds. A. Huici Miranda and M. Desamparados Cabanes Pecourt, 5 vols. to date. Valencia, 1976–   .

"Documents de juifs barcelonnais au XIe siècle," eds. J. Miret i Sans and M. Schwab, *Boletín de la Real Academia de la Historia*, 69 (1916), 569–583.

Documents hebraics de jueus catalans, ed. José María Millás y Vallicrosa. Barcelona, 1927.

"Documents sur les juifs catalans aux XIe, XIIe et XIIIe siècles," eds. J. Miret i Sans and M. Schwab, *Revue des études juives*, 68 (1914), 52–83, 175–197.

"Dos documentos latino-hebraicos del Archivo del monasterio de San Pedro de las Puellas de Barcelona," eds. J. M. Millás Vallicrosa and F. Udina Martorell, *Sefarad*, 7 (1947), 123–36.

España sagrada, eds. E. Flórez et al., 51 vols. Madrid, 1787–1849.

Ferrer i Mallol, Maria Teresa and Garcia i Sanz, Arcadi. *Assegurances i canvis marítims medievals a Barcelona*, 2 vols. Barcelona, 1983.

Font Rius, José María. *Cartas de población y franquicia de Cataluña*, 2 vols. Barcelona and Madrid, 1969–83.

Garcia i Sanz, Arcadi and Madurell i Marimon, Josep. *Comandas comerciales barcelonesas de la baja edad media*. Barcelona, 1973.

Societats mercantils medievals a Barcelona, 2 vols. Barcelona, 1986.

Guicciardini, Francesco. *Diario del viaggio in Spagna*, in *Ricordi, diari, memorie*, ed. M. Spinella. Rome, 1981.

Guillem de Berguedà, ed. M. de Riquer. Poblet, 1971.

Bibliography

Jaume I. *Llibre dels feits*, in *Les quatre grans cròniques*, ed. F. Soldevila. Barcelona, 1971.

Leges Langobardorum, ed. F. Bluhme, in *Monumenta Germaniae Historica, Leges*, IV. Hanover, 1869.

Lex Wisigothorum, ed. K. Zeumer, in *Monumenta Germaniae Historica, Leges*, I. Hanover and Leipzig, 1902.

Liber feudorum maior: cartulario real que se conserva en el Archivo de la Corona de Aragón, ed. F. Miquel Rosell, 2 vols. Barcelona, 1945–47.

Liber iurium reipublicae genuensis. Monumentae historiae patriae. Turin, 1854.

El "Llibre blanch" de Santas Creus (cartulario del siglo XII), ed. F. Udina Martorell. Barcelona, 1947.

Madurell i Marimón, José María. "El monasterio de Santa María de Valldaura del Vallés (1150–79)," *Analecta sacra tarraconensia*, 25 (1952), 115–63.

Marca Hispanica, sive Limes Hispanicus, hoc est, geographica et historica descriptio Cataloniae, Ruscionis, et circumjacentium populorum, ed. P. de Marca. Paris, 1688.

Muntaner, Ramon. *Crònica*, in *Les quartre grans cròniques*, ed. F. Soldevila. Barcelona, 1971.

"Nouveaux documents des juifs barcelonnais au XIIᵉ siècle," eds. J. Miret i Sans and M. Schwab, *Boletín de la Real Academia de la Historia*, 68 (1916), 563–78.

Oliveras Caminal, José. *Archivo Capitular de la Santa Iglesia Catedral de Barcelona. Cartas reales (siglos XII–XV). Catálogo*. Barcelona, 1946.

Pi y Arimón, Andrés. *Barcelona antigua y moderna o descripción e historia de esta ciudad desde su fundación hasta nuestros días*, 2 vols. Barcelona, 1854.

Puig y Puig, Sebastián. *Episcopologio de la sede barcinonense*. Barcelona, 1929.

Les quatre grans cròniques, ed. F. Soldevila. Barcelona, 1971.

Riu Riu, Manuel. "La documentación del siglo XIII conservada en el archivo de la basílica de Santa María del Mar (Barcelona)," *X CHCA* (Zaragoza, 1980–82), II, 591–606.

Sanpere y Miquel, S. *Topografía antigua de Barcelona*, 2 vols. Barcelona, 1890.

Udina i Abelló, Antoni M. *La successió testada a la Catalunya altomedieval*. Barcelona, 1984.

Usatges de Barcelona i commemoracions de Pere Albert, ed. J. Rovira i Ermengol. Barcelona, 1933.

Viage literario a las iglesias de España, ed. J. Villanueva, 22 vols. Madrid and Valencia, 1806–1902.

SECONDARY WORKS

Abadal i de Vinyals, Ramon d'. "A propos de la domination de la maison comtale de Barcelone sur le Midi français," *AM*, 76 (1964), 315–45.

Dels visigots als catalans, 2 vols. Barcelona, 1969.

"La institució comtal carolíngia en la pre-Catalunya del segle IX," *AEM*, 1 (1964), 29–75.

Els primers comtes catalans. Barcelona, 1958.

Abel, Wilhelm. *Agricultural fluctuations in Europe*, trans. O. Ordish. London, 1980.

Bibliography

Abrams, Philip. "Towns and economic growth: some theories and problems," in *Towns in societies: essays in economic history and historical sociology*, eds. P. Abrams and E. W. Wrigley. Cambridge, 1978, 9–33.

Abulafia, David. "Catalan merchants and the western Mediterranean, 1236–1300: studies in the notarial acts of Barcelona and Sicily," *Viator*, 16 (1985), 209–42.

Italy, Sicily and the Mediterranean, 1100–1400. London, 1987.

"The Norman kingdom of Africa and the Norman expeditions to Majorca and the Muslim Mediterranean," *Anglo-Norman studies*, 7 (1985), 26–49.

"The problem of the Kingdom of Majorca (1229/1276–1343). 2. Economic identity," *Mediterranean Historical Review*, 6 (1991), 35–61.

The two Sicilies: economic relations between the Norman Kingdom of Sicily and the northern communes. Cambridge, 1977.

Amari, Michelle. *Storia dei musulmani di Sicilia*, 3 vols., 2nd ed. Catania, 1933–39.

Amelang, James S. *Honored citizens of Barcelona: patrician culture and class relations, 1490–1714*. Princeton, 1986.

Aragó Cabañas, Antonio. "La institución 'baiulus regis' en Cataluña, en la época de Alfonso el Casto," *VII CHCA* (Barcelona, 1962), III, 137–42.

Ashtor, Eliyahu. *Levant trade in the later Middle Ages*. Princeton, 1983.

Aubenas, R. *Cours d'histoire du droit privé*, III. *Testaments et successions dans les anciens pays de droit écrit au moyen âge et sous l'ancien régime*. Aix-en-Provence, 1954.

"Réflexions sur les 'fraternités artificielles' au moyen âge," in *Etudes historiques à la mémoire de Noël Didier*. Paris, 1960, 1–10.

Aurell i Cardona, Martin. *Une famille de la noblesse provençale au moyen âge: les Porcelet*. Avignon, 1986.

Bach, Erik. *La Cité de Gênes au XIIe siècle*. Copenhagen, 1955.

Baer, Fritz (Yitzhak). *A history of the Jews of Christian Spain*, trans. L. Schoffman, 2 vols. Philadelphia, 1961.

Bagué, E., Cabestany, J., and Schramm, Percy E. *Els primers comtes-reis*. Barcelona, 1960.

Balaguer, Anna M. "Statutes governing coinage in Iberian kingdoms during the Middle Ages," in *Medieval coinage and the Iberian area*, ed. M. Gomes Marques. Santarém, 1984–88, I, 121–38.

Balaguer, Anna M. and Crusafont i Sabater, M. "Els comtats catalans: les seves encunyacions i àrees d'influència," *Symposium numismático de Barcelona I*. Barcelona, 1979, 377–508.

Balard, Michel. *La Romanie génoise (XIIe – début du XVe siècle)*, 2 vols. Rome, 1978.

Balari Jovany, José. *Orígenes históricos de Cataluña*, 2 vols. 2nd ed., San Cugat del Vallés, 1964.

Baldwin, John W. *Masters, princes, and merchants: the social views of Peter Chanter and his circle*, 2 vols. Princeton, 1970.

Banks, Philip. "Alguns immigrants del Llenguadoc al Barcelona del segle XII," *Misel·lània d'homenatge a Enric Moreu-Rey*. Barcelona, 1989, I, 153–72.

" 'Burgus,' 'suburbium' and 'villanova': the extramural growth of Barcelona before A.D. 1200," in *Història urbana del Pla de Barcelona. Actes del II Congrés d'Història del Pla de Barcelona celebrat a l'Institut Municipal d'Història els dies 6 i 7 de desembre de 1985* (Barcelona, 1989–90), II, 106–33.

"The inhabitants of Barcelona in 1145," *Acta mediaevalia*, 9 (1988), 143–66.

"Mensuration in early medieval Barcelona," *Medievalia*, 7 (1987), 37–56.

"The north-western gate of the city of Barcelona," *Cuadernos de arqueología e historia de la ciudad*, 17 (1977), 117–27.

"The origins of the 'Gremi de Sabaters' of Barcelona," *Quaderns d'arqueologia e història de la ciutat*, 18 (1980), 109–18.

"The Roman inheritance and topographical transitions in early medieval Barcelona," in *Papers in Iberian archaeology*, eds. T. F. C. Blagg, R. F. J. Jones, and S.J. Keay. Oxford, 1984, 600–33.

"The topography of Barcelona and its urban context in eastern Catalonia from the third to the twelfth centuries," 5 vols. Unpublished Ph.D. thesis, University of Nottingham, 1980.

Barel, Yves. *La Ville médiévale: système social, système urbain*. Grenoble, 1977.

Bastardas i Parera, Joan. *Sobre la problemàtica dels Usatges de Barcelona*. Barcelona, 1977.

Bastier, J. "Le Testament en Catalogne du IXe au XIIe siècle: une survivance wisigothique," *Revue historique de droit français et étranger*, 51 (1973), 372–417.

Batlle i Gallart, Carme. "La burguesía de Barcelona a mediados del siglo XIII," *X CHCA* (Zaragoza, 1980–82), II, 7–19.

"La casa barcelonina en el segle XIII: l'exemple de la família Durfort," in *La ciudad hispánica durante los siglos XIII al XVI*. Madrid, 1985, II, 1347–60.

"La casa burguesa en la Barcelona del siglo XIII," in *La societat barcelonina a la baixa edat mitjana. Annexos d'història medieval*, I. Barcelona, 1983, 9–51.

"La casa i les béns de Bernat Durfort, ciutadà de Barcelona, a la fi del segle XIII," *Acta mediaevalia*, 9 (1988), 9–51.

La crisis social y económica de Barcelona a mediados del siglo XV, 2 vols. Barcelona, 1973.

"En torn de la fira de Barcelona," *Cuadernos de arqueología e historia de la ciudad*, 18 (1977), 129–39.

"La família i la casa d'un draper de Barcelona, Burget de Banyeres (primera meitat del segle XIII)," *Acta mediaevalia*, 2 (1981), 69–91.

"Els prohoms de la Ribera de Barcelona i llurs atribucions en matèria d'urbanisme (segona meitat del segle XIII)," in *El Pla de Barcelona i la seva història*. Barcelona, 1984, II, 155–60.

"Les relacions entre Barcelona i Sicília a la segona meitat del segle XIII," *XI CHCA*, (Palermo, 1983), II, 147–85.

"La vida y las actividades de los mercaderes de Barcelona dedicados al comercio marítimo (siglo XIII)," in *Le genti del mare mediterraneo*. Naples, 1981, I, 291–339.

Batlle, Carme, Busqueta, Joan J., and Cuadrada, Coral "Notes sobre l'eix comercial Barcelona-Mallorca-Barbaria, a la segona meitat del s. XIII," *XIII CHCA* (Palma, 1987–89), I, 33–47.

Bibliography

Batlle, C., Busquets, A., and Navarro, I. "Aproximació a l'estudi d'una família barcelonina els segles XIII i XIV: els Grony," *AEM*, 19 (1989), 285–310.

Batlle i Gallart, Carme and Casas i Nadal, Montserrat. "La caritat privada i les institucions benèfiques de Barcelona (segle XIII)," in *La pobreza y la asistencia a los pobres en la Cataluña medieval*, ed. M. Riu. Barcelona, 1980–82, I, 117–90.

Bátori, Ingrid. "Das Patriziat der deutschen Stadt. Zu den Forschungsergebnisse über das Patriziat besonders der süddeutschen Städte," *Zeitschrift für Stadtgeschichte, Stadtsoziologie und Denkmahlpflege*, 2 (1975), 1–30.

Baucells i Reig, Josep. *El Baix Llobregat i la Pia Almoina de la Seu de Barcelona: inventari dels pergamins*. Barcelona, 1984.

Bauer, Johannes Josef. "Rechtsverhältnisse der katalanischen Klöster in ihren Klosterverbände (9.–12. Jahrhundert)," *GAKS*, 23 (1967), 69–130.

Bellomo, Manlio. *Profili della famiglia italiana nell'età dei comuni*. Catania, 1966.

Below, M. von. *Der Ursprung der deutschen Stadtverfassung*. Dusseldorf, 1892.

Beneviste, E. "Termes de parenté dans les langues indo-européennes," *L'Homme*, 5 (1965), 5–16.

Bensch, Stephen P. "Early Catalan contacts with Byzantium," in *Iberia and the Mediterranean world of the Middle Ages: essays in honor of Robert I. Burns* (forthcoming).

"La primera crisis bancaria de Barcelona," *AEM*, 19 (1989), 311–28.

"From prizes of war to domestic merchandise: the changing face of slavery in Catalonia and Aragon, 1000–1300," *Viator*, 25 (1994).

Berner, Leila. "A modest enterprise: Jewish moneylenders in thirteenth-century Barcelona," paper presented to 100th Meeting of the American Historical Association, December 27–30, 1985.

Berthold, Brigette. "Charakter und Entwicklung des Patriziats in mittelalterlichen deutschen Städten," *Jahrbuch für Geschichte des Feudalismus*, 6 (1982), 195–241.

"Zur Heiratspolitik des mittelalterlichen Städteburgertums," *Magdeburger Beiträge zur Stadtgeschichte*, 3 (1981), 3–19.

Bisson, Thomas N. *Conservation of coinage: monetary exploitation and its restraint in France, Catalonia and Aragon c. A.D. 1000 – c. 1225*. Oxford, 1979.

"Feudalism in twelfth-century Catalonia," in *Structures féodales et féodalisme dans l'Occident méditerranéen (X^e–XIIIe siècles): bilan et perspectives*. Rome, 1980, 173–92.

"Las finanzas del joven Jaime I (1213–28)," *X CHCA* (Zaragoza, 1980–82), I, 161–208.

The medieval Crown of Aragon: a short history. Oxford, 1986.

Medieval France and her Pyrenean neighbours: studies in early institutional history. London and Ronceverte, WV, 1989.

"Nobility and family in medieval France: a review essay," *French historical studies*, 16 (1990), 597–613.

"Prelude to power: kingship and constitution in the realms of Aragon, 1175–1250," in *The worlds of Alfonso the Learned and James the Conqueror: intellect and force in the Middle Ages*, ed. R. I. Burns. Princeton, 1985, 23–40.

Bibliography

"Ramon de Caldes (c. 1135–1199): dean of Barcelona and king's minister," in *Law, Church, and society: essays in honor of Stephan Kuttner*, ed. K. J. Pennington and R. Somerville. Philadelphia, 1977, 281–92.

"Some characteristics of Mediterranean territorial power in the twelfth century," *Proceedings of the American Philosophical Society*, 123 (1975), 143–50.

"Unheroed pasts: history and commemoration in south Frankland before the Albigensian Crusades," *Speculum*, 65 (1990), 281–308.

Bloch, Marc. *Feudal society*, trans. L. A. Manyon, 2 vols. London, 1961.

Bofarull i Sans, Francesc. "Jaime I y los judíos," *CHCA* (Barcelona, 1909), II, 819–943.

Bois, Guy. *La Mutation de l'an mil*. Paris, 1989 [*The tranformation of the year one thousand: the village of Lournand from antiquity to feudalism*, trans. J. Birrell. Manchester and New York, 1992].

Bongert, Yvonne. *Recherches sur les cours laïques du Xᵉ au XIIIᵉ siècle*. Paris, 1949.

Bonnassie, Pierre. *La Catalogne du milieu de Xᵉ à la fin du XIᵉ siècle: croissance et mutations d'une société*, 2 vols. Toulouse, 1975–76.

"Les Conventions féodales dans la Catalogne du XIᵉ siècle," in *Les Structures sociales de l'Aquitaine, du Languedoc et de l'Espagne au premier âge féodal*. Paris, 1969, 187–219.

"Du Rhône à la Galice: genèse et modalité du régime féodal," in *Structures féodales et féodalisme dans l'Occident méditerranéen (Xᵉ – XIIIᵉ siècles): bilan et perspectives*. Rome, 1980, 17–56.

"Une famille de la campagne barcelonnaise et ses activités économiques aux alentours de l'an mil," *AM*, 75 (1964), 261–307 ["A family of the Barcelona countryside and its economic activities around the year 1000," in *Early medieval society*, ed. and trans. S. Thrupp. New York, 1967, 103–25].

From slavery to feudalism in south-western Europe, trans. J. Birrel. Cambridge, 1991.

La organización del trabajo en Barcelona a fines del siglo XV. Barcelona, 1975.

Bono, José. *Historia del derecho notarial español*, 1 vol. to date. Madrid, 1979– .

Bordone, Renato. "Tema cittadino e 'ritorno alla terra' nella storiografia comunale recente," *Quaderni storici*, 52 (1983), 255–78.

Botet y Sisó, Joaquím. *Les monedes catalanes: estudi y descripció de les monedes carolingies, comtals, senyorials, reyals y locals propries de Catalunya*, 3 vols. Barcelona, 1908–11.

Bouchard, Constance B. *Sword, miter, and cloister: nobility and the Church in Burgandy, 980–1198*. Ithaca, 1987.

Bourin, Monique. *Villages médiévaux en Bas-Languedoc: genèse d'une sociabilité*, 2 vols. Paris, 1987.

Brady, Thomas. *Ruling class, regime, and Reformation at Strasbourg, 1520–55*. Leiden, 1978.

Braudel, Fernand. *The Mediterranean and the Mediterranean world in the age of Philip II*, trans. S. Reynolds, 2 vols., 2nd ed., New York, 1973.

Bibliography

Bresc, Henri. *Un monde méditerranéen: économie et société en Sicile, 1300–1450*, 2 vols. Rome, 1986.

Brett, Michael. "Ifriqiya as a market for Saharan trade from the tenth to the twelfth century AD," *Journal of African history*, 10 (1969), 347–64.

Breuer, Stefan. "Blockierte Rationalisierung: Max Weber und die italiensiche Stadt des Mittelalters," *Archiv für Kulturgeschichte*, 71 (1984), 47–85.

Brocá y Montagut, Guillermo María de, and Arnell y Llopis, Juan. *Instituciones de derecho civil catalan vigente*, 2 vols., 2nd ed., Barcelona, 1886.

Broussolle, Jean. "Les Impositions municipales de Barcelone de 1328 à 1462," *Estudios de historia moderna*, 5 (1955), 3–164.

Brucker, Gene. "Tales of two cities: Florence and Venice in the Renaissance," *American historical review*, 83 (1983), 599–616.

Bruniquer, Esteve Gilabert. *Rúbriques de ceremonial dels magnífichs consellers y regiment de la ciutat de Barcelona*, eds. F. Carreras Candi and B. Gunyalons y Bou, 5 vols. Barcelona, 1912–16.

Brutails, J. A. *Etude sur la condition des populations rurales en Roussillon au moyen âge*. Paris, 1891.

Bullough, Donald. "Early medieval social groupings: the terminology of kinship," *Past and present*, 45 (1969), 3–18.

Burns, Robert I. *The crusader kingdom of Valencia: reconstruction on a thirteenth century frontier*, 2 vols. Cambridge, MA, 1967.

Moors and crusaders in Mediterranean Spain. London, 1978.

"Piracy: Islamic-Christian interface in conquered Valencia," *Muslims, Christians, and Jews in the Crusader Kingdom of Valencia*. Cambridge, 1984, 109–25.

"The realms of Aragon: new directions in medieval history," *The Midwest quarterly*, 18 (1977), 225–39.

"The spiritual life of James the Conqueror, King of Arago-Catalonia, 1208–1276: portrait and self-portrait," *The Catholic historical review*, 62 (1976), 1–35.

Busqueta i Riu, Joan J. *Una vila del Territori de Barcelona: Sant Andreu de Palomar als segles XIII–XIV*. Barcelona, 1991.

The Cambridge economic history of Europe, ed. M. M. Postan, 6 vols. Cambridge, 1941–87.

Cammarosano, Paolo. "Structures familiales dans les villes de l'Italie communale," in *Famille et parenté dans l'Occident médiéval*, eds. G. Duby and J. Le Goff. Rome, 1977, 181–94.

Carreras Candi, Francesc. "Los ciutadans de Barcelona," *BRABLB*, 9 (1921), 137–40.

"Desentrollament de la institució notarial a Catalunya en lo segle XIII," *Miscelánea histórica catalana*. Barcelona, 1905–6, 1, 323–60.

Geografia general de Catalunya. La ciutat de Barcelona. Barcelona, nd [1916].

"Itinerari del rei Anfós II," *BRABLB*, 10 (1921–22), 61–83.

"Notes sobre los origens de la enfitiusis en lo territori de Barcelona," *Revista jurídica de Catalunya*, 15 (1909), 1–92.

Carrère, Claude. *Barcelone: centre économique à l'époque des difficultés 1380–1462*, 2 vols. Paris, 1967.

Caruana, Jaime. "Itinerario de Alfonso II de Aragón," *EEMCA*, 7 (1962), 73–298.

Bibliography

Casey, James. *The history of the family*. Oxford, 1989.

Castaing-Sicard, Mireille. *Monnaies féodales et circulation monétaire en Languedoc (XIe au XIIIe siècles)*. Toulouse, 1961.

Els castells catalans, ed. R. Dalmau, 6 vols. Barcelona, 1967–80.

Català i Roca, Pere. *Extinció del Vescomtat de Barcelona*. Barcelona, 1974.

Charles Edwards, T.M. "Some Celtic kinship terms," *Bulletin of Celtic studies*, 24 (1971), 105–22.

Chédeville, André. *Chartres et ses campagnes, XIe au XIIIe siècles*. Paris, 1977.

Chiffoleau, Jacques. *La Compatabilité de l'au-delà: les hommes, la mort et la religion dans la région d'Avignon à la fin du Moyen Age, vers 1320–vers 1480*. Paris, 1980.

Chojnacki, Stanley. "Marriage legislation and patrician society in Venice," in *Law, custom, and the social fabric in medieval Europe: essays in honor of Bryce Lyon*, eds. B. S. Bachrach and D. Nicholas. Kalamazoo, 1990, 163–86.

Clanchy, M. T. *From memory to written record, England, 1066–1307*. Cambridge, MA, 1979.

Codina, Jaume. *Els pagesos de Provençana (984–1807): societat i economia a l'Hospitalet pre-industrial*, 3 vols. Barcelona, 1987.

Cohn, Samuel K. *Death and property in Siena, 1205–1800: strategies for the afterlife*. Baltimore, 1988.

Collins, Roger J. H. "Charles the Bald and Wifrid the Hairy," in *Charles the Bald: court and kingdom*, eds. M. T. Gisbon and J. L. Nelson. 2nd ed., London, 1990, 169–88.

"Literacy and the laity in early mediaeval Spain," in *The uses of literacy in early mediaeval Europe*, ed. R. McKitterick. Cambridge, 1990, 109–33.

" 'Sicut lex Gothorum continet': law and charters in ninth- and tenth-century León and Catalonia," *English historical review*, 100 (1985), 487–512.

"Visigothic law and regional custom in disputes in early medieval Spain," in *The settlement of disputes in early medieval Europe*, eds. W. Davies and P. Fouracre. Cambridge, 1986, 85–104.

Conde y Delgado de Molina, Rafael. "Los Llull: una familia de la burgesía barcelonesa del siglo XIII," *XI CHCA* (Montpellier, 1983), II, 371–408.

Crusafont i Sabater, M. *Numismática de la Corona catalano-aragonesa medieval*. Madrid, 1982.

Cuadrada, Coral. *El Maresme medieval: les jurisdiccions baronals de Mataró i Sant Vicenç/Vilassar (hàbitat, economia i societat, segles X–XIV)*. Barcelona, 1988.

"Sobre les relacions camp-ciutat a la Baixa Edat Mitjana: Barcelona i les comarques de l'entorn," *Acta mediaevalia*, 11–12 (1990–91), 161–85.

Cunchillos Plano, Sara. "Breves extractos de los documentos contenidos en la caja primera de Jaime I, de 'Cartas reales', conservadas en el Archivo de la Corona de Aragón," *X CHCA* (Zaragoza, 1980–82), II, 485–508.

Cuvillier, Jean-Pierre. "Barcelone, Gênes et le commerce du blé de Sicile vers le milieu du XIIIe siècle," *Atti del I.° congresso storico Liguria-Catalogna*. Bordighera, 1974, 220–34.

Dameron, George W. *Episcopal power and Florentine society, 1000–1320*. Cambridge, MA, 1991.

Delcor, Mathias. "Les Juifs de Puigcerdà au XIIIe siècle," *Sefarad*, 26 (1966), 17–46.

Bibliography

Delort, Robert. *Le Commerce des fourrures en Occident à la fin du moyen âge*, 2 vols. Rome, 1978.

Díaz, M. C. "La *Lex Visigothorum* y sus manuscritos – un ensayo de reinterpretación," *AHDE*, 46 (1976), 163–223.

Dickey, Sara A. and Harrell, Steven. "Dowry systems in complex societies," *Ethnology*, 24 (1985), 111–19.

Dilcher, Gerhard. *Die Entstehung der lombardischen Stadtkommune: eine rechtsgeschichtliche Untersuchung.* Aalen, 1967.

Dillard, Heath. *Daughters of the Reconquest: women in Castilian town society, 1100–1300.* Cambridge, 1984.

Duby, Georges. "Le Budget de l'abbaye de Cluny, 1075–1155: économie domaniale et économie monétaire," *AESC*, 7 (1952), 155–71.

Le Chevalier, la femme et le prêtre: le mariage dans la France féodale. Paris, 1981.

The chivalrous society, trans. C. Postan. Berkeley and Los Angeles, 1980.

"La Diffusion du titre chevaleresque sur le versant méditerranéen de la chrétienté latine," in *La Noblesse au moyen âge, XIe au XVe siècles: essais à la mémoire de Robert Boutrouche*, ed. P. Contamine. Paris, 1976, 39–70.

The early growth of the European economy, trans. H.B. Clarke. London, 1974.

L'Economie rurale et la vie des campagnes dans l'Occident médiéval, 2 vols. Paris, 1962 [*Rural economy and country life in the medieval West*, trans. C. Postan. Columbia, SC, 1968].

Hommes et structures du moyen âge: recueil d'articles. The Hague and Paris, 1973.

"Lignages, noblesse et chevalerie au XIIe siècles dans la région mâconnaise: une révision," *AESC*, 27 (1972), 802–23.

"Remarques sur la littérature généalogique en France aux XIe et XIIe siècle," *Académie des Inscriptions et Belles-lettres: comptes rendus des séances de l'année (avril–juin)* (Paris, 1967), 335–45.

La Société aux XIe et XIIe siècles dans la région mâconnaise. 2nd ed., Paris, 1982.

The three orders: feudal society imagined, trans. A. Goldhammer. Chicago, 1980.

"Les Villes du sud-est de la Gaule du VIIIe au XIe siècle," *La città nell'alto medioevo. Settimane di studio del centro italiano di studi sull'alto medioevo*, VI. Spoleto, 1959, 231–58.

"La Vulgarisation des modèles culturels dans la société féodale," in *Niveaux de culture et groupes sociaux: actes du colloque réuni du 7 au 9 mai 1966 à l'Ecole normale supériure.* The Hague and Paris, 1967, 33–41.

Dufourcq, Charles-Emmanuel. "Les Consulats catalans de Tunis et de Bougie au temps de Jacques le Conquérant," *AEM*, 3 (1966), 469–79.

L'Espagne catalane et le Maghrib aux XIIIe et XIVe siècles de la bataille de Las Navas de Tolosa (1212) à l'avènement du sultan mérinide Abou-l-Hasan (1331). Paris, 1966.

" 'Honrats,' 'mercaders' et autres dans le Conseil des Cent au XIVe siècle," in *La ciudad hispánica durante los siglos XIII al XVI* (Madrid, 1985), II, 1361–95.

L'Ibérie chrétienne et le Maghreb XIIe – XVe siècles. London, 1990.

"Vers la Mediterranée orientale et l'Afrique," *X CHCA. Ponencias* (Zaragoza, 1980–82), 7–90.

Dupont, André. *Les Relations commerciales entre les cités maritimes de Languedoc et les cités méditerranéennes d'Espagne et d'Italie du Xe au XIIIe siècle.* Nîmes, 1943.

Bibliography

Dupré-Theseider, Eugenio. "Vescovi e città nell'Italia precomunale," *Atti del II convegno di storia della Chiesa in Italia*. Padua, 1964, 55–110.

Duran i Sanpere, Augustí. *Barcelona i la seva història*, 3 vols. Barcelona, 1973–75.

Emery, Richard W. "Flemish cloth and Flemish merchants in Perpignan in the thirteenth century," in *Essays in medieval life and thought in honor of A. P. Evans*. New York, 1955, 153–66.

The Jews of Perpignan in the thirteenth century: an economic study based on notarial records. New York, 1959.

English, Edward D. *Enterprise and liability in Sienese banking, 1230–1350*. Cambridge, MA, 1988.

Ennen, Edith. "Les Différents types de formation des villes européennes," *Le Moyen âge*, 62 (1956), 397–412.

Epstein, Steven. *Wills and wealth in medieval Genoa, 1150–1250*. Cambridge, MA, 1984.

Farmer, D. L. "Some price fluctuations in Angevin England," *Economic history review*, 9 (1956), 34–43.

Feliu i Montfort, Gaspar. "Els inicis del domini territorial de la Seu de Barcelona," *CHEC*, 11 (1976), 45–61.

Fernández-Armesto, Felipe. *Before Columbus: exploration and colonization from the Mediterranean to the Atlantic, 1229–1492*. Philadelphia, 1987.

Ferrer i Mallol, Maria Teresa. "Els italians a terres catalanes (segles XII–XV)," *AEM* (1980), 393–467.

"Nous documents sobre els catalans a les fires de la Xampanya," *X CHCA* (Zaragoza, 1980–82), II, 151–59.

Fietier, R. *La Cité de Besançon de la fin du XIIᵉ au milieu du XIVᵉ siècle*, 3 vols. Lille, 1978.

Fiumi, E. "Sui rapporti tra città e contado nell'età comunale," *Archivio storico italiano*, 114 (1956), 18–68.

Font Bayell, Josefina. "Documents escrits en català durant el regnat de Jaume I," *X CHCA* (Zaragoza, 1980–82), II, 517–26.

Font Rius, José María. "La administración financiera en los municipios medievales catalanes," in *Historia de la hacienda española (épocas antigua y medieval): homenaje al Profesor García de Valdeavellano*. Madrid, 1982, 194–231.

"El desarrollo general del derecho en los territorios de la Corona de Aragón (siglos XII–XIV)," *VII CHCA* (Barcelona, 1962), I, 289–326.

Estudis sobre els drets i institucions locals en la Catalunya medieval. Barcelona, 1985.

"Jaume I i la municipalitat de Barcelona," *Discurs inaugural de l'any 1977–78 de la Universitat de Barcelona*. Barcelona, 1977.

Orígenes del régimen municipal de Cataluña. Madrid, 1940.

"Un problème de rapports: gouvernements urbains en France et en Catalogne (XIIᵉ et XIIIᵉ siècles)," *AM*, 69 (1957), 293–306.

"La universidad de prohombres de Ribera de Barcelona y sus ordenanzas marítimas (1258)," in *Estudios de derecho mercantil en homenaje al Profesor Antonio Polo*. Madrid, 1981, 198–240.

"Valencia y Barcelona en los orígenes del régimen municipal," in *Estudios jurídicos en homenaje al Profesor Santa Cruz Teijeiro*. Valencia, 1974, I, 291–336.

Bibliography

Forey, A. J. *The Templars in the Corona de Aragón.* London, 1973.

Fossier, Robert. *Enfance de l'Europe,* 2 vols. Paris, 1982.

La Terre et les hommes en Picardie jusqu'à la fin du XIIIᵉ siècle, 2 vols. Paris, 1968.

Fourquin, Guy. *The anatomy of popular rebellion in the Middle Ages,* trans. A. Chester. Amsterdam, New York, and Oxford, 1978.

Freedman, Paul H. *The diocese of Vic: tradition and regeneration in medieval Catalonia.* New Brunswick, NJ, 1983.

The origins of peasant servitude in medieval Catalonia. Cambridge, 1991.

"An unsuccessful attempt at urban organization in medieval Catalonia," *Speculum,* 54 (1979), 479–91.

Garcia i Sanz, Arcadi. *Història de la marina catalana.* Barcelona, 1977.

Garí, Blanca. *El linaje de los Castellvell en los siglos XI y XII. Medievalia, monografías* 5. Barcelona, 1985.

Gaudemet, Jean. *Les Communautés familiales.* Paris, 1963.

Gautier-Dalché, Jean. "Les Colonies étrangères en Castille," *AEM,* 10 (1980), 469–86.

"L'Histoire monétaire de l'Espagne septentrionale et centrale du XIᵉ et XIIᵉ siècles: quelques réflexions sur divers problèmes," *AEM,* 6 (1969), 43–95.

Génestal, R. *Le Rôle des monastères comme établissements de crédit étudié en Norman- die du XIᵉ à la fin du XIIIᵉ siècle.* Paris, 1901.

Genicot, Léopolde. "Villes et campagnes dans les Pays-Bas médiévaux," *Acta mediaevalia,* 7–8 (1986–87), 163–92.

Geografia de Catalunya, III. *La ciutat de Barcelona.* Barcelona, 1974.

Giunta, Francesco. *Aragonesi e catalani nel Mediterraneo,* 2 vols. Palermo, 1956–59.

Goetz, W. *Die Entstehung der italienischen Kommunen im Frühen Mittelalter.* Munich, 1944.

Goitein, S. D. *A Mediterranean society: the Jewish communities of the Arab world as portrayed in the documents of the Cairo Geniza,* 5 vols. Berkeley and Los Angeles, 1969–88.

Goody, Jack. *The development of the family and marriage in Europe.* Cambridge, 1983.

"Inheritance, property and women," in *Family and inheritance,* eds. J. Goody, J. Thirsk, and E. P. Thompson. Cambridge, 1976, 10–36.

The oriental, the ancient and the primitive: systems of marriage and the family in the pre-industrial societies of Eurasia. Cambridge, 1990.

Gouron, André. "Les Consuls de Barcelone en 1130: la plus ancienne organi- sation municipale à l'ouest des Alpes?" *AHDE,* 60 (1991), 205–13.

"Diffusion des consulats méridionaux et expansion du droit romain aux XIIᵉ et XIIIᵉ siècles," *Bibliothèque de l'Ecole des Chartes,* 121 (1963), 30–54.

Grand, Roger. "La 'complantatio' en el derecho medieval español," *AHDE,* 23 (1953), 737–67.

Grierson, Philip. "Commerce in the Dark Ages: a critique of the evidence," *Transactions of the Royal Historical Society,* 9 (1959), 123–40.

Grundmann, Herbert. "*Litteratus–Illitteratus,*" *Archiv für Kulturgeschichte,* 40 (1958), 1–65.

Guarni, Sanches. *Aproximació a la història de la llengua catalana: creixença i esplendor.* Barcelona, 1980.

Bibliography

Guasch i Dalmau, David. *Els Durforts, senyors del Baix Llobregat al segle XIII.* *Quaderns d'estudis santjustencs*, 1. Barcelona, 1984.

Guenée, Bernard. *Histoire et culture historique dans l'Occident médiéval.* Paris, 1980.

Guia dels arxius eclesiàstics de Catalunya-València-Balears. Barcelona, 1968.

Guilleré, Christian. "Les Finances royales à la fin du regne d'Alfonso IV el Benigno (1335–36)," *MCV*, 18 (1982), 33–60.

"Ville et féodalité dans la Catalogne au bas moyen-âge," in *La formació i expansió del feudalisme català. Actes del col·loqui organitzat pel Col·legi Universitari de Girona (8–11 de gener de 1985)* [*Estudi General. Revista del Col·legi Universitari de Girona*, 5–6]. Girona, 1986, 447–66.

Hajnal, J. "European marriage patterns in perspective," in *Population in history*, eds. D. V. Glass and E. C. Eversely. London, 1965, 101–43.

Hauk, Karl. "Haus- und sippengebundene Literatur mittelalterlichen Adelsgeschlechter von Adelssatiren des 11. und 12. Jahrhunderts hier erläutert" *Mitteilungen des Instituts für österreichische Geschichte*, 62 (1954), 121–45.

Hauptmeyer, C. H. "Vor- und Frühformen des Patriziats mitteleuropäischer Städte: Theorien zur Patriziatsentstehung," *Die alte Stadt*, 1 (1979), 1–20.

Haverkamp, Alfred. "Die Städte im Herrschafts- und Sozialgefüge Reichsitaliens," *Stadt und Herrschaft: Römische Kaiserzeit und hohes Mittelalter. Historische Zeitschrift.* Beiheft 7. Munich, 1982, 149–245.

Heers, Jacques. *Le Clan familial au moyen âge: étude sur les structures politiques et sociales des milieux urbains.* Paris, 1974 [*Family clans in the Middle Ages: a study of political and social structure in urban areas*, trans. B. Herbert. Amsterdam, London, and New York, 1977].

Les Partis et la vie politique dans l'Occident médiéval. Paris, 1981 [*Parties and political life in the medieval West*, trans. D. Nicholas. Amsterdam, London, and New York, 1977].

Herlihy, David. "Church property on the European continent, 701–1200," *Speculum*, 36 (1961), 81–105.

"Family solidarity in medieval Italian history," in *Economy, society and government in medieval Italy*, eds. D. Herlihy, R. S. Lopez, and V. Slessarev. Kent, OH, 1969, 173–84.

"Land, family, and women in Continental Europe, 701–1200," *Traditio*, 18 (1962), 89–120.

Medieval households. Cambridge, MA, 1984.

"The medieval marriage market," *Medieval and Renaissance studies*, 6 (1976), 1–27.

The social history of Italy and Western Europe, 700–1500. London, 1978.

"Società e spazio nella città italiana del medioevo," *La storiografia urbanistica. Atti del 1.° convegno internazionale di storia urbanistica. Lucca 24–28 settembre 1975.* Lucca, 1976, 174–90.

"Tuscan names, 1200–1530," *Renaissance quarterly*, 41 (1988), 561–82.

Herlihy, David and Klapisch-Zuber, Christiane. *Les Toscans et leurs familles.* Paris, 1978.

Herzfeld, M. *Anthropology through the looking glass: critical ethnography in the margins of Europe.* Cambridge, 1987.

436

Bibliography

Heyd, Wilhelm von. *Histoire du commerce du Levant au moyen-âge*, trans. F. Raynaud, 2 vols. Leipzig, 1885–86.

Hibbert, A. B. "The origins of the medieval town patriciate," *Past and present*, 3 (1953), 15–27 [repr. in *Towns in societies: essays in economic history and historical sociology*, eds. P. Abrams and E. A. Wrigley. Cambridge, 1978, 91–104].

Higounet, Charles. "Un grand chapitre de l'histoire du XIIᵉ siècle: la rivalité des maisons de Toulouse et de Barcelone pour la prépondérance méridionale," in *Mélanges d'histoire du moyen âge dédiés à la mémoire de Louis Halphen*. Paris, 1951, 313–22.

Hillgarth, Jocelyn N. *The problem of a Catalan Mediterranean empire*. Supplement to the *English historical review*, 8. London, 1975.

Hilton, R. H. *English and French towns in feudal society: a comparative study*. Cambridge, 1992.

Histoire de la France urbaine, ed. G. Duby, 5 vols. Paris, 1980–85.

Història de Barcelona. De la prehistòria al segle XVI, ed. A. Duran i Sanpere. Barcelona, 1975.

Historia social y económica de España y América, ed. J. Vicens Vives, 5 vols. Barcelona, 1957–59.

Hodges, Richard. *Dark Age economics*. London, 1982.

Primitive and peasant markets. Cambridge, 1988.

Hohenberg, Paul M. and Lees, Lynn H. *The making of urban Europe*. Cambridge, MA, 1985.

Hughes, Diane Owen. "From brideprice to dowry in Mediterranean Europe," *Journal of family history*, 3 (1978), 262–96.

"Struttura familiare e sistemi di successione ereditaria nei testamenti dell'Europa medievale," *Quaderni storici*, 33 (1976), 928–52.

"Urban growth and family structure in medieval Genoa," *Past and present*, 66 (1975), 3–28 [repr. in *Towns in societies: essays in economic history and historical sociology*, eds. P. Abrams and E. A. Wrigley. Cambridge, 1978, 105–30].

Ibanès, Jean. *La Doctrine de l'Eglise et les réalités économiques au XIIIᵉ siècle*. Paris, 1967.

Iglesia Ferreirós, Aquilino. "La creación del derecho en Cataluña," *AHDE*, 47 (1977), 99–423.

Iglésies Fort, Josep. "La cursa demògrafica de les principals ciutats catalanes," *Memorias de la Real Academia de Ciencias y Artes de Barcelona*, 43 (1977), 451–74.

"El fogatge de 1365–70," *Memorias de la Real Academia de Ciencias y Artes de Barcelona*, 34 (1962), 247–356.

Isenmann, Eberhard. *Die deutsche Stadt im Spätmittelalter*. Stuttgart, 1988.

Jones, Philip. "Economia e società nell'Italia medievale: il mito della borghesia," *Economia e società nell'Italia medievale*. Turin, 1980, 1–189.

"From manor to mezzadria: a Tuscan case-study in the medieval origins of modern agrarian society," in *Florentine studies*, ed. N. Rubinstein. Evanston, IL, 1968, 193–241.

Kehr, Paul. "Das Papstum und der katalanische Prinzipat bis zur Vereinigung mit Aragon," *Abhandlungen der preußischen Akademie der Wissenschaften (Philosophisch-historische Klasse)* (1926), 1–91.

Bibliography

Keller, Hagen. *Adelsherrschaft und städtische Geschichte in Oberitalien 9. bis 12. Jahrhundert.* Tübingen, 1979.

"Die Enstehung der italienischen Stadtkommunen als Problem der Sozialgeschichte," *Frühmittelalterliche Studien*, 10 (1976), 169–211.

Kienast, Walter. "La pervivencia del derecho godo en el sur de Francia y Cataluña," *BRABLB*, 35 (1973–74), 265–95.

King, P. D. *Law and society in the Visigothic kingdom.* Cambridge, 1972.

Klapisch-Zuber, Christiane. "Le Complexe de Griselda," *Mélanges de l'Ecole française de Rome*, 94 (1982), 7–43.

"Women and the family," in *Medieval callings*, ed. J. Le Goff, trans. L. Cochrane. Chicago, 1990, 284–311.

Women, family, and ritual in Renaissance Florence, trans. L. G. Cochrane. Chicago, 1985.

Klocke, F. von. *Das Patriziatsproblem und die Werler Erbsälzer.* Münster, 1965.

Kuper, Adam. "Lineage theory: a critical retrospect," *Annual review of anthropology*, 11 (1982), 71–95.

Kuttner, Stephan. "Zur Entstehungsgeschichte der 'Summa de casibus poenitentiae' des hl. Raymund von Penyafort," *Zeitschrift der Savigny-Stiftung für Rechtsgeschichte. Kanonistische Abteilung*, 39 (1953), 419–34.

Lacarra, José María. "Aspectos económicos de la sumisión de los reinos de taifas (1010–1102)," in *Homenaje a Jaime Vicens Vives.* Barcelona, 1965, I, 255–77.

Colonización, parias, repoblación y otros estudios. Zaragoza, 1981.

"Desarrollo urbano de Jaca en la edad media," *EEMCA*, 4 (1951), 139–55.

"Panorama de la historia urbana en la península ibérica desde el siglo V a X," *La città nell'alto medioevo. Settimane di studio del centro italiano di studi sull'alto medioevo*, VI. Spoleto, 1959, 319–58.

Lalinde Abadía, Jesús. "El derecho sucesoria en el 'Recognoverunt proceres'," *Revista jurídica catalana*, 62 (1963), 651–64.

La jurisdicción real inferior en Cataluña ("corts, verguers, batlles"). Barcelona, 1966.

"Los pactos matrimoniales catalanes (esquema histórico)," *AHDE*, 33 (1963), 132–266.

"La recepción española del senadoconsulto Velleyano," *AHDE*, 41 (1971), 335–72.

Lambert, A. "Barcelone (diocèse de)," *Dictionnaire d'histoire et de géographie ecclésiastique*, VI, cols. 671–715.

Lane, Frederic C. "Economic consequences of organized violence," *Journal of economic history*, 18 (1958), 401–17.

"The economic meaning of war and protection," *Journal of social philosophy and jurisprudence*, 7 (1942), 254–70.

Venice and history: the collected papers of Frederic C. Lane. Baltimore, 1966.

Lansing, Carol. *The Florentine magnates: lineage and faction in a medieval commune.* Princeton, 1991.

Le Goff, Jacques. "Ludwig IX. und der Ursprung der feudalen Monarchie in Frankreich," *Jahrbuch für Geschichte des Feudalismus*, 14 (1990), 106–14.

"Travail, techniques et artisans dans les systèmes de valeur du haut moyen âge (V^e au Xe siècle)," *Pour un autre moyen âge.* Paris, 1977, 108–30.

Bibliography

"Warriors and conquering bourgeois: the image of the city in twelfth-century French literature," *The medieval imagination*, trans. A. Goldhammer. Chicago, 1988, 151–76.

Lestocquoy, Jean. *Aux origines de la bourgeoisie: les villes de Flandres et d'Italie sous le gouvernement des patriciens, XIe – XVe siècles*. Paris, 1952.

Lévi-Provençal, E. *Histoire de l'Espagne musulmane*, 3 vols. Leiden and Paris, 1950–53.

Lewis, Archibald R. *Naval power and trade in the Mediterranean A.D. 500–1100*. Princeton, 1951.

Linehan, Peter. "Religion and national identity in medieval Spain," *Studies in Church history*, 18 (1982), 161–99.

The Spanish Church and the papacy in the thirteenth century. Cambridge, 1971.

Little, Lester K. *Religious poverty and the profit economy in medieval Europe*. London, 1978.

Lombard, Maurice. "La Chasse et le produit de la chasse dans le monde musulman (VIIIe–XIe siècle)," *AESC*, 25 (1969), 572–93.

Lombard-Jourdan, Anne. "Du problème de la continuité: y-a-t-il une protohistoire urbaine en France?" *AESC*, 25 (1970), 1121–42.

Lopez, Robert S. "An aristocracy of money in the early Middle Ages," *Speculum*, 28 (1953), 1–43.

The commercial revolution of the Middle Ages. Englewood Cliffs, NJ, 1971.

La primera crisis della banca di Genova (1250–59). Milan, 1956.

Lourie, Elena. *Crusade and colonisation: Muslims, Christians and Jews in medieval Aragon*. London, 1990.

"A society organized for war: medieval Spain," *Past and present*, 35 (1966), 54–76.

Luzzati, Michelle. "Familles nobles et familles marchandes à Pise et en Toscane dans le Bas Moyen Âge," in *Famille et parenté dans l'Occident médiéval*. Rome, 1977, 275–96.

McCrank, Lawrence J. "Restauración canónica e intento de reconquista de la sede tarraconense, 1076–1108," *Cuadernos de historia de España*, 61–62 (1977), 145–245.

McKitterick, Rosamund. *The Carolingians and the written word*. Cambridge, 1989.

Madurell i Marimon, Josep Maria. "Marimón de Plegamans y de Montoliu (1256–1295)," *Hidalguía*, 103 (1970), 941–50.

"Romeo de Marimón de Plegamans y de Montoliu (1256–1309), señor de Sant Marçal," *Hidalguía*, 99 (1970), 251–88.

Magnou-Nortier, Elisabeth. *La Société laique et l'Eglise dans la province ecclésiastique de Narbonne (zone cispyrénéenne) de la fin du VIIIe à la fin du XIe siècle*. Toulouse, 1974.

Malafosse, J. de. "Contribution à l'étude du crédit dans le Midi aux Xe et XIe siècles: les sûretés réeles," *AM*, 63 (1951), 105–48.

Manaresi, C. "Alle origini del potere dei vescovi sul territorio esterno delle città," *Bollettino dell'istituto storico italiano per il medioevo ed archivio muratoriano*, 88 (1944), 221–334

Martínez Ferrando, Jesús M. *El Archivo de la Corona de Aragón*. Barcelona, 1944.

Mas, Josep. *Notes històriques del bisbat de Barcelona*, 12 vols. Barcelona, 1906–15.

Maschke, Erich. "Die Wirtschaftspolitik Kaiser Friedrichs II. im Königreich Sizilien," *Vierteljahrschrift für Sozial- und Wirtschaftsgeschichte*, 53 (1966), 289–328.

The medieval nobility: studies on the ruling classes of France and Germany from the sixth to the twelfth century, ed. and trans. T. Reuter. Amsterdam, London, and New York, 1979.

Menéndez Pidal, Ramón. *La España del Cid*, 2 vols. 3rd ed., Madrid, 1947.

Meynen, Emil. "Einleitung" to *Zentralität als Problem der mittelalterlichen Stadtge-schichtsforschung*, ed. E. Meynen. Cologne and Vienna, 1979.

Miret i Sans, Joaquím. "Escolars catalans al estudi de Bolonia en la XIIIª centuria," *BRABLB*, 8 (1915), 137–55.

Itinerari de Jaume I "el Conqueridor." Barcelona, 1918.

"Itinerario del rey Pedro I de Cataluña, II en Aragón," *BRABLB*, 3 (1905–6), 79–87, 151–60, 238–49, 265–84, 365–87, 435–50, 497–519; 4 (1907–8), 15–36, 91–114.

"Un missatge de Yarmoraced de Tremecen a Jaume I," *BRABLB*, 9 (1915), 48–51.

Mitjá Sagué, Marina. "Condado y ciudad de Barcelona: capítulos de su historia en los siglos IX y X," *EHDAP*, 3 (1955), 267–81.

Moore, R. I. "Duby's eleventh century," *History*, 69 (1984), 36–49.

Moreu-Rey, Enric. "Antropònims a Barcelona als segles XIV i XV," *Estudis d'història medieval*, 3 (1970), 113–20.

Mundó, Anscari M. "Moissac, Cluny et les mouvements monastiques de l'est des Pyrénées," *AM*, 75 (1963), 551–70 ["Monastic movements in the East Pyrenees," in *Cluniac monasticism in the central Middle Ages*, ed. and trans. N. Hunt. London, 1971, 98–122].

Mundy, John H. *Liberty and political power in Toulouse, 1050–1230.* New York, 1954.

Men and women of Toulouse in the age of the Cathars. Toronto, 1990.

"Urban society and culture: Toulouse and its region," in *Renaissance and renewal in the twelfth century*, eds. G. Constable and R. Benson. Cambridge, MA, 1982, 229–47.

Murray, Alexander. *Reason and society in the Middle Ages.* Oxford, 1978.

Mutgé Vives, Josefa. *La ciudad de Barcelona durante el reinado de Alfonso el Benigno (1327–1336).* Barcelona, 1987.

Nadal, Josep and Prats, Modest. *Història de la llengua catalana*, 1 vol. to date. Barcelona, 1982– .

Nehlsen-von Stryk, K. *Die boni homines des frühen Mittelalters. Freiburger rechtsgeschichtliche Abhandlungen*, new series II. Freiburg, 1981.

Niccolai, R. "I consorzi nobiliari ed comune nell'alta e media Italia," *Rivista di storia del diritto italiano*, 13 (1940), 116–17, 292–342, 397–477.

Nicholas, David. *The domestic life of a medieval city: women, children, and the family in fourteenth century Ghent.* Lincoln, NE, 1985.

"Of poverty and primacy: demand, liquidity, and the Flemish economic miracle, 1050–1200," *American historical review*, 96 (1991), 17–41.

Bibliography

Town and countryside: social, economic, and political tensions in fourteenth-century Flanders. Bruges, 1971.

Ollich i Castanyer, Immaculada. "Aspects econòmics de l'activitat dels jueus de Vic, segon els 'Libri judeorum' (1266–1278)," *Miscel·lània de textos medievals*, 3 (1985), 7–118.

Olwer, Lluís Nicolau d'. *L'expansió de Catalunya en la Mediterrània oriental*. 3rd ed., Barcelona, 1974.

Otero, A. "La mejora," *AHDE*, 32 (1963), 5–131.

Palacio, J. M. de. "Contribución al estudio de los burgueses y ciudadanos honrados de Cataluña," *Hidalguía*, 5 (1957), 305–12.

Palacios Martín, Bonifacio. *La coronación de los reyes de Aragón*. Valencia, 1975.

Pauli Meléndez, A. *El real monasterio de San Pedro de las Puellas de Barcelona*. Barcelona, 1945.

Pella y Forgas, Josep. "Establement per Jaume I del Concell de Cent de Barcelona," *CHCA* (Barcelona, 1909), I, 37–49.

Pérez de Benavides, Manuel de. *El testamento visigótico: una contribución al estudio del derecho romano vulgar*. Granada, 1975.

Pirenne, Henri. *Early democracies in the Low Countries*, trans. J.V. Saunders. New York, 1963.

Medieval towns, trans. F. D. Halsey. Princeton, 1925.

"L'Origine des constitutions urbaines au moyen âge," *Revue historique*, 53 (1893), 57–98, 293–327.

"The stages in the social history of capitalism," *American historical review*, 19 (1914), 494–514.

Les Villes et les institutions urbaines, 2 vols. Paris and Brussels, 1939.

Pistarino, Geo. "Genova e Barcelona: incontro e scontro di due civiltà," *Atti di 1.° congresso storico Liguria–Catalogna*. Bordighera, 1974, 81–122.

"Genova e l'Occitania nel secolo XII," *Actes du 1ᵉʳ congrès historique Provence-Ligurie*. Aix, Bordighera, and Marseilles, 1966, 64–129.

Planitz, Hans. "Zur Geschichte des städtischen Meliorats," *Zeitschrift der Savigny-Stiftung für Rechtsgeschichte. Germanistische Abteilung*, 75 (1950), 141–75.

Polanyi, Karl. "The economy as instituted process," in *Trade and markets in archaic societies*, eds. K. Polanyi, C. Arensbert, and H. Pearson. Glencoe, 1957, 243–69.

Poly, Jean-Pierre. *La Provence et la société féodale (879–1166)*. Paris, 1976.

Pons i Guri, J. M. "Característiques paleogràfiques dels llibres notarials catalans fins el 1351," *VII CHCA* (Barcelona, 1962), III, 225–48.

"Entre l'emfeuteusi i el feudalisme (Els reculls de dret gironins)," in *La formació i expansió del feudalisme català. Actes del col·loqui organitzat pel Col·legi Universitari de Girona (8–11 de gener de 1985)* [*Estudi General. Revista del Col·legi Universitari de Girona*, 5–6]. Girona, 1986, 411–18.

"Sentència arbitral sobre lluïsmes, subestabliments i altres drets emfitèutics a Sant Celoni," *Recull d'estudis d'història jurídica catalana*. Barcelona, 1989, I, 235–47.

Powers, James F. *A society organized for war: the Iberian municipal militias in the central Middle Ages*, 1000–1284. Berkeley and Los Angeles, 1988.

Bibliography

Proctor, Evelyn. "The development of the Catalan Corts in the thirteenth century," in *Homenatge a Rubió i Lluch*. Barcelona, 1935, III, 525–36.

Pryor, John H. *Geography, technology and war: studies in the maritime history of the Mediterranean 649–1571*. Cambridge, 1988.

Racine, Pierre. *Plaisance du Xᵉ à la fin du XIIIᵉ siècle: essaie d'histoire urbaine*, 3 vols. Lille and Paris, 1980.

Rashdall, Hastings. *The universities of Europe in the Middle Ages*, eds. F. M. Powicke and A. B. Emden, 3 vols., 2nd ed., Oxford, 1936.

Razi, Zvi. *Life, marriage, and death in a medieval parish: economy, society and demography in Halesowen, 1270–1400*. Cambridge, 1980.

Reglà Campistol, J. "El comercio entre Francia y la Corona de Aragón en los siglos XIII y XIV y sus relaciones con el desenvolvimiento de la industria textil catalana," *Actas del primer congreso internacional de pireneístas*, 1 (1950), 3–25.

Renouard, Yves. *Les Hommes d'affaires italiens*, 3rd ed., Paris, 1968.

"Les Principaux aspects économiques et sociaux de l'histoire des pays de la couronne d'Aragón au XIIᵉ, XIIIᵉ, et XIVᵉ siècles," *VII CHCA. Ponencias* (Barcelona, 1962), 231–66.

Reyerson, Kathryn L. "Le Rôle de Montpellier dans le commerce des draps de laine avant 1350," *AM*, 94 (1982), 17–40.

Reynolds, Susan. *Kingdoms and communities in Western Europe, 900–1300*. Oxford, 1984.

Riquer, Martí de. *Història de la literatura catalana*, 4 vols. Barcelona, 1964–72.

Riu Riu, Manuel. "La financión de la vivienda, propiedad horizontal y pisos de alquiler en la Barcelona del siglo XIV," in *La ciudad hispánica durante los siglos XIII al XVI*. Barcelona, 1985, II, 1397–1405.

Rius Serra, José. "El derecho visigodo en Cataluña," *GAKS*, 8 (1940), 65–80.

Romano, David. *Patricians and popolani: the social foundations of the Venetian Renaissance state*. Baltimore and London, 1987.

Rösch, Gerhard. *Der venezianische Adel bis zur Schließung des Großen Rats*. Sigmaringen, 1989.

Rossetti, Gabriella. "Histoire familiale et structures sociales et politiques à Pise aux XIᵉ et XIIᵉ siècles," in *Famille et parenté dans l'Occident médiéval*, eds. G. Duby and J. Le Goff. Rome, 1977, 159–80.

Pisa nei secoli XI e XII: formazione e caratteri di una classe di governo. Pisa, 1979.

Roustit, Yvan. "La Consolidation de la dette publique à Barcelone au milieu du XIVᵉ siècle," *Estudios de historia moderna*, 4 (1954), 13–156.

Rubiés, Joan Pau and Salrach, Josep M. "Entorn de la mentalitat i la ideologia del bloc de poder feudal a través de la historiografia medieval fins a les *Quatre grans cròniques*," in *La formació i expansió del feudalisme català. Actes del col·loqui organitzat pel Col·legi Universitari de Girona (8–11 de gener de 1985)* [*Estudi General. Revista del Col·legi Universitari de Girona*, 5–6]. Girona, 1986, 467–506.

Ruiz Doménec, José E. "La ciudad de Barcelona durante la Edad Media: de los orígenes a la formación de un sistema urbano," *Quaderns d'arqueologia i història de la ciutat*, 18 (1980), 67–97.

Bibliography

"En torno a un tratado comercial entre las ciudades de Génova y Barcelona en la primera mitad del siglo XII," *Atti del 1.° congresso storico Liguria–Catalogna.* Bordighera, 1974, 151–59.

L'estructura feudal: sistema de parentiu i teoria de l'aliança en la societat catalana (c. 980–c. 1220). Barcelona, 1985.

"Génova y Barcelona en el siglo XII: la estructura básica de su realidad," *Saggi i documenti,* 4 (1983), 25–86.

"Introducción al estudio del crédito en la ciudad de Barcelona durante los siglos XI y XII," *Miscellanea barcinonensia,* 42 (1975), 17–33.

"El origen del capital comercial en Barcelona," *Miscellanea barcinonensia,* 31 (1972), 55–88.

"La primera estructura feudal (consideraciones sobre la producción, el poder y el parentesco en Cataluña) (c. 980–1060)," *Quaderni catanensi di studi classici e medievali,* 4 (1982), 301–68.

"Ruta de las especias / ruta de las islas: apuntes para una nueva periodización," *AEM,* 10 (1980), 689–97.

"Système de parenté et théorie de l'alliance dans la société catalane (env. 1000–env. 1240)," *Revue historique,* 532 (1976), 305–26.

"The urban origins of Barcelona: agricultural revolution or commercial development?" *Speculum,* 52 (1977), 265–86.

Sabean, David. "Aspects of kinship behaviour and property in rural Western Europe before 1800," in *Family and inheritance,* eds. J. Goody, J. Thirsk, and E. P. Thompson. Cambridge, 1976, 96–112.

Salavert, Vicente. "Nuevamente sobre la expansión mediterránea de la Corona de Aragón," in *Segundo congreso internacional de estudios sobre las culturas del Mediterráneo occidental.* Barcelona, 1978, 359–88.

Salin, Edouard. *La Civilisation mérovingienne d'après les sépultures, les textes et le laboratoire,* 4 vols. Paris, 1949–57.

Salrach i Marés, Josep Maria. *Història de Catalunya,* II. *El procés de feudalització.* Barcelona, 1987.

El procés de formació nacional de Catalunya (segles VIII–IX), 2 vols. Barcelona, 1978.

Sanches Guarni, Manuel. *Aproximació a la història de la llengua catalana: creixença i esplendor.* Barcelona, 1980.

Sánchez Albornoz, Claudio. *Una ciudad de la España cristiana hace mil años: estampas de la vida en León.* 9th ed., Madrid, 1982.

Santamaría, Alvaro. "Los consells municipales de la Corona de Aragón mediado el siglo XIII. El sistema de cooptación," *AHDE,* 51 (1981), 291–364.

Sayous, André. "Les Méthodes commerciales de Barcelone au XIIIe siècle, d'après des documents inédits des archives de sa cathédrale," *Estudis universitaris catalans,* 16 (1931), 155–98.

Els mètodes comercials a la Catalunya medieval, trans. and intr. A. Garcia i Sanz and G. Feliu i Montfort. Barcelona, 1975.

Schadek, Hans. "Tunis oder Sizilien? Die Ziele der aragonishen Mittelmeerspolitik unter Pere III. von Aragon," *GAKS,* 28 (1975), 335–49.

Schaube, Adolf. *Handelsgeschichte der romanischen Völker.* Munich and Berlin, 1906.

Bibliography

Schneider, Jean. *La Ville de Metz aux XIIIe et XIVe siècles*. Nancy, 1950.

Schulz, K. "Stadt und Ministerialität in rheinischen Bischofsstädten," in *Stadt und Ministerialität. Protokoll der IX. Arbeitstagung des Arbeitskreises für südwestdeutsche Stadtgeschichtsforschung*, eds. E. Maschke and J. Sydow. Baden-Württemberg, 1973, 16–42.

Schwarzmaier, Hansmartin. *Lucca und das Reich bis zum Ende des 11. Jahrhunderts.* Sigmaringen, 1972.

Septimus, Bernard. "Piety and power in thirteenth-century Catalonia," in *Studies in medieval Jewish history*, ed. I. Twersky. Cambridge, MA, 1979, I, 197–230.

Sevillano Colom, Francisco. *Historia del Puerto de Palma de Mallorca*. Palma, 1974.

Shatzmiller, Joseph. *Shylock reconsidered: Jews, moneylending, and medieval society.* Berkeley and Los Angeles, 1990.

Shideler, John C. *A medieval Catalan noble family: the Montcadas (1000–1230).* Berkeley and Los Angeles, 1983.

Shneidman, J. Lee. *The rise of the Aragonese–Catalan empire, 1200–1350*, 2 vols. London and New York, 1970.

Singer, Charles. *A history of technology*, 8 vols. Oxford, 1954–84.

Sivéry, Gérard. *L'Économie du Royaume de France au siècle de Saint Louis.* Lille, 1983.

Sobrequés i Callicó, Jaume and Riera i Viade, Sebastià. "La lleuda de Barcelona del segle XII," *Miscel·lània Aramon i Serra. Estudis de llengua i literatura catalanes ofertes a R. Aramon i Serra en el seu setantè aniversari.* Barcelona, 1984, IV, 329–346.

Sobrequés i Vidal, Santiago. *Els barons del Catalunya*. Barcelona, 1957.

Els grans comtes de Barcelona. Barcelona, 1961.

Soldevila, Ferran. "A pròposit del servei del bovatge," *AEM*, I (1964). 573–87.

El amirall Ramon Marquet. Barcelona, 1953.

Història de Catalunya. 2nd ed., Barcelona, 1963.

Jaume I, Pere el Gran. Barcelona, 1955.

Els primers temps de Jaume I. Barcelona, 1968.

Spufford, Peter. *Handbook of medieval exchange*. London, 1986.

Money and its use in medieval Europe. Cambridge, 1988.

Steensgaard, Niels. "Violence and the rise of capitalism: Frederic C. Lane's theory of protection and tribute," *Fernand Braudel center for the study of economics, historical systems, and civilizations. Review*, 2 (1981), 247–73.

Stephenson, Carl. *Borough and town: a study of urban origins in England*. Cambridge, MA, 1933.

Stock, Brian. *The implications of literacy: written language and models of interpretation in the eleventh and twelfth century.* Princeton, 1983.

Stouff, Louis. *Arles à la fin du moyen-âge*, 2 vols. Aix-en-Provence, 1986.

Tabacco, Giovanni. *Egemonie sociali e strutture del potere nel medioevo italiano.* Turin, 1974.

"Fief et seigneurie dans l'Italie communale: l'évolution d'un thème historiographique," *Le Moyen âge*, 75 (1969), 5–37, 203–18.

Tangheroni, M. "Famiglie nobili e ceto dirigente a Pisa nel XIII secolo," in *I ceti dirigenti dell'età comunale nei secoli XII e XIII*. Pisa, 1982, II, 323–46.

444

Bibliography

Toubert, Pierre. *Les Structures du Latium médiéval: le Latium méridional et la Sabine du IX⁰ à la fin du XII⁰ siècle*, 2 vols. Rome, 1973.

Trenchs Odena, José. "'De Alexandriis' (el comercio prohibido con los musulmanes y el Papado de Aviñón durante la primera mitad del siglo XIV)," *AEM*, 10 (1980), 237–320.

Treppo, Mario del. "L'espansione catalano-aragonese nel Mediterraneo," in *Nuove questioni di storia medievale*. Milan, 1969, 259–300.

I mercanti catalani e l'espansione della Corona d'Aragon nel secolo XV. Naples, 1972 [*Els mercaders catalans i l'expansió de la Corona catalano-aragonesa al segle XV*, trans. J. Riera Sans. Barcelona, 1976].

Udina Martorell, Federico. "La expansión mediterránea catalano-aragonesa," in *Segundo congreso internacional de estudios sobre las culturas del Mediterráneo occidental*. Barcelona, 1978, 209–24.

"Noms catalans de persona als documents dels segles X–XI," *Miscelánea filológica dedicada a Mons. A. Greiera*. Barcelona, 1962, II, 387–402.

Uytven, R. van. "Les Origines des villes dans les anciens Pays-Bas (jusque vers 1300)," in *La fortune historiographique des thèses d'Henri Pirenne*, eds. G. Despy and A. Verhulst. Brussels, 1986, 13–26.

Valls Taberner, F. "El *liber iudicum popularis* de Homobonus de Barcelona," *AHDE*, 2 (1925), 200–12.

Vanacker, C. "Géographie économique de l'Afrique du Nord du IX⁰ siècle au milieu du XII⁰ siècle," *AESC*, 28 (1973), 659–80.

Ventura, Jordi. *Alfons el 'Cast.'* Barcelona, 1961.

Pere el Catòlic i Simó de Montfort. Barcelona, 1960.

Verhulst, Adriaan. "The 'agricultural revolution' of the Middle Ages reconsidered," in *Law, custom, and the social fabric in medieval Europe: essays in honor of Bryce Lyon*, eds. B.S. Bachrach and D. Nicholas. Kalamazoo, 1990, 17–28.

"The origins of towns in the Low Countries and the Pirenne thesis," *Past and present*, 122 (1989), 3–35.

Verlinden, Charles. "Marchands ou tisserands? A propos des origines urbaines," *AESC*, 27 (1972), 396–406.

"La Place de la Catalogne dans l'histoire commerciale du monde méditerranéen médiéval," *Revue des cours et conférences* (1937–38), 586–605, 737–54.

"The rise of Spanish trade in the Middle Ages," *Economic history review*, 10 (1940), 44–59.

Vicens Vives, Jaume. *Aproximación a la historia de España*. Barcelona, 1952.

España: geopolítica del estado y del imperio. Barcelona, 1940.

Ferran II i la ciutat de Barcelona, 3 vols. Barcelona, 1936.

Manual de historia económica de España. 5th ed., Barcelona, 1967 [*An economic history of Spain*, trans. F. M. López-Morillas. Princeton, 1969].

Vilar, Pierre. *La Catalogne dans l'Espagne moderne*, 3 vols. Paris, 1962.

Vincke, Johannes. "Königtum und Sklaverei im aragonischen Staatenbund während des 14. Jahrhunderts," *GAKS*, 25 (1970), 19–119.

Vinyoles i Vidal, Teresa-Maria, *La vida quotidiana a Barcelona vers 1400*. Barcelona, 1985.

Violante, Cinzio. "Les Prêts sur gage foncier dans la vie économique et sociale de

Bibliography

Milan au XIe siècle," *Cahiers de civilisation médiévale*, 5 (1962), 146–68, 437–59.

La società milanese nell'età precomunale. Bari, 1953.

Volpe, Gioacchino. *Medio evo italiano*, 2nd ed., Florence, 1961.

Waley, Daniel. *The Italian city-republics.* New York and Toronto, 1969.

Walsh, Thomas J. "Spelling lapses in early medieval Latin documents and the reconstruction of primitive Romance phonology," in *Latin and Romance languages in the early Middle Ages*, ed. R. Wright. London and New York, 1991, 206–18.

Ward-Perkins, Bryan. "The towns of northern Italy: rebirth or renewal?" in *The rebirth of towns in the West, A.D. 700–1050*, eds. R. Hodges and B. Hobley. Oxford, 1988, 16–27.

Wasserstein, David. *The rise of the party kings.* Princeton, 1985.

Watson, Andrew. "Back to gold – and silver," *Economic history review*, 2nd series, 20 (1967), 1–34.

Weber, Max. *The city*, trans. D. Martindale and G. Neuwirth. New York, 1958.

Werveke, H. van. "Le Mort-gage et son rôle économique en Flandre et en Lotharingie," *Revue belge de philologie et d'histoire*, 8 (1929), 53–91.

White, Stephen. *Custom, kinship, and gifts to saints.* Chapel Hill and London, 1988.

Wickham, C. J. *The mountains and the city: the Tuscan Appennines in the early Middle Ages.* Oxford, 1988.

Wolff, Philippe. "Barcelone et Toulouse aux XIIe et XIIIe siècles: esquisse d'une comparison," *VII CHCA* (Barcelona, 1962), II, 586–92.

"L'Episode de Berenguer Oller à Barcelone en 1285: essai d'interprétation sociale," *AEM*, 5 (1968), 207–22.

"Quidam homo nomine Roberto negociatore," *Le Moyen âge*, 69 (1963), 129–39.

Wright, Roger. *Late Latin and early Romance in Spain and Carolingian France.* Liverpool, 1982.

Zimmerman, Michel. "La Prise de Barcelone par Al-Mansûr et la naissance de l'historiographie catalane," *Annales de Bretagne et des pays de l'Ouest*, 87 (1980), 191–218.

"L'Usage du droit visigothique en Catalogne du IXe au XIIe siècle: approche d'une signification culturelle," *MCV*, 9 (1973), 233–81.

INDEX

Index

Arsendis, 136
artisans: *see* economy, craft sector

Bag, 157
bailiffs, 65, 69–72, 187, 294, 320–21,
    323–25, 328, 340, 343, 354, 409–11
Baix Llobregat, 29, 69, 112, 145, 211, 214,
    304–5, 348, 358
Balari Jovany, José, 13, 241
Balearics, 19, 53, 55, 116, 222, 227, 229,
    277–80, 290–91, 293–96, 303, 322,
    324–29, 338, 354, 384, 403
Balluvin, 142
banks, bankers, 295, 332–35, 383; *see also*
    credit
Banks, Philip, 21, 66–67
Banyeres, Arbert de, 381
Banyeres, Bernat de, 369
Banyeres, Burget de, 17
Banyeres, Guillem de, 297
Banyeres, Joan de, 241, 286, 300
Banyeres, Ramon de, 293
Banyuls, 210
Barbot, Arnau, 271
Barcino (Roman *colonia*), 24, 28
Barel, Yves, 11–12
baths: *see* topography, baths
Batlle i Gallart, Carme, 14, 150, 280, 371
Bell-lloc, Pere Bertran de, 136, 138
Benevist de Porta, 70–71, 323–24, 410–11
Benjamin of Tudela 1, 2, 4, 297, 404
Benvenist, Gombau de, 408
Berenguer Bernat, 63, 136, 138, 142, 145,
    190, 347, 405
Berenguer de Barcelona, 65, 190, 218–19,
    232, 414–15
Berenguer de Soler, 198
Berenguer de Tarragona, 215
Berenguer Ramon I "the Bent"
    (1017–35), count of Barcelona, 59, 124,
    129
Berenguer Ramon II "the Fratricide"
    (1076–96), 61–63, 99, 116, 131
Berenguer Ramon de Castellet, 64–65, 68,
    76–77, 81, 218, 405
Berenguera, daughter of Roman de La
    Granada, 357
Berenguera, sister of Berenguer Donuç,
    352
Berenguera, sister of Bernat Marcús, 353
Berenguera, wife of Bernat Durfort, 356
Berenguera, wife of Guillem de Vic, 305,
    317, 337
Bernat, bishop of Barcelona, 54–55
Bernat de Barberà, 145

Bernat de Tallada, 79
Bernat Ramon, 152–54, 156–59, 162, 164
Bernat Ricart, 157
Bernat Udalard, 264
Besòs River, 28–30, 31 n. 12, 125, 162
Béziers, 228 n. 143
bishop of Barcelona, 33, 37, 51–56, 77, 81,
    213 n. 93, 214, 341, 386
Bishop's Gate, 33, 35–36, 53, 131; *see also*
    topography, castle-gates
Blanche, queen of Aragon, 326
Bleda, 142
Bofill, 163
Bofill, Pere, 162, 195, 203, 255
Bologna, 381
Bonadona, 142
Bonafos, Salamó, 70, 410
Bonhom, 374
boni homines: *see* constitution, *boni homines*
Bonmacip, 163
Bonnassie, Pierre, 15, 59, 61, 88, 91, 116,
    134, 150, 368, 399
Boquer, Ramon, 200
Borday, Guillem de, 300
Borotí, Bernat, 215, 406
Borrell II (947–92), count of Barcelona,
    128
Bosa, Guillem, 328
Bosc, Pere de, 299
Botet y Sisó, Joaquím, 13, 104
Bou, Arnau, 390
Bou, Berenguer, 68, 79, 180, 208, 229,
    405–6
Bougie, 289–92, 294–95, 302–3, 393
bovatge: *see* taxation, *bovatge*
Braudel, Fernand, 2–3
Bruniquer, Esteve Gilabert, 177
Brunisenda, daughter of Bernat Burget,
    357
Burgès, Arnau, 37
Burgès, Bernat, 339
Burgès, Guillem, 317
Burget, 190, 229
Burget, Berenguer, 296, 301 n. 67, 326,
    328, 406
Burget, Bernat, 357
Burget, Guillem, 352
burial, 385, 389–92
Byzantine Empire, trade with, 1, 288,
    297–99, 302, 334

Cabrera, 128, 130, 155
Caffaro, 224
Cagalell, 218
Calders, Guillem de, 408

448

Index

Index

Index

Guillema, wife of Pere Adarró, 260–61, 263, 275
Guillemona, daughter of Berenguer de Tornamira, 326, 367
Guisalbert, bishop of Barcelona, 60, 129–30
Guisla, countess of Barcelona, 129–30
Guitard, viscount of Barcelona, 128
Guitard, Esteve, 229
Gurb, 159

Ḥafṣids, 292, 328
Heers, Jacques, 10, 123, 127
hereu, 257
Homdedeu, Joan, 296
Horta, 29
Hospital of En Colom, 36
Hospitallers, 213, 390
House of Barcelona, 6, 42–43, 48–51, 83–84, 117, 129–30, 167, 221–25, 290, 334
Huesca, 42–43
Hughes, Diane Owen, 123, 127, 262

Inforcats, 28
inheritance: age of emancipation for heirs, 367–69; female, 246, 248–51, 253–54, 260, 392, 401; joint heirship, 252, 255, 258–60, 275–76, 363; legal limits on, 245–46; male, 140, 145–46, 252–60, 262, 392, 401; of spouses, 250–52; promotion of single heir, 256–57, 259–60, 402; strategies of, 157–58, 169, 248–60, 347–48, 363–69; *see also* dowry, *frarisca*, *hereu*, *melioratio*, premortem transfers.
irrigation, 29–30, 88
Italy: bankers, 287, 332; comparisons with Italian urbanism, 4, 7–8, 32, 46, 81, 83–84, 87, 115, 119–20, 123–24, 164, 391, 396, 398, 402–4; dotal regime in, 271, 360; family structure in Italian towns, 127, 148–49, 234, 236, 275–76, 348, 370, 373; households in, 361–62; immigrants from, 228, 231; inheritance in, 251, 253; trade with, 293, 296–97; *see also* Sicily.
iurisperiti, 381

Jaén, 330, 336
Játiva, 98, 382
Jaume I (1213–76) "the Conqueror," king of Aragon, 20, 38 n. 26, 67, 81, 176, 202, 208–9, 216, 232, 270, 277–80, 282, 290, 292, 314–16, 318, 321–23, 325–27, 332, 366, 378–79, 381, 384, 402

Jaume II (1291–1327), king of Aragon, 326, 332, 381
Jews, 34, 62, 70–71, 117, 125, 137, 144, 195, 202, 210, 284–86, 321, 323–24, 342
Jirba, 290
Joan de Cascai, 69, 406
Joan Martí, 161–63
Jordà de Sant Martí, 132
justice, 49, 58–60, 62, 73–80, 316–17, 341, 344, 371

knights: *see* nobility, knights

Lacera, Berenguer de, 319, 341, 355, 387
Lacera, Guillem de, 325, 336, 354–55, 357, 371, 391 n. 85, 410
landholding: ecclesiastical, 53, 310–12; emphyteusis, 306–13; leases, 36, 90, 110, 184, 189, 342; rents, 104, 182, 190, 199–200, 304–13, 342
Lepers' House, 36, 137
Leteric, Guillem, 163
Levant: *see* Ultramar
Liber iudiciorum, 75, 374, 382
literacy, 373–80
Lleida, 24, 41–43, 50, 65, 81, 98–99, 170, 324, 381
Llibre del Consolat de Mar, 339, 381
Lliçà, 63
Llobell, 70, 409
Llobregat River, 28–30, 50, 125, 299, 354
Lluçà, Berenguer de, bishop of Vic, 54–55
lluisme, 306–13, 230, 342; *see also* landholding, emphyteusis
Llull, Domènec, 328
Llull, Ramon, 301, 375, 382
Lobeta, 265
lordship: banal, 33, 58–61, 167, 217, 399; limitations on, 65–68, 73, 83–84; over town, 32–33, 45–68, 175, 210, 396–401
Louis I "the Pious," emperor, 48
Louis II "the Stammerer," emperor, 50, 52
Lucca, 332–33

Mahalta, 132
Majorca; *see* Balearics
Málaga, 294
Malla, Pere de, 299
Mallol, Berenguer, 299, 329–331
Mallol, Ferrer, 321, 330, 408, 411
Mallol, Pere, 297, 329
mancus: *see* coinage, mancus
Manfred, king of Sicily, 290
Manresa, Bonet de, 256

Index

Index

Index

Index

Udalard II, viscount of Barcelona, 60,
128–31
Udalard Bernat, 165
Ultramar, 222, 322; trade with, 1, 232,
288, 297–99, 330
Usatges de Barcelona, 78, 80, 125, 141, 368,
382

Vacarisses, 212
Valencia, 19, 41–43, 53, 55, 98–99, 102,
116, 279, 293–94, 299, 315, 318, 322,
327–28, 379, 403
Vallès, 25, 53, 63, 145, 152, 155, 158, 186,
205, 212, 320
Venice, 107, 115, 283, 298, 398, 402–3
Vic, 51 n. 15, 65, 81, 214–15
Vic, Berenguer de, 390
Vic, Bernat de, 190, 299, 344
Vic, Guillem de, 242, 305, 337
Vic, Jaume de, 272
Vic, Pere de, 190, 406
Vic, Ramon de, 387
Vic, Simó de, 333–34, 344
Vic, Tomàs de, 296
vicars, 33, 59, 61, 63–65, 68–69, 76–77,
79–80, 82, 160, 167, 219, 299, 315–16,
320–22, 325–26, 328, 340, 342, 365, 371,
383, 400, 405–8

Vicens Vives, Jaume, 14, 221, 298
Viladecols, Guillem de, 213–14, 217, 219
Viladecols, Pere de, 270, 336, 339
vilae, vilanovae: see topography, *vilae,
vilanovae*
Vilafranca, Bartomeu de, 411
Vilafranca del Penedès, 323–24, 371
Vilar, Pere de, 328
viscount of Béarn, 329
viscounts of Barcelona, 59–62, 128–35,
167, 397
Visigothic law, 60, 74, 78, 80, 196, 244–45,
248, 253–58, 261–63, 266, 275, 368, 378
viticulture: *see* agriculture
Vives, 70, 409

walls: new, 38–39, 41, 331; Roman, 24,
31–32, 34–35, 37, 125, 133, 137, 145,
147, 164, 362–63
Weber, Max, 7, 10
widows, 265, 272–74, 276, 356, 372
will: forms of, 244–47, 367–68, 373;
nature of testators, 247–48; pious
donations, 248–49, 285–392

Yaghmurāsan, emir of Tlemcen, 293

Zaragoza, 42–43, 50, 98–99, 107

457

Cambridge studies in medieval life and thought
Fourth series

★ *Also published as a paperback*

DATE DUE

			Printed in USA

HIGHSMITH #45230